PRENTICE HALL
CUSTOM BUSINESS RESOURCES

Compiled by

Operations Management

Custom Edition for
San Francisco State University

Director of Database Publishing: Michael Payne
Senior Sponsoring Editor: Robin J. Lazrus
Development Editor: Catherine O'Keefe
Marketing Manager: Amy Dawson
Assistant Editor: Ana Díaz-Caneja
Operations Manager: Eric M. Kenney
Production Product Manager: Jennifer Berry
Cover Designer: Renée Sartell

Cover Art: Courtesy of EyeWire/Getty Images and PhotoDisc/Getty Images. Photodisc, "Globe surrounded by business people on computer monitors," courtesy of Photodisc/Getty Images. Dave Cutler (Artist), "Man Dropping Coins Into Glass Jar," courtesy of David Cutler/Images.com. Dave Cutler (Artist), "Three Coins in Glass Jar," courtesy of David Cutler/Images.com.

Copyright © 2008 by Pearson Custom Publishing.
All rights reserved.

Permission in writing must be obtained from the publisher before any part of this work may be reproduced or transmitted in any form or by any means, electronic or mechanical, including photocopying and recording, or by any information storage or retrieval system.

Additional copyright information is included, where applicable, as a footnote at the beginning of each chapter.

This special edition published in cooperation with Pearson Custom Publishing.

Printed in the United States of America.

Please visit our web site at *www.pearsoncustom.com*

Attention bookstores: For permission to return unused stock, call 800-777-6872.

ISBN–13: 978-0-558-09183-5

ISBN–10: 0-558-09183-0

Package ISBN–13: 978-0-558-09184-2

Package ISBN–10: 0-558-09184-9

PEARSON CUSTOM PUBLISHING
501 Boylston Street, Suite 900
Boston, MA 02116

Editorial Advisory Board

James M. Olver, Ph.D.
School of Business
College of William and Mary
Marketing

Theresa K. Lant, Ph.D.
Leonard N. Stern School of Business
New York University
Management - Strategy

Robert Plant, Ph.D.
School of Business Administration
University of Miami
MIS/CIS

Karl D. Majeske, Ph.D.
Ross School of Business
University of Michigan
Decision Science

Steven R. Kursh, Ph.D., CSDP
College of Business Administration
Northeastern University
Finance/MIS

Contents

Chapter 1

Operations and Productivity

Operations and Productivity

Outline

Learning Objectives

When you complete this selection you should be able to

1. Define operations management
2. Explain the distinction between goods
   and services
3. Explain the difference between
   production and productivity

4. Compute single-factor productivity
5. Compute multifactor productivity
6. Identify the critical variables in
   enhancing productivity

From *Operations Management*, 9/e. Jay Heizer. Barry Render. Copyright © 2008 by
Pearson Education. All rights reserved.

Global Company Profile: Hard Rock Cafe

Operations Management at Hard Rock Cafe

Operations managers throughout the world are producing products every day to provide for the well-being of society. These products take on a multitude of forms. They may be washing machines at Whirlpool, motion pictures at Dreamworks, rides at Disney World, or food at Hard Rock Cafe. These firms produce thousands of complex products every day— to be delivered as the customer ordered them, when the customers wants them, and where the customer wants them. Hard Rock does this for over 35 million guests worldwide every year. This is a challenging task, and the operations manager's job, whether at Whirlpool, Dreamworks, Disney, or Hard Rock, is demanding.

Orlando-based Hard Rock Cafe opened its first restaurant in London in 1971, making it over 35 years old and the granddaddy of theme restaurants. Although other theme restaurants have come and gone, Hard Rock is still going strong, with 121 restaurants in more than 40 countries—and new restaurants opening each year. Hard Rock made its name with rock music memorabilia, having started when Eric Clapton, a regular customer, marked his favorite bar stool by hanging his guitar on the wall in the London cafe. Now Hard Rock has millions of dollars invested in memorabilia. To keep customers coming back time and again, Hard Rock creates value in the form of good food and entertainment.

The operations managers at Hard Rock Cafe at Universal Studios in Orlando provide more than

Hard Rock Café

3,500 custom products, in this case meals, every day. These products are designed, tested, and then analyzed for cost of ingredients, labor requirements, and customer satisfaction. On approval, menu items are put into production—and then only if the ingredients are available from qualified suppliers. The production process, from receiving, to cold storage, to grilling or baking or frying, and a dozen other steps, is designed and maintained to yield a quality

▶ *Operations managers are interested in the attractiveness of the layout, but they must be sure that the facility contributes to the efficient movement of people and material with the necessary controls to ensure that proper portions are served.*

Lots of work goes into designing, testing, and costing meals. Then suppliers deliver quality products on time, every time, for well-trained cooks to prepare quality meals. But none of that matters unless an enthusiastic wait staff, such as the one shown here, is doing its job.

Hard Rock Cafe in Orlando, Florida, prepares over 3,500 meals each day. Seating over 1,500 people, it is one of the largest restaurants in the world. But Hard Rock's operations managers serve the hot food hot and the cold food cold.

Hard Rock Café

Efficient kitchen layouts, motivated personnel, tight schedules, and the right ingredients at the right place at the right time are required to delight the customer.

meal. Operations managers, using the best people they can recruit and train, also prepare effective employee schedules and design efficient layouts.

Managers who successfully design and deliver goods and services throughout the world understand operations. In this text, we look not only at how Hard Rock's managers create value but also how operations managers in other services, as well as in manufacturing, do so. Operations management is demanding, challenging, and exciting. It affects our lives every day. Ultimately, operations managers determine how well we live.

Video 1.1

Operations Management
at Hard Rock

Operations management (OM) is a discipline that applies to restaurants like Hard Rock Cafe as well as to factories like Sony, Ford, and Whirlpool. The techniques of OM apply throughout the world to virtually all productive enterprises. It doesn't matter if the application is in an office, a hospital, a restaurant, a department store, or a factory—the production of goods and services requires operations management. And the *efficient* production of goods and services requires effective applications of the concepts, tools, and techniques of OM.

In this selection, we first define *operations management*, explaining its heritage and exploring the exciting role operations managers play in a huge variety of businesses. Then we discuss production and productivity in both goods- and service-producing firms. This is followed by a discussion of operations in the service sector and the challenge of managing an effective production system.

WHAT IS OPERATIONS MANAGEMENT?

Learning Objective

1. Define operations management

Production
The creation of goods and services.

Operations management (OM)
Activities that relate to the creation of goods and services through the transformation of inputs to outputs.

Production is the creation of goods and services. **Operations management (OM)** is the set of activities that creates value in the form of goods and services by transforming inputs into outputs. Activities creating goods and services take place in all organizations. In manufacturing firms, the production activities that create goods are usually quite obvious. In them, we can see the creation of a tangible product such as a Sony TV or a Harley-Davidson motorcycle.

In an organization that does not create a tangible good or product, the production function may be less obvious. We often call these activities *services*. The services may be "hidden" from the public and even from the customer. The product may take such forms as the transfer of funds from a savings account to a checking account, the transplant of a liver, the filling of an empty seat on an airplane, or the education of a student. Regardless of whether the end product is a good or service, the production activities that go on in the organization are often referred to as operations, or *operations management*.

ORGANIZING TO PRODUCE GOODS AND SERVICES

To create goods and services, all organizations perform three functions (see Figure 1). These functions are the necessary ingredients not only for production but also for an organization's survival. They are:

1. *Marketing*, which generates the demand, or at least takes the order for a product or service (nothing happens until there is a sale).
2. *Production/operations*, which creates the product.
3. *Finance/accounting*, which tracks how well the organization is doing, pays the bills, and collects the money.

Universities, churches or synagogues, and businesses all perform these functions. Even a volunteer group such as the Boy Scouts of America is organized to perform these three basic functions. Figure 1 shows how a bank, an airline, and a manufacturing firm organize themselves to perform these functions. The blue-shaded areas of Figure 1 show the operations functions in these firms.

WHY STUDY OM?

We study OM for four reasons:

1. OM is one of the three major functions of any organization, and it is integrally related to all the other business functions. All organizations market (sell), finance (account), and produce (operate), and it is important to know how the OM activity functions. Therefore, we study *how people organize themselves for productive enterprise.*
2. We study OM because we want to know *how goods and services are produced.* The production function is the segment of our society that creates the products and services we use.
3. We study OM to *understand what operations managers do.* By understanding what these managers do, you can develop the skills necessary to become such a manager. This will help you explore the numerous and lucrative career opportunities in OM.

4. We study OM *because it is such a costly part of an organization.* A large percentage of the revenue of most firms is spent in the OM function. Indeed, OM provides a major opportunity for an organization to improve its profitability and enhance its service to society. Example 1 considers how a firm might increase its profitability via the production function.

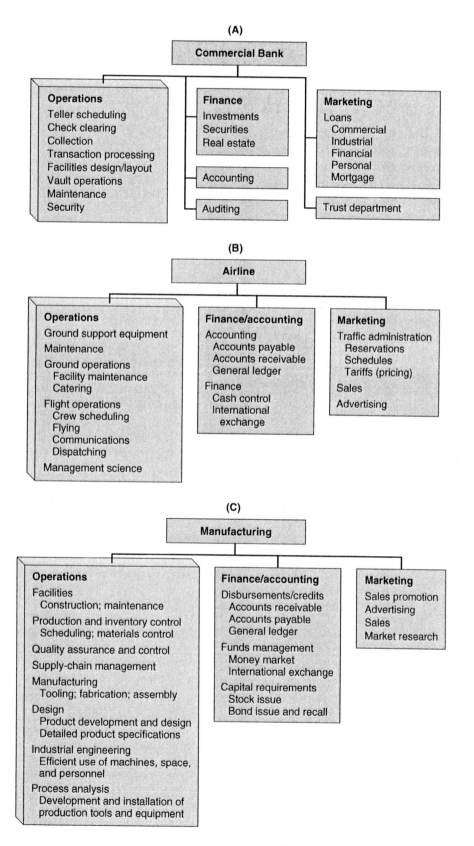

Figure 1

Organization Charts for Two Service Organizations and One Manufacturing Organization

(A) A bank, (B) an airline, and (C) a manufacturing organization. The blue areas are OM activities.

7

EXAMPLE 1

Examining the options for increasing contribution

Fisher Technologies is a small firm that must double its dollar contribution to fixed cost and profit in order to be profitable enough to purchase the next generation of production equipment. Management has determined that if the firm fails to increase contribution, its bank will not make the loan and the equipment cannot be purchased. If the firm cannot purchase the equipment, the limitations of the old equipment will force Fisher to go out of business and, in doing so, put its employees out of work and discontinue producing goods and services for its customers.

Approach: Table 1 shows a simple profit-and-loss statement and three strategic options (marketing, finance/accounting, and operations) for the firm. The first option is a *marketing option*, where good marketing management may increase sales by 50%. By increasing sales by 50%, contribution will in turn increase 71%. But increasing sales 50% may be difficult; it may even be impossible.

▶ **Table 1**

Options for Increasing Contribution

	Current	Marketing Option[a] Increase Sales Revenue 50%	Finance/ Accounting Option[b] Reduce Finance Costs 50%	OM Option[c] Reduce Production Costs 20%
Sales	$100,000	$150,000	$100,000	$100,000
Costs of goods	−80,000	−120,000	−80,000	−64,000
Gross margin	20,000	30,000	20,000	36,000
Finance costs	−6,000	−6,000	−3,000	−6,000
Subtotal	14,000	24,000	17,000	30,000
Taxes at 25%	−3,500	−6,000	−4,250	−7,500
Contribution[d]	$10,500	$18,000	$12,750	$22,500

[a]Increasing sales 50% increases contribution by $7,500, or 71% (7,500/10,500).
[b]Reducing finance costs 50% increases contribution by $2,250, or 21% (2,250/10,500).
[c]Reducing production costs 20% increases contribution by $12,000, or 114% (12,000/10,500).
[d]Contribution to fixed cost (excluding finance costs) and profit.

The second option is a *finance/accounting option*, where finance costs are cut in half through good financial management. But even a reduction of 50% is still inadequate for generating the necessary increase in contribution. Contribution is increased by only 21%.

The third option is an *OM option*, where management reduces production costs by 20% and increases contribution by 114%.

Solution: Given the conditions of our brief example, Fisher Technologies has increased contribution from $10,500 to $22,500. It may now have a bank willing to lend it additional funds.

Insight: The OM option not only yields the greatest improvement in contribution but also may be the only feasible option. Increasing sales by 50% and decreasing finance cost by 50% may both be virtually impossible. Reducing operations cost by 20% may be difficult but feasible.

Learning exercise: What is the impact of only a 15% decrease in costs in the OM option? [Answer: A $19,500 contribution.]

Example 1 underscores the importance of an effective operations activity of a firm. Development of increasingly effective operations is the approach taken by many companies as they face growing global competition.[1]

---

[1]See related discussion in Michael Hammer, "Deep Change: How Operational Innovation Can Transform Your Company," *Harvard Business Review* 82, no. 4 (2004): 85–93.

WHAT OPERATIONS MANAGERS DO

All good managers perform the basic functions of the management process. The **management process** consists of *planning, organizing, staffing, leading,* and *controlling.* Operations managers apply this management process to the decisions they make in the OM function. The 10 major decisions of OM are shown in Table 2. Successfully addressing each of these decisions requires planning, organizing, staffing, leading, and controlling. Typical issues relevant to these decisions and the chapter where each is discussed are also shown.

Management process
The application of planning, organizing, staffing, leading, and controlling to the achievement of objectives.

How This Book Is Organized

The 10 decisions shown in Table 2 are activities required of operations managers. The ability to make good decisions in these areas and allocate resources to ensure their effective execution goes a long way toward an efficient operations function. The text is structured around these 10 decisions. Throughout the book, we discuss the issues and tools that help managers make these 10 decisions. We also consider the impact that these decisions can have on the firm's strategy and productivity.

Where Are the OM Jobs? How does one get started on a career in operations? The 10 OM decisions identified in Table 2 are made by individuals who work in the disciplines shown in the blue areas of Figure 1. Competent business students who know their accounting, statistics, finance, and OM have an opportunity to assume entry-level positions in all of these areas. As you read this text, identify disciplines that can assist you in making these decisions. Then take courses in those areas. The more background an OM student has in accounting, statistics, information systems, and mathematics, the more job opportunities will be available. About 40% of *all* jobs are in OM. Figure 2 shows some recent job opportunities.

Ten OM Strategy Decisions

Design of Goods and Services

Managing Quality

Process Strategy

Location Strategies

Layout Strategies

Human Resources

Supply Chain Management

Inventory Management

Scheduling

Maintenance

◄ **Table 2**

Ten Critical Decisions of Operations Management

Ten Decision Areas	Issues	Chapter(s)
Design of goods and services	What good or service should we offer? How should we design these products?	5
Managing quality	How do we define the quality? Who is responsible for quality?	6, Supplement 6
Process and capacity design	What process and what capacity will these products require? What equipment and technology is necessary for these processes?	7, Supplement 7
Location strategy	Where should we put the facility? On what criteria should we base the location decision?	8
Layout strategy	How should we arrange the facility? How large must the facility be to meet our plan?	9
Human resources and job design	How do we provide a reasonable work environment? How much can we expect our employees to produce?	10, Supplement 10
Supply chain management	Should we make or buy this component? Who are our suppliers and who can integrate into our e-commerce program?	11, Supplement 11
Inventory, material requirements planning, and JIT (just-in-time)	How much inventory of each item should we have? When do we reorder?	12, 14, 16
Intermediate and short-term scheduling	Are we better off keeping people on the payroll during slowdowns? Which job do we perform next?	13, 15
Maintenance	Who is responsible for maintenance? When do we do maintenance?	17

PLANT MANAGER

Division of Fortune 1000 company seeks plant manager for plant located in the upper Hudson Valley area. This plant manufactures loading dock equipment for commercial markets. The candidate must be experienced in plant management including expertise in production planning, purchasing, and inventory management. Good written and oral communication skills are a must along with excellent understanding of and application skills in managing people.

Operations Analyst

Expanding national coffee shop; top 10 "Best Places to Work" wants junior level systems analyst to join our excellent store improvement team. Business or I.E. degree, work methods, labor standards, ergonomics, cost accounting knowledge a plus. This is a hands on job and excellent opportunity for team player with good people skills. West Coast location. Some travel required.

Quality Manager

Several openings exist in our small package processing facilities in the Northeast, Florida, and Southern California for quality managers. These highly visible positions require extensive use of statistical tools to monitor all aspects of service timeliness and workload measurement. The work involves (1) a combination of hands-on applications and detailed analysis using databases and spreadsheets, (2) process audits to identify areas for improvement, and (3) management of implementation of changes. Positions involve night hours and weekends. Send resume.

Supply Chain Manager and Planner

Responsibilities entail negotiating contracts and establishing long-term relationships with suppliers. We will rely on the selected candidate to maintain accuracy in the purchasing system, invoices, and product returns. A bachelor's degree and up to 2 years related experience are required. Working knowledge of MRP, ability to use feedback to master scheduling and suppliers and consolidate orders for best price and delivery are necessary. Proficiency in all PC Windows applications, particularly Excel and Word, is essential. Knowledge of Oracle business system I is a plus. Effective verbal and written communication skills are essential.

Process Improvement Consultants

An expanding consulting firm is seeking consultants to design and implement lean production and cycle time reduction plans in both service and manufacturing processes. Our firm is currently working with an international bank to improve its back office operations, as well as with several manufacturing firms. A business degree required; APICS certification a plus.

▲ **Figure 2**   Many Opportunities Exist for Operations Managers

THE HERITAGE OF OPERATIONS MANAGEMENT

The field of OM is relatively young, but its history is rich and interesting. Our lives and the OM discipline have been enhanced by the innovations and contributions of numerous individuals. We now introduce a few of these people, and we provide a summary of significant events in operations management in Figure 3.

Eli Whitney (1800) is credited for the early popularization of interchangeable parts, which was achieved through standardization and quality control. Through a contract he signed with the U.S. government for 10,000 muskets, he was able to command a premium price because of their interchangeable parts.

Frederick W. Taylor (1881), known as the father of scientific management, contributed to personnel selection, planning and scheduling, motion study, and the now popular field of ergonomics. One of his major contributions was his belief that management should be much more resourceful and aggressive in the improvement of work methods. Taylor and his colleagues, Henry L. Gantt and Frank and Lillian Gilbreth, were among the first to systematically seek the best way to produce.

Another of Taylor's contributions was the belief that management should assume more responsibility for:

1. Matching employees to the right job.
2. Providing the proper training.
3. Providing proper work methods and tools.
4. Establishing legitimate incentives for work to be accomplished.

By 1913, Henry Ford and Charles Sorensen combined what they knew about standardized parts with the quasi-assembly lines of the meatpacking and mail-order industries and added the revolutionary concept of the assembly line, where men stood still and material moved.[2]

Quality control is another historically significant contribution to the field of OM. Walter Shewhart (1924) combined his knowledge of statistics with the need for quality control and provided the foundations for statistical sampling in quality control. W. Edwards Deming (1950)

Taylor revolutionized manufacturing: his scientific approach to the analysis of daily work and the tools of industry frequently increased productivity 400%.

Charles Sorensen towed an automobile chassis on a rope over his shoulders through the Ford plant while others added parts.

---

[2]Jay Heizer, "Determining Responsibility for the Development of the Moving Assembly Line," *Journal of Management History* 4, no. 2 (1998): 94–103.

Customization Focus

**Mass Customization Era
1995–2010**
Globalization
Internet/E-Commerce
Enterprise Resource Planning
Learning Organization
International Quality Standards
Finite Scheduling
Supply Chain Management
Mass Customization
Build-to-Order

Quality Focus

Cost Focus

**Early Concepts
1776–1880**
Labor Specialization
    (Smith, Babbage)
Standardized Parts (Whitney)

**Scientific Management Era
1880–1910**
Gantt Charts (Gantt)
Motion & Time Studies
    (Gilbreth)
Process Analysis (Taylor)
Queuing Theory (Erlang)

**Mass Production Era
1910–1980**
Moving Assembly Line
    (Ford/Sorensen)
Statistical Sampling
    (Shewhart)
Economic Order
    Quantity (Harris)
Linear Programming
    PERT/CPM (DuPont)
Material Requirements
    Planning

**Lean Production Era
1980–1995**
Just-in-Time
Computer-Aided Design
Electronic Data Interchange
Total Quality Management
Baldrige Award
Empowerment
Kanbans

Henry Ford Museum & Greenfield Village

▲ **Figure 3** **Significant Events in Operations Management**

believed, as did Frederick Taylor, that management must do more to improve the work environment and processes so that quality can be improved.

Operations management will continue to progress with contributions from other disciplines, including *industrial engineering* and *management science*. These disciplines, along with statistics, management, and economics, contribute to improved models and decision making.

Innovations from the *physical sciences* (biology, anatomy, chemistry, physics) have also contributed to advances in OM. These innovations include new adhesives, faster integrated circuits, gamma rays to sanitize food products, and higher-quality glass for LCD and plasma TVs. Innovation in products and processes often depends on advances in the physical sciences.

Especially important contributions to OM have come from *information technology*, which we define as the systematic processing of data to yield information. Information technology—with wireless links, Internet, and e-commerce—is reducing costs and accelerating communication.

Decisions in operations management require individuals who are well versed in management science, in information technology, and often in one of the biological or physical sciences. In this textbook, we look at the diverse ways a student can prepare for a career in operations management.

OPERATIONS IN THE SERVICE SECTOR

Manufacturers produce a tangible product, while service products are often intangible. But many products are a combination of a good and a service, which complicates the definition of a service. Even the U.S. government has trouble generating a consistent definition. Because definitions vary, much of the data and statistics generated about the service sector are inconsistent. However, we define **services** as including repair and maintenance, government, food and

Services
Economic activities that typically produce an intangible product (such as education, entertainment, lodging, government, financial, and health services).

lodging, transportation, insurance, trade, financial, real estate, education, legal, medical, entertainment, and other professional occupations.[3]

Differences between Goods and Services

Learning Objective

2. Explain the distinction between goods and services

Let's examine some of the differences between goods and services:

- Services are usually *intangible* (for example, your purchase of a ride in an empty airline seat between two cities) as opposed to a tangible good.
- Services are often *produced and consumed simultaneously*; there is no stored inventory. For instance, the beauty salon produces a haircut that is "consumed" simultaneously, or the doctor produces an operation that is "consumed" as it is produced. We have not yet figured out how to inventory haircuts or appendectomies.
- Services are often *unique*. Your mix of financial coverage, such as investments and insurance policies, may not be the same as anyone else's, just as the medical procedure or a haircut produced for you is not exactly like anyone else's.
- Services have *high customer interaction*. Services are often difficult to standardize, automate, and make as efficient as we would like because customer interaction demands uniqueness. In fact, in many cases this uniqueness is what the customer is paying for; therefore, the operations manager must ensure that the product is designed (i.e., customized) so that it can be delivered in the required unique manner.
- Services have *inconsistent product definition*. Product definition may be rigorous, as in the case of an auto insurance policy, but inconsistent because policyholders change cars and mature.
- Services are often *knowledge based*, as in the case of educational, medical, and legal services, and therefore hard to automate.
- Services are frequently *dispersed*. Dispersion occurs because services are frequently brought to the client/customer via a local office, a retail outlet, or even a house call.

Table 3 indicates some additional differences between goods and services that affect OM decisions. Although service products are different from goods, the operations function continues to transform resources into products. Indeed, the activities of the operations function are often very similar for both goods and services. For instance, both goods and services must have quality standards established, and both must be designed and processed on a schedule in a facility where human resources are employed.

Having made the distinction between goods and services, we should point out that in many cases, the distinction is not clear-cut. In reality, almost all services and almost all goods are a mixture of a service and a tangible product. Even services such as consulting may require a tangible report. Similarly, the sale of most goods includes a service. For instance, many products have the service components of financing and delivery (e.g., automobile sales). Many also require after-sale training and maintenance (e.g., office copiers and machinery). "Service" activ-

▷ **Table 3**

Differences between Goods and Services

Attributes of Goods (tangible product)	Attributes of Services (intangible product)
Product can be resold.	Reselling a service is unusual.
Product can be inventoried.	Many services cannot be inventoried.
Some aspects of quality are measurable.	Many aspects of quality are difficult to measure.
Selling is distinct from production.	Selling is often a part of the service.
Product is transportable.	Provider, not product, is often transportable.
Site of facility is important for cost.	Site of facility is important for customer contact.
Often easy to automate.	Service is often difficult to automate.
Revenue is generated primarily from the tangible product.	Revenue is generated primarily from the intangible services.

[3]This definition is similar to the categories used by the U.S. Bureau of Labor Statistics.

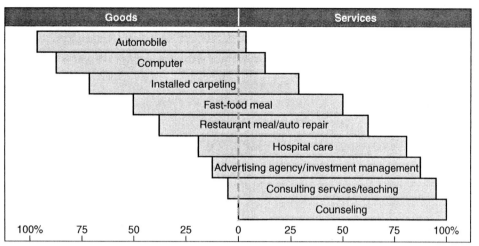

◀ **Figure 4**

Most Goods Contain a Service, and Most Services Contain a Good

ities may also be an integral part of production. Human resource activities, logistics, accounting, training, field service, and repair are all service activities, but they take place within a manufacturing organization.

When a tangible product is *not* included in the service, we may call it a **pure service**. Although there are not very many pure services, in some instances counseling may be an example. Figure 4 shows the range of *services* in a product. The range is extensive and shows the pervasiveness of service activities.

Pure service
A service that does not include a tangible product.

Growth of Services

Services now constitute the largest economic sector in postindustrial societies. Until about 1900, most Americans were employed in agriculture. Increased agricultural productivity allowed people to leave the farm and seek employment in the city. Similarly, manufacturing employment has decreased somewhat in the last 25 years. The changes in manufacturing and service employment, in millions, are shown in Figure 5(a). Interestingly, as Figure 5(b)

▼ **Figure 5** Development of the Service Economy and Manufacturing Productivity

Sources: U.S. Bureau of Labor Statistics; Federal Reserve Board, Industrial Production and Capacity Utilization (2003); Statistical Abstract of the United States (2005).

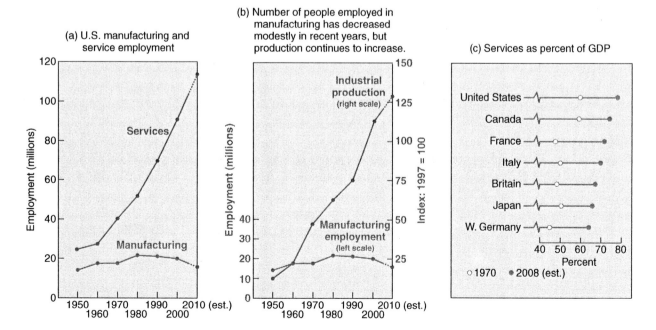

Source: Statistical Abstract of the United States (2007), Table 606 and Bureau of Labor Statistics, 2007.

> **Table 4**

Examples of Organizations in Each Sector

Sector	Example	Percent of All Jobs
Service Sector		
Education, Legal, Medical, and other services	Notre Dame University, San Diego Zoo, Arnold Palmer Hospital	25.5
Trade (retail, wholesale)	Walgreen's, Wal-Mart, Nordstrom	15.1
Utilities, Transportation	Pacific Gas & Electric, American Airlines, Santa Fe R.R., Roadway Express	5.2
Professional and Business Services	Snelling and Snelling, Waste Management, Inc., Pitney-Bowes	10.1
Finance, Information, Real Estate	Citicorp, American Express, Prudential, Aetna, Trammell Crow, EDS, IBM	9.6
Food, Lodging, Entertainment	Olive Garden, Hard Rock Cafe, Motel 6, Hilton Hotels, Walt Disney, Paramount Pictures	8.5
Public Administration	U.S., State of Alabama, Cook County	4.6
Manufacturing Sector	General Electric, Ford, U.S. Steel, Intel	11.5
Construction Sector	Bechtel, McDermott	7.9
Agriculture	King Ranch	1.6
Mining Sector	Homestake Mining	.4
Grand Total		100.0

The Service Sector subtotals (25.5 through 4.6) are bracketed together to total 78.6.

indicates, while the *number* of people employed in manufacturing has held relatively steady since 1950, each person is now producing about 20 times more than in 1950. Services became the dominant employer in the early 1920s, with manufacturing employment peaking at about 32% in 1950. The huge productivity increases in agriculture and manufacturing have allowed more of our economic resources to be devoted to services, as shown in Figure 5(c). Consequently, much of the world can now enjoy the pleasures of education, health services, entertainment, and myriad other things that we call services. Examples of firms and percentage of employment in the U.S. **service sector** are shown in Table 4. Table 4 also provides employment percentages for the nonservice sectors of manufacturing, construction, agriculture, and mining on the bottom four lines.

Service sector

The segment of the economy that includes trade, financial, lodging, education, legal, medical, and other professional occupations.

Service Pay

Although there is a common perception that service industries are low paying, in fact, many service jobs pay very well. Operations managers in the maintenance facility of an airline are very well paid, as are the operations managers who supervise computer services to the financial community. About 42% of all service workers receive wages above the national average. However, the service-sector average is driven down because 14 of the U.S. Department of Commerce categories of the 33 service industries do indeed pay below the all-private industry average. Of these, retail trade, which pays only 61% of the national private industry average, is large. But even considering the retail sector, the average wage of all service workers is about 96% of the average of all private industries.[4]

EXCITING NEW TRENDS IN OPERATIONS MANAGEMENT

One of the reasons OM is such an exciting discipline is that the operations manager is confronted with an ever-changing world. Both the approach to and the results of the 10 OM decisions in Table 2 are subject to change. These dynamics are the result of a variety of forces, from globalization of world trade to the transfer of ideas, products, and money at electronic speeds. The

[4]Herbert Stein and Murray Foss, *The New Illustrated Guide to the American Economy* (Washington, DC: The AIE Press, 1995): 30.

Past	Causes	Future
Local or national focus	Reliable worldwide communication and transportation networks	Global focus, moving production offshore
Batch (large) shipments	Short product life cycles and cost of capital put pressure on reducing inventory	Just-in-time performance
Low-bid purchasing	Supply chain competition requires that suppliers be engaged in a focus on the end customer	Supply-chain partners, collaboration, alliances, outsourcing
Lengthy product development	Shorter life cycles, Internet, rapid international communication, computer-aided design, and international collaboration	Rapid product development, alliances, collaborative designs
Standardized products	Affluence and worldwide markets; increasingly flexible production processes	Mass customization with added emphasis on quality
Job specialization	Changing sociocultural milieu; increasingly a knowledge and information society	Empowered employees, teams, and lean production
Low-cost focus	Environmental issues, ISO 14000, increasing disposal costs	Environmentally sensitive production, green manufacturing, recycled materials, remanufacturing
Ethics not at forefront	Businesses operate more openly; public and global review of ethics; opposition to child labor, bribery, pollution	High ethical standards and social responsibility expected

▲ **Figure 6** Changing Challenges for the Operations Manager

direction now being taken by OM—where it has been and where it is going—is shown in Figure 6. We now introduce some of the challenges shown in Figure 6:

- *Global focus:* The rapid decline in communication and transportation costs has made markets global. At the same time, resources in the form of capital, materials, talent, and labor have also become global. Contributing to this rapid globalization are countries throughout the world that are vying for economic growth and industrialization. Operations managers are responding with innovations that generate and move ideas, production, and finished goods rapidly.
- *Just-in-time performance:* Vast financial resources are committed to inventory, making it costly. Inventory also impedes response to rapid changes in the marketplace. Operations managers are viciously cutting inventories at every level, from raw materials to finished goods.
- *Supply chain partnering:* Shorter product life cycles, driven by demanding customers, as well as rapid changes in material and processes, require suppliers to be more in tune with the needs of the end user. And because suppliers often have unique expertise, operations managers are outsourcing and building long-term partnerships with critical players in the supply chain.
- *Rapid product development:* Rapid international communication of news, entertainment, and lifestyles is dramatically chopping away at the life span of products. Operations managers are responding with management structures and technology that are faster and alliances (partners) that are more effective.
- *Mass customization:* Once managers begin to recognize the world as the marketplace, then the individual differences become quite obvious. Cultural differences, compounded by individual differences, in a world where consumers are increasingly aware of innovation and options, places substantial pressure on firms to respond. Operations managers are responding with production processes that are flexible enough to cater to individual whims of consumers. The goal is to produce customized products, whenever and wherever needed.

- *Empowered employees:* The knowledge explosion and a more technical workplace have combined to require more competence at the workplace. Operations managers are responding by moving more decision making to the individual worker.
- *Environmentally sensitive production:* The operation manager's continuing battle to improve productivity is increasingly concerned with designing products and processes that are environmentally friendly. That means designing products that are biodegradable, or automobile components that can be reused or recycled, or making packaging more efficient.
- *Ethics:* Operations managers are taking their place in the continuing challenge to enhance ethical behavior.

These and many more topics that are part of the exciting challenges to operations managers are discussed in this text.

THE PRODUCTIVITY CHALLENGE

Productivity

The ratio of outputs (goods and services) divided by one or more inputs (such as labor, capital, or management).

The creation of goods and services requires changing resources into goods and services. The more efficiently we make this change, the more productive we are and the more value is added to the good or service provided. **Productivity** is the ratio of outputs (goods and services) divided by the inputs (resources, such as labor and capital) (see Figure 7). The operations manager's job is to enhance (improve) this ratio of outputs to inputs. Improving productivity means improving efficiency.[5]

This improvement can be achieved in two ways: reducing inputs while keeping output constant or increasing output while keeping inputs constant. Both represent an improvement in productivity. In an economic sense, inputs are labor, capital, and management, which are integrated into a production system. Management creates this production system, which provides the conversion of inputs to outputs. Outputs are goods and services, including such diverse items as guns, butter, education, improved judicial systems, and ski resorts. *Production* is the making of goods and services. High production may imply only that more people are working and that employment levels are high (low unemployment), but it does not imply high *productivity*.

Learning Objective

3. Explain the difference between production and productivity

Measurement of productivity is an excellent way to evaluate a country's ability to provide an improving standard of living for its people. *Only through increases in productivity can the standard of living improve.* Moreover, only through increases in productivity can labor, capital, and management receive additional payments. If returns to labor, capital, or management are increased without increased productivity, prices rise. On the other hand, downward pressure is placed on prices when productivity increases, because more is being produced with the same resources.

The benefits of increased productivity are illustrated in the *OM in Action* box "Improving Productivity at Starbucks."

▶ **Figure 7**

The Economic System Adds Value by Transforming Inputs to Outputs

An effective feedback loop evaluates process performance against a plan or standard. It also evaluates customer satisfaction and sends signals to managers controlling the inputs and process.

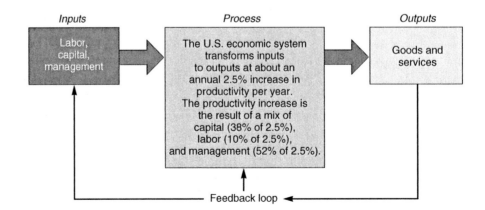

[5]*Efficiency* means doing the job well—with a minimum of resources and waste. Note the distinction between being *efficient*, which implies doing the job well, and *effective*, which means doing the right thing. A job well done—say, by applying the 10 decisions of operations management—helps us be *efficient*; developing and using the correct strategy helps us be *effective*.

OM in Action Improving Productivity at Starbucks

"This is a game of seconds . . . " says Silva Peterson, whom Starbucks has put in charge of saving seconds. Her team of 10 analysts is constantly asking themselves: "How can we shave time off this?"

Peterson's analysis suggested that there were some obvious opportunities. First, stop requiring signatures on credit-card purchases under $25. This sliced 8 seconds off the transaction time at the cash register.

Then analysts noticed that Starbucks's largest cold beverage, the Venti size, required two bending and digging motions to scoop up enough ice. The scoop was too small. Redesign of the scoop provided the proper amount in one motion and cut 14 seconds off the average time of one minute.

Third were new espresso machines; with the push of a button, the machines grind coffee beans and brew. This allowed the server, called a "barista" in Starbucks's vocabulary, to do other things. The savings: about 12 seconds per espresso shot.

As a result, operations improvements at Starbucks outlets have increased the average yearly volume by nearly $200,000, to about $940,000 in the past 6 years. This is a 27% improvement in productivity—about 4.5% per year. In the service industry, a 4.5% per year increase is very tasty.

Sources: The Wall Street Journal (April 12, 2005): B2:B7; *Knight Ridder Tribune Business News* (July 25, 2003):1; **www.finfacts.com**, October 6, 2005.

For well over a century (from about 1869), the U.S. has been able to increase productivity at an average rate of almost 2.5% per year. Such growth has doubled U.S. wealth every 30 years. The manufacturing sector, although a decreasing portion of the U.S. economy, has recently seen annual productivity increases exceeding 4%, and the service sector, with increases of almost 1%, has also shown some improvement. The combination has moved U.S. annual productivity growth in this early part of the 21st century slightly above the 2.5% range for the economy as a whole.[6]

In this selection, we examine how to improve productivity through the operations function. Productivity is a significant issue for the world and one that the operations manager is uniquely qualified to address.

> **Video 1.2**
>
> The Transformation Process at Regal Marine

Productivity Measurement

The measurement of productivity can be quite direct. Such is the case when productivity is measured by labor-hours per ton of a specific type of steel. Although labor-hours is a common measure of input, other measures such as capital (dollars invested), materials (tons of ore), or energy (kilowatts of electricity) can be used.[7] An example of this can be summarized in the following equation:

$$\text{Productivity} = \frac{\text{Units produced}}{\text{Input used}} \qquad (1)$$

For example, if units produced = 1,000 and labor-hours used is 250, then:

$$\text{Productivity} = \frac{\text{Units produced}}{\text{Labor-hours used}} = \frac{1{,}000}{250} = 4 \text{ units per labor-hour}$$

The use of just one resource input to measure productivity, as shown in Equation (1), is known as **single-factor productivity**. However, a broader view of productivity is **multifactor productivity**, which includes all inputs (e.g., capital, labor, material, energy). Multifactor productivity is also known as *total factor productivity*. Multifactor productivity is calculated by combining the input units as shown here:

$$\text{Productivity} = \frac{\text{Output}}{\text{Labor} + \text{Material} + \text{Energy} + \text{Capital} + \text{Miscellaneous}} \qquad (2)$$

> **Learning Objective**
>
> 4. Compute single-factor productivity

> **Single-factor productivity**
> Indicates the ratio of one resource (input) to the goods and services produced (outputs).

> **Multifactor productivity**
> Indicates the ratio of many or all resources (inputs) to the goods and services produced (outputs).

[6]According to the *Statistical Abstract of the United States*, non-farm business sector productivity increase for 1995 was 0.9%; 1996, 2.5%; 1997, 2.0%; 1998, 2.6%; 1999, 2.4%; 2000, 2.9%; 2001, 1.1%; 2002, 4.8%; (see Table 633). Productivity increase for 2003, 4.5%; 2004, 4.0%; 2005, 2.9%; and 2006, 1.6% (U.S. Dept. of Labor, April 2007). **www.bls.gov/newsreleases/archives**.

[7]The quality and time period are assumed to remain constant.

To aid in the computation of multifactor productivity, the individual inputs (the denominator) can be expressed in dollars and summed as shown in Example 2.

EXAMPLE 2

Computing single- and multifactor gains in productivity

Collins Title wants to evaluate its labor and multifactor productivity with a new computerized title-search system. The company has a staff of four, each working 8 hours per day (for a payroll cost of $640/day) and overhead expenses of $400 per day. Collins processes and closes on 8 titles each day. The new computerized title-search system will allow the processing of 14 titles per day. Although the staff, their work hours, and pay are the same, the overhead expenses are now $800 per day.

Approach: Collins uses Equation (1) to compute labor productivity and Equation (2) to compute multifactor productivity.

Solution:

Labor productivity with the old system: $\dfrac{8 \text{ titles per day}}{32 \text{ labor-hours}} = .25$ titles per labor-hour

Labor productivity with the new system: $\dfrac{14 \text{ titles per day}}{32 \text{ labor-hours}} = .4375$ titles per labor-hour

Multifactor productivity with the old system: $\dfrac{8 \text{ titles per day}}{\$640 + 400} = .0077$ titles per dollar

Multifactor productivity with the new system: $\dfrac{14 \text{ titles per day}}{\$640 + 800} = .0097$ titles per dollar

Labor productivity has increased from .25 to .4375. The change is .4375/.25 = 1.75, or a 75% increase in labor productivity. Multifactor productivity has increased from .0077 to .0097. This change is .0097/.0077 = 1.26, or a 26% increase in multifactor productivity.

Insight: Both the labor (single-factor) and multifactor productivity measures show an increase in productivity. However, the multifactor measure provides a better picture of the increase because it includes all the costs connected with the increase in output.

Learning exercise: If the overhead goes to $960 (rather than $800), what is the multifactor productivity? [Answer: .00875.]

Related problems: 1, 2, 5, 6, 7, 8, 9, 11, 12, 14, 15

Learning Objective

5. Compute multifactor productivity

Use of productivity measures aids managers in determining how well they are doing. But results from the two measures can be expected to vary. If labor productivity growth is entirely the result of capital spending, measuring just labor distorts the results. Multifactor productivity is usually better, but more complicated. Labor productivity is the more popular measure. The multifactor-productivity measures provide better information about the trade-offs among factors, but substantial measurement problems remain. Some of these measurement problems are listed here:

1. *Quality* may change while the quantity of inputs and outputs remains constant. Compare an HDTV of this decade with a black-and-white TV of the 1950s. Both are TVs, but few people would deny that the quality has improved. The unit of measure—a TV—is the same, but the quality has changed.
2. *External elements*[8] may cause an increase or a decrease in productivity for which the system under study may not be directly responsible. A more reliable electric power service may greatly improve production, thereby improving the firm's productivity because of this support system rather than because of managerial decisions made within the firm.
3. *Precise units of measure* may be lacking. Not all automobiles require the same inputs: Some cars are subcompacts, others are 911 Turbo Porsches.

Video 1.3

Productivity at Whirlpool

Productivity measurement is particularly difficult in the service sector, where the end product can be hard to define. For example, economic statistics ignore the quality of your haircut, the outcome of a court case, or service at a retail store. In some cases, adjustments are made for the quality of the product sold but *not* the quality of the sales presentation or the advantage of a

[8]These are exogenous variables—that is, variables outside the system under study that influence it.

broader product selection. Productivity measurements require specific inputs and outputs, but a free economy is producing worth—what people want—which includes convenience, speed, and safety. Traditional measures of outputs may be a very poor measure of these other measures of worth. Note the quality-measurement problems in a law office, where each case is different, altering the accuracy of the measure "cases per labor-hour" or "cases per employee."

Productivity Variables

As we saw in Figure 7, productivity increases are dependent on three **productivity variables**:

1. *Labor*, which contributes about 10% of the annual increase.
2. *Capital*, which contributes about 38% of the annual increase.
3. *Management*, which contributes about 52% of the annual increase.

These three factors are critical to improved productivity. They represent the broad areas in which managers can take action to improve productivity.[9]

Productivity variables
The three factors critical to productivity improvement—labor, capital, and the art and science of management.

Labor   Improvement in the contribution of labor to productivity is the result of a healthier, better-educated, and better-nourished labor force. Some increase may also be attributed to a shorter workweek. Historically, about 10% of the annual improvement in productivity is attributed to improvement in the quality of labor. Three key variables for improved labor productivity are:

1. Basic education appropriate for an effective labor force.
2. Diet of the labor force.
3. Social overhead that makes labor available, such as transportation and sanitation.

Learning Objective

6. Identify the critical variables in enhancing productivity

Illiteracy and poor diets are a major impediment to productivity, costing countries up to 20% of their productivity.[10] Infrastructure that yields clean drinking water and sanitation is also an opportunity for improved productivity, as well as an opportunity for better health, in much of the world.

In developed nations, the challenge becomes *maintaining and enhancing the skills of labor* in the midst of rapidly expanding technology and knowledge. Recent data suggest that the average American 17-year-old knows significantly less mathematics than the average Japanese at the same age, and about half cannot answer the questions in Figure 8. Moreover, more than 38% of American job applicants tested for basic skills were deficient in reading, writing, or math.[11]

Overcoming shortcomings in the quality of labor while other countries have a better labor force is a major challenge. Perhaps improvements can be found not only through increasing competence of labor but also via *better utilized labor with a stronger commitment*. Training, motivation, team building, and the human resource strategies discussed in further Chapter, as well as improved education, may be among the many techniques that will contribute to increased labor productivity. Improvements in labor productivity are possible; however, they can be expected to be increasingly difficult and expensive.

Many American high schools exceed a 50% dropout rate in spite of offering a wide variety of programs.

Between 20% and 30% of U.S. workers lack the basic skills they need for their current jobs.

(Source: Nan Stone, Harvard Business Review.)

6 yds
4 yds

What is the area of this rectangle?

_____ 4 square yds
_____ 6 square yds
_____ 10 square yds
_____ 20 square yds
_____ 24 square yds

If $9y + 3 = 6y + 15$ then $y =$

_____ 1   _____ 4
_____ 2   _____ 6

Which of the following is true about 84% of 100?

_____ It is greater than 100
_____ It is less than 100
_____ It is equal to 100

◁ **Figure 8**

About Half of the 17-Year-Olds in the U.S. Cannot Correctly Answer Questions of This Type

[9]The percentages are from Herbert Stein and Murray Foss, *The New Illustrated Guide to the American Economy* (Washington, DC: AIE Press, 1995): 67.

[10]See report by Christopher Wanjek, "Food at Work: Workplace Solutions for Malnutrition, Obesity, and Chronic Diseases," *International Labor Office*, 2005.

[11]"Can't Read, Can't Count," *Scientific American* (October 2001): 24; and "Economic Time Bomb: U.S. Teens are Among Worst at Math," *The Wall Street Journal* (December 7, 2004):B1.

Capital Human beings are tool-using animals. Capital investment provides those tools. Capital investment has increased in the U.S. every year except during a few very severe recession periods. Annual capital investment in the U.S. has increased at an annual rate of 1.5% after allowances for depreciation.

Inflation and taxes increase the cost of capital, making capital investment increasingly expensive. When the capital invested per employee drops, we can expect a drop in productivity. Using labor rather than capital may reduce unemployment in the short run, but it also makes economies less productive and therefore lowers wages in the long run. Capital investment is often a necessary, but seldom a sufficient ingredient in the battle for increased productivity.

The trade-off between capital and labor is continually in flux. The higher the interest rate, the more projects requiring capital are "squeezed out": they are not pursued because the potential return on investment for a given risk has been reduced. Managers adjust their investment plans to changes in capital cost.

Management Management is a factor of production and an economic resource. Management is responsible for ensuring that labor and capital are effectively used to increase productivity. Management accounts for over half of the annual increase in productivity. This increase includes improvements made through the use of knowledge and the application of technology.

Knowledge society
A society in which much of the labor force has migrated from manual work to work based on knowledge.

Using knowledge and technology is critical in postindustrial societies. Consequently, postindustrial societies are also known as knowledge societies. **Knowledge societies** are those in which much of the labor force has migrated from manual work to technical and information-processing tasks requiring ongoing education. The required education and training are important high-cost items that are the responsibility of operations managers as they build organizations and workforces. The expanding knowledge base of contemporary society requires that managers use *technology and knowledge effectively*.

More effective use of capital also contributes to productivity. It falls to the operations manager, as a productivity catalyst, to select the best new capital investments as well as to improve the productivity of existing investments.

The productivity challenge is difficult. A country cannot be a world-class competitor with second-class inputs. Poorly educated labor, inadequate capital, and dated technology are second-class inputs. High productivity and high-quality outputs require high-quality inputs, including good operations managers.

▼ *The effective use of capital often means finding the proper trade-off between investment in capital assets (automation, left) and human assets (a manual process, right). While there are risks connected with any investment, the cost of capital and physical investments is fairly clear-cut, but the cost of employees has many hidden costs including fringe benefits, social insurance, and legal constraints on hiring, employment, and termination.*

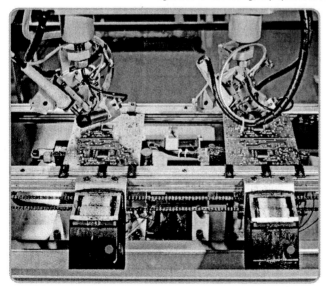

TEK Image/Photo Researchers, Inc.

John McLean, Photo Researchers, Inc.

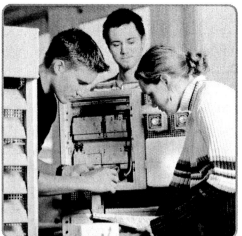

◁ *Siemens, the multi-billion-dollar German conglomerate, has long been known for its apprentice programs in its home country. Because education is often the key to efficient operations in a technological society, Siemens has spread its apprentice-training programs to its U.S. plants. These programs are laying the foundation for the highly skilled workforce that is essential for global competitiveness.*

Siemens AG

Productivity and the Service Sector

The service sector provides a special challenge to the accurate measurement of productivity and productivity improvement. The traditional analytical framework of economic theory is based primarily on goods-producing activities. Consequently, most published economic data relate to goods production. But the data do indicate that, as our contemporary service economy has increased in size, we have had slower growth in productivity.

Productivity of the service sector has proven difficult to improve because service-sector work is:

1. Typically labor-intensive (for example, counseling, teaching).
2. Frequently focused on unique individual attributes or desires (for example, investment advice).
3. Often an intellectual task performed by professionals (for example, medical diagnosis).
4. Often difficult to mechanize and automate (for example, a haircut).
5. Often difficult to evaluate for quality (for example, performance of a law firm).

The more intellectual and personal the task, the more difficult it is to achieve increases in productivity. Low-productivity improvement in the service sector is also attributable to the growth of low-productivity activities in the service sector. These include activities not previously a part of the measured economy, such as child care, food preparation, house cleaning, and laundry service. These activities have moved out of the home and into the measured economy as more and more women have joined the workforce. Inclusion of these activities has probably resulted in lower measured productivity for the service sector, although, in fact, actual productivity has probably increased because these activities are now more efficiently produced than previously.[12]

However, in spite of the difficulty of improving productivity in the service sector, improvements are being made. And this text presents a multitude of ways to make these improvements. Indeed, what can be done when management pays attention to how work actually gets done is astonishing![13]

Although the evidence indicates that all industrialized countries have the same problem with service productivity, the U.S. remains the world leader in overall productivity *and* service productivity. Retailing is twice as productive in the U.S. as in Japan, where laws protect shopkeepers from discount chains. The U.S. telephone industry is at least twice as productive as Germany's. The U.S. banking system is also 33% more efficient than Germany's banking oligopolies. However, because productivity is central to the operations manager's job and because the service sector is so large, we take special note in this text of how to improve productivity in the service sector. (See, for instance, the *OM in Action* box "Taco Bell Improves Productivity to Lower Costs.")

[12]Allen Sinai and Zaharo Sofianou, "The Service Economy—Productivity Growth Issues" (CSI Washington, DC), *The Service Economy* (January 1992): 11–16.
[13]These conclusions are not unique. See the work of Michael van Biema and Bruce Greenwald, "Managing Our Way to Higher Service-Sector Productivity," *Harvard Business Review* 75, no. 4 (July–August 1997): 89.

OM IN ACTION Taco Bell Improves Productivity to Lower Costs

Founded in 1962 by Glenn Bell, Taco Bell is seeking competitive advantage via low cost. Like many other services, Taco Bell increasingly relies on its operations function to improve productivity and reduce cost.

First, it revised its menu and designed meals that were easy to prepare. Taco Bell then shifted a substantial portion of food preparation to suppliers who could perform food processing more efficiently than a standalone restaurant. Ground beef is now precooked prior to arrival and then reheated, as are many dishes that arrive in plastic boil bags for easy sanitary reheating. Similarly, tortillas arrive already fried and onions prediced. Efficient layout and automation has cut to 8 seconds the time needed to prepare tacos and burritos and has cut time in the drive-thru lines by one minute.

These advances have been combined with training and empowerment to increase the span of management from one supervisor for 5 restaurants to one supervisor for 30 or more.

Operations managers at Taco Bell believe they have cut in-store labor by 15 hours per day and reduced floor space by more than 50%. The result is a store that can handle twice the volume with half the labor. Effective operations management has resulted in productivity increases that support Taco Bell's low-cost strategy. Taco Bell is now the fast-food low-cost leader and has a 73% share of the Mexican fast-food market.

Sources: Jackie Hueter and William Swart, *Interfaces* (January–February 1998): 75–91; and *Nation's Restaurant News* (August 15, 2005):68–70.

ETHICS AND SOCIAL RESPONSIBILITY

Operations managers are subjected to constant changes and challenges. The systems they build to convert resources into goods and services are complex. The physical and social environment changes, as do laws and values. These changes present a variety of challenges that come from the conflicting perspectives of stakeholders such as customers, distributors, suppliers, owners, lenders, and employees. These stakeholders, as well as government agencies at various levels, require constant monitoring and thoughtful responses.

Identifying ethical and socially responsible responses while building productive systems is not always clear-cut. Among the many ethical challenges facing operations managers are:

- Efficiently developing and producing safe, quality products.
- Maintaining a clean environment.
- Providing a safe workplace.
- Honoring community commitments.

Managers must do all of this in an ethical and socially responsible way while meeting the demands of the marketplace. If operations managers have a *moral awareness and focus on increasing productivity* in a system where all stakeholders have a voice, then many of the ethical challenges will be successfully addressed. The organization will use fewer resources, the employees will be committed, the market will be satisfied, and the ethical climate will be enhanced. Throughout this text, we note a variety of ways in which operations managers can take ethical and socially responsible actions to successfully address these challenges. We also end each chapter with an *Ethical Dilemma* exercise.

Summary

Operations, marketing, and finance/accounting are the three functions basic to all organizations. The operations function creates goods and services. Much of the progress of operations management has been made in the twentieth century, but since the beginning of time, humankind has been attempting to improve its material well-being. Operations managers are key players in the battle for improved productivity.

However, as societies become increasingly affluent, more of their resources are devoted to services. In the U.S., more than three-quarters of the workforce is employed in the service sector. Productivity improvements are difficult to achieve, but operations managers are the primary vehicle for making improvements.

Key Terms

Production	Pure service	Multifactor productivity
Operations management (OM)	Service sector	Productivity variables
Management process	Productivity	Knowledge society
Services	Single-factor productivity	

Solved Problems

⊙ **Virtual Office Hours help is available on Student DVD.**

Solved Problem 1

Productivity can be measured in a variety of ways, such as by labor, capital, energy, material usage, and so on. At Modern Lumber, Inc., Art Binley, president and producer of apple crates sold to growers, has been able, with his current equipment, to produce 240 crates per 100 logs. He currently purchases 100 logs per day, and each log requires 3 labor-hours to process. He believes that he can hire a professional buyer who can buy a better-quality log at the same cost. If this is the case, he can increase his production to 260 crates per 100 logs. His labor-hours will increase by 8 hours per day.

What will be the impact on productivity (measured in crates per labor-hour) if the buyer is hired?

solution

(a)
$$\text{Current labor productivity} = \frac{240 \text{ crates}}{100 \text{ logs} \times 3 \text{ hours/log}}$$
$$= \frac{240}{300}$$
$$= .8 \text{ crates per labor-hour}$$

(b)
$$\begin{array}{l}\text{Labor productivity} \\ \text{with buyer}\end{array} = \frac{260 \text{ crates}}{(100 \text{ logs} \times 3 \text{ hours/log}) + 8 \text{ hours}}$$
$$= \frac{260}{308}$$
$$= .844 \text{ crates per labor-hour}$$

Using current productivity (.80 from [a]) as a base, the increase will be 5.5% (.844/.8 = 1.055, or a 5.5% increase).

Solved Problem 2

Art Binley has decided to look at his productivity from a multifactor (total factor productivity) perspective (refer to Solved Problem 1). To do so, he has determined his labor, capital, energy, and material usage and decided to use dollars as the common denominator. His total labor-hours are now 300 per day and will increase to 308 per day. His capital and energy costs will remain constant at $350 and $150 per day, respectively. Material costs for the 100 logs per day are $1,000 and will remain the same. Because he pays an average of $10 per hour (with fringes), Binley determines his productivity increase as follows:

solution

	Current System		System with Professional Buyer	
Labor:	300 hrs. @ $10 =	$3,000	308 hrs. @ $10 =	$3,080
Material:	100 logs/day	1,000		1,000
Capital:		350		350
Energy:		150		150
Total Cost:		$4,500		$4,580

Multifactor productivity of current system:
= 240 crates/4,500 = .0533 crates/dollar

Multifactor productivity of proposed system:
= 260 crates/4,580 = .0568 crates/dollar

Using current productivity (.0533) as a base, the increase will be .066. That is, .0568/.0533 = 1.066, or a 6.6% increase.

Self-Test

- **Before taking the self-test**, refer to the learning objectives listed at the beginning of the selection and the key terms listed at the end of the selection.
- Use the key at the back of the text to **correct** your answers.
- **Restudy** pages that correspond to any questions you answered incorrectly or material you feel uncertain about.

1. OM jobs constitute what percentage of all jobs?
   a) 20%
   b) 35%
   c) 18%
   d) 40%

2. Productivity increases when:
   a) inputs increase while outputs remain the same.
   b) inputs decrease while outputs remain the same.
   c) outputs decrease while inputs remain the same.
   d) inputs and outputs increase proportionately.
   e) inputs increase at the same rate as outputs.

3. The capital investment each year in the U.S. usually:
   a) decreases.
   b) remains constant.
   c) increases.
   d) decreases unless favorably taxed.
   e) is very cyclical.

4. Productivity increases each year in the U.S. are the result of three factors:
   a) labor, capital, management
   b) engineering, labor, capital
   c) engineering, capital, quality control
   d) engineering, labor, data processing
   e) engineering, capital, data processing

5. Which appears to provide the best opportunity for increases in productivity?
   a) labor
   b) capital
   c) management
   d) engineering

6. When returns to labor, capital, or management are increased without increased productivity, prices:
   a) rise.
   b) fall.
   c) stay the same.
   d) unable to determine.

7. Problems in the measurement of productivity include:
   a) the unknown effect of external elements.
   b) the absence of precise units of measure.
   c) the effects of quality over time.
   d) all of the above.

8. The person who introduced standardized, interchangeable parts was:
   a) Eli Whitney.
   b) Henry Ford.
   c) Adam Smith.
   d) W. Edwards Deming.
   e) Frederick W. Taylor.

Internet and Student CD-ROM/DVD Exercises

Visit our Companion Web site or use your student CD-ROM/DVD to help with material in this chapter.

 On Our Companion Web site, www.prenhall.com/heizer
- Self-Study Quizzes
- Practice Problems
- Virtual Company Tour
- Power Point Lecture

⊙ **On Your Student CD-ROM**
- Practice Problems
- POM for Windows

⊙ **On Your Student DVD**
- Video Clips and Video Case
- Virtual Office Hours for Solved Problems

Discussion Questions

1. Why should one study operations management?
2. Identify four people who have contributed to the theory and techniques of operations management.
3. Briefly describe the contributions of the four individuals identified in the preceding question.
4. Figure 1 outlines the operations, finance/accounting, and marketing functions of three organizations. Prepare a chart similar to Figure 1 outlining the same functions for one of the following:
   (a) a newspaper
   (b) a drugstore
   (c) a college library
   (d) a summer camp
   (e) a small costume-jewelry factory
5. Answer question 4 for some other organization, perhaps an organization where you have worked.
6. What are the three basic functions of a firm?
7. Name the 10 decision areas of operations management.
8. Name four areas that are significant to improving labor productivity.
9. The U.S., and indeed much of the world, has been described as a "knowledge society." How does this affect productivity measurement and the comparison of productivity between the U.S. and other countries?
10. What are the measurement problems that occur when one attempts to measure productivity?
11. Mass customization and rapid product development were identified as current trends in modern manufacturing operations. What is the relationship, if any, between these trends? Can you cite any examples?
12. What are the five reasons productivity is difficult to improve in the service sector?
13. Describe some of the actions taken by Taco Bell to increase productivity that have resulted in Taco Bell's ability to serve "twice the volume with half the labor."

Ethical Dilemma

Major corporations with overseas subcontractors (such as Ikea in Bangladesh, Unilever in India, and Nike in China) have been criticized, often with substantial negative publicity, when children as young as 10 have been found working in the subcontractor's facilities. The standard response is to perform an audit and then enhance controls so it does not happen again. In one such case, a 10-year-old was terminated. Shortly thereafter, the family, without the 10-year-old's contribution to the family income, lost its modest home, and the 10-year-old was left to scrounge in the local dump for scraps of metal. Was the decision to hire the 10-year-old ethical? Was the decision to terminate the 10-year-old ethical?

Problems*

• 1 John Lucy makes wooden boxes in which to ship motorcycles. John and his three employees invest a total of 40 hours per day making the 120 boxes.
a) What is their productivity?
b) John and his employees have discussed redesigning the process to improve efficiency. If they can increase the rate to 125 per day, what will be their new productivity?
c) What will be their percentage *increase* in productivity and percentage change? P×

• 2 Riverside Metal Works produces cast bronze valves on a 10-person assembly line. On a recent day, 160 valves were produced during an 8-hour shift. Calculate the labor productivity of the line. P×

• 3 This year, Benson, Inc., will produce 57,600 hot water heaters at its plant in Yulee, Florida, in order to meet expected global demand. To accomplish this, each laborer at the Yulee plant will work 160 hours per month. If the labor productivity at the plant is 0.15 hot water heaters per labor hour, how many laborers are employed at the plant?

• 4 As a library or Internet assignment, find the U.S. productivity rate (increase) last year for the (a) national economy, (b) manufacturing sector, and (c) service sector.

• 5 Lori produces "Final Exam Care Packages" for resale by her sorority. She is currently working a total of 5 hours per day to produce 100 care packages.
a) What is Lori's productivity?
b) Lori thinks that by redesigning the package, she can increase her total productivity to 133 care packages per day. What will be her new productivity?
c) What will be the percentage increase in productivity if Lori makes the change? P×

•• 6 Eric Johnson makes billiard balls in his New England plant. With recent increases in his costs, he has a newfound interest in efficiency. Eric is interested in determining the productivity of his organization. He would like to know if his organization is maintaining the manufacturing average of 3% increase in productivity. He has the following data representing a month from last year and an equivalent month this year:

	Last Year	Now
Units produced	1,000	1,000
Labor (hours)	300	275
Resin (pounds)	50	45
Capital invested ($)	10,000	11,000
Energy (BTU)	3,000	2,850

*Note: P× means the problem may be solved with POM for Windows and/or Excel OM.

Show the productivity percentage change for each category and then determine the improvement for labor-hours, the typical standard for comparison. P×

•• 7 Eric Johnson (using data from Problem 6) determines his costs to be as follows:
• *Labor:* $10 per hour
• *Resin:* $5 per pound
• *Capital expense:* 1% per month of investment
• *Energy:* $.50 per BTU.
Show the percent change in productivity for one month last year versus one month this year, on a multifactor basis with dollars as the common denominator. P×

• 8 Kleen Karpet cleaned 65 rugs in October, consuming the following resources:

Labor:	520 hours at $13 per hour
Solvent:	100 gallons at $5 per gallon
Machine rental:	20 days at $50 per day

a) What is the labor productivity per dollar?
b) What is the multifactor productivity? P×

•• 9 David Upton is president of Upton Manufacturing, a producer of Go-Kart tires. Upton makes 1,000 tires per day with the following resources:

Labor:	400 hours per day @ $12.50 per hour
Raw material:	20,000 pounds per day @ $1 per pound
Energy:	$5,000 per day
Capital:	$10,000 per day

a) What is the labor productivity per labor-hour for these tires at Upton Manufacturing?
b) What is the multifactor productivity for these tires at Upton Manufacturing?
c) What is the percent change in multifactor productivity if Upton can reduce the energy bill by $1,000 per day without cutting production or changing any other inputs? P×

•• 10 Sawyer's, a local bakery, is worried about increased costs—particularly energy. Last year's records can provide a fairly good estimate of the parameters for this year. Judy Sawyer, the owner, does not believe things have changed much, but she did invest an additional $3,000 for modifications to the bakery's ovens to make them more energy-efficient. The modifications were supposed to make the ovens at least 15% more efficient. Sawyer has asked you to check the energy savings of the new ovens and also to look over other measures of the bakery's productivity to see if the

Andreas Buck/Das Fotoarchiv, Peter Arnold, Inc.

modifications were beneficial. You have the following data to work with:

	Last Year	Now
Production (dozen)	1,500	1,500
Labor (hours)	350	325
Capital investment ($)	15,000	18,000
Energy (BTU)	3,000	2,750

•• 11 Cunningham Performance Auto, Inc., modifies 375 autos per year. The manager, Peter Cunningham, is interested in obtaining a measure of overall performance. He has asked you to provide him with a multifactor measure of last year's performance as a benchmark for future comparison. You have assembled the following data. Resource inputs were: labor, 10,000 hours; 500 suspension and engine modification kits; and energy, 100,000 kilowatt-hours. Average labor cost last year was $20 per hour, kits cost $1,000 each, and energy costs were $3 per kilowatt-hour. What do you tell Mr. Cunningham?

•• 12 Lake Charles Seafood makes 500 wooden packing boxes for fresh seafood per day, working in two 10-hour shifts. Due to increased demand, plant managers have decided to operate three 8-hour shifts instead. The plant is now able to produce 650 boxes per day. Calculate the company's productivity before the change in work rules and after the change. What is the percent increase in productivity?

••• 13 Charles Lackey operates a bakery in Idaho Falls, Idaho. Because of its excellent product and excellent location, demand has increased by 25% in the last year. On far too many occasions, customers have not been able to purchase the bread of their choice. Because of the size of the store, no new ovens can be added. At a staff meeting, one employee suggested ways to load the ovens differently so that more loaves of bread can be baked at one time. This new process will require that the ovens be loaded by hand, requiring additional manpower. This is the only thing to be changed. If the bakery makes 1,500 loaves per month with a labor productivity of 2.344 loaves per labor-hour, how many workers will Lackey need to add? (*Hint:* Each worker works 160 hours per month.)

•• 14 Refer to Problem 13. The pay will be $8 per hour for employees. Charles Lackey can also improve the yield by purchasing a new blender. The new blender will mean an increase in his investment. This added investment has a cost of $100 per month, but he will achieve the same output (an increase to 1,875) as the change in labor hours. Which is the better decision?
a) Show the productivity change, in loaves per dollar, with an increase in labor cost (from 640 to 800 hours).
b) Show the new productivity, in loaves per dollar, with only an increase in investment ($100 per month more).
c) Show the percent productivity change for labor and investment.

••• 15 Refer to Problems 13 and 14. If Charles Lackey's utility costs remain constant at $500 per month, labor at $8 per hour, and cost of ingredients at $0.35 per loaf, but Charles does not purchase the blender suggested in Problem 14, what will be the productivity of the bakery be? What will be the percent increase or decrease?

•• 16 In December, General Motors produced 6,600 customized vans at its plant in Detroit. The labor productivity at this plant is known to have been 0.10 vans per labor-hour during that month. If 300 laborers were employed at the plant that month, how many hours did the average laborer work that month?

•• 17 Natalie Attired runs a small job shop where garments are made. The job shop employs eight workers. Each worker is paid $10 per hour. During the first week of March, each worker worked 45 hours. Together, they produced a batch of 132 garments. Of these garments, 52 were "seconds" (meaning that they were flawed). The seconds were sold for $90 each at a factory outlet store. The remaining 80 garments were sold to retail outlets at a price of $198 per garment. What was the labor productivity, in dollars per labor-hour, at this job shop during the first week of March?

Case Studies

National Air Express

National Air is a competitive air-express firm with offices around the country. Frank Smith, the Chattanooga, Tennessee, station manager, is preparing his quarterly budget report, which will be presented at the Southeast regional meeting next week. He is very concerned about adding capital expense to the operation when business has not increased appreciably. This has been the worst first quarter he can remember: snowstorms, earthquakes, and bitter cold. He has asked Martha Lewis, field services supervisor, to help him review the available data and offer possible solutions.

Service Methods

National Air offers door-to-door overnight air-express delivery within the U.S. Smith and Lewis manage a fleet of 24 trucks to handle freight in the Chattanooga area. Routes are assigned by area, usually delineated by zip code boundaries, major streets, or key geographical features, such as the Tennessee River. Pickups are generally handled between 3:00 P.M. and 6:00 P.M., Monday through Friday. Driver routes are a combination of regularly scheduled daily stops and pickups that the customer calls in as needed. These call-in pickups are dispatched by radio to the driver. Most call-in customers want as late a pickup as possible, just before closing (usually at 5:00 P.M.).

When the driver arrives at each pickup location, he or she provides supplies as necessary (an envelope or box if requested) and must receive a completed air waybill for each package. Because the industry is extremely competitive, a professional, courteous driver is essential to retaining customers. Therefore, Smith has always been concerned that drivers not rush a customer to complete his or her package and paperwork.

Budget Considerations

Smith and Lewis have found that they have been unable to meet their customers' requests for a scheduled pickup on many occasions in the past quarter. Although, on average, drivers are not handling any more business, they are unable on some days to arrive at each location on time. Smith does not think he can justify increasing costs by $1,200 per week for additional trucks and drivers while productivity (measured in shipments per truck/day) has remained flat. The company has established itself as the low-cost operator in the industry but has at the same time committed itself to offering quality service and value for its customers.

Discussion Questions

1. Is the productivity measure of shipments per day per truck still useful? Are there alternatives that might be effective?
2. What, if anything, can be done to reduce the daily variability in pickup call-ins? Can the driver be expected to be at several locations at once at 5:00 P.M.?
3. How should package pickup performance be measured? Are standards useful in an environment that is affected by the weather, traffic, and other random variables? Are other companies having similar problems?

Source: Adapted from a case by Phil Pugliese under the supervision of Professor Marilyn M. Helms, University of Tennessee at Chattanooga. Reprinted by permission.

Zychol Chemicals Corporation

Bob Richards, the production manager of Zychol Chemicals, in Houston, Texas, is preparing his quarterly report, which is to include a productivity analysis for his department. One of the inputs is production data prepared by Sharon Walford, his operations analyst. The report, which she gave him this morning, showed the following:

	2006	2007
Production (units)	4,500	6,000
Raw material used (barrels of petroleum by-products)	700	900
Labor hours	22,000	28,000
Capital cost applied to the department ($)	$375,000	$620,000

Bob knew that his labor cost per hour had increased from an average of $13 per hour to an average of $14 per hour, primarily due to a move by management to become more competitive with a new company that had just opened a plant in the area. He also knew that his average cost per barrel of raw material had increased from $320 to $360. He was concerned about the accounting procedures that increased his capital cost from $375,000 to $620,000, but earlier discussions with his boss suggested that there was nothing that could be done about that allocation.

Bob wondered if his productivity had increased at all. He called Sharon into the office and conveyed the above information to her and asked her to prepare this part of the report.

Discussion Questions

1. Prepare the productivity part of the report for Mr. Richards. He probably expects some analysis of productivity inputs for all factors, as well as a multifactor analysis for both years with the change in productivity (up or down) and the amount noted.
2. The producer price index had increased from 120 to 125, and this fact seemed to indicate to Mr. Richards that his costs were too high. What do you tell him are the implications of this change in the producer price index?
3. Management's expectation for departments such as Mr. Richards's is an annual productivity increase of 5%. Did he reach this goal?

Source: Professor Hank Maddux III, Sam Houston State University.

Hard Rock Cafe: Operations Management in Services

Video Case

In its 37 years of existence, Hard Rock has grown from a modest London pub to a global power managing 121 cafes, 5 hotels, casinos, live music venues, and a huge annual Rockfest concert. This puts Hard Rock firmly in the service industry—a sector that employs over 75% of the people in the U.S. Hard Rock moved its world headquarters to Orlando, Florida, in 1988 and has expanded to more than 40 locations throughout the U.S., serving over 100,000 meals each day. Hard Rock chefs are modifying the menu from classic American—burgers and chicken wings—to include higher-end items such as stuffed veal chops and lobster tails. Just as taste in music changes over time, so does Hard Rock Cafe, with new menus, layouts, memorabilia, services, and strategies.

At Orlando's Universal Studios, a traditional tourist destination, Hard Rock Cafe serves over 3,500 meals each day. The cafe employs about 400 people. Most are employed in the restaurant, but some work in the retail shop. Retail is now a standard and increasingly prominent feature in Hard Rock Cafes (since close to 48% of revenue comes from this source). Cafe employees include kitchen and wait staff, hostesses, and bartenders. Hard Rock employees are not only competent in their job skills but are also passionate about music and have engaging personalities. Cafe staff is scheduled down to 15-minute intervals to meet seasonal and daily demand changes in the tourist environment of Orlando. Surveys are done on a regular basis to evaluate quality of food and service at the cafe.

Scores are rated on a 1 to 7 scale, and if the score is not a 7, the food or service is a failure.

Hard Rock is adding a new emphasis on live music and is redesigning its restaurants to accommodate the changing tastes. Since Eric Clapton hung his guitar on the wall to mark his favorite bar stool, Hard Rock has become the world's leading collector and exhibitor of rock 'n' roll memorabilia, with changing exhibits at its cafes throughout the world. The collection includes 1,000's of pieces, valued at $40 million. In keeping with the times, Hard Rock also maintains a Web site, **www.hardrock.com**, which receives over 100,000 hits per week, and a weekly cable television program on VH-1. Hard Rock's brand recognition, at 92%, is one of the highest in the world.

Discussion Questions*

1. From your knowledge of restaurants, from the video, from the *Global Company Profile* that opens this chapter, and from the case itself, identify how each of the 10 decisions of operations management is applied at Hard Rock Cafe.
2. How would you determine the productivity of the kitchen staff and wait staff at Hard Rock?
3. How are the 10 decisions of OM different when applied to the operations manager of a service operation such as Hard Rock versus an automobile company such as Ford Motor Company?

*You may wish to play this video case on your DVD before addressing these questions.

Additional Case Study

Harvard has selected this Harvard Business School case to accompany this chapter:

harvardbusinessonline.hbsp.harvard.edu

- **Taco Bell Corp.** (#692-058): Illustrates the power of breakthrough thinking in a service industry.

Bibliography

Deo, Balbinder S., and Doug Strong. "Cost: The Ultimate Measure of Productivity." *Industrial Management* 42, no. 3 (May–June 2000): 20–23.

Dewan, Sanjeev. "Information Technology and Productivity: Evidence from Country-Level Data." *Management Science* 46, no. 4 (April 2000): 548–562.

Hounshell, D. A. *From the American System to Mass Production 1800–1932: The Development of Manufacturing.* Baltimore: Johns Hopkins University Press, 1985.

Lewis, William W., *The Power of Productivity.* Chicago: University of Chicago Press, 2004.

Sahay, B. S. "Multi-factor Productivity Measurement Model for Service Organization." *International Journal of*

Productivity and Performance Management 54, no. 1–2 (2005):7–23.

Tangen, S. "Demystifying Productivity and Performance." *International Journal of Productivity and Performance Measurement* 54, no. 1–2 (2005):34–47.

Taylor, F. W. *The Principles of Scientific Management.* New York: Harper & Brothers, 1911.

van Biema, Michael, and Bruce Greenwald. "Managing Our Way to Higher Service-Sector Productivity." *Harvard Business Review* 75, no. 4 (July–August 1997): 87–95.

Wrege, C. D. *Frederick W. Taylor, the Father of Scientific Management: Myth and Reality.* Homewood, IL: Business One Irwin, 1991.

Internet Resources

American Productivity and Quality Center: **www.apqc.org**

American Statistical Association (ASA) offers business and economics DataLinks, a searchable index of statistical data: **www.econ-datalinks.org**

Economics and Statistics Administration: **www.esa.doc.gov**

Federal Statistics: **www.fedstats.gov**

National Bureau of Economic Research: **www.nber.org**

U.S. Bureau of Labor Statistics: **stats.bls.gov**

U.S. Census Bureau: **www.census.gov**

Solutions to Even Numbered Problems

2 2 valves/hr.
4 Varies by site and source.
6 Productivity of labor: 9.3%
   Productivity of resin: 11.1%
   Productivity of capital: −10.0%
   Productivity of energy: 6.1%
8 **(a)** .0096 rugs/labor-dollar
   (b) .00787 rugs/dollar
10 Productivity of capital dropped; labor and energy productivity increased.

12 Before: 25 boxes/hr.
   After: 27.08 boxes/hr.
   Increase: 8.3%
14 **(a)** .293 loaves/dollar
   (b) .359 loaves/dollar
   (c) Labor change: 0%; Investment change: 22.5%
16 220 hours per laborer; 66,000 labor hours

Solutions to Self Test

1. d; **2.** b; **3.** c; **4.** a; **5.** c; **6.** a; **7.** d, **8.** a.

Chapter 2

Operations Strategy in a Global Environment

Operations Strategy in a Global Environment

Outline

Global Company Profile: Boeing

A Global View of Operations
- Cultural and Ethical Issues

Developing Missions and Strategies
- Mission
- Strategy

Achieving Competitive Advantage Through Operations
- Competing on Differentiation
- Competing on Cost
- Competing on Response

Ten Strategic OM Decisions

Issues in Operations Strategy
- Research
- Preconditions
- Dynamics

Strategy Development and Implementation
- Critical Success Factors and Core Competencies
- Build and Staff the Organization
- Integrate OM with Other Activities

Learning Objectives

When you complete this selection you should be able to

1. Define mission and strategy
2. Identify and explain three strategic approaches to competitive advantage
3. Identify and define the 10 decisions of operations management
4. Identify five OM strategy insights provided by PIMS research
5. Identify and explain four global operations strategy options

From *Operations Management*, 9/e. Jay Heizer. Barry Render. Copyright © 2008 by Pearson Education. All rights reserved.

Boeing's Global Strategy Yields Competitive Advantage

Boeing's strategy for its 787 Dreamliner is unique from both an engineering and global perspective.

The Dreamliner incorporates the latest in a wide range of aerospace technologies, from airframe and engine design to superlightweight titanium graphite laminate, carbon fiber and epoxy, and composites. Another innovation is the electronic monitoring system that allows the airplane to report maintenance requirements to ground-based computer systems. Boeing has also worked with General Electric and Rolls-Royce to develop more efficient engines. The advances in engine technology contribute as much as 8% of the increased fuel/payload efficiency of the new airplane, representing a nearly two-generation jump in technology.

Boeing Commercial Airplane Group

▲ With the 787's state-of-the-art design, more spacious interior, and global suppliers, Boeing has garnered record sales worldwide.

Some of the International Suppliers of Boeing 787 Components

Latecoere	France	Passenger doors
Labinel	France	Wiring
Dassault	France	Design and PLM software
Messier-Bugatti	France	Electric brakes
Thales	France	Electrical power conversion system and integrated standby flight display
Messier-Dowty	France	Landing gear structure
Diehl	Germany	Interior lighting
Cobham	UK	Fuel pumps and valves
Rolls-Royce	UK	Engines
Smiths Aerospace	UK	Central computer system
BAE Systems	UK	Electronics
Alenia Aeronautica	Italy	Upper center fuselage and horizontal stabilizer
Toray Industries	Japan	Carbon fiber for wing and tail units
Fuji Heavy Industries	Japan	Center wing box
Kawasaki Heavy Industries	Japan	Forward fuselage, fixed sections of wing, landing gear wheel well
Teijin Seiki	Japan	Hydraulic actuators
Mitsubishi Heavy Industries	Japan	Wing box
Chengdu Aircraft Group	China	Rudder
Hafei Aviation	China	Parts
Korean Airlines	South Korea	Wingtips
Saab	Sweden	Cargo and access doors

This state-of-the-art Boeing 787 is also *global*. Led by Boeing at its Everett, Washington, facility, an international team of aerospace companies developed the airplane. New technologies, new design, new manufacturing processes, and committed international suppliers are helping Boeing and its partners achieve unprecedented levels of performance in design, manufacture, and operation.

The 787 is global with a range of 8,300 miles. And it is global because it is being built across the world. With a huge financial risk of over $5 billion, Boeing needed partners. The global nature of both technology and the aircraft market meant finding exceptional developers and suppliers, wherever they might be. It also meant finding firms willing to step up to the risk associated with a very expensive new product. These partners not only spread the risk but also bring commitment to the table. Countries that have a stake in the 787 are more likely to buy from Boeing than from the European competitor Airbus Industries.

Boeing teamed with more than 20 international systems suppliers to develop technologies and design concepts for the 787. Boeing found its 787 partners in over a dozen countries; a few of them are shown in the table on the left.

The Japanese companies Toray, Teijin Seiki, Fuji, Kawasaki, and Mitsubishi are producing over 35% of the project, providing whole composite fuselage sections. Italy's Alenia Aeronautica is building an additional 10% of the plane.

Many U.S. companies, including Crane Aerospace, Fairchild Controls, Goodrich, General Dynamics, Hamilton Sundstrand, Honeywell, Moog, Parker Hannifin, Rockwell Collins, Vought Aircraft, and Triumph Group are also suppliers. Boeing has 70% to 80% of the Dreamliner built by other companies. And even some of the portion built by Boeing is produced at Boeing facilities outside the U.S., in Australia and Canada.

The global Dreamliner is efficient, has a global range, and is made from components produced around the world. The result: a state-of-the-art airplane reflecting the global nature of business in the 21st century and one of the fastest-selling commercial jets in history.

Boeing Commercial Airplane Group

▲ *Boeing's collaborative technology enables a "virtual workspace" that allows engineers on the 787, including partners in Australia, Japan, Italy, Canada and across the United States, to make concurrent design changes to the airplane in real time. Designing, building, and testing the 787 digitally before production reduced design errors and improved production efficiencies.*

◄ *Components from Boeing's worldwide supply chain come together on an assembly line in Everett, Washington. Although components come from throughout the world, about 35% of the 787 structure comes from Japanese companies.*

▶ *State-of-the-art composite sections of the 787 such as this fuselage section are built around the world and shipped to Boeing for final assembly.*

Today's operations manager must have a global view of operations strategy. Since the early 1990s, nearly 3 billion people in developing countries have overcome the cultural, religious, ethnic, and political barriers that constrain productivity and are now players on the global economic stage. As these barriers disappear, simultaneous advances are being made in technology, reliable shipping, and cheap communication. The unsurprising result is the growth of world trade, global capital markets, and the international movement of people; see Figure 1(a), (b), and (c). This means: increasing economic integration and interdependence of countries—in a word, globalization.[1] In response, organizations are hastily extending their operations globally with innovative strategies. For instance:

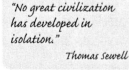

"No great civilization has developed in isolation."

Thomas Sewell

- Boeing is competitive because both its sales and production are worldwide.
- Italy's Benetton moves inventory to stores around the world faster than its competition by building flexibility into design, production, and distribution.
- Sony purchases components from suppliers in Thailand, Malaysia, and elsewhere around the world for assembly in its electronic products.
- Volvo, considered a Swedish company, is controlled by a U.S. company, Ford. But the current Volvo S40 is built in Belgium on a platform shared with the Mazda 3 (built in Japan) and the Ford Focus (built and sold in Europe.)
- China's Haier (pronounced "higher") is now producing compact refrigerators (it has one-third of the U.S. market) and refrigerated wine cabinets (it has half of the U.S. market) in South Carolina.

Globalization means that domestic production and exporting may no longer be a viable business model; local production and exporting no longer guarantee success or even survival. There are new standards of global competitiveness that impact quality, variety, customization, convenience, timeliness, and cost. The globalization of strategy contributes efficiency and adds value to products and services, but it also complicates the operations manager's job. Complexity, risk and competition are intensified; companies must carefully account for them.

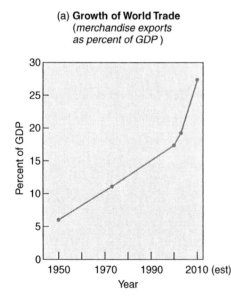

(a) Growth of World Trade (*merchandise exports as percent of GDP*)

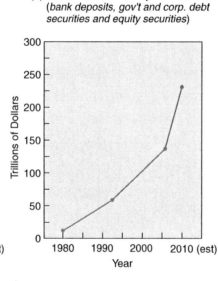

(b) Growth of Global Capital Markets (*bank deposits, gov't and corp. debt securities and equity securities*)

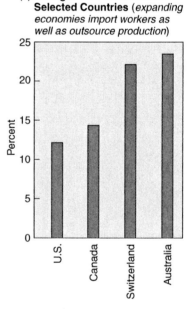

(c) Foreign Born Residents in Selected Countries (*expanding economies import workers as well as outsource production*)

▲ **Figure 1** Movement of Goods, Capital, and People is Reflected in (a) Growth of World Trade, (b) Growth of Global Capital Markets, and (c) Foreign-Born Residents

Sources: Federal Reserve Bank of Dallas (May–June 2006) and (July–August 2005); *McKinsey Quarterly* (July 26, 2006); and Organization for Economic Cooperation and Development (OECD).

[1]See Thomas Friedman's *The World Is Flat: A Brief History of the Twenty-first Century*, Farrar, Straus, and Giroux, 2005, for his stimulating discussion of how new players, new playing field, and new processes ensure the rapid expansion of globalization.

A GLOBAL VIEW OF OPERATIONS

We have identified six reasons domestic business operations decide to change to some form of international operation. They are:

1. Reduce costs (labor, taxes, tariffs, etc.).
2. Improve supply chain.
3. Provide better goods and services.
4. Understand markets.
5. Learn to improve operations.
6. Attract and retain global talent.

Let us examine, in turn, each of the six reasons.

Reduce Costs Many international operations seek to take advantage of the tangible opportunities to reduce their costs. Foreign locations with lower wages can help lower both direct and indirect costs. (See the *OM in Action* box "U.S. Cartoon Production at Home in Manila.") Less stringent government regulations on a wide variety of operation practices (e.g., environmental control, health and safety, etc.) reduce costs. Opportunities to cut the cost of taxes and tariffs also encourage foreign operations. In Mexico, the creation of **maquiladoras** (free trade zones) allows manufacturers to cut their costs of taxation by paying only on the value added by Mexican workers. If a U.S. manufacturer, such as GM, brings a $500 engine to a maquiladora operation for assembly work costing $25, tariff duties will be charged only on the $25 of work performed in Mexico.

Shifting low-skilled jobs to another country has several potential advantages. First, and most obviously, the firm may reduce costs. Second, moving the lower skilled jobs to a lower cost location frees higher cost workers for more valuable tasks. Third, reducing wage costs allows the savings to be invested in improved products and facilities (and the retraining of existing workers, if necessary) at the home location. The impact of this approach is shown in the *OM in Action* box "Going Global to Compete."

Trade agreements have also helped reduce tariffs and thereby reduce the cost of operating facilities in foreign countries. The **World Trade Organization (WTO)** has helped reduce tariffs from 40% in 1940 to less than 3% today. Another important trade agreement is the **North American Free Trade Agreement (NAFTA)**. NAFTA seeks to phase out all trade and tariff barriers among Canada, Mexico, and the U.S. Other trade agreements that are accelerating global trade include APEC (the Pacific Rim countries), SEATO (Australia, New Zealand, Japan, Hong Kong, South Korea, New Guinea, and Chile), and MERCOSUR (Argentina, Brazil, Paraguay, and Uruguay).

Maquiladoras
Mexican factories located along the U.S.–Mexico border that receive preferential tariff treatment.

World Trade Organization (WTO)
An international organization that promotes world trade by lowering barriers to the free flow of goods across borders.

NAFTA
A free trade agreement between Canada, Mexico, and the U.S.

OM in Action U.S. Cartoon Production at Home in Manila

Fred Flintstone is not from Bedrock. He is actually from Manila, capital of the Philippines. So are Tom and Jerry, Aladdin, and Donald Duck. More than 90% of American television cartoons are produced in Asia and India, with the Philippines leading the way. With their natural advantage of English as an official language and a strong familiarity with U.S. culture, animation companies in Manila now employ more than 1,700 people. Filipinos think Western, and "you need to have a group of artists that can understand the humor that goes with it," says Bill Dennis, a Hanna-Barbera executive.

Major studios like Disney, Marvel, Warner Brothers, and Hanna-Barbera send *storyboards*—cartoon action outlines—and voice tracks to the Philippines. Artists there draw, paint, and film about 20,000 sketches for a 30-minute episode. The cost of $130,000 to produce an episode in the Philippines compares with $160,000 in Korea and $500,000 in the U.S.

Sources: The New York Times (February 26, 2004): A29; and *The Wall Street Journal* (August 9, 2005): D8.

European Union (EU)

A European trade group that has 27 member states.

Another trading group is the **European Union (EU)**.[2] The European Union has reduced trade barriers among the participating European nations through standardization and a common currency, the euro. However, this major U.S. trading partner, with 490 million people, is also placing some of the world's most restrictive conditions on products sold in the EU. Everything from recycling standards to automobile bumpers to hormone-free farm products must meet EU standards, complicating international trade.

Improve the Supply Chain   The supply chain can often be improved by locating facilities in countries where unique resources are available. These resources may be expertise, labor, or raw material. For example, auto-styling studios from throughout the world are migrating to the auto mecca of southern California to ensure the necessary expertise in contemporary auto design. Similarly, world athletic shoe production has migrated from South Korea to Guangzhou, China: this location takes advantage of the low-cost labor and production competence in a city where 40,000 people work making athletic shoes for the world. And a perfume essence manufacturer wants a presence in Grasse, France, where much of the world's perfume essences are prepared from the flowers of the Mediterranean.

Provide Better Goods and Services   Although the characteristics of goods and services can be objective and measurable (e.g., number of on-time deliveries), they can also be subjective and less measurable (e.g., sensitivity to culture). We need an ever better understanding of differences in culture and of the way business is handled in different countries. Improved understanding as the result of a local presence permits firms to customize products and services to meet unique cultural needs in foreign markets.

Another reason for international operations is to reduce response time to meet customers' changing product and service requirements. Customers who purchase goods and services from U.S. firms are increasingly located in foreign countries. Providing them with quick and adequate service is often improved by locating facilities in their home countries.

Understand Markets   Because international operations require interaction with foreign customers, suppliers, and other competitive businesses, international firms inevitably learn about opportunities for new products and services. Europe led the way with cell phone innovations, and now the Japanese lead with the latest cell phone fads. Knowledge of these markets not only helps firms understand where the market is going but also helps firms diversify their customer base, add production flexibility, and smooth the business cycle.

OM in Action   Going Global to Compete

Banking giant Wachovia Corp. of Charlotte, North Carolina, has inked a $1.1 billion deal with India's Genpact to outsource finance and accounting jobs. Wachovia has also handed over administration of its human resources programs to Illinois-based Hewitt Associates. This is "what we need to do to become a great customer-relationship company," says Wachovia executive P. J. Sidebottom. The expected cost savings of $600 million to $1 billion over the next three years will be invested in the U.S. to boost the core banking business. These investments will be made in new ATMs, branches, and personnel.

Similarly, Dana Corp. of Toledo, Ohio, is also taking a global approach. Dana established a joint venture with Cardanes S.A. to produce truck transmissions in Queretaro, Mexico. Then Dana switched 288 U.S. employees in its Jonesboro, Arkansas, plant from producing truck transmissions at breakeven to axle production at a profit. Productivity is up in Jonesboro, and the Mexican joint venture is making money. Employees in both Jonesboro and Queretaro, as well as stockholders, came out ahead on the move. Dana is also moving operations to China, India, Eastern Europe, and South America.

Resourceful organizations like Wachovia and Dana use a global perspective to become more efficient, which allows them to develop new products, retrain employees, and invest in new plant and equipment.

Sources: Business Week (January 30, 2006): 50–64; *Forbes* (May 8, 2006): 58; and **www.dana.com/news/**.

---

[2]The 27 members of the European Union (EU) as of 2007 were Austria, Belgium, Bulgaria, Cyprus, Czech Republic, Denmark, Estonia, Finland, France, Germany, Greece, Hungary, Ireland, Italy, Latvia, Lithuania, Luxembourg, Malta, the Netherlands, Poland, Portugal, Romania, Slovakia, Slovenia, Spain, Sweden, United Kingdom: not all have adopted the Euro.

A worldwide strategy places added burdens on operations management. Because of economic and lifestyle differences, designers must target products to each market. For instance, clothes washers sold in northern countries must spin-dry clothes much better than those in warmer climates, where consumers are likely to line-dry them. Similarly, as shown here, Whirlpool refrigerators sold in Bangkok are manufactured in bright colors because they are often put in living rooms.

Kraipit Phanvut, SIPA Press

Another reason to go into foreign markets is the opportunity to expand the *life cycle* (i.e., stages a product goes through) of an existing product. While some products in the U.S. are in a "mature" stage of their product life cycle, they may represent state-of-the-art products in less developed countries. For example, the U.S. market for personal computers could be characterized as "mature" but as in the "introductory" stage in many developing countries, such as Albania, Vietnam, and Myanmar (Burma).

Learn to Improve Operations   Learning does not take place in isolation. Firms serve themselves and their customers well when they remain open to the free flow of ideas. For example, GM found that it could improve operations by jointly building and running, with the Japanese, an auto assembly plant in San Jose, California. This strategy allows GM to contribute its capital and knowledge of U.S. labor and environmental laws while the Japanese contribute production and inventory ideas. GM also used its employees and experts from Japan to help design its U.S. Saturn plant around production ideas from Japan. Similarly, operations managers have improved equipment and layout by learning from the ergonomic competence of the Scandinavians.

Attract and Retain Global Talent   Global organizations can attract and retain better employees by offering more employment opportunities. They need people in all functional areas and areas of expertise worldwide. Global firms can recruit and retain good employees because they provide both greater growth opportunities and insulation against unemployment during times of economic downturn. During economic downturns in one country or continent, a global firm has the means to relocate unneeded personnel to more prosperous locations. Global organizations also provide incentives for people who like to travel or take vacations in foreign countries.

So, to recap, successfully achieving a competitive advantage in our shrinking world means maximizing all of the possible opportunities, from tangible to intangible, that international operations can offer.

Globalization may take us to the floating factory: A six-person crew will take a factory from port to port to obtain the best market, material, labor, and tax advantages. The service industry, by way of the floating resort (the cruise ship), already provides such an example.

Cultural and Ethical Issues

One of the great challenges as operations go global is reconciling differences in social and cultural behavior. With issues ranging from bribery, to child labor, to the environment, managers sometimes do not know how to respond when operating in a different culture. What one country's culture deems acceptable may be considered unacceptable or illegal in another.

In the last decade, changes in international laws, agreements, and codes of conduct have been applied to define ethical behavior among managers around the world. The World Trade Organization, for example, helps to make uniform the protection of both governments and industries from foreign firms that engage in unethical conduct. Even on issues where significant differences between cultures exist, as in the area of bribery or the protection of intellectual property, global uniformity is slowly being accepted by most nations.

"The ethics of the world market are very clear. Manufacturers will move wherever it is cheapest or most convenient to their interests."

Carlos Arias Macelli, owner of a Guatemala plant that supplies JCPenney

In spite of cultural and ethical differences, we live in a period of extraordinary mobility of capital, information, goods, and even people. We can expect this to continue. The financial sector, the telecommunications sector, and the logistics infrastructure of the world are healthy institutions that foster efficient and effective use of capital, information, and goods. Globalization, with all its opportunities and risks, is here and will continue. It must be embraced as managers develop their missions and strategies.

DEVELOPING MISSIONS AND STRATEGIES

Learning Objective

1. Define mission and strategy

Mission

The purpose or rationale for an organization's existence.

An effective operations management effort must have a *mission* so it knows where it is going and a *strategy* so it knows how to get there. This is the case for a small or domestic organization, as well as a large international organization.

Mission

Economic success, indeed survival, is the result of identifying missions to satisfy a customer's needs and wants. We define the organization's **mission** as its purpose—what it will contribute to society. Mission statements provide boundaries and focus for organizations and the concept around which the firm can rally. The mission states the rationale for the organization's existence. Developing a good strategy is difficult, but it is much easier if the mission has been well defined. Figure 2 provides examples of mission statements.

Once an organization's mission has been decided, each functional area within the firm determines its supporting mission. By *functional area* we mean the major disciplines required by the firm, such as marketing, finance/accounting, and production/operations. Missions for each function are developed to support the firm's overall mission. Then within that function lower-level supporting missions are established for the OM functions. Figure 3 provides such a hierarchy of sample missions.

▶ **Figure 2**

Mission Statements for Four Organizations

Sources: Annual reports: courtesy of FedEx and Merck; Hard Rock Cafe: *Employee Handbook.* Arnold Palmer Hospital.

FedEx
FedEx is committed to our People-Service-Profit philosophy. We will produce outstanding financial returns by providing totally reliable, competitively superior, global air–ground transportation of high-priority goods and documents that require rapid, time-certain delivery. Equally important, positive control of each package will be maintained utilizing real time electronic tracking and tracing systems. A complete record of each shipment and delivery will be presented with our request for payment. We will be helpful, courteous, and professional to each other and the public. We will strive to have a completely satisfied customer at the end of each transaction.
Merck
The mission of Merck is to provide society with superior products and services—innovations and solutions that improve the quality of life and satisfy customer needs—to provide employees with meaningful work and advancement opportunities and investors with a superior rate of return.
Hard Rock Cafe
Our Mission: To spread the spirit of Rock 'n' Roll by delivering an exceptional entertainment and dining experience. We are committed to being an important, contributing member of our community and offering the Hard Rock family a fun, healthy, and nurturing work environment while ensuring our long-term success.
Arnold Palmer Hospital
Arnold Palmer Hospital is a healing environment providing family-centered care with compassion, comfort and respect ... when it matters most.

Sample Company Mission
To manufacture and service an innovative, growing, and profitable worldwide microwave communications business that exceeds our customers' expectations.

Sample Operations Management Mission
To produce products consistent with the company's mission as the worldwide low-cost manufacturer.

Sample OM Department Missions	
Product design	To design and produce products and services with outstanding quality and inherent customer value.
Quality management	To attain the exceptional value that is consistent with our company mission and marketing objectives by close attention to design, procurement, production, and field service opportunities.
Process design	To determine and design or produce the production process and equipment that will be compatible with low-cost product, high quality, and a good quality of work life at economical cost.
Location	To locate, design, and build efficient and economical facilities that will yield high value to the company, its employees, and the community.
Layout design	To achieve, through skill, imagination, and resourcefulness in layout and work methods, production effectiveness and efficiency while supporting a high quality of work life.
Human resources	To provide a good quality of work life, with well-designed, safe, rewarding jobs, stable employment, and equitable pay, in exchange for outstanding individual contribution from employees at all levels.
Supply-chain management	To collaborate with suppliers to develop innovative products from stable, effective, and efficient sources of supply.
Inventory	To achieve low investment in inventory consistent with high customer service levels and high facility utilization.
Scheduling	To achieve high levels of throughput and timely customer delivery through effective scheduling.
Maintenance	To achieve high utilization of facilities and equipment by effective preventive maintenance and prompt repair of facilities and equipment.

◀ **Figure 3**

Sample Missions for a Company, the Operations Function, and Major OM Departments

Strategy

With the mission established, strategy and its implementation can begin. **Strategy** is an organization's action plan to achieve the mission. Each functional area has a strategy for achieving its mission and for helping the organization reach the overall mission. These strategies exploit opportunities and strengths, neutralize threats, and avoid weaknesses. In the following sections we will describe how strategies are developed and implemented.

Firms achieve missions in three conceptual ways: (1) differentiation, (2) cost leadership, and (3) response.[3] This means operations managers are called on to deliver goods and services that are (1) *better*, or at least different, (2) *cheaper*, and (3) more *responsive*. Operations managers translate these *strategic concepts* into tangible tasks to be accomplished. Any one or combination

Strategy

How an organization expects to achieve its missions and goals.

Learning Objective

2. Identify and explain three strategic approaches to competitive advantage

---

[3]See related discussion in Michael E. Porter, *Competitive Strategy: Techniques for Analyzing Industries and Competitors* (New York: The Free Press, 1980). Also see Donald C. Hambrick and James W. Fredrickson, "Are You Sure You Have a Strategy?" *Academy of Management Executive* 15, no. 4 (November 2001): 48–59.

Video 2.1

Operations Strategy at Regal Marine

of these three strategic concepts can generate a system that has a unique advantage over competitors. For example, Hunter Fan has differentiated itself as a premier maker of quality ceiling fans that lower heating and cooling costs for its customers. Nucor Steel, on the other hand, satisfies customers by being the lowest-cost steel producer in the world. And Dell achieves rapid response by building personal computers with each customer's requested software in a matter of hours.

Clearly, strategies differ. And each strategy puts different demands on operations management. Hunter Fan's strategy is one of *differentiating* itself via quality from others in the industry. Nucor focuses on value at *low cost*, and Dell's dominant strategy is quick, reliable *response*.

ACHIEVING COMPETITIVE ADVANTAGE THROUGH OPERATIONS

Competitive advantage

The creation of a unique advantage over competitors.

Each of the three strategies provides an opportunity for operations managers to achieve competitive advantage. **Competitive advantage** implies the creation of a system that has a unique advantage over competitors. The idea is to create customer value in an efficient and sustainable way. Pure forms of these strategies may exist, but operations managers will more likely be called on to implement some combination of them. Let us briefly look at how managers achieve competitive advantage via *differentiation*, *low cost*, and *response*.

Competing on Differentiation

Safeskin Corporation is number one in latex exam gloves because it has differentiated itself and its products. It did so by producing gloves that were designed to prevent allergic reactions about which doctors were complaining. When other glove makers caught up, Safeskin developed hypoallergenic gloves. Then it added texture to its gloves. Then it developed a synthetic disposable glove for those allergic to latex—always staying ahead of the competition. Safeskin's strategy is to develop a reputation for designing and producing reliable state-of-the-art gloves, thereby differentiating itself.

Differentiation

Distinguishing the offerings of an organization in a way that the customer perceives as adding value.

Differentiation is concerned with providing *uniqueness*. A firm's opportunities for creating uniqueness are not located within a particular function or activity but can arise in virtually everything the firm does. Moreover, because most products include some service, and most services include some product, the opportunities for creating this uniqueness are limited only by imagination. Indeed, **differentiation** should be thought of as going beyond both physical characteristics and service attributes to encompass everything about the product or service that influences the value that the customers derive from it. Therefore, effective operations managers assist in defining everything about a product or service that will influence the potential value to the customer. This may be the convenience of a broad product line, product features, or a service related to the product. Such services can manifest themselves through convenience (location of distribution centers, stores, or branches), training, product delivery and installation, or repair and maintenance services.

In the service sector, one option for extending product differentiation is through an *experience*. Differentiation by experience in services is a manifestation of the growing "experience economy."[4] The idea of **experience differentiation** is to engage the customer—to use people's five senses so they become immersed, or even an active participant, in the product. Disney does this with the Magic Kingdom. People no longer just go on a ride; they are immersed in the Magic Kingdom—surrounded by a dynamic visual and sound experience that complements the physical ride. Some rides further engage the customer by having them steer the ride or shoot targets or villains.

Experience differentiation

Engaging the customer with a product through imaginative use of the five senses, so the customer "experiences" the product.

Theme restaurants, such as Hard Rock Cafe, likewise differentiate themselves by providing an "experience." Hard Rock engages the customer with classic rock music, big-screen rock videos, memorabilia, and staff who can tell stories. In many instances, a full-time guide is available to explain the displays, and there is always a convenient retail store so the guest can take home a tangible part of the experience. The result is a "dining experience" rather than just a

Video 2.2

Hard Rock's Global Strategy

---

[4]For an engaging book on the experience economy, see Joseph Pine II and James H. Gilmore, *The Experience Economy*, (Boston: Harvard Business School Press, 1999). Also see Leonard L. Berry, Lewis P. Carbone, and Stephan H. Haeckel, "Managing the Total Customer Experience," *MIT Sloan Management Review* (spring 2002): 85–90.

meal. In a less dramatic way, your local supermarket delivers an experience when it provides music and the aroma of freshly baked bread, and when it has samples for you to taste.

Competing on Cost

Southwest Airlines has been a consistent moneymaker while other U.S. airlines have lost billions. Southwest has done this by fulfilling a need for low-cost and short-hop flights. Its operations strategy has included use of secondary airports and terminals, first-come, first-served seating, few fare options, smaller crews flying more hours, snacks-only or no-meal flights, and no downtown ticket offices.

Additionally, and less obviously, Southwest has very effectively matched capacity to demand and effectively utilized this capacity. It has done this by designing a route structure that matches the capacity of its Boeing 737, the only plane in its fleet. Second, it achieves more air miles than other airlines through faster turnarounds—its planes are on the ground less.

One driver of a low-cost strategy is a facility that is effectively utilized. Southwest and others with low-cost strategies understand this and utilize resources effectively. Identifying the optimum size (and investment) allows firms to spread overhead costs, providing a cost advantage. For instance, Wal-Mart continues to pursue its low-cost strategy with superstores, open 24 hours a day. For 20 years, it has successfully grabbed market share. Wal-Mart has driven down store overhead costs, shrinkage, and distribution costs. Its rapid transportation of goods, reduced warehousing costs, and direct shipment from manufacturers have resulted in high inventory turnover and made it a low-cost leader. Franz Colruyt, as discussed in the *OM in Action* box, is also winning with a low-cost strategy.

Low-cost leadership entails achieving maximum *value* as defined by your customer. It requires examining each of the 10 OM decisions in a relentless effort to drive down costs while meeting customer expectations of value. A low-cost strategy does *not* imply low value or low quality.

Low-cost leadership
Achieving maximum value as perceived by the customer.

Competing on Response

The third strategy option is response. Response is often thought of as *flexible* response, but it also refers to *reliable* and *quick* response. Indeed, we define **response** as including the entire range of values related to timely product development and delivery, as well as reliable scheduling and flexible performance.

Response
A set of values related to rapid, flexible, and reliable performance.

OM in Action — Low-Cost Strategy Wins at Franz Colruyt

Belgian discount food retailer Franz Colruyt NV is so obsessed with cutting costs that there are no shopping bags at its checkout counters, the lighting at its stores is dimmed to save money on electricity, and employees clock out when they go on 5-minute coffee breaks. And to keep costs down at the company's spartan headquarters on the outskirts of Brussels, employees don't have voice mail on their phones. Instead, two receptionists take messages for nearly 1,000 staffers. The messages are bellowed out every few minutes from loudspeakers peppered throughout the building.

This same approach is evident at all 160 of Colruyt's shopping outlets, which are converted factory warehouses, movie theaters, or garages, with black concrete floors, exposed electrical wires, metal shelves, and discarded boxes strewn about. There is no background music (estimated annual cost saving: 2 million euros or $2.5 million), nor are there bags for packing groceries (estimated annual cost saving: 5 million euros). And all the store's freezers have doors, so the company can save about 3 million euros a year on electricity for refrigeration.

The company also employs a team of 30 "work simplifiers"—in Colruyt jargon—whose job is to come up with new ways to improve productivity. One recently discovered that 5 seconds could be shaved from every minute it takes customers to check out if they paid at a separate station from where groceries are scanned, so that when one customer steps away from the scanner, another can step up right away.

Chief Executive Rene De Wit says Colruyt's strategy is simple: cut costs at every turn and undersell your competitors. In an industry where margins of 1% to 2% are typical, Colruyt's cost cutting is so effective that a profit margin of 6.5% dwarfs those of rivals.

A low-cost strategy places significant demands on operations management, but Franz Colruyt, like Wal-Mart, makes it work.

Sources: The Wall Street Journal (September 22, 2003): R3, R7; and DC Velocity (September 2004): 38–40.

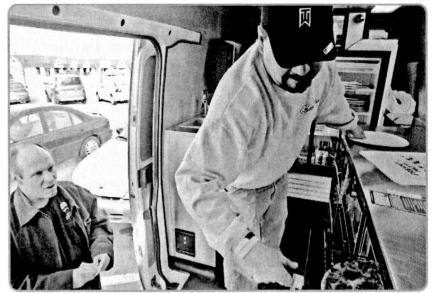

▶ *Response strategy wins orders at Super Fast Pizza. Using a wireless connection, orders are transmitted to $20,000 kitchens in vans. The driver, who works solo, receives a printed order, goes to the kitchen area, pulls premade pizzas from the cooler, and places them in the oven— it takes about 1 minute. The driver then delivers the pizza—sometimes even arriving before the pizza is ready.*

AP Wide World Photos

Flexible response may be thought of as the ability to match changes in a marketplace where design innovations and volumes fluctuate substantially.

Hewlett-Packard is an exceptional example of a firm that has demonstrated flexibility in both design and volume changes in the volatile world of personal computers. HP's products often have a life cycle of months, and volume and cost changes during that brief life cycle are dramatic. However, HP has been successful at institutionalizing the ability to change products and volume to respond to dramatic changes in product design and costs—thus building a *sustainable competitive advantage.*

The second aspect of response is the *reliability* of scheduling. One way the German machine industry has maintained its competitiveness despite having the world's highest labor costs is through reliable response. This response manifests itself in reliable scheduling. German machine firms have meaningful schedules—and they perform to these schedules. Moreover, the results of these schedules are communicated to the customer and the customer can, in turn, rely on them. Consequently, the competitive advantage generated through reliable response has value to the end customer.

The third aspect of response is *quickness.* Johnson Electric, discussed in the *OM in Action* box, competes on speed—speed in design, production, and delivery. Whether it is a production

OM in Action — Response Strategy at Hong Kong's Johnson Electric

Patrick Wang, managing director of Johnson Electric Holdings, Ltd., walks through his Hong Kong headquarters with a micromotor in his hand. This tiny motor, about twice the size of his thumb, powers a Dodge Viper power door lock. Although most people have never heard of Johnson Electric, we all have several of its micromotors nearby. This is because Johnson is the world's leading producer of micromotors for cordless tools, household appliances (such as coffee grinders and food processors), personal care items (such as hair dryers and electric shavers), and cars. A luxury Mercedes, with its headlight wipers, power windows, power seat adjustments, and power side mirrors, may use 50 Johnson micromotors.

Like all truly global businesses, Johnson spends liberally on communications to tie together its global network of factories, R&D facilities, and design centers. For example, Johnson Electric installed a $20 million videoconfer-

encing system that allows engineers in Cleveland, Ohio, and Stuttgart, Germany, to monitor trial production of their micromotors in China.

Johnson's first strength is speed in product development, speed in production, and speed in delivering—13 million motors a month, mostly assembled in China but delivered throughout the world. Its second strength is the ability to stay close to its customers. Johnson has design and technical centers scattered across the U.S., Europe, and Japan. "The physical limitations of the past are gone" when it comes to deciding where to locate a new center, says Patrick Wang. "Customers talk to us where they feel most comfortable, but products are made where they are most competitive."

Sources: Hoover's Company Records (January 1, 2006): 58682; *Far Eastern Economic Review* (May 16, 2002): 44–45; and *The Economist* (June 22, 1996): 65.

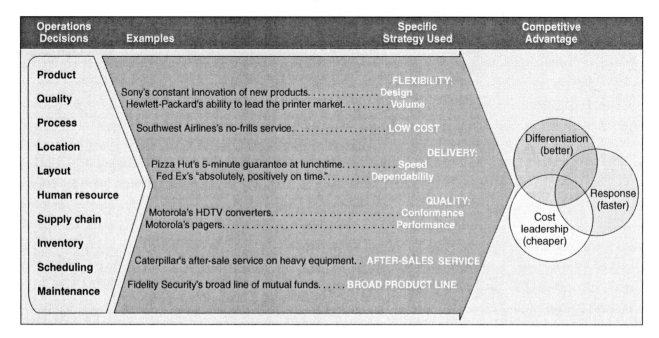

Operations Decisions	Examples	Specific Strategy Used	Competitive Advantage

Product
Quality
Process
Location
Layout
Human resource
Supply chain
Inventory
Scheduling
Maintenance

FLEXIBILITY:
Sony's constant innovation of new products. . . . . Design
Hewlett-Packard's ability to lead the printer market. . . . . Volume

Southwest Airlines's no-frills service. . . . . LOW COST

DELIVERY:
Pizza Hut's 5-minute guarantee at lunchtime. . . . . Speed
Fed Ex's "absolutely, positively on time.". . . . . Dependability

QUALITY:
Motorola's HDTV converters. . . . . Conformance
Motorola's pagers. . . . . Performance

Caterpillar's after-sale service on heavy equipment. . AFTER-SALES SERVICE

Fidelity Security's broad line of mutual funds. . . . . . BROAD PRODUCT LINE

Differentiation (better)
Response (faster)
Cost leadership (cheaper)

▲ **Figure 4** **Operations Management's Contribution to Strategy**

system at Johnson Electric, a lunch delivered in 15 minutes at Bennigan's, or customized pagers delivered in three days from Motorola, the operations manager who develops systems that respond quickly can have a competitive advantage.

In practice, these three *concepts* —differentiation, low cost, and response—are often implemented via the six *specific strategies* shown in Figure 4: (1) flexibility in design and volume, (2) low cost, (3) delivery, (4) quality, (5) after-sales service, and (6) a broad product line. Through these six specific strategies, OM can increase productivity and generate a sustainable competitive advantage. Proper implementation of the following decisions by operations managers will allow these strategies to be achieved.

> *"In the future, there will be just two kinds of firms: those who disrupt their markets and those who don't survive the assault."*
>
> *Professor Richard D'Aveni, author of Hypercompetition*

TEN STRATEGIC OM DECISIONS

Differentiation, low cost, and response can be achieved when managers make effective decisions in 10 areas of OM. These are collectively known as **operations decisions**. The 10 decisions of OM that support missions and implement strategies follow:

1. *Goods and service design:* Designing goods and services defines much of the transformation process. Costs, quality, and human resource decisions are often determined by design decisions. Designs usually determine the lower limits of cost and the upper limits of quality.
2. *Quality:* The customer's quality expectations must be determined and policies and procedures established to identify and achieve that quality.
3. *Process and capacity design:* Process options are available for products and services. Process decisions commit management to specific technology, quality, human resource use, and maintenance. These expenses and capital commitments determine much of the firm's basic cost structure.
4. *Location selection:* Facility location decisions for both manufacturing and service organizations may determine the firm's ultimate success. Errors made at this juncture may overwhelm other efficiencies.
5. *Layout design:* Material flows, capacity needs, personnel levels, technology decisions, and inventory requirements influence layout.
6. *Human resources and job design:* People are an integral and expensive part of the total system design. Therefore, the quality of work life provided, the talent and skills required, and their costs must be determined.

Learning Objective

3. Identify and define the 10 decisions of operations management

Operations decisions
The strategic decisions of OM are goods and service design, quality, process design, location selection, layout design, human resources and job design, supply chain management, inventory, scheduling, and maintenance.

7. *Supply chain management:* These decisions determine what is to be made and what is to be purchased. Consideration is also given to quality, delivery, and innovation, all at a satisfactory price. Mutual trust between buyer and supplier is necessary for effective purchasing.

8. *Inventory:* Inventory decisions can be optimized only when customer satisfaction, suppliers, production schedules, and human resource planning are considered.

9. *Scheduling:* Feasible and efficient schedules of production must be developed; the demands on human resources and facilities must be determined and controlled.

10. *Maintenance:* Decisions must be made regarding desired levels of reliability and stability, and systems must be established to maintain that reliability and stability.

> *"Operations is typically thought of as an execution of strategy; for us it is the strategy."*
>
> Joe R. Lee,
> Former chairman of
> Darden Restaurants

Operations managers implement these 10 decisions by identifying key tasks and the staffing needed to achieve them. However, the implementation of decisions is influenced by a variety of issues, including a product's proportion of goods and services (see Table 1). Few products are either all goods or all services. Although the 10 decisions remain the same for both goods and services, their relative importance and method of implementation depend on this ratio of goods and services. Throughout this text, we discuss how strategy is selected and implemented for both goods and services through these 10 operations management decisions.

Let's look at an example of strategy development through one of the 10 decisions.

EXAMPLE 1

Strategy development

Pierre Alexander has just completed chef school and is ready to open his own restaurant. After examining both the external environment and his prospective strengths and weaknesses, he makes a decision on the mission for his restaurant, which he defines as "To provide outstanding French fine dining for the people of Chicago."

Approach: Alexander's supporting operations strategy is to ignore the options of *cost leadership* and *quick response* and focus on *differentiation*. Consequently, his operations strategy requires him to evaluate product designs (menus and meals) and selection of process, layout, and location. He must also evaluate the human resources, suppliers, inventory, scheduling, and maintenance that will support his mission and a differentiation strategy.

Solution: Examining just one of these 10 decisions, *process design*, requires that Alexander consider the issues presented in the following figure.

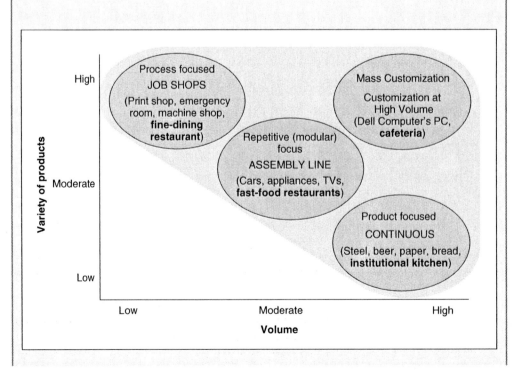

The first option is to operate in the lower right corner of the preceding figure, where he could produce high volumes of food with a limited variety, much as in an institutional kitchen. Such a process could produce large volumes of standard items such as baked goods and mashed potatoes prepared with state-of-the-art automated equipment. Alexander concludes that this is not an acceptable process option.

Alternatively, he can move to the middle of the figure, where he could produce more variety and lower volumes. Here he would have less automation and use prepared modular components for meals, much as a fast-food restaurant does. Again, he deems such process designs inappropriate for his mission.

Another option is to move to the upper right corner and produce a high volume of customized meals, but neither Alexander nor anyone else knows how to do this with gourmet meals.

Finally, Alexander can design a process that operates in the upper left corner of the figure, which requires little automation but lends itself to high variety. This process option suggests that he build an extremely flexible kitchen suitable for a wide variety of custom meals catering to the whims of each customer. With little automation, such a process would be suitable for a huge variety. This process strategy will support his mission and desired product differentiation. Only with a process such as this can he provide the fine French-style gourmet dining that he has in mind.

Insight: By considering the options inherent in each of the 10 OM decisions, managers—Alexander, in this case—can make decisions that support the mission.

Learning exercise: If Alexander's mission were to offer less expensive meals and reduce the variety offered but still do so with a French flair, what might his process strategy be? [Answer: Alexander might try a repetitive (modular) strategy and mimic the La Madeleine cafeteria-style restaurants.]

▼ **Table 1**   **The Differences Between Goods and Services Influence How the 10 Operations Management Decisions Are Applied**

Operations Decisions	Goods	Services
Goods and service design	Product is usually tangible.	Product is not tangible. A new range of product attributes—a smile.
Quality	Many objective quality standards.	Many subjective quality standards—nice color.
Process and capacity design	Customer is not involved in most of the process.	Customer may be directly involved in the process—a haircut.
		Capacity must match demand to avoid lost sales—customers often avoid waiting.
Location selection	May need to be near raw materials or labor force.	May need to be near customer—car rental.
Layout design	Layout can enhance production efficiency.	Can enhance product as well as production—layout of a fine-dining restaurant.
Human resources and job design	Workforce focused on technical skills. Labor standards can be consistent. Output-based wage system possible.	Direct workforce usually needs to be able to interact well with customer—bank teller. Labor standards vary depending on customer requirements—legal cases.
Supply chain management	Supply chain relationships critical to final product.	Supply chain relationships important but may not be critical
Inventory	Raw materials, work-in-process, and finished goods may be inventoried.	Most services cannot be stored; so other ways must be found to accommodate fluctuations in demand—can't store haircuts.
Scheduling	Ability to inventory may allow leveling of production rates.	Often concerned with meeting the customer's immediate schedule with human resources.
Maintenance	Maintenance is often preventive and takes place at the production site.	Maintenance is often "repair" and takes place at the customer's site.

▼ **Table 2** Operations Strategies of Two Drug Companies

	Brand Name Drugs, Inc.	Generic Drug Corp.
Competitive Advantage	**Product Differentiation**	**Low Cost**
Product Selection and Design	Heavy R&D investment; extensive labs; focus on development in a broad range of drug categories	Low R&D investment; focus on development of generic drugs
Quality	Quality is major priority, standards exceed regulatory requirements	Meets regulatory requirements on a country-by-country basis as necessary
Process	Product and modular production process; tries to have long product runs in specialized facilities; builds capacity ahead of demand	Process focused; general production processes; "jobshop" approach, short-run production; focus on high utilization
Location	Still located in city where it was founded	Recently moved to low-tax, low-labor-cost environment
Layout	Layout supports automated product-focused production	Layout supports process-focused "job shop" practices
Human Resources	Hire the best; nationwide searches	Very experienced top executives provide direction; other personnel paid below industry average
Supply Chain	Long-term supplier relationships	Tends to purchase competitively to find bargains
Inventory	Maintains high finished goods inventory primarily to ensure all demands are met	Process focus drives up work-in-process inventory; finished goods inventory tends to be low
Scheduling	Centralized production planning	Many short-run products complicate scheduling
Maintenance	Highly trained staff; extensive parts inventory	Highly trained staff to meet changing demands

The 10 decisions of operations management are implemented in ways that provide competitive advantage, not just for fine-dining restaurants, but for all the goods and services that enrich our lives. How this might be done for two drug companies, one seeking a competitive advantage via differentiation, and the other via low cost, is shown in Table 2.

ISSUES IN OPERATIONS STRATEGY

Once a firm has formed a mission, developing and implementing a specific strategy requires that the operations manager consider a number of issues. We will examine these issues in three ways. First, we look at what *research* tells us about effective operations management strategies. Second, we identify some of the *preconditions* to developing effective OM strategy. Third, we look at the *dynamics* of OM strategy development.

Research

PIMS

A program established in cooperation with GE to identify characteristics of high-return-on-investment firms.

Learning Objective

4. Identify five OM strategy insights provided by PIMS research

Strategic insight has been provided by the findings of the Strategic Planning Institute.[5] Its **PIMS** program (profit impact of market strategy) was established in cooperation with the General Electric Corporation. PIMS has collected nearly 100 data items from about 3,000 cooperating organizations. Using the data collected and high *return on investment* (ROI)[6] as a measure of success, PIMS has been able to identify some characteristics of high-ROI firms. Among those characteristics that affect strategic OM decisions are:

1. High product quality (relative to the competition).
2. High capacity utilization.
3. High operating efficiency (the ratio of expected to actual employee productivity).
4. Low investment intensity (the amount of capital required to produce a dollar of sales).
5. Low direct cost per unit (relative to the competition).

[5]See B. Leavy, "Assessing Your Strategic Alternatives," *Strategy and Leadership* (2003): 29, or R. D. Buzzel and B. T. Gale, *The PIMS Principles* (New York: The Free Press, 1987).

[6]Like other performance measures, *return on investment* (ROI) has limitations, including sensitivity to the business cycle, depreciation policies and schedules, book value (goodwill), and transfer pricing.

These five findings support a high return on investment and should therefore be considered as an organization develops a strategy. In the analysis of a firm's relative strengths and weaknesses, these characteristics can be measured and evaluated. The specific strategic approaches suggested earlier, in Figure 4, indicate where an operations manager may want to go, but without achieving the five characteristics of firms with a high return on investment, that journey may not be successful.

Another research study indicates the significant role that OM can play in competitive strategy. When a wide mix of 248 businesses were asked to evaluate the importance of 32 categories in obtaining a sustainable competitive advantage, 28% of the categories selected fell under operations management. When quality/service is added, the total goes to 44%. The study supports the major role OM strategy plays in developing a competitive advantage.[7]

Preconditions

Before establishing and attempting to implement a strategy, the operations manager needs to understand that the firm is operating in an open system in which a multitude of factors exists. These factors influence strategy development and execution. The more thorough the analysis and understanding of both the external and internal factors, the more the likelihood of success. Although the list of factors to be considered is extensive, at a minimum it entails an understanding of:

1. Strengths and weaknesses of competitors, as well as possible new entrants into the market, substitute products, and commitment of suppliers and distributors.
2. Current and prospective environmental, technological, legal, and economic issues.
3. Product life cycle, which may dictate the limitations of operations strategy.
4. Resources available within the firm and within the OM function.
5. Integration of the OM strategy with the company's strategy and other functional areas.

"To the Japanese, strategy is so dynamic as to be thought of as 'accommodation' or 'adaptive persistence.'"
Richard Pascale, MIT Sloan Management Review

Dynamics

Strategies change for two reasons. First, strategy is dynamic because of *changes within the organization*. All areas of the firm are subject to change. Changes may occur in a variety of areas, including personnel, finance, technology, and product life. All may make a difference in an organization's strengths and weaknesses and therefore its strategy. Figure 5 shows possible change in both overall strategy and OM strategy during the product's life. For instance, as a product moves from introduction to growth, product and process design typically move from development to stability. As the product moves to the growth stage, forecasting and capacity planning become issues.

Strategy is also dynamic because of *changes in the environment*.[8] Boeing provides an example, in the opening *Global Company Profile* in this chapter, of how strategy must change as the environment changes. Its strategies, like many OM strategies, are increasingly global. Microsoft also had to adapt quickly to a changing environment. Microsoft's shift in strategy was caused by changing customer demand, security, and the Internet. Microsoft moved from operating systems to office products, to Internet service provider, and now to an integrator of computers and television.

STRATEGY DEVELOPMENT AND IMPLEMENTATION

Once firms understand the issues involved in developing an effective strategy, they evaluate their internal strengths and weaknesses as well as the opportunities and threats of the environment. This is known as **SWOT analysis** (for *S*trengths, *W*eaknesses, *O*pportunities, and *T*hreats). Beginning with SWOT analyses, firms position themselves, through their strategy, to have a competitive advantage. The firm may have excellent design skills or great talent at identifying outstanding locations. However, the firm may recognize limitations of its manufacturing process or in finding good suppliers. The idea is to maximize opportunities and minimize threats in the environment while maximizing the advantages of the organization's strengths and minimizing the weaknesses. Any preconceived ideas about mission are then reevaluated to ensure they are consistent with the SWOT analysis. Subsequently, a strategy for achieving the mission is developed. This strategy is continually evaluated against the value provided customers and competi-

SWOT analysis
A method of determining internal strengths and weaknesses and external opportunities and threats.

---

[7]See David A. Aaker, "Creating a Sustainable Competitive Advantage," *California Management Review* (winter 1989): 91–106.
[8]Anita M. McGahan, "How Industries Change," *Harvard Business Review* 82, no. 10 (October 11, 2004): 87–94.

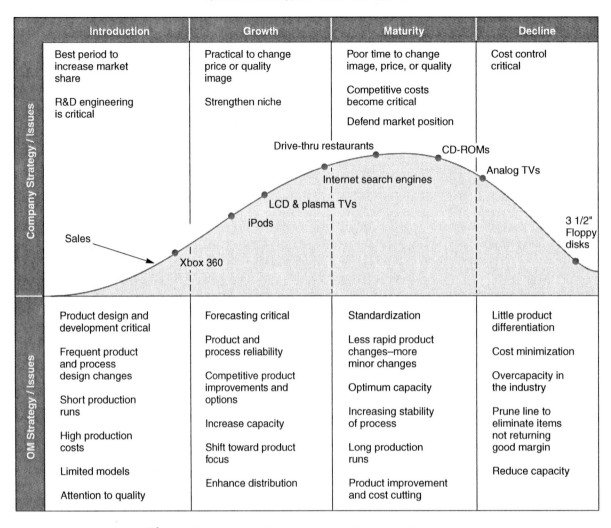

	Introduction	Growth	Maturity	Decline
Company Strategy / Issues	Best period to increase market share R&D engineering is critical	Practical to change price or quality image Strengthen niche	Poor time to change image, price, or quality Competitive costs become critical Defend market position	Cost control critical
OM Strategy / Issues	Product design and development critical Frequent product and process design changes Short production runs High production costs Limited models Attention to quality	Forecasting critical Product and process reliability Competitive product improvements and options Increase capacity Shift toward product focus Enhance distribution	Standardization Less rapid product changes–more minor changes Optimum capacity Increasing stability of process Long production runs Product improvement and cost cutting	Little product differentiation Cost minimization Overcapacity in the industry Prune line to eliminate items not returning good margin Reduce capacity

Curve labels: Sales, Xbox 360, iPods, LCD & plasma TVs, Internet search engines, Drive-thru restaurants, CD-ROMs, Analog TVs, 3 1/2" Floppy disks

▲ **Figure 5** **Strategy and Issues During a Product's Life**

tive realities. The process is shown in Figure 6. From this process critical success factors are identified.

Critical Success Factors and Core Competencies

Critical success factors (CSFs)

Activities or factors that are *key* to achieving competitive advantage.

Because no firm does everything exceptionally well, a successful strategy requires determining the firm's critical success factors and core competencies. **Critical success factors (CSFs)** are those activities that are necessary for a firm to achieve its goals. Critical success factors can be so significant that a firm must get them right to survive in the industry. A CSF for McDonald's, for example,

▶ **Figure 6**

Strategy Development Process

Environmental Analysis
Identify the strengths, weaknesses, opportunities, and threats.
Understand the environment, customers, industry, and competitors.

Determine Corporate Mission
State the reason for the firm's existence and identify the value it wishes to create.

Form a Strategy
Build a competitive advantage, such as low price, design or volume flexibility, quality, quick delivery, dependability, after-sale services, or broad product lines.

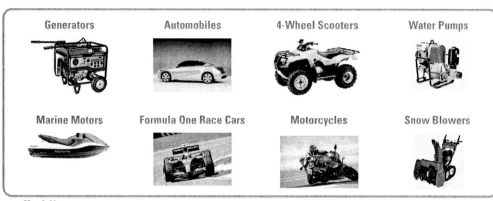

Generators   Automobiles   4-Wheel Scooters   Water Pumps

Marine Motors   Formula One Race Cars   Motorcycles   Snow Blowers

www.HondaNews.com

◀ *Honda's core competence is the design and manufacture of gas-powered engines. This competence has allowed Honda to become a leader in the design and manufacture of a wide range of gas-powered products. Tens of millions of these products are produced and shipped around the world.*

is layout. Without a play area, an effective drive-thru, and an efficient kitchen, McDonald's cannot be successful. CSFs are often necessary, but not sufficient for competitive advantage. On the other hand, **core competencies** are the set of unique skills, talents, and capabilities that a firm does at a world-class standard. They allow a firm to set itself apart and develop a competitive advantage. Organizations that prosper identify their core competencies and nurture them. While McDonald's CSFs may include layout, its core competency may be consistency and quality. Honda Motors's core competence is gas-powered engines—engines for automobiles, motorcycles, lawn mowers, generators, snow blowers, and more. The idea is to build CSFs and core competencies that provide a competitive advantage and support a successful strategy and mission. A core competence may be a subset of CSFs or a combination of CSFs. The operations manager begins this inquiry by asking:

Core competencies
A set of skills, talents, and activities that a firm does particularly well.

- "What tasks must be done particularly well for a given strategy to succeed?"
- "Which activities will help the OM function provide a competitive advantage?"
- "Which elements contain the highest likelihood of failure, and which require additional commitment of managerial, monetary, technological, and human resources?"

Only by identifying and strengthening critical success factors and core competencies can an organization achieve sustainable competitive advantage.

In this text we focus on the 10 OM decisions that typically include the CSFs. Potential CSFs for marketing, finance, and operations are shown in Figure 7. The 10 operations management

◀ **Figure 7**

Implement Strategy by Identifying and Executing Critical Success Factors and Supporting the Core Competence

Support a Core Competence and Implement Strategy by Identifying and Executing the Critical Success Factors in the Functional Areas

Marketing
Service
Distribution
Promotion
Price
Channels of distribution
Product positioning (image, functions)

Finance/Accounting
Leverage
Cost of capital
Working capital
Receivables
Payables
Financial control
Lines of credit

Operations

Decisions	Sample Options	Chapter
Product	Customized or standardized	5
Quality	Define customer expectations and how to achieve them	6,S6
Process	Facility design, capacity	7,S7
Location	Near supplier or near customer	8
Layout	Work cells or assembly line	9
Human resource	Specialized or enriched jobs	10,S10
Supply chain	Single or multiple suppliers	11,S11
Inventory	When to reorder; how much to keep on hand	12,14,16
Schedule	Stable or fluctuating production rate	13,15
Maintenance	Repair as required or preventive maintenance	17

decisions we develop in this text provide an excellent initial checklist for determining CSFs and identifying core competencies within the operations function. For instance, the 10 decisions, related CSFs, and core competencies can allow a firm to differentiate its product or service. That differentiation may be via a core competence of innovation and new products, where the CSFs are product design and speed to market, as is the case for 3M and Rubbermaid. Similarly, differentiation may be via quality, where the core competence is institutionalizing quality, as at Toyota. Differentiation may also be via maintenance, where the CSFs are product reliability and after-sale service, as is the case at IBM and Canon.

Activity map

A graphical link of competitive advantage, CSFs, and supporting activities.

Whatever the CSFs and core competences, they must be supported by the related activities. One approach to identifying the activities is an **activity map**, which links competitive advantage, CSFs, and supporting activities. For example, Figure 8 shows how Southwest Airlines, whose core competence is operations, built a set of integrated activities to support its low-cost competitive advantage. Notice how the CSFs support operations and in turn are supported by other activities.[9] The activities fit together and reinforce each other. And the better they fit and reinforce each other, the more sustainable the competitive advantage. By focusing on enhancing its core competence and CSFs with a supporting set of activities, Southwest Airlines has become one of the great airline success stories.

Build and Staff the Organization

The operations manager's job is a three-step process. Once a strategy and critical success factors have been identified, the second step is to group the necessary activities into an organizational structure. The third step is to staff it with personnel who will get the job done. The manager

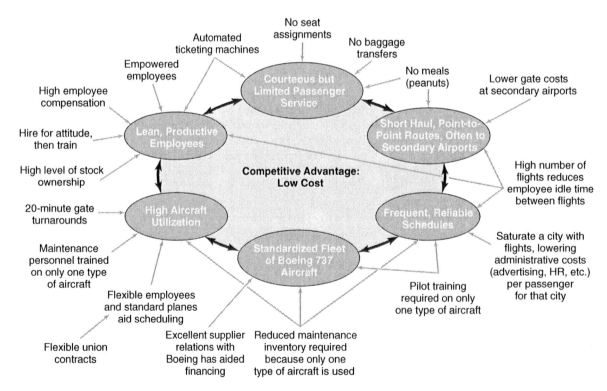

▲ **Figure 8**   Activity Mapping of Southwest Airlines's Low-Cost Competitive Advantage

To achieve a low-cost competitive advantage, Southwest has identified a number of critical success factors (connected by red arrows) and support activities (shown by blue arrows). As this figure indicates, a low-cost advantage is highly dependent on a very well run operations function.

[9]Michael E. Porter and C. Roland Christensen, "What Is Strategy?" *Harvard Business Review* (November–December 1996): 61–75.

works with subordinate managers to build plans, budgets, and programs that will successfully implement strategies that achieve missions. Firms tackle this organization of the operations function in a variety of ways.

Integrate OM with Other Activities

The organization of the operations function and its relationship to other parts of the organization vary with the OM mission. Moreover, the operations function is most likely to be successful when the operations strategy is integrated with other functional areas of the firm, such as marketing, finance, information technology, and human resources. In this way, all of the areas support the company's objectives. For example, short-term scheduling in the airline industry is dominated by volatile customer travel patterns. Day-of-week preference, holidays, seasonality, college schedules, and so on, all play a role in changing flight schedules. Consequently, airline scheduling, although an OM activity, can be a part of marketing. Effective scheduling in the trucking industry is reflected in the amount of time trucks travel loaded. However, scheduling of trucks requires information from delivery and pickup points, drivers, and other parts of the organization. When the OM function results in effective scheduling in the air passenger and commercial trucking industries, a competitive advantage can exist.

The operations manager provides a means of transforming inputs into outputs. The transformations may be in terms of storage, transportation, manufacturing, dissemination of information, and utility of the product or service. *The operations manager's job is to implement an OM strategy, provide competitive advantage, and increase productivity.*

"The manufacturing business of tomorrow will not be run by financial executives, marketers, or lawyers inexperienced in manufacturing, as so many U.S. companies are today."

Peter Drucker

GLOBAL OPERATIONS STRATEGY OPTIONS

As we suggested early in this chapter, many operations strategies now require an international dimension. We tend to call a firm with an international dimension an international business or a multinational corporation. An **international business** is any firm that engages in international trade or investment. This is a very broad category and is the opposite of a domestic, or local, firm.

A **multinational corporation (MNC)** is a firm with *extensive* international business involvement. MNCs buy resources, create goods or services, and sell goods or services in a variety of countries. The term *multinational corporation* applies to most of the world's large, well-known businesses. Certainly IBM is a good example of an MNC. It imports electronics components to the U.S. from over 50 countries, exports computers to over 130 countries, has facilities in 45 countries, and earns more than half its sales and profits abroad.

Operations managers of international and multinational firms approach global opportunities with one of four operations strategies: *international*, *multidomestic*, *global*, and *transnational* (see Figure 9). The matrix of Figure 9 has a vertical axis of cost reduction and a horizontal axis of local responsiveness. Local responsiveness implies quick response and/or the differentiation necessary for the local market. The operations manager must know how to position the firm in this matrix. Let us briefly examine each of the four strategies.

International business
A firm that engages in cross-border transactions.

Multinational corporation (MNC)
A firm that has extensive involvement in international business, owning or controlling facilities in more than one country.

International Strategy

An **international strategy** uses exports and licenses to penetrate the global arena. As Figure 9 suggests, the international strategy is the least advantageous, with little local responsiveness and little cost advantage. There is little responsiveness because we are exporting or licensing a good from the home country. And the cost advantages may be few because we are using the existing production process at some distance from the new market. However, an international strategy is often the easiest, as exports can require little change in existing operations, and licensing agreements often leave much of the risk to the licensee.

International strategy
A strategy in which global markets are penetrated using exports and licenses.

Multidomestic Strategy

The **multidomestic strategy** has decentralized authority with substantial autonomy at each business. Organizationally these are typically subsidiaries, franchises, or joint ventures with substantial independence. The advantage of this strategy is maximizing a competitive response for the

Multidomestic strategy
A strategy in which operating decisions are decentralized to each country to enhance local responsiveness.

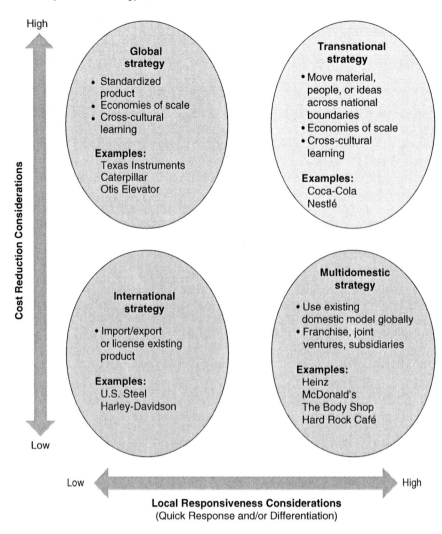

Figure 9

Four International Operations Strategies

Sources: See a similar presentation in M. Hitt, R. D. Ireland, and R. E. Hoskisson, *Strategic Management, Competitiveness and Globalization,* 6th ed. (Cincinnati: Southwestern College Publishing, 2006).

Learning Objective

5. Identify and explain four global operations strategy options

local market; however, the strategy has little or no cost advantage. Many food producers, such as Heinz, use a multidomestic strategy to accommodate local tastes because global integration of the production process is not critical. The concept is one of "we were successful in the home market, let's export the management talent and processes, not necessarily the product, to accommodate another market." McDonald's is operating primarily as a multidomestic, which gives it the local responsiveness needed to modify its menu country by country. McDonald's can then serve beer in Germany, wine in France, McHuevo (poached egg hamburger) in Uruguay, and hamburgers without beef in India. With over 2,000 restaurants in Japan and a presence of more than a generation, the average Japanese family thinks Japan invented McDonald's. Interestingly, McDonald's prefers to call itself *multilocal*.[10]

Global Strategy

Global strategy

A strategy in which operating decisions are centralized and headquarters coordinates the standardization and learning between facilities.

A **global strategy** has a high degree of centralization, with headquarters coordinating the organization to seek out standardization and learning between plants, thus generating economies of scale. This strategy is appropriate when the strategic focus is cost reduction but has little to recommend it when the demand for local responsiveness is high. Caterpillar, the world leader in earth-moving equipment, and Texas Instruments, a world leader in semiconductors, pursue global strategies. Caterpillar and Texas Instruments find this strategy advantageous because the end products are similar throughout the world. Earth-moving equipment is the same in Nigeria as

[10]James L. Watson, ed., *Golden Arches East: McDonald's in East Asia* (Stanford University Press, 1997): 12. *Note:* McDonald's also operates with some of the advantages of a global organization. By using very similar product lines throughout the world, McDonald's obtains some of the standardization advantages of a global strategy. However, it manages to retain the advantages of a multidomestic strategy.

Komatsu Ltd.

Louis Psihoyos. Science Faction Images

⚠ *In a continuing fierce worldwide battle, both Komatsu and Caterpillar seek global advantage in the heavy equipment market. As Komatsu (left) moved west to the UK, Caterpillar (right) moved east, with 13 facilities and joint ventures in China. Both firms are building equipment throughout the world as cost and logistics dictate. Their global strategies allow production to move as markets, risk, and exchange rates dictate.*

in Iowa, which allows Caterpillar to have individual factories focus on a limited line of products to be shipped worldwide. This results in economies of scale and learning within each facility. A global strategy also allows Texas Instruments to build optimum-size plants with similar process and to then maximize learning by aggressive communication between plants. The result is an effective cost reduction advantage for Texas Instruments.

Transnational Strategy

A **transnational strategy** exploits the economies of scale and learning, as well as pressure for responsiveness, by recognizing that core competence does not reside in just the "home" country but can exist anywhere in the organization. *Transnational* describes a condition in which material, people, and ideas cross—or *transgress*—national boundaries. These firms have the potential to pursue all three operations strategies (i.e., differentiation, low cost, and response). Such firms can be thought of as "world companies" whose country identity is not as important as its interdependent network of worldwide operations. Key activities in a transnational company are neither centralized in the parent company nor decentralized so that each subsidiary can carry out its own tasks on a local basis. Instead, the resources and activities are dispersed, but specialized, so as to be both efficient and flexible in an interdependent network. Nestlé is a good example of such a company. Although it is legally Swiss, 95% of its assets are held and 98% of its sales are made outside Switzerland. Fewer than 10% of its workers are Swiss. Similarly, service firms such as Asea Brown Boveri (an engineering firm that is Swedish but headquartered in Switzerland), Reuters (a news agency), Bertelsmann (a publisher), and Citicorp (a banking corporation) can be viewed as transnationals. We can expect the national identities of these transnationals to continue to fade.

Transnational strategy
A strategy that combines the benefits of global-scale efficiencies with the benefits of local responsiveness.

Summary

Global operations provide an increase in both the challenges and opportunities for operations managers. Although the task is challenging, operations managers can and do improve productivity. They can build and manage OM functions that contribute in a significant way to competitiveness. Organizations identify their strengths and weaknesses. They then develop effective missions and strategies that account for these strengths and weaknesses and complement the opportunities and threats in the environment. If this procedure is performed well, the organization can have competitive advantage through some combination of product differentiation, low cost, and response. This competitive advantage is often achieved via a move to international, multidomestic, global, or transnational strategies.

Effective use of resources, whether domestic or international, is the responsibility of the professional manager, and professional managers are among the few in our society who *can* achieve this performance. The challenge is great, and the rewards to the manager and to society substantial.

Key Terms

Maquiladoras
World Trade Organization (WTO)
North American Free Trade Agreement
    (NAFTA)
European Union (EU)
Mission
Strategy
Competitive advantage

Differentiation
Experience differentiation
Low-cost leadership
Response
Operations decisions
PIMS
SWOT analysis
Critical success factors

Core competencies
Activity map
International business
Multinational corporation (MNC)
International strategy
Multidomestic strategy
Global strategy
Transnational strategy

Solved Problem

 Virtual Office Hours help is available on Student DVD.

Solved Problem 1

Strategy at Pirelli SpA The global tire industry continues to consolidate. Michelin buys Goodrich and Uniroyal and builds plants throughout the world. Bridgestone buys Firestone, expands its research budget, and focuses on world markets. Goodyear spends almost 4% of its sales revenue on research. These three aggressive firms have come to dominate the world tire market, with total market share approaching 60%. And the German tire maker Continental AG has strengthened its position as fourth in the world, with a dominant presence in Germany. Against this formidable array, the old-line Italian tire company Pirelli SpA found it difficult to respond effectively. Although Pirelli still had 5% of the market, it was losing millions a year while the competition was getting stronger. Tires are a tough, competitive business that rewards companies having strong market shares and long production runs. Pirelli has some strengths: an outstanding reputation for excellent high-performance tires and an innovative manufacturing function.

Use a SWOT analysis to establish a feasible strategy for Pirelli.

Solution

First, find an opportunity in the world tire market that avoids the threat of the mass-market onslaught by the big three tire makers. Second, utilize the internal marketing strength represented by Pirelli's strong brand name and history of winning World Rally Championships. Third, maximize the internal innovative capabilities of the operations function.

To achieve these goals, Pirelli made a strategic shift out of low-margin standard tires and into higher-margin performance tires. Pirelli established deals with luxury brands Jaguar, BMW, Maserati, Ferrari, Bentley, and Lotus Elise and established itself as a provider of a large share of tires on new Porsches, S-class Mercedes, and Saabs. As a result, more than 70% of the company's tire production is now high-performance tires. People are willing to pay a premium for Pirellis.

The operations function continued to focus its design efforts on performance tires and developing a system of modular tire manufacture that allows much faster switching between models. This modular system, combined with investments in new manufacturing flexibility, has driven batch sizes down to as small as 150 to 200, making small-lot performance tires economically feasible. Manufacturing innovations at Pirelli have streamlined the production process, moving it from a 14-step process to a 3-step process. A threat from the big three going after the performance market remains, but Pirelli has bypassed its weakness of having a small market share. The firm now has a presence in 120 countries and sales exceeding $3.5 billion.

Sources: Just Auto (September 2005): 8–14; *Hoover's Company Records* (October 15, 2005): 41369; and *Frankfurter Allgemeine Zeitung* (February 11, 2002): 5.

Discussion Questions

1. Based on the descriptions and analyses in this chapter, would Boeing be better described as a global firm or a transnational firm? Discuss.
2. List six reasons to internationalize operations.
3. Coca-Cola is called a global product. Does this mean that Coca-Cola is formulated in the same way throughout the world? Discuss.
4. Define *mission*.
5. Define *strategy*.
6. Describe how an organization's *mission* and *strategy* have different purposes.
7. Identify the mission and strategy of your automobile repair garage. What are the manifestations of the 10 OM decisions at the garage? That is, how is each of the 10 decisions accomplished?
8. As a library or Internet assignment, identify the mission of a firm and the strategy that supports that mission.
9. How does an OM strategy change during a product's life cycle?
10. There are three primary ways to achieve competitive advantage. Provide an example, not included in the text, of each. Support your choices.
11. Describe PIMS's five characteristics of high-return-on-investment (ROI) firms.
12. Given the discussion of Southwest Airlines in the text, define an *operations* strategy for that firm.
13. How must an operations strategy integrate with marketing and accounting?

Self-Test

- **Before taking the self-test**, refer to the learning objectives listed at the beginning of the selection and the key terms listed at the end of the selection.
- Use the key at the back of the text to **correct** your answers.
- **Restudy** pages that correspond to any questions you answered incorrectly or material you feel uncertain about.

1. Among the ways for a firm to effectively use its OM function to yield competitive advantage are:
   a) rapid design changes.
   b) speed of delivery.
   c) maintain a variety of product options.
   d) all of the above.

2. A mission statement is beneficial to an organization because it:
   a) is a statement of the organization's economic purpose.
   b) provides a basis for the organization's culture.
   c) identifies important constituencies.
   d) establishes a basis for strategy formulation.
   e) ensures profitability.

3. A strategy is:
   a) a functional area of the firm.
   b) the purpose for which an organization is established.
   c) the goal that is to be achieved.
   d) an action plan to achieve a mission.
   e) a critical success factor.

4. The PIMS program developed a number of criteria that were based on evaluating firms who did well at:
   a) profitability.
   b) sustained sales growth.
   c) achieving their mission.
   d) high return on investments.
   e) establishing goals.

5. Which of the following are not characteristics of high return-on-investment firms?
   a) high variety of product options
   b) high product quality relative to the competition
   c) high capacity utilization
   d) low investment intensity
   e) all are characteristic of high ROI firms

6. A company that is organized across international boundaries with decentralized authority and substantial autonomy at each business via subsidiaries, franchises, or joint ventures has:
   a) a global strategy.
   b) a transnational strategy.
   c) an international straetgy.
   d) a multidomestic strategy.
   e) a regional strategy.

7. The relatively few activities that make a difference between a firm having and not having a competitive advantage are known as:
   a) activity maps.
   b) SWOT.
   c) critical success factors.
   d) global profile.
   e) response strategy.

8. The three strategic approaches to competitive advantage are _____, _____, and _____.

Internet and Student CD-ROM/DVD Exercises

Visit our Companion Web site or use your student CD-ROM/DVD to help with material in this chapter.

 On Our Companion Web site, www.prenhall.com/heizer
- Self-Study Quizzes
- Practice Problems
- Virtual Company Tour
- Internet Case
- Power Point Lecture

⊙ **On Your Student CD-ROM**
- Practice Problems

⊙ **On Your Student DVD**
- Video Clips and Video Cases
- Virtual Office Hours for Solved Problem

Ethical Dilemma

As a manufacturer of athletic shoes whose image, indeed performance, is widely regarded as socially responsible, you find your costs increasing. Traditionally, your athletic shoes have been made in Indonesia and South Korea. Although the ease of doing business in those countries has been improving, wage rates have also been increasing. The labor-cost differential between your present suppliers and a contractor who will get the shoes made in China now exceeds $1 per pair. Your sales next year are projected to be 10 million pairs, and your analysis suggests that this cost differential is not offset by any other tangible costs; you face only the political risk and potential damage to your commitment to social responsibility. Thus, this $1 per pair savings should flow directly to your bottom line. There is no doubt that the Chinese government engages in censorship, remains repressive, and is a long way from a democracy. Moreover, you will have little or no control over working conditions, sexual harassment, and pollution. What do you do and on what basis do you make your decision?

Problems

• 1 The text provides three primary ways—strategic approaches (differentiation, cost, and response)—for achieving competitive advantage. Provide an example of each not given in the text. Support your choices. (*Hint:* Note the examples provided in the text.)

•• 2 Within the food service industry (restaurants that serve meals to customers, but not just fast food), find examples of firms that have sustained competitive advantage by competing on the basis of (1) cost leadership, (2) response, and (3) differentiation. Cite one example in each category; provide a sentence or two in

support of each choice. Do not use fast-food chains for all categories. (*Hint:* A "99¢ menu" is very easily copied and is not a good source of sustained advantage.)

•• 3 Browse through *The Wall Street Journal*, the financial section of a daily paper, or read business news online. Seek articles that constrain manufacturing innovation and productivity—workers aren't allowed to do this, workers are not or cannot be trained to do that, this technology is not allowed, this material cannot be handled by workers, and so forth. Be prepared to share your articles in class discussion.

•• 4 Match the product with the proper parent company and country in the table below:

Product	Parent Company	Country
Arrow Shirts	**a.** Volkswagen	**1.** France
Braun Household Appliances	**b.** Bidermann International	**2.** Great Britain
Lotus Autos	**c.** Bridgestone	**3.** Germany
Firestone Tires	**d.** Campbell Soup	**4.** Japan
Godiva Chocolate	**e.** Credit Lyonnais	**5.** U.S.
Häagen-Daz Ice Cream (USA)	**f.** Ford Motor Company	**6.** Switzerland
Jaguar Autos	**g.** Procter & Gamble	**7.** Malaysia
MGM Movies	**h.** Michelin	
Lamborghini Autos	**i.** Nestlé	
Goodrich Tires	**j.** Proton	
Alpo Pet Foods		

••• 5 Identify how changes within an organization affect the OM strategy for a company. For instance, discuss what impact the following internal factors might have on OM strategy:
a) Maturing of a product.
b) Technology innovation in the manufacturing process.
c) Changes in laptop computer design that move disk drives from CD-ROM drives to DVD drives.

••• 6 Identify how changes in the external environment affect the OM strategy for a company. For instance, discuss what impact the following external factors might have on OM strategy:
a) Major increases in oil prices.
b) Water- and air-quality legislation.
c) Fewer young prospective employees entering the labor market.

d) Inflation versus stable prices.
e) Legislation moving health insurance from a pretax benefit to taxable income.

•• 7 Develop a ranking for corruption in the following countries: Mexico, Turkey, Denmark, the U.S., Taiwan, Brazil, and another country of your choice. (*Hint:* See sources such as *Transparency International*, *Asia Pacific Management News*, and *The Economist*.)

•• 8 Develop a ranking for competitiveness and/or business environment for Britain, Singapore, the U.S., Hong Kong, and Italy. (*Hint:* See the *Global Competitive Report*, *World Economic Forum*, Geneva, and *The Economist*.)

Case Studies

Minit-Lube

A substantial market exists for automobile tune-ups, oil changes, and lubrication service for more than 200 million cars on U.S. roads. Some of this demand is filled by full-service auto dealerships, some by Sears and Firestone, and some by other tire/service dealers. However, Minit-Lube, Mobil-Lube, Jiffy-Lube and others have also developed strategies to accommodate this opportunity.

Minit-Lube stations perform oil changes, lubrication, and interior cleaning in a spotless environment. The buildings are clean,

painted white, and often surrounded by neatly trimmed landscaping. To facilitate fast service, cars can be driven through three abreast. At Minit-Lube, the customer is greeted by service representatives who are graduates of Minit-Lube U. The Minit-Lube school is not unlike McDonald's Hamburger University near Chicago or Holiday Inn's training school in Memphis. The greeter takes the order, which typically includes fluid checks (oil, water, brake fluid, transmission fluid, differential grease) and the necessary lubrication, as well as filter changes for air and oil. Service personnel in neat uniforms then move into action. The standard three-person team has one person checking fluid levels under the hood, another assigned interior vacuuming and window cleaning, and the third in the garage pit, removing the oil filter, draining the oil, checking the differential and transmission, and lubricating as necessary. Precise task assignments and good training are designed to move the car into and out of the bay in 10 minutes. The idea is to charge no more, and hopefully less, than gas stations, automotive repair chains, and auto dealers, while providing better service.

Discussion Questions

1. What constitutes the mission of Minit-Lube?
2. How does the Minit-Lube operations strategy provide competitive advantage? (*Hint:* Evaluate how Minit-Lube's traditional competitors perform the 10 decisions of operations management vs. how Minit-Lube performs them.)
3. Is it likely that Minit-Lube has increased productivity over its more traditional competitors? Why? How would we measure productivity in this industry?

Strategy at Regal Marine

Video Case

Regal Marine, one of the U.S.'s 10 largest power-boat manufacturers, achieves its mission—providing luxury performance boats to customers worldwide—using the strategy of differentiation. It differentiates its products through constant innovation, unique features, and high quality. Increasing sales at the Orlando, Florida, family-owned firm suggest that the strategy is working.

As a quality boat manufacturer, Regal Marine starts with continuous innovation, as reflected in computer-aided design (CAD), high-quality molds, and close tolerances that are controlled through both defect charts and rigorous visual inspection. In-house quality is not enough, however. Because a product is only as good as the parts put into it, Regal has established close ties with a large number of its suppliers to ensure both flexibility and perfect parts. With the help of these suppliers, Regal can profitably produce a product line of 22 boats, ranging from the $14,000 19-foot boat to the $500,000 44-foot Commodore yacht.

"We build boats," says VP Tim Kuck, "but we're really in the 'fun' business. Our competition includes not only 300 other boat, canoe, and yacht manufacturers in our $17 billion industry, but home theaters, the Internet, and all kinds of alternative family enter-

tainment." Fortunately for Regal, with the strong economy and the repeal of the boat luxury tax on its side, it has been paying down debt and increasing market share.

Regal has also joined with scores of other independent boat makers in the American Boat Builders Association. Through economies of scale in procurement, Regal is able to navigate against billion-dollar competitor Brunswick (makers of the Sea Ray and Bayliner brands). The *Global Company Profile* featuring Regal Marine provides further background on Regal and its strategy.

Discussion Questions*

1. State Regal Marine's mission in your own words.
2. Identify the strengths, weaknesses, opportunities, and threats that are relevant to the strategy of Regal Marine.
3. How would you define Regal's strategy?
4. How would each of the 10 operations management decisions apply to operations decision making at Regal Marine?

*You may wish to play this video case on your DVD before addressing these questions.

Hard Rock Cafe's Global Strategy

Video Case

Hard Rock is bringing the concept of the "experience economy" to its cafe operation. The strategy is to incorporate a unique "experience" into its operations. This innovation is somewhat akin to mass customization in manufacturing. At Hard Rock, the experience concept is to provide not only a custom meal from the menu but a dining event that includes a unique visual and sound experience not duplicated anywhere else in the world. This strategy is succeeding. Other theme restaurants have come and gone while Hard Rock continues to grow. As Professor C. Markides of the London Business School says, "The trick is not to play the game better than the competition, but to develop and play an altogether different game."* At Hard Rock, the different game is the experience game.

From the opening of its first cafe in London in 1971, during the British rock music explosion, Hard Rock has been serving food and rock music with equal enthusiasm. Hard Rock Cafe has 40 U.S. locations, about a dozen in Europe, and the remainder scattered throughout the world, from Bangkok and Beijing to Beirut. New construction, leases, and investment in remodeling are long term; so a global strategy means special consideration of political risk, currency risk, and social norms in a context of a brand fit. Although

Hard Rock is one of the most recognized brands in the world, this does not mean its cafe is a natural everywhere. Special consideration must be given to the supply chain for the restaurant and its accompanying retail store. About 48% of a typical cafe's sales are from merchandise.

The Hard Rock Cafe business model is well defined, but because of various risk factors and differences in business practices and employment law, Hard Rock elects to franchise about half of its cafes. Social norms and preferences often suggest some tweaking of menus for local taste. For instance, Europeans, particularly the British, still have some fear of mad cow disease; therefore, Hard Rock is focusing less on hamburgers and beef and more on fish and lobster in its British cafes.

Because 70% of Hard Rock's guests are tourists, recent years have found it expanding to "destination" cities. While this has been a winning strategy for decades, allowing the firm to grow from 1 London cafe to 110 facilities in 41 countries, it has made Hard Rock susceptible to economic fluctuations that hit the tourist business hardest. So Hard Rock is signing a long-term lease for a new location in Nottingham, England, to join recently opened cafes in Manchester and Birmingham—cities that are not standard tourist destinations. At the same time, menus are being upgraded. Hopefully, repeat business from locals in these cities will smooth demand and make Hard Rock less dependent on tourists.

Discussion Questions[†]

1. Identify the strategy changes that have taken place at Hard Rock Cafe since its founding in 1971.

2. As Hard Rock Cafe has changed its strategy, how has its responses to some of the 10 decisions of OM changed?

3. Where does Hard Rock fit in the four international operations strategies outlined in Figure 9? Explain your answer.

*Constantinos Markides, "Strategic Innovation," *MIT Sloan Management Review* 38, no. 3 (spring 1997): 9.

†You may wish to play this video case on your DVD before addressing these questions.

Additional Case Studies

Internet Case Study: Visit our Companion Web site at www.prenhall.com/heizer for this free case study:

- **Motorola's Global Strategy:** Focuses on Motorola's international strategy.

Harvard has selected these Harvard Business School cases to accompany this chapter.

harvardbusinessonline.hbsp.harvard.edu

- **Eli Lilly and Co.: Manufacturing Process Technology Strategy—1991** (#692056): Manufacturing pursues comparative advantage in an industry where R&D is the primary competitive advantage.
- **Fresh Connections** (#600-022): Investigates how to structure operations to take advantage of the continued growth in the home meal replacement market.
- **Hitting the Wall: Nike and International Labor Practices** (#7000047): Nike must deal with a spate of alarmingly bad publicity regarding wages in developing countries.
- **Hewlett-Packard Singapore (A)** (#694035): Product development issues when source and recipients of knowledge are separated both geographically and culturally.
- **Komatsu Ltd.** (#398-016): Describes strategic and organizational transformations at Komatsu, a major Japan-based producer of construction equipment.
- **McDonald's Corp.** (#693028): Changing environment and competition forces McDonald's to rethink its operating strategy.
- **Southwest Airlines—1993 (A)** (#694023): Provides insight into Southwest's strategy, operations, marketing, and culture.
- **Toys "Я" Us Japan** (#796-077): Documents Toys "Я" Us difficulties as it enters the Japanese toy market.
- **Lenzing AG: Expanding in Indonesia** (#796-099): Presents the issues surrounding expansion in a foreign country.

Bibliography

Bhagwati, J. *In Defense of Globalization.* Oxford, UK: Oxford University Press, 2004.

Crotts, J. C., D. R. Dickson, and R. C. Ford. "Aligning Organizational Processes with Mission: The Case of Service Excellence." *Academy of Management Executive* 19, no. 3 (August 2005): 54–68.

Drucker, P. F. "The Emerging Theory of Manufacturing." *Harvard Business Review* 68, no. 3 (May–June 1990): 94–103.

Flynn, B. B., R. G. Schroeder, and E. J. Flynn. "World Class Manufacturing: An Investigation of Hayes and Wheelwright's Foundation." *Journal of Operations Management* 17, no. 3 (March 1999): 249–269.

Friedman, Thomas. *The World Is Flat: A Brief History of the Twenty-first Century.* New York: Farrar, Straus, and Giroux, 2005.

Greenwald, Bruce, and Judd Kahn. "All Strategy Is Local." *Harvard Business Review*, 83, no. 9 (September 2005): 94–104.

Kaplan, Robert S., and David P. Norton. *Strategy Maps.* Boston: Harvard Business School Publishing, 2003.

Luke, Royce D., Stephen L. Walston, and Patrick Michael Plummer. *Healthcare Strategy: In Pursuit of Competitive Advantage.* Chicago: Health Administration Press, 2003.

Porter, M. E. *The Competitive Advantage of Nations.* New York: The Free Press, 1990.

Wolf, Martin. *Why Globalization Works.* London: Yale University Press, 2004.

Womack, J. P., D. T. Jones, and D. Roos. *The Machine That Changed the World.* New York: Rawson Associates, 1990.

Internet Resources

Business Policy and Strategy, Division of the Academy of Management: **www.aom.pace.edu/bps**
European Union: **europa.eu.int/index_en.htm**
International Trade Administration: **www.ita.doc.gov**
Manufacturing Strategies, maintained at Cranfield University: **www.cranfield.ac.uk/som**

Transparency International maintains a Bribe Payers Perception Index (BPI) and a Corruption Perceptions Index: **www.transparency.de**, **www.globalcorruptionreport.org**
World Bank: **www.worldbank.org**
World Economic Forum: **www.weforum.org**
World Trade Organization: **www.wto.org**

Solutions to Even Numbered Problems

2 Cost leadership: Sodexho
Response: a catering firm
Differentiation: a fine-dining restaurant

4 The first few:
Arrow; Bidermann International, France
Braun; Procter & Gamble, U.S.
Lotus Autos; Proton, Malaysia
Firestone; Bridgestone, Japan
Godiva; Campbell Soup, U.S.

6 Some general thoughts to get you going:
(a) Energy costs change the cost structure of airlines.
(b) Environmental constraints force changes in process technology (paint manufacturing and application) and product design (autos).

8 Look at current ranking at **www.weforum.org**.

Solutions to Self Test

1. d; **2.** a; **3.** d; **4.** d; **5.** a; **6.** d; **7.** c; **8.** differentiation, cost, response.

Chapter 3

Project Management

Project Management

Outline

Learning Objectives

When you complete this selection you should be able to

1. Create a work breakdown structure
2. Draw AOA and AON networks
3. Complete both forward and backward passes for a project
4. Determine a critical path
5. Calculate the variance of activity times
6. Crash a project
7. Use Microsoft Project software to create a project

From *Operations Management*, 9/e. Jay Heizer. Barry Render. Copyright © 2008 by Pearson Education. All rights reserved.

Global Company Profile: Bechtel Group

Project Management Provides a Competitive Advantage for Bechtel

Now in its 110th year, the San Francisco–based Bechtel Group (**www.bechtel.com**) is the world's premier manager of massive construction and engineering projects. Known for billion-dollar projects, Bechtel is famous for its construction feats on the Hoover Dam, the Boston Central Artery/Tunnel project, and rebuilding of Kuwait's oil and gas infrastructure after the invasion by Iraq in 1990.

Conditions weren't what Bechtel expected when it won a series of billion-dollar contracts from the U.S. government to help reconstruct Iraq in 2003–2006. Saddam Hussein's defeat by Allied forces hadn't caused much war damage. Instead, what Bechtel found was a country that had been crumbling for years. None of the sewage plants in Baghdad worked. Power flicked on and off. Towns

QA Photos Ltd.

▲ Workers wrestle with a 1,500-ton boring machine, measuring 25 feet in diameter, that was used to dig the Eurotunnel between England and France in the early 1990s. With overruns that boosted the cost of the project to $13 billion, a Bechtel Group VP was brought in to head operations.

◀ A massive dredge hired by Bechtel removes silt from Iraq's port at Umm Qasr. This paved the way for large-scale deliveries of U.S. food and the return of commercial shipping.

Bechtel Corporation, Inc.

and cities in the anti-Hussein south had been left to decay as punishment. And to complicate matters even more, scavengers were stealing everything from museum artifacts to electric power lines. Bechtel's job was to oversee electric power, sewage, transportation, and airport repairs.

Bechtel's crews travelled under armed escort and slept in trailers surrounded by razor wire. But the company's efforts have paid off. Iraq's main seaport, Umm Qasr, was reopened when Bechtel dredged the water and repaired the grain elevators. Electrical generation was back to prewar levels in 10 months. Bechtel refurbished more than 1,200 schools.

With a global procurement program, Bechtel easily tapped the company's network of suppliers and

▶ Managing massive construction projects such as this is the strength of Bechtel. With large penalties for late completion and incentives for early completion, a good project manager is worth his or her weight in gold.

Bill Pogue/Getty Images Inc.—Stone Allstock

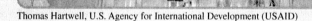

Thomas Hartwell, U.S. Agency for International Development (USAID)

▲ *Reconstructed terminal at Baghdad International Airport*

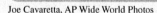

▶ Bechtel was the construction contractor for the Hoover Dam. This dam, on the Colorado River, is the highest in the Western Hemisphere.

Joe Cavaretta, AP Wide World Photos

buyers worldwide to help rebuild Iraq's infrastructure. Other interesting recent Bechtel projects include:

- Building 26 massive distribution centers, in just 2 years, for the Internet company Webvan Group ($1 billion).
- Constructing 30 high-security data centers worldwide for Equinix, Inc. ($1.2 billion).
- Building and running a rail line between London and the Channel Tunnel ($4.6 billion).
- Developing an oil pipeline from the Caspian Sea region to Russia ($850 million).
- Expanding the Dubai Airport in the United Arab Emirates ($600 million) and the Miami International Airport ($2 billion).

- Building liquefied natural gas plants in Trinidad, West Indies ($1 billion).
- Building a new subway for Athens, Greece ($2.6 billion).
- Constructing a natural gas pipeline in Thailand ($700 million).
- Building 30 plants for iMotors.com, a company that sells refurbished autos online ($300 million).
- Building a highway to link the north and south of Croatia ($303 million).

When companies or countries seek out firms to manage massive projects, they go to Bechtel, which, again and again, through outstanding project management, has demonstrated its competitive advantage.

THE IMPORTANCE OF PROJECT MANAGEMENT

- When the Bechtel project management team entered Iraq after the 2003 war, it quickly had to mobilize an international force of manual workers, construction professionals, cooks, medical personnel, and security forces. It had to access millions of tons of supplies to rebuild ports, roads, schools, and electrical systems.

- When Microsoft Corporation set out to develop Windows Vista—its biggest, most complex, and most important program to date—time was the critical factor for the project manager. With hundreds of programmers working on millions of lines of code in a program costing hundreds of millions of dollars to develop, immense stakes rode on timely delivery of the project.

Project Management at Hard Rock's Rockfest

- When Hard Rock Cafe sponsors Rockfest, hosting 100,000 plus fans at its annual concert, the project manager begins planning some 9 months earlier. Using the software package Microsoft Project, described in this chapter, each of the hundreds of details can be monitored and controlled. When a band can't reach the Rockfest site by bus because of massive traffic jams, Hard Rock's project manager is ready with a helicopter backup.

Bechtel, Microsoft, and Hard Rock are just three examples of firms that face a modern phenomenon: growing project complexity and collapsing product/service life cycles. This change stems from awareness of the strategic value of time-based competition and a quality mandate for continuous improvement. Each new product/service introduction is a unique event—a project. In addition, projects are a common part of our everyday life. We may be planning a wedding or a surprise birthday party, remodeling a house, or preparing a semester-long class project.

Scheduling projects is a difficult challenge for operations managers. The stakes in project management are high. Cost overruns and unnecessary delays occur due to poor scheduling and poor controls.

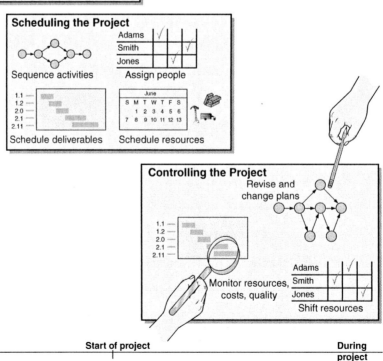

Figure 1 Project Planning, Scheduling, and Controlling

66

Projects that take months or years to complete are usually developed outside the normal production system. Project organizations within the firm may be set up to handle such jobs and are often disbanded when the project is complete. On other occasions, managers find projects just a part of their job. The management of projects involves three phases (see Figure 1):

1. *Planning:* This phase includes goal setting, defining the project, and team organization.
2. *Scheduling:* This phase relates people, money, and supplies to specific activities and relates activities to each other.
3. *Controlling:* Here the firm monitors resources, costs, quality, and budgets. It also revises or changes plans and shifts resources to meet time and cost demands.

We begin this selection with a brief overview of these functions. Three popular techniques to allow managers to plan, schedule, and control—Gantt charts, PERT, and CPM—are also described.

PROJECT PLANNING

Projects can be defined as a series of related tasks directed toward a major output. In some firms a **project organization** is developed to make sure existing programs continue to run smoothly on a day-to-day basis while new projects are successfully completed.

For companies with multiple large projects, such as a construction firm, a project organization is an effective way of assigning the people and physical resources needed. It is a temporary organization structure designed to achieve results by using specialists from throughout the firm. NASA and many other organizations use the project approach. You may recall Project Gemini and Project Apollo. These terms were used to describe teams that NASA organized to reach space exploration objectives.

The project organization works best when:

1. Work can be defined with a specific goal and deadline.
2. The job is unique or somewhat unfamiliar to the existing organization.
3. The work contains complex interrelated tasks requiring specialized skills.
4. The project is temporary but critical to the organization.
5. The project cuts across organizational lines.

Project organization

An organization formed to ensure that programs (projects) receive the proper management and attention.

The Project Manager

An example of a project organization is shown in Figure 2. Project team members are temporarily assigned to a project and report to the project manager. The manager heading the project coordinates activities with other departments and reports directly to top management. Project managers receive high visibility in a firm and are responsible for making sure that (1) all necessary activities are finished in proper sequence and on time; (2) the project comes in within budget; (3) the project meets its quality goals; and (4) the people assigned to the project receive the motivation, direction, and information needed to do their jobs. This means that project managers should be good coaches and communicators, and be able to organize activities from a variety of disciplines.

When a project organization is made permanent, it is usually called a "matrix organization."

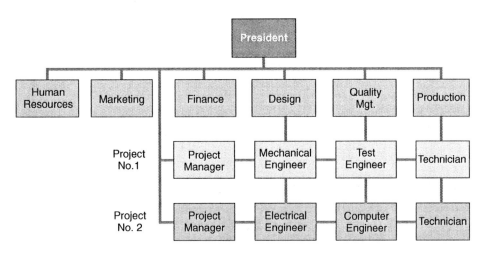

◄ **Figure 2**

A Sample Project Organization

Ethical Issues Faced in Project Management   Project managers not only have high visibility but they also face ethical decisions on a daily basis. How they act establishes the code of conduct for everyone on their project. On the personal level, project managers often deal with (1) offers of gifts from contractors, (2) pressure to alter status reports to mask the reality of delays, (3) false reports for charges of time and expenses, and (4) pressures to compromise quality to meet bonus or penalty schedules.

Other major problems in projects large and small are:

- Bid rigging—divulging confidential information to some bidders to give them an unfair advantage.
- "Low-balling" contractors—who try to "buy" the project by bidding low with the hope of recovering costs later by contract renegotiations or by simply cutting corners.
- Bribery—particularly on international projects.
- Expense account padding, use of substandard materials, compromising health/safety standards, withholding needed information.
- Failure to admit project failure at the close of the project.

Codes of ethics such as those established by the Project Management Institute (**www.pmi.org**) are one means of trying to establish standards. Research has shown that without good leadership and a strong organizational culture most people follow their own set of ethical standards and values.[1]

Learning Objective

1. Create a work breakdown structure

Work breakdown structure (WBS)

Division of a project into more and more detailed components.

Work Breakdown Structure

The project management team begins its task well in advance of project execution so that a plan can be developed. One of its first steps is to carefully establish the project's objectives, then break the project down into manageable parts. This **work breakdown structure (WBS)** defines the project by dividing it into its major subcomponents (or tasks), which are then subdivided into more detailed components, and finally into a set of activities and their related costs. The division of the project into smaller and smaller tasks can be difficult, but is critical to managing the project and to scheduling success. Gross requirements for people, supplies, and equipment are also estimated in this planning phase.

The work breakdown structure typically decreases in size from top to bottom and is indented like this:

Level
1 Project
2   Major tasks in the project
3   Subtasks in major tasks
4   Activities (or "work packages") to be completed

This hierarchical framework can be illustrated with the development of Microsoft's operating system Windows Vista. As we see in Figure 3, the project, creating a new operating system, is labeled 1.0. The first step is to identify the major tasks in the project (level 2). Two examples would be development of graphic user interfaces or GUIs (1), and creating compatibility with

▶ **Figure 3**

Work Breakdown Structure

Level	Level ID Number	Activity
1	1.0	Develop/launch Windows Vista operating system
2	1.1	Develop GUIs
2	1.2	Ensure compatibility with earlier Windows versions
3	1.21	Compatibility with Windows ME
3	1.22	Compatibility with Windows XP
3	1.23	Compatibility with Windows 2000
4	1.231	Ensure ability to import files

[1] See P. J. Rutland, "Ethical Codes and Personal Values," *Cost Engineering* 44 (December 2002): 22; and K. K. Humphreys, *What Every Engineer Should Know About Ethics* (New York: Marcel Dekker, 2004).

previous versions of Windows (2). The major subtasks for 2 are creating a team to handle compatibility with Windows ME (1.21), a compatibility team for Windows XP (1.22), and compatibility with Windows 2000 (1.23). Then, each major subtask is broken down into level-4 activities that need to be done, such as "importing files" created in Windows 2000 (1.231). There are usually many level-4 activities.

PROJECT SCHEDULING

Project scheduling involves sequencing and allotting time to all project activities. At this stage, managers decide how long each activity will take and compute how many people and materials will be needed at each stage of production. Managers also chart separate schedules for personnel needs by type of skill (management, engineering, or pouring concrete, for example). Charts also can be developed for scheduling materials.

One popular project scheduling approach is the Gantt chart. **Gantt charts** are low-cost means of helping managers make sure that (1) all activities are planned for, (2) their order of performance is accounted for, (3) the activity time estimates are recorded, and (4) the overall project time is developed. As Figure 4 shows, Gantt charts are easy to understand. Horizontal bars are drawn for each project activity along a time line. This illustration of a routine servicing of a Delta jetliner during a 40-minute layover shows that Gantt charts also can be used for scheduling repetitive operations. In this case, the chart helps point out potential delays. The *OM in Action* box on Delta provides additional insights.

On simple projects, scheduling charts such as these can be used alone. They permit managers to observe the progress of each activity and to spot and tackle problem areas. Gantt charts, though, do not adequately illustrate the interrelationships between the activities and the resources.

PERT and CPM, the two widely used network techniques that we shall discuss shortly, *do* have the ability to consider precedence relationships and interdependency of activities. On complex projects, the scheduling of which is almost always computerized, PERT and CPM thus have an edge over the simpler Gantt charts. Even on huge projects, though, Gantt charts can be used as summaries of project status and may complement the other network approaches.

To summarize, whatever the approach taken by a project manager, project scheduling serves several purposes:

1. It shows the relationship of each activity to others and to the whole project.
2. It identifies the precedence relationships among activities.
3. It encourages the setting of realistic time and cost estimates for each activity.
4. It helps make better use of people, money, and material resources by identifying critical bottlenecks in the project.

Gantt charts
Planning charts used to schedule resources and allocate time.

Gnatt charts are an example of a widely used, nonmathematical technique that is very popular with managers because it is simple and visual.

Passengers	Deplaning					
	Baggage claim					
Baggage	Container offload					
Fueling	Pumping					
	Engine injection water					
Cargo and mail	Container offload					
Galley servicing	Main cabin door					
	Aft cabin door					
Lavatory servicing	Aft, center, forward					
Drinking water	Loading					
Cabin cleaning	First-class section					
	Economy section					
Cargo and mail	Container/bulk loading					
Flight service	Galley/cabin check					
	Receive passengers					
Operating crew	Aircraft check					
Baggage	Loading					
Passengers	Boarding					

	0	10	20	30	40

Time, minutes

◀ **Figure 4**

Gantt Chart of Service Activities for a Delta Jet during a 40-Minute Layover

Delta hopes to save $50 million a year with this turnaround time, which is a reduction from its traditional 60-minute routine.

Flight 574's engines screech its arrival as the jet lumbers down Richmond's taxiway with 140 passengers arriving from Atlanta. In 40 minutes, the plane is to be airborne again.

However, before this jet can depart, there is business to attend to: passengers, luggage, and cargo to unload and load; thousands of gallons of jet fuel and countless drinks to restock; cabin and restrooms to clean; toilet holding tanks to drain; and engines, wings, and landing gear to inspect.

The 10-person ground crew knows that a miscue anywhere—a broken cargo loader, lost baggage, misdirected passengers—can mean a late departure and trigger a chain reaction of headaches from Richmond to Atlanta to every destination of a connecting flight.

Carla Sutera, the operations manager for Delta's Richmond International Airport, views the turnaround operation like a pit boss awaiting a race car. Trained crews

are in place for Flight 574 with baggage carts and tractors, hydraulic cargo loaders, a truck to load food and drinks, another to lift the cleanup crew, another to put fuel on, and a fourth to take water off. The "pit crew" usually performs so smoothly that most passengers never suspect the proportions of the effort. Gantt charts, such as the one in Figure 4, aid Delta and other airlines with the staffing and scheduling that are needed for this task.

Sources: Knight Ridder Tribune Business News (July 16, 2005): 1 and (November 21, 2002): 1.

PROJECT CONTROLLING

The control of large projects, like the control of any management system, involves close monitoring of resources, costs, quality, and budgets. Control also means using a feedback loop to revise the project plan and having the ability to shift resources to where they are needed most. Computerized PERT/CPM reports and charts are widely available today on personal computers. Some of the more popular of these programs are Primavera (by Primavera Systems, Inc.), MacProject (by Apple Computer Corp.), Pertmaster (by Westminster Software, Inc.), VisiSchedule (by Paladin Software Corp.), Time Line (by Symantec Corp.), and Microsoft Project (by Microsoft Corp.), which we illustrate in this chapter.

These programs produce a broad variety of reports, including (1) detailed cost breakdowns for each task, (2) total program labor curves, (3) cost distribution tables, (4) functional cost and hour summaries, (5) raw material and expenditure forecasts, (6) variance reports, (7) time analysis reports, and (8) work status reports.

 Video 3.2

Project Management at Arnold Palmer Hospital

▲ *Construction of the new 11-story building at Arnold Palmer Hospital in Orlando, Florida, was an enormous project for the hospital administration. The photo on the left shows the first six floors under construction. The photo on the right shows the building as completed in 2006, two years later. Prior to beginning actual construction, regulatory and funding issues added, as they do with most projects, substantial time to the overall project. Cities have zoning and parking issues, the EPA has drainage and waste issues, and regulatory authorities have their own requirements, as do issuers of bonds. The $100 million, four-year project at Arnold Palmer Hospital is discussed in the Video Case Study at the end of this chapter.*

PROJECT MANAGEMENT TECHNIQUES: PERT AND CPM

Program evaluation and review technique (PERT) and the **critical path method (CPM)** were both developed in the 1950s to help managers schedule, monitor, and control large and complex projects. CPM arrived first, in 1957, as a tool developed by J. E. Kelly of Remington Rand and M. R. Walker of duPont to assist in the building and maintenance of chemical plants at duPont. Independently, PERT was developed in 1958 by Booz, Allen, and Hamilton for the U.S. Navy.

The Framework of PERT and CPM

PERT and CPM both follow six basic steps:

1. Define the project and prepare the work breakdown structure.
2. Develop the relationships among the activities. Decide which activities must precede and which must follow others.
3. Draw the network connecting all the activities.
4. Assign time and/or cost estimates to each activity.
5. Compute the *longest* time path through the network. This is called the **critical path**.
6. Use the network to help plan, schedule, monitor, and control the project.

Step 5, finding the critical path, is a major part of controlling a project. The activities on the critical path represent tasks that will delay the entire project if they are not completed on time. Managers can gain the flexibility needed to complete critical tasks by identifying noncritical activities and replanning, rescheduling, and reallocating labor and financial resources.

Although PERT and CPM differ to some extent in terminology and in the construction of the network, their objectives are the same. Furthermore, the analysis used in both techniques is very similar. The major difference is that PERT employs three time estimates for each activity. These time estimates are used to compute expected values and standard deviations for the activity. CPM makes the assumption that activity times are known with certainty and hence requires only one time factor for each activity.

For purposes of illustration, the rest of this section concentrates on a discussion of PERT. Most of the comments and procedures described, however, apply just as well to CPM.

PERT and CPM are important because they can help answer questions such as the following about projects with thousands of activities:

1. When will the entire project be completed?
2. What are the critical activities or tasks in the project—that is, which activities will delay the entire project if they are late?
3. Which are the noncritical activities—the ones that can run late without delaying the whole project's completion?
4. What is the probability that the project will be completed by a specific date?
5. At any particular date, is the project on schedule, behind schedule, or ahead of schedule?
6. On any given date, is the money spent equal to, less than, or greater than the budgeted amount?
7. Are there enough resources available to finish the project on time?
8. If the project is to be finished in a shorter amount of time, what is the best way to accomplish this goal at the least cost?

Network Diagrams and Approaches

The first step in a PERT or CPM network is to divide the entire project into significant activities in accordance with the work breakdown structure. There are two approaches for drawing a project network: **activity on node (AON)** and **activity on arrow (AOA)**. Under the AON convention, *nodes* designate activities. Under AOA, *arrows* represent activities. Activities consume time and resources. The basic difference between AON and AOA is that the nodes in an AON diagram represent activities. In an AOA network, the nodes represent the starting and finishing times of an activity and are also called *events*. So nodes in AOA consume neither time nor resources.

Figure 5 illustrates both conventions for a small portion of the airline turnaround Gantt chart (in Figure 4). The examples provide some background for understanding six common activity

Program evaluation and review technique (PERT)
A project management technique that employs three time estimates for each activity.

Critical path method (CPM)
A project management technique that uses only one time factor per activity.

Critical path
The computed *longest* time path(s) through a network.

Activity-on-node (AON)
A network diagram in which nodes designate activities.

Activity-on-arrow (AOA)
A network diagram in which arrows designate activities.

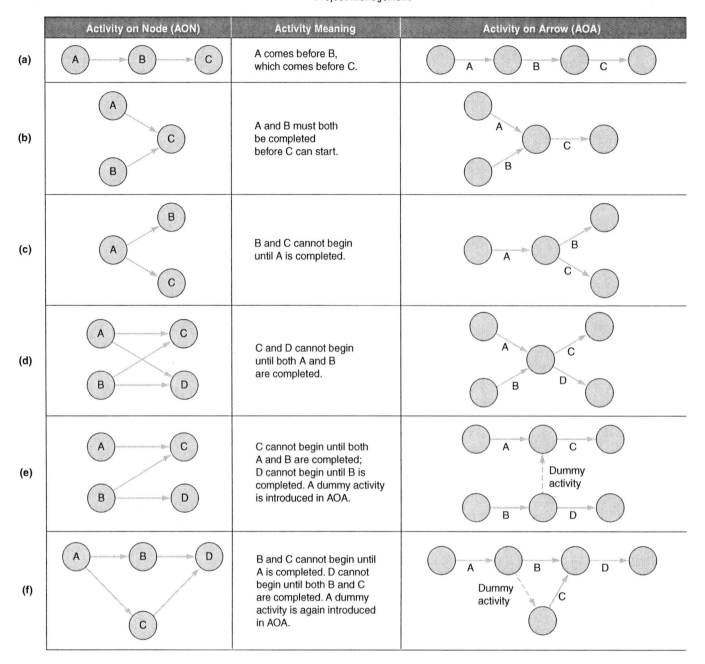

▲ **Figure 5** A Comparison of AON and AOA Network Conventions

relationships in networks. In Figure 5(a), activity A must be finished before activity B is started, and B must, in turn, be completed before C begins. Activity A might represent "deplaning passengers," while B is "cabin cleaning," and C is "boarding new passengers."

Figures 5(e) and 5(f) illustrate that the AOA approach sometimes needs the addition of a **dummy activity** to clarify relationships. A dummy activity consumes no time or resources, but is required when a network has two activities with identical starting and ending events, or when two or more follow some, but not all, "preceding" activities. The use of dummy activities is also important when computer software is employed to determine project completion time. A dummy activity has a completion time of zero.

Although both AON and AOA are popular in practice, many of the project management software packages, including Microsoft Project, use AON networks. For this reason, although we illustrate both types of networks in the next example, we focus on AON networks in subsequent discussions in this chapter.

Dummy activity

An activity having no time that is inserted into a network to maintain the logic of the network.

Activity-on-Node Example

EXAMPLE 1

Activity-on-node
for EPA problem at
Milwaukee Paper

Milwaukee Paper Manufacturing, Inc., located near downtown Milwaukee, has long been trying to avoid the expense of installing air pollution control equipment in its facility. The Environmental Protection Agency (EPA) has recently given the manufacturer 16 weeks to install a complex air filter system. Milwaukee Paper has been warned that it may be forced to close the facility unless the device is installed in the allotted period. Joni Steinberg, the plant manager, wants to make sure that installation of the filtering system progresses smoothly and on time.

Given the following information, develop a table showing activity precedence relationships.

Approach: Milwaukee Paper has identified the eight activities that need to be performed in order for the project to be completed. When the project begins, two activities can be simultaneously started: building the internal components for the device (activity A) and the modifications necessary for the floor and roof (activity B). The construction of the collection stack (activity C) can begin when the internal components are completed. Pouring the concrete floor and installation of the frame (activity D) can be started as soon as the internal components are completed and the roof and floor have been modified.

After the collection stack has been constructed, two activities can begin: building the high-temperature burner (activity E) and installing the pollution control system (activity F). The air pollution device can be installed (activity G) after the concrete floor has been poured, the frame has been installed, and the high-temperature burner has been built. Finally, after the control system and pollution device have been installed, the system can be inspected and tested (activity H).

Solution: Activities and precedence relationships may seem rather confusing when they are presented in this descriptive form. It is therefore convenient to list all the activity information in a table, as shown in Table 1. We see in the table that activity A is listed as an *immediate predecessor* of activity C. Likewise, both activities D and E must be performed prior to starting activity G.

◁ **Table 1**

Milwaukee Paper Manufacturing's Activities and Predecessors

Activity	Description	Immediate Predecessors
A	Build internal components	—
B	Modify roof and floor	—
C	Construct collection stack	A
D	Pour concrete and install frame	A, B
E	Build high-temperature burner	C
F	Install pollution control system	C
G	Install air pollution device	D, E
H	Inspect and test	F, G

Insight: To complete a network, all predecessors must be clearly defined.

Learning exercise: What is the impact on the sequence of activities if EPA approval is required after *Inspect and Test?* [Answer: The immediate predecessor for the new activity would be H, *Inspect and Test*, with *EPA approval* as the last activity.]

Related problem: 27

Note that in Example 1, it is enough to list just the *immediate predecessors* for each activity. For instance, in Table 1, since activity A precedes activity C, and activity C precedes activity E, the fact that activity A precedes activity E is *implicit*. This relationship need not be explicitly shown in the activity precedence relationships.

When there are many activities in a project with fairly complicated precedence relationships, it is difficult for an individual to comprehend the complexity of the project from just the tabular information. In such cases, a visual representation of the project, using a *project network*, is convenient and useful. A project network is a diagram of all the activities and the precedence relationships that exist between these activities in a project. Example 2 illustrates how to construct a project network for Milwaukee Paper Manufacturing.

Networks consist of nodes that are connected by lines (or arcs).

OM in Action   Rebuilding the Pentagon after 9/11

On September 11, 2001, American Airlines Flight 77 slammed into the Pentagon. The world was shocked by this and the other terrorist attacks on the Twin Towers in New York City. One hundred and twenty-five people died when a large portion of the Pentagon was severely damaged. Among the first to react were construction workers renovating another portion of the Pentagon. Their heroism saved lives and eased suffering. Within hours of the disaster, heavy equipment began arriving on the site, accompanied by hundreds of volunteer construction workers driven by patriotism and pride.

Just four days after the attack, Walker Lee Evey, named program manager for "Project Phoenix," promised to rebuild the damaged portions of the Pentagon "faster than anyone has a right to expect . . . and to have people back in the damaged portion of the building, right where the plane hit, by September 11, 2002."

Preliminary construction reports estimated it would take 3 to 4 years and $3/4 billion to rebuild. By directing the project with teamwork, handshake contracts, creativity, and ingenuity—not to mention emotional 20-hour days 6 to 7 days a week—Evey's Project Phoenix met its psychological and physical goal. In less than 11 months,

Mai/Mai, Getty Images/Time Life Pictures

and for only $501 million, workers demolished and rebuilt the damaged sections—400,000 square feet of structure, 2 million square feet of offices, 50,000 tons of debris—using 1,000 construction workers from 80 companies. By September 9, 2002, over 600 military and civilian personnel were sitting at their desks in rebuilt Pentagon offices.

Outside, the blackened gash is long gone. Instead, some 4,000 pieces of limestone—mined from the same Indiana vein that the Pentagon's original stone came from 65 years ago—have been placed on the building's façade. For this impressive accomplishment, the Pentagon and Walker Evey were nominated for the Project Management Institute's 2003 Project of the Year Award.

Sources: Knight-Ridder Tribune Business News (February 1, 2004): 1; *ENR* (September 2, 2002): 6; *U.S. News & World Report* (September 16, 2002): 35.

EXAMPLE 2

AON graph for Milwaukee Paper

Draw the AON network for Milwaukee Paper, using the data in Example 1.

Approach: In the AON approach, we denote each activity by a node. The lines, or arcs, represent the precedence relationships between the activities.

Solution: In this example, there are two activities (A and B) that do not have any predecessors. We draw separate nodes for each of these activities, as shown in Figure 6. Although not required, it is usually convenient to have a unique starting activity for a project. We have therefore included a *dummy activity* called *Start* in Figure 6. This dummy activity does not really exist and takes up zero time and resources. Activity *Start* is an immediate predecessor for both activities A and B, and serves as the unique starting activity for the entire project.

▶ **Figure 6**

Beginning AON Network for Milwaukee Paper

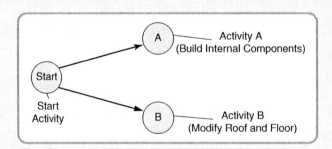

We now show the precedence relationships using lines with arrow symbols. For example, an arrow from activity Start to activity A indicates that Start is a predecessor for activity A. In a similar fashion, we draw an arrow from Start to B.

Next, we add a new node for activity C. Since activity A precedes activity C, we draw an arc from node A to node C (see Figure 7). Likewise, we first draw a node to represent activity D. Then, since activities A and B both precede activity D, we draw arrows from A to D and from B to D (see Figure 7).

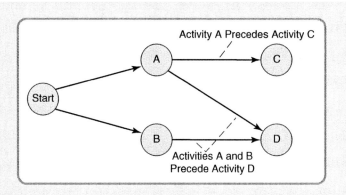

◀ **Figure 7**

Intermediate AON Network
for Milwaukee Paper

We proceed in this fashion, adding a separate node for each activity and a separate line for each precedence relationship that exists. The complete AON project network for the Milwaukee Paper Manufacturing project is shown in Figure 8.

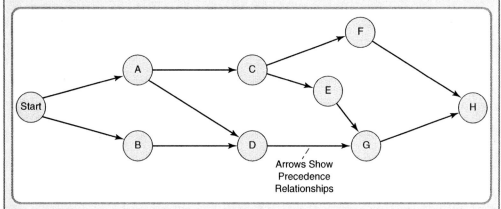

◀ **Figure 8**

Complete AON Network
for Milwaukee Paper

Insight: Drawing a project network properly takes some time and experience. We would like the lines to be straight and arrows to move to the right when possible.

Learning exercise: If *EPA Approval* occurs after *Inspect and Test*, what is the impact on the graph? [Answer: A straight line is extended to the right beyond H to reflect the additional activity.]

Related problems: 3, 6, 7, 9a, 10, 12, 15a

When we first draw a project network, it is not unusual that we place our nodes (activities) in the network in such a fashion that the arrows (precedence relationships) are not straight lines. That is, the lines could be intersecting each other, and even facing in opposite directions. For example, if we had switched the location of the nodes for activities E and F in Figure 8, the lines from F to H and E to G would have intersected. Although such a project network is perfectly valid, it is good practice to have a well-drawn network. One rule that we especially recommend is to place the nodes in such a fashion that all arrows point in the same direction. To achieve this, we suggest that you first draw a rough draft of the network, making sure all the relationships are shown. Then you can redraw the network to make appropriate changes in the location of the nodes.

As with the unique starting node, it is convenient to have the project network finish with a unique ending node. In the Milwaukee Paper example, it turns out that a unique activity, H, is the last activity in the project. We therefore automatically have a unique ending node.

In situations in which a project has multiple ending activities, we include a "dummy" ending activity. This dummy activity has all the multiple ending activities in the project as immediate predecessors. We illustrate this type of situation in Solved Problem 2 at the end of this chapter.

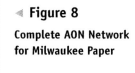

It is convenient, but not required, to have unique starting and ending activities in a project.

Activity-on-Arrow Example

We saw earlier that in an AOA project network we can represent activities by arrows. A node represents an *event*, which marks the start or completion time of an activity. We usually identify an event (node) by a number.

EXAMPLE 3

Activity-on-arrow for
Milwaukee Paper

Draw the complete AOA project network for Milwaukee Paper's problem.

Approach: Using the data from Table 1 in Example 1, draw one activity at a time, starting with A.

Solution: We see that activity A starts at event 1 and ends at event 2. Likewise, activity B starts at event 1 and ends at event 3. Activity C, whose only immediate predecessor is activity A, starts at node 2 and ends at node 4. Activity D, however, has two predecessors (i.e., A and B). Hence, we need both activities A and B to end at event 3, so that activity D can start at that event. However, we cannot have multiple activities with common starting and ending nodes in an AOA network. To overcome this difficulty, in such cases, we may need to add a dummy line (activity) to enforce the precedence relationship. The dummy activity, shown in Figure 9 as a dashed line, is inserted between events 2 and 3 to make the diagram reflect the precedence between A and D. The remainder of the AOA project network for Milwaukee Paper's example is also shown.

▶ **Figure 9**

**Complete AOA Network
(with Dummy Activity)
for Milwaukee Paper**

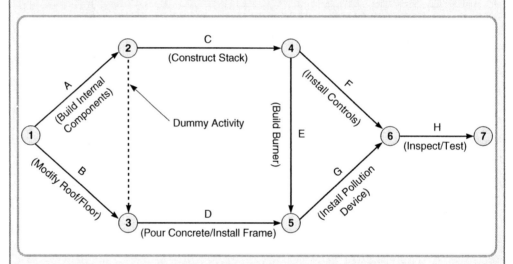

Insight: Dummy activities are common in AOA networks. They do not really exist in the project and take zero time.

Learning exercise: A new activity, *EPA Approval*, follows activity H. Add it to Figure 9. [Answer: Insert an arrowed line from node 7, which ends at a new node 8, and is labeled I (EPA Approval).]

Related problems: 4, 5, 9b

DETERMINING THE PROJECT SCHEDULE

Look back to Figure 8 (in Example 2) for a moment to see Milwaukee Paper's completed AON project network. Once this project network has been drawn to show all the activities and their precedence relationships, the next step is to determine the project schedule. That is, we need to identify the planned starting and ending time for each activity.

Let us assume Milwaukee Paper estimates the time required for each activity, in weeks, as shown in Table 2. The table indicates that the total time for all eight of the company's activities is 25 weeks. However, since several activities can take place simultaneously, it is clear that the total project completion time may be less than 25 weeks. To find out just how long the project will take, we perform the **critical path analysis** for the network.

Critical path analysis
A process that helps determine a project schedule.

Activity	Description	Time (weeks)
A	Build internal components	2
B	Modify roof and floor	3
C	Construct collection stack	2
D	Pour concrete and install frame	4
E	Build high-temperature burner	4
F	Install pollution control system	3
G	Install air pollution device	5
H	Inspect and test	2
	Total time (weeks)	25

◀ **Table 2**

Time Estimates for Milwaukee Paper Manufacturing

As mentioned earlier, the critical path is the *longest* time path through the network. To find the critical path, we calculate two distinct starting and ending times for each activity. These are defined as follows:

Earliest start (ES) = earliest time at which an activity can start, assuming all predecessors have been completed

Earliest finish (EF) = earliest time at which an activity can be finished

Latest start (LS) = latest time at which an activity can start so as to not delay the completion time of the entire project

Latest finish (LF) = latest time by which an activity has to finish so as to not delay the completion time of the entire project

We use a two-pass process, consisting of a forward pass and a backward pass, to determine these time schedules for each activity. The early start and finish times (ES and EF) are determined during the **forward pass**. The late start and finish times (LS and LF) are determined during the backward pass.

Forward pass
A process that identifies all the earliest times.

Forward Pass

To clearly show the activity schedules on the project network, we use the notation shown in Figure 10. The ES of an activity is shown in the top left corner of the node denoting that activity. The EF is shown in the top right corner. The latest times, LS and LF, are shown in the bottom-left and bottom-right corners, respectively.

Learning Objective

3. Complete both forward and backward passes for a project

Earliest Start Time Rule Before an activity can start, *all* its immediate predecessors must be finished:

- If an activity has only a single immediate predecessor, its ES equals the EF of the predecessor.
- If an activity has multiple immediate predecessors, its ES is the maximum of all EF values of its predecessors. That is,

$$ES = \text{Max}\{EF \text{ of all immediate predecessors}\} \qquad (1)$$

All predecessor activities must be completed before an activity can begin.

Earliest Finish Rule The earliest finish time (EF) of an activity is the sum of its earliest start time (ES) and its activity time. That is,

$$EF = ES + \text{Activity time} \qquad (2)$$

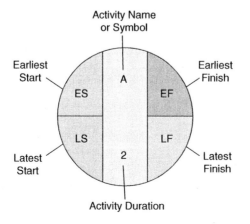

◀ **Figure 10**

Notation Used in Nodes for Forward and Backward Pass

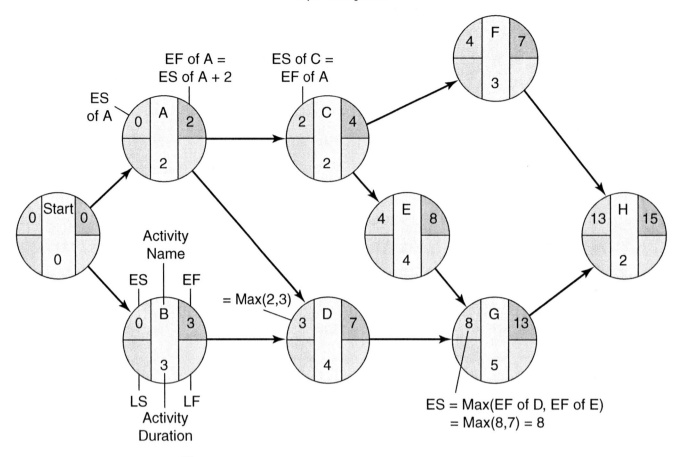

▲ **Figure 11** Earliest Start and Earliest Finish Times for Milwaukee Paper

EXAMPLE 4

Computing earliest
start and finish times
for Milwaukee paper

Excel OM Data File
Ch03Ex4.xls

Calculate the earliest start and finish times for the activities in the Milwaukee Paper Manufacturing project.

Approach: Use Table 2, which contains the activity times. Complete the project network for the company's project, along with the ES and EF values for all activities.

Solution: With the help of Figure 11, we describe how these values are calculated.

Since activity Start has no predecessors, we begin by setting its ES to 0. That is, activity Start can begin at the *end* of week 0, which is the same as the beginning of week 1.[2] If activity Start has an ES of 0, its EF is also 0, since its activity time is 0.

Next, we consider activities A and B, both of which have only Start as an immediate predecessor. Using the earliest start time rule, the ES for both activities A and B equals zero, which is the EF of activity Start. Now, using the earliest finish time rule, the EF for A is 2 (= 0 + 2), and the EF for B is 3 (= 0 + 3).

Since activity A precedes activity C, the ES of C equals the EF of A (= 2). The EF of C is therefore 4 (= 2 + 2).

We now come to activity D. Both activities A and B are immediate predecessors for B. Whereas A has an EF of 2, activity B has an EF of 3. Using the earliest start time rule, we compute the ES of activity D as follows:

$$\text{ES of D} = \text{Max(EF of A, EF of B)} = \text{Max}(2, 3) = 3$$

The EF of D equals 7 (= 3 + 4). Next, both activities E and F have activity C as their only immediate predecessor. Therefore, the ES for both E and F equals 4 (= EF of C). The EF of E is 8 (= 4 + 4), and the EF of F is 7 (= 4 + 3).

[2]In writing all earliest and latest times, we need to be consistent. For example, if we specify that the ES value of activity *i* is week 4, do we mean the *beginning* of week 4 or the *end* of week 4? Note that if the value refers to the *beginning* of week 4, it means that week 4 is also available for performing activity *i*. In our discussions, *all* earliest and latest time values correspond to the *end* of a period. That is, if we specify that the ES of activity *i* is week 4, it means that activity *i* starts work only at the beginning of week 5.

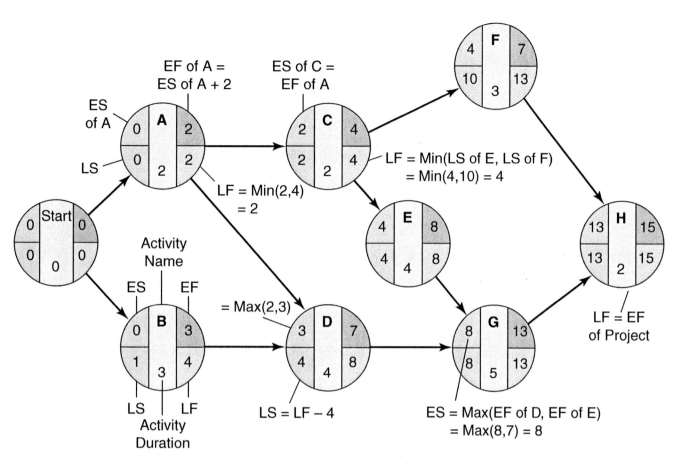

Latest Start and Finish Times for Milwaukee Paper

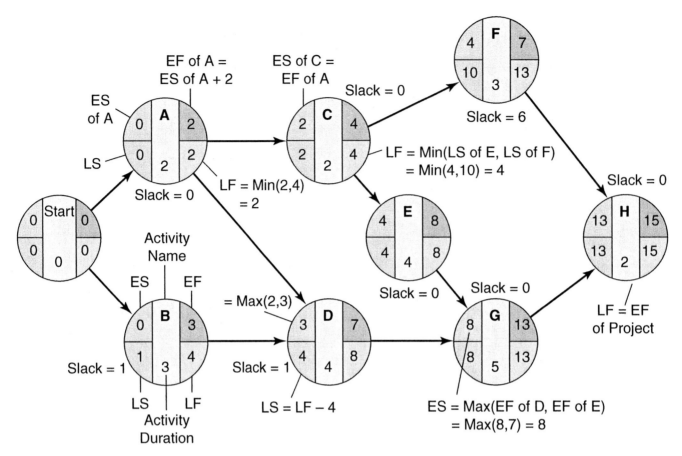

Slack Times for Milwaukee Paper

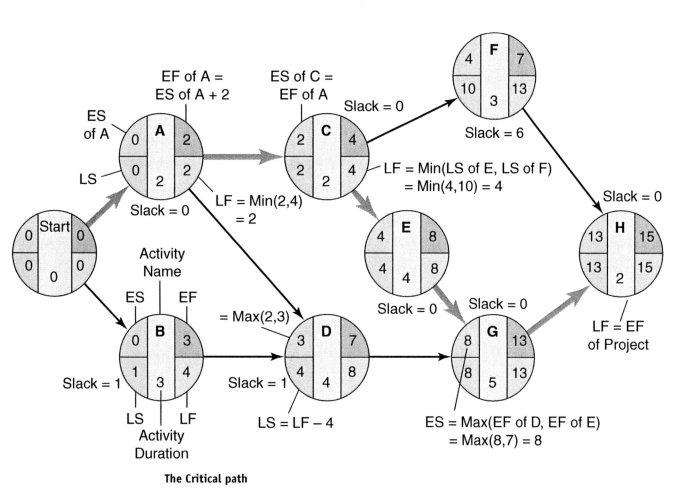

The Critical path

Activity G has both activities D and E as predecessors. Using the earliest start time rule, its ES is therefore the maximum of the EF of D and the EF of E. Hence, the ES of activity G equals 8 (= maximum of 7 and 8), and its EF equals 13 (= 8 + 5).

Finally, we come to activity H. Since it also has two predecessors, F and G, the ES of H is the maximum EF of these two activities. That is, the ES of H equals 13 (= maximum of 13 and 7). This implies that the EF of H is 15 (= 13 + 2). Since H is the last activity in the project, this also implies that the earliest time in which the entire project can be completed is 15 weeks.

Insight: The ES of an activity that has only one predecessor is simply the EF of that predecessor. For an activity with more than one predecessor, we must carefully examine the EFs of all immediate predecessors and choose the largest one.

Learning exercise: A new activity I, *EPA Approval*, takes 1 week. Its predecessor is activity H. What are I's ES and EF? [Answer: 15, 16]

Related problems: 11, 14c

Although the forward pass allows us to determine the earliest project completion time, it does not identify the critical path. To identify this path, we need to now conduct the backward pass to determine the LS and LF values for all activities.

Backward Pass

Just as the forward pass began with the first activity in the project, the **backward pass** begins with the last activity in the project. For each activity, we first determine its LF value, followed by its LS value. The following two rules are used in this process.

Backward pass
An activity that finds all the latest times.

Latest Finish Time Rule This rule is again based on the fact that before an activity can start, all its immediate predecessors must be finished:

- If an activity is an immediate predecessor for just a single activity, its LF equals the LS of the activity that immediately follows it.
- If an activity is an immediate predecessor to more than one activity, its LF is the minimum of all LS values of all activities that immediately follow it. That is,

$$LF = Min\{LS \text{ of all immediate following activities}\} \quad (3)$$

LF of an activity = minimum LS of all activities that follow.

Latest Start Time Rule The latest start time (LS) of an activity is the difference of its latest finish time (LF) and its activity time. That is,

$$LS = LF - \text{Activity time} \quad (4)$$

EXAMPLE 5

Computing latest start and finish times for Milwaukee Paper

Calculate the latest start and finish times for each activity in Milwaukee Paper's pollution project.

Approach: Use Figure 11 as a beginning point. Overlay 1 of Figure 11 shows the complete project network for Milwaukee Paper, along with LS and LF values for all activities. In what follows, we see how these values were calculated.

Solution: We begin by assigning an LF value of 15 weeks for activity H. That is, we specify that the latest finish time for the entire project is the same as its earliest finish time. Using the latest start time rule, the LS of activity H is equal to 13 (= 15 − 2).

Since activity H is the lone succeeding activity for both activities F and G, the LF for both F and G equals 1 This implies that the LS of G is 8 (= 13 − 5), and the LS of F is 10 (= 13 − 3).

Proceeding in this fashion, we see that the LF of E is 8 (= LS of G), and its LS is 4 (= 8 − 4). Likewise, the LF of D is 8 (= LS of G), and its LS is 4 (= 8 − 4).

We now consider activity C, which is an immediate predecessor to two activities: E and F. Using the latest finish time rule, we compute the LF of activity C as follows:

$$LF \text{ of } C = Min(LS \text{ of } E, LS \text{ of } F) = Min(4, 10) = 4$$

The LS of C is computed as 2 (= 4 − 2). Next, we compute the LF of B as 4 (= LS of D), and its LS as 1 (= 4 − 3).

We now consider activity A. We compute its LF as 2 (= minimum of LS of C and LS of D). Hence, the LS of activity A is 0 (= 2 − 2). Finally, both the LF and LS of activity Start are equal to 0.

Insight: The LF of an activity that is the predecessor of only one activity is just the LS of that following activity. If the activity is the predecessor to more than one activity, its LF is the smallest LS value of all activities that follow immediately.

Learning exercise: A new activity I, *EPA Approval*, takes 1 week. Its predecessor is activity H, What are I's LS and LF? [Answer: 15, 16]

Related problems: 11, 14c

Calculating Slack Time and Identifying the Critical Path(s)

Slack time

Free time for an activity.

After we have computed the earliest and latest times for all activities, it is a simple matter to find the amount of **slack time**, or free time, that each activity has. Slack is the length of time an activity can be delayed without delaying the entire project. Mathematically,

$$\text{Slack} = \text{LS} - \text{ES} \quad \text{or} \quad \text{Slack} = \text{LF} - \text{EF} \tag{5}$$

EXAMPLE 6

Calculating slack times for Milwaukee Paper

Calculate the slack for the activities in the Milwaukee Paper project.

Approach: Start with the data in Overlay 1 of Figure 11 in Example 5 and develop Table 3 one line at a time.

Solution: Table 3 summarizes the ES, EF, LS, LF, and slack time for all of the firm's activities. Activity B, for example, has 1 week of slack time since its LS is 1 and its ES is 0 (alternatively, its LF is 4 and its EF is 3). This means that activity B can be delayed by up to 1 week, and the whole project can still be finished in 15 weeks.

▶ **Table 3**

Milwaukee Paper's Schedule and Slack Times

Activity	Earliest Start ES	Earliest Finish EF	Latest Start LS	Latest Finish LF	Slack LS – ES	On Critical Path
A	0	2	0	2	0	Yes
B	0	3	1	4	1	No
C	2	4	2	4	0	Yes
D	3	7	4	8	1	No
E	4	8	4	8	0	Yes
F	4	7	10	13	6	No
G	8	13	8	13	0	Yes
H	13	15	13	15	0	Yes

Active Model 3.1

This example is further illustrated in Active Model 1 on the Student CD-ROM and in the exercise located on page 91.

On the other hand, activities A, C, E, G, and H have *no* slack time. This means that none of them can be delayed without delaying the entire project. Conversely, if plant manager Joni Steinberg wants to reduce the total project times, she will have to reduce the length of one of these activities.

Overlay 2 of Figure 11 shows the slack computed for each activity.

Insight: Slack may be computed from either early/late starts or early/late finishes. The key is to find which activities have zero slack.

Learning exercise: A new activity I, *EPA Approval*, follows activity H and takes 1 week. Is it on the critical path? [Answer: Yes, it's LS – ES = 0]

Related problems: 6, 11, 27

Learning Objective

4. Determine a critical path

The activities with zero slack are called *critical activities* and are said to be on the critical path. The critical path is a continuous path through the project network that:

- Starts at the first activity in the project (Start in our example).
- Terminates at the last activity in the project (H in our example).
- Includes only critical activities (i.e., activities with no slack time).

EXAMPLE 7

Showing critical path
with blue arrows

Show Milwaukee Paper's critical path and find the project completion time.

Approach: We use Table 3 and Overlay 3 of Figure 11. Overlay 3 of Figure 11 indicates that the total project completion time of 15 weeks corresponds to the longest path in the network. That path is start-A-C-E-G-H in network form. It is shown with thick blue arrows.

Insight: The critical path follows the activities with slack = 0. This is considered the longest path through the network.

Learning exercise: Why are activities B, D, and F not on the path with the thick blue line? [Answer: They are not critical and have slack values of 1, 1, and 6 weeks, respectively.]

Related problems: 3, 4, 5, 6, 7, 12, 14b, 15, 17, 20a, 22a, 23, 26, 27

> *Critical path is the longest path through the network.*

Total Slack Time versus Free Slack Time Look again at the project network in Overlay 3 of Figure 11. Consider activities B and D, which have slack of 1 week each. Does it mean that we can delay *each* activity by 1 week, and still complete the project in 15 weeks? The answer is no.

Let's assume that activity B is delayed by 1 week. It has used up its slack of 1 week and now has an EF of 4. This implies that activity D now has an ES of 4 and an EF of 8. Note that these are also its LS and LF values, respectively. That is, activity D also has no slack time now. Essentially, the slack of 1 week that activities B and D had is, for that path, *shared* between them. Delaying either activity by 1 week causes not only that activity, but also the other activity, to lose its slack. This type of a slack time is referred to as **total slack**. Typically, when two or more non-critical activities appear successively in a path, they share total slack.

In contrast, consider the slack time of 6 weeks in activity F. Delaying this activity decreases only its slack time and does not affect the slack time of any other activity. This type of a slack time is referred to as **free slack**. Typically, if a noncritical activity has critical activities on either side of it in a path, its slack time is free slack.

Total slack
Time shared among more than one activity.

Free slack
Time associated with a single activity.

VARIABILITY IN ACTIVITY TIMES

In identifying all earliest and latest times so far, and the associated critical path(s), we have adopted the CPM approach of assuming that all activity times are known and fixed constants. That is, there is no variability in activity times. However, in practice, it is likely that activity completion times vary depending on various factors.

Hard Rock Café

> ◄ *To plan, monitor, and control the huge number of details involved in sponsoring a rock festival attended by more than 100,000 fans, Hard Rock Cafe uses Microsoft Project and the tools discussed in this chapter. The Video Case Study "Managing Hard Rock's Rockfest," at the end of the chapter, provides more details of the management task.*

For example, building internal components (activity A) for Milwaukee Paper Manufacturing is estimated to finish in 2 weeks. Clearly, factors such as late arrival of raw materials, absence of key personnel, and so on, could delay this activity. Suppose activity A actually ends up taking 3 weeks. Since A is on the critical path, the entire project will now be delayed by 1 week to 16 weeks. If we had anticipated completion of this project in 15 weeks, we would obviously miss our deadline.

Although some activities may be relatively less prone to delays, others could be extremely susceptible to delays. For example, activity B (modify roof and floor) could be heavily dependent on weather conditions. A spell of bad weather could significantly affect its completion time.

This means that we cannot ignore the impact of variability in activity times when deciding the schedule for a project. PERT addresses this issue.

Three Time Estimates in PERT

In PERT, we employ a probability distribution based on three time estimates for each activity, as follows:

Optimistic time
The "best" activity completion time that could be obtained in a PERT network.

Pessimistic time
The "worst" activity time that could be expected in a PERT network.

Most likely time
The most probable time to complete an activity in a PERT network.

Optimistic time (a) = time an activity will take if everything goes as planned. In estimating this value, there should be only a small probability (say, 1/100) that the activity time will be $< a$.

Pessimistic time (b) = time an activity will take assuming very unfavorable conditions. In estimating this value, there should also be only a small probability (also, 1/100) that the activity time will be $> b$.

Most likely time (m) = most realistic estimate of the time required to complete an activity.

When using PERT, we often assume that activity time estimates follow the beta probability distribution (see Figure 12). This continuous distribution is often appropriate for determining the expected value and variance for activity completion times.

To find the *expected activity time*, t, the beta distribution weights the three time estimates as follows:

$$t = (a + 4m + b)/6 \tag{6}$$

That is, the most likely time (m) is given four times the weight as the optimistic time (a) and pessimistic time (b). The time estimate t computed using Equation 6 for each activity is used in the project network to compute all earliest and latest times.

To compute the *dispersion* or *variance of activity completion time*, we use the formula[3]:

$$\text{Variance} = [(b - a)/6]^2 \tag{7}$$

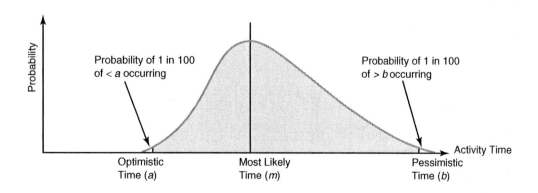

> **Figure 12**

Beta Probability Distribution with Three Time Estimates

[3]This formula is based on the statistical concept that from one end of the beta distribution to the other is 6 standard deviations (±3 standard deviations from the mean). Since $(b - a)$ is 6 standard deviations, the variance is $[(b - a/6]^2$.

EXAMPLE 8

Joni Steinberg and the project management team at Milwaukee Paper want an expected time and variance for Activity F (Installing the Pollution Control System) where:

$$a = 1 \text{ week}, m = 2 \text{ weeks}, b = 9 \text{ weeks}$$

Approach: Use Equations 6 and 7 to compute the expected time and variance for F.

Solution: The expected time for Activity F is

$$t = \frac{a + 4m + b}{6} = \frac{1 + 4(2) + 9}{6} = \frac{18}{6} = 3 \text{ weeks}$$

The variance for Activity F is

$$\text{Variance} = \left[\frac{(b-a)}{6}\right]^2 = \left[\frac{(9-1)}{6}\right]^2 = \left(\frac{8}{6}\right)^2 = \frac{64}{36} = 1.78$$

Insight: Steinberg now has information that allows her to understand and manage Activity F. The expected time is, in fact, the activity time used in our earlier computation and identification of the critical path.

Learning exercise: Review the expected times and variances for all of the other activities in the project. These are shown in Table 4.

Learning Objective

5. Calculate the variance of activity times

◁ **Table 4**

Time Estimates (in weeks) for Milwaukee Paper's Project

Activity	Optimistic a	Most Likely m	Pessimistic b	Expected Time $t = (a + 4m + b)/6$	Variance $[(b - a)/6]^2$
A	1	2	3	2	$[(3 - 1)/6]^2 = 4/36 = .11$
B	2	3	4	3	$[(4 - 2)/6]^2 = 4/36 = .11$
C	1	2	3	2	$[(3 - 1)/6]^2 = 4/36 = .11$
D	2	4	6	4	$[(6 - 2)/6]^2 = 16/36 = .44$
E	1	4	7	4	$[(7 - 1)/6]^2 = 36/36 = 1.00$
F	1	2	9	3	$[(9 - 1)/6]^2 = 64/36 = 1.78$
G	3	4	11	5	$[(11 - 3)/6]^2 = 64/36 = 1.78$
H	1	2	3	2	$[(3 - 1)/6]^2 = 4/36 = .11$

Excel OM Data FileCh03Ex8.xls

Related problems: 13, 14a, 17a,b, 21a

◁ We see here a ship being built at the Hyundi shipyard, Asia's largest shipbuilder, in Korea. Managing this project uses the same techniques as managing the remodeling of a store or installing a new production line.

Paul Chesley, Getty Images Inc.—Stone Allstock

Probability of Project Completion

We compute the project variance by summing variances of only those activities on the critical path.

The critical path analysis helped us determine that Milwaukee Paper's expected project completion time is 15 weeks. Joni Steinberg knows, however, that there is significant variation in the time estimates for several activities. Variation in activities that are on the critical path can affect the overall project completion time—possibly delaying it. This is one occurrence that worries the plant manager considerably.

PERT uses the variance of critical path activities to help determine the variance of the overall project. Project variance is computed by summing variances of *critical* activities:

$$\sigma_p^2 = \text{Project variance} = \Sigma \text{ (variances of activities on critical path)} \qquad (8)$$

EXAMPLE 9

Computing project variance and standard deviation for Milwaukee Paper

Milwaukee Paper's managers now wish to know the project's variance and standard deviation.

Approach: Because the activities are independent, we can add the variances of the activities on the critical path and then take the square root to determine the project's standard deviation.

Solution: From Example 8 (Table 4), we have the variances of all of the activities on the critical path. Specifically, we know that the variance of activity A is 0.11, variance of activity C is 0.11, variance of activity E is 1.00, variance of activity G is 1.78, and variance of activity H is 0.11.

Compute the total project variance and project standard deviation:

$$\text{Project variance } (\sigma_p^2) = 0.11 + 0.11 + 1.00 + 1.78 + 0.11 = 3.11$$

which implies:

$$\text{Project standard deviation } (\sigma_p) = \sqrt{\text{Project variance}} = \sqrt{3.11} = 1.76 \text{ weeks}$$

Insight: Management now has an estimate not only of expected completion time for the project but also of the standard deviation of that estimate.

Learning exercise: If the variance for activity A is actually 0.30 (instead of 0.11), what is the new project standard deviation? [Answer: 1.817.]

Related problem: 17e

How can this information be used to help answer questions regarding the probability of finishing the project on time? PERT makes two more assumptions: (1) total project completion times follow a normal probability distribution, and (2) activity times are statistically independent. With these assumptions, the bell-shaped normal curve shown in Figure 13 can be used to represent project completion dates. This normal curve implies that there is a 50% chance that the manufacturer's project completion time will be less than 15 weeks and a 50% chance that it will exceed 15 weeks.

▶ **Figure 13**

Probability Distribution for Project Completion Times at Milwaukee Paper

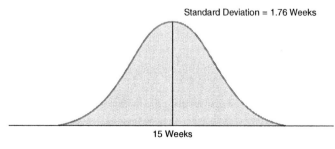

Standard Deviation = 1.76 Weeks

15 Weeks

(Expected Completion Time)

EXAMPLE 10

Probability of completing a project on time

Joni Steinberg would like to find the probability that her project will be finished on or before the 16-week deadline.

Approach: To do so, she needs to determine the appropriate area under the normal curve. This is the area to the left of the 16th week.

Solution: The standard normal equation can be applied as follows:

$$Z = (\text{Due date} - \text{expected date of completion})/\sigma_p \qquad (9)$$

$$= (16 \text{ weeks} - 15 \text{ weeks})/1.76 \text{ weeks} = 0.57$$

where Z is the number of standard deviations the due date or target date lies from the mean or expected date.

Referring to the Normal Table in Appendix: Normal Curve Areas, we find a Z value of 0.57 to the right of the mean indicates a probability of 0.7157. Thus, there is a 71.57% chance that the pollution control equipment can be put in place in 16 weeks or less. This is shown in Figure 14.

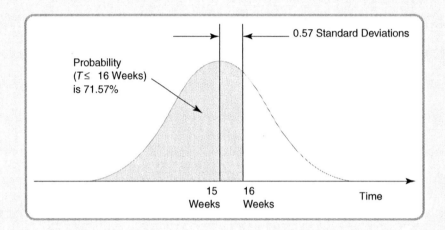

Insight: The shaded area to the left of the 16th week (71.57%) represents the probability that the project will be completed in less than 16 weeks.

Learning exercise: What is the probability that the project will be completed on or before the 17th week? [Answer: About 87.2%.]

Related problems: 14d, 17f, 21d,e, 22b, 24

Determining Project Completion Time for a Given Confidence Level Let's say Joni Steinberg is worried that there is only a 71.57% chance that the pollution control equipment can be put in place in 16 weeks or less. She thinks that it may be possible to plead with the environmental group for more time. However, before she approaches the group, she wants to arm herself with sufficient information about the project. Specifically, she wants to find the deadline by which she has a 99% chance of completing the project. She hopes to use her analysis to convince the group to agree to this extended deadline.

Clearly, this due date would be greater than 16 weeks. However, what is the exact value of this new due date? To answer this question, we again use the assumption that Milwaukee Paper's project completion time follows a normal probability distribution with a mean of 15 weeks and a standard deviation of 1.76 weeks.

EXAMPLE 11

Computing probability for any completion date

Joni Steinberg wants to find the due date that gives her company's project a 99% chance of *on-time* completion.

Approach: She first needs to compute the Z-value corresponding to 99%, as shown in Figure 15. Mathematically, this is similar to Example 10, except the unknown is now Z rather than the due date.

▶ Figure 15

Z-Value for 99% Probability of Project Completion at Milwaukee Paper

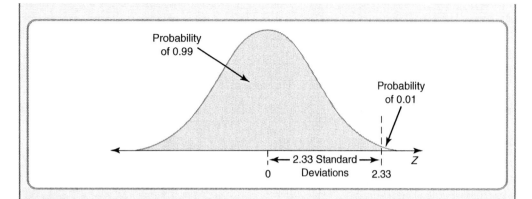

Solution: Referring again to the Normal Table in the Appendix: Normal Curve Areas, we identify a Z-value of 2.33 as being closest to the probability of 0.99. That is, Joni Steinberg's due date should be 2.33 standard deviations above the mean project completion time. Starting with the standard normal equation (see Equation 9), we can solve for the due date and rewrite the equation as:

$$\text{Due date} = \text{Expected completion time} + (Z \times \sigma_p) \tag{10}$$

$$= 15 + (2.33 \times 1.76) = 19.1 \text{ weeks}$$

Insight: If Steinberg can get the environmental group to agree to give her a new deadline of 19.1 weeks (or more), she can be 99% sure of finishing the project on time.

Learning exercise: What due date gives the project a 95% chance of on-time completion? [Answer: About 17.9 weeks.]

Related problems: 22c, 24e

Variability in Completion Time of Noncritical Paths In our discussion so far, we have focused exclusively on the variability in the completion times of activities on the critical path. This seems logical since these activities are, by definition, the more important activities in a project network. However, when there is variability in activity times, it is important that we also investigate the variability in the completion times of activities on *noncritical* paths.

Consider, for example, activity D in Milwaukee Paper's project. Recall from Overlay 3 in Figure 11 (in Example 7) that this is a noncritical activity, with a slack time of 1 week. We have therefore not considered the variability in D's time in computing the probabilities of project completion times. We observe, however, that D has a variance of 0.44 (see Table 4 in Example 8). In fact, the pessimistic completion time for D is 6 weeks. This means that if D ends up taking its pessimistic time to finish, the project will not finish in 15 weeks, even though D is not a critical activity.

For this reason, when we find probabilities of project completion times, it may be necessary for us to not focus only on the critical path(s). Indeed, some research has suggested that expending project resources to reduce the variability of activities not on the critical path can be an effective element in project management.[4] We may need also to compute these probabilities for noncritical paths, especially those that have relatively large variances. It is possible for a noncritical path to have a smaller probability of completion within a due date, when compared with the critical path. Determining the variance and probability of completion for a noncritical path is done in the same manner as Examples 9 and 10.

Noncritical paths with large variances should also be closely monitored.

What Project Management Has Provided So Far Project management techniques have thus far been able to provide Joni Steinberg with several valuable pieces of management information:

1. The project's expected completion date is 15 weeks.
2. There is a 71.57% chance that the equipment will be in place within the 16-week deadline. PERT analysis can easily find the probability of finishing by any date Steinberg is interested in.

[4]F. M. Pokladnik, T. F. Anthony, R. R. Hill, G. Ulrich, "A Fresh Look at Estimated Project Duration: Noncritical Path Activity Contribution to Project Variance in PERT/CPM," *Proceedings of the 2003 Southwest Decision Science Conference*, Houston.

3. Five activities (A, C, E, G, and H) are on the critical path. If any one of these is delayed for any reason, the entire project will be delayed.

4. Three activities (B, D, F) are not critical and have some slack time built in. This means that Steinberg can borrow from their resources, and, if necessary, she may be able to speed up the whole project.

5. A detailed schedule of activity starting and ending dates has been made available (see Table 3 in Example 6).

COST–TIME TRADE-OFFS AND PROJECT CRASHING

While managing a project, it is not uncommon for a project manager to be faced with either (or both) of the following situations: (1) the project is behind schedule, and (2) the scheduled project completion time has been moved forward. In either situation, some or all of the remaining activities need to be speeded up to finish the project by the desired due date. The process by which we shorten the duration of a project in the cheapest manner possible is called project **crashing**.

CPM is a technique in which each activity has a *normal* or *standard* time that we use in our computations. Associated with this normal time is the *normal* cost of the activity. However, another time in project management is the *crash time*, which is defined as the shortest duration required to complete an activity. Associated with this crash time is the *crash cost* of the activity. Usually, we can shorten an activity by adding extra resources (e.g., equipment, people) to it. Hence, it is logical for the crash cost of an activity to be higher than its normal cost.

The amount by which an activity can be shortened (i.e., the difference between its normal time and crash time) depends on the activity in question. We may not be able to shorten some activities at all. For example, if a casting needs to be heat-treated in the furnace for 48 hours, adding more resources does not help shorten the time. In contrast, we may be able to shorten some activities significantly (e.g., frame a house in 3 days instead of 10 days by using three times as many workers).

Likewise, the cost of crashing (or shortening) an activity depends on the nature of the activity. Managers are usually interested in speeding up a project at the least additional cost. Hence, when choosing which activities to crash, and by how much, we need to ensure the following:

- The amount by which an activity is crashed is, in fact, permissible
- Taken together, the shortened activity durations will enable us to finish the project by the due date
- The total cost of crashing is as small as possible

Crashing a project involves four steps:

Step 1: Compute the crash cost per week (or other time period) for each activity in the network. If crash costs are linear over time, the following formula can be used:

$$\text{Crash cost per period} = \frac{(\text{Crash cost} - \text{Normal cost})}{(\text{Normal time} - \text{Crash time})} \tag{11}$$

Step 2: Using the current activity times, find the critical path(s) in the project network. Identify the critical activities.

Step 3: If there is only one critical path, then select the activity on this critical path that (a) can still be crashed and (b) has the smallest crash cost per period. Crash this activity by one period.

If there is more than one critical path, then select one activity from each critical path such that (a) each selected activity can still be crashed and (b) the total crash cost per period of *all* selected activities is the smallest. Crash each activity by one period. Note that the same activity may be common to more than one critical path.

Step 4: Update all activity times. If the desired due date has been reached, stop. If not, return to Step 2.

We illustrate project crashing in Example 12.

Crashing
Shortening activity time in a network to reduce time on the critical path so total completion time is reduced.

We want to find the cheapest way of crashing a project to the desired due date.

Learning Objective
6. Crash a project

EXAMPLE 12

Project crashing to meet a deadline at Milwaukee Paper

Suppose that Milwaukee Paper Manufacturing has been given only 13 weeks (instead of 16 weeks) to install the new pollution control equipment or face a court-ordered shutdown. As you recall, the length of Joni Steinberg's critical path was 15 weeks, but she must now complete the project in 13.

Approach: Steinberg needs to determine which activities to crash, and by how much, to meet this 13-week due date. Naturally, Steinberg is interested in speeding up the project by 2 weeks, at the least additional cost.

Solution: The company's normal and crash times, and normal and crash costs, are shown in Table 5. Note, for example, that activity B's normal time is 3 weeks (the estimate used in computing the critical path), and its crash time is 1 week. This means that activity B can be shortened by up to 2 weeks if extra resources are provided. The cost of these additional resources is $4,000 (= difference between the crash cost of $34,000 and the normal cost of $30,000). If we assume that the crashing cost is linear over time (i.e., the cost is the same each week), activity B's crash cost per week is $2,000 (= $4,000/2).

▶ **Table 5**

Normal and Crash Data for Milwaukee Paper Manufacturing

	Time (Weeks)		Cost ($)			
Activity	Normal	Crash	Normal	Crash	Crash Cost Per Week ($)	Critical Path?
A	2	1	22,000	22,750	750	Yes
B	3	1	30,000	34,000	2,000	No
C	2	1	26,000	27,000	1,000	Yes
D	4	3	48,000	49,000	1,000	No
E	4	2	56,000	58,000	1,000	Yes
F	3	2	30,000	30,500	500	No
G	5	2	80,000	84,500	1,500	Yes
H	2	1	16,000	19,000	3,000	Yes

This calculation for Activity B is shown in Figure 16. Crash costs for all other activities can be computed in a similar fashion.

▶ **Figure 16**

Crash and Normal Times and Costs for Activity B

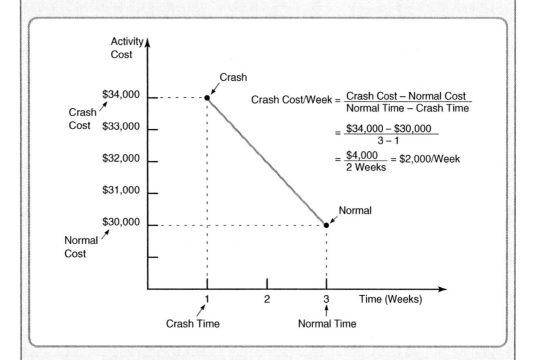

Steps 2, 3, and 4 can now be applied to reduce Milwaukee Paper's project completion time at a minimum cost. We show the project network for Milwaukee Paper again in Figure 17.

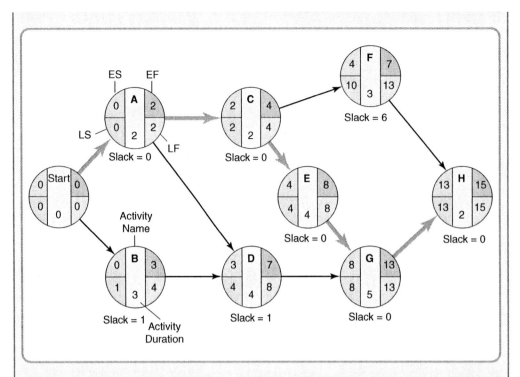

◀ **Figure 17**

Critical Path and Slack Times for Milwaukee Paper

The current critical path (using normal times) is Start-A-C-E-G-H, in which Start is just a dummy starting activity. Of these critical activities, activity A has the lowest crash cost per week of $750. Joni Steinberg should therefore crash activity A by 1 week to reduce the project completion time to 14 weeks. The cost is an additional $750. Note that activity A cannot be crashed any further, since it has reached its crash limit of 1 week.

At this stage, the original path Start-A-C-E-G-H remains critical with a completion time of 14 weeks. However, a new path Start-B-D-G-H is also critical now, with a completion time of 14 weeks. Hence, any further crashing must be done to both critical paths.

On each of these critical paths, we need to identify one activity that can still be crashed. We also want the total cost of crashing an activity on each path to be the smallest. We might be tempted to simply pick the activities with the smallest crash cost per period in each path. If we did this, we would select activity C from the first path and activity D from the second path. The total crash cost would then be $2,000 (= $1,000 + $1,000).

But we spot that activity G is common to both paths. That is, by crashing activity G, we will simultaneously reduce the completion time of both paths. Even though the $1,500 crash cost for activity G is higher than that for activities C and D, we would still prefer crashing G, since the total cost will now be only $1,500 (compared with the $2,000 if we crash C and D).

Insight: To crash the project down to 13 weeks, Steinberg should crash activity A by 1 week, and activity G by 1 week. The total additional cost will be $2,250 (= $750 + $1,500). This is important because many contracts for projects include bonuses or penalties for early or late finishes.

Learning exercise: Say the crash cost for activity B is $31,000 instead of $34,000. How does this change the answer? [Answer: no change.]

Related problems: 16, 18, 19, 20, 25

A CRITIQUE OF PERT AND CPM

As a critique of our discussions of PERT, here are some of its features about which operations managers need to be aware:

Advantages
1. Especially useful when scheduling and controlling large projects.
2. Straightforward concept and not mathematically complex.
3. Graphical networks help highlight relationships among project activities.

OM in Action The Mismanagement of Amtrak's Massive Acela Project

With pressure from Congress to break Amtrak into smaller, less-government-dependent pieces, the U.S. passenger rail service embarked in 1996 on a huge project: Acela. Acela's goal was to become the first U.S. train service to compete with airlines in the Washington DC–New York–Boston corridor. One key component was the Acela Express, a sleek 150-mile-per-hour train, with Internet connections at every seat and microbrews on tap. The $32 billion project, when complete, was expected to cut the New York–Boston run by almost 2 hours and add $180 million in annual profits to the besieged Amtrak Corporation.

But according to the U.S. General Accounting Office (GAO) (the nation's auditing arm) both Amtrak and its major suppliers mismanaged the project. "Amtrak's management was not comprehensive, and it was focused primarily on the short term," states a recent GAO report. Amtrak spokesman Cliff Black says "The GAO report is accurate . . . as it relates to project planning and management." Amtrak was faulted for not tackling infrastructure problems like track improvements, bridges, and overhead electrical wires. As a result Acela makes the journey much more slowly than planned.

Stew Milne, AP Wide World Photos

It didn't help the project that the firms jointly building the $1 billion worth of Acela trains, Bombardier of Quebec and Britain's GEC Alston, produced a locomotive with defective wheels. As in most large projects, the penalties for late delivery were painful. The fines started at $1,000 per train per day and escalated to $13,500 per train per day.

Now, having redefined the scope of the project, clarified the work breakdown structure, addressed many of the infrastructure problems, and invested billions more, Amtrak reports that Acela's speed is finally increasing. The train may one day beat the plane.

Sources: The Wall Street Journal (April 21, 2005): D3; Knight Ridder Tribune Business News (March 19, 2004): 1; and The New York Times (July 17, 2004): C7.

4. Critical path and slack time analyses help pinpoint activities that need to be closely watched.
5. Project documentation and graphs point out who is responsible for various activities.
6. Applicable to a wide variety of projects.
7. Useful in monitoring not only schedules but costs as well.

Limitations

1. Project activities have to be clearly defined, independent, and stable in their relationships.
2. Precedence relationships must be specified and networked together.
3. Time estimates tend to be subjective and are subject to fudging by managers who fear the dangers of being overly optimistic or not pessimistic enough.
4. There is the inherent danger of placing too much emphasis on the longest, or critical, path. Near-critical paths need to be monitored closely as well.

In large networks there are too many activities to monitor closely, but managers can concentrate on the critical and near critical activities.

USING MICROSOFT PROJECT TO MANAGE PROJECTS

Learning Objective

7. Use Microsoft Project software to create a project

The approaches discussed so far are effective for managing small projects. However, for large or complex projects, specialized project management software is much preferred. In this section, we provide a brief introduction to the most popular example of such specialized software, Microsoft Project.

We should note that at this introductory level, our intent here is not to describe the full capabilities of this program. Rather, we illustrate how it can be used to perform some of the basic calculations in managing projects. We leave it to you to explore the advanced capabilities and functions of Microsoft Project (or any other project management software) in greater detail. A time-limited version of Microsoft Project may be requested with this text.

Microsoft Project is useful for project scheduling and control.

Microsoft Project is extremely useful in drawing project networks, identifying the project schedule, and managing project costs and other resources. It does not, however, perform PERT probability calculations.

Creating a Project Schedule Using Microsoft Project

First, we define a new project.

Let us again consider the Milwaukee Paper Manufacturing project. Recall that this project has eight activities. The first step is to define the activities and their precedence relationships. To do so, we start Microsoft Project and click File|New to open a blank project. We can now enter the

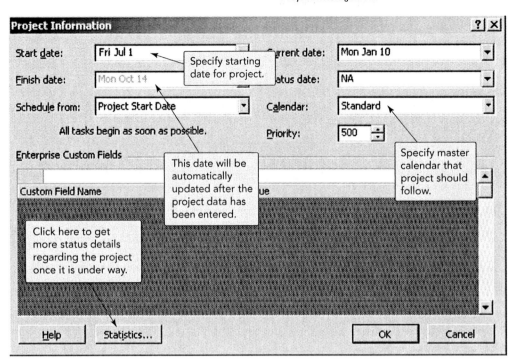

Durations	
Activity	**Time in Weeks**
A	2
B	3
C	2
D	4
E	4
F	3
G	5
H	2

project start date in the summary information that is first presented (see Program 1). Note that dates are referred to by actual calendar dates rather than as day 0, day 1, and so on. For example, we have used July 1 as our project starting date in Program 1. Microsoft Project will automatically update the project finish date once we have entered all the project information. In Program 1, we have specified the current date as January 10.

Entering Activity Information After entering the summary information, we now use the window shown in Program 2 to enter all activity information. For each activity (or task, as Microsoft Project calls it), we enter its name and duration. Microsoft Project identifies tasks by numbers (e.g., 1, 2) rather than letters. Hence, for convenience, we have shown both the letter

Next, we enter the activity information.

▼ **Program 2**   **Activity Entry in Microsoft Project for Milwaukee Paper Manufacturing**

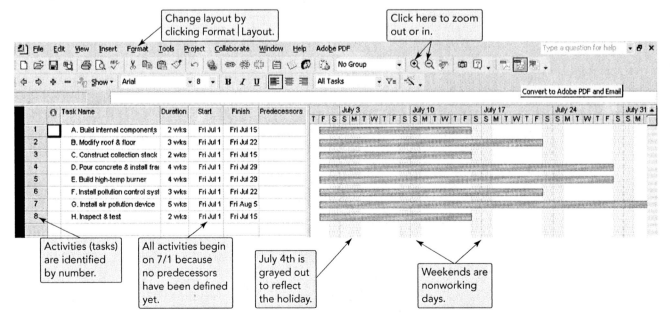

(e.g., A, B) and the description of the activity in the *Task Name* column in Program 2. By default, the duration is measured in days. To specify weeks, we include the letter "*w*" after the duration of each activity. For example, we enter the duration of activity A as 2*w*.

As we enter the activities and durations, the software automatically inserts start and finish dates. Note that all activities have the same start date (i.e., July 1), since we have not yet defined the precedence relationships. Also, as shown in Program 2, if the *Gantt Chart* option is selected in the *View* menu, a horizontal bar corresponding to the duration of each activity appears on the right pane of the window.

Observe that Saturdays and Sundays are automatically grayed out in the Gantt chart to reflect that these are nonworking days. In most project management software, the entire project is linked to a master calendar (or alternatively, each activity is linked to its own specific calendar). Additional nonworking days can be defined using these calendars. For example, we have used *Tools|Change Working Time* to specify July 4 as a nonworking day in Program 2. This automatically extends all activity completion times by one day. Since activity A starts on Friday, July 1, and takes 2 weeks (i.e., 10 working days), its finish time is now Friday, July 15 (rather than Thursday, July 14).

> *The schedule automatically takes nonworking days into account.*

Defining Precedence Relationships The next step is to define precedence relationships (or links) between these activities. There are two ways of specifying these links. The first is to enter the relevant activity numbers (e.g., 1, 2) in the *Predecessor* column, as shown in Program 3 for activities C and D. The other approach uses the *Link* icon. For example, to specify the precedence relationship between activities C and E, we click activity C first, hold the Ctrl key down, and then click activity E. We then click the Link icon, as shown in Program 3. As soon as we define a link, the bars in the Gantt chart are automatically repositioned to reflect the new start and finish times for the linked activities. Further, the link itself is shown as an arrow extending from the predecessor activity.

Viewing the Project Schedule When all links have been defined, the complete project schedule can be viewed as a Gantt chart, as shown in Program 4. We can also select *View|Network Diagram* to view the schedule as a project network (shown in Program 5). The critical path is shown in red on the screen (bold in Program 5) in the network diagram. We can click on any of the activities in the project network to view details of the activities. Likewise, we can easily add or remove activities and/or links from the project network. Each time we do so, Microsoft Project automatically updates all start dates, finish dates, and the critical path(s). If desired, we can manually change the layout of the network (e.g., reposition activities) by changing the options in *Format|Layout*.

> *The project can be viewed either as a Gantt chart or as a network.*

Precedences

Activity	Predecessors
A	—
B	—
C	A
D	A, B
E	C
F	C
G	D, E
H	F, G

▼ **Program 3** Defining Links Between Activities in Microsoft Project

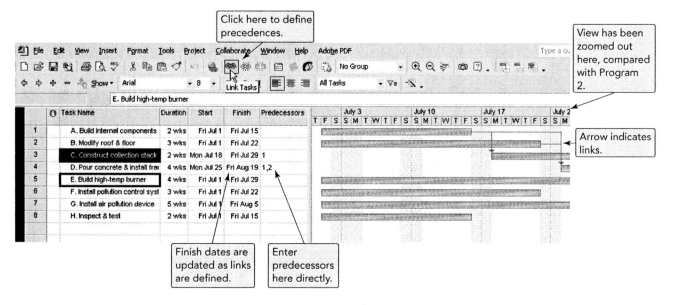

95

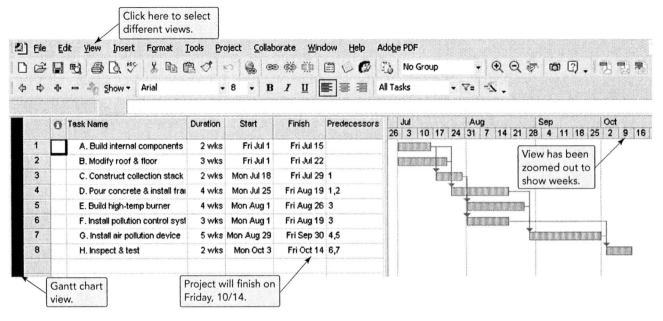

▲ **Program 4**   Gantt Chart in Microsoft Project for Milwaukee Paper Manufacturing

Programs 4 and 5 show that if Milwaukee Paper's project starts on July 1, it can be finished on October 14. The start and finish dates for all activities are also clearly identified. This schedule takes into account the nonworking days on all weekends, and on July 4. These programs illustrate how the use of specialized project management software can greatly simplify the scheduling procedures discussed earlier in this chapter.

PERT Analysis   As mentioned, Microsoft Project does not perform the PERT probability calculations discussed in Examples 10 and 11. However, by clicking View|Toolbars|PERT Analysis, we can get Microsoft Project to allow us to enter optimistic, most likely, and pessimistic times for each activity. We can then choose to view Gantt charts based on any of these three times for each activity.

▼ **Program 5**   Project Network in Microsoft Project for Milwaukee Paper Manufacturing

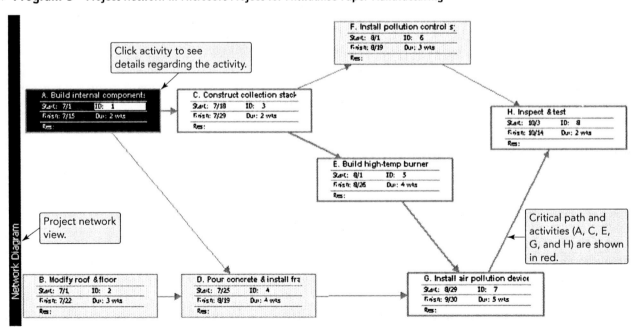

> Using PERT/CPM, Taco Bell built and opened this fast-food restaurant in Compton, California, in just 2 days! Typically, 2 months are needed to accomplish such a task. Good project management means a faster revenue stream instead of money tied up in construction.

David Young-Wolff, PhotoEdit Inc.

Tracking Progress and Managing Costs Using Microsoft Project

Perhaps the biggest advantage of using specialized software to manage projects is that they can track the progress of the project. In this regard, Microsoft Project has many features available to track individual activities in terms of time, cost, resource usage, and so on. In this section, we illustrate how we can track the progress of a project in terms of time.

Pollution Project Percent Completed on Aug. 12

Activity	Completed
A	100
B	100
C	100
D	10
E	20
F	20
G	0
H	0

Tracking the Time Status of a Project   An easy way to track the time progress of tasks is to enter the percent of work completed for each task. One way to do so is to double-click on any activity in the *Task Name* column in Program 4. A window, like the one shown in Program 6 is displayed. Let us now enter the percent of work completed for each task.

The table in the margin provides data regarding the percent of each of Milwaukee Paper's activities as of today. (Assume today is Friday, August 12, i.e., the end of the sixth week of the project schedule.)[5] Program 6 shows that activity A is 100% complete. We enter the percent completed for all other activities in a similar fashion.

> **Program 6**

Updating Activity Progress in Microsoft Project

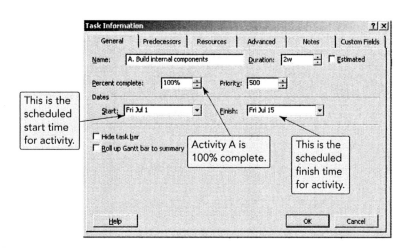

[5]Remember that the nonworking day on July 4 has moved all schedules by one day. Therefore, activities end on Fridays rather than on Thursdays.

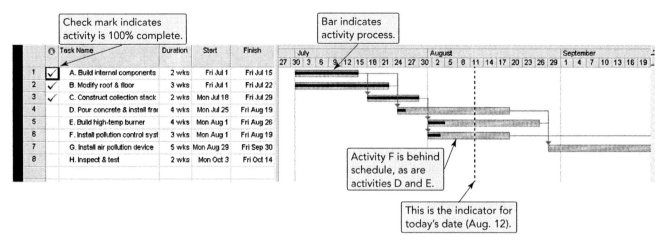

Check mark indicates activity is 100% complete.

Bar indicates activity process.

		Task Name	Duration	Start	Finish
1	✓	A. Build internal components	2 wks	Fri Jul 1	Fri Jul 15
2	✓	B. Modify roof & floor	3 wks	Fri Jul 1	Fri Jul 22
3	✓	C. Construct collection stack	2 wks	Mon Jul 18	Fri Jul 29
4		D. Pour concrete & install fra	4 wks	Mon Jul 25	Fri Aug 19
5		E. Build high-temp burner	4 wks	Mon Aug 1	Fri Aug 26
6		F. Install pollution control syst	3 wks	Mon Aug 1	Fri Aug 19
7		G. Install air pollution device	5 wks	Mon Aug 29	Fri Sep 30
8		H. Inspect & test	2 wks	Mon Oct 3	Fri Oct 14

Activity F is behind schedule, as are activities D and E.

This is the indicator for today's date (Aug. 12).

▲ **Program 7**   **Tracking Project Progress in Microsoft Project**

As shown in Program 7, the Gantt chart immediately reflects this updated information by drawing a thick line within each activity's bar. The length of this line is proportional to the percent of that activity's work that has been completed.

How do we know if we are on schedule? Notice that there is a vertical line shown on the Gantt chart corresponding to today's date. Microsoft Project will automatically move this line to correspond with the current date. If the project is on schedule, we should see all bars to the *left* of today's line indicate that they have been completed. For example, Program 7 shows that activities A, B, and C are on schedule. In contrast, activities D, E, and F appear to be behind schedule. These activities need to be investigated further to determine the reason for the delay. This type of easy *visual* information is what makes such software so useful in practice for project management.

In addition to reading this section on Microsoft Project, we encourage you to load the software from the CD-ROM that may be ordered with your text and try these procedures.

> *"Poorly managed projects are costly, not only financially, but also in wasted time and demoralized personnel. But failure is almost never the result of poor software."*
>
> *C. Fujinami and A. Marshall, consultants at Kepner Tregoe, Inc.*

Summary

PERT, CPM, and other scheduling techniques have proven to be valuable tools in controlling large and complex projects. With these tools, managers understand the status of each activity and know which activities are critical and which have slack; in addition, they know where crashing makes the most sense. Projects are segmented into discrete activities, and specific resources are identified. This allows project managers to respond aggressively to global competition. Effective project management also allows firms to create products and services for global markets. As with Microsoft Project illustrated in this chapter, a wide variety of software packages are available to help managers handle network modeling problems.

PERT and CPM do not, however, solve all the project scheduling and management problems. Good management practices, clear responsibilities for tasks, and straightforward and timely reporting systems are also needed. It is important to remember that the models we described in this chapter are only tools to help managers make better decisions.

Key Terms

Project organization
Work breakdown structure (WBS)
Gantt charts
Program evaluation and review technique (PERT)
Critical path method (CPM)
Critical path

Activity-on-node (AON)
Activity-on-arrow (AOA)
Dummy activity
Critical path analysis
Forward pass
Backward pass
Slack time

Total slack
Free slack
Optimistic time
Pessimistic time
Most likely time
Crashing

Using Software to Solve Project Management Problems

In addition to the Microsoft Project software just illustrated, both Excel OM and POM for Windows are available to readers of this text as project management tools.

✖ Using Excel OM

Excel OM has a Project Scheduling module. Program 8 uses the data from the Milwaukee Paper Manufacturing example in this chapter (see Examples 4 and 5). The PERT/CPM analysis also handles activities with three time estimates.

ℙ Using POM for Windows

POM for Window's Project Scheduling module can also find the expected project completion time for a CPM and PERT network with either one or three time estimates. POM for Windows also performs project crashing.

▶ **Program 8**

Excel OM's Use of Milwaukee Paper Manufacturing's Data from Examples 4 and 5

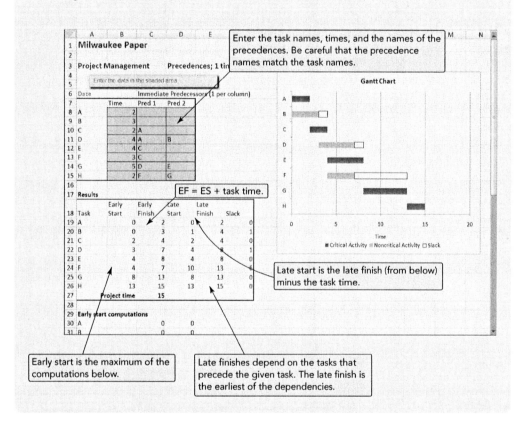

Solved Problems

Virtual Office Hours help is available on Student DVD.

Solved Problem 1

Construct an AON network based on the following:

Activity	Immediate Predecessor(s)
A	—
B	—
C	—
D	A, B
E	C

Solution

Solved Problem 2

Insert a dummy activity and event to correct the following AOA network:

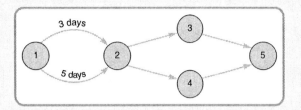

solution

Since we cannot have two activities starting and ending at the same node, we add the following dummy activity and dummy event to obtain the correct AOA network:

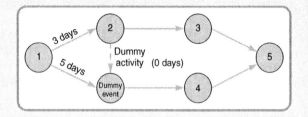

Solved Problem 3

Calculate the critical path, project completion time T, and project variance σ_p^2, based on the following AON network information:

Activity	Time	Variance	ES	EF	LS	LF	Slack
A	2	$\frac{2}{6}$	0	2	0	2	0
B	3	$\frac{2}{6}$	0	3	1	4	1
C	2	$\frac{4}{6}$	2	4	2	4	0
D	4	$\frac{4}{6}$	3	7	4	8	1
E	4	$\frac{2}{6}$	4	8	4	8	0
F	3	$\frac{1}{6}$	4	7	10	13	6
G	5	$\frac{1}{6}$	8	13	8	13	0

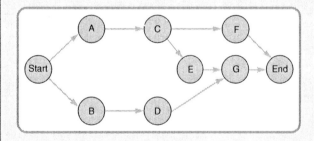

solution

We conclude that the critical path is Start-A-C-E-G-End:

$$\text{Total project time} = T = 2 + 2 + 4 + 5 = 13$$

and

$$\sigma_p^2 = \Sigma \text{ Variances on the critical path} = \frac{2}{6} + \frac{4}{6} + \frac{2}{6} + \frac{1}{6} = \frac{9}{6} = 1.5$$

Solved Problem 4

To complete the wing assembly for an experimental aircraft, Jim Gilbert has laid out the seven major activities involved. These activities have been labeled A through G in the following table, which also shows their estimated completion times (in weeks) and immediate predecessors. Determine the expected time and variance for each activity:

Activity	a	m	b	Immediate Predecessors
A	1	2	3	—
B	2	3	4	—
C	4	5	6	A
D	8	9	10	B
E	2	5	8	C, D
F	4	5	6	D
G	1	2	3	E

solution

Expected times and variances can be computed using Equations and (7) presented in this chapter. The results are summarized in the following table:

Activity	Expected Time (in weeks)	Variance
A	2	$\frac{1}{9}$
B	3	$\frac{1}{9}$
C	5	$\frac{1}{9}$
D	9	$\frac{1}{9}$
E	5	1
F	5	$\frac{1}{9}$
G	2	$\frac{1}{9}$

Solved Problem 5

Referring to Solved Problem 4, now Jim Gilbert would like to determine the critical path for the entire wing assembly project as well as the expected completion time for the total project. In addition, he would like to determine the earliest and latest start and finish times for all activities.

solution

The AON network for Gilbert's project is shown in Figure 18. Note that this project has multiple activities (A and B) with no immediate predecessors, and multiple activities (F and G) with no successors. Hence, in addition to a unique starting activity (Start), we have included a unique finishing activity (End) for the project.

Figure 18 shows the earliest and latest times for all activities. The results are also summarized in the following table:

		Activity Time			
Activity	**ES**	**EF**	**LS**	**LF**	**Slack**
A	0	2	5	7	5
B	0	3	0	3	0
C	2	7	7	12	5
D	3	12	3	12	0
E	12	17	12	17	0
F	12	17	14	19	2
G	17	19	17	19	0

Expected project length = 19 weeks

Variance of the critical path = 1.333

Standard deviation of the critical path = 1.155 weeks

The activities along the critical path are B, D, E, and G. These activities have zero slack as shown in the table.

▶ Figure 18

Critical Path for Solved Problem 5

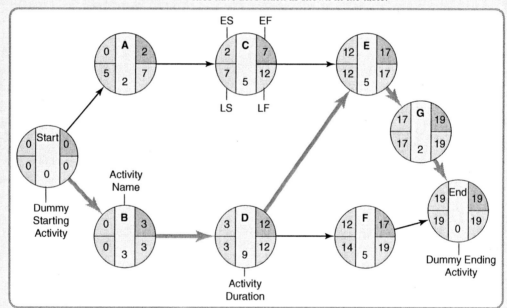

Solved Problem 6

The following information has been computed from a project:

Expected total project time = T = 62 weeks

Project variance $\left(\sigma_p^2\right) = 81$

What is the probability that the project will be completed 18 weeks *before* its expected completion date?

solution

The desired completion date is 18 weeks before the expected completion date, 62 weeks. The desired completion date is 44 (or 62 − 18) weeks:

$$\sigma_p = \sqrt{\text{Project variance}}$$

$$Z = \frac{\text{Due date} - \text{Expected completion date}}{\sigma_p}$$

$$= \frac{44 - 62}{9} = \frac{-18}{9} = -2.0$$

The normal curve appears as follows:

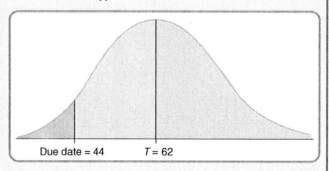

Because the normal curve is symmetrical and table values are calculated for positive values of Z, the area desired is equal to 1 − (table value). For Z = +2.0, the area from the table is .97725. Thus, the area corresponding to a Z value of −2.0 is .02275 (or 1 − .97725). Hence, the probability of completing the project 18 weeks before the expected completion date is approximately .023, or 2.3%.

101

Solved Problem 7

Determine the least cost of reducing the project completion date by 3 months based on the following information:

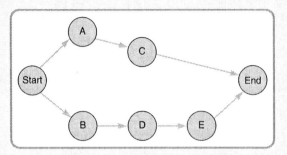

Activity	Normal Time (months)	Crash Time (months)	Normal Cost	Crash Cost
A	6	4	$2,000	$2,400
B	7	5	3,000	3,500
C	7	6	1,000	1,300
D	6	4	2,000	2,600
E	9	8	8,800	9,000

solution

The first step in this problem is to compute ES, EF, LS, LF, and slack for each activity:

Activity	ES	EF	LS	LF	Slack
A	0	6	9	15	9
B	0	7	0	7	0
C	6	13	15	22	9
D	7	13	7	13	0
E	13	22	13	22	0

The critical path consists of activities B, D, and E.

Next, crash cost/month must be computed for each activity:

Activity	Normal Time – Crash Time	Crash Cost – Normal Cost	Crash Cost/ Month	Critical Path?
A	2	$400	$200/month	No
B	2	500	250/month	Yes
C	1	300	300/month	No
D	2	600	300/month	Yes
E	1	200	200/month	Yes

Finally, we will select that activity on the critical path with the smallest crash cost/month. This is activity E. Thus, we can reduce the total project completion date by 1 month for an additional cost of $200. We still need to reduce the project completion date by 2 more months. This reduction can be achieved at least cost along the critical path by reducing activity B by 2 months for an additional cost of $500. This solution is summarized in the following table:

Activity	Months Reduced	Cost
E	1	$200
B	2	500
		Total: $700

Active Model Exercise

Milwaukee Paper Manufacturing. This Active Model allows you to evaluate changes in important elements on the hospital network we saw in this chapter, using your CD-ROM. See Active Model 1.

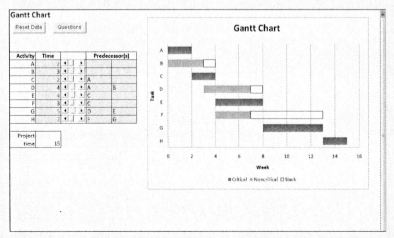

◄ **Active Model 3.1**

Project Management

This graph contains a Gantt chart for the single time estimate Milwaukee Paper project. The critical activities appear in red in both the data table and the Gantt chart. Noncritical activities appear in green in the Gantt chart, and the right side of these noncritical activities displays the amount of slack they have. You can use the scrollbars to change the times of the individual activities. For critical activities, when you change the times the project times will change. For noncritical activities, if you increase the time, then they will eventually become critical.

Questions

1. Both A and H are critical activities. Describe the difference between what happens on the graph when you increase A vs. increasing H.

2. Activity F is not critical. By how many weeks can you increase activity F until it becomes critical?

3. Activity B is not critical. By how many weeks can you increase activity B until it becomes critical? What happens when B becomes critical?

4. What happens when you increase B by 1 more week after it becomes critical?

5. Suppose that building codes change and as a result activity B would have to be completed before activity C could be started. How would this affect the project?

Self-Test

- **Before taking the self-test**, *refer to the learning objectives listed at the beginning of the chapter and the key terms listed at the end of the chapter.*
- *Use the key at the back of the text to* **correct** *your answers.*
- **Restudy** *pages that correspond to any questions you answered incorrectly or material you feel uncertain about.*

1. With respect to PERT and CPM, an event:
   a) marks the start or completion of a task.
   b) is a task or subproject that must be completed.
   c) is the amount of time a task may be delayed without affecting any other task in the network.
   d) is the amount of time a task may be delayed without changing the overall project completion time.

2. With respect to PERT and CPM, free slack:
   a) marks the start or completion of a task.
   b) is a task or subproject that must be completed.
   c) is the amount of time a task may be delayed without affecting any other task in the network.
   d) is the amount of time a task may be delayed without changing the overall project completion time.

3. A dummy activity is required when:
   a) the network contains two or more activities that have identical starting and ending events.
   b) two or more activities have the same starting events.
   c) two or more activities have the same ending events.
   d) all of the above are true.

4. Critical path analysis is used to determine:
   a) the earliest activity start time.
   b) the latest activity start time.
   c) activity slack time.
   d) all of the above.

5. The critical path of a network is the:
   a) shortest time path through the network.
   b) path with the fewest activities.
   c) path with the most activities.
   d) longest time path through the network.

6. Slack time equals:
   a) $ES + t$.
   b) $LS - ES$.
   c) zero.
   d) $EF - ES$.

7. If an activity with free slack time of 2 weeks is delayed by 1 week:
   a) the project will be delayed by 1 week.
   b) the slack time of all activities that follow this activity is reduced by 1 week.
   c) no other activity in the project is affected.
   d) the probability of completing the project on time decreases.

8. In PERT, if the pessimistic time was 14 weeks, the optimistic time was 8 weeks, and the most likely time was 11 weeks:
   a) the variance would be 1 week.
   b) the variance would be 11 weeks.
   c) the expected time would be 6 weeks.
   d) the expected time would be $5\frac{1}{2}$ weeks.
   e) there is not enough information.

9. The crash cost per week:
   a) is the difference in costs divided by the difference in times (crash and normal).
   b) is considered to be linear in the range between normal and crash.
   c) needs to be determined so that the smallest cost values on the critical path may be considered for time reduction first.
   d) all of the above.

10. PERT analysis computes the variance of the total project completion time as:
    a) the sum of the variances of all activities in the project.
    b) the sum of the variances of all activities on the critical path.
    c) the sum of the variances of all activities not on the critical path.
    d) the variance of the final activity of the project.

Internet and Student CD-ROM/DVD Exercises

Visit our Companion Web site or use your student CD-ROM/DVD to help with the material in this chapter.

On Our Companion Web site,
www.prenhall.com/heizer
- Self-Study Quizzes
- Practice Problems
- Virtual Company Tour
- Internet Cases
- PowerPoint Lecture
- Microsoft Project (upon request)

On Your Student CD-ROM
- Practice Problems
- ExcelOM
- Excel OM Data Files
- Active Model Exercise
- POM for Windows

On Your Student DVD
- Video Clips and Video Cases
- Virtual Office Hours for Solved Problems

Discussion Questions

1. Give an example of a situation in which project management is needed.
2. Explain the purpose of project organization.
3. What are the three phases involved in the management of a large project?
4. What are some of the questions that can be answered with PERT and CPM?
5. Define *work breakdown structure*. How is it used?
6. What is the use of Gantt charts in project management?
7. What is the difference between an activity-on-arrow (AOA) network and an activity-on-node (AON) network? Which is primarily used in this chapter?
8. What is the significance of the critical path?
9. What would a project manager have to do to crash an activity?
10. Describe how expected activity times and variances can be computed in a PERT network.
11. Define *early start*, *early finish*, *late finish*, and *late start* times.

12. Students are sometimes confused by the concept of critical path, and want to believe that it is the *shortest* path through a network. Convincingly explain why this is not so.
13. What are dummy activities? Why are they used in activity-on-arrow (AOA) project networks?
14. What are the three time estimates used with PERT?
15. Would a project manager ever consider crashing a noncritical activity in a project network? Explain convincingly.
16. How is the variance of the total project computed in PERT?
17. Describe the meaning of slack, and discuss how it can be determined.
18. How can we determine the probability that a project will be completed by a certain date? What assumptions are made in this computation?
19. Name some of the widely used project management software programs.

Ethical Dilemma

Two examples of massively mismanaged projects are TAURUS and the "Big Dig." The first, formally called the London Stock Exchange Automation Project, cost $575 million before it was finally abandoned. Although most IT projects have a reputation for cost overruns, delays, and underperformance, TAURUS set a new standard.

But even TAURUS paled next to the biggest, most expensive public works project in U.S. history—Boston's 15-year-long Central Artery/Tunnel Project. Called the Big Dig, this was perhaps the poorest and most felonious case of project mismanagement in decades. From a starting $2 billion budget to a final price tag of $15 billion, the Big Dig cost more than the Panama Canal, Hoover Dam, or Interstate 95, the 1,919-mile highway between Maine and Florida.

Read about one of these two projects (or another of your choice) and explain why it faced such problems. How and why do project managers allow such massive endeavors to fall into such a state? What do you think are the causes?

Problems*

* 1 The work breakdown structure for building a house (levels 1 and 2) is shown below:

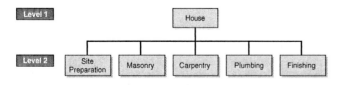

Note: **PX** means the problem may be solved with POM for Windows and/or Excel OM.

a) Add two level-3 activities to each of the level-2 activities to provide more detail to the WBS.
b) Select one of your level-3 activities and add two level-4 activities below it.

** 2 Robert Mefford has decided to run for a seat as Congressman from the House of Representative district 34 in California. He views his 8-month campaign for office as a major project and wishes to create a work breakdown structure (WBS) to help control the detailed scheduling. So far, he has developed the following pieces of the WBS:

Level	Level ID No.	Activity
1	1.0	Develop political campaign
2	1.1	Fund-raising plan
3	1.11	_____
3	1.12	_____
3	1.13	_____
2	1.2	Develop a position on major issues
3	1.21	_____
3	1.22	_____
3	1.23	_____
2	1.3	Staffing for campaign
3	1.31	_____
3	1.32	_____
3	1.33	_____
3	1.34	_____
2	1.4	Paperwork compliance for candidacy
3	1.41	_____
3	1.42	_____
2	1.5	Ethical plan/issues
3	1.51	_____

Help Mr. Mefford by providing details where the blank lines appear. Are there any other major (level-2) activities to create? If so, add an ID no. 1.6 and insert them.

• **3** Draw the activity-on-node (AON) project network associated with the following activities for Dave Carhart's consulting company project. How long should it take Dave and his team to complete this project? What are the critical path activities?

Activity	Immediate Predecessor(s)	Time (days)
A	—	3
B	A	4
C	A	6
D	B	6
E	B	4
F	C	4
G	D	6
H	E, F	8

• **4** Given the activities whose sequence is described by the following table, draw the appropriate activity-on-arrow (AOA) network diagram.
a) Which activities are on the critical path?
b) What is the length of the critical path?

Activity	Immediate Predecessor(s)	Time (days)
A	—	5
B	A	2
C	A	4
D	B	5
E	B	5
F	C	5
G	E, F	2
H	D	3
I	G, H	5

• **5** Using AOA, diagram the network described below for Sarah McComb's construction project. Calculate its critical path. How long is the minimum duration of this network?

Activity	Nodes	Time (weeks)	Activity	Nodes	Time (weeks)
J	1–2	10	N	3–4	2
K	1–3	8	O	4–5	7
L	2–4	6	P	3–5	5
M	2–3	3			

•• **6** Shirley Hopkins is developing a program in leadership training for middle-level managers. Shirley has listed a number of activities that must be completed before a training program of this nature could be conducted. The activities, immediate predecessors, and times appear in the accompanying table:

Activity	Immediate Predecessor(s)	Time (days)
A	—	2
B	—	5
C	—	1
D	B	10
E	A, D	3
F	C	6
G	E, F	8

a) Develop an AON network for this problem.
b) What is the critical path?
c) What is the total project completion time?
d) What is the slack time for each individual activity?

•• **7** Task time estimates for a production line setup project at Robert Klassen's Ontario factory are as follows:

Activity	Time (in hours)	Immediate Predecessors
A	6.0	—
B	7.2	—
C	5.0	A
D	6.0	B, C
E	4.5	B, C
F	7.7	D
G	4.0	E, F

a) Draw the project network using AON.
b) Identify the critical path.
c) What is the expected project length?
d) Draw a Gantt chart for the project.

•• **8** The City Commission of Nashville has decided to build a botanical garden and picnic area in the heart of the city for the recreation of its citizens. The precedence table for all the activities required to construct this area successfully is given on page 95. Draw the Gantt chart for the whole construction activity.

105

Code	Activity	Description	Time (in hours)	Immediate Predecessor(s)
A	Planning	Find location; determine resource requirements	20	None
B	Purchasing	Requisition of lumber and sand	60	Planning
C	Excavation	Dig and grade	100	Planning
D	Sawing	Saw lumber into appropriate sizes	30	Purchasing
E	Placement	Position lumber in correct locations	20	Sawing, excavation
F	Assembly	Nail lumber together	10	Placement
G	Infill	Put sand in and under the equipment	20	Assembly
H	Outfill	Put dirt around the equipment	10	Assembly
I	Decoration	Put grass all over the garden, landscape, paint	30	Infill, outfill

•• 9 Refer to the table in Problem 8.
a) Draw the AON network for the construction activity.
b) Draw the AOA network for the construction activity.

• 10 The activities needed to build an experimental chemical contaminant tracking machine at Charlie Cook Corp. are listed in the following table. Construct an AON network for these activities.

Activity	Immediate Predecessor(s)	Activity	Immediate Predecessor(s)
A	—	E	B
B	—	F	B
C	A	G	C, E
D	A	H	D, F

• 11 Charlie Cook (see Problem 10) was able to determine the activity times for constructing his chemical contaminant tracking machine. Cook would like to determine ES, EF, LS, LF, and slack for each activity. The total project completion time and the critical path should also be determined. Here are the activity times:

Activity	Time (weeks)	Activity	Time (weeks)
A	6	E	4
B	7	F	6
C	3	G	10
D	2	H	7

• 12 The activities described by the following table are given for the Duplaga Corporation:

Activity	Immediate Predecessor(s)	Time
A	—	9
B	A	7
C	A	3
D	B	6
E	B	9
F	C	4
G	E, F	6
H	D	5
I	G, H	3

a) Draw the appropriate AON PERT diagram for Ed Duplaga's management team.
b) Find the critical path.
c) What is the project completion time?

• 13 A small renovation of a Hard Rock Cafe gift shop has six activities (in hours). For the following estimates of a, m, and b, calculate the expected time and the standard deviation for each activity:

Activity	a	m	b
A	11	15	19
B	27	31	41
C	18	18	18
D	8	13	19
E	17	18	20
F	16	19	22

•• 14 McGee Carpet and Trim installs carpet in commercial offices. Andrea McGee has been very concerned with the amount of time it took to complete several recent jobs. Some of her workers are very unreliable. A list of activities and their optimistic completion time, the most likely completion time, and the pessimistic completion time (all in days) for a new contract are given in the following table:

Activity	Time (days)			Immediate Predecessor(s)
	a	m	b	
A	3	6	8	—
B	2	4	4	—
C	1	2	3	—
D	6	7	8	C
E	2	4	6	B, D
F	6	10	14	A, E
G	1	2	4	A, E
H	3	6	9	F
I	10	11	12	G
J	14	16	20	C
K	2	8	10	H, I

a) Determine the expected completion time and variance for each activity.
b) Determine the total project completion time and the critical path for the project.
c) Determine ES, EF, LS, LF, and slack for each activity.
d) What is the probability that McGee Carpet and Trim will finish the project in 40 days or less?

•• 15 The following is a table of activities associated with a project at Bill Figg Enterprises, their durations and what activities each must precede:

Activity	Duration (weeks)	Precedes
A (start)	1	B, C
B	1	E
C	4	F
E	2	F
F (end)	2	—

a) Draw an AON diagram of the project, including activity durations.
b) Define the critical path, listing all critical activities in chronological order.
c) What is the project duration (in weeks)?
d) What is the slack (in weeks) associated with any and all noncritical paths through the project? **Px**

•• 16 Assume that the activities in Problem 15 have the following costs to shorten: A, $300/week; B, $100/week; C, $200/week; E, $100/week; and F, $400/week. Assume also that you can crash an activity down to 0 weeks in duration and that every week you can shorten the project is worth $250 to you. What activities would you crash? What is the total crashing cost?

••• 17 Bill Fennema, president of Fennema Construction, has developed the tasks, durations, and predecessor relationships in the following table for building new motels. Draw the AON network and answer the questions that follow.

		Time Estimates (in weeks)		
Activity	Immediate Predecessor(s)	Optimistic	Most Likely	Pessimistic
A	—	4	8	10
B	A	2	8	24
C	A	8	12	16
D	A	4	6	10
E	B	1	2	3
F	E, C	6	8	20
G	E, C	2	3	4
H	F	2	2	2
I	F	6	6	6
J	D, G, H	4	6	12
K	I, J	2	2	3

a) What is the expected (estimated) time for activity C?
b) What is the variance for activity C?
c) Based on the calculation of estimated times, what is the critical path?
d) What is the estimated time of the critical path?
e) What is the activity variance along the critical path?
f) What is the probability of completion of the project before week 36? **Px**

••• 18 What is the minimum cost of crashing the following project that James Walters manages at Ball State University by 4 days?

Activity	Normal Time (days)	Crash Time (days)	Normal Cost	Crash Cost	Immediate Predecessor(s)
A	6	5	$ 900	$1,000	—
B	8	6	300	400	—
C	4	3	500	600	—
D	5	3	900	1,200	A
E	8	5	1,000	1,600	C

Px

•• 19 Three activities are candidates for crashing on a project network for a large computer installation (all are, of course, critical). Activity details are in the following table:

Activity	Predecessor	Normal Time	Normal Cost	Crash Time	Crash Cost
A	—	7 days	$6,000	6 days	$6,600
B	A	4 days	1,200	2 days	3,000
C	B	11 days	4,000	9 days	6,000

a) What action would you take to reduce the critical path by 1 day?
b) Assuming no other paths become critical, what action would you take to reduce the critical path one additional day?
c) What is the total cost of the 2-day reduction? **Px**

••• 20 Development of a new deluxe version of a particular software product is being considered by Ravi Behara's software house. The activities necessary for the completion of this project are listed in the following table:

Activity	Normal Time (weeks)	Crash Time (weeks)	Normal Cost	Crash Cost	Immediate Predecessor(s)
A	4	3	$2,000	$2,600	—
B	2	1	2,200	2,800	—
C	3	3	500	500	—
D	8	4	2,300	2,600	A
E	6	3	900	1,200	B
F	3	2	3,000	4,200	C
G	4	2	1,400	2,000	D, E

a) What is the project completion date?
b) What is the total cost required for completing this project on normal time?
c) If you wish to reduce the time required to complete this project by 1 week, which activity should be crashed, and how much will this increase the total cost?
d) What is the maximum time that can be crashed? How much would costs increase? **Px**

••• 21 The estimated times and immediate predecessors for the activities in a project at Caesar Douglas's retinal scanning company are given in the following table. Assume that the activity times are independent.

	Immediate	Time (weeks)		
Activity	Predecessor	a	m	b
A	—	9	10	11
B	—	4	10	16
C	A	9	10	11
D	B	5	8	11

107

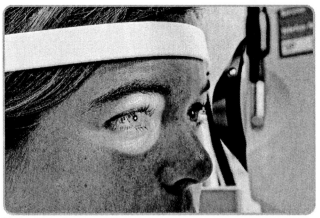

Markus Diohy, Peter Arnold Inc.

a) Calculate the expected time and variance for each activity.
b) What is the expected completion time of the critical path? What is the expected completion time of the other path in the network?
c) What is the variance of the critical path? What is the variance of the other path in the network?
d) If the time to complete path A–C is normally distributed, what is the probability that this path will be finished in 22 weeks or less?
e) If the time to complete path B–D is normally distributed, what is the probability that this path will be finished in 22 weeks or less?
f) Explain why the probability that the *critical path* will be finished in 22 weeks or less is not necessarily the probability that the *project* will be finished in 22 weeks or less. **Px**

• • • 22 Jack Kanet Manufacturing produces custom-built pollution control devices for medium-size steel mills. The most recent project undertaken by Jack requires 14 different activities.
a) Jack's managers would like to determine the total project completion time (in days) and those activities that lie along the critical path. The appropriate data are shown in the following table.
b) What is the probability of being done in 53 days?
c) What date results in a 99% probability of completion?

Activity	Immediate Predecessor(s)	Optimistic Time	Most Likely Time	Pessimistic Time
A	—	4	6	7
B	—	1	2	3
C	A	6	6	6
D	A	5	8	11
E	B, C	1	9	18
F	D	2	3	6
G	D	1	7	8
H	E, F	4	4	6
I	G, H	1	6	8
J	I	2	5	7
K	I	8	9	11
L	J	2	4	6
M	K	1	2	3
N	L, M	6	8	10

Px

• • • 23 Dream Team Productions, a firm hired to coordinate the release of the movie *Paycheck* (starring Uma Thurman and Ben Affleck), identified 16 activities to be completed before the release of the film.
a) How many weeks in advance of the film release should Dream Team have started its marketing campaign? What is the critical path? The tasks (in time units of weeks) are as follows:

Activity	Immediate Predecessors	Optimistic Time	Most Likely Time	Pessimistic Time
A	—	1	2	4
B	—	3	3.5	4
C	—	10	12	13
D	—	4	5	7
E	—	2	4	5
F	A	6	7	8
G	B	2	4	5.5
H	C	5	7.7	9
I	C	9.9	10	12
J	C	2	4	5
K	D	2	4	6
L	E	2	4	6
M	F, G, H	5	6	6.5
N	J, K, L	1	1.1	2
O	I, M	5	7	8
P	N	5	7	9

b) If activities I and J were not necessary, what impact would this have on the critical path and the number of weeks needed to complete the marketing campaign? **Px**

Paramount/Dreamworks, Picture Desk, Inc./Kobal Collection

• • 24 Using PERT, Harold Benson was able to determine that the expected project completion time for the construction of a pleasure yacht is 21 months, and the project variance is 4.
a) What is the probability that the project will be completed in 17 months?
b) What is the probability that the project will be completed in 20 months?

c) What is the probability that the project will be completed in 23 months?

d) What is the probability that the project will be completed in 25 months?

e) What is the due date that yields a 95% chance of completion? Px

••• 25 Bolling Electronics manufactures DVD players for commercial use. W. Blaker Bolling, president of Bolling Electronics, is contemplating producing DVD players for home use. The activities necessary to build an experimental model and related data are given in the following table:

Activity	Normal Time (weeks)	Crash Time (weeks)	Normal Cost ($)	Crash Cost ($)	Immediate Predecessor(s)
A	3	2	1,000	1,600	—
B	2	1	2,000	2,700	—
C	1	1	300	300	—
D	7	3	1,300	1,600	A
E	6	3	850	1,000	B
F	2	1	4,000	5,000	C
G	4	2	1,500	2,000	D, E

a) What is the project completion date?

b) Crash this project to 10 weeks at the least cost.

c) Crash this project to 7 weeks (which is the maximum it can be crashed) at the least cost. Px

••• 26 The Maser is a new custom-designed sports car. An analysis of the task of building the Maser reveals the following list of relevant activities, their immediate predecessors, and their duration[6]:

Job Letter	Description	Immediate Predecessor(s)	Normal Time (days)
A	Start	—	0
B	Design	A	8
C	Order special accessories	B	0.1
D	Build frame	B	1
E	Build doors	B	1
F	Attach axles, wheels, gas tank	D	1
G	Build body shell	B	2
H	Build transmission and drivetrain	B	3
I	Fit doors to body shell	G, E	1
J	Build engine	B	4
K	Bench-test engine	J	2
L	Assemble chassis	F, H, K	1
M	Road-test chassis	L	0.5
N	Paint body	I	2
O	Install wiring	N	1
P	Install interior	N	1.5
Q	Accept delivery of special accessories	C	5
R	Mount body and accessories on chassis	M, O, P, Q	1
S	Road test car	R	0.5
T	Attach exterior trim	S	1
U	Finish	T	0

a) Draw a network diagram for the project.

b) Mark the critical path and state its length.

c) If the Maser had to be completed 2 days earlier, would it help to:
   i) Buy preassembled transmissions and drivetrains?
   ii) Install robots to halve engine-building time?
   iii) Speed delivery of special accessories by 3 days?

d) How might resources be borrowed from activities on the noncritical path to speed activities on the critical path? Px

••• 27 You are asked to manage the morning seminars at Miami's South Beach Wine and Food Festival next year. There are three seminars, each requiring several tasks. You must begin by recruiting a committee of six people to help you. You must also recruit one assistant. This is task A and you expect it will take 12 hours. Then, you will concurrently work on developing ideas for each of the seminars. The business college dean, Bill Quain, says two of the seminars will be on "Dining in South Beach." You know this won't take you long. In fact, you plan to divide your committee into two groups to define the topic and then recruit a speaker. You think that these two groups, working concurrently, will take about 4 hours each to complete the task.

The third seminar is more difficult. Dean Quain wants something on "Great Wines I Found in Cheap Restaurants." You are going to work on this yourself, along with your most trusted assistant. This will be done at the same time as the planning for the other two seminars. It will probably take about 12 hours to complete. All three tasks must be completed before moving on to the next phase.

The next phase (task E) will require only you and your assistant. You will write the material for the programs. This will take about 6 hours to complete. For task F, your assistant faxes the program material to four printers, asking them for bids (1 hour). You will use specifications that were developed last year. You receive the bids, make copies, and provide them to the committee members (3 hours). In tasks H and I, the committee again splits up into two groups. Each group reviews all four bids and rates them (4 hours). Then, in task J, the committee members all meet and discuss the bids (2 hours). They then vote on the winning bid. This takes an additional hour.

After you and your assistant receive the vote, you both meet with the winning printer (task L), another hour. After the printer returns the proof, you and your assistant are required to have another 1-hour meeting with the printer to give your final approval. Two members of the committee make final arrangements for the venue (5 hours). The printer takes 10 hours to print the programs. Finally, the three seminars are run, concurrently. Each of them takes 2 hours and requires two committee members to be present at each seminar. After it is all over, your entire committee, including you and your assistant, meet for a 1-hour debriefing.

a) How long does the project take?

b) Which task has the *most* slack time?

c) Which tasks have no slack time?

d) What is the slack time for the critical path?

e) How many different tasks are there in this project?

f) Calculate how many hours you, your assistant, and the committee spend on this project.

g) You value your time, your assistant's time, and the time of your committee members at $25/hour. A consultant has bid $5,000 to take over the whole project (excluding the actual printing) and do all the work. Should you accept the bid? Px

[6]Source: James A. D. Stoner and Charles Wankel, *Management*, 3rd ed. (Upper Saddle River, NJ: Prentice Hall): 195.

Case Studies

Southwestern University: (A)*

Southwestern University (SWU), a large state college in Stephenville, Texas, 30 miles southwest of the Dallas/Fort Worth metroplex, enrolls close to 20,000 students. In a typical town–gown relationship, the school is a dominant force in the small city, with more students during fall and spring than permanent residents.

A longtime football powerhouse, SWU is a member of the Big Eleven conference and is usually in the top 20 in college football rankings. To bolster its chances of reaching the elusive and long-desired number-one ranking, in 2001, SWU hired the legendary Bo Pitterno as its head coach.

One of Pitterno's demands on joining SWU had been a new stadium. With attendance increasing, SWU administrators began to face the issue head-on. After 6 months of study, much political arm wrestling, and some serious financial analysis, Dr. Joel Wisner, president of Southwestern University, had reached a decision to expand the capacity at its on-campus stadium.

Adding thousands of seats, including dozens of luxury skyboxes, would not please everyone. The influential Pitterno had argued the need for a first-class stadium, one with built-in dormitory rooms for his players and a palatial office appropriate for the coach of a future NCAA champion team. But the decision was made, and *everyone*, including the coach, would learn to live with it.

The job now was to get construction going immediately after the 2007 season ended. This would allow exactly 270 days until the 2008 season opening game. The contractor, Hill Construction (Bob Hill being an alumnus, of course), signed his contract. Bob Hill looked at the tasks his engineers had outlined and looked President Wisner in the eye. "I guarantee the team will be able to take the field on schedule next year," he said with a sense of confidence. "I sure hope so," replied Wisner. "The contract penalty of $10,000 per day for running late is nothing compared to what Coach Pitterno will do to you if our opening game with Penn State is delayed or canceled." Hill, sweating slightly, did not need to respond. In football-crazy Texas, Hill Construction would be *mud* if the 270-day target was missed.

Back in his office, Hill again reviewed the data (see Table 6) and noted that optimistic time estimates can be used as crash times. He then gathered his foremen. "Folks, if we're not 75% sure we'll finish this stadium in less than 270 days, I want this project crashed! Give me the cost figures for a target date of 250 days—also for 240 days. I want to be *early*, not just on time!"

▼ **Table 6** Southwestern University Project

| Activity | Description | Predecessor(s) | Time Estimates (days) | | | Crash Cost/Day |
			Optimistic	Most Likely	Pessimistic	
A	Bonding, insurance, tax structuring	—	20	30	40	$1,500
B	Foundation, concrete footings for boxes	A	20	65	80	3,500
C	Upgrading skybox stadium seating	A	50	60	100	4,000
D	Upgrading walkways, stairwells, elevators	C	30	50	100	1,900
E	Interior wiring, lathes	B	25	30	35	9,500
F	Inspection approvals	E	0.1	0.1	0.1	0
G	Plumbing	D, E	25	30	35	2,500
H	Painting	G	10	20	30	2,000
I	Hardware/AC/metal workings	H	20	25	60	2,000
J	Tile/carpeting/windows	H	8	10	12	6,000
K	Inspection	J	0.1	0.1	0.1	0
L	Final detail work/cleanup	I, K	20	25	60	4,500

Discussion Questions

1. Develop a network drawing for Hill Construction and determine the critical path. How long is the project expected to take?
2. What is the probability of finishing in 270 days?
3. If it is necessary to crash to 250 or 240 days, how would Hill do so, and at what costs? As noted in the case, assume that optimistic time estimates can be used as crash times.

*This integrated case study runs throughout the text. Other issues facing Southwestern's football stadium include: (A) Managing the renovation project; (B) Forecasting game attendance; (C) Quality of facilities; (D) Break-even analysis of food services; (E) Locating the new stadium; (F) Inventory palnning of football programs; and (G) Scheduling of campus security officers/staff for game days.

Project Management at Arnold Palmer Hospital

Video Case

The equivalent of a new kindergarten class is born every day at Orlando's Arnold Palmer Hospital. With more than 12,300 births in 2005 in a hospital that was designed in 1989 for a capacity of 6,500 births a year, the newborn intensive care unit was stretched to the limit. Moreover, with continuing strong population growth in central Florida, the hospital was often full. It was clear that new facilities were needed. After much analysis, forecasting, and discussion, the management team decided to build a new 273-bed building across the street from the existing hospital. But the facility had to be built in accordance with the hospital's Guiding Principles and its uniqueness as a health center dedicated to the specialized needs of women and infants. Those Guiding Principles are: *Family-centered focus, a healing environment where privacy and dignity are respected, sanctuary of caring that includes warm, serene surroundings with natural lighting, sincere and dedicated staff providing the highest quality care, and patient-centered flow and function.*

The vice president of business development, Karl Hodges, wanted a hospital that was designed from the inside out by the people who understood the Guiding Principles, who knew most about the current system, and who were going to use the new system, namely, the doctors and nurses. Hodges and his staff spent 13 months discussing expansion needs with this group, as well as with patients and the community before developing a proposal for the new facility on December 17, 2001. An administrative team created 35 user groups, which held over 1,000 planning meetings (lasting from 45 minutes to a whole day). They even created a "Supreme Court" to deal with conflicting views on the multifaceted issues facing the new hospital.

Funding and regulatory issues added substantial complexity to this major expansion, and Hodges was very concerned that the project stay on time and within budget. Tom Hyatt, director of facility development, was given the task of onsite manager of the $100 million project, in addition to overseeing ongoing renovations, expansions, and other projects. The activities in the multiyear project for the new building at Arnold Palmer are shown in Table 7.

▼ Table 7   Expansion Planning and Arnold Palmer Hospital Construction Activities and Times[a]

Activity	Scheduled Time	Precedence Activity(ies)
1. Proposal and review	1 month	—
2. Establish master schedule	2 weeks	1
3. Architect selection process	5 weeks	1
4. Survey whole campus and its needs	1 month	1
5. Conceptual architect's plans	6 weeks	3
6. Cost estimating	2 months	2, 4, 5
7. Deliver plans to board for consideration/decision	1 month	6
8. Surveys/regulatory review	6 weeks	6
9. Construction manager selection	9 weeks	6
10. State review of need for more hospital beds ("Certificate of Need")	3.5 months	7, 8
11. Design drawings	4 months	10
12. Construction documents	5 months	9, 11
13. Site preparation/demolish existing building	9 weeks	11
14. Construction start/building pad	2 months	12, 13
15. Relocate utilities	6 weeks	12
16. Deep foundations	2 months	14
17. Building structure in place	9 months	16
18. Exterior skin/roofing	4 months	17
19. Interior buildout	12 months	17
20. Building inspections	5 weeks	15, 19
21. Occupancy	1 month	20

[a]This list of activities is abbreviated for purposes of this case study. For simplification, assume each week = .25 months (i.e., 2 weeks = .5 month, 6 weeks = 1.5 months, etc.).

Discussion Questions*

1. Develop the network for planning and construction of the new hospital at Arnold Palmer.
2. What is the critical path and how long is the project expected to take?
3. Why is the construction of this 11-story building any more complex than construction of an equivalent office building?
4. What percent of the whole project duration was spent in planning that occurred prior to the proposal and reviews? Prior to the actual building construction? Why?

*You may wish to review this video case on your DVD before answering these questions.

Source: Professors Barry Render (Rollins College), Jay Heizer (Texas Lutheran University), and Beverly Amer (Northern Arizona University).

Managing Hard Rock's Rockfest

Video Case

At the Hard Rock Cafe, like many organizations, project management is a key planning tool. With Hard Rock's constant growth in hotels and cafes, remodeling of existing cafes, scheduling for Hard Rock Live concert and event venues, and planning the annual Rockfest, managers rely on project management techniques and software to maintain schedule and budget performance.

"Without Microsoft Project," says Hard Rock Vice-President Chris Tomasso, "there is no way to keep so many people on the same page." Tomasso is in charge of the Rockfest event, which is attended by well over 100,000 enthusiastic fans. The challenge is pulling it off within a tight 9-month planning horizon. As the event approaches, Tomasso devotes greater energy to its activities. For the first 3 months, Tomasso updates his Microsoft Project charts monthly. Then

at the 6-month mark, he updates his progress weekly. At the 9-month mark, he checks and corrects his schedule twice a week.

Early in the project management process, Tomasso identifies 10 major tasks (called level-2 activities in a work breakdown structure, or WBS)[†]: talent booking, ticketing, marketing/PR, online promotion, television, show production, travel, sponsorships, operations, and merchandising. Using a WBS, each of these is further divided into a series of subtasks. Table 8 identifies 26 of the major activities and subactivities, their immediate predecessors, and time estimates. Tomasso enters all these into the Microsoft Project software.[‡] Tomasso alters the Microsoft Project document and the time line as the project progresses. "It's okay to change it as long as you keep on track," he states.

Activity	Description	Predecessor(s)	Time (weeks)
A	Finalize site and building contracts	—	7
B	Select local promoter	A	3
C	Hire production manager	A	3
D	Design promotional Web site	B	5
E	Set TV deal	D	6
F	Hire director	E	4
G	Plan for TV camera placement	F	2
H	Target headline entertainers	B	4
I	Target support entertainers	H	4
J	Travel accommodations for talent	I	10
K	Set venue capacity	C	2
L	Ticketmaster contract	D, K	3
M	On-site ticketing	L	8
N	Sound and staging	C	6
O	Passes and stage credentials	G, R	7
P	Travel accommodations for staff	B	20
Q	Hire sponsor coordinator	B	4
R	Finalize sponsors	Q	4
S	Define/place signage for sponsors	R, X	3
T	Hire operations manager	A	4
U	Develop site plan	T	6
V	Hire security director	T	7
W	Set police/fire security plan	V	4
X	Power, plumbing, AC, toilet services	U	8
Y	Secure merchandise deals	B	6
Z	Online merchandise sales	Y	6

◀ **Table 8**

Some of the Major Activities and Subactivities in the Rockfest Plan

The day of the rock concert itself is not the end of the project planning. "It's nothing but surprises. A band not being able to get to the venue because of traffic jams is a surprise, but an 'anticipated' surprise. We had a helicopter on stand-by ready to fly the band in," says Tomasso.

On completion of Rockfest in July, Tomasso and his team have a 3-month reprieve before starting the project planning process again.

Discussion Questions[§]

1. Identify the critical path and its activities for Rockfest. How long does the project take?
2. Which activities have a slack time of 8 weeks or more?

3. Identify five major challenges a project manager faces in events such as this one.
4. Why is a work breakdown structure useful in a project such as this? Take the 26 activities and break them into what you think should be level-2, level-3, and level-4 tasks.

[†]The level-1 activity is the Rockfest concert itself.

[‡]There are actually 127 activities used by Tomasso; the list is abbreviated for this case study.

[§]You may wish to play this video case on your DVD before addressing these questions.

Source: Professors Barry Render (Rollins College), Jay Heizer (Texas Lutheran University), and Beverly Amer (Northern Arizona University).

Additional Case Studies

Internet Case Study: Visit our Companion Web site at www.prenhall.com/heizer *for this free case study:*
- **Shale Oil Company:** This oil refinery must shut down for maintenance of a major piece of equipment.

Harvard has selected these Harvard Business School cases to accompany this chapter:

harvardbusinessonline.hbsp.harvard.edu

- **Microsoft Office 2000** (#600-097): An analysis of the evolution of the Office 2000 project.
- **Chrysler and BMW: Tritec Engine Joint Venture** (#600-004): A gifted project leader defines a new product strategy.
- **BAE Automated Systems (A): Denver International Baggage-Handling System** (#396-311): The project management of the construction of Denver's baggage-handling system.
- **Turner Construction Co.** (#190-128): Deals with the project management control system at a construction company.

Bibliography

Balakrishnan, R., B. Render, and R. M. Stair. *Managerial Decision Modeling with Spreadsheets*, 2nd ed. Upper Saddle River, NJ: Prentice Hall (2007).

Barkley, B. T. *Integrated Project Management.* New York: McGraw-Hill/Irwin (2006).

Cleland, D. L., and L. R. Ireland. *Project Management*, 5th ed. New York: McGraw-Hill/Irwin (2007).

Dusenberry, W. "CPM for New Product Introductions." *Harvard Business Review* (July–August 1967): 124–139.

Gray, C. L., and E. W. Larson. *Project Management: The Management Process.* New York: McGraw-Hill/Irwin (2006).

Herroslen, W., and R. Leus. "Project Scheduling Under Uncertainty: Survey and Research Potentials." *European Journal of Operations Research* 165, no. 2 (September, 2005): 289.

Kerzner, H. *Using the Project Management Maturity Model*, 2nd ed. New York: Wiley (2005).

Kumar, P. P. "Effective Use of Gantt Chart for Managing Large-Scale Projects." *Cost Engineering* 47, no. 7 (July 2005): 14–21.

Meredith, J. R., and S. Mantel. *Project Management*, 6th ed. New York: Wiley (2006).

Matta, N. F., and R. N. Ashkenas. "Why Good Projects Fail Anyways." *Harvard Business Review* (September 2003): 109–114.

Oates, David. "Understanding and Solving the Causes of Project Failure." *Knowledge Management Review* 9, no. 5 (May–June 2006): 5.

Render, B., R. M. Stair, and M. Hanna. *Quantitative Analysis for Management*, 10th ed. Upper Saddle River, NJ: Prentice Hall (2009).

Shtub, A. F., et al. *Project Management*, 2nd ed. Upper Saddle River, NJ: Prentice Hall (2005).

Vanhoucke, M., and E. Demeulemeester. "The Application of Project Scheduling Techniques in a Real-Life Environment." *Project Management Journal* (March 2003): 30–43.

Wysocki, R. K. *Effective Project Management.* New York: Wiley (2007).

Internet Resources

E-Business Solutions for project management:
www.eprojectcentral.com
PERT Chart EXPERT is an add-on product for Microsoft Project that adds extensive PERT charting: **www.criticaltools.com**
PERT Chart and WBS Chart add-on products for Microsoft Project: **www.criticaltools.com**
Project Management Forum: **www.pmforum.org**

Project Management Institute, Inc.: **www.pmi.org**
Project Management Software: **www.project-management-software.org**
Project workspace for the construction industry:
www.buzzsaw.com
Project time collection: **www.journeyx.com**

Solutions to Even Numbered Problems

2 Here are some detailed activities for the first two activities for Mefford's WBS:

11 Set initial goals for fundraising.
12 Set strategy, including identifying sources and solicitation place.
13 Raise the funds.
21 Identify voters' concerns.
22 Analyze competitor's voting record.
23 Establish position on issues.

4

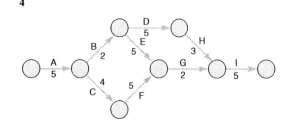

A–C–F–G–I is critical path; 21 days.
This is an AOA network.

6 (a)

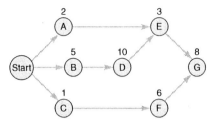

(b) B–D–E–G

(c) 26 days

(d)

Activity	Slack
A	13
B	0
C	11
D	0
E	0
F	11
G	0

8

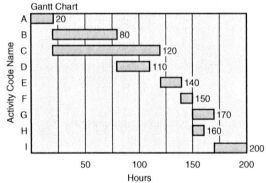

10

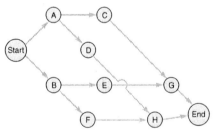

12 (a)

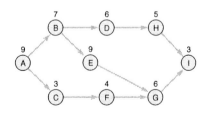

(b) A–B–E–G–I, is critical path.

(c) 34

14 (a)

A, 5.83, 0.69	G, 2.17, 0.25
B, 3.67, 0.11	H, 6.00, 1.00
C, 2.00, 0.11	I, 11.00, 0.11
D, 7.00, 0.11	J, 16.33, 1.00
E, 4.00, 0.44	K, 7.33, 1.78
F, 10.00, 1.78	

(b) C.P. is C–D–E–F–H–K. Time = 36.33 days.

(c) Slacks are 7.17, 5.33, 0, 0, 0, 0, 2.83, 0, 2.83, 18, and 0, respectively, for A through K.

(d) $P = .946$

16 Crash C to 3 weeks at $200 total for one week. Now both paths are critical. Not worth it to crash further.

18 Critical path currently is C–E for 12 days. $1,100 to crash by 4 days. Watch for parallel critical paths as you crash.

20 (a) 16 (A–D–G)

(b) $12,300

(c) D; 1 wk. for $75

(d) 7 wk.; $1,600

22 (a) A–C–E–H–I–K–M–N; 50 days

(b) 82.1%

(c) 58 days

24 (a) .0228

(b) .3085

(c) .8413

(d) .9772

(e) 24 mo.

26 (a)

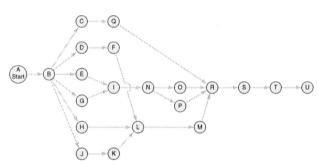

(b) Critical path is A–B–J–K–L–M–R–S–T–U for 18 days.

(c) i No, transmissions and drivetrains are not on the critical path.

ii No, halving engine-building time will reduce the critical path by only 1 day.

iii No, it is not on the critical path.

(d) Reallocating workers not involved with critical-path activities to activities along the critical path will reduce the critical path length.

Solutions to Self Test

1. a; **2.** c; **3.** a; **4.** d; **5.** d; **6.** b; **7.** c; **8.** a; **9.** d; **10.** b.

Chapter 4

Forecasting

Forecasting

Outline

Learning Objectives

When you complete this selection you should be able to

1. Understand the three time horizons and which models apply for each
2. Explain when to use each of the four qualitative models
3. Apply the naive, moving average, exponential smoothing, and trend methods

4. Compute three measures of forecast accuracy
5. Develop seasonal indexes
6. Conduct a regression and correlation analysis
7. Use a tracking signal

From *Operations Management*, 9/e. Jay Heizer. Barry Render. Copyright © 2008 by Pearson Education. All rights reserved.

Forecasting Provides a Competitive Advantage for Disney

When it comes to the world's most respected global brands, Walt Disney Parks & Resorts is a visible leader. Although the monarch of this magic kingdom is no man but a mouse—Mickey Mouse—it's CEO Robert Iger who daily manages the entertainment giant.

Disney's global portfolio includes Hong Kong Disneyland (opened 2005), Disneyland Paris (1992), and Tokyo Disneyland (1983). But it is Disney World (in Florida) and Disneyland (in California) that drive profits in this $32 billion corporation, which is ranked 54th in the *Fortune* 500 and 79th in the *Financial Times* Global 500.

Revenues at Disney are all about people—how many visit the parks and how they spend money while there. When Iger receives a daily report from his six theme parks in Orlando, the report contains only two numbers: the *forecast* of yesterday's attendance at the parks (Magic Kingdom, Epcot, Animal Kingdom, MGM Studios, Typhoon Lagoon, and Blizzard Beach) and the *actual* attendance. An error close to zero is expected. Iger takes his forecasts very seriously.

The forecasting team at Disney World doesn't just do a daily prediction, however, and Iger is not its only customer. The team also provides daily,

▲ Mickey and Minnie Mouse, and other Disney characters, with Cinderella's Castle in the background, provide the public image of Disney to the world. Forecasts drive the work schedules of 56,000 cast members working at Disney World's Orlando parks.

Kelly-Mooney Photography, Corbis/Bettmann

◀ The giant sphere is the symbol of Epcot, one of Disney's six Orlando parks, for which forecasts of meals, lodging, entertainment, and transportation must be made. This Disney monorail moves guests among parks and the 20 hotels on the massive 47-square-mile property (about the size of San Francisco and twice the size of Manhattan).

Jeff Greenberg, PhotoEdit, Inc.

Kevin Fleming, CORBIS-NY

A daily forecast of attendance is made by adjusting Disney's annual operating plan for weather forecasts, the previous day's crowds, conventions, and seasonal variations. One of the two water parks at Disney World, Typhoon Lagoon, is shown here.

Peter Cosgrove, AP Wide World Photos

◄ Forecasts are critical to making sure rides are not overcrowded. Disney is good at "managing demand" with techniques such as adding more street activities to reduce long lines for rides.

weekly, monthly, annual, and 5-year forecasts to the labor management, maintenance, operations, finance, and park scheduling departments. Forecasters use judgmental models, econometric models, moving-average models, and regression analysis.

With 20% of Disney World's customers coming from outside the United States, its economic model includes such variables as gross domestic product, cross-exchange rates, and arrivals into the U.S. Disney also uses 35 analysts and 70 field people to survey 1 million people each year. The surveys, administered to guests at the parks and its 20 hotels, to employees, and to travel industry professionals, examine future travel plans and experiences at the parks. This helps forecast not only attendance but behavior at each ride (e.g., how long people will wait, how many times they will ride). Inputs to the monthly forecasting model include airline specials, speeches by the chair of the Federal Reserve, and Wall Street trends. Disney even monitors 3,000 school districts inside and outside the U.S. for holiday/vacation schedules. With this approach, Disney's 5-year attendance forecast yields just a 5% error on average. Its annual forecasts have a 0% to 3% error.

Attendance forecasts for the parks drive a whole slew of management decisions. For example, capacity on any day can be increased by opening at 8 A.M. instead of the usual 9 A.M., by opening more shows or rides, by adding more food/beverage carts (9 million hamburgers and 50 million Cokes are sold per year!), and by bringing in more employees

Joe Raedle, Getty Images

▲ Disney uses characters such as Minnie Mouse to entertain customers when lines are forecast to be long. On slow days, Disney calls fewer cast members to work.

(called "cast members"). Cast members are scheduled in 15-minute intervals throughout the parks for flexibility. Demand can be managed by limiting the number of guests admitted to the parks, with the "fast pass" reservation system, and by shifting crowds from rides to more street parades.

At Disney, forecasting is a key driver in the company's success and competitive advantage.

Every day, managers like those at Disney make decisions without knowing what will happen in the future. They order inventory without knowing what sales will be, purchase new equipment despite uncertainty about demand for products, and make investments without knowing what profits will be. Managers are always trying to make better estimates of what will happen in the future in the face of uncertainty. Making good estimates is the main purpose of forecasting.

In this selection, we examine different types of forecasts and present a variety of forecasting models. Our purpose is to show that there are many ways for managers to forecast. We also provide an overview of business sales forecasting and describe how to prepare, monitor, and judge the accuracy of a forecast. Good forecasts are an *essential* part of efficient service and manufacturing operations.

WHAT IS FORECASTING?

Forecasting

The art and science of predicting future events.

Forecasting is the art and science of predicting future events. Forecasting may involve taking historical data and projecting them into the future with some sort of mathematical model. It may be a subjective or intuitive prediction. Or it may involve a combination of these—that is, a mathematical model adjusted by a manager's good judgment.

As we introduce different forecasting techniques in this selection, you will see that there is seldom one superior method. What works best in one firm under one set of conditions may be a complete disaster in another organization, or even in a different department of the same firm. In addition, you will see that there are limits as to what can be expected from forecasts. They are seldom, if ever, perfect. They are also costly and time-consuming to prepare and monitor.

Few businesses, however, can afford to avoid the process of forecasting by just waiting to see what happens and then taking their chances. Effective planning in both the short run and long run depends on a forecast of demand for the company's products.

Forecasting Time Horizons

Learning Objective

1. Understand the three time horizons and which models apply for each

A forecast is usually classified by the *future time horizon* that it covers. Time horizons fall into three categories:

1. *Short-range forecast:* This forecast has a time span of up to 1 year but is generally less than 3 months. It is used for planning purchasing, job scheduling, workforce levels, job assignments, and production levels.
2. *Medium-range forecast:* A medium-range, or intermediate, forecast generally spans from 3 months to 3 years. It is useful in sales planning, production planning and budgeting, cash budgeting, and analysis of various operating plans.
3. *Long-range forecast:* Generally 3 years or more in time span, long-range forecasts are used in planning for new products, capital expenditures, facility location or expansion, and research and development.

Medium and long-range forecasts are distinguished from short-range forecasts by three features:

1. First, intermediate and long-run forecasts *deal with more comprehensive issues* and support management decisions regarding planning and products, plants, and processes. Implementing some facility decisions, such as GM's decision to open a new Brazilian manufacturing plant, can take 5 to 8 years from inception to completion.
2. Second, short-term forecasting usually *employs different methodologies* than longer-term forecasting. Mathematical techniques, such as moving averages, exponential smoothing, and trend extrapolation (all of which we shall examine shortly), are common to short-run projections. Broader, *less* quantitative methods are useful in predicting such issues as whether a new product, like the optical disk recorder, should be introduced into a company's product line.
3. Finally, as you would expect, short-range forecasts *tend to be more accurate* than longer-range forecasts. Factors that influence demand change every day. Thus, as the time horizon lengthens, it is likely that forecast accuracy will diminish. It almost goes without saying, then, that sales forecasts must be updated regularly to maintain their value and integrity. After each sales period, forecasts should be reviewed and revised.

Our forecasting ability has improved, but it has been outpaced by an increasingly complex world economy.

120

The Influence of Product Life Cycle

Another factor to consider when developing sales forecasts, especially longer ones, is product life cycle. Products, and even services, do not sell at a constant level throughout their lives. Most successful products pass through four stages: (1) introduction, (2) growth, (3) maturity, and (4) decline.

Products in the first two stages of the life cycle (such as virtual reality and LCD TVs) need longer forecasts than those in the maturity and decline stages (such as $3\frac{1}{2}$" floppy disks and skateboards). Forecasts that reflect life cycle are useful in projecting different staffing levels, inventory levels, and factory capacity as the product passes from the first to the last stage.

TYPES OF FORECASTS

Organizations use three major types of forecasts in planning future operations:

1. **Economic forecasts** address the business cycle by predicting inflation rates, money supplies, housing starts, and other planning indicators.
2. **Technological forecasts** are concerned with rates of technological progress, which can result in the birth of exciting new products, requiring new plants and equipment.
3. **Demand forecasts** are projections of demand for a company's products or services. These forecasts, also called *sales forecasts*, drive a company's production, capacity, and scheduling systems and serve as inputs to financial, marketing, and personnel planning.

Economic and technological forecasting are specialized techniques that may fall outside the role of the operations manager. The emphasis in this book will therefore be on demand forecasting.

Economic forecasts
Planning indicators that are valuable in helping organizations prepare medium- to long-range forecasts.

Technological forecasts
Long-term forecasts concerned with the rates of technological progress.

Demand forecasts
Projections of a company's sales for each time period in the planning horizon.

THE STRATEGIC IMPORTANCE OF FORECASTING

Good forecasts are of critical importance in all aspects of a business: *The forecast is the only estimate of demand until actual demand becomes known.* Forecasts of demand therefore drive decisions in many areas. Let's look at the impact of product forecast on three activities: (1) human resources, (2) capacity, and (3) supply chain management.

Human Resources

Hiring, training, and laying off workers all depend on anticipated demand. If the human resources department must hire additional workers without warning, the amount of training declines and the quality of the workforce suffers. A large Louisiana chemical firm almost lost its biggest customer when a quick expansion to around-the-clock shifts led to a total breakdown in quality control on the second and third shifts.

Video 4.1

Forecasting at Hard Rock Cafe

Capacity

When capacity is inadequate, the resulting shortages can mean undependable delivery, loss of customers, and loss of market share. This is exactly what happened to Nabisco when it underestimated the huge demand for its new low-fat Snackwell Devil's Food Cookies. Even with production lines working overtime, Nabisco could not keep up with demand, and it lost customers. When excess capacity is built, on the other hand, costs can skyrocket.

Supply Chain Management

Good supplier relations and the ensuing price advantages for materials and parts depend on accurate forecasts. For example, auto manufacturers who want TRW Corp. to guarantee sufficient airbag capacity must provide accurate forecasts to justify TRW plant expansions. In the global marketplace, where expensive components for Boeing 787 jets are manufactured in dozens of countries, coordination driven by forecasts is critical. Scheduling transportation to Seattle for final assembly at the lowest possible cost means no last-minute surprises that can harm already-low profit margins.

SEVEN STEPS IN THE FORECASTING SYSTEM

Forecasting follows seven basic steps. We use Disney World, the focus of this selection's *Global Company Profile*, as an example of each step:

1. *Determine the use of the forecast:* Disney uses park attendance forecasts to drive staffing, opening times, ride availability, and food supplies.
2. *Select the items to be forecasted:* For Disney World, there are six main parks. A forecast of daily attendance at each is the main number that determines labor, maintenance, and scheduling.
3. *Determine the time horizon of the forecast:* Is it short, medium, or long term? Disney develops daily, weekly, monthly, annual, and 5-year forecasts.
4. *Select the forecasting model(s):* Disney uses a variety of statistical models that we shall discuss, including moving averages, econometrics, and regression analysis. It also employs judgmental, or nonquantitative, models.
5. *Gather the data needed to make the forecast:* Disney's forecasting team employs 35 analysts and 70 field personnel to survey 1 million people/businesses every year. It also uses a firm called Global Insights for travel industry forecasts and gathers data on exchange rates, arrivals into the U.S., airline specials, Wall Street trends, and school vacation schedules.
6. *Make the forecast.*
7. *Validate and implement the results:* At Disney, forecasts are reviewed daily at the highest levels to make sure that the model, assumptions, and data are valid. Error measures are applied; then the forecasts are used to schedule personnel down to 15-minute intervals.

These seven steps present a systematic way of initiating, designing, and implementing a forecasting system. When the system is to be used to generate forecasts regularly over time, data must be routinely collected. Then actual computations are usually made by computer.

Regardless of the system that firms like Disney use, each company faces several realities:

1. Forecasts are seldom perfect. This means that outside factors that we cannot predict or control often impact the forecast. Companies need to allow for this reality.
2. Most forecasting techniques assume that there is some underlying stability in the system. Consequently, some firms automate their predictions using computerized forecasting software, then closely monitor only the product items whose demand is erratic.
3. Both product family and aggregated forecasts are more accurate than individual product forecasts. Disney, for example, aggregates daily attendance forecasts by park. This approach helps balance the over- and underpredictions of each of the six attractions.

FORECASTING APPROACHES

There are two general approaches to forecasting, just as there are two ways to tackle all decision modeling. One is a quantitative analysis; the other is a qualitative approach. **Quantitative forecasts** use a variety of mathematical models that rely on historical data and/or causal variables to forecast demand. Subjective or **qualitative forecasts** incorporate such factors as the decision maker's intuition, emotions, personal experiences, and value system in reaching a forecast. Some firms use one approach and some use the other. In practice, a combination of the two is usually most effective.

Overview of Qualitative Methods

In this section, we consider four different *qualitative* forecasting techniques:

1. **Jury of executive opinion:** Under this method, the opinions of a group of high-level experts or managers, often in combination with statistical models, are pooled to arrive at a group estimate of demand. Bristol-Meyers Squibb Company, for example, uses 220 well-known research scientists as its jury of executive opinion to get a grasp on future trends in the world of medical research.
2. **Delphi method:** There are three different types of participants in the Delphi method: decision makers, staff personnel, and respondents. Decision makers usually consist of a group of

Quantitative forecasts
Forecasts that employ one or more mathematical models that rely on historical data and/or causal variables to forecast demand.

Qualitative forecasts
Forecasts that incorporate such factors as the decision maker's intuition, emotions, personal experiences, and value system.

Jury of executive opinion
A forecasting technique that takes the opinion of a small group of high-level managers and results in a group estimate of demand.

Delphi method
A forecasting technique using a group process that allows experts to make forecasts.

Learning Objective

2. Explain when to use each of the four qualitative models

5 to 10 experts who will be making the actual forecast. Staff personnel assist decision makers by preparing, distributing, collecting, and summarizing a series of questionnaires and survey results. The respondents are a group of people, often located in different places, whose judgments are valued. This group provides inputs to the decision makers before the forecast is made.

The state of Alaska, for example, has used the Delphi method to develop its long-range economic forecast. An amazing 90% of the state's budget is derived from 1.5 million barrels of oil pumped daily through a pipeline at Prudhoe Bay. The large Delphi panel of experts had to represent all groups and opinions in the state and all geographic areas. Delphi was the perfect forecasting tool because panelist travel could be avoided. It also meant that leading Alaskans could participate because their schedules were not affected by meetings and distances.

3. **Sales force composite:** In this approach, each salesperson estimates what sales will be in his or her region. These forecasts are then reviewed to ensure that they are realistic. Then they are combined at the district and national levels to reach an overall forecast. A variation of this approach occurs at Lexus, where every quarter Lexus dealers have a "make meeting." At this meeting, they talk about what is selling, in what colors, and with what options, so the factory knows what to build.[1]

4. **Consumer market survey:** This method solicits input from customers or potential customers regarding future purchasing plans. It can help not only in preparing a forecast but also in improving product design and planning for new products. The consumer market survey and sales force composite methods can, however, suffer from overly optimistic forecasts that arise from customer input. The 2001 crash of the telecommunication industry was the result of overexpansion to meet "explosive customer demand." Where did these data come from? Oplink Communications, a Nortel Networks supplier, says its "company forecasts over the last few years were based mainly on informal conversations with customers."[2]

Sales force composite
A forecasting technique based on salespersons' estimates of expected sales.

Consumer market survey
A forecasting method that solicits input from customers or potential customers regarding future purchasing plans.

Overview of Quantitative Methods

Five quantitative forecasting methods, all of which use historical data, are described in this chapter. They fall into two categories:

1. Naive approach
2. Moving averages
3. Exponential smoothing } **time-series models**
4. Trend projection
5. Linear regression } **associative model**

Time-Series Models **Time-series** models predict on the assumption that the future is a function of the past. In other words, they look at what has happened over a period of time and use a series of past data to make a forecast. If we are predicting sales of lawn mowers, we use the past sales for lawn mowers to make the forecasts.

Time series
A forecasting technique that uses a series of past data points to make a forecast.

Associative Models Associative models, such as linear regression, incorporate the variables or factors that might influence the quantity being forecast. For example, an associative model for lawn mower sales might use factors such as new housing starts, advertising budget, and competitors' prices.

TIME-SERIES FORECASTING

A time series is based on a sequence of evenly spaced (weekly, monthly, quarterly, and so on) data points. Examples include weekly sales of Nike Air Jordans, quarterly earnings reports of Microsoft stock, daily shipments of Coors beer, and annual consumer price indices. Forecasting

[1]Jonathan Fahey, "The Lexus Nexus," *Forbes* (June 21, 2004): 68–70.
[2]"Lousy Sales Forecasts Helped Fuel the Telecom Mess," *The Wall Street Journal* (July 9, 2001): B1–B4.

time-series data implies that future values are predicted *only* from past values and that other variables, no matter how potentially valuable, may be ignored.

Decomposition of a Time Series

Analyzing time series means breaking down past data into components and then projecting them forward. A time series has four components:

1. *Trend* is the gradual upward or downward movement of the data over time. Changes in income, population, age distribution, or cultural views may account for movement in trend.
2. *Seasonality* is a data pattern that repeats itself after a period of days, weeks, months, or quarters. There are six common seasonality patterns:

Period of Pattern	"Season" Length	Number of "Seasons" in Pattern
Week	Day	7
Month	Week	$4–4\frac{1}{2}$
Month	Day	28–31
Year	Quarter	4
Year	Month	12
Year	Week	52

Restaurants and barber shops, for example, experience weekly seasons, with Saturday being the peak of business. See the *OM in Action* box "Forecasting at Olive Garden and Red Lobster." Beer distributors forecast yearly patterns, with monthly seasons. Three "seasons"—May, July, and September—each contain a big beer-drinking holiday.

3. *Cycles* are patterns in the data that occur every several years. They are usually tied into the business cycle and are of major importance in short-term business analysis and planning. Predicting business cycles is difficult because they may be affected by political events or by international turmoil.
4. *Random variations* are "blips" in the data caused by chance and unusual situations. They follow no discernible pattern, so they cannot be predicted.

Figure 1 illustrates a demand over a 4-year period. It shows the average, trend, seasonal components, and random variations around the demand curve. The average demand is the sum of the demand for each period divided by the number of data periods.

Naive Approach

The simplest way to forecast is to assume that demand in the next period will be equal to demand in the most recent period. In other words, if sales of a product—say, Nokia cell phones—were 68 units in January, we can forecast that February's sales will also be 68

Two famous quotes:

"You can never plan the future from the past."

Sir Edmund Burke

"I know of no way of judging the future but by the past."

Patrick Henry

During stable times, forecasting is easy; it is just this year's performance plus or minus a few percentage points.

▶ **Figure 1**

Product Demand Charted over 4 Years with a Growth Trend and Seasonality Indicated

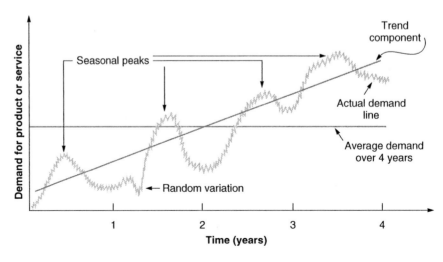

OM in Action   Forecasting at Olive Garden and Red Lobster

It's Friday night in the college town of Gainesville, Florida, and the local Olive Garden restaurant is humming. Customers may wait an average of 30 minutes for a table, but they can sample new wines and cheeses and admire scenic paintings of Italian villages on the restaurant's walls. Then comes dinner with portions so huge that many people take home a doggie bag. The typical bill: under $15 per person.

Crowds flock to the Darden restaurant chain's Olive Garden, Red Lobster, Seasons 52, and Bahama Breeze for value and consistency *and* they get it.

Every night, Darden's computers crank out forecasts that tell store managers what demand to anticipate the next day. The forecasting software generates a total meal forecast and breaks that down into specific menu items. The system tells a manager, for instance, that if 625 meals will be served the next day, "you will serve these items in these quantities. So before you go home, pull 25 pounds of shrimp and 30 pounds of crab out, and tell your operations

Fred Prouser, Corbis/Reuters America LLC

people to prepare 42 portion packs of chicken, 75 scampi dishes, 8 stuffed flounders, and so on." Managers often fine tune the quantities based on local conditions, such as weather or a convention, but they know what their customers are going to order.

By relying on demand history, the forecasting system has cut millions of dollars of waste out of the system. The forecast also reduces labor costs by providing the necessary information for improved scheduling. Labor costs decreased almost a full percent in the first year, translating in additional millions in savings for the Darden chain. In the low-margin restaurant business, every dollar counts.

Source: Interviews with Darden executives, 2006, 2007.

phones. Does this make any sense? It turns out that for some product lines, this **naive approach** is the most cost-effective and efficient objective forecasting model. At least it provides a starting point against which more sophisticated models that follow can be compared.

Naive approach

A forecasting technique that assumes demand in the next period is equal to demand in the most recent period.

Moving Averages

A **moving-average** forecast uses a number of historical actual data values to generate a forecast. Moving averages are useful *if we can assume that market demands will stay fairly steady over time*. A 4-month moving average is found by simply summing the demand during the past 4 months and dividing by 4. With each passing month, the most recent month's data are added to the sum of the previous 3 months' data, and the earliest month is dropped. This practice tends to smooth out short-term irregularities in the data series.

Mathematically, the simple moving average (which serves as an estimate of the next period's demand) is expressed as

$$\text{Moving average} = \frac{\Sigma \text{ Demand in previous } n \text{ periods}}{n} \qquad (1)$$

where *n* is the number of periods in the moving average—for example, 4, 5, or 6 months, respectively, for a 4-, 5-, or 6-period moving average.

Example 1 shows how moving averages are calculated.

Moving averages

A forecasting method that uses an average of the *n* most recent periods of data to forecast the next period.

Learning Objective

3. Apply the naive, moving average, exponential smoothing, and trend methods

---

Donna's Garden Supply wants a 3-month moving-average forecast, including a forecast for next January, for shed sales.

Approach: Storage shed sales are shown in the middle column of the table below. A 3-month moving average appears on the right.

EXAMPLE 1

Determining the moving average

Excel OM Data File
Ch04Ex1.xls

Month	Actual Shed Sales	3-Month Moving Average
January	10	
February	12	
March	13	
April	16	$(10 + 12 + 13)/3 = 11\frac{2}{3}$
May	19	$(12 + 13 + 16)/3 = 13\frac{2}{3}$
June	23	$(13 + 16 + 19)/3 = 16$
July	26	$(16 + 19 + 23)/3 = 19\frac{1}{3}$
August	30	$(19 + 23 + 26)/3 = 22\frac{2}{3}$
September	28	$(23 + 26 + 30)/3 = 26\frac{1}{3}$
October	18	$(26 + 30 + 28)/3 = 28$
November	16	$(30 + 28 + 18)/3 = 25\frac{1}{3}$
December	14	$(28 + 18 + 16)/3 = 20\frac{2}{3}$

Solution: The forecast for December is $20\frac{2}{3}$. To project the demand for sheds in the coming January, we sum the October, November, and December sales and divide by 3: January forecast = $(18 + 16 + 14)/3 = 16$.

Insight: Management now has a forecast that averages sales for the last 3 months. It is easy to use and understand.

Learning exercise: If actual sales in December were 18 (rather than 14), what is the new January forecast? [Answer: $17\frac{1}{3}$.]

Related problems: 1a, 2b, 5a, 6, 8a,b, 10a, 13b, 15, 47

Active Model 4.1

Example 1 is further illustrated as Active Model 4.1 on your CD-ROM.

When a detectable trend or pattern is present, *weights* can be used to place more emphasis on recent values. This practice makes forecasting techniques more responsive to changes because more recent periods may be more heavily weighted. Choice of weights is somewhat arbitrary because there is no set formula to determine them. Therefore, deciding which weights to use requires some experience. For example, if the latest month or period is weighted too heavily, the forecast may reflect a large unusual change in the demand or sales pattern too quickly.

A weighted moving average may be expressed mathematically as:

$$\text{Weighted moving average} = \frac{\Sigma\ (\text{Weight for period } n)(\text{Demand in period } n)}{\Sigma\ \text{Weights}} \qquad (2)$$

Example 2 shows how to calculate a weighted moving average.

EXAMPLE 2

Determining the weighted moving average

Excel OM Data File
Ch04Ex2.xls

Donna's Garden Supply (see Example 1) wants to forecast storage shed sales by weighting the past 3 months, with more weight given to recent data to make them more significant.

Approach: Assign more weight to recent data, as follows:

Weights Applied	Period
3	Last month
2	Two months ago
1	Three months ago
$\overline{6}$	Sum of weights

$$\text{Forecast for this month} = \frac{3 \times \text{Sales last mo.} + 2 \times \text{Sales 2 mos. ago} + 1 \times \text{Sales 3 mos. ago}}{\text{Sum of the weights}}$$

Solution: The results of this weighted-average forecast are as follows:

Month	Actual Shed Sales	Three-Month Weighted Moving Average
January	10	
February	12	
March	13	
April	16	$[(3 \times 13) + (2 \times 12) + (10)]/6 = 12\frac{1}{6}$
May	19	$[(3 \times 16) + (2 \times 13) + (12)]/6 = 14\frac{1}{3}$
June	23	$[(3 \times 19) + (2 \times 16) + (13)]/6 = 17$
July	26	$[(3 \times 23) + (2 \times 19) + (16)]/6 = 20\frac{1}{2}$
August	30	$[(3 \times 26) + (2 \times 23) + (19)]/6 = 23\frac{5}{6}$
September	28	$[(3 \times 30) + (2 \times 26) + (23)]/6 = 27\frac{1}{2}$
October	18	$[(3 \times 28) + (2 \times 30) + (26)]/6 = 28\frac{1}{3}$
November	16	$[(3 \times 18) + (2 \times 28) + (30)]/6 = 23\frac{1}{3}$
December	14	$[(3 \times 16) + (2 \times 18) + (28)]/6 = 18\frac{2}{3}$

Insight: In this particular forecasting situation, you can see that more heavily weighting the latest month provides a much more accurate projection.

Learning exercise: If the assigned weights were 4, 2, and 1 (instead of 3, 2, and 1) what is the forecast for January's weighted moving average? [Answer: $15\frac{1}{7}$.]

Related problems: 1b, 2c, 5c, 6, 7, 10b

Both simple and weighted moving averages are effective in smoothing out sudden fluctuations in the demand pattern to provide stable estimates. Moving averages do, however, present three problems:

1. Increasing the size of *n* (the number of periods averaged) does smooth out fluctuations better, but it makes the method less sensitive to *real* changes in the data.
2. Moving averages cannot pick up trends very well. Because they are averages, they will always stay within past levels and will not predict changes to either higher or lower levels. That is, they *lag* the actual values.
3. Moving averages require extensive records of past data.

> *Data that are 20 years old may not be so useful. It is not always necessary to use all data.*

Figure 2, a plot of the data in Examples 1 and 2, illustrates the lag effect of the moving-average models. Note that both the moving-average and weighted-moving-average lines lag the actual demand. The weighted moving average, however, usually reacts more quickly to demand changes. Even in periods of downturn (see November and December), it more closely tracks the demand.

Exponential Smoothing

Exponential smoothing is a sophisticated weighted-moving-average forecasting method that is still fairly easy to use. It involves very *little* record keeping of past data. The basic exponential smoothing formula can be shown as follows:

> **Exponential smoothing**
> A weighted-moving-average forecasting technique in which data points are weighted by an exponential function.

$$\text{New forecast} = \text{Last period's forecast} + \alpha\,(\text{Last period's actual demand} - \text{Last period's forecast}) \quad (3)$$

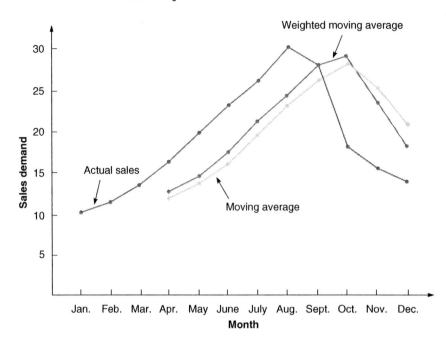

▷ **Figure 2**

Actual Demand vs. Moving-Average and Weighted-Moving-Average Methods for Donna's Garden Supply

Smoothing constant

The weighting factor used in an exponential smoothing forecast, a number between 0 and 1.

where α is a weight, or **smoothing constant**, chosen by the forecaster, that has a value between 0 and 1. Equation (3) can also be written mathematically as:

$$F_t = F_{t-1} + \alpha(A_{t-1} - F_{t-1}) \tag{4}$$

where F_t = new forecast
F_{t-1} = previous period's forecast
α = smoothing (or weighting) constant ($0 \le \alpha \le 1$)
A_{t-1} = previous period's actual demand

The concept is not complex. The latest estimate of demand is equal to the old estimate adjusted by a fraction of the difference between the last period's actual demand and the old estimate. Example 3 shows how to use exponential smoothing to derive a forecast.

EXAMPLE 3

Determining a forecast via exponential smoothing

In January, a car dealer predicted February demand for 142 Ford Mustangs. Actual February demand was 153 autos. Using a smoothing constant chosen by management of $\alpha = .20$, the dealer wants to forecast March demand using the exponential smoothing model.

Approach: The exponential smoothing model in Equations 3 and 4 can be applied.

Solution: Substituting the sample data into the formula, we obtain:

New forecast (for March demand) $= 142 + .2(153 - 142) = 142 + 2.2$

$= 144.2$

Thus, the March demand forecast for Ford Mustangs is rounded to 144.

Insight: Using just two pieces of data, the forecast and the actual demand, plus a smoothing constant, we developed a forecast of 144 Ford Mustangs for March.

Learning exercise: If the smoothing constant is changed to .30, what is the new forecast? [Answer: 145.3]

Related problems: 1c, 3, 4, 5d, 6, 9d, 11, 12, 13a, 17, 18, 37, 43, 47, 49

The *smoothing constant*, α, is generally in the range from .05 to .50 for business applications. It can be changed to give more weight to recent data (when α is high) or more weight to past data (when α is low). When α reaches the extreme of 1.0, then in Equation (4), $F_t = 1.0A_{t-1}$. All the older values drop out, and the forecast becomes identical to the naive model mentioned earlier in this chapter. That is, the forecast for the next period is just the same as this period's demand.

The following table helps illustrate this concept. For example, when $\alpha = .5$, we can see that the new forecast is based almost entirely on demand in the last three or four periods. When $\alpha = .1$, the forecast places little weight on recent demand and takes many periods (about 19) of historical values into account.

Exponential smoothing is widely used in business and is an important part of many computerized inventory control systems.

			Weight Assigned to		
Smoothing Constant	Most Recent Period (α)	2nd Most Recent Period $\alpha(1-\alpha)$	3rd Most Recent Period $\alpha(1-\alpha)^2$	4th Most Recent Period $\alpha(1-\alpha)^3$	5th Most Recent Period $\alpha(1-\alpha)^4$
$\alpha = .1$	.1	.09	.081	.073	.066
$\alpha = .5$	.5	.25	.125	.063	.031

Selecting the Smoothing Constant The exponential smoothing approach is easy to use, and it has been successfully applied in virtually every type of business. However, the appropriate value of the smoothing constant, α, can make the difference between an accurate forecast and an inaccurate forecast. High values of α are chosen when the underlying average is likely to change. Low values of α are used when the underlying average is fairly stable. In picking a value for the smoothing constant, the objective is to obtain the most accurate forecast.

Measuring Forecast Error

The overall accuracy of any forecasting model—moving average, exponential smoothing, or other—can be determined by comparing the forecasted values with the actual or observed values. If F_t denotes the forecast in period t, and A_t denotes the actual demand in period t, the *forecast error* (or deviation) is defined as:

The forecast error tells us how well the model performed against itself using past data.

$$\text{Forecast error} = \text{Actual demand} - \text{Forecast value}$$
$$= A_t - F_t$$

Several measures are used in practice to calculate the overall forecast error. These measures can be used to compare different forecasting models, as well as to monitor forecasts to ensure they are performing well. Three of the most popular measures are mean absolute deviation (MAD), mean squared error (MSE), and mean absolute percent error (MAPE). We now describe and give an example of each.

Learning Objective

4. Compute three measures of forecast accuracy

Mean Absolute Deviation The first measure of the overall forecast error for a model is the **mean absolute deviation (MAD)**. This value is computed by taking the sum of the absolute values of the individual forecast errors and dividing by the number of periods of data (n):

$$\text{MAD} = \frac{\Sigma |\text{Actual} - \text{Forecast}|}{n} \tag{5}$$

Mean absolute deviation (MAD)
A measure of the overall forecast error for a model.

Example 4 applies MAD, as a measure of overall forecast error, by testing two values of α.

EXAMPLE 4

Determining the mean absolute deviation (MAD)

During the past 8 quarters, the Port of Baltimore has unloaded large quantities of grain from ships. The port's operations manager wants to test the use of exponential smoothing to see how well the technique works in predicting tonnage unloaded. He guesses that the forecast of grain unloaded in the first quarter was 175 tons. Two values of α are to be examined: $\alpha = .10$ and $\alpha = .50$.

Approach: Compare the actual data with the data we forecast (using each of the two α values) and then find the absolute deviation and MADs.

Excel OM Data Files
Ch04Ex4a.xls,
Ch04Ex4b.xls

Solution: The following table shows the *detailed* calculations for $\alpha = .10$ only:

Quarter	Actual Tonnage Unloaded	Forecast with $\alpha = .10$	Forecast with $\alpha = .50$
1	180	175	175
2	168	175.50 = 175.00 + .10(180 − 175)	177.50
3	159	174.75 = 175.50 + .10(168 − 175.50)	172.75
4	175	173.18 = 174.75 + .10(159 − 174.75)	165.88
5	190	173.36 = 173.18 + .10(175 − 173.18)	170.44
6	205	175.02 = 173.36 + .10(190 − 173.36)	180.22
7	180	178.02 = 175.02 + .10(205 − 175.02)	192.61
8	182	178.22 = 178.02 + .10(180 − 178.02)	186.30
9	?	178.59 = 178.22 + .10(182 − 178.22)	184.15

To evaluate the accuracy of each smoothing constant, we can compute forecast errors in terms of absolute deviations and MADs:

Quarter	Actual Tonnage Unloaded	Forecast with $\alpha = .10$	Absolute Deviation for $\alpha = .10$	Forecast with $\alpha = .50$	Absolute Deviation for $\alpha = .50$
1	180	175	5.00	175	5.00
2	168	175.50	7.50	177.50	9.50
3	159	174.75	15.75	172.75	13.75
4	175	173.18	1.82	165.88	9.12
5	190	173.36	16.64	170.44	19.56
6	205	175.02	29.98	180.22	24.78
7	180	178.02	1.98	192.61	12.61
8	182	178.22	3.78	186.30	4.30
		Sum of absolute deviations:	82.45		98.62
	$MAD = \dfrac{\Sigma \lvert Deviations \rvert}{n}$		10.31		12.33

Insight: On the basis of this comparison of the two MADs, a smoothing constant of $\alpha = .10$ is preferred to $\alpha = .50$ because its MAD is smaller.

Learning exercise: If the smoothing constant is changed from $\alpha = .10$ to $\alpha = .20$, what is the new MAD? [Answer: 10.21.]

Related problems: 5b, 8c, 9c, 14, 23, 37a

Active Model 4.2

Example 4 is further illustrated in Active Model 4.2 on the CD-ROM.

Most computerized forecasting software includes a feature that automatically finds the smoothing constant with the lowest forecast error. Some software modifies the α value if errors become larger than acceptable.

Mean squared error (MSE)
The average of the squared differences between the forecasted and observed values.

Mean Squared Error The **mean squared error (MSE)** is a second way of measuring overall forecast error. MSE is the average of the squared differences between the forecasted and observed values. Its formula is:

$$MSE = \frac{\Sigma(\text{Forecast errors})^2}{n} \tag{6}$$

Example 5 finds the MSE for the Port of Baltimore introduced in Example 4.

EXAMPLE 5

Determining the
mean squared error
(MSE)

The operations manager for the Port of Baltimore now wants to compute MSE for $\alpha = .10$.

Approach: Use the same forecast data for $\alpha = .10$ from Example 4, then compute the MSE using Equation (6).

Solution:

Quarter	Actual Tonnage Unloaded	Forecast for $\alpha = .10$	(Error)^2
1	180	175	$5^2 = 25$
2	168	175.50	$(-7.5)^2 = 56.25$
3	159	174.75	$(-15.75)^2 = 248.06$
4	175	173.18	$(1.82)^2 = 3.33$
5	190	173.36	$(16.64)^2 = 276.89$
6	205	175.02	$(29.98)^2 = 898.70$
7	180	178.02	$(1.98)^2 = 3.92$
8	182	178.22	$(3.78)^2 = 14.31$
			Sum of errors squared = 1,526.46

$$\text{MSE} = \frac{\Sigma(\text{Forecast errors})^2}{n} = 1{,}526.54/8 = 190.8$$

Insight: Is this MSE = 190.8 good or bad? It all depends on the MSEs for other forecasting approaches. A low MSE is better because we want to minimize MSE. MSE exaggerates errors because it squares them.

Learning exercise: Find the MSE for $\alpha = .50$. [Answer: MSE = 195.24. The result indicates that $\alpha = .10$ is a better choice because we seek a lower MSE. Coincidentally, this is the same conclusion we reached using MAD in Example 4]

Related problems: 8d, 14, 20

A drawback of using the MSE is that it tends to accentuate large deviations due to the squared term. For example, if the forecast error for period 1 is twice as large as the error for period 2, the squared error in period 1 is four times as large as that for period 2. Hence, using MSE as the measure of forecast error typically indicates that we prefer to have several smaller deviations rather than even one large deviation.

Mean Absolute Percent Error A problem with both the MAD and MSE is that their values depend on the magnitude of the item being forecast. If the forecast item is measured in thousands, the MAD and MSE values can be very large. To avoid this problem, we can use the **mean absolute percent error (MAPE)**. This is computed as the average of the absolute difference between the forecasted and actual values, expressed as a percentage of the actual values. That is, if we have forecasted and actual values for n periods, the MAPE is calculated as:

Mean absolute percent error (MAPE)
The average of the absolute differences between the forecast and actual values, expressed as a percent of actual values.

$$\text{MAPE} = \frac{\sum_{i=1}^{n} 100 \left| \text{Actual}_i - \text{Forecast}_i \right| / \text{Actual}_i}{n} \tag{7}$$

Example 6 illustrates the calculations using the data from Examples 4 and 5.

EXAMPLE 6

Determining the mean absolute percent error (MAPE)

The Port of Baltimore wants to now calculate the MAPE when $\alpha = .10$.

Approach: Equation (7) is applied to the forecast data computed in Example 4.

Solution:

Quarter	Actual Tonnage Unloaded	Forecast for $\alpha = .10$	Absolute Percent Error 100 (lerrorl/actual)
1	180	175.00	$100(5/180) = 2.78\%$
2	168	175.50	$100(7.5/168) = 4.46\%$
3	159	174.75	$100(15.75/159) = 9.90\%$
4	175	173.18	$100(1.82/175) = 1.05\%$
5	190	173.36	$100(16.64/190) = 8.76\%$
6	205	175.02	$100(29.98/205) = 14.62\%$
7	180	178.02	$100(1.98/180) = 1.10\%$
8	182	178.22	$100(3.78/182) = 2.08\%$
			Sum of % errors = 44.75%

$$\text{MAPE} = \frac{\Sigma \text{ Absolute percent errors}}{n} = \frac{44.75\%}{8} = 5.59\%$$

Insight: MAPE expresses the error as a percent of the actual values, undistorted by a single large value.

Learning exercise: What is MAPE when α is .50? [Answer: MAPE = 6.75%. As was the case with MAD and MSE, the $\alpha = .1$ was preferable for this series of data.]

Related problems: 8e, 33c

The MAPE is perhaps the easiest measure to interpret. For example, a result that the MAPE is 6% is a clear statement that is not dependent on issues such as the magnitude of the input data.

Exponential Smoothing with Trend Adjustment

Simple exponential smoothing, the technique we just illustrated in Examples 3 to 6, is like any other moving-average technique: It fails to respond to trends. Other forecasting techniques that can deal with trends are certainly available. However, because exponential smoothing is such a popular modeling approach in business, let us look at it in more detail.

Here is why exponential smoothing must be modified when a trend is present. Assume that demand for our product or service has been increasing by 100 units per month and that we have been forecasting with $\alpha = 0.4$ in our exponential smoothing model. The following table shows a severe lag in the 2nd, 3rd, 4th, and 5th months, even when our initial estimate for month 1 is perfect:

Month	Actual Demand	Forecast for Month $T(F_T)$
1	100	$F_1 = 100$ (given)
2	200	$F_2 = F_1 + \alpha(A_1 - F_1) = 100 + .4(100 - 100) = 100$
3	300	$F_3 = F_2 + \alpha(A_2 - F_2) = 100 + .4(200 - 100) = 140$
4	400	$F_4 = F_3 + \alpha(A_3 - F_3) = 140 + .4(300 - 140) = 204$
5	500	$F_5 = F_4 + \alpha(A_4 - F_4) = 204 + .4(400 - 204) = 282$

To improve our forecast, let us illustrate a more complex exponential smoothing model, one that adjusts for trend. The idea is to compute an exponentially smoothed average of the data and then adjust for positive or negative lag in trend. The new formula is:

$$\text{Forecast including trend}(FIT_t) = \text{Exponentially smoothed forecast}(F_t) + \text{Exponentially smoothed trend}(T_t) \tag{8}$$

With trend-adjusted exponential smoothing, estimates for both the average and the trend are smoothed. This procedure requires two smoothing constants: α for the average and β for the trend. We then compute the average and trend each period:

F_t = α(Actual demand last period) + (1 − α)(Forecast last period + Trend estimate last period)

or:

$$F_t = \alpha(A_{t-1}) + (1 - \alpha)(F_{t-1} + T_{t-1}) \qquad (9)$$

$T_t = \beta$(Forecast this period − Forecast last period)
    $+ (1 - \beta)$(Trend estimate last period)

or:

$$T_t = \beta(F_t - F_{t-1}) + (1 - \beta)T_{t-1} \qquad (10)$$

where F_t = exponentially smoothed forecast of the data series in period t
    T_t = exponentially smoothed trend in period t
    A_t = actual demand in period t
    α = smoothing constant for the average ($0 \le \alpha \le 1$)
    β = smoothing constant for the trend ($0 \le \beta \le 1$)

So the three steps to compute a trend-adjusted forecast are:

Step 1: Compute F_t, the exponentially smoothed forecast for period t, using Equation (9).
Step 2: Compute the smoothed trend, T_t, using Equation (10).
Step 3: Calculate the forecast including trend, FIT_t, by the formula $FIT_t = F_t + T_t$.

Example 7 shows how to use trend-adjusted exponential smoothing.

A large Portland manufacturer wants to forecast demand for a piece of pollution-control equipment. A review of past sales, as shown below, indicates that an increasing trend is present:

Month (t)	Actual Demand (A_t)	Month (t)	Actual Demand (A_t)
1	12	6	21
2	17	7	31
3	20	8	28
4	19	9	36
5	24	10	?

Smoothing constants are assigned the values of α = .2 and β = .4. The firm assumes the initial forecast for month 1 (F_1) was 11 units and the trend over that period (T_1) was 2 units.

Approach: A trend-adjusted exponential smoothing model, using Equations (9) and (10) and the three steps above, is employed.

Solution:

Step 1: Forecast for month 2:

$$F_2 = \alpha A_1 + (1 - \alpha)(F_1 + T_1)$$
$$F_2 = (.2)(12) + (1 - .2)(11 + 2)$$
$$= 2.4 + (.8)(13) = 2.4 + 10.4 = 12.8 \text{ units}$$

Step 2: Compute the trend in period 2:

$$T_2 = \beta(F_2 - F_1) + (1 - \beta)T_1$$
$$= .4(12.8 - 11) + (1 - .4)(2)$$
$$= (.4)(1.8) + (.6)(2) = .72 + 1.2 = 1.92$$

Step 3: Compute the forecast including trend (FIT_t):

$$FIT_2 = F_2 + T_2$$
$$= 12.8 + 1.92$$
$$= 14.72 \text{ units}$$

EXAMPLE 7

Computing a trend-adjusted exponential smoothing forecast

Active Model 4.3

Example 7 is further illustrated in Active Model 4.3 on the CD-ROM.

We will also do the same calculations for the third month:

Step 1. $F_3 = \alpha A_2 + (1 - \alpha)(F_2 + T_2) = (.2)(17) + (1 - .2)(12.8 + 1.92)$
$= 3.4 + (.8)(14.72) = 3.4 + 11.78 = 15.18$

Step 2. $T_3 = \beta(F_3 - F_2) + (1 - \beta)T_2 = (.4)(15.18 - 12.8) + (1 - .4)(1.92)$
$= (.4)(2.38) + (.6)(1.92) = .952 + 1.152 = 2.10$

Step 3. $FIT_3 = F_3 + T_3$
$= 15.18 + 2.10 = 17.28.$

Table 1 completes the forecasts for the 10-month period.

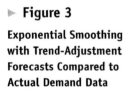

▷ Table 1

Forecast with $\alpha = .2$ and $\beta = .4$

Month	Actual Demand	Smoothed Forecast, F_t	Smoothed Trend, T_t	Forecast Including Trend FIT_t
1	12	11	2	13.00
2	17	12.80	1.92	14.72
3	20	15.18	2.10	17.28
4	19	17.82	2.32	20.14
5	24	19.91	2.23	22.14
6	21	22.51	2.38	24.89
7	31	24.11	2.07	26.18
8	28	27.14	2.45	29.59
9	36	29.28	2.32	31.60
10	—	32.48	2.68	35.16

Insight: Figure 3 compares actual demand (A_t) to an exponential smoothing forecast that includes trend (FIT_t). FIT picks up the trend in actual demand. A simple exponential smoothing model (like we saw in Examples 3 and 4) trails far behind.

▷ Figure 3

Exponential Smoothing with Trend-Adjustment Forecasts Compared to Actual Demand Data

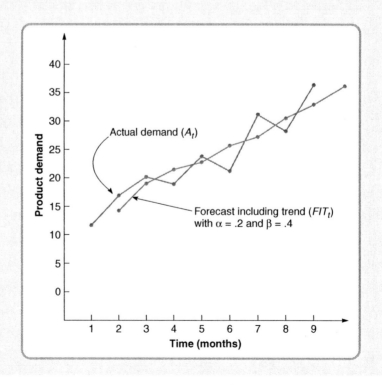

Learning exercise: Using the data for actual demand for the 9 months, compute the exponentially smoothed forecast *without* trend (using Equation (4) as we did earlier in Examples 3 and 4). Apply $\alpha = .2$ and assume an initial forecast for month 1 of 11 units. Then plot the months 2–10 forecast values on Figure 3. What do you notice? [Answer: Month 10 forecast = 24.65. All the points are below and lag the trend-adjusted forecast.]

Related problems: 19, 20, 21, 22, 44

The value of the trend-smoothing constant, β, resembles the α constant because a high β is more responsive to recent changes in trend. A low β gives less weight to the most recent trends and tends to smooth out the present trend. Values of β can be found by the trial-and-error approach or by using sophisticated commercial forecasting software, with the MAD used as a measure of comparison.

Simple exponential smoothing is often referred to as *first-order smoothing*, and trend-adjusted smoothing is called *second-order*, or *double smoothing*. Other advanced exponential-smoothing models are also used, including seasonal-adjusted and triple smoothing.[3]

Trend Projections

The last time-series forecasting method we will discuss is **trend projection**. This technique fits a trend line to a series of historical data points and then projects the line into the future for medium to long-range forecasts. Several mathematical trend equations can be developed (for example, exponential and quadratic), but in this section, we will look at *linear* (straight-line) trends only.

Trend projection

A time-series forecasting method that fits a trend line to a series of historical data points and then projects the line into the future for forecasts.

If we decide to develop a linear trend line by a precise statistical method, we can apply the *least-squares method*. This approach results in a straight line that minimizes the sum of the squares of the vertical differences or deviations from the line to each of the actual observations. Figure 4 illustrates the least-squares approach.

A least-squares line is described in terms of its *y*-intercept (the height at which it intercepts the *y*-axis) and its slope (the angle of the line). If we can compute the *y*-intercept and slope, we can express the line with the following equation:

$$\hat{y} = a + bx \tag{11}$$

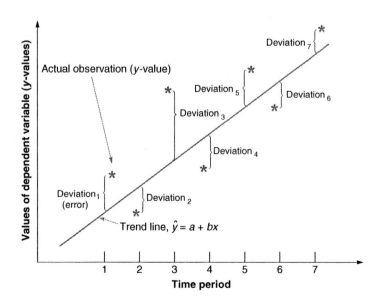

◁ **Figure 4**

The Least-Squares Method for Finding the Best-Fitting Straight Line, Where the Asterisks Are the Locations of the Seven Actual Observations or Data Points

[3]For more details, see D. Groebner, P. Shannon, P. Fry, and K. Smith, *Business Statistics*, 7th ed. (Upper Saddle River, NJ: Prentice Hall, 2008).

where $\hat{y}$ (called "y hat") = computed value of the variable to be predicted (called the
dependent variable)
a = y-axis intercept
b = slope of the regression line (or the rate of change in y for given changes in x)
x = the independent variable (which in this case is *time*)

Statisticians have developed equations that we can use to find the values of a and b for any regression line. The slope b is found by:

$$b = \frac{\Sigma xy - n\bar{x}\,\bar{y}}{\Sigma x^2 - n\bar{x}^2} \qquad (12)$$

where b = slope of the regression line
Σ = summation sign
x = known values of the independent variable
y = known values of the dependent variable
$\bar{x}$ = average of the x-values
$\bar{y}$ = average of the y-values
n = number of data points or observations

We can compute the y-intercept a as follows:

$$a = \bar{y} - b\bar{x} \qquad (13)$$

Example 8 shows how to apply these concepts.

EXAMPLE 8

Forecasting with least squares

Excel OM Data File Ch04Ex8.xls

Active Model 4.4

Example 8 is further illustrated in Active Model 4.4 on the CD-ROM.

The demand for electric power at N.Y. Edison over the period 2001 to 2007 is shown in the following table, in megawatts. The firm wants to forecast 2008 demand by fitting a straight-line trend to these data.

Year	Electrical Power Demand	Year	Electrical Power Demand
2001	74	2005	105
2002	79	2006	142
2003	80	2007	122
2004	90		

Approach: With a series of data over time, we can minimize the computations by transforming the values of x (time) to simpler numbers. Thus, in this case, we can designate 2001 as year 1, 2002 as year 2, and so on. Then Equations (12) and (13) can be used to create the trend projection model.

Solution:

Year	Time Period (x)	Electric Power Demand (y)	x^2	xy
2001	1	74	1	74
2002	2	79	4	158
2003	3	80	9	240
2004	4	90	16	360
2005	5	105	25	525
2006	6	142	36	852
2007	7	122	49	854
	$\Sigma x = 28$	$\Sigma y = 692$	$\Sigma x^2 = 140$	$\Sigma xy = 3{,}063$

$$\bar{x} = \frac{\Sigma x}{n} = \frac{28}{7} = 4 \qquad \bar{y} = \frac{\Sigma y}{n} = \frac{692}{7} = 98.86$$

$$b = \frac{\Sigma xy - n\bar{x}\,\bar{y}}{\Sigma x^2 - n\bar{x}^2} = \frac{3{,}063 - (7)(4)(98.86)}{140 - (7)(4^2)} = \frac{295}{28} = 10.54$$

$$a = \bar{y} - b\bar{x} = 98.86 - 10.54(4) = 56.70$$

Thus, the least squares trend equation is $\hat{y} = 56.70 + 10.54x$. To project demand in 2008, we first denote the year 2008 in our new coding system as $x = 8$:

$$\text{Demand in } 2008 = 56.70 + 10.54(8)$$
$$= 141.02, \text{ or } 141 \text{ megawatts}$$

Insight: To evaluate the model, we plot both the historical demand and the trend line in Figure 5. In this case, we may wish to be cautious and try to understand the 2006 to 2007 swing in demand.

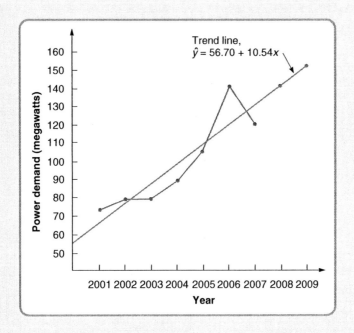

◁ Figure 5

Electrical Power and the Computed Trend Line

Learning exercise: Estimate demand for 2009. [Answer: 151.56 or 152 megawatts.]

Related problems: 6, 13c, 16, 25, 39, 49

Notes on the Use of the Least-Squares Method Using the least-squares method implies that we have met three requirements:

1. We always plot the data because least-squares data assume a linear relationship. If a curve appears to be present, curvilinear analysis is probably needed.
2. We do not predict time periods far beyond our given database. For example, if we have 20 months' worth of average prices of Microsoft stock, we can forecast only 3 or 4 months into the future. Forecasts beyond that have little statistical validity. Thus, you cannot take 5 years' worth of sales data and project 10 years into the future. The world is too uncertain.
3. Deviations around the least-squares line (see Figure 4) are assumed to be random. They are normally distributed, with most observations close to the line and only a smaller number farther out.

Seasonal Variations in Data

Seasonal variations in data are regular up-and-down movements in a time series that relate to recurring events such as weather or holidays. Demand for coal and fuel oil, for example, peaks during cold winter months. Demand for golf clubs or sunscreen may be highest in summer.

Seasonality may be applied to hourly, daily, weekly, monthly, or other recurring patterns. Fast-food restaurants experience *daily* surges at noon and again at 5 P.M. Movie theaters see higher demand on Friday and Saturday evenings. The post office, Toys "Я" Us, The Christmas Store, and Hallmark Card Shops also exhibit seasonal variation in customer traffic and sales.

Seasonal variations
Regular upward or downward movements in a time series that tie to recurring events.

Yamaha Motor Corp., USA

> Demand for many products is seasonal. Yamaha, the manufacturer of these jet skis and snowmobiles, produces products with complementary demands to address seasonal fluctuations.

Learning Objective

5. Develop seasonal indexes

Because John Deere understands seasonal variations in sales, it has been able to obtain 70% of its orders in advance of seasonal use (through price reductions and incentives such as 0% interest) so it can smooth production.

Similarly, understanding seasonal variations is important for capacity planning in organizations that handle peak loads. These include electric power companies during extreme cold and warm periods, banks on Friday afternoons, and buses and subways during the morning and evening rush hours.

Time-series forecasts like those in Example 8 involve reviewing the trend of data over a series of time periods. The presence of seasonality makes adjustments in trend-line forecasts necessary. Seasonality is expressed in terms of the amount that actual values differ from average values in the time series. Analyzing data in monthly or quarterly terms usually makes it easy for a statistician to spot seasonal patterns. Seasonal indices can then be developed by several common methods.

In what is called a *multiplicative seasonal model*, seasonal factors are multiplied by an estimate of average demand to produce a seasonal forecast. Our assumption in this section is that trend has been removed from the data. Otherwise, the magnitude of the seasonal data will be distorted by the trend.

Here are the steps we will follow for a company that has "seasons" of 1 month:

1. Find the *average historical demand each season* (or month in this case) by summing the demand for that month in each year and dividing by the number of years of data available. For example, if, in January, we have seen sales of 8, 6, and 10 over the past 3 years, average January demand equals (8 + 6 + 10)/3 = 8 units.
2. Compute the *average demand over all months* by dividing the total average annual demand by the number of seasons. For example, if the total average demand for a year is 120 units and there are 12 seasons (each month), the average monthly demand is 120/12 = 10 units.
3. Compute a *seasonal index* for each season by dividing that month's actual historical demand (from step 1) by the average demand over all months (from step 2). For example, if the average historical January demand over the past 3 years is 8 units and the average demand over all months is 10 units, the seasonal index for January is 8/10 = .80. Likewise, a seasonal index of 1.20 for February would mean that February's demand is 20% larger than the average demand over all months.
4. Estimate next year's total annual demand.
5. Divide this estimate of total annual demand by the number of seasons, then multiply it by the seasonal index for that month. This provides the *seasonal forecast*.

Example 9 illustrates this procedure as it computes seasonal indices from historical data.

EXAMPLE 9

Determining seasonal indices

A Des Moines distributor of Sony laptop computers wants to develop monthly indices for sales. Data from 2005–2007, by month, are available.

Approach: Follow the five steps listed above.

Solution:

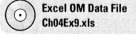
Excel OM Data File
Ch04Ex9.xls

Month	Demand 2005	Demand 2006	Demand 2007	Average 2005–2007 Demand	Average Monthly Demand[a]	Seasonal Index[b]
Jan.	80	85	105	90	94	.957 (= 90/94)
Feb.	70	85	85	80	94	.851 (= 80/94)
Mar.	80	93	82	85	94	.904 (= 85/94)
Apr.	90	95	115	100	94	1.064 (= 100/94)
May	113	125	131	123	94	1.309 (= 123/94)
June	110	115	120	115	94	1.223 (= 115/94)
July	100	102	113	105	94	1.117 (= 105/94)
Aug.	88	102	110	100	94	1.064 (= 100/94)
Sept.	85	90	95	90	94	.957 (= 90/94)
Oct.	77	78	85	80	94	.851 (= 80/94)
Nov.	75	82	83	80	94	.851 (= 80/94)
Dec.	82	78	80	80	94	.851 (= 80/94)

Total average annual demand = 1,128

[a]Average monthly demand = $\dfrac{1,128}{12 \text{ months}} = 94$.   [b]Seasonal index = $\dfrac{\text{Average 2005–2007 monthly demand}}{\text{Average monthly demand}}$.

If we expected the 2008 annual demand for computers to be 1,200 units, we would use these seasonal indices to forecast the monthly demand as follows:

Month	Demand	Month	Demand
Jan.	$\dfrac{1,200}{12} \times .957 = 96$	July	$\dfrac{1,200}{12} \times 1.117 = 112$
Feb.	$\dfrac{1,200}{12} \times .851 = 85$	Aug.	$\dfrac{1,200}{12} \times 1.064 = 106$
Mar.	$\dfrac{1,200}{12} \times .904 = 90$	Sept.	$\dfrac{1,200}{12} \times .957 = 96$
Apr.	$\dfrac{1,200}{12} \times 1.064 = 106$	Oct.	$\dfrac{1,200}{12} \times .851 = 85$
May	$\dfrac{1,200}{12} \times 1.309 = 131$	Nov.	$\dfrac{1,200}{12} \times .851 = 85$
June	$\dfrac{1,200}{12} \times 1.223 = 122$	Dec.	$\dfrac{1,200}{12} \times .851 = 85$

Insight: Think of these indices as percentages of average sales. The average sales (without seasonality) would be 94, but with seasonality, sales fluctuate from 85% to 131% of average.

Learning exercise: If 2008 annual demand is 1,150 laptops (instead of 1,200), what will the January, February, and March forecasts be? [Answer: 92, 82, and 87.]

Related problems: 27, 28

For simplicity, only 3 periods are used for each monthly index in the preceding example. Example 10 illustrates how indices that have already been prepared can be applied to adjust trend-line forecasts for seasonality.

San Diego Hospital wants to improve its forecasting by applying both trend and seasonal indices to 66 months of data it has collected. It will then forecast "patient-days" over the coming year.

Approach: A trend line is created; then monthly seasonal indices are computed. Finally, a multiplicative seasonal model is used to forecast months 67 to 78.

EXAMPLE 10

Applying both trend and seasonal indices

Solution: Using 66 months of adult inpatient hospital days, the following equation was computed:

$$\hat{y} = 8,090 + 21.5x$$

where

$\hat{y}$ = patient days
x = time, in months

Based on this model, which reflects only trend data, the hospital forecasts patient days for the next month (period 67) to be:

Patient days = 8,090 + (21.5)(67) = 9,530 (trend only)

While this model, as plotted in Figure 6, recognized the upward trend line in the demand for inpatient services, it ignored the seasonality that the administration knew to be present.

> **Figure 6**

Trend Data for San Diego Hospital

Source: From "Modern Methods Improve Hospital Forecasting" by W. E. Sterk and E. G. Shryock from *Healthcare Financial Management*, Vol. 41, no. 3, p. 97. Reprinted by permission of Healthcare Financial Management Association.

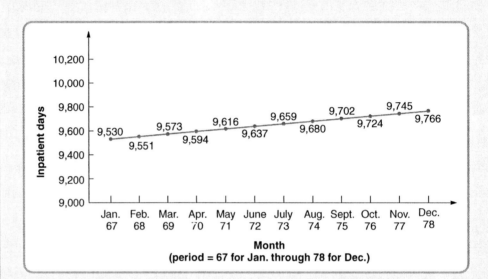

The following table provides seasonal indices based on the same 66 months. Such seasonal data, by the way, were found to be typical of hospitals nationwide.

Seasonality Indices for Adult Inpatient Days at San Diego Hospital

Month	Seasonality Index	Month	Seasonality Index
January	1.04	July	1.03
February	0.97	August	1.04
March	1.02	September	0.97
April	1.01	October	1.00
May	0.99	November	0.96
June	0.99	December	0.98

These seasonal indices are graphed in Figure 7. Note that January, March, July, and August seem to exhibit significantly higher patient days on average, while February, September, November, and December experience lower patient days.

However, neither the trend data nor the seasonal data alone provide a reasonable forecast for the hospital. Only when the hospital multiplied the trend-adjusted data times the appropriate seasonal index did it obtain good forecasts. Thus, for period 67 (January):

Patient days = (Trend-adjusted forecast) (Monthly seasonal index) = (9,530)(1.04) = 9,911

The patient days for each month are:

Period	67	68	69	70	71	72	73	74	75	76	77	78
Month	Jan.	Feb.	March	April	May	June	July	Aug.	Sept.	Oct.	Nov.	Dec.
Forecast with Trend & Seasonal	9,911	9,265	9,764	9,691	9,520	9,542	9,949	10,068	9,411	9,724	9,355	9,572

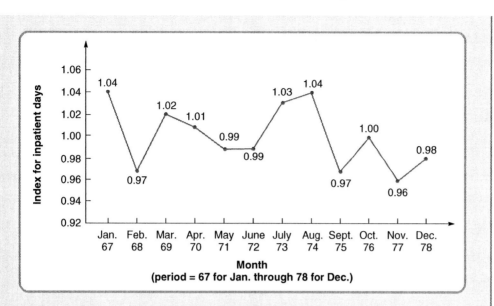

◀ **Figure 7**

Seasonal Index for San Diego Hospital

A graph showing the forecast that combines both trend and seasonality appears in Figure 8.

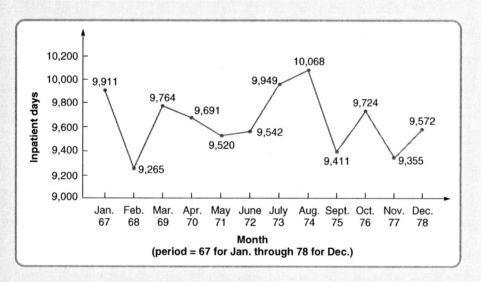

◀ **Figure 8**

Combined Trend and Seasonal Forecast

Insight: Notice that with trend only, the September forecast is 9,702, but with both trend and seasonal adjustments the forecast is 9,411. By combining trend and seasonal data the hospital was better able to forecast inpatient days and the related staffing and budgeting vital to effective operations.

Learning exercise: If the slope of the trend line for patient-days is 22.0 (rather than 21.5) and the index for December is .99 (instead of .98), what is the new forecast for December inpatient days? [Answer: 9,708.]

Related problems: 26, 29

Example 11 further illustrates seasonality for quarterly data at a department store.

EXAMPLE 11

Adjusting trend data with seasonal indices

Management at Davis's Department Store has used time-series regression to forecast retail sales for the next 4 quarters. Sales estimates are $100,000, $120,000, $140,000, and $160,000 for the respective quarters. Seasonal indices for the 4 quarters have been found to be 1.30, .90, .70, and 1.15, respectively.

Approach: To compute a seasonalized or adjusted sales forecast, we just multiply each seasonal index by the appropriate trend forecast:

$$\hat{y}_{seasonal} = Index \times \hat{y}_{trend\ forecast}$$

Solution:

Quarter I:	$\hat{y}_{I} = (1.30)(\$100,000)$	$= \$130,000$
Quarter II:	$\hat{y}_{II} = (.90)(\$120,000)$	$= \$108,000$
Quarter III:	$\hat{y}_{III} = (.70)(\$140,000)$	$= \$98,000$
Quarter IV:	$\hat{y}_{IV} = (1.15)(\$160,000)$	$= \$184,000$

Insight: The straight-line trend forecast is now adjusted to reflect the seasonal changes.

Learning exercise: If the sales forecast for Quarter IV was 180,000 (rather than 160,000), what would be the seasonally adjusted forecast? [Answer: $207,000.]

Related problems: 26, 29

Cyclical Variations in Data

Cycles
Patterns in the data that occur every several years.

Cycles are like seasonal variations in data but occur every several *years*, not weeks, months, or quarters. Forecasting cyclical variations in a time series is difficult. This is because cycles include a wide variety of factors that cause the economy to go from recession to expansion to recession over a period of years. These factors include national or industrywide overexpansion in times of euphoria and contraction in times of concern. Demand forecasting cycles for individual products can also be driven by product life cycles—the stages products go through from introduction through decline. Life cycles exist for virtually all products; striking examples include floppy disks, video recorders, and the original Game Boy. We leave cyclical analysis to forecasting texts.

Developing associative techniques of variables that affect one another is our next topic.

ASSOCIATIVE FORECASTING METHODS: REGRESSION AND CORRELATION ANALYSIS

Unlike time-series forecasting, *associative forecasting* models usually consider *several* variables that are related to the quantity being predicted. Once these related variables have been found, a statistical model is built and used to forecast the item of interest. This approach is more powerful than the time-series methods that use only the historical values for the forecasted variable.

Many factors can be considered in an associative analysis. For example, the sales of Dell PCs may be related to Dell's advertising budget, the company's prices, competitors' prices and promotional strategies, and even the nation's economy and unemployment rates. In this case, PC sales would be called the *dependent variable*, and the other variables would be called *independent variables*. The manager's job is to develop *the best statistical relationship between PC sales and the independent variables*. The most common quantitative associative forecasting model is **linear-regression analysis**.

Linear-regression analysis
A straight-line mathematical model to describe the functional relationships between independent and dependent variables.

Using Regression Analysis for Forecasting

Learning Objective

6. Conduct a regression and correlation analysis

We can use the same mathematical model that we employed in the least squares method of trend projection to perform a linear-regression analysis. The dependent variables that we want to forecast will still be $\hat{y}$. But now the independent variable, x, need no longer be time. We use the equation:

$$\hat{y} = a + bx$$

where
$\hat{y}$ = value of the dependent variable (in our example, sales)
a = y-axis intercept
b = slope of the regression line
x = independent variable

142

Example 12 shows how to use linear regression.

EXAMPLE 12

Computing a linear
regression equation

Nodel Construction Company renovates old homes in West Bloomfield, Michigan. Over time, the company has found that its dollar volume of renovation work is dependent on the West Bloomfield area payroll. Management wants to establish a mathematical relationship to help predict sales.

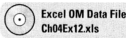

Excel OM Data File
Ch04Ex12.xls

Approach: Nodel's VP of operations has prepared the following table, which lists company revenues and the amount of money earned by wage earners in West Bloomfield during the past 6 years:

Nodel's Sales (in $ millions), y	Local Payroll (in $ billions), x	Nodel's Sales (in $ millions), y	Local Payroll (in $ billions), x
2.0	1	2.0	2
3.0	3	2.0	1
2.5	4	3.5	7

The VP needs to determine whether there is a straight-line (linear) relationship between area payroll and sales. He plots the known data on a scatter diagram:

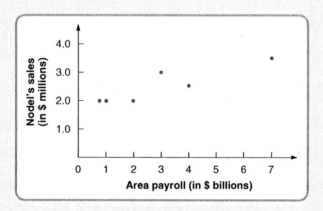

It appears from the six data points that there is a slight positive relationship between the independent variable (payroll) and the dependent variable (sales): As payroll increases, Nodel's sales tend to be higher.

Solution: We can find a mathematical equation by using the least-squares regression approach:

Sales, y	Payroll, x	x^2	xy
2.0	1	1	2.0
3.0	3	9	9.0
2.5	4	16	10.0
2.0	2	4	4.0
2.0	1	1	2.0
3.5	7	49	24.5
$\Sigma y = 15.0$	$\Sigma x = 18$	$\Sigma x^2 = 80$	$\Sigma xy = 51.5$

$$\bar{x} = \frac{\Sigma x}{6} = \frac{18}{6} = 3$$

$$\bar{y} = \frac{\Sigma y}{6} = \frac{15}{6} = 2.5$$

$$b = \frac{\Sigma xy - n\bar{x}\bar{y}}{\Sigma x^2 - n\bar{x}^2} = \frac{51.5 - (6)(3)(2.5)}{80 - (6)(3^2)} = .25$$

$$a = \bar{y} - b\bar{x} = 2.5 - (.25)(3) = 1.75$$

The estimated regression equation, therefore, is:

$$\hat{y} = 1.75 + .25x$$

or:

$$\text{Sales} = 1.75 + .25 \text{ (payroll)}$$

If the local chamber of commerce predicts that the West Bloomfield area payroll will be $6 billion next year, we can estimate sales for Nodel with the regression equation:

$$\text{Sales (in \$ millions)} = 1.75 + .25(6)$$

$$= 1.75 + 1.50 = 3.25$$

or:

$$\text{Sales} = \$3,250,000$$

Insight: Given our assumptions of a straight-line relationship between payroll and sales, we now have an indication of the slope of that relationship: Sales increases at the rate of a million dollars for every quarter billion dollars in the local payroll. This is because $b = .25$.

Learning exercise: What are Nodel's sales when the local payroll is $8 billion? [Answer: $3.75 million.]

Related problems: 24, 30, 31, 32, 33, 35, 38, 40, 41, 46, 48, 49

The final part of Example 12 shows a central weakness of associative forecasting methods like regression. Even when we have computed a regression equation, we must provide a forecast of the independent variable x—in this case, payroll—before estimating the dependent variable y for the next time period. Although this is not a problem for all forecasts, you can imagine the difficulty of determining future values of *some* common independent variables (such as unemployment rates, gross national product, price indices, and so on).

Standard Error of the Estimate

The forecast of $3,250,000 for Nodel's sales in Example 12 is called a *point estimate* of y. The point estimate is really the *mean*, or *expected value*, of a distribution of possible values of sales. Figure 9 illustrates this concept.

To measure the accuracy of the regression estimates, we must compute the **standard error of the estimate**, $S_{y,x}$. This computation is called the *standard deviation of the regression:* It measures the error from the dependent variable, y, to the regression line, rather than to the mean. Equation (14) is a similar expression to that found in most statistics books for computing the standard deviation of an arithmetic mean:

Standard error of the estimate

A measure of variability around the regression line—its standard deviation.

$$S_{y,x} = \sqrt{\frac{\Sigma(y - y_c)^2}{n - 2}} \qquad (14)$$

where
$y = y$-value of each data point
$y_c = $ computed value of the dependent variable, from the regression equation
$n = $ number of data points

▶ **Figure 9**

Distribution about the Point Estimate of $3.25 Million Sales

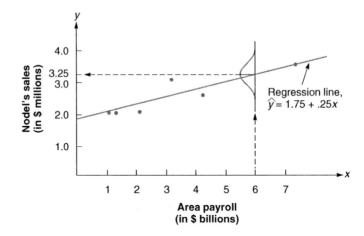

Glidden Paints' assembly lines fill thousands of cans per hour. To predict demand, the firm uses associative forecasting methods such as linear regression, with independent variables such as disposable personal income and GNP. Although housing starts would be a natural variable, Glidden found that it correlated poorly with past sales. It turns out that most Glidden paint is sold through retailers to customers who already own homes or businesses.

ICI Paints

Equation (15) may look more complex, but it is actually an easier-to-use version of Equation (14). Both formulas provide the same answer and can be used in setting up prediction intervals around the point estimate.[4]

$$S_{y,x} = \sqrt{\frac{\Sigma y^2 - a\Sigma y - b\Sigma xy}{n-2}} \qquad (15)$$

Example 13 shows how we would calculate the standard error of the estimate in Example 12.

EXAMPLE 13

Computing the standard error of the estimate

Nodel's VP of operations now wants to know the error associated with the regression line computed in Example 12.

Approach: Compute the standard error of the estimate, $S_{y,x}$, using Equation (15).

Solution: The only number we need that is not available to solve for $S_{y,x}$ is Σy^2. Some quick addition reveals $\Sigma y^2 = 39.5$. Therefore:

$$\begin{aligned} S_{y,x} &= \sqrt{\frac{\Sigma y^2 - a\Sigma y - b\Sigma xy}{n-2}} \\ &= \sqrt{\frac{39.5 - 1.75(15.0) - .25(51.5)}{6-2}} \\ &= \sqrt{.09375} = .306 \text{ (in \$ millions)} \end{aligned}$$

The standard error of the estimate is then \$306,000 in sales.

Insight: The interpretation of the standard error of the estimate is similar to the standard deviation; namely, ±1 standard deviation = .6827. So there is a 68.27% chance of sales being ±\$306,000 from the point estimate of \$3,250,000.

Learning exercise: What is the probability sales will exceed \$3,556,000? [Answer: About 16%.]

Related problems: 41e, 48b

Correlation Coefficients for Regression Lines

The regression equation is one way of expressing the nature of the relationship between two variables. Regression lines are not "cause-and-effect" relationships. They merely describe the relationships among variables. The regression equation shows how one variable relates to the value and changes in another variable.

Another way to evaluate the relationship between two variables is to compute the **coefficient of correlation**. This measure expresses the degree or strength of the linear relationship. Usually

Coefficient of correlation

A measure of the strength of the relationship between two variables.

---

[4]When the sample size is large ($n > 30$), the prediction interval value of y can be computed using normal tables. When the number of observations is small, the *t*-distribution is appropriate. See D. Groebner et al., *Business Statistics*, 7th ed. (Upper Saddle River, NJ: Prentice Hall, 2008).

▶ **Figure 10**

Four Values of the Correlation Coefficient

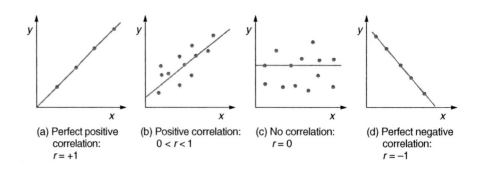

(a) Perfect positive correlation: $r = +1$

(b) Positive correlation: $0 < r < 1$

(c) No correlation: $r = 0$

(d) Perfect negative correlation: $r = -1$

identified as r, the coefficient of correlation can be any number between $+1$ and -1. Figure 10 illustrates what different values of r might look like.

To compute r, we use much of the same data needed earlier to calculate a and b for the regression line. The rather lengthy equation for r is:

$$r = \frac{n\Sigma xy - \Sigma x\Sigma y}{\sqrt{[n\Sigma x^2 - (\Sigma x)^2][n\Sigma y^2 - (\Sigma y)^2]}}$$

(16)

Example 14 shows how to calculate the coefficient of correlation for the data given in Examples 12 and 13.

EXAMPLE 14

Determining the coefficient of correlation

A high r doesn't always mean one variable will be a good predictor of the other. Skirt lengths and stock market prices may be correlated, but a rise in one doesn't mean the other will also go up.

In Example 12, we looked at the relationship between Nodel Construction Company's renovation sales and payroll in its hometown of West Bloomfield. The VP now wants to know the strength of the association between local payroll and sales.

Approach: We compute the r value using Equation 16. We need to first add one more column of calculations—for y^2.

Solution: The data, including the column for y^2 and the calculations, are shown here:

y	x	x^2	xy	y^2
2.0	1	1	2.0	4.0
3.0	3	9	9.0	9.0
2.5	4	16	10.0	6.25
2.0	2	4	4.0	4.0
2.0	1	1	2.0	4.0
3.5	7	49	24.5	12.25
$\Sigma y = 15.0$	$\Sigma x = 18$	$\Sigma x^2 = 80$	$\Sigma xy = 51.5$	$\Sigma y^2 = 39.5$

$$r = \frac{(6)(51.5) - (18)(15.0)}{\sqrt{[(6)(80) - (18)^2][(6)(39.5) - (15.0)^2]}}$$

$$= \frac{309 - 270}{\sqrt{(156)(12)}} = \frac{39}{\sqrt{1,872}}$$

$$= \frac{39}{43.3} = .901$$

Insight: This r of .901 appears to be a significant correlation and helps confirm the closeness of the relationship between the two variables.

Learning exercise: If the coefficient of correlation was $-.901$ rather than $+.901$, what would this tell you? [Answer: The negative correlation would tell you that as payroll went up, Nodel's sales went down—a rather unlikely occurrence that would suggest you recheck your math.]

Related problems: 24d, 35d, 38c, 41f, 48b

Although the coefficient of correlation is the measure most commonly used to describe the relationship between two variables, another measure does exist. It is called the **coefficient of determination** and is simply the square of the coefficient of correlation—namely, r^2. The value of r^2 will always be a positive number in the range $0 \le r^2 \le 1$. The coefficient of determination is the percent of variation in the dependent variable (y) that is explained by the regression equation. In Nodel's case, the value of r^2 is .81, indicating that 81% of the total variation is explained by the regression equation.

Coefficient of determination
A measure of the amount of variation in the dependent variable about its mean that is explained by the regression equation.

Multiple-Regression Analysis

Multiple regression is a practical extension of the simple regression model we just explored. It allows us to build a model with several independent variables instead of just one variable. For example, if Nodel Construction wanted to include average annual interest rates in its model for forecasting renovation sales, the proper equation would be:

$$\hat{y} = a + b_1 x_1 + b_2 x_2 \qquad (17)$$

Multiple regression
An associative forecasting method with more than one independent variable.

where

$\hat{y}$ = dependent variable, sales
a = a constant, the y intercept
x_1 and x_2 = values of the two independent variables, area payroll and interest rates, respectively
b_1 and b_2 = coefficients for the two independent variables

The mathematics of multiple regression becomes quite complex (and is usually tackled by computer), so we leave the formulas for a, b_1, and b_2 to statistics textbooks. However, Example 15 shows how to interpret Equation (17) in forecasting Nodel's sales.

EXAMPLE 15

Using a multiple-regression equation

Nodel Construction wants to see the impact of a second independent variable, interest rates, on its sales.

Approach: The new multiple-regression line for Nodel Construction, calculated by computer software, is:

$$\hat{y} = 1.80 + .30 x_1 - 5.0 x_2$$

We also find that the new coefficient of correlation is .96, implying the inclusion of the variable x_2, interest rates, adds even more strength to the linear relationship.

Solution: We can now estimate Nodel's sales if we substitute values for next year's payroll and interest rate. If West Bloomfield's payroll will be $6 billion and the interest rate will be .12 (12%), sales will be forecast as:

$$\text{Sales (\$ millions)} = 1.80 + .30(6) - 5.0(.12)$$
$$= 1.8 + 1.8 - .6$$
$$= 3.00$$

or:

$$\text{Sales} = \$3,000,000$$

Insight: By using both variables, payroll and interest rates, Nodel now has a sales forecast of $3 million and a higher coefficient of correlation. This suggests a stronger relationship between the two variables and a more accurate estimate of sales.

Learning exercise: If interest rates were only 6%, what would be the sales forecast? [Answer: $3,300,000.]

Related problems: 34, 36

MONITORING AND CONTROLLING FORECASTS

Once a forecast has been completed, it should not be forgotten. No manager wants to be reminded that his or her forecast is horribly inaccurate, but a firm needs to determine why actual demand (or whatever variable is being examined) differed significantly from that projected.

If the forecaster is accurate, that individual usually makes sure that everyone is aware of his or her talents. Very seldom does one read articles in *Fortune*, *Forbes*, or *The Wall Street Journal*, however, about money managers who are consistently off by 25% in their stock market forecasts.

One way to monitor forecasts to ensure that they are performing well is to use a tracking signal. A **tracking signal** is a measurement of how well a forecast is predicting actual values. As forecasts are updated every week, month, or quarter, the newly available demand data are compared to the forecast values.

The tracking signal is computed as the *running sum of the forecast errors (RSFE)* divided by the *mean absolute deviation (MAD)*:

$$\left(\begin{array}{c} \text{Tracking} \\ \text{signal} \end{array} \right) = \frac{\text{RSFE}}{\text{MAD}}$$

$$= \frac{\Sigma(\text{Actual demand in period } i - \text{Forecast demand in period } i)}{\text{MAD}}$$

(18)

where

$$\text{MAD} = \frac{\Sigma |\text{Actual} - \text{Forecast}|}{n}$$

as seen earlier in Equation (5).

Positive tracking signals indicate that demand is *greater* than forecast. *Negative* signals mean that demand is *less* than forecast. A good tracking signal—that is, one with a low RSFE—has about as much positive error as it has negative error. In other words, small deviations are okay, but positive and negative errors should balance one another so that the tracking signal centers closely around zero. A consistent tendency for forecasts to be greater or less than the actual values (that is, for a high RSFE) is called a **bias** error. Bias can occur if, for example, the wrong variables or trend line are used or if a seasonal index is misapplied.

Once tracking signals are calculated, they are compared with predetermined control limits. When a tracking signal exceeds an upper or lower limit, there is a problem with the forecasting method, and management may want to reevaluate the way it forecasts demand. Figure 11 shows the graph of a tracking signal that is exceeding the range of acceptable variation. If the model being used is exponential smoothing, perhaps the smoothing constant needs to be readjusted.

How do firms decide what the upper and lower tracking limits should be? There is no single answer, but they try to find reasonable values—in other words, limits not so low as to be triggered with every small forecast error and not so high as to allow bad forecasts to be regularly overlooked. One MAD is equivalent to approximately .8 standard deviation, ± 2 MADs = ± 1.6 standard deviations, ± 3 MADs = ± 2.4 standard deviations, and ± 4 MADs = ± 3.2 standard deviations. This fact suggests that for a forecast to be "in control," 89% of the errors are expected to fall within ± 2 MADs, 98% within ± 3 MADs, or 99.9% within ± 4 MADs.[5]

Example 16 shows how the tracking signal and RSFE can be computed.

Tracking signal

A measurement of how well the forecast is predicting actual values.

Bias

A forecast that is consistently higher or consistently lower than actual values of a time series.

Learning Objective

7. Use a tracking signal

▶ **Figure 11**

A Plot of Tracking Signals

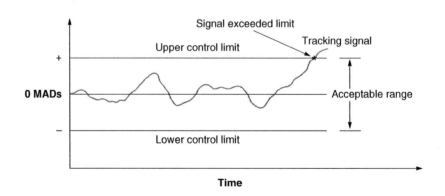

---

[5]To prove these three percentages to yourself, just set up a normal curve for ± 1.6 standard deviations (*z*-values). Using the normal table in Appendix I, you find that the area under the curve is .89. This represents ± 2 MADs. Likewise, ± 3 MADs = ± 2.4 standard deviations encompass 98% of the area, and so on for ± 4 MADs.

EXAMPLE 16

Computing the
tracking signal
at Carlson Bakery

Carlson's Bakery wants to evaluate performance of its croissant forecast.

Approach: Develop a tracking signal for the forecast and see if it stays within acceptable limits, which we define as ±4 MADs.

Solution: Using the forecast and demand data for the last 6 quarters for croissant sales, we develop a tracking signal in the table below:

Quarter	Actual Demand	Forecast Demand	Error	RSFE	Absolute Forecast Error	Cumulative Absolute Forecast Error	MAD	Tracking Signal (RSFE/MAD)
1	90	100	−10	−10	10	10	10.0	−10/10 = −1
2	95	100	−5	−15	5	15	7.5	−15/7.5 = −2
3	115	100	+15	0	15	30	10.0	0/10 = 0
4	100	110	−10	−10	10	40	10.0	−10/10 = −1
5	125	110	+15	+5	15	55	11.0	+5/11 = +0.5
6	140	110	+30	+35	30	85	14.2	+35/14.2 = +2.5

$$\text{At the end of quarter 6, MAD} = \frac{\Sigma\,|\text{Forecast errors}|}{n} = \frac{85}{6} = 14.2$$

$$\text{and Tracking signal} = \frac{\text{RSFE}}{\text{MAD}} = \frac{35}{14.2} = 2.5 \text{ MADs}$$

Insight: Because the tracking signal drifted from −2 MAD to +2.5 MAD (between 1.6 and 2.0 standard deviations), we can conclude that it is within acceptable limits.

Learning exercise: If actual demand in quarter 6 was 130 (rather than 140), what would be the MAD and resulting tracking signal? [Answer: MAD for quarter 6 would be 12.5, and the tracking signal for period 6 would be 2 MADs.]

Related problems: 37, 45

Adaptive Smoothing

Adaptive forecasting refers to computer monitoring of tracking signals and self-adjustment if a signal passes a preset limit. For example, when applied to exponential smoothing, the α and β coefficients are first selected on the basis of values that minimize error forecasts and then adjusted accordingly whenever the computer notes an errant tracking signal. This process is called **adaptive smoothing**.

Adaptive smoothing
An approach to exponential smoothing forecasting in which the smoothing constant is automatically changed to keep errors to a minimum.

Focus Forecasting

Rather than adapt by choosing a smoothing constant, computers allow us to try a variety of forecasting models. Such an approach is called focus forecasting. **Focus forecasting** is based on two principles:

1. Sophisticated forecasting models are not always better than simple ones.
2. There is no single technique that should be used for all products or services.

Focus forecasting
Forecasting that tries a variety of computer models and selects the best one for a particular application.

Bernard Smith, inventory manager for American Hardware Supply, coined the term *focus forecasting.* Smith's job was to forecast quantities for 100,000 hardware products purchased by American's 21 buyers.[6] He found that buyers neither trusted nor understood the exponential smoothing model then in use. Instead, they used very simple approaches of their own. So Smith developed his new computerized system for selecting forecasting methods.

[6]Bernard T. Smith, *Focus Forecasting: Computer Techniques for Inventory Control* (Boston: CBI Publishing, 1978).

Famous forecasts somewhat lacking in accuracy:

"I think there is a world market for maybe five computers."

Thomas Watson, chairman of IBM, 1943

"640,000 bytes of memory ought to be enough for anybody."

Bill Gates, 1981

"The Internet will catastrophically collapse in 1996."

Robert Metcalfe, inventor of the Internet

Smith chose seven forecasting methods to test. They ranged from the simple ones that buyers used (such as the naive approach) to statistical models. Every month, Smith applied the forecasts of all seven models to each item in stock. In these simulated trials, the forecast values were subtracted from the most recent actual demands, giving a simulated forecast error. The forecast method yielding the least error is selected by the computer, which then uses it to make next month's forecast. Although buyers still have an override capability, American Hardware finds that focus forecasting provides excellent results.

FORECASTING IN THE SERVICE SECTOR

Forecasting in the service sector presents some unusual challenges. A major technique in the retail sector is tracking demand by maintaining good short-term records. For instance, a barbershop catering to men expects peak flows on Fridays and Saturdays. Indeed, most barbershops are closed on Sunday and Monday, and many call in extra help on Friday and Saturday. A downtown restaurant, on the other hand, may need to track conventions and holidays for effective short-term forecasting. The *OM in Action* box "Forecasting at FedEx's Customer Service Center" provides an example of a major service-sector industry, the call center.

Specialty Retail Shops Specialty retail facilities, such as flower shops, may have other unusual demand patterns, and those patterns will differ depending on the holiday. When Valentine's Day falls on a weekend, for example, flowers can't be delivered to offices, and those romantically inclined are likely to celebrate with outings rather than flowers. If a holiday falls on a Monday, some of the celebration may also take place on the weekend, reducing flower sales. However, when Valentine's Day falls in midweek, busy midweek schedules often make flowers the optimal way to celebrate. Because flowers for Mother's Day are to be delivered on Saturday or Sunday, this holiday forecast varies less. Due to special demand patterns, many service firms maintain records of sales, noting not only the day of the week but also unusual events, including the weather, so that patterns and correlations that influence demand can be developed.

Fast-Food Restaurants Fast-food restaurants are well aware not only of weekly, daily, and hourly but even 15-minute variations in demands that influence sales. Therefore, detailed forecasts of demand are needed. Figure 12(a) shows the hourly forecast for a typical fast-food restau-

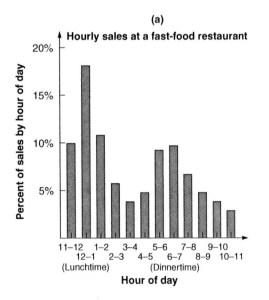

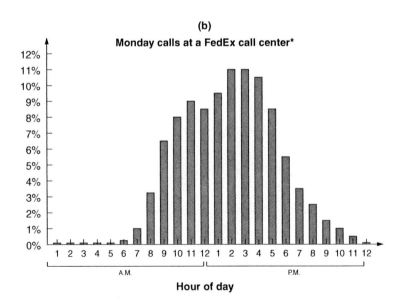

▲ **Figure 12** Forecasts Are Unique: Note the Variations Between (a) Hourly Sales at a Fast-Food Restaurant and (b) Hourly Call Volume at FedEx

*Based on historical data: see *Journal of Business Forecasting* (Winter 1999–2000): 6–11.

OM in Action   Forecasting at FedEx's Customer Service Centers

The world's largest express shipping company, FedEx, generates $30 billion in revenues, using 650 planes, 42,000 trucks, and a workforce of 145,000 in 210 countries. To support this global network, the company has 51 customer service call centers, whose service goal is to answer 90% of all calls within 20 seconds. With a half-million daily calls just in the U.S., FedEx makes extensive use of forecasting models for staffing decisions and to ensure that customer satisfaction levels stay the highest in the industry.

FedEx's Forecasting & Modeling department makes several different forecasts. *One-year* and *five-year* models predict number of calls, average handle time, and staffing needs. They break forecasts into weekday, Saturday, and Sunday and then use the Delphi method and time-series analysis.

FedEx's *tactical forecasts* are monthly and use 8 years of historical daily data. This time-series model addresses

Anton Vengo, Superstock, Inc.

month, day of week, and day of month to predict caller volume. Finally, the *operational forecast* uses a weighted moving average and 6 weeks of data to project the number of calls on a half-hourly basis.

FedEx's forecasts are consistently accurate to within 1% to 2% of actual call volumes. This means coverage needs are met, service levels are maintained, and costs are controlled.

Sources: Baseline (January 2005): 54; and *Journal of Business Forecasting* (Winter 1999–2000): 7–11.

rant. Note the lunchtime and dinnertime peaks. This contrasts to the 10:30 A.M. and 4:30 P.M. peaks at FedEx's call center in Figure 12(b).

Firms like Taco Bell now use point-of-sale computers that track sales every quarter hour. Taco Bell found that a 6-week moving average was the forecasting technique that minimized its mean squared error (MSE) of these quarter-hour forecasts. Building this forecasting methodology into each of Taco Bell's 6,500 stores' computers, the model makes weekly projections of customer transactions. These in turn are used by store managers to schedule staff, who begin in 15-minute increments, not 1-hour blocks as in other industries. The forecasting model has been so successful that Taco Bell has increased customer service while documenting more than $50 million in labor cost savings in 4 years of use.[7]

Summary

Forecasts are a critical part of the operations manager's function. Demand forecasts drive a firm's production, capacity, and scheduling systems and affect the financial, marketing, and personnel planning functions.

There are a variety of qualitative and quantitative forecasting techniques. Qualitative approaches employ judgment, experience, intuition, and a host of other factors that are difficult to quantify. Quantitative forecasting uses historical data and causal, or associative, relations to project future demands. Table 2 summarizes the formulas we introduced in quantita-

tive forecasting. Forecast calculations are seldom performed by hand. Most operations managers turn to software packages such as Forecast PRO, SAP, tsMetrix, AFS, SAS, SPSS, or Excel.

No forecasting method is perfect under all conditions. And even once management has found a satisfactory approach, it must still monitor and control forecasts to make sure errors do not get out of hand. Forecasting can often be a very challenging, but rewarding, part of managing.

[7]J. Hueter and W. Swart, "An Integrated Labor Management System for Taco Bell," *Interfaces* 28, no. 1 (January-February 1998): 75–91.

Table 2

Summary of Forecasting Formulas

Moving averages—forecasts based on an average of recent values

$$\text{Moving average} = \frac{\Sigma \text{ Demand in previous } n \text{ periods}}{n} \tag{1}$$

Weighted moving averages—a moving average with weights that vary

$$\text{Weighted moving average} = \frac{\Sigma \text{ (Weight for period } n)(\text{Demand in period } n)}{\Sigma \text{ Weights}} \tag{2}$$

Exponential smoothing—a moving average with weights following an exponential distribution

$$\text{New forecast} = \text{Last period's forecast} + \alpha \text{ (Last period's actual demand} - \text{Last period's forecast)} \tag{3}$$

$$F_t = F_{t-1} + \alpha(A_{t-1} - F_{t-1}) \tag{4}$$

Mean absolute deviation—a measure of overall forecast error

$$\text{MAD} = \Sigma \,|\, \text{Actual} - \text{Forecast} \,|\, /n = \frac{\Sigma \,|\text{Forecast Errors}|}{n} \tag{5}$$

Mean squared error—a second measure of forecast error

$$\text{MSE} = \frac{\Sigma(\text{Forecast errors})^2}{n} \tag{6}$$

Mean absolute percent error—a third measure of forecast error

$$\text{MAPE} = \frac{\sum_{i=1}^{n} 100\,|\text{Actual}_i - \text{Forecast}_i|\big/\text{Actual}_i}{n} \tag{7}$$

Exponential smoothing with trend adjustment—an exponential smoothing model that can accommodate trend

$$\text{Forecast including trend}(FIT_t) = \text{Exponentially smoothed forecast}(F_t) + \text{Exponentially smoothed trend}(T_t) \tag{8}$$

$$F_t = \alpha(A_{t-1}) + (1 - \alpha)(F_{t-1} + T_{t-1}) \tag{9}$$

$$T_t = \beta(F_t - F_{t-1}) + (1 - \beta)T_{t-1} \tag{10}$$

Trend projection and regression analysis—fitting a trend line to historical data or a regression line to an independent variable

$$\hat{y} = a + bx \tag{11}$$

$$b = \frac{\Sigma xy - n\bar{x}\,\bar{y}}{\Sigma x^2 - n\bar{x}^2} \tag{12}$$

$$a = \bar{y} - b\bar{x} \tag{13}$$

Multiple regression analysis—a regression model with more than one independent (predicting) variable

$$\hat{y} = a + b_1 x_1 + b_2 x_2 + \quad + b_n x_n \tag{17}$$

Tracking signal—a measurement of how well the forecast is predicting actual values

$$\text{Tracking signal} = \frac{\text{RSFE}}{\text{MAD}} = \frac{\Sigma(\text{Actual demand in period } i - \text{Forecast demand in period } i)}{\text{MAD}} \tag{18}$$

Key Terms

Forecasting	Naive approach	Standard error of the estimate
Economic forecasts	Moving averages	Coefficient of correlation
Technological forecasts	Exponential smoothing	Coefficient of determination
Demand forecasts	Smoothing constant	Multiple regression
Quantitative forecasts	Mean absolute deviation (MAD)	Tracking signal
Qualitative forecasts	Mean squared error (MSE)	Bias
Jury of executive opinion	Mean absolute percent error (MAPE)	Adaptive smoothing
Delphi method	Trend projection	Focus forecasting
Sales force composite	Seasonal variations	
Consumer market survey	Cycles	
Time series	Linear-regression analysis	

Using Software in Forecasting

This section presents three ways to solve forecasting problems with computer software. First, you can create your own Excel spreadsheets to develop forecasts. Second, you can use the Excel OM software that comes with the text and is found on the student CD. Third, POM for Windows is another program that is located on the student CD.

Creating Your Own Excel Spreadsheets

Excel spreadsheets (and spreadsheets in general) are frequently used in forecasting. Exponential smoothing, trend analysis, and regression analysis (simple and multiple) are supported by built-in Excel functions.

Program 1 illustrates how to build an Excel forecast for the data in Example 8. The goal for N.Y. Edison is to create a trend analysis of the 2001–2007 data. Note that in cell D4 you can enter either = $B\$16 + \$B\$17 * C4$ *or* = TREND ($B\$4: \$B\$10, \$C\$4: \$C\$10, C4$).

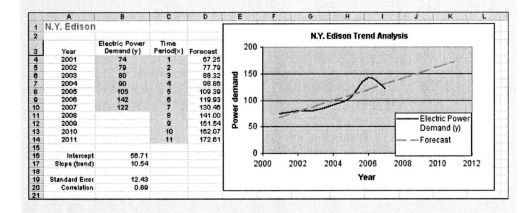

◁ **Program 1**

Using Excel to Develop Your Own Forecast with Data from Example 8

Computations

Value	Cell	Excel Formula	Action
Trend line column	D4	=$B$16+$B$17*C4 (or =TREND($B$4:$B$10,$C$4:$C$10,C4))	Copy to D5:D14
Intercept	B16	=INTERCEPT(B4:B10, C4:C10)	
Slope (trend)	B17	=SLOPE(B4:B10, C4:C10)	
Standard error	B19	=STEYX(B4:B10, C4:C10)	
Correlation	B20	=CORREL(B4:B10, C4:C10)	

As an alternative, you may want to experiment with Excel's built-in regression analysis. To do so, under the *Tools* menu bar selection choose *Data Analysis*, then *Regression*. Enter your Y and X data into two columns (say B and C). When the regression window appears, enter the Y and X ranges, then select *OK*. Excel offers several plots and tables to those interested in more rigorous analysis of regression problems.

X Using Excel OM

Excel OM's forecasting module has five components: (1) moving averages, (2) weighted moving averages, (3) exponential smoothing, (4) regression (with one variable only), and (5) decomposition. Excel OM's error analysis is much more complete than that available with the Excel add-in.

Program 2 illustrates Excel OM's input and output, using Example 2's weighted moving-average data.

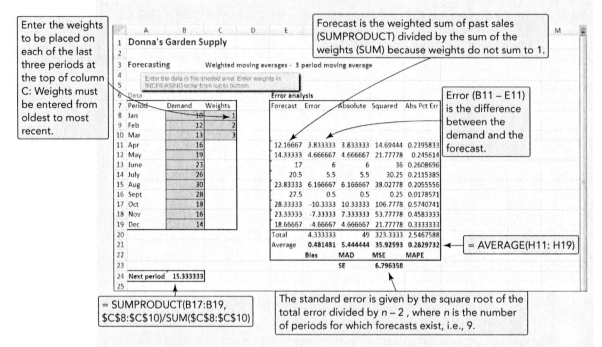

Enter the weights to be placed on each of the last three periods at the top of column C: Weights must be entered from oldest to most recent.

Forecast is the weighted sum of past sales (SUMPRODUCT) divided by the sum of the weights (SUM) because weights do not sum to 1.

Error (B11 – E11) is the difference between the demand and the forecast.

= AVERAGE(H11: H19)

= SUMPRODUCT(B17:B19, $C$8:$C$10)/SUM($C$8:$C$10)

The standard error is given by the square root of the total error divided by $n - 2$, where n is the number of periods for which forecasts exist, i.e., 9.

▲ **Program 2** Analysis of Excel OM's Weighted Moving-Average Program, Using Data from Example 2 as Input

P Using POM for Windows

POM for Windows can project moving averages (both simple and weighted), handle exponential smoothing (both simple and trend adjusted), forecast with least squares trend projection, and solve linear-regression (associative) models. A summary screen of error analysis and a graph of the data can also be generated. As a special example of exponential smoothing adaptive forecasting, when using an α of 0, POM for Windows will find the α value that yields the minimum MAD.

Solved Problems

Virtual Office Hours help is available on Student DVD.

Solved Problem 1

Sales of Volkswagen's popular Beetle have grown steadily at auto dealerships in Nevada during the past 5 years (see table below). The sales manager had predicted in 2002 that 2003 sales would be 410 VWs. Using exponential smoothing with a weight of $\alpha = .30$, develop forecasts for 2004 through 2008.

Year	Sales	Forecast
2003	450	410
2004	495	
2005	518	
2006	563	
2007	584	
2008	?	

Solution

Year	Forecast
2003	410.0
2004	$422.0 = 410 + .3\,(450 - 410)$
2005	$443.9 = 422 + .3\,(495 - 422)$
2006	$466.1 = 443.9 + .3\,(518 - 443.9)$
2007	$495.2 = 466.1 + .3\,(563 - 466.1)$
2008	$521.8 = 495.2 + .3\,(584 - 495.2)$

Solved Problem 2

In Example 7, we applied trend-adjusted exponential smoothing to forecast demand for a piece of pollution-control equipment for months 2 and 3 (out of 9 months of data provided). Let us now continue this process for month 4. We want to confirm the forecast for month 4 shown in Table 1 (p. 120) and Figure 3 (p. 120).

For month 4, $A_4 = 19$, with $\alpha = .2$, and $\beta = .4$

Solution

$$F_4 = \alpha A_3 + (1 - \alpha)(F_3 + T_3)$$
$$= (.2)(20) + (1 - .2)(15.18 + 2.10)$$
$$= 4.0 + (.8)(17.28)$$
$$= 4.0 + 13.82$$
$$= 17.82$$

$$T_4 = \beta(F_4 - F_3) + (1 - \beta)T_3$$
$$= (.4)(17.82 - 15.18) + (1 - .4)(2.10)$$
$$= (.4)(2.64) + (.6)(2.10)$$
$$= 1.056 + 1.26$$
$$= 2.32$$

$$FIT_4 = 17.82 + 2.32$$
$$= 20.14$$

Solved Problem 3

Room registrations in the Toronto Towers Plaza Hotel have been recorded for the past 9 years. To project future occupancy, management would like to determine the mathematical trend of guest registration. This estimate will help the hotel determine whether future expansion will be needed. Given the following time-series data, develop a regression equation relating registrations to time (e.g., a trend equation). Then forecast 2009 registrations. Room registrations are in the thousands:

1999: 17   2000: 16   2001: 16   2002: 21   2003: 20
2004: 20   2005: 23   2006: 25   2007: 24

Solution

Year	Transformed Year, x	Registrants, y (in thousands)	x^2	xy
1999	1	17	1	17
2000	2	16	4	32
2001	3	16	9	48
2002	4	21	16	84
2003	5	20	25	100
2004	6	20	36	120
2005	7	23	49	161
2006	8	25	64	200
2007	9	24	81	216
	$\Sigma x = 45$	$\Sigma y = 182$	$\Sigma x^2 = 285$	$\Sigma xy = 978$

$$b = \frac{\Sigma xy - n\bar{x}\bar{y}}{\Sigma x^2 = n\bar{x}^2} = \frac{978 - (9)(5)(20.22)}{285 - (9)(25)} = \frac{978 - 909.9}{285 - 225} = \frac{68.1}{60} = 1.135$$

$$a = \bar{y} - b\bar{x} = 20.22 - (1.135)(5) = 20.22 - 5.675 = 14.545$$

$$\hat{y}(\text{registrations}) = 14.545 + 1.135x$$

The projection of registrations in the year 2009 (which is $x = 11$ in the coding system used) is:

$$\hat{y} = 14.545 + (1.135)(11) = 27.03$$

or 27,030 guests in 2009

Solved Problem 4

Quarterly demand for Ford F150 pickups at a New York auto dealer is forecast with the equation:

$$\hat{y} = 10 + 3x$$

where x = quarters, and:

Quarter I of 2006 = 0
Quarter II of 2006 = 1
Quarter III of 2006 = 2
Quarter IV of 2006 = 3
Quarter I of 2007 = 4
and so on

and:

$$\hat{y} = \text{quarterly demand}$$

The demand for trucks is seasonal, and the indices for Quarters I, II, III, and IV are 0.80, 1.00, 1.30, and 0.90, respectively. Forecast demand for each quarter of 2008. Then, seasonalize each forecast to adjust for quarterly variations.

Solution

Quarter II of 2007 is coded $x = 5$; Quarter III of 2007, $x = 6$; and Quarter IV of 2007, $x = 7$. Hence, Quarter I of 2008 is coded $x = 8$; Quarter II, $x = 9$; and so on.

$$\hat{y}(2008 \text{ Quarter I}) = 10 + 3(8) = 34$$
$$\hat{y}(2008 \text{ Quarter II}) = 10 + 3(9) = 37$$
$$\hat{y}(2008 \text{ Quarter III}) = 10 + 3(10) = 40$$
$$\hat{y}(2008 \text{ Quarter IV}) = 10 + 3(11) = 43$$

Adjusted forecast = $(.80)(34) = 27.2$
Adjusted forecast = $(1.00)(37) = 37$
Adjusted forecast = $(1.30)(40) = 52$
Adjusted forecast = $(.90)(43) = 38.7$

Active Model Exercise

This active model, as well as the three others in this chapter, appears on your CD-ROM. It allows you to evaluate important elements of an exponential smoothing forecast.

▶ **Active Model 4.2**

Exponential Smoothing Using Data from Example 4

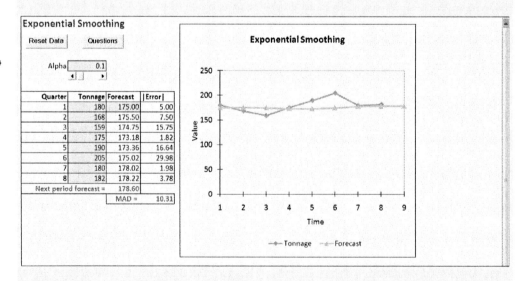

Questions

1. What happens to the graph when $\alpha = 0$?

2. What happens to the graph when $\alpha = 1$?

3. Generalize what happens to a forecast as alpha increases.

4. At what level of alpha is the mean absolute deviation (MAD) minimized?

Self-Test

- **Before taking the self-test,** *refer to the learning objectives at the beginning of the chapter, the notes in the margins, and the glossary at the end of the selection.*
- *Use the key at the back of the selection to* **correct** *your answers.*
- **Restudy** *pages that correspond to any questions you answered incorrectly or material you feel uncertain about.*

1. Forecasting time horizons include:
 a) long range
 b) medium range
 c) short range
 d) all of the above

2. Quantitative methods of forecasting include:
 a) sales force composite
 b) jury of executive opinion
 c) consumer market survey
 d) exponential smoothing
 e) all are quantitative methods

3. The method that considers the relationship between data and the variable being predicted is:
 a) exponential smoothing
 b) associative forecasting
 c) weighted moving average
 d) all of the above

4. Three popular measures of forecast accuracy are:
 a) total error, average error, and mean error
 b) average error, median error, and maximum error
 c) median error, minimum error, and maximum absolute error
 d) mean absolute error, mean squared error, and mean absolute percent error

5. In exponential smoothing, when the smoothing constant is high:
 a) more weight is placed on the more recent data
 b) less weight is placed on the more recent data
 c) the forecast will be a high number
 d) the forecast is a number between -1 and $+1$

6. With regard to a regression-based forecast, the *standard error of the estimate* gives a measure of:
 a) the overall accuracy of the forecast
 b) the time period for which the forecast is valid
 c) the time required to derive the forecast equation
 d) the maximum error of the forecast
 e) all of the above

7. The main difference between simple and multiple regression is _____.

8. The difference between a *moving average* model and an *exponential smoothing* model is that _____.

9. The purpose of drawing a scatter diagram is to _____.

Internet and Student CD-ROM/DVD Exercises

Visit our Companion Web site or use your student CD-ROM/DVD to help with material in this chapter.

 On Our Companion Web Site,
 www.prenhall.com/heizer
- Self-Study Quizzes
- Practice Problems
- Virtual Company Tour
- Internet Case
- PowerPoint Lecture

⊙ **On Your Student CD-ROM**
- Practice Problems
- Active Model Exercises
- Excel OM
- Excel OM Data Files
- POM for Windows

⊙ **On Your Student DVD**
- Video Clip and Video Case
- Virtual Office Hours for Solved Problems

Discussion Questions

1. What is a qualitative forecasting model, and when is its use appropriate?
2. Identify and briefly describe the two general forecasting approaches.
3. Identify the three forecasting time horizons. State an approximate duration for each.
4. Briefly describe the steps that are used to develop a forecasting system.
5. A skeptical manager asks what medium-range forecasts can be used for. Give the manager three possible uses/purposes.
6. Explain why such forecasting devices as moving averages, weighted moving averages, and exponential smoothing are not well suited for data series that have trends.
7. What is the basic difference between a weighted moving average and exponential smoothing?

8. What three methods are used to determine the accuracy of any given forecasting method? How would you determine whether time-series regression or exponential smoothing is better in a specific application?
9. Research and briefly describe the Delphi technique. How would it be used by an employer you have worked for?
10. What is the primary difference between a time-series model and an associative model?
11. Define time series.
12. What effect does the value of the smoothing constant have on the weight given to the recent values?
13. Explain the value of seasonal indices in forecasting. How are seasonal patterns different from cyclical patterns?
14. Which forecasting technique can place the most emphasis on recent values? How does it do this?

15. In your own words, explain adaptive forecasting.
16. What is the purpose of a tracking signal?
17. Explain, in your own words, the meaning of the correlation coefficient. Discuss the meaning of a negative value of the correlation coefficient.
18. What is the difference between a dependent and an independent variable?

19. Give examples of industries that are affected by seasonality. Why would these businesses want to filter out seasonality?
20. Give examples of industries in which demand forecasting is dependent on the demand for other products.
21. What happens to the ability to forecast for periods farther into the future?

Ethical Dilemma

In 2006, the board of regents responsible for all public higher education funding in a large Midwestern state hired a consultant to develop a series of enrollment forecasting models, one for each college. These models used historical data and exponential smoothing to forecast the following year's enrollments. Based on the model, which included a smoothing constant (α) for each school, each college's budget was set by the board. The head of the board personally selected each smoothing constant, based on what she called her "gut reactions and political acumen."

What do you think the advantages and disadvantages of this system are? Answer from the perspective of (a) the board of regents and (b) the president of each college. How can this model be abused and what can be done to remove any biases? How can a *regression model* be used to produce results that favor one forecast over another?

Problems*

• 1 The following gives the number of pints of type A blood used at Woodlawn Hospital in the past 6 weeks:

Week Of	Pints Used
August 31	360
September 7	389
September 14	410
September 21	381
September 28	368
October 5	374

a) Forecast the demand for the week of October 12 using a 3-week moving average.
b) Use a 3-week weighted moving average, with weights of .1, .3, and .6, using .6 for the most recent week. Forecast demand for the week of October 12.
c) Compute the forecast for the week of October 12 using exponential smoothing with a forecast for August 31 of 360 and $\alpha = .2$. **Px**

•• 2

Year	1	2	3	4	5	6	7	8	9	10	11
Demand	7	9	5	9	13	8	12	13	9	11	7

a) Plot the above data on a graph. Do you observe any trend, cycles, or random variations?
b) Starting in year 4 and going to year 12, forecast demand using a 3-year moving average. Plot your forecast on the same graph as the original data.
c) Starting in year 4 and going to year 12, forecast demand using a 3-year moving average with weights of .1, .3, and .6, using .6 for the most recent year. Plot this forecast on the same graph.
d) As you compare forecasts with the original data, which seems to give the better results? **Px**

*Note: **Px** means the problem may be solved with POM for Windows and/or Excel OM.

• 3 Refer to Problem 2. Develop a forecast for years 2 through 12 using exponential smoothing with $\alpha = .4$ and a forecast for year 1 of 6. Plot your new forecast on a graph with the actual data and the naive forecast. Based on a visual inspection, which forecast is better? **Px**

• 4 A check-processing center uses exponential smoothing to forecast the number of incoming checks each month. The number of checks received in June was 40 million, while the forecast was 42 million. A smoothing constant of .2 is used.
a) What is the forecast for July?
b) If the center received 45 million checks in July, what would be the forecast for August?
c) Why might this be an inappropriate forecasting method for this situation? **Px**

•• 5 The Carbondale Hospital is considering the purchase of a new ambulance. The decision will rest partly on the anticipated mileage to be driven next year. The miles driven during the past 5 years are as follows:

Year	Mileage
1	3,000
2	4,000
3	3,400
4	3,800
5	3,700

a) Forecast the mileage for next year using a 2-year moving average.
b) Find the MAD based on the 2-year moving average forecast in part (a). (Hint: You will have only 3 years of matched data.)
c) Use a weighted 2-year moving average with weights of .4 and .6 to forecast next year's mileage. (The weight of .6 is for the most recent year.) What MAD results from using this approach to forecasting? (Hint: You will have only 3 years of matched data.)
d) Compute the forecast for year 6 using exponential smoothing, an initial forecast for year 1 of 3,000 miles, and $\alpha = .5$. **Px**

6 The monthly sales for Telco Batteries, Inc., were as follows:

Month	Sales
January	20
February	21
March	15
April	14
May	13
June	16
July	17
August	18
September	20
October	20
November	21
December	23

a) Plot the monthly sales data.
b) Forecast January sales using each of the following:
   i) Naive method.
   ii) A 3-month moving average.
   iii) A 6-month weighted average using .1, .1, .1, .2, .2, and .3, with the heaviest weights applied to the most recent months.
   iv) Exponential smoothing using an $\alpha = .3$ and a September forecast of 18.
   v) A trend projection.
c) With the data given, which method would allow you to forecast next March's sales? P✗

7 The actual demand for the patients at Omaha Emergency Medical Clinic for the first six weeks of this year follows:

Week	Actual No. of Patients
1	65
2	62
3	70
4	48
5	63
6	52

Clinic administrator Marc Schniederjans wants you to forecast patient demand at the clinic for week 7 by using this data. You decide to use a weighted moving average method to find this forecast. Your method uses four actual demand levels, with weights of 0.333 on the present period, 0.25 one period ago, 0.25 two periods ago, and 0.167 three periods ago.

What is the value of your forecast? P✗

8 Daily high temperatures in St. Louis for the last week were as follows: 93, 94, 93, 95, 96, 88, 90 (yesterday).
a) Forecast the high temperature today, using a 3-day moving average.
b) Forecast the high temperature today, using a 2-day moving average.
c) Calculate the mean absolute deviation based on a 2-day moving average.
d) Compute the mean squared error for the 2-day moving average.
e) Calculate the mean absolute percent error for the 2-day moving average. P✗

9 Dell uses the CR5 chip in some of its laptop computers. The prices for the chip during the last 12 months were as follows:

Month	Price per Chip	Month	Price per Chip
January	$1.80	July	1.80
February	1.67	August	1.83
March	1.70	September	1.70
April	1.85	October	1.65
May	1.90	November	1.70
June	1.87	December	1.75

a) Use a 2-month moving average on all the data and plot the averages and the prices.
b) Use a 3-month moving average and add the 3-month plot to the graph created in part (a).
c) Which is better (using the mean absolute deviation): the 2-month average or the 3-month average?
d) Compute the forecasts for each month using exponential smoothing, with an initial forecast for January of $1.80. Use $\alpha = .1$, then $\alpha = .3$, and finally $\alpha = .5$. Using MAD, which α is the best? P✗

10 Data collected on the yearly registrations for a Six Sigma seminar at the Quality College are shown in the following table:

Year	1	2	3	4	5	6	7	8	9	10	11
Registrations (000)	4	6	4	5	10	8	7	9	12	14	15

a) Develop a 3-year moving average to forecast registrations from year 4 to year 12.
b) Estimate demand again for years 4 to 12 with a 3-year weighted moving average in which registrations in the most recent year are given a weight of 2, and registrations in the other 2 years are each given a weight of 1.
c) Graph the original data and the two forecasts. Which of the two forecasting methods seems better? P✗

11 a) Use exponential smoothing with a smoothing constant of 0.3 to forecast the registrations at the seminar given in Problem 10. To begin the procedure, assume that the forecast for year 1 was 5,000 people signing up.
b) What is the MAD? P✗

12 Consider the following actual and forecast demand levels for Big Mac hamburgers at a local McDonald's restaurant:

Day	Actual Demand	Forecast Demand
Monday	88	88
Tuesday	72	88
Wednesday	68	84
Thursday	48	80
Friday		

The forecast for Monday was derived by observing Monday's demand level and setting Monday's forecast level equal to this demand level. Subsequent forecasts were derived by using exponential smoothing with a smoothing constant of 0.25. Using this exponential smoothing method, what is the forecast for Big Mac demand for Friday? P✗

13 As you can see in the following table, demand for heart transplant surgery at Washington General Hospital has increased steadily in the past few years:

Year	1	2	3	4	5	6
Heart Transplants	45	50	52	56	58	?

The director of medical services predicted 6 years ago that demand in year 1 would be 41 surgeries.

Jim Olive, Peter Arnold, Inc.

Time Period	Actual Demand	Forecast Demand
t	A_t	F_t
1	50	50
2	42	50
3	56	48
4	46	50
5		

The first forecast, F_1, was derived by observing A_1 and setting F_1 equal to A_1. Subsequent forecasts were derived by exponential smoothing. Using the exponential smoothing method, find the forecast for time period 5. (Hint: You need to first find the smoothing constant, α.)

••• **19** Income at the law firm of Smith and Wesson for the period February to July was as follows:

Month	February	March	April	May	June	July
Income (in $ thousand)	70.0	68.5	64.8	71.7	71.3	72.8

Use trend-adjusted exponential smoothing to forecast the law firm's August income. Assume that the initial forecast for February is $65,000 and the initial trend adjustment is 0. The smoothing constants selected are $\alpha = .1$ and $\beta = .2$. **Px**

••• **20** Resolve Problem 19 with $\alpha = .1$ and $\beta = .8$. Using MSE, determine which smoothing constants provide a better forecast. **Px**

• **21** Refer to the trend-adjusted exponential smoothing illustration in Example 7 on pages 119–121. Using $\alpha = .2$ and $\beta = .4$, we forecast sales for 9 months, showing the detailed calculations for months 2 and 3. In Solved Problem 2, we continued the process for month 4.

In this problem, show your calculations for months 5 and 6 for F_t, T_t, and FIT_t. **Px**

• **22** Refer to Problem 21. Complete the trend-adjusted exponential-smoothing forecast computations for periods 7, 8, and 9. Confirm that your numbers for F_t, T_t, and FIT_t match those in Table 1. **Px**

•• **23** Sales of vegetable dehydrators at Bud Banis's discount department store in St. Louis over the past year are shown below. Management prepared a forecast using a combination of exponential smoothing and its collective judgment for the 4 months (March, April, May, and June of 2007):

Month	2006–2007 Unit Sales	Management's Forecast
July	100	
August	93	
September	96	
October	110	
November	124	
December	119	
January	92	
February	83	
March	101	120
April	96	114
May	89	110
June	108	108

a) Use exponential smoothing, first with a smoothing constant of .6 and then with one of .9, to develop forecasts for years 2 through 6.

b) Use a 3-year moving average to forecast demand in years 4, 5, and 6.

c) Use the trend-projection method to forecast demand in years 1 through 6.

d) With MAD as the criterion, which of the four forecasting methods is best? **Px**

•• **14** Following are two weekly forecasts made by two different methods for the number of gallons of gasoline, in thousands, demanded at a local gasoline station. Also shown are actual demand levels, in thousands of gallons:

	Forecasts		
Week	Method 1	Method 2	Actual Demand
1	0.90	0.80	0.70
2	1.05	1.20	1.00
3	0.95	0.90	1.00
4	1.20	1.11	1.00

What are the MAD and MSE for each method?

• **15** Refer to Solved Problem 1 on page 139. Use a 3-year moving average to forecast the sales of Volkswagen Beetles in Nevada through 2008. What is the MAD? **Px**

• **16** Refer to Solved Problem 1. Using the trend projection method, develop a forecast for the sales of Volkswagen Beetles in Nevada through 2008. What is the MAD? **Px**

• **17** Refer to Solved Problem 1. Using smoothing constants of .6 and .9, develop forecasts for the sales of VW Beetles. What effect did the smoothing constant have on the forecast? Use MAD to determine which of the three smoothing constants (.3, .6, or .9) gives the most accurate forecast. **Px**

•••• **18** Consider the following actual (A_t) and forecast (F_t) demand levels for a product:

a) Compute MAD and MAPE for management's technique.

b) Do management's results outperform (i.e., have smaller MAD and MAPE than) a naive forecast?

c) Which forecast do you recommend, based on lower forecast error?

•• 24   Howard Weiss, owner of a musical instrument distributorship, thinks that demand for bass drums may be related to the number of television appearances by the popular group Stone Temple Pilots during the previous month. Weiss has collected the data shown in the following table:

Demand for Bass Drums	3	6	7	5	10	7
Stone Temple Pilots' TV Appearances	3	4	7	6	8	5

a) Graph these data to see whether a linear equation might describe the relationship between the group's television shows and bass drum sales.

b) Use the least-squares regression method to derive a forecasting equation.

c) What is your estimate for bass drum sales if the Stone Temple Pilots performed on TV nine times last month?

d) What are the correlation coefficient (r) and the coefficient of determination (r^2) for this model, and what do they mean? Px

• 25   The following gives the number of accidents that occurred on Florida State Highway 101 during the last 4 months:

Month	Number of Accidents
January	30
February	40
March	60
April	90

Forecast the number of accidents that will occur in May, using least-squares regression to derive a trend equation. Px

• 26   In the past, Arup Mukherjee's tire dealership in Pensacola sold an average of 1,000 radials each year. In the past 2 years, 200 and 250, respectively, were sold in fall, 350 and 300 in winter, 150 and 165 in spring, and 300 and 285 in summer. With a major expansion planned, Mukherjee projects sales next year to increase to 1,200 radials. What will be the demand during each season?

•• 27   Mark Cotteleer owns a company that manufactures sailboats. Actual demand for Mark's sailboats during each season in 2004 through 2007 was as follows:

	Year			
Season	2004	2005	2006	2007
Winter	1,400	1,200	1,000	900
Spring	1,500	1,400	1,600	1,500
Summer	1,000	2,100	2,000	1,900
Fall	600	750	650	500

Mark has forecasted that annual demand for his sailboats in 2009 will equal 5,600 sailboats. Based on this data and the multiplicative seasonal model, what will the demand level be for Mark's sailboats in the spring of 2009?

•• 28   Attendance at Los Angeles's newest Disneylike attraction, Vacation World, has been as follows:

Quarter	Guests (in thousands)	Quarter	Guests (in thousands)
Winter '05	73	Summer '06	124
Spring '05	104	Fall '06	52
Summer '05	168	Winter '07	89
Fall '05	74	Spring '07	146
Winter '06	65	Summer '07	205
Spring '06	82	Fall '07	98

Compute seasonal indices using all of the data. Px

• 29   Central States Electric Company estimates its demand trend line (in millions of kilowatt hours) to be:

$$D = 77 + 0.43Q$$

where Q refers to the sequential quarter number and $Q = 1$ for winter 1984. In addition, the multiplicative seasonal factors are as follows:

Quarter	Factor (Index)
Winter	.8
Spring	1.1
Summer	1.4
Fall	.7

Forecast energy use for the four quarters of 2009, beginning with winter.

• 30   Brian Buckley has developed the following forecasting model:

$$\hat{y} = 36 + 4.3x$$

where $\hat{y} =$ demand for Aztec air conditioners and
$x =$ the outside temperature (°F)

a) Forecast demand for the Aztec when the temperature is 70°F.

b) What is demand when the temperature is 80°F?

c) What is demand when the temperature is 90°F? Px

•• 31   Coffee Palace's manager, Joe Felan, suspects that demand for mocha latte coffees depends on the price being charged. Based on historical observations, Joe has gathered the following data, which show the numbers of these coffees sold over six different price values:

Price	Number Sold
$2.70	760
$3.50	510
$2.00	980
$4.20	250
$3.10	320
$4.05	480

Using these data, how many mocha latte coffees would be forecast to be sold according to simple linear regression if the price per cup were $1.80? Px

• 32   The following data relate the sales figures of the bar in Marty and Polly Starr's small bed-and-breakfast inn in Marathon, Florida, to the number of guests registered that week:

Week	Guests	Bar Sales
1	16	$330
2	12	270
3	18	380
4	14	300

a) Perform a linear regression that relates bar sales to guests (not to time).
b) If the forecast is for 20 guests next week, what are the sales expected to be? **P**×

• 33   The number of transistors (in millions) made at a plant in Japan during the past 5 years follows:

Year	Transistors
1	140
2	160
3	190
4	200
5	210

a) Forecast the number of transistors to be made next year, using linear regression.
b) Compute the mean squared error (MSE) when using linear regression.
c) Compute the mean absolute percent error (MAPE). **P**×

• 34   The number of auto accidents in a certain region is related to the regional number of registered automobiles in thousands (X_1), alcoholic beverage sales in $10,000s ($X_2$), and rainfall in inches (X_3). Furthermore, the regression formula has been calculated as:

$$Y = a + b_1X_1 + b_2X_2 + b_3X_3$$

where Y = number of automobile accidents
         $a = 7.5$
         $b_1 = 3.5$
         $b_2 = 4.5$
         $b_3 = 2.5$

Calculate the expected number of automobile accidents under conditions a, b, and c:

	X_1	X_2	X_3
(a)	2	3	0
(b)	3	5	1
(c)	4	7	2	**P**×

•• 35   John Howard, a Mobile, Alabama, real estate developer, has devised a regression model to help determine residential housing prices in South Alabama. The model was developed using recent sales in a particular neighborhood. The price (Y) of the house is based on the size (square footage = X) of the house. The model is:

$$Y = 13,473 + 37.65X$$

The coefficient of correlation for the model is 0.63.
a) Use the model to predict the selling price of a house that is 1,860 square feet.

b) An 1,860-square-foot house recently sold for $95,000. Explain why this is not what the model predicted.
c) If you were going to use multiple regression to develop such a model, what other quantitative variables might you include?
d) What is the value of the coefficient of determination in this problem? **P**×

• 36   Accountants at the firm Michael Vest, CPAs, believed that several traveling executives were submitting unusually high travel vouchers when they returned from business trips. First, they took a sample of 200 vouchers submitted from the past year. Then they developed the following multiple-regression equation relating expected travel cost to number of days on the road (x_1) and distance traveled (x_2) in miles:

$$\hat{y} = \$90.00 + \$48.50x_1 + \$.40x_2$$

The coefficient of correlation computed was .68.
a) If Wanda Fennell returns from a 300-mile trip that took her out of town for 5 days, what is the expected amount she should claim as expenses?
b) Fennell submitted a reimbursement request for $685. What should the accountant do?
c) Should any other variables be included? Which ones? Why? **P**

•• 37   Sales of music stands at Johnny Ho's music store in Columbus, Ohio, over the past 10 weeks are shown in the table below. Forecast demand for each week, including week 10, using exponential smoothing with $\alpha = .5$ (initial forecast = 20):

Week	Demand	Week	Demand
1	20	6	29
2	21	7	36
3	28	8	22
4	37	9	25
5	25	10	28

a) Compute the MAD.
b) Compute the tracking signal. **P**×

•• 38   City government has collected the following data on annual sales tax collections and new car registrations:

Annual Sales Tax Collections (in millions)	1.0	1.4	1.9	2.0	1.8	2.1	2.3
New Car Registrations (in thousands)	10	12	15	16	14	17	20

Determine the following:
a) The least-squares regression equation.
b) Using the results of part (a), find the estimated sales tax collections if new car registrations total 22,000.
c) The coefficients of correlation and determination. **P**×

•• 39   Dr. Susan Sweeney, a Providence psychologist, specializes in treating patients who are agoraphobic (i.e., afraid to leave their homes). The following table indicates how many patients Dr. Sweeney has seen each year for the past 10 years. It also indicates what the robbery rate was in Providence during the same year:

Year	1	2	3	4	5	6	7	8	9	10
Number of Patients	36	33	40	41	40	55	60	54	58	61
Robbery Rate per 1,000 Population	58.3	61.1	73.4	75.7	81.1	89.0	101.1	94.8	103.3	116.2

Using trend analysis, predict the number of patients Dr. Sweeney will see in years 11 and 12. How well does the model fit the data? **P**×

•• **40** Using the data in Problem 39, apply linear regression to study the relationship between the robbery rate and Dr. Sweeney's patient load. If the robbery rate increases to 131.2 in year 11, how many phobic patients will Dr. Sweeney treat? If the robbery rate drops to 90.6, what is the patient projection? **P**×

••• **41** Bus and subway ridership for the summer months in London, England, is believed to be tied heavily to the number of tourists visiting the city. During the past 12 years, the following data have been obtained:

Year (summer months)	Number of Tourists (in millions)	Ridership (in millions)
1	7	1.5
2	2	1.0
3	6	1.3
4	4	1.5
5	14	2.5
6	15	2.7
7	16	2.4
8	12	2.0
9	14	2.7
10	20	4.4
11	15	3.4
12	7	1.7

a) Plot these data and decide if a linear model is reasonable.
b) Develop a regression relationship.
c) What is expected ridership if 10 million tourists visit London in a year?
d) Explain the predicted ridership if there are no tourists at all.
e) What is the standard error of the estimate?
f) What is the model's correlation coefficient and coefficient of determination? **P**×

Alan Copson, Photolibrary.com.

••• **42** Des Moines Power and Light has been collecting data on demand for electric power in its western subregion for only the past 2 years. Those data are shown in the following table:

Demand in Megawatts		
Month	Last Year	This Year
January	5	17
February	6	14
March	10	20
April	13	23
May	18	30
June	15	38
July	23	44
August	26	41
September	21	33
October	15	23
November	12	26
December	14	17

To plan for expansion and to arrange to borrow power from neighboring utilities during peak periods, the utility needs to be able to forecast demand for each month next year. However, the standard forecasting models discussed in this chapter will not fit the data observed for the 2 years.

a) What are the weaknesses of the standard forecasting techniques as applied to this set of data?
b) Because known models are not appropriate here, propose your own approach to forecasting. Although there is no perfect solution to tackling data such as these (in other words, there are no 100% right or wrong answers), justify your model.
c) Forecast demand for each month next year using the model you propose.

••• **43** Emergency calls to the 911 system of Gainesville, Florida, for the past 24 weeks are shown in the following table:

Week	1	2	3	4	5	6	7	8	9	10	11	12
Calls	50	35	25	40	45	35	20	30	35	20	15	40

Week	13	14	15	16	17	18	19	20	21	22	23	24
Calls	55	35	25	55	55	40	35	60	75	50	40	65

a) Compute the exponentially smoothed forecast of calls for each week. Assume an initial forecast of 50 calls in the first week, and use $\alpha = .2$. What is the forecast for week 25?
b) Reforecast each period using $\alpha = .6$.
c) Actual calls during week 25 were 85. Which smoothing constant provides a superior forecast? Explain and justify the measure of error you used. **P**×

••• **44** Using the 911 call data in Problem 43, forecast calls for weeks 2 through 25 with a trend-adjusted exponential smoothing model. Assume an initial forecast for 50 calls for week 1 and an initial trend of zero. Use smoothing constants of $\alpha = .3$ and $\beta = .2$. Is this model better than that of Problem 43? What adjustment might be useful for further improvement? (Again, assume that actual calls in week 25 were 85.) **P**×

••• **45** The following are monthly actual and forecast demand levels for May through December for units of a product manufactured by the N. Tamimi Pharmaceutical Company:

Month	Actual Demand	Forecast Demand
May	100	100
June	80	104
July	110	99
August	115	101
September	105	104
October	110	104
November	125	105
December	120	109

What is the value of the tracking signal as of the end of December?

•• 46 Thirteen students entered the business program at Hillcrest College 2 years ago. The following table indicates what each student scored on the high school SAT math exam and their grade-point averages (GPAs) after students were in the Hillcrest program for 2 years.

a) Is there a meaningful relationship between SAT math scores and grades?
b) If a student scores a 350, what do you think his or her GPA will be?
c) What about a student who scores 800?

Student	A	B	C	D	E	F	G
SAT Score	421	377	585	690	608	390	415
GPA	2.90	2.93	3.00	3.45	3.66	2.88	2.15
Student	H	I	J	K	L	M	
SAT Score	481	729	501	613	709	366	
GPA	2.53	3.22	1.99	2.75	3.90	1.60	

Px

••• 47 City Cycles has just started selling the new Z-10 mountain bike, with monthly sales as shown in the table. First, co-owner Amit wants to forecast by exponential smoothing by initially setting February's forecast equal to January's sales with $\alpha = .1$. Co-owner, Barbara wants to use a three-period moving average.

	Sales	Amit	Barbara	Amit's Error	Barbara's Error
January	400	—			
February	380	400			
March	410				
April	375				
May					

a) Is there a strong linear trend in sales over time?
b) Fill in the table with what Amit and Barbara each forecast for May and the earlier months, as relevant.
c) Assume that May's actual sales figure turns out to be 405. Complete the table's columns and then calculate the mean absolute deviation for both Amit's and Barbara's methods.
d) Based on these calculations, which method seems more accurate? Px

•• 48 Sundar Balakrishnan, the general manager of Precision Engineering Corporation (PEC), thinks that his firm's engineering services contracted to highway construction firms are directly related to the volume of highway construction business contracted with companies in his geographic area. He wonders if this is really so, and if it is, can this information help him plan his operations better by forecasting the quantity of his engineering services

required by construction firms in each quarter of the year? The following table presents the sales of his services and total amounts of contracts for highway construction over the last 8 quarters:

Quarter	1	2	3	4	5	6	7	8
Sales of PEC Services (in $ thousands)	8	10	15	9	12	13	12	16
Contracts Released (in $ thousands)	153	172	197	178	185	199	205	226

a) Using this data, develop a regression equation for predicting the level of demand of Precision's services.
b) Determine the coefficient of correlation and the standard error of the estimate. Px

••••49 Salinas Savings and Loan is proud of its long tradition in Topeka, Kansas. Begun by Teresita Salinas 18 years after World War II, the S&L has bucked the trend of financial and liquidity problems that has plagued the industry since 1985. Deposits have increased slowly but surely over the years, despite recessions in 1983, 1988, 1991, and 2001. Ms. Salinas believes it is necessary to have a long-range strategic plan for her firm, including a 1-year forecast and preferably even a 5-year forecast of deposits. She examines the past deposit data and also peruses Kansas's gross state product (GSP), over the same 44 years. (GSP is analogous to gross national product [GNP] but on the state level.) The resulting data are in the following table:

Year	Deposits[a]	GSP[b]	Year	Deposits[a]	GSP[b]
1964	.25	.4	1986	6.2	2.5
1965	.24	.4	1987	4.1	2.8
1966	.24	.5	1988	4.5	2.9
1967	.26	.7	1989	6.1	3.4
1968	.25	.9	1990	7.7	3.8
1969	.30	1.0	1991	10.1	4.1
1970	.31	1.4	1992	15.2	4.0
1971	.32	1.7	1993	18.1	4.0
1972	.24	1.3	1994	24.1	3.9
1973	.26	1.2	1995	25.6	3.8
1974	.25	1.1	1996	30.3	3.8
1975	.33	.9	1997	36.0	3.7
1976	.50	1.2	1998	31.1	4.1
1977	.95	1.2	1999	31.7	4.1
1978	1.70	1.2	2000	38.5	4.0
1979	2.3	1.6	2001	47.9	4.5
1980	2.8	1.5	2002	49.1	4.6
1981	2.8	1.6	2003	55.8	4.5
1982	2.7	1.7	2004	70.1	4.6
1983	3.9	1.9	2005	70.9	4.6
1984	4.9	1.9	2006	79.1	4.7
1985	5.3	2.3	2007	94.0	5.0

[a]In $ millions.
[b]In $ billions.

a) Using exponential smoothing, with $\alpha = .6$, then trend analysis, and finally linear regression, discuss which forecasting model fits best for Salinas's strategic plan. Justify the selection of one model over another.
b) Carefully examine the data. Can you make a case for excluding a portion of the information? Why? Would that change your choice of model? Px

Case Studies

Southwestern University: (B)*

Southwestern University (SWU), a large state college in Stephenville, Texas, enrolls close to 20,000 students. The school is a dominant force in the small city, with more students during fall and spring than permanent residents.

Always a football powerhouse, SWU is usually in the top 20 in college football rankings. Since the legendary Bo Pitterno was hired as its head coach in 2001 (in hopes of reaching the elusive number 1 ranking), attendance at the five Saturday home games each year increased. Prior to Pitterno's arrival, attendance generally averaged 25,000 to 29,000 per game. Season ticket sales bumped up by 10,000 just with the announcement of the new coach's arrival. Stephenville and SWU were ready to move to the big time!

The immediate issue facing SWU, however, was not NCAA ranking. It was capacity. The existing SWU stadium, built in 1953, has seating for 54,000 fans. The following table indicates attendance at each game for the past 6 years.

One of Pitterno's demands upon joining SWU had been a stadium expansion, or possibly even a new stadium. With attendance increasing, SWU administrators began to face the issue head-on. Pitterno had wanted dormitories solely for his athletes in the stadium as an additional feature of any expansion.

SWU's president, Dr. Joel Wisner, decided it was time for his vice president of development to forecast when the existing stadium would "max out." The expansion was, in his mind, a given. But Wisner needed to know how long he could wait. He also sought a revenue projection, assuming an average ticket price of $20 in 2008 and a 5% increase each year in future prices.

Discussion Questions

1. Develop a forecasting model, justifying its selection over other techniques, and project attendance through 2009.
2. What revenues are to be expected in 2008 and 2009?
3. Discuss the school's options.

*This integrated case study runs throughout the text. Other issues facing Southwestern's football stadium include (A) managing the stadium project; (C) quality of facilities; (D) break-even analysis of food services (Supplement 7 web site); (E) locating the new stadium; (F) inventory planning of football programs; and (G) scheduling of campus security officers/staff for game days.

Southwestern University Football Game Attendance, 2002–2007

Game	2002 Attendees	Opponent	2003 Attendees	Opponent	2004 Attendees	Opponent
1	34,200	Baylor	36,100	Oklahoma	35,900	TCU
2[a]	39,800	Texas	40,200	Nebraska	46,500	Texas Tech
3	38,200	LSU	39,100	UCLA	43,100	Alaska
4[b]	26,900	Arkansas	25,300	Nevada	27,900	Arizona
5	35,100	USC	36,200	Ohio State	39,200	Rice

Game	2005 Attendees	Opponent	2006 Attendees	Opponent	2007 Attendees	Opponent
1	41,900	Arkansas	42,500	Indiana	46,900	LSU
2[a]	46,100	Missouri	48,200	North Texas	50,100	Texas
3	43,900	Florida	44,200	Texas A&M	45,900	Prairie View A&M
4[b]	30,100	Miami	33,900	Southern	36,300	Montana
5	40,500	Duke	47,800	Oklahoma	49,900	Arizona State

[a]Homecoming games.

[b]During the 4th week of each season, Stephenville hosted a hugely popular southwestern crafts festival. This event brought tens of thousands of tourists to the town, especially on weekends, and had an obvious negative impact on game attendance.

Digital Cell Phone, Inc.

Paul Jordan has just been hired as a management analyst at Digital Cell Phone, Inc. Digital Cell manufactures a broad line of phones for the consumer market. Paul's boss, John Smithers, chief operations officer, has asked Paul to stop by his office this morning. After a brief exchange of pleasantries over a cup of coffee, he says he has a special assignment for Paul: "We've always just made an educated guess about how many phones we need to make each month. Usually we just look at how many we sold last month and plan to produce about the same number. This sometimes works fine. But most months we either have too many phones in inventory or we are out of stock. Neither situation is good."

Handing Paul the table shown here, Smithers continues, "Here are our actual orders entered for the past 36 months. There are 144 phones per case. I was hoping that since you graduated recently from the University of Alaska, you might have studied some techniques that would help us plan better. It's been awhile since I was in college—I think I forgot most of the details I learned then. I'd like you to analyze these data and give me an idea of what our business will look like over the next 6 to 12 months. Do you think you can handle this?"

"Of course," Paul replies, sounding more confident than he really is. "How much time do I have?"

"I need your report on the Monday before Thanksgiving—that would be November 20th. I plan to take it home with me and read it during the holiday. Since I'm sure you will not be around during the holiday, be sure that you explain things carefully so that I can understand your recommendation without having to ask you any more questions. Since you are new to the company, you should know that I like to see all the details and complete justification for recommendations from my staff."

With that, Paul was dismissed. Arriving back at his office, he began his analysis.

Orders Received by Month

Month	Cases 2005	Cases 2006	Cases 2007
January	480	575	608
February	436	527	597
March	482	540	612
April	448	502	603
May	458	508	628
June	489	573	605
July	498	508	627
August	430	498	578
September	444	485	585
October	496	526	581
November	487	552	632
December	525	587	656

Discussion Question

1. Prepare Paul Jordan's report to John Smithers using regression analysis. Provide a summary of the cell phone industry outlook as part of Paul's response.
2. Adding seasonality into your model, how does the analysis change?

Source: Professor Victor E. Sower, Sam Houston State University.

Forecasting at Hard Rock Cafe

Video Case

With the growth of Hard Rock Cafe—from one pub in London in 1971 to more than 110 restaurants in more than 40 countries today—came a corporatewide demand for better forecasting. Hard Rock uses long-range forecasting in setting a capacity plan and intermediate-term forecasting for locking in contracts for leather goods (used in jackets) and for such food items as beef, chicken, and pork. Its short-term sales forecasts are conducted each month, by cafe, and then aggregated for a headquarters view.

The heart of the sales forecasting system is the point-of-sale system (POS), which, in effect, captures transaction data on nearly every person who walks through a cafe's door. The sale of each entrée represents one customer; the entrée sales data are transmitted daily to the Orlando corporate headquarters' database. There, the financial team, headed by Todd Lindsey, begins the forecast process. Lindsey forecasts monthly guest counts, retail sales, banquet sales, and concert sales (if applicable) at each cafe. The general managers of individual cafes tap into the same database to prepare a daily forecast for their sites. A cafe manager pulls up prior years' sales for that day, adding information from the local Chamber of Commerce or Tourist Board on upcoming events such as a major convention, sporting event, or concert in the city where the cafe is located. The daily forecast is further broken into hourly sales, which drives employee scheduling. An hourly forecast of $5,500 in sales translates into 19 workstations, which are further broken down into a specific number of wait staff, hosts, bartenders, and kitchen staff. Computerized scheduling software plugs in people based on their availability. Variances between forecast and actual sales are then examined to see why errors occurred.

Hard Rock doesn't limit its use of forecasting tools to sales. To evaluate managers and set bonuses, a 3-year weighted moving average is applied to cafe sales. If cafe general managers exceed their

targets, a bonus is computed. Todd Lindsey, at corporate headquarters, applies weights of 40% to the most recent year's sales, 40% to the year before, and 20% to sales 2 years ago in reaching his moving average.

An even more sophisticated application of statistics is found in Hard Rock's menu planning. Using multiple regression, managers can compute the impact on demand of other menu items if the price of one item is changed. For example, if the price of a cheeseburger increases from $7.99 to $8.99, Hard Rock can predict the effect this will have on sales of chicken sandwiches, pork sandwiches, and salads. Managers do the same analysis on menu placement, with the center section driving higher sales volumes. When an item such as a hamburger is moved off the center to one of the side flaps, the corresponding effect on related items, say french fries, is determined.

Hard Rock's Moscow Cafe[a]

Month	1	2	3	4	5	6	7	8	9	10
Guest count (in thousands)	21	24	27	32	29	37	43	43	54	66
Advertising (in $ thousand)	14	17	25	25	35	35	45	50	60	60

[a]These figures are used for purposes of this case study.

Discussion Questions*

1. Describe three different forecasting applications at Hard Rock. Name three other areas in which you think Hard Rock could use forecasting models.
2. What is the role of the POS system in forecasting at Hard Rock?

3. Justify the use of the weighting system used for evaluating managers for annual bonuses.
4. Name several variables besides those mentioned in the case that could be used as good predictors of daily sales in each cafe.
5. At Hard Rock's Moscow restaurant, the manager is trying to evaluate how a new advertising campaign affects guest counts.

Using data for the past 10 months (see the table) develop a least squares regression relationship and then forecast the expected guest count when advertising is $65,000.

*You may wish to review this video case on your DVD before answering these questions.

Additional Case Studies

Internet Case Study: Visit our Companion Web site at www.prenhall.com/heizer for this free case study:

- **North–South Airline:** Reflects the merger of two airlines and addresses their maintenance costs.

Harvard has selected these Harvard Business School case studies to accompany this chapter:

harvardbusinessonline.hbsp.harvard.edu

- **Merchandising at Nine West Retail Stores** (# 698-098): This large retail shoe store chain faces a merchandising decision.
- **New Technologies, New Markets: The Launch of Hong Kong Telecom's Video-on-Demand** (# HKU-011): Asks students to examine the forecasting behind a new technology.
- **Sport Obermeyer Ltd.** (# 695-022): This skiwear company has short-life-cycle products with uncertain demand and a globally dispersed supply chain.
- **L.L. Bean, Inc.** (# 893-003): L.L. Bean must forecast and manage thousands of inventory items sold through its catalogs.

Bibliography

Balakrishnan, R., B. Render, and R. M. Stair. *Managerial Decision Modeling with Spreadsheets*, 2nd ed. Upper Saddle River, NJ: Prentice Hall, 2007.

Berenson, Mark, Tim Krehbiel, and David Levine. *Basic Business Statistics*, 10th ed. Upper Saddle River, NJ: Prentice Hall, 2006.

Diebold, F. X. *Elements of Forecasting*, 4th ed. Cincinnati: Southwestern College Publishing, 2007.

Georgoff, D. M., and R. G. Murdick. "Manager's Guide to Forecasting." *Harvard Business Review* 64 (January–February 1986): 110–120.

Gilliland, M. "Is Forecasting a Waste of Time?" *Supply Chain Management Review* 1 (July 2002).

Gilliland, M., and M. Leonard. "Forecasting Software—The Past and the Future." *The Journal of Business Forecasting* 25, no. 1 (Spring 2006): 33–36.

Hanke, J. E., A. G. Reitsch, and D. W. Wichern. *Business Forecasting*, 9th ed. Upper Saddle River, NJ: Prentice Hall, 2007.

Heizer, Jay. "Forecasting with Stagger Charts." *IIE Solutions* 34 (June 2002): 46–49.

Jain, C. L. "Benchmarking Forecasting Models." *The Journal of Business Forecasting* 24, no. 4 (Winter 2005/2006): 9–11.

Lapide, Larry. "Evolution of the Forecasting Function." *The Journal of Business Forecasting* 25, no. 1 (Spring 2006): 22–24.

Meade, Nigel. "Evidence for the Selection of Forecasting Models." *Journal of Forecasting* 19, no. 6 (November 2000): 515–535.

Portougal, V. "Demand Forecast for a Catalog Retailing Company." *Production and Inventory Management Journal* (first–second quarter 2002): 29–34.

Render, B., R. M. Stair, and M. Hanna. *Quantitative Analysis for Management*, 9th ed. Upper Saddle River, NJ: Prentice Hall, 2006.

Sanders, N. R., and K. B. Manrodt. "Forecasting Software in Practice." *Interfaces* 33 (September–October 2003): 90–93.

Snyder, Ralph D., and Roland G. Shami. "Exponential Smoothing of Seasonal Data." *Journal of Forecasting* 20, no. 3 (April 2001): 197–202.

Wilson, J. H., B. Keating, and J. Galt. *Business Forecasting with Forecast X Software*. New York: McGraw-Hill, 2007.

Internet Resources

American Statistical Association: **www.amstat.org**
Institute of Business Forecasting: **www.ibf.org**
International Institute of Forecasters: **www.forecasters.org**

Journal of Time Series Analysis: **www.blackwellpublishers.co.uk**
Royal Statistical Society: **www.rss.org.uk**

Solutions to Even Numbered Problems

2 **(a)** None obvious.
(b) 7, 7.67, 9, 10, 11, 11, 11.33, 11, 9
(c) 6.4, 7.8, 11, 9.6, 10.9, 12.2, 10.5, 10.6, 8.4
(d) The 3-yr. moving average.

4 **(a)** 41.6
(b) 42.3
(c) Banking industry's seasonality.

6 **(b)** Naive = 23; 3-mo. moving = 21.33; 6-mo. weighted = 20.6; trend = 20.67
(c) Trend projection.

8 **(a)** 91.3
(b) 89
(c) MAD = 2.7
(d) MSE = 13.35
(e) MAPE = 2.99%

10 **(a)** 4.67, 5.00, 6.33, 7.67, 8.33, 8.00, 9.33, 11.67, 13.7
(b) 4.50, 5.00, 7.25, 7.75, 8.00, 8.25, 10.00, 12.25, 14.0
(c) Forecasts are about the same.

12 72

14 Method 1: MAD = .5; MSE = .085
Method 2: MAD = .51; MSE = .0721

16 $y = 421 + 33.6x$. When $x = 6$, $y = 622.8$.

18 49

20 $\alpha = .1$, $\beta = .8$, August forecast = $71,303; MSE = 12.7 for $\beta = .8$ vs. MSE = 18.87 for $\beta = .2$ in Problem 4.19.

22 Confirm that you match the numbers in Table 1.

24 **(a)** Observations do not form a straight line but do cluster about one.
(b) $y = .676 + 1.03x$
(c) 10 drums
(d) $r^2 = .68$; $r = .825$

26 270, 390, 189, 351 for fall, winter, spring, and summer, respectively.

28 Index is 0.709, winter; 1.037, spring; 1.553, summer; 0.700, fall.

30 **(a)** 337
(b) 380
(c) 423

32 **(a)** $y = 50 + 18x$
(b) $410

34 **(a)** 28
(b) 43
(c) 58

36 **(a)** $452.50
(b) Request is higher than predicted, so seek additional documentation.
(c) Include other variables (such as a destination cost index) to try to increase r and r^2.

38 **(a)** $y = -.158 + .1308x$
(b) 2.719
(c) $r = .966$; $r^2 = .934$

40 $131.2 \rightarrow 72.7$ patients; $90.6 \rightarrow 50.6$ patients

42 **(a)** They need more data and must be able to address seasonal *and* trend factors.
(b) Try to create your own naive model because seasonality is strong.
(c) Compute and graph your forecast.

44 Trend adjustment does not appear to give any significant improvement.

46 **(a)** $y = 1.03 + .0034x$, $r^2 = .479$
(b) For $x = 350$; $Y = 2.22$
(c) For $x = 800$; $Y = 3.75$
(Some rounding may occur, depending on software.)

48 **(a)** Sales (y) = $-9.349 + .1121$ (contracts)
(b) $r = .8963$; $S_{xy} = 1.3408$

Solutions to Self Test

1. d; **2.** d; **3.** b; **4.** d; **5.** a; **6.** a; **7.** simple regression has only one independent variable; **8.** exponential smoothing is a weighted moving average model in which all prior values are weighted with a set of exponentially declining weight; **9.** spot relationships between two variables.

Chapter 6

Managing Quality

Managing Quality

Outline

Ten OM Strategy Decisions

Design of Goods and Services

Managing Quality

Process Strategy

Location Strategies

Layout Strategies

Human Resources

Supply Chain Management

Inventory Management

Scheduling

Maintenance

Learning Objectives

When you complete this selection you should be able to

1. Define quality and TQM
2. Describe the ISO international quality standards
3. Explain Six Sigma
4. Explain how benchmarking is used
5. Explain quality robust products and Taguchi concepts
6. Use the seven tools of TQM

From *Operations Management*, 9/e. Jay Heizer. Barry Render. Copyright © 2008 by Pearson Education. All rights reserved.

Managing Quality Provides a Competitive Advantage at Arnold Palmer Hospital

Since 1989, the Arnold Palmer Hospital, named after its famous golfing benefactor, has touched the lives of over 7 million children and women and their families. Its patients come not only from its Orlando location but from all 50 states and around the world. More than 13,000 babies are delivered every year at Arnold Palmer, and its huge neonatal intensive care unit boasts one of the highest survival rates in the U.S.

Every hospital professes quality health care, but at Arnold Palmer quality is the mantra—practiced in a fashion like the Ritz-Carlton practices it in the hotel industry. The hospital typically scores in the top 10% of national benchmark studies in terms of patient satisfaction. And its managers follow patient questionnaire results daily. If anything is amiss, corrective action takes place immediately.

Virtually every quality management technique we present in this chapter is employed at Arnold Palmer Hospital:

- *Continuous improvement:* The hospital constantly seeks new ways to lower infection rates, readmission rates, deaths, costs, and hospital stay times.
- *Employee empowerment:* When employees see a problem, they are trained to take care of it. Just like at the Ritz, staff are empowered to give gifts to patients displeased with some aspect of service.
- *Benchmarking:* The hospital belongs to a 2,000-member organization that monitors standards in many areas and provides monthly feedback to the hospital.
- *Just-in-time:* Supplies are delivered to Arnold Palmer on a JIT basis. This keeps inventory costs low and keeps quality problems from hiding.

▼ *The lobby of Arnold Palmer Hospital, with its 20-foot-high Genie, is clearly intended as a warm and friendly place for children.*

▼ *The Storkboard is a visible chart of the status of each baby about to be delivered, so all nurses and doctors are kept up-to-date at a glance.*

Jonathan Bailey Associates

This PYXIS inventory station gives nurses quick access to medicines and supplies needed in their departments. When the nurse removes an item for patient use, the item is automatically billed to that account, and usage is noted at the main supply area.

Cardinal Health Supply Technologies

The Mark Twain quote on the board reads "Always Do Right. This will gratify some people and astonish most." The hospital has redesigned its neonatal rooms. In the old system, there were 16 neonatal beds in an often noisy and large room. The new rooms are semiprivate, with a quiet simulated-night atmosphere. These rooms have proven to help babies develop and improve more quickly.

Jonathan Bailey Associates

When Arnold Palmer Hospital began planning for a new 11-story hospital across the street from its existing building, it decided on a circular pod design, creating a patient-centered environment. Rooms use warm colors, have pull-down Murphy beds for family members, 14-foot ceilings, and natural lighting with oversized windows. The pod concept also means there is a nursing station within a few feet of each 10-bed pod, saving much wasted walking time by nurses to reach the patient. The Video Case Study in next Chapter examines this layout in detail.

Jonathan Bailey Associates

- *Tools such as Pareto charts and flowcharts:* These tools monitor processes and help the staff graphically spot problem areas and suggest ways they can be improved.

From their first day of orientation, employees from janitors to nurses learn that the patient comes first. Staff standing in hallways will never be heard discussing their personal lives or commenting on confidential issues of health care. This culture of quality at Arnold Palmer Hospital makes a hospital visit, often traumatic to children and their parents, a warmer and more comforting experience.

QUALITY AND STRATEGY

Video 6.1

The Culture of Quality at Arnold Palmer Hospital

As Arnold Palmer Hospital and many other organizations have found, quality is a wonderful tonic for improving operations. Managing quality helps build successful strategies of *differentiation*, *low cost*, and *response*. For instance, defining customer quality expectations has helped Bose Corp. successfully *differentiate* its stereo speakers as among the best in the world. Nucor has learned to produce quality steel at *low cost* by developing efficient processes that produce consistent quality. And Dell Computers rapidly *responds* to customer orders because quality systems, with little rework, have allowed it to achieve rapid throughput in its plants. Indeed, quality may be the critical success factor for these firms just as it is at Arnold Palmer Hospital.

As Figure 1 suggests, improvements in quality help firms increase sales and reduce costs, both of which can increase profitability. Increases in sales often occur as firms speed response, lower selling prices as a result of economies of scale, and improve their reputation for quality products. Similarly, improved quality allows costs to drop as firms increase productivity and lower rework, scrap, and warranty costs. One study found that companies with the highest quality were five times as productive (as measured by units produced per labor-hour) as companies with the poorest quality. Indeed, when the implications of an organization's long-term costs and the potential for increased sales are considered, total costs may well be at a minimum when 100% of the goods or services are perfect and defect free.

Quality, or the lack of quality, affects the entire organization from supplier to customer and from product design to maintenance. Perhaps more importantly, *building* an organization that can achieve quality also affects the entire organization—and it is a demanding task. Figure 2 lays out the flow of activities for an organization to use to achieve total quality management (TQM). A successful quality strategy begins with an organizational environment that fosters quality, followed by an understanding of the principles of quality, and then an effort to engage employees in the necessary activities to implement quality. When these things are done well, the organization typically satisfies its customers and obtains a competitive advantage. The ultimate goal is to win customers. Because quality causes so many other good things to happen, it is a great place to start.

DEFINING QUALITY

Quality

The ability of a product or service to meet customer needs.

The operations manager's objective is to build a total quality management system that identifies and satisfies customer needs. Total quality management takes care of the customer. Consequently, we accept the definition of **quality** as adopted by the American Society for Quality: "The totality of features and characteristics of a product or service that bears on its ability to satisfy stated or implied needs."[1]

Others, however, believe that definitions of quality fall into several categories. Some definitions are *user based*. They propose that quality "lies in the eyes of the beholder." Marketing people like this approach and so do customers. To them, higher quality means better performance, nicer features, and other (sometimes costly) improvements. To production managers, quality is *manufacturing based*. They believe that quality means conforming to standards and "making it right the first time." Yet a third approach is *product based*, which views quality as a precise and measurable variable. In this view, for example, really good ice cream has high butterfat levels.

Learning Objective

1. Define quality and TQM

▶ **Figure 1**

Ways Quality Improves Profitability

[1]See the American Society for Quality Web site, at **www.asq.org**.

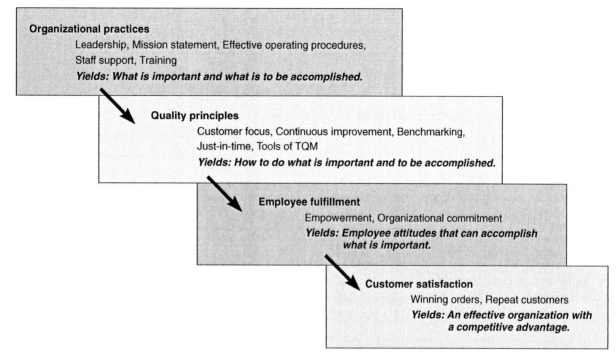

Organizational practices
Leadership, Mission statement, Effective operating procedures, Staff support, Training
Yields: What is important and what is to be accomplished.

Quality principles
Customer focus, Continuous improvement, Benchmarking, Just-in-time, Tools of TQM
Yields: How to do what is important and to be accomplished.

Employee fulfillment
Empowerment, Organizational commitment
Yields: Employee attitudes that can accomplish what is important.

Customer satisfaction
Winning orders, Repeat customers
Yields: An effective organization with a competitive advantage.

▲ **Figure 2** The Flow of Activities that Are Necessary to Achieve Total Quality Management

This text develops approaches and techniques to address all three categories of quality. The characteristics that connote quality must first be identified through research (a user-based approach to quality). These characteristics are then translated into specific product attributes (a product-based approach to quality). Then, the manufacturing process is organized to ensure that products are made precisely to specifications (a manufacturing-based approach to quality). A process that ignores any one of these steps will not result in a quality product.

Quality may be in the eyes of the beholder, but to create a good or a service, operations managers must define what the beholder (the consumer) expects.

Implications of Quality

In addition to being a critical element in operations, quality has other implications. Here are three other reasons why quality is important:

1. *Company reputation:* An organization can expect its reputation for quality—be it good or bad—to follow it. Quality will show up in perceptions about the firm's new products, employment practices, and supplier relations. Self-promotion is not a substitute for quality products.

2. *Product liability:* The courts increasingly hold organizations that design, produce, or distribute faulty products or services liable for damages or injuries resulting from their use. Legislation such as the Consumer Product Safety Act sets and enforces product standards by banning products that do not reach those standards. Impure foods that cause illness, nightgowns that burn, tires that fall apart, or auto fuel tanks that explode on impact can all lead to huge legal expenses, large settlements or losses, and terrible publicity.

3. *Global implications:* In this technological age, quality is an international, as well as OM, concern. For both a company and a country to compete effectively in the global economy, products must meet global quality, design, and price expectations. Inferior products harm a firm's profitability and a nation's balance of payments.

Malcolm Baldrige National Quality Award

The global implications of quality are so important that the U.S. has established the *Malcolm Baldrige National Quality Award* for quality achievement. The award is named for former Secretary of Commerce Malcolm Baldrige. Winners include such firms as Motorola, Milliken, Xerox, FedEx, Ritz-Carlton Hotels, AT&T, Cadillac, and Texas Instruments.

The Japanese have a similar award, the Deming Prize, named after an American, Dr. W. Edwards Deming.

For further information regarding the Baldrige Award and its 1,000-point scoring system, visit **www.quality.nist.gov.**

OM in Action   The Very High Cost of Quality at Mercedes

Perhaps it was Mercedes's merger with Chrysler that first diverted management's attention from quality. Or perhaps it was the $4.7 billion operating loss at Chrysler in 2001. But Mercedes made the difficult decision—squeeze costs to pump out better corporate profits and demand lower prices from suppliers. The result: suppliers cut corners on quality. By 2003, Mercedes had fallen to the bottom of the J.D. Power reliability survey.

Mercedes is still reeling from a series of recalls from its $50,000 E-Class sedan. In 2004, the company suffered a spate of problems with brake control systems; 680,000 cars were recalled. Then in 2005, Mercedes announced the biggest recall in its history—1.3 million cars with faulty fuel pumps made by supplier Robert Bosch. Software problems and interfaces that failed to let complex electronics systems talk to each other were to blame for many

Koichi Kamoshida/Liaison, Getty Images
Mercedes E-Class on fire in Tokyo.

other defects. All totaled, Mercedes spent $600 million in one year to cover warranty costs.

The cost of the quality fiasco takes a toll in sales, of course, as well. Market shares in the U.S. and Europe are down. And rival BMW has just overtaken Mercedes as the world's number-one luxury carmaker. BMW's strategy: build only premium quality cars . . . and don't get diverted.

Sources: Business Week (August 15, 2005): 31–38; *Motor Trend* (November 2005): 4; *The Wall Street Journal* (January 30, 2006): B4; and *Automotive News* (May 2, 2005): 3.

Cost of Quality (COQ)

Cost of quality (COQ)
The cost of doing things wrong—that is, the price of nonconformance.

Four major categories of costs are associated with quality. Called the **cost of quality (COQ)**, they are:

- *Prevention costs:* costs associated with reducing the potential for defective parts or services (e.g., training, quality improvement programs).
- *Appraisal costs:* costs related to evaluating products, processes, parts, and services (e.g., testing, labs, inspectors).
- *Internal failure:* costs that result from production of defective parts or services before delivery to customers (e.g., rework, scrap, downtime).
- *External costs:* costs that occur after delivery of defective parts or services (e.g., rework, returned goods, liabilities, lost goodwill, costs to society).

The first three costs can be reasonably estimated, but external costs are very hard to quantify. When GE had to recall 3.1 million dishwashers recently (because of a defective switch alleged to have started seven fires), the cost of repairs exceeded the value of all the machines. This leads to the belief by many experts that the cost of poor quality is consistently underestimated. The *OM in Action* box "The Very High Cost of Quality at Mercedes" certainly reinforces that point.

Observers of quality management believe that, on balance, the cost of quality products is only a fraction of the benefits. They think the real losers are organizations that fail to work aggressively at quality. For instance, Philip Crosby stated that quality is free. "What costs money are the unquality things—all the actions that involve not doing it right the first time."[2]

TAKUMI

Takumi is a Japanese character that symbolizes a broader dimension than quality, a deeper process than education, and a more perfect method than persistence.

Leaders in Quality   Besides Crosby there are several other giants in the field of quality management, including Deming, Feigenbaum, and Juran. Table 1 summarizes their philosophies and contributions.

Ethics and Quality Management

For operations managers, one of the most important jobs is to deliver healthy, safe, and quality products and services to customers. The development of poor-quality products, because of inadequate design and production processes, results not only in higher production costs but also leads to injuries, lawsuits, and increased government regulation.

[2]Philip B. Crosby, *Quality Is Free* (New York: McGraw-Hill, 1979). Further, J. M. Juran states, in his book *Juran on Quality by Design* (The Free Press 1992, p. 119), that costs of poor quality "are huge, but the amounts are not known with precision. In most companies the accounting system provides only a minority of the information needed to quantify this cost of poor quality. It takes a great deal of time and effort to extend the accounting system so as to provide full coverage."

176

▼ **Table 1** Leaders in the Field of Quality Management

Leader	Philosophy/Contribution
W. Edwards Deming	Deming insisted management accept responsibility for building good systems. The employee cannot produce products that on average exceed the quality of what the process is capable of producing. His 14 points for implementing quality improvement are presented in this chapter.
Joseph M. Juran	A pioneer in teaching the Japanese how to improve quality, Juran believes strongly in top-management commitment, support, and involvement in the quality effort. He is also a believer in teams that continually seek to raise quality standards. Juran varies from Deming somewhat in focusing on the customer and defining quality as fitness for use, not necessarily the written specifications.
Armand Feigenbaum	His 1961 book, *Total Quality Control*, laid out 40 steps to quality improvement processes. He viewed quality not as a set of tools but as a total field that integrated the processes of a company. His work in how people learn from each other's successes led to the field of cross-functional teamwork.
Philip B. Crosby	*Quality is Free* was Crosby's attention-getting book published in 1979. Crosby believed that in the traditional trade-off between the cost of improving quality and the cost of poor quality, the cost of poor quality is understated. The cost of poor quality should include all of the things that are involved in not doing the job right the first time. Crosby coined the term *zero defects* and stated, "There is absolutely no reason for having errors or defects in any product or service."

If a firm believes that it has introduced a questionable product, ethical conduct must dictate the responsible action. This may be a worldwide recall, as conducted by both Johnson & Johnson (for Tylenol) and Perrier (for sparkling water), when each of these products was found to be contaminated. A manufacturer must accept responsibility for any poor-quality product released to the public. Neither Ford (the Explorer SUV maker) nor Firestone (the radial tire maker) did this. In recent years, both firms have been accused of failing to issue product recalls, of withholding damaging information, and of handling complaints on an individual basis.[3]

There are many stakeholders involved in the production and marketing of poor-quality products, including stockholders, employees, customers, suppliers, distributors, and creditors. As a matter of ethics, management must ask if any of these stakeholders are being wronged. Every company needs to develop core values that become day-to-day guidelines for everyone from the CEO to production-line employees.

High-quality products and services are the most profitable.

Tim Boyle, Getty Images, Inc.—Liaison

◄ *The ISO 9000 Certified sign is up, but this Bridgestone/Firestone plant in Decatur, Illinois, produced millions of defective tires that resulted in thousands of accidents and 271 deaths. After lying before Congress, the firm was forced to admit that the Firestone 500 radial had 17.5% return rates (vs. 2.9% for competitor Goodyear). Before the investigation became public knowledge, Firestone held a half-price clearance sale of defective tires in the Southeast U.S. Congress later discovered that Firestone continued to manufacture the 500 radial tire after claiming it had stopped production. This case of unethical conduct eventually resulted in the recall of 14.4 million tires and cost Bridgestone/Firestone hundreds of millions of dollars.*

[3]For further reading, see M. R. Nayebpour and D. Koehn, "The Ethics of Quality: Problems and Preconditions" *Journal of Business Ethics* 44 (April, 2003): 37–48.

INTERNATIONAL QUALITY STANDARDS

ISO 9000

ISO 9000

A set of quality standards developed by the International Organization for Standardization (ISO).

Quality is so important globally that the world is uniting around a single quality standard, **ISO 9000**. ISO 9000 is the only quality standard with international recognition. In 1987, 91 member nations (including the U.S.) published a series of quality assurance standards, known collectively as ISO 9000. The U.S., through the American National Standards Institute, has adopted the ISO 9000 series as the ANSI/ASQ Q9000 series.[4] The focus of the standards is to establish quality management procedures, through leadership, detailed documentation, work instructions, and recordkeeping. These procedures, we should note, say nothing about the actual quality of the product—they deal entirely with standards to be followed.

"ISO" is Greek for equal or uniform, as in uniform throughout the world.

To become ISO 9000 certified, organizations go through a 9- to 18-month process that involves documenting quality procedures, an on-site assessment, and an ongoing series of audits of their products or services. To do business globally—and especially in Europe—being listed in the ISO directory is critical. As of 2007, there were well over 600,000 certifications awarded to firms in 158 countries. About 50,000 U.S. firms are ISO 9000 certified.

Visit the Web sites www.iso.ch and www.asq.org to learn more about ISO standards.

ISO revised its standards in 2000 into more of a quality management system, which is detailed in its ISO 9001: 2000 component. Leadership by top management and customer requirements and satisfaction play a much larger role, while documented procedures receive less emphasis under ISO 9001: 2000.

Learning Objective

2. Describe the ISO international quality standards

ISO 14000

ISO 14000

An environmental management standard established by the International Organization for Standardization (ISO).

The continuing internationalization of quality is evident with the development of **ISO 14000**. ISO 14000 is an environmental management standard that contains five core elements: (1) environmental management, (2) auditing, (3) performance evaluation, (4) labeling, and (5) life cycle assessment. The new standard could have several advantages:

- Positive public image and reduced exposure to liability.
- Good systematic approach to pollution prevention through the minimization of ecological impact of products and activities.
- Compliance with regulatory requirements and opportunities for competitive advantage.
- Reduction in need for multiple audits.

This standard is being accepted worldwide.

TOTAL QUALITY MANAGEMENT

Total quality management (TQM)

Management of an entire organization so that it excels in all aspects of products and services that are important to the customer.

Total quality management (TQM) refers to a quality emphasis that encompasses the entire organization, from supplier to customer. TQM stresses a commitment by management to have a continuing companywide drive toward excellence in all aspects of products and services that are important to the customer.

TQM is important because quality decisions influence each of the 10 decisions made by operations managers. Each of those 10 decisions deals with some aspect of identifying and meeting customer expectations. Meeting those expectations requires an emphasis on TQM if a firm is to compete as a leader in world markets.

Quality expert W. Edwards Deming used 14 points (see Table 2) to indicate how he implemented TQM. We develop these into seven concepts for an effective TQM program: (1) continuous improvement, (2) Six Sigma, (3) employee empowerment, (4) benchmarking, (5) just-in-time (JIT), (6) Taguchi concepts, and (7) knowledge of TQM tools.

Continuous Improvement

Respect for people is a cornerstone of continuous improvement.

Total quality management requires a never-ending process of continuous improvement that covers people, equipment, suppliers, materials, and procedures. The basis of the philosophy is that every aspect of an operation can be improved. The end goal is perfection, which is never achieved but always sought.

[4]ASQ is the American Society for Quality.

1. Create consistency of purpose.
2. Lead to promote change.
3. Build quality into the product; stop depending on inspections to catch problems.
4. Build long-term relationships based on performance instead of awarding business on the basis of price.
5. Continuously improve product, quality, and service.
6. Start training.
7. Emphasize leadership.
8. Drive out fear.
9. Break down barriers between departments.
10. Stop haranguing workers.
11. Support, help, and improve.
12. Remove barriers to pride in work.
13. Institute a vigorous program of education and self-improvement.
14. Put everybody in the company to work on the transformation.

◀ Table 2

Deming's 14 Points for Implementing Quality Improvement

Source: Deming revised his 14 points a number of times over the years. See J. Spigener and P. J. Angelo, "What Would Deming Say?" *Quality Progress* (March 2001): 61–65.

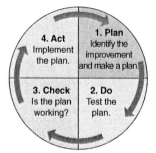

▲ Figure 3 PDCA Cycle

Plan-Do-Check-Act Walter Shewhart, another pioneer in quality management, developed a circular model known as **PDCA** (plan, do, check, act) as his version of continuous improvement. Deming later took this concept to Japan during his work there after World War II. The PDCA cycle is shown in Figure 3 as a circle to stress the continuous nature of the improvement process.

The Japanese use the word *kaizen* to describe this ongoing process of unending improvement—the setting and achieving of ever-higher goals. In the U.S., *TQM* and *zero defects* are also used to describe continuous improvement efforts. But whether it's PDCA, *kaizen*, TQM, or zero defects, the operations manager is a key player in building a work culture that endorses continuous improvement.

PDCA
A continuous improvement model of plan, do, check. act.

Six Sigma

The term **Six Sigma**, popularized by Motorola, Honeywell, and General Electric, has two meanings in TQM. In a *statistical* sense, it describes a process, product, or service with an extremely high capability (99.9997% accuracy). For example, if 1 million passengers pass through the St. Louis Airport with checked baggage each month, a Six Sigma program for baggage handling will result in only 3.4 passengers with misplaced luggage. The more common three-sigma program (which we address in the supplement to this chapter) would result in 2,700 passengers with misplaced bags every month. See Figure 4.

The second TQM definition of Six Sigma is a program designed to reduce defects to help lower costs, save time, and improve customer satisfaction. Six Sigma is a comprehensive system—a strategy, a discipline, and a set of tools—for achieving and sustaining business success:

- It is a *strategy* because it focuses on total customer satisfaction.
- It is a *discipline* because it follows the formal Six Sigma Improvement Model known as DMAIC. This five-step process improvement model (1) Defines the project's purpose, scope, and outputs and then identifies the required process information, keeping in mind the customer's definition of quality; (2) Measures the process and collects data; (3) Analyzes the data, ensuring repeatability (the results can be duplicated), and reproducibility (others get the

Six Sigma
A program to save time, improve quality, and lower costs.

Learning Objective

3. Explain what Six Sigma is

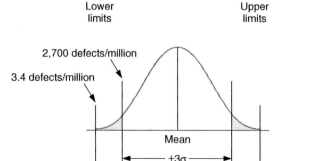

◀ Figure 4

Defects per Million for ±3σ vs. ± 6σ

same result); (4) *Improves*, by modifying or redesigning, existing processes and procedures; and (5) *Controls* the new process to make sure performance levels are maintained.

- It is a *set of seven tools* that we introduce shortly in this chapter: check sheets, scatter diagrams, cause-and-effect diagrams, Pareto charts, flowcharts, histograms, and statistical process control.

Motorola developed Six Sigma in the 1980s in response to customer complaints about its products, and to stiff competition. The company first set a goal of reducing defects by 90%. Within 1 year it had achieved such impressive results—through benchmarking competitors, soliciting new ideas from employees, changing reward plans, adding training, revamping critical processes—that it documented the procedures into what it called Six Sigma. Although the concept was rooted in manufacturing, GE later expanded Six Sigma into services, including human resources, sales, customer services, and financial/credit services. The concept of wiping out defects turns out to be the same in both manufacturing and services.

Implementing Six Sigma Implementing Six Sigma "is a big commitment," says the head of that program at Praxair, a major industrial gas company. "We're asking our executives to spend upward of 15% of their time on Six Sigma. If you don't spend the time you don't get the results."[5] Indeed, successful Six Sigma programs in every firm, from GE to Motorola to DuPont to Texas Instruments require a major time commitment, especially from top management. These leaders have to formulate the plan, communicate their buy-in and the firm's objectives, and take a visible role in setting the example for others.

Successful Six Sigma projects are clearly related to the strategic direction of a company. It is a management-directed, team-based, and expert-led approach.[6]

Employee Empowerment

Employee empowerment means involving employees in every step of the production process. Consistently, business literature suggests that some 85% of quality problems have to do with materials and processes, not with employee performance. Therefore, the task is to design equipment and processes that produce the desired quality. This is best done with a high degree of involvement by those who understand the shortcomings of the system. Those dealing with the system on a daily basis understand it better than anyone else. One study indicated that TQM programs that delegate responsibility for quality to shop-floor employees tend to be twice as likely to succeed as those implemented with "top-down" directives.[7]

When nonconformance occurs, the worker is seldom wrong. Either the product was designed wrong, the system that makes the product was designed wrong, or the employee was improperly trained. Although the employee may be able to help solve the problem, the employee rarely causes it.

Techniques for building employee empowerment include (1) building communication networks that include employees; (2) developing open, supportive supervisors; (3) moving responsibility from both managers and staff to production employees; (4) building high-morale organizations; (5) and creating such formal organization structures as teams and quality circles.

Teams can be built to address a variety of issues. One popular focus of teams is quality. Such teams are often known as quality circles. A **quality circle** is a group of employees who meet regularly to solve work-related problems. The members receive training in group planning, problem solving, and statistical quality control. They generally meet once a week (usually after work but sometimes on company time). Although the members are not rewarded financially, they do

Employee empowerment
Enlarging employee jobs so that the added responsibility and authority is moved to the lowest level possible in the organization.

Quality circle
A group of employees meeting regularly with a facilitator to solve work-related problems in their work area.

---

[5]B. Schmitt, "Expanding Six Sigma," *Chemical Week* (February 21, 2001): 21–24.

[6]To train employees in how to improve quality and its relationship to customers, there are three other key players in the Six Sigma program: Master Black Belts, Black Belts, and Green Belts. Master Black Belts are full-time teachers who have extensive training in statistics, quality tools, and leadership. They mentor Black Belts, who in turn are project team leaders, directing perhaps a half-dozen projects per year (with average savings of $175,000 per project, according to the Six Sigma Academy). They receive about 4 weeks of Six Sigma training but must also have solid "people skills," so as to be able to see their changes through. Green Belts spend part of their time on team projects and the rest on their normal jobs. Dow Chemical and DuPont have more than 1,000 Black Belts each in their global operations. DuPont also has 160 Master Black Belts and introduces over 2,000 Green Belts per year into its ranks.

[7]"The Straining of Quality," *The Economist* (January 14, 1995): 55. We also see that this is one of the strengths of Southwest Airlines, which offers bare-bones domestic service but whose friendly and humorous employees help it obtain number one ranking for quality. (See *Fortune* [March 6, 2006]: 65–69.)

Workers at this TRW airbag manufacturing plant in Marshall, Illinois, are their own inspectors. Empowerment is an essential part of TQM. This man is checking the quality of a crash sensor he built.

TRW Automobile, General Manley Ford

receive recognition from the firm. A specially trained team member, called the *facilitator*, usually helps train the members and keeps the meetings running smoothly. Teams with a quality focus have proven to be a cost-effective way to increase productivity as well as quality.

Benchmarking

Benchmarking is another ingredient in an organization's TQM program. **Benchmarking** involves selecting a demonstrated standard of products, services, costs, or practices that represent the very best performance for processes or activities very similar to your own. The idea is to develop a target at which to shoot and then to develop a standard or benchmark against which to compare your performance. The steps for developing benchmarks are:

Benchmarking
Selecting a demonstrated standard of performance that represents the very best performance for a process or an activity.

1. Determine what to benchmark.
2. Form a benchmark team.
3. Identify benchmarking partners.
4. Collect and analyze benchmarking information.
5. Take action to match or exceed the benchmark.

Typical performance measures used in benchmarking include percentage of defects, cost per unit or per order, processing time per unit, service response time, return on investment, customer satisfaction rates, and customer retention rates. When considering company Web sites, this benchmark list is quite different, as we see in Table 3.

In the ideal situation, you find one or more similar organizations that are leaders in the particular areas you want to study. Then you compare yourself (benchmark yourself) against them. The company need not be in your industry. Indeed, to establish world-class standards, it may be best

Learning Objective

4. Explain how benchmarking is used in TQM

1. Use of meta tags (keywords)	Yes: 70%, No: 30%
2. A meaningful homepage title	Yes: 97%, No: 3%
3. Unique domain name	Yes: 91%, No: 9%
4. Search engine site registration	Above 96%
5. Average speed of homepage loading (in seconds)	28K: 19.31; 56K: 10.88; T1: 2.59
6. Average number of spelling errors	0.16
7. Visibility of contact information	Yes: 74%, No: 26%
8. Presence of a search engine	Yes: 59%, No: 41%
9. Translation to multiple languages	Yes: 11%; No: 89%

◁ **Table 3**

Benchmarking Factors Deemed Critical to Quality at *Fortune* 500 Company Web Sites (and survey results)

Sources: Adopted from M. Jenamani, P. K. J. Mohapatra, and S. Ghose, *Internet Research* 16, no. 3 (2006): 248; and N. Tamini, M. Rajan, and R. Sebastianelli, *Quality Progress* 33, no. 7 (July 2000): 47–51.

▷ **Table 4**

**Best Practices for
Resolving Customer
Complaints**

- *Make it easy for clients to complain:* It is free market research.
- *Respond quickly to complaints:* It adds customers and loyalty.
- *Resolve complaints on the first contact:* It reduces cost.
- *Use computers to manage complaints:* Discover trends, share them, and align your services.
- *Recruit the best for customer service jobs:* It should be part of formal training and career advancement.

Source: Canadian Government Guide on Complaint Mechanism.

to look outside your industry. If one industry has learned how to compete via rapid product development while yours has not, it does no good to study your industry.

This is exactly what Xerox and Mercedes Benz did when they went to L.L. Bean for order-filling and warehousing benchmarks. Xerox noticed that L.L. Bean was able to "pick" orders three times as fast as it could. After benchmarking, it was immediately able to pare warehouse costs by 10%. Mercedes Benz observed that L.L. Bean warehouse employees used flowcharts to spot wasted motions. The auto giant followed suit and now relies more on problem solving at the worker level.

Benchmarks often take the form of "best practices" found in other firms or in other divisions. Table 4 illustrates best practices for resolving customer complaints.

Likewise, British computer manufacturer ICL benchmarked Marks and Spencer (the food and clothing retailer) to improve its distribution system.

Internal Benchmarking When an organization is large enough to have many divisions or business units, a natural approach is the internal benchmark. Data are usually much more accessible than from outside firms. Typically, one internal unit has superior performance worth learning from.

Xerox's almost religious belief in benchmarking has paid off not only by looking outward to L.L. Bean but by examining the operations of its various country divisions. For example, Xerox Europe, a $6 billion subsidiary of Xerox Corp., formed teams to see how better sales could result through internal benchmarking. Somehow, France sold five times as many color copiers as did other divisions in Europe. By copying France's approach, namely, better sales training and use of dealer channels to supplement direct sales, Norway increased sales by 152%, Holland by 300%, and Switzerland by 328%!

Benchmarks can and should be established in a variety of areas. Total quality management requires no less.[8]

⊙ **Video 6.2**

Xerox's Benchmarking Strategy

Just-in-Time (JIT)

The philosophy behind just-in-time (JIT) is one of continuing improvement and enforced problem solving. JIT systems are designed to produce or deliver goods just as they are needed. JIT is related to quality in three ways:

- *JIT cuts the cost of quality:* This occurs because scrap, rework, inventory investment, and damage costs are directly related to inventory on hand. Because there is less inventory on hand with JIT, costs are lower. Additionally, inventory hides bad quality, whereas JIT immediately *exposes* bad quality.
- *JIT improves quality:* As JIT shrinks lead time it keeps evidence of errors fresh and limits the number of potential sources of error. JIT creates, in effect, an early warning system for quality problems, both within the firm and with vendors.
- *Better quality means less inventory and a better, easier-to-employ JIT system:* Often the purpose of keeping inventory is to protect against poor production performance resulting from unreliable quality. If consistent quality exists, JIT allows firms to reduce all the costs associated with inventory.

---

[8]Note that benchmarking is good for evaluating how well you are doing the thing you are doing compared with the industry, but the more imaginative approach to process improvement is to ask, Should we be doing this at all? Comparing your warehousing operations to the marvelous job that L.L. Bean does is fine, but maybe you should be outsourcing the warehousing function (see Supplement 11).

Taguchi Concepts

Most quality problems are the result of poor product and process design. Genichi Taguchi has provided us with three concepts aimed at improving both product and process quality: *quality robustness*, *quality loss function*, and *target-oriented quality*.[9]

Quality robust products are products that can be produced uniformly and consistently in adverse manufacturing and environmental conditions. Taguchi's idea is to remove the *effects* of adverse conditions instead of removing the causes. Taguchi suggests that removing the effects is often cheaper than removing the causes and more effective in producing a robust product. In this way, small variations in materials and process do not destroy product quality.

A **quality loss function (QLF)** identifies all costs connected with poor quality and shows how these costs increase as the product moves away from being exactly what the customer wants. These costs include not only customer dissatisfaction but also warranty and service costs; internal inspection, repair, and scrap costs; and costs that can best be described as costs to society. Notice that Figure 5(a) shows the quality loss function as a curve that increases at an increasing rate. It takes the general form of a simple quadratic formula:

$$L = D^2 C$$

where
L = loss to society
D^2 = square of the distance from the target value
C = cost of the deviation at the specification limit

All the losses to society due to poor performance are included in the loss function. The smaller the loss, the more desirable the product. The farther the product is from the target value, the more severe the loss.

Taguchi observed that traditional conformance-oriented specifications (i.e., the product is good as long as it falls within the tolerance limits) are too simplistic. As shown in Figure 5(b), conformance-oriented quality accepts all products that fall within the tolerance limits, producing more units farther from the target. Therefore, the loss (cost) is higher in terms of customer satisfaction and benefits to society. Target-oriented quality, on the other hand, strives to keep the product at the desired specification, producing more (and better) units near the target. **Target-oriented quality** is a philosophy of continuous improvement to bring the product exactly on target.

Quality robust
Products that are consistently built to meet customer needs in spite of adverse conditions in the production process.

Quality loss function (QLF)
A mathematical function that identifies all costs connected with poor quality and shows how these costs increase as product quality moves from what the customer wants.

Learning Objective

5. Explain quality robust products and Taguchi concepts

Target-oriented quality
A philosophy of continuous improvement to bring the product exactly on target.

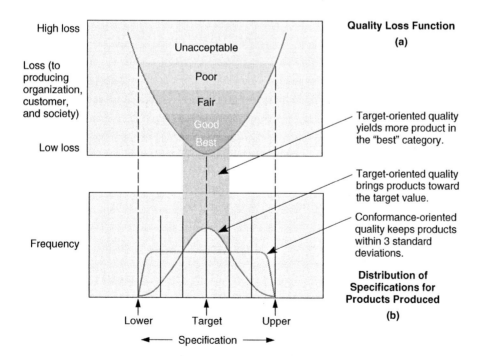

Quality Loss Function
(a)

Target-oriented quality yields more product in the "best" category.

Target-oriented quality brings products toward the target value.

Conformance-oriented quality keeps products within 3 standard deviations.

Distribution of Specifications for Products Produced
(b)

◁ **Figure 5**

(a) Quality Loss Function and (b) Distribution of Products Produced

Taguchi aims for the target because products produced near the upper and lower acceptable specifications result in higher quality loss function.

[9]G. Taguchi, S. Chowdhury, and Y. Wu, *Taguchi's Quality Engineering Handbook* (New York: Wiley, 2004).

"Quality is never an accident; it is always the result of intelligent effort."

John Ruskin

Knowledge of TQM Tools

To empower employees and implement TQM as a continuing effort, everyone in the organization must be trained in the techniques of TQM. In the following section, we focus on some of the diverse and expanding tools that are used in the TQM crusade.

TOOLS OF TQM

Seven tools that are particularly helpful in the TQM effort are shown in Figure 6. We will now introduce these tools.

Learning Objective

6. Use the seven tools of TQM

Check Sheets

A check sheet is any kind of a form that is designed for recording data. In many cases, the recording is done so the patterns are easily seen while the data are being taken (see Figure 6[a]). Check sheets help analysts find the facts or patterns that may aid subsequent analysis. An example might be a drawing that shows a tally of the areas where defects are occurring or a check sheet showing the type of customer complaints.

Tools for Generating Ideas

(a) *Check Sheet:* An organized method of recording data

Defect	Hour							
	1	2	3	4	5	6	7	8
A	///	/		/	/	/	///	/
B	//	/	/	/			//	///
C	/	//					//	////

(b) *Scatter Diagram:* A graph of the value of one variable vs. another variable

(c) *Cause-and-Effect Diagram:* A tool that identifies process elements (causes) that may effect an outcome

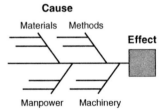

Tools for Organizing the Data

(d) *Pareto Chart:* A graph to identify and plot problems or defects in descending order of frequency

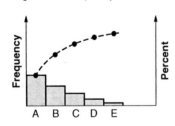

(e) *Flow Chart (Process Diagram):* A chart that describes the steps in a process

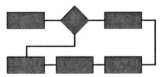

Tools for Identifying Problems

(f) *Histogram:* A distribution showing the frequency of occurrences of a variable

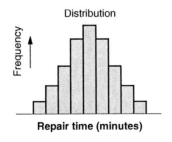

(g) *Statistical Process Control Chart:* A chart with time on the horizontal axis for plotting values of a statistic

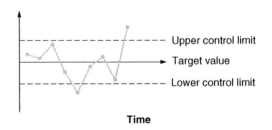

▲ **Figure 6** Seven Tools of TQM

OM in Action   TQM Improves Copier Service

In the copier industry, technology in copier design has blurred the distinction between most companies' products. Savin, a copier manufacturer owned by Japan's Ricoh Corp., believes that competitive advantage is to be found in service and is stressing customer service rather than product specifications. Says Savin VP Robert Williams: "A company's fortunes ride on the quality of its service."

Here are two ways in which Savin reduced expenses while improving service quality:

- Using the tools of TQM, Savin found that significant time on service calls was being wasted when engineers had to go back to their trucks for spare parts. The firm assembled a "call kit," which allows engineers to carry onto customer premises all parts with highest probability for use. Now service calls are faster and cost less, and more can be made per day.

- The Pareto principle, that 20% of your staff causes 80% of your errors, was used to tackle the "callback" problem. Callbacks meant the job was not done right the first time and that a second visit, at Savin's expense, was needed. Retraining only the 11% of customer engineers with the most callbacks resulted in a 19% drop in return visits.

"Total quality management," according to Williams, "is an approach to doing business that should permeate every job in the service industry."

Sources: Fortune (July 24, 2006): S16–S17; and *The Wall Street Journal* (May 19, 1998): B8.

Scatter Diagrams

Scatter diagrams show the relationship between two measurements. An example is the positive relationship between length of a service call and the number of trips the repairperson makes back to the truck for parts (as discussed in the *OM in Action* box "TQM Improves Copier Service"). Another example might be a plot of productivity and absenteeism, as shown in Figure 6(b). If the two items are closely related, the data points will form a tight band. If a random pattern results, the items are unrelated.

Cause-and-Effect Diagrams

Another tool for identifying quality issues and inspection points is the **cause-and-effect diagram**, also known as an **Ishikawa diagram** or a **fish-bone chart**. Figure 7 illustrates a chart (note the shape resembling the bones of a fish) for a basketball quality control problem—missed free throws. Each "bone" represents a possible source of error.

Cause-and-effect diagram
A schematic technique used to discover possible locations of quality problems.

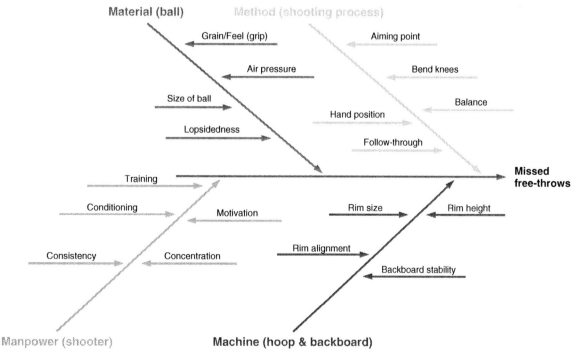

▲ **Figure 7**   Fish-Bone Chart (or Cause-and-Effect Diagram) for Problems with Missed Free Throws

Source: Adapted from MoreSteam.com, 2007.

The operations manager starts with four categories: material, machinery/equipment, manpower, and methods. These four *M*s are the "causes." They provide a good checklist for initial analysis. Individual causes associated with each category are tied in as separate bones along that branch, often through a brainstorming process. For example, the method branch in Figure 7 has problems caused by hand position, follow-through, aiming point, bent knees, and balance. When a fish-bone chart is systematically developed, possible quality problems and inspection points are highlighted.

Pareto Charts

Pareto charts are a method of organizing errors, problems, or defects to help focus on problem-solving efforts. They are based on the work of Vilfredo Pareto, a nineteenth-century economist. Joseph M. Juran popularized Pareto's work when he suggested that 80% of a firm's problems are a result of only 20% of the causes.

Example 1 indicates that of the five types of complaints identified, the vast majority were of one type, poor room service.

Pareto charts

Graphics that identify the few critical items as opposed to many less important ones.

EXAMPLE 1

A Pareto chart at the Hard Rock Hotel

The Hard Rock Hotel in Bali has just collected the data from 75 complaint calls to the general manager during the month of October. The manager wants to prepare an analysis of the complaints. The data provided are room service, 54; check-in delays, 12; hours the pool is open, 4; minibar prices, 3; and miscellaneous, 2.

Approach: A Pareto chart is an excellent choice for this analysis.

Solution: The Pareto chart shown below indicates that 72% of the calls were the result of one cause: room service. The majority of complaints will be eliminated when this one cause is corrected.

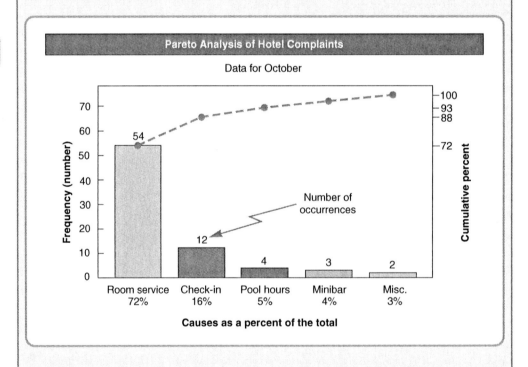

Active Model 6.1

Example 1 is further illustrated in Active Model 6.1 in the CD-ROM.

Insight: This visual means of summarizing data is very helpful—particularly with large amounts of data, as in the Southwestern University case study at the end of this chapter. We can immediately spot the top problems and prepare a plan to address them.

Learning exercise: Hard Rock's bar manager decides to do a similar analysis on complaints she has collected over the past year: too expensive, 22; weak drinks, 15; slow service, 65; short hours, 8; unfriendly bartender, 12. Prepare a Pareto chart. [Answer: slow service, 53%; expensive, 18%; drinks, 12%; bartender, 10%; hours, 7%.]

Related problems: 1, 3, 7b, 12, 13, 16c

Pareto analysis indicates which problems may yield the greatest payoff. Pacific Bell discovered this when it tried to find a way to reduce damage to buried phone cable, the number-one cause of phone outages. Pareto analysis showed that 41% of cable damage was caused by construction work. Armed with this information, Pacific Bell was able to devise a plan to reduce cable cuts by 24% in one year, saving $6 million.

Flowcharts

Flowcharts graphically present a process or system using annotated boxes and interconnected lines (see Figure 6[e]). They are a simple, but great tool for trying to make sense of a process or explain a process. Example 2 uses a flowchart to show the process of completing an MRI at a hospital.

Flowcharts
Block diagrams that graphically describe a process or system.

EXAMPLE 2

A flowchart for hospital MRI service

Arnold Palmer Hospital has undertaken a series of process improvement initiatives. One of these is to make the MRI service efficient for patient, doctor, and hospital. The first step, the administrator believes, is to develop a flowchart for this process.

Approach: A process improvement staffer observed a number of patients and followed them (and information flow) from start to end. Here are the 11 steps:

1. Physician schedules MRI after examining patient (START).
2. Patient taken to the MRI lab with test order and copy of medical records.
3. Patient signs in, completes required paperwork.
4. Patient is prepped by technician for scan.
5. Technician carries out the MRI scan.
6. Technician inspects film for clarity.
7. If MRI not satisfactory (20% of time), steps 5 and 6 are repeated.
8. Patient taken back to hospital room.
9. MRI is read by radiologist and report is prepared.
10. MRI and report are transferred electronically to physician.
11. Patient and physician discuss report (END).

Solution: Here is the flowchart:

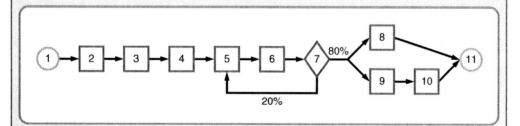

Insight: With the flowchart in hand, the hospital can analyze each step and identify value-added activities and activities that can be improved or eliminated.

Learning exercise: If the patient's blood pressure is over 200/120 when being prepped for the MRI, she is taken back to her room for 2 hours and the process returns to step 2. How does the flowchart change? Answer:

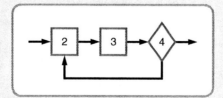

Related problems: 6, 15

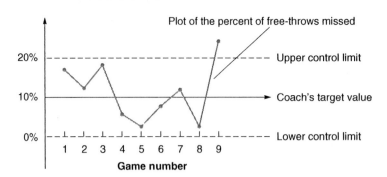

▶ Figure 8

Control Chart for Percentage of Free Throws Missed by the Chicago Bulls in Their First Nine Games of the New Season

Histograms

Histograms show the range of values of a measurement and the frequency with which each value occurs (see Figure 6[f]). They show the most frequently occurring readings as well as the variations in the measurements. Descriptive statistics, such as the average and standard deviation, may be calculated to describe the distribution. However, the data should always be plotted so the shape of the distribution can be "seen." A visual presentation of the distribution may also provide insight into the cause of the variation.

Statistical Process Control (SPC)

Statistical process control (SPC)

A process used to monitor standards, make measurements and take corrective action as a product or service is being produced.

Statistical process control monitors standards, makes measurements, and takes corrective action as a product or service is being produced. Samples of process outputs are examined; if they are within acceptable limits, the process is permitted to continue. If they fall outside certain specific ranges, the process is stopped and, typically, the assignable cause located and removed.

Control charts

Graphic presentations of process data over time, with predetermined control limits.

Control charts are graphic presentations of data over time that show upper and lower limits for the process we want to control (see Figure 6[g]). Control charts are constructed in such a way that new data can be quickly compared with past performance data. We take samples of the process output and plot the average of these samples on a chart that has the limits on it. The upper and lower limits in a control chart can be in units of temperature, pressure, weight, length, and so on.

Figure 8 shows the plot of percentages of a sample in a control chart. When the average of the samples falls within the upper and lower control limits and no discernible pattern is present, the process is said to be in control with only natural variation present. Otherwise, the process is out of control or out of adjustment.

The supplement to this chapter details how control charts of different types are developed. It also deals with the statistical foundation underlying the use of this important tool.

THE ROLE OF INSPECTION

To make sure a system is producing at the expected quality level, control of the process is needed. The best processes have little variation from the standard expected. The operations manager's task is to build such systems and to verify, often by inspection, that they are performing to standard. This **inspection** can involve measurement, tasting, touching, weighing, or testing of the product (sometimes even destroying it when doing so). Its goal is to detect a bad process immediately. Inspection does not correct deficiencies in the system or defects in the products; nor does it change a product or increase its value. Inspection only finds deficiencies and defects, and it is expensive.

Inspection

A means of ensuring that an operation is producing at the quality level expected.

Inspection should be thought of as an audit. Audits do not add value to the product. However, operations managers, like financial managers, need audits, and they need to know when and where to audit. Thus there are two basic issues relating to inspection: (1) *when to inspect* and (2) *where to inspect*.

When and Where to Inspect

Deciding when and where to inspect depends on the type of process and the value added at each stage. Inspections (audits) can take place at any of the following points:

1. At your supplier's plant while the supplier is producing.
2. At your facility upon receipt of goods from your supplier.

188

3. Before costly or irreversible processes.
4. During the step-by-step production process.
5. When production or service is complete.
6. Before delivery to your customer.
7. At the point of customer contact.

The seven tools of TQM discussed in the previous section aid in this "when and where to inspect" decision. However, inspection is not a substitute for a robust product produced by well-trained employees in a good process. In one well-known experiment conducted by an independent research firm, 100 defective pieces were added to a "perfect" lot of items and then subjected to 100% inspection.[10] The inspectors found only 68 of the defective pieces in their first inspection. It took another three passes by the inspectors to find the next 30 defects. The last two defects were never found. So the bottom line is that there is variability in the inspection process. Additionally, inspectors are only human: They become bored, they become tired, and the inspection equipment itself has variability. Even with 100% inspection, inspectors cannot guarantee perfection. Therefore, good processes, employee empowerment, and source control are a better solution than trying to find defects by inspection.

For example, at Velcro Industries, as in many organizations, quality was viewed by machine operators as the job of "those quality people." Inspections were based on random sampling, and if a part showed up bad, it was thrown out. The company decided to pay more attention to operators, machine repair and design, measurement methods, communications, and responsibilities, and to invest more money in training. Over time as defects declined, Velcro was able to pull half its quality control people out of the process.

One of the themes of our treatment of quality is that "quality cannot be inspected into a product."

Source Inspection

The best inspection can be thought of as no inspection at all; this "inspection" is always done at the source—it is just doing the job properly with the operator ensuring that this is so. This may be called **source inspection** (or source control) and is consistent with the concept of employee empowerment, where individual employees self-check their own work. The idea is that each supplier, process, and employee *treats the next step in the process as the customer*, ensuring perfect product to the next "customer." This inspection may be assisted by the use of checklists and controls such as a fail-safe device called a *poka-yoke*, a name borrowed from the Japanese.

A **poka-yoke** is a foolproof device or technique that ensures production of good units every time.[11] These special devices avoid errors and provide quick feedback of problems. A simple example of a poka-yoke device is the diesel or leaded gas pump nozzle that will not fit into the "unleaded" gas tank opening on your car. In McDonald's, the french fry scoop and standard-size

Source inspection
Controlling or monitoring at the point of production or purchase—at the source.

Poka-yoke
Literally translated, "foolproof"; it has come to mean a device or technique that ensures the production of a good unit every time.

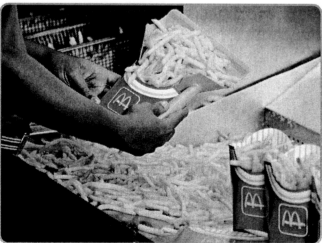

Ralf-Finn Hestoft, Corbis/SABA Press Photos, Inc.

◄ *Good methods analysis and the proper tools can result in poka-yokes that improve both quality and speed. Here, two poka-yokes are demonstrated. First, the aluminum scoop automatically positions the French fries vertically, and second, the properly sized container ensures that the portion served is correct. This combination also speeds delivery, ensuring that french fries are delivered just as the customer requests them.*

[10] *Statistical Quality Control* (Springfield, MA: Monsanto Chemical Company, n.d.): 19.
[11] For further discussion, see D. M. Stewart and S. A. Melnyk, "Effective Process Improvement Developing Poka-Yoke Procedures," *Production & Inventory Management Journal* 41, no. 4 (4th quarter, 2000): 11–17.

> **Table 5**

Examples of Inspection in Services

Organization	What Is Inspected	Standard
Jones Law Offices	Receptionist performance	Phone answered by the second ring
	Billing	Accurate, timely, and correct format
	Attorney	Promptness in returning calls
Hard Rock Hotel	Reception desk	Use customer's name
	Doorman	Greet guest in less than 30 seconds
	Room	All lights working, spotless bathroom
	Minibar	Restocked and charges accurately posted to bill
Arnold Palmer Hospital	Billing	Accurate, timely, and correct format
	Pharmacy	Prescription accuracy, inventory accuracy
	Lab	Audit for lab-test accuracy
	Nurses	Charts immediately updated
	Admissions	Data entered correctly and completely
Olive Garden Restaurant	Busboy	Serves water and bread within 1 minute
	Busboy	Clears all entrée items and crumbs prior to dessert
	Waiter	Knows and suggests specials, desserts
Nordstrom Department Store	Display areas	Attractive, well organized, stocked, good lighting
	Stockrooms	Rotation of goods, organized, clean
	Salesclerks	Neat, courteous, very knowledgeable

bag used to measure the correct quantity are poka-yokes. Similarly, in a hospital, the prepackaged surgical coverings that contain exactly the items needed for a medical procedure are poka-yokes. Checklists are another type of poka-yoke. The idea of source inspection and poka-yokes is to ensure that 100% good product or service is provided at each step in the process.

Service Industry Inspection

In *service*-oriented organizations, inspection points can be assigned at a wide range of locations, as illustrated in Table 5. Again, the operations manager must decide where inspections are justified and may find the seven tools of TQM useful when making these judgments.

Inspection of Attributes versus Variables

Attribute inspection

An inspection that classifies items as being either good or defective.

Variable inspection

Classifications of inspected items as falling on a continuum scale, such as dimension, size, or strength.

When inspections take place, quality characteristics may be measured as either *attributes* or *variables*. **Attribute inspection** classifies items as being either good or defective. It does not address the *degree* of failure. For example, the lightbulb burns or it does not. **Variable inspection** measures such dimensions as weight, speed, height, or strength to see if an item falls within an acceptable range. If a piece of electrical wire is supposed to be 0.01 inch in diameter, a micrometer can be used to see if the product is close enough to pass inspection.

Knowing whether attributes or variables are being inspected helps us decide which statistical quality control approach to take, as we will see in the supplement to this chapter.

TQM IN SERVICES

The personal component of services is more difficult to measure than the quality of the tangible component. Generally, the user of a service, like the user of a good, has features in mind that form a basis for comparison among alternatives. Lack of any one feature may eliminate the service from further consideration. Quality also may be perceived as a bundle of attributes in which many lesser characteristics are superior to those of competitors. This approach to product comparison differs little between goods and services. However, what is very different about the selection of services is the poor definition of the (1) *intangible differences between products* and (2) *the intangible expectations customers have of those products*.[12] Indeed, the intangible attributes may not

---

[12] V. Zeithaml, L. Berry, and A. Parasuraman, "The Behavioral Consequence of Service Quality," *Journal of Marketing* (April 1996): 31–47.

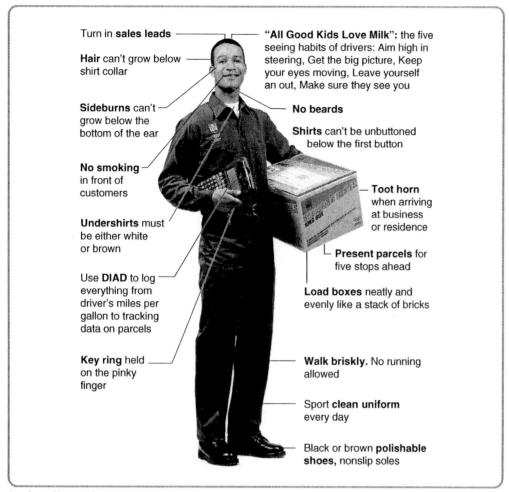

Turn in **sales leads**

Hair can't grow below shirt collar

Sideburns can't grow below the bottom of the ear

No smoking in front of customers

Undershirts must be either white or brown

Use **DIAD** to log everything from driver's miles per gallon to tracking data on parcels

Key ring held on the pinky finger

"All Good Kids Love Milk": the five seeing habits of drivers: Aim high in steering, Get the big picture, Keep your eyes moving, Leave yourself an out, Make sure they see you

No beards

Shirts can't be unbuttoned below the first button

Toot horn when arriving at business or residence

Present parcels for five stops ahead

Load boxes neatly and evenly like a stack of bricks

Walk briskly. No running allowed

Sport **clean uniform** every day

Black or brown **polishable shoes**, nonslip soles

Ann States Photography

UPS drivers are taught 340 precise methods of how to correctly deliver a package. Regimented? Absolutely. But UPS credits its uniformity and efficiency with laying the foundation for its high-quality service.

Source: Forbes (January 10, 2000): 80.

be defined at all. They are often unspoken images in the purchaser's mind. This is why all of those marketing issues such as advertising, image, and promotion can make a difference (see the photo of the UPS driver).

The operations manager plays a significant role in addressing several major aspects of service quality. First, the *tangible component of many services is important.* How well the service is designed and produced does make a difference. This might be how accurate, clear, and complete your checkout bill at the hotel is, how warm the food is at Taco Bell, or how well your car runs after you pick it up at the repair shop.

Second, another aspect of service and service quality is the process. Notice in Table 6 that 9 out of 10 of the determinants of service quality are related to *the service process.* Such things as reliability and courtesy are part of the process. An operations manager can *design processes (service products) that have these attributes* and can ensure their quality through the TQM techniques discussed in this chapter.

Third, the operations manager should realize that the customer's expectations are the standard against which the service is judged. Customers' perceptions of service quality result from a comparison of their before-service expectations with their actual-service experience. In other words, service quality is judged on the basis of whether it meets expectations. The *manager may be able to influence both the quality of the service and the expectation.* Don't promise more than you can deliver.

Fourth, the manager must expect exceptions. There is a standard quality level at which the regular service is delivered, such as the bank teller's handling of a transaction. However, there are "exceptions" or "problems" initiated by the customer or by less-than-optimal operating conditions (e.g., the computer "crashed"). This implies that the quality control system must recognize and *have a set of alternative plans for less-than-optimal operating conditions.*

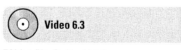

Video 6.3

TQM at Ritz-Carlton Hotels

▶ **Table 6**

Determinants of Service Quality

Reliability involves consistency of performance and dependability. It means that the firm performs the service right the first time and that the firm honors its promises.

Responsiveness concerns the willingness or readiness of employees to provide service. It involves timeliness of service.

Competence means possession of the required skills and knowledge to perform the service.

Access involves approachability and ease of contact.

Courtesy involves politeness, respect, consideration, and friendliness of contact personnel (including receptionists, telephone operators, etc.).

Communication means keeping customers informed in language they can understand and listening to them. It may mean that the company has to adjust its language for different consumers—increasing the level of sophistication with a well-educated customer and speaking simply and plainly with a novice.

Credibility involves trustworthiness, believability, and honesty. It involves having the customer's best interests at heart.

Security is the freedom from danger, risk, or doubt.

Understanding/knowing the customer involves making the effort to understand the customer's needs.

Tangibles include the physical evidence of the service.

Source: Adapted from A. Parasuranam, Valarie A. Zeithaml, and Leonard L. Berry, *Delivering Quality Service and Balancing Customer Expectations* (New York: The Free Press, 1990).

Service recovery

Training and empowering frontline workers to solve a problem immediately.

Well-run companies have **service recovery** strategies. This means they train and empower frontline employees to immediately solve a problem. Staff at Marriott Hotels are drilled in the LEARN routine—*L*isten, *E*mpathize, *A*pologize, *R*eact, *N*otify—with the final step ensuring that the complaint is fed back into the system. The Ritz-Carlton trains its staff not to say merely "sorry" but "please accept my apology" and gives them a budget for reimbursing upset guests.

Designing the product, managing the service process, matching customer expectations to the product, and preparing for the exceptions are keys to quality services. The *OM in Action* box "Richey International's Spies" provides another glimpse of how OM managers improve quality in services.

OM in Action   Richey International's Spies

How do luxury hotels maintain quality? They inspect. But when the product is one-on-one service, largely dependent on personal behavior, how do you inspect? You hire spies!

Richey International is the spy. Preferred Hotels and Resorts Worldwide and Intercontinental Hotels have both hired Richey to do quality evaluations via spying. Richey employees posing as customers perform the inspections. However, even then management must have established what the customer expects and specific services that yield customer satisfaction. Only then do managers know where and how to inspect. Aggressive training and objective inspections reinforce behavior that will meet those customer expectations.

The hotels use Richey's undercover inspectors to ensure performance to exacting standards. The hotels do not know when the evaluators will arrive or what aliases they will use. More than 50 different standards are evaluated before the inspectors even check in at a luxury hotel. Over the next 24 hours, using checklists, tape recordings, and photos, written reports are prepared and include evaluation of standards such as the following:

- Does the doorman greet each guest in less than 30 seconds?
- Does the front-desk clerk use the guest's name during check-in?
- Is the bathroom tub and shower spotlessly clean?
- How many minutes does it take to get coffee after the guest sits down for breakfast?
- Did the waiter make eye contact?
- Were minibar charges posted correctly on the bill?

Established standards, aggressive training, and inspections are part of the TQM effort at these hotels. Quality does not happen by accident.

Sources: Hotel and Motel Management (August 2002): 128; *The Wall Street Journal* (May 12, 1999): B1, B12; and *Forbes* (October 5, 1998): 88–89.

Summary

Quality is a term that means different things to different people. It is defined in this chapter as "the totality of features and characteristics of a product or service that bears on its ability to satisfy stated or implied needs." Defining quality expectations is critical to effective and efficient operations.

Quality requires building a total quality management (TQM) environment because quality cannot be inspected into a product. The selection also addresses seven TQM *concepts* : continuous improvement, Six Sigma, employee empowerment, benchmarking, just-in-time, Taguchi concepts, and knowledge of TQM tools. The seven TQM *tools* introduced in this chapter are check sheets, scatter diagrams, cause-and-effect diagrams, Pareto charts, flowcharts, histograms, and statistical process control (SPC).

Key Terms

Quality
Cost of quality (COQ)
ISO 9000
ISO 14000
Total quality management (TQM)
PDCA
Six Sigma
Employee empowerment
Quality circle

Benchmarking
Quality robust
Quality loss function (QLF)
Target-oriented quality
Cause-and-effect diagram, Ishikawa
    diagram, or fish-bone chart
Pareto charts
Flowcharts
Statistical process control (SPC)

Control charts
Inspection
Source inspection
Poka-yoke
Attribute inspection
Variable inspection
Service recovery

Active Model Exercise

This Active Model appears on your CD-ROM. It allows you to evaluate important elements in the Pareto chart.

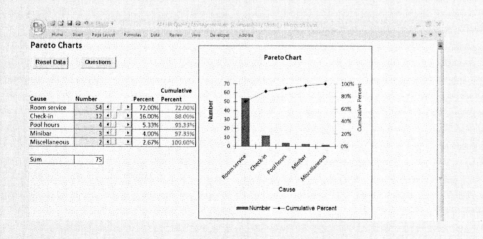

◁ **Active Model 6.1**

Pareto Analysis of Hotel Data from Example 1

Questions

1. What percentage of overall defects do the room service complaints account for?

2. If we could reduce the room service complaints in half how would this affect the chart?

Self-Test

- *Before taking the self-test*, refer to the learning objectives listed at the beginning of the chapter and the key terms listed at the end of the selection.
- *Use the key at the back of the text to **correct** your answers.*
- *Restudy pages that correspond to any questions you answered incorrectly or material you feel uncertain about.*

1. In this selection, *quality* is defined as:
   a) the degree of excellence at an acceptable price and the control of variability at an acceptable cost
   b) how well a product fits patterns of consumer preferences
   c) the totality or features and characteristics of a product or service that bears on its ability to satisfy stated or implied needs
   d) even though it cannot be defined, you know what it is

2. 100% inspection:
   a) will always catch all of the defective parts
   b) means that only good parts will be shipped to a customer
   c) is practical and generally a good idea
   d) means that every part is checked to see whether or not it is defective

3. The seven basic concepts of TQM are _____, _____, _____, _____, _____, _____, and _____.

4. ISO 14000 is an EC standard to address _____.

5. The seven tools of total quality management are _____, _____, _____, _____, _____, _____, and _____.

6. Cause-and-effect diagrams are also known as:
   a) quality loss charts
   b) target specification graphs
   c) fish-bone charts
   d) Ishikawa diagrams
   e) a and b
   f) c and d

7. The Taguchi method includes all except which of the following major concepts:
   a) employee involvement
   b) remove the effects of adverse conditions
   c) quality loss function
   d) target specifications

8. Quality cannot be _____ into a product.

Internet and Student CD-ROM/DVD Exercises

Visit our Companion Web site or your student CD-ROM/DVD to help with material in this chapter.

On Our Companion Web Site, www.prenhall.com/heizer
- Self-Study Quizzes
- Practice Problems
- Virtual Company Tour
- Internet Case
- PowerPoint Lecture

On Your Student CD-ROM
- Practice Problems
- Active Model Exercise

On Your Student DVD
- Video Clips and Video Cases

Discussion Questions

1. Explain how improving quality can lead to reduced costs.
2. As an Internet exercise, determine the Baldrige Award Criteria. See the Web site **www.quality.nist.gov**.
3. Which 3 of Deming's 14 points do you feel are most critical to the success of a TQM program? Why?
4. List the seven concepts that are necessary for an effective TQM program. How are these related to Deming's 14 points?
5. Name three of the important people associated with the quality concepts of this chapter. In each case, write a short sentence about each one summarizing their primary contribution to the field of quality management.
6. What are seven tools of TQM?
7. How does fear in the workplace (and in the classroom) inhibit learning?
8. How can a university control the quality of its output (that is, its graduates)?
9. Philip Crosby said that quality is free. Why?
10. List the three concepts central to Taguchi's approach.
11. What is the purpose of using a Pareto chart for a given problem?
12. What are the four broad categories of "causes" to help initially structure an Ishikawa diagram or cause-and-effect diagram?
13. Of the several points where inspection may be necessary, which apply especially well to manufacturing?
14. What roles do operations managers play in addressing the major aspects of service quality?
15. Explain, in your own words, what is meant by *source inspection*.
16. What are 10 determinants of service quality?
17. Name several products that do not require high quality.
18. What does the formula $L = D^2 C$ mean?
19. In this chapter, we have suggested that building quality into a process and its people is difficult. Inspections are also difficult. To indicate just how difficult inspections are, count the number of *E*s (both capital *E* and lowercase *e*) in the *OM in Action* box "Richey International's Spies" (include the title but not the footnote). How many did you find? If each student does this individually, you are very likely to find a distribution rather than a single number!

Ethical Dilemma

A lawsuit a few years ago made headlines worldwide when a McDonald's drive-through customer spilled a cup of scalding hot coffee on herself. Claiming the coffee was too hot to be safely consumed in a car, the badly burned 80-year-old woman won $2.9 million in court. (The judge later reduced the award to $640,000.) McDonald's claimed the product was served to the correct specifications and was of proper quality. Further, the cup read "Caution—Contents May Be Hot." McDonald's coffee, at 180°, is substantially hotter (by corporate rule) than typical restaurant coffee,

despite hundreds of coffee-scalding complaints in the past 10 years. Similar court cases, incidentally, resulted in smaller verdicts, but again in favor of the plaintiffs. For example, Motor City Bagel Shop was sued for a spilled cup of coffee by a drive-through patron, and Starbucks by a customer who spilled coffee on her own ankle.

Are McDonald's, Motor City, and Starbucks at fault in situations such as these? How do quality and ethics enter into these cases?

Problems

• **1** An avant-garde clothing manufacturer runs a series of high-profile, risqué ads on a billboard on Highway 101 and regularly collects protest calls from people who are offended by them. The company has no idea how many people in total see the ad, but it has been collecting statistics on the number of phone calls from irate viewers:

Type	Description	Number of Complaints
R	Offensive racially/ethnically	10
M	Demeaning to men	4
W	Demeaning to women	14
I	Ad is Incomprehensible	6
O	Other	2

a) Depict this data with a Pareto chart. Also depict the cumulative complaint line.
b) What percent of the total complaints can be attributed to the most prevalent complaint?

• **2** Develop a scatter diagram for two variables of interest (say pages in the newspaper by day of the week; see example in Figure 6b).

• **3** Develop a Pareto chart of the following causes of poor grades on an exam:

Reason for Poor Grade	Frequency
Insufficient time to complete	15
Late arrival to exam	7
Difficulty understanding material	25
Insufficient preparation time	2
Studied wrong material	2
Distractions in exam room	9
Calculator batteries died during exam	1
Forgot exam was scheduled	3
Felt ill during exam	4

• **4** Develop a histogram of the time it took for you or your friends to receive six recent orders at a fast-food restaurant.

•• **5** Theresa Shotwell's restaurant in Tallahassee, Florida, has recorded the following data for eight recent customers:

Customer Number, i	Minutes from Time Food Ordered Until Food Arrived (y_i)	No. of Trips to Kitchen by Waitress (x_i)
1	10.50	4
2	12.75	5
3	9.25	3
4	8.00	2
5	9.75	3
6	11.00	4
7	14.00	6
8	10.75	5

a) Theresa wants you to graph the eight points (x_i, y_i), $i = 1, 2, \ldots 8$. She has been concerned because customers have been waiting too long for their food, and this graph is intended to help her find possible causes of the problem.
b) This is an example of what type of graph?

•• **6** Develop a flowchart (as in Figure 6[e] and Example 2) showing all the steps involved in planning a party.

•• **7** Consider the types of poor driving habits that might occur at a traffic light. Make a list of the 10 you consider most likely to happen. Add the category of "other" to that list.
a) Compose a check sheet (like that in Figure 6[a]) to collect the frequency of occurrence of these habits. Using your check sheet, visit a busy traffic light intersection at four different times of the day, with two of these times being during high-traffic periods (rush hour, lunch hour). For 15 to 20 minutes each visit, observe the frequency with which the habits you listed occurred.
b) Construct a Pareto chart showing the relative frequency of occurrence of each habit.

•• **8** Draw a fish-bone chart detailing reasons why an airline customer might be dissatisfied.

•• **9** Consider the everyday task of getting to work on time or arriving at your first class on time in the morning. Draw a fish-bone chart showing reasons why you might arrive late in the morning.

•• **10** Construct a cause-and-effect diagram to reflect "student dissatisfied with university registration process." Use the "four Ms" or create your own organizing scheme. Include at least 12 causes.

•• **11** Draw a fish-bone chart depicting the reasons that might give rise to an incorrect fee statement at the time you go to pay for your registration at school.

• • • 12   Mary Beth Marrs, the manager of an apartment complex, feels overwhelmed by the number of complaints she is receiving. Below is the check sheet she has kept for the last 12 weeks. Develop a Pareto chart using this information. What recommendations would you make?

Week	Grounds	Parking/ Drives	Pool	Tenant Issues	Electrical/ Plumbing
1	✓✓✓	✓✓	✓	✓✓✓	
2	✓	✓✓✓	✓✓	✓✓	✓
3	✓✓✓	✓✓✓	✓✓	✓	
4	✓	✓✓✓✓	✓	✓	✓✓
5	✓✓	✓✓✓	✓✓✓✓	✓✓	
6	✓	✓✓✓✓	✓✓		
7		✓✓✓	✓✓	✓✓	
8	✓	✓✓✓✓	✓✓	✓✓✓	✓
9	✓	✓✓	✓		
10	✓	✓✓✓✓	✓✓	✓✓	
11		✓✓✓	✓✓	✓	
12	✓✓	✓✓✓	✓✓✓	✓	

• 13   Use Pareto analysis to investigate the following data collected on a printed-circuit-board assembly line:

Defect	Number of Defect Occurrences
Components not adhering	143
Excess adhesive	71
Misplaced transistors	601
Defective board dimension	146
Mounting holes improperly positioned	12
Circuitry problems on final test	90
Wrong component	212

a) Prepare a graph of the data.
b) What conclusions do you reach?

• • 14   A list of 16 issues that led to incorrect formulations in Richard Dulski's jam manufacturing unit is provided below:

List of Issues

1. Incorrect measurement	9. Variability
2. Antiquated scales	10. Equipment in disrepair
3. Lack of clear instructions	11. Technician calculation off
4. Damaged raw material	12. Jars mislabeled
5. Operator misreads display	13. Temperature controls off
6. Inadequate cleanup	14. Incorrect weights
7. Incorrect maintenance	15. Priority miscommunication
8. Inadequate flow controls	16. Inadequate instructions

Create a fish-bone diagram and categorize each of these issues correctly, using the "four *M*s" method.

• • 15   Develop a flowchart for one of the following:
a) Filling up with gasoline at a self-serve station.
b) Determining your account balance and making a withdrawal at an ATM.
c) Getting a cone of yogurt or ice cream from an ice cream store.

• • • • 16   Boston Electric Generators has been getting many complaints from its major customer, Home Station, about the quality of its shipments of home generators. Daniel Shimshak, the plant manager, is alarmed that a customer is providing him with the only information the company has on shipment quality. He decides to collect information on defective shipments through a form he has asked his drivers to complete

on arrival at customers' stores. The forms for the first 279 shipments have been turned in. They show the following over the last 8 weeks:

		Reason for Defective Shipment			
Week	No. of Ship- ments	No. of Ship- ments with Defects	Incorrect Bill of Lading	Incorrect Truck- load	Damaged Product	Trucks Late
1	23	5	2	2	1	
2	31	8	1	4	1	2
3	28	6	2	3	1	
4	37	11	4	4	1	2
5	35	10	3	4	2	1
6	40	14	5	6	3	
7	41	12	3	5	3	1
8	44	15	4	7	2	2

Even though Daniel increased his capacity by adding more workers to his normal contingent of 30, he knew that for many weeks he exceeded his regular output of 30 shipments per week. A review of his turnover over the last 8 weeks shows the following:

Week	No. of New Hires	No. of Terminations	Total No. of Workers
1	1	0	30
2	2	1	31
3	3	2	32
4	2	0	34
5	2	2	34
6	2	4	32
7	4	1	35
8	3	2	36

a) Develop a scatter diagram using total number of shipments and number of defective shipments. Does there appear to be any relationship?
b) Develop a scatter diagram using the variable "turnover" (number of new hires plus number of terminations) and the number of defective shipments. Does the diagram depict a relationship between the two variables?
c) Develop a Pareto chart for the type of defects that have occurred.
d) Draw a fish-bone chart showing the possible causes of the defective shipments.

Bill Aron, PhotoEdit Inc.

Case Study

Southwestern University: (C)*

The popularity of Southwestern University's football program under its new coach, Bo Pitterno, surged in each of the 5 years since his arrival at the Stephenville, Texas, college. With a football stadium close to maxing out at 54,000 seats and a vocal coach pushing for a new stadium, SWU president Joel Wisner faced some difficult decisions. After a phenomenal upset victory over its archrival, the University of Texas, at the homecoming game in the fall, Dr. Wisner was not as happy as one would think. Instead of ecstatic alumni, students, and faculty, all Wisner heard were complaints. "The lines at the concession stands were too long"; "Parking was harder to find and farther away than in the old days" (that is, before the team won regularly); "Seats weren't comfortable"; "Traffic was backed up halfway to Dallas"; and on

and on. "A college president just can't win," muttered Wisner to himself.

At his staff meeting the following Monday, Wisner turned to his VP of administration, Leslie Gardner. "I wish you would take care of these football complaints, Leslie," he said. "See what the *real* problems are and let me know how you've resolved them." Gardner wasn't surprised at the request. "I've already got a handle on it, Joel," she replied. "We've been randomly surveying 50 fans per game for the past year to see what's on their minds. It's all part of my campuswide TQM effort. Let me tally things up and I'll get back to you in a week."

When she returned to her office, Gardner pulled out the file her assistant had compiled (see Table 7). "There's a lot of information here," she thought.

		Overall Grade				
		A	B	C	D	E
Game Day	A. Parking	90	105	45	5	5
	B. Traffic	50	85	48	52	15
	C. Seating	45	30	115	35	25
	D. Entertainment	160	35	26	10	19
	E. Printed Program	66	34	98	22	30
Tickets	A. Pricing	105	104	16	15	10
	B. Season Ticket Plans	75	80	54	41	0
Concessions	A. Prices	16	116	58	58	2
	B. Selection of Foods	155	60	24	11	0
	C. Speed of Service	35	45	46	48	76

Respondents

Alumnus	113
Student	83
Faculty/Staff	16
None of the above	38

Open-Ended Comments on Survey Cards:

Parking a mess	More hot dog stands	Put in bigger seats	My company will buy a
Add a skybox	Seats are all metal	Friendly ushers	skybox—build it!
Get better cheerleaders	Need skyboxes	Need better seats	Programs overpriced
Double the parking attendants	Seats stink	Expand parking lots	Want softer seats
Everything is okay	Go SWU!	Hate the bleacher seats	Beat those Longhorns!
Too crowded	Lines are awful	Hot dogs cold	I'll pay for a skybox
Seats too narrow	Seats are uncomfortable	$3 for a coffee? No way!	Seats too small
Great food	I will pay more for better view	Get some skyboxes	Band was terrific
Joe P. for President!	Get a new stadium	Love the new uniforms	Love Pitterno
I smelled drugs being smoked	Student dress code needed	Took an hour to park	Everything is great
Stadium is ancient	I want cushioned seats	Coach is terrific	Build new stadium
Seats are like rocks	Not enough police	More water fountains	Move games to Dallas
Not enough cops for traffic	Students too rowdy	Better seats	No complaints
Game starts too late	Parking terrible	Seats not comfy	Dirty bathroom
Hire more traffic cops	Toilets weren't clean	Bigger parking lot	
Need new band	Not enough handicap spots in lot	I'm too old for bench seats	
Great!	Well done, SWU	Cold coffee served at game	

▲ **Table 7** Fan Satisfaction Survey Results (*N* = 250)

Discussion Questions

1. Using at least two different quality tools, analyze the data and present your conclusions.
2. How could the survey have been more useful?
3. What is the next step?

*This integrated case study runs throughout the text. Other issues facing Southwestern's football stadium include: (A) Managing the renovation project; (B) Forecasting game attendance; (C) Quality of facilities; (D) Break-even analysis of food services; (E) Locating the new stadium; (F) Inventory planning of football programs; and (G) Scheduling of campus security officers/staff for game days.

The Culture of Quality at Arnold Palmer Hospital

Video Case

Founded in 1989, Arnold Palmer Hospital is one of the largest hospitals for women and children in the U.S., with 431 beds in two facilities totaling 676,000 square feet. Located in downtown Orlando, Florida, and named after its famed golf benefactor, the hospital, with more than 2,000 employees serves an 18-county area in central Florida and is the only Level 1 trauma center for children in that region. Arnold Palmer Hospital provides a broad range of medical services including neonatal and pediatric intensive care, pediatric oncology and cardiology, care for high-risk pregnancies, and maternal intensive care.

The Issue of Assessing Quality Health Care

Quality health care is a goal all hospitals profess, but Arnold Palmer Hospital has actually developed comprehensive and scientific means of asking customers to judge the quality of care they receive. Participating in a national benchmark comparison against other hospitals, Arnold Palmer Hospital consistently scores in the top 10% in overall patient satisfaction. Executive Director Kathy Swanson states, "Hospitals in this area will be distinguished largely on the basis of their customer satisfaction. We must have accurate information about how our patients and their families judge the quality of our care, so I follow the questionnaire results daily. The in-depth survey helps me and others on my team to gain quick knowledge from patient feedback." Arnold Palmer Hospital employees are empowered to provide gifts in value up to $200 to patients who find reason to complain about any hospital service such as food, courtesy, responsiveness, or cleanliness.

Swanson doesn't focus just on the customer surveys, which are mailed to patients one week after discharge, but also on a variety of internal measures. These measures usually start at the grassroots level, where the staff sees a problem and develops ways to track performance. The hospital's longstanding philosophy supports the concept that each patient is important and respected as a person. That patient has the right to comprehensive, compassionate family-centered health care provided by a knowledgeable physician-directed team.

Some of the measures Swanson carefully monitors for continuous improvement are morbidity, infection rates, readmission rates, costs per case, and length of stays. The tools she uses daily include Pareto charts, flowcharts and process charts, in addition to benchmarking against hospitals both nationally and in the southeast region.

The result of all of these efforts has been a quality culture as manifested in Arnold Palmer's high ranking in patient satisfaction and one of the highest survival rates of critically ill babies.

Discussion Questions*

1. Why is it important for Arnold Palmer Hospital to get a patient's assessment of health care quality? Does the patient have the expertise to judge the health care she receives?
2. How would you build a culture of quality in an organization, such as Arnold Palmer Hospital?
3. What techniques does Arnold Palmer Hospital practice in its drive for quality and continuous improvement?
4. Develop a fish-bone diagram illustrating the quality variables for a patient who just gave birth at Arnold Palmer Hospital (or any other hospital).

*You may wish to review this video case on your DVD before answering these questions.

Quality at the Ritz-Carlton Hotel Company

Video Case

Ritz-Carlton. The name alone evokes images of luxury and quality. As the first hotel company to win the Malcolm Baldrige National Quality Award, the Ritz treats quality as if it is the heartbeat of the company. This means a daily commitment to meeting customer expectations and making sure that each hotel is free of any deficiency.

In the hotel industry, quality can be hard to quantify. Guests do not purchase a product when they stay at the Ritz: They buy an experience. Thus, creating the right combination of elements to make the experience stand out is the challenge and goal of every employee, from maintenance to management.

Before applying for the Baldrige Award, company management undertook a rigorous self-examination of its operations in an attempt to measure and quantify quality. Nineteen processes were studied, including room service delivery, guest reservation and registration, message delivery, and breakfast service. This period of self-study included statistical measurement of process work flows and cycle times for areas ranging from room service delivery times

and reservations to valet parking and housekeeping efficiency. The results were used to develop performance benchmarks against which future activity could be measured.

With specific, quantifiable targets in place, Ritz-Carlton managers and employees now focus on continuous improvement. The goal is 100% customer satisfaction: If a guest's experience does not meet expectations, the Ritz-Carlton risks losing that guest to competition.

One way the company has put more meaning behind its quality efforts is to organize its employees into "self-directed" work teams. Employee teams determine work scheduling, what work needs to be done, and what to do about quality problems in their own areas. In order that they can see the relationship of their specific area to the overall goals, employees are also given the opportunity to take additional training in hotel operations. Ritz-Carlton believes that a more educated and informed employee is in a better position to make decisions in the best interest of the organization.

198

Discussion Questions*

1. In what ways could the Ritz-Carlton monitor its success in achieving quality?
2. Many companies say that their goal is to provide quality products or services. What actions might you expect from a company that intends quality to be more than a slogan or buzzword?
3. Why might it cost the Ritz-Carlton less to "do things right" the first time?
4. How could control charts, Pareto diagrams, and cause-and-effect diagrams be used to identify quality problems at a hotel?
5. What are some nonfinancial measures of customer satisfaction that might be used by the Ritz-Carlton?

*You may wish to view this video case on your DVD before addressing these questions.

Source: Adapted from C. T. Horngren, S. M. Datar, and G. Foster, *Cost Accounting*, 12th ed. (Upper Saddle River, NJ: Prentice Hall, 2006).

Additional Case Studies

Internet Case Study: Visit our Companion Web site at www.prenhall.com/heizer for this free case study:

- **Westover Electrical, Inc.:** This electric motor manufacturer has a large log of defects in its wiring process.

Harvard has selected these Harvard Business School cases to accompany this chapter:

harvardbusinessonline.hbsp.harvard.edu

- **GE: We Bring Good Things to Life (A) (#899-162):** Illustrates the complexity of managing change and the momentum that initiatives can provide.
- **Wainwright Industries (A): Beyond the Baldrige (#396-219):** Traces the growth of an auto supply company and its culture of quality.
- **Romeo Engine Plant (#197-100):** The employees at this auto engine plant must solve problems and ensure quality, not watch parts being made.
- **Motorola-Penang (#494-135):** The female manager of this Malaysia factory is skeptical of empowerment efforts at other Motorola sites.
- **Measure of Delight: The Pursuit of Quality at AT&T Universal Card Service (A) (#694-047):** Links performance measurement and compensation policies to precepts of quality management.

Bibliography

Aikens, C. *Quality*. Upper Saddle River, NJ: Prentice Hall, 2006.

Beer, M. "Why Total Quality Management Programs Do Not Persist." *Decision Sciences* 34, no. 4 (Fall 2003): 623–642.

Brown, Mark G. *Baldrige Award Winning Quality*, 13th ed. University Park, IL: Productivity Press, 2004.

Crosby, P. B. *Quality Is Still Free.* New York: McGraw-Hill, 1996.

Evans, J. R., and W. M. Lindsay. *An Introduction to Six Sigma and Process Improvement.* Mason, OH: Thompson-Southwestern, 2005.

Foster, S. Thomas. *Managing Quality*, 3rd ed. Upper Saddle River, NJ: Prentice Hall, 2007.

Gitlow, H. S., et al. *Quality Management*, 3rd ed. New York: McGraw-Hill, 2005.

Goetsch, David L., and Stanley B. Davis. *Quality Management*, 5th ed. Upper Saddle River, NJ: Prentice Hall, 2006.

Gryna, F. M., R. C. H. Chua, and J. A. DeFeo. *Juran's Quality Planning and Analysis for Enterprise Quality*, 5th ed. New York: McGraw-Hill, 2007.

Henderson, G. R. *Six Sigma Quality Improvement with Minitab.* New York: Wiley, 2006.

King, J., and R. Cichy. *Managing for Quality in the Hospitality Industry.* Upper Saddle River, NJ: Prentice Hall, 2006.

Pande, P. S., R. P. Neuman, R. R. Cavanagh. *What Is Design for Six Sigma?* New York: McGraw-Hill, 2005.

Pil, F. K., and S. Rothenberg. "Environmental Performance as a Driver of Superior Quality." *Production and Operations Management* 12, no. 3 (Fall 2003): 404–415.

Prahalad, C. K., and M. S. Krishnan. "The New Meaning of Quality in the Information Age." *Harvard Business Review* (September–October, 1999): 109–118.

Stewart, D. M. "Piecing Together Service Quality: A Framework for Robust Service." *Production and Operations Management* (Summer 2003): 246–265.

Summers, Donna. *Quality.* 4th ed. Upper Saddle River, NJ: Prentice Hall, 2006.

Tonkin, L. P. "Supercharging Business Improvements: Motorola's Six Sigma Leadership Tools." *Target: Innovation at Work* 20, no. 1 (first issue 2004): 50–53.

Vastag, Gyula. "Revisiting ISO 14000 Diffusion: A New 'Look' at the Drivers of Certification." *Production and Operations Management* 13, no. 3 (Fall 2004): 260–267.

Internet Resources

American Society for Quality: **www.asq.org/**
ISO Central Secretariat: **www.iso.ch/**
Juran Institute: **www.juran.com/**
Links to benchmarking sites: **www.ebenchmarking.com**

National Institute of Standards and Technology: **www.quality.nist.gov/**
Quality Assurance Institute: **www.qai.worldwide.org**
Quality Digest: **www. qualitydigest.com**
Quality Progress: **www.qualityprogress.asq.org**

2 Individual answer, in the style of Figure 6(b).

4 Individual answer, in the style of Figure 6(f).

6 Partial flowchart for planning a party:

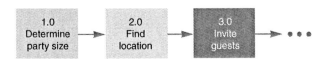

8 See figure on next page.

10 Individual answer, in the style of Figure 7 in the chapter.

12 Pareto chart, in the style of Example 1 with parking/drives most frequent, pool second, etc.

14 See figure on next page.
Materials: 4, 12, 14; Methods: 3, 7, 15, 16; Manpower: 1, 5, 6, 11; Machines: 2, 8, 9, 10, 13.

16 (a) A scatter diagram in the style of Figure 6(b) that shows a strong positive relationship between shipments and defects

(b) A scatter diagram in the style of Figure 6(b) that shows a mild relationship between shipments and turnover

▼ *Figure for problem 8.*

Fish-Bone Chart for Dissatisfied Airline Customer

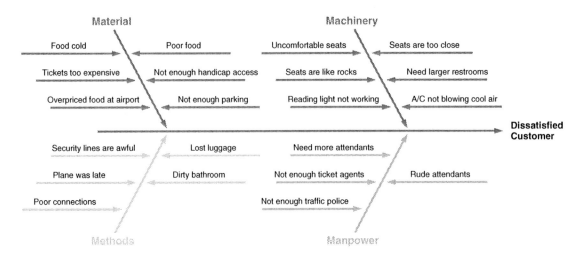

▼ *Figure for problem 14.*

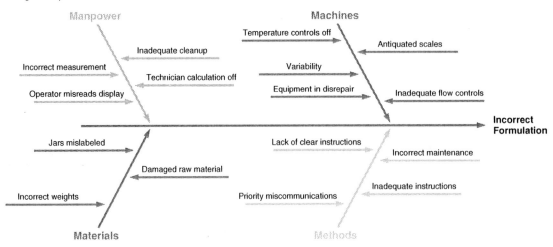

    (c) A Pareto chart in the style of Figure 6(d) that shows frequency of each type of defect

    (d) A fishbone chart in the style of Figure 6(c) with the 4 *M*s showing possible causes of increasing defects in shipments

Solutions to Self Test

1. c; **2.** d; **3.** continuous improvement; Six Sigma; Taguchi concepts; empowerment; benchmarking; JIT; TQM tools; **4.** environmental procedures; **5.** check sheets, scatter diagrams, cause-and-effect diagrams, Pareto charts, flowcharts, histograms, SPC charts; **6.** f; **7.** a; **8.** inspected.

Supplement 6

Statistical Process Control

Statistical Process Control

Outline

Learning Objectives

When you complete this selection you should be able to

1. Explain the purpose of a control chart
2. Explain the role of the central limit theorem in SPC
3. Build $\bar{x}$-charts and R-charts
4. List the five steps involved in building control charts
5. Build p-charts and c-charts
6. Explain process capability and compute C_p and C_{pk}
7. Explain acceptance sampling
8. Compute the AOQ

From *Operations Management*, 9/e. Jay Heizer. Barry Render. Copyright © 2008 by Pearson Education. All rights reserved.

P.L. Vidor, BetzDearborn, Inc.

▶ *BetzDearborn, A Division of Hercules Incorporated, is headquartered in Trevose, Pennsylvania. It is a global supplier of specialty chemicals for the treatment of industrial water, wastewater, and process systems. The company uses statistical process control to monitor the performance of treatment programs in a wide variety of industries throughout the world. BetzDearborn's quality assurance laboratory (shown here) also uses statistical sampling techniques to monitor manufacturing processes at all of the company's production plants.*

Statistical process control (SPC)

A process used to monitor standards by taking measurements and corrective action as a product or service is being produced.

In this supplement, we address statistical process control—the same techniques used at BetzDearborn, at IBM, at GE, and at Motorola to achieve quality standards. We also introduce acceptance sampling. **Statistical process control** is the application of statistical techniques to the control of processes. *Acceptance sampling* is used to determine acceptance or rejection of material evaluated by a sample.

STATISTICAL PROCESS CONTROL (SPC)

Statistical process control (SPC) is a statistical technique that is widely used to ensure that processes meet standards. All processes are subject to a certain degree of variability. While studying process data in the 1920s, Walter Shewhart of Bell Laboratories made the distinction between the common and special causes of variation. Many people now refer to these variations as *natural* and *assignable* causes. He developed a simple but powerful tool to separate the two—the **control chart**.

Control chart

A graphical presentation of process data over time.

We use statistical process control to measure performance of a process. A process is said to be operating *in statistical control* when the only source of variation is common (natural) causes. The process must first be brought into statistical control by detecting and eliminating special (assignable) causes of variation.[1] Then its performance is predictable, and its ability to meet customer expectations can be assessed. The *objective* of a process control system is to *provide a statistical signal when assignable causes of variation are present*. Such a signal can quicken appropriate action to eliminate assignable causes.

Natural variations

Variability that affects every production process to some degree and is to be expected; also known as common cause.

Natural Variations Natural variations affect almost every production process and are to be expected. **Natural variations** are the many sources of variation that occur within a process that is in statistical control. Natural variations behave like a constant system of chance causes. Although individual values are all different, as a group they form a pattern that can be described as a *distribution*. When these distributions are *normal*, they are characterized by two parameters:

- Mean, μ (the measure of central tendency—in this case, the average value)
- Standard deviation, σ (the measure of dispersion)

As long as the distribution (output measurements) remains within specified limits, the process is said to be "in control," and natural variations are tolerated.

[1]Removing assignable causes is work. Quality expert W. Edwards Deming observed that a state of statistical control is not a natural state for a manufacturing process. Deming instead viewed it as an achievement, arrived at by elimination, one by one, by determined effort, of special causes of excessive variation. See J. R. Thompson and J. Koronacki, *Statistical Process Control, The Deming Paradigm and Beyond*. Boca Raton, FL: Chapman and Hall, 2002.

Assignable Variations **Assignable variation** in a process can be traced to a specific reason. Factors such as machine wear, misadjusted equipment, fatigued or untrained workers, or new batches of raw material are all potential sources of assignable variations.

Natural and assignable variations distinguish two tasks for the operations manager. The first is to *ensure that the process is capable* of operating under control with only natural variation. The second is, of course, to *identify and eliminate assignable variations* so that the processes will remain under control.

Samples Because of natural and assignable variation, statistical process control uses averages of small samples (often of four to eight items) as opposed to data on individual parts. Individual pieces tend to be too erratic to make trends quickly visible.

Figure 1 provides a detailed look at the important steps in determining process variation. The horizontal scale can be weight (as in the number of ounces in boxes of cereal) or length (as in fence posts) or any physical measure. The vertical scale is frequency. The samples of five boxes of cereal in Figure 1 (**a**) are weighed; (**b**) form a distribution, and (**c**) can vary. The distributions formed in (**b**) and (**c**) will fall in a predictable pattern (**d**) if only natural variation is present. If assignable causes of variation are present, then we can expect either the mean to vary or the dispersion to vary, as is the case in (**e**).

Control Charts The process of building control charts is based on the concepts presented in Figure 2. This figure shows three distributions that are the result of outputs from three types of processes. We plot small samples and then examine characteristics of the resulting data to see if the process is within "control limits." The purpose of control charts is to help distinguish between natural variations and variations due to assignable causes. As seen in Figure 2, a process is (**a**) in control *and the process is capable of producing within established control limits*, (**b**) in control *but the process is not capable of producing within established limits*, or (**c**) out of control. We now look at ways to build control charts that help the operations manager keep a process under control.

Assignable variation
Variation in a production process that can be traced to specific causes.

 Video S6.1

SPC at Harley-Davidson

Learning Objective

1. Explain the purpose of a control chart

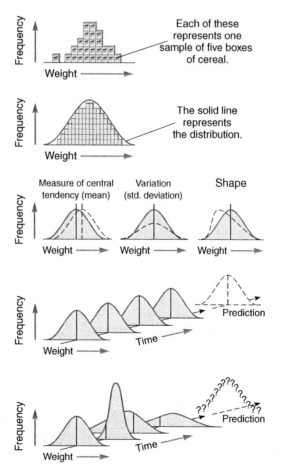

(a) Samples of the product, say five boxes of cereal taken off the filling machine line, vary from one another in weight.

Each of these represents one sample of five boxes of cereal.

(b) After enough samples are taken from a stable process, they form a pattern called a *distribution*.

The solid line represents the distribution.

(c) There are many types of distributions, including the normal (bell-shaped) distribution, but distributions do differ in terms of central tendency (mean), standard deviation or variance, and shape.

(d) If only natural causes of variation are present, the output of a process forms a distribution that is stable over time and is predictable.

(e) If assignable causes of variation are present, the process output is not stable over time and is not predictable. That is, when causes that are not an expected part of the process occur, the samples will yield unexpected distributions that vary by central tendency, standard deviation, and shape.

◁ **Figure 1**

Natural and Assignable Variation

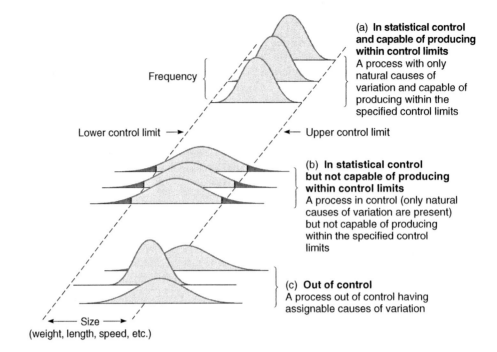

▶ Figure 2

Process Control: Three Types of Process Outputs

Frequency

Lower control limit → ← Upper control limit

(a) **In statistical control and capable of producing within control limits**
A process with only natural causes of variation and capable of producing within the specified control limits

(b) **In statistical control but not capable of producing within control limits**
A process in control (only natural causes of variation are present) but not capable of producing within the specified control limits

(c) **Out of control**
A process out of control having assignable causes of variation

← Size →
(weight, length, speed, etc.)

x̄-chart

A quality control chart for variables that indicates when changes occur in the central tendency of a production process.

R-chart

A control chart that tracks the "range" within a sample; it indicates that a gain or loss in uniformity has occurred in dispersion of a production process.

Central limit theorem

The theoretical foundation for x̄-charts, which states that regardless of the distribution of the population of all parts or services, the distribution of x̄s will tend to follow a normal curve as the number of samples increases.

Control Charts for Variables

The variables of interest here are those that have continuous dimensions. They have an infinite number of possibilities. Examples are weight, speed, length, or strength. Control charts for the mean, $\bar{x}$ or x-bar, and the range, R, are used to monitor processes that have continuous dimensions. The **x̄-chart** tells us whether changes have occurred in the central tendency (the mean, in this case) of a process. These changes might be due to such factors as tool wear, a gradual increase in temperature, a different method used on the second shift, or new and stronger materials. The **R-chart** values indicate that a gain or loss in dispersion has occurred. Such a change may be due to worn bearings, a loose tool, an erratic flow of lubricants to a machine, or to sloppiness on the part of a machine operator. The two types of charts go hand in hand when monitoring variables because they measure the two critical parameters: central tendency and dispersion.

The Central Limit Theorem

The theoretical foundation for $\bar{x}$-charts is the **central limit theorem**. This theorem states that regardless of the distribution of the population, the distribution of $\bar{x}$s (each of which is a mean of a sample drawn from the population) will tend to follow a normal curve as the number of samples increases. Fortunately, even if the sample (n) is fairly small (say, 4 or 5), the distributions of the averages will still roughly follow a normal curve. The theorem also states that: (1) the mean of the distribution of the $\bar{x}$s (called $\bar{\bar{x}}$) will equal the mean of the overall population (called μ); and (2) the standard deviation of the *sampling distribution*, $\sigma_{\bar{x}}$, will be the *population standard deviation*, σ, divided by the square root of the sample size, n. In other words:[2]

$$\bar{\bar{x}} = \mu \qquad (1)$$

and:

$$\sigma_{\bar{x}} = \frac{\sigma}{\sqrt{n}} \qquad (2)$$

Figure 3 shows three possible population distributions, each with its own mean, μ, and standard deviation, σ. If a series of random samples ($\bar{x}_1, \bar{x}_2, \bar{x}_3, \bar{x}_4$, and so on), each of size n, is drawn

[2]*Note:* The standard deviation is easily calculated as $\sigma = \sqrt{\dfrac{\sum\limits_{i=1}^{n}(x_i - \bar{x})^2}{n-1}}$.

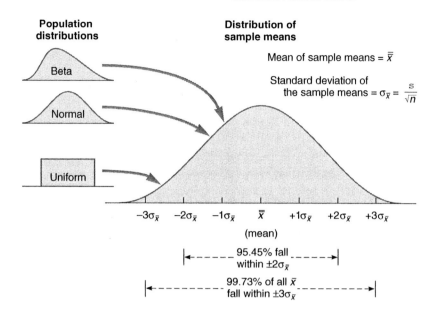

The Relationship between Population and Sampling Distributions

Regardless of the population distribution (e.g., normal, beta, uniform), each with its own mean (μ) and standard deviation (σ), the distribution of sample means is normal.

from any population distribution (which could be normal, beta, uniform, and so on), the resulting distribution of $\bar{x}_i$s will appear as they do in Figure 3.

Moreover, the sampling distribution, as is shown in Figure 4, will have less variability than the process distribution. Because the sampling distribution is normal, we can state that:

- 95.45% of the time, the sample averages will fall within $\pm 2\sigma_{\bar{x}}$ if the process has only natural variations.
- 99.73% of the time, the sample averages will fall within $\pm 3\sigma_{\bar{x}}$ if the process has only natural variations.

If a point on the control chart falls outside of the $\pm 3\sigma_{\bar{x}}$ control limits, then we are 99.73% sure the process has changed. This is the theory behind control charts.

Learning Objective

2. Explain the role of the central limit theorem in SPC

Setting Mean Chart Limits ($\bar{x}$-Charts)

If we know, through past data, the standard deviation of the process population, σ, we can set upper and lower control limits by using these formulas:

$$\text{Upper control limit (UCL)} = \bar{\bar{x}} + z\sigma_{\bar{x}} \qquad (3)$$

$$\text{Lower control limit (LCL)} = \bar{\bar{x}} - z\sigma_{\bar{x}} \qquad (4)$$

where $\bar{\bar{x}}$ = mean of the sample means or a target value set for the process

z = number of normal standard deviations (2 for 95.45% confidence, 3 for 99.73%)

$\sigma_{\bar{x}}$ = standard deviation of the sample means = $\sigma / \sqrt{n}$

σ = population (process) standard deviation

n = sample size

Learning Objective

3. Build $\bar{x}$-charts and R-charts

Example 1 shows how to set control limits for sample means using standard deviations.

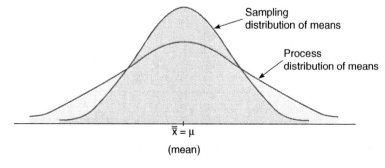

The Sampling Distribution of Means Is Normal and Has Less Variability Than the Process Distribution

In this figure, the process distribution from which the sample was drawn was also normal, but it could have been any distribution.

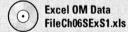

EXAMPLE 1

Setting control limits using samples

⊙ **Excel OM Data**
FileCh06SExS1.xls

The weights of boxes of Oat Flakes within a large production lot are sampled each hour. Managers want to set control limits that include 99.73% of the sample means.

Approach: Randomly select and weigh nine ($n = 9$) boxes each hour. Then find the overall mean and use Equations (3) and (4) to compute the control limits. Here are the nine boxes chosen for Hour 1:

Solution: The average weight in the first sample = $\dfrac{17+13+16+18+17+16+15+17+16}{9}$

$= 16.1$ oz.

Also, the *population* standard deviation (σ) is known to be 1 ounce. We do not show each of the boxes randomly selected in hours 2 through 12, but here are all twelve hourly samples:

	Weight of Sample		Weight of Sample		Weight of Sample
Hour	**(Avg. of 9 Boxes)**	**Hour**	**(Avg. of 9 Boxes)**	**Hour**	**(Avg. of 9 Boxes)**
1	16.1	5	16.5	9	16.3
2	16.8	6	16.4	10	14.8
3	15.5	7	15.2	11	14.2
4	16.5	8	16.4	12	17.3

The average mean of the 12 samples is calculated to be exactly 16 ounces. We therefore have $\bar{\bar{x}} = 16$ ounces, $\sigma = 1$ ounce, $n = 9$, and $z = 3$. The control limits are:

$$\text{UCL}_{\bar{x}} = \bar{\bar{x}} + z\sigma_{\bar{x}} = 16 + 3\left(\frac{1}{\sqrt{9}}\right) = 16 + 3\left(\frac{1}{3}\right) = 17 \text{ ounces}$$

$$\text{LCL}_{\bar{x}} = \bar{\bar{x}} - z\sigma_{\bar{x}} = 16 - 3\left(\frac{1}{\sqrt{9}}\right) = 16 - 3\left(\frac{1}{3}\right) = 15 \text{ ounces}$$

The 12 samples are then plotted on the following control chart:

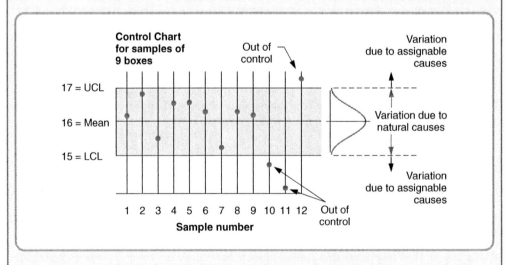

Insight: Because the means of recent sample averages fall outside the upper and lower control limits of 17 and 15, we can conclude that the process is becoming erratic and is *not* in control.

Learning exercise: If Oat Flakes's population standard deviation (σ) is 2 (instead of 1), what is your conclusion? [Answer: LCL = 14, UCL = 18; the process would be in control.]

Related problems: 1, 2, 4, 8, 10a,b

Sample Size, n	Mean Factor, A_2	Upper Range, D_4	Lower Range, D_3
2	1.880	3.268	0
3	1.023	2.574	0
4	.729	2.282	0
5	.577	2.115	0
6	.483	2.004	0
7	.419	1.924	0.076
8	.373	1.864	0.136
9	.337	1.816	0.184
10	.308	1.777	0.223
12	.266	1.716	0.284

◄ **Table 1**

Factors for Computing Control Chart Limits (3 sigma)

Source: Reprinted by permission of American Society for Testing Materials. Copyright 1951. Taken from Special Technical Publication 15-C, "Quality Control of Materials," pp. 63 and 72.

Because process standard deviations are either not available or difficult to compute, we usually calculate control limits based on the average *range* values rather than on standard deviations. Table 1 provides the necessary conversion for us to do so. The *range* is defined as the difference between the largest and smallest items in one sample. For example, the heaviest box of Oat Flakes in Hour 1 of Example S1 was 18 ounces and the lightest was 13 ounces, so the range for that hour is 5 ounces. We use Table 1 and the equations:

> *The range is the difference between the largest and the smallest items in a sample.*

$$UCL_{\bar{x}} = \bar{\bar{x}} + A_2 \bar{R} \qquad (5)$$

and:

$$LCL_{\bar{x}} = \bar{\bar{x}} - A_2 \bar{R} \qquad (6)$$

where $\bar{R}$ = average range of the samples

A_2 = value found in Table 1

$\bar{\bar{x}}$ = mean of the sample means

Example 2 shows how to set control limits for sample means by using Table 1 and the average range.

Super Cola bottles soft drinks labeled "net weight 12 ounces." Indeed, an overall process average of 12 ounces has been found by taking many samples, in which each sample contained 5 bottles. The average range of the process is .25 ounce. The OM team wants to determine the upper and lower control limits for averages in this process.

Approach: Super Cola applies Equations (5) and (6) and uses the A_2 column of Table 1.

Solution: Looking in Table 1 for a sample size of 5 in the mean factor A_2 column, we find the value .577. Thus, the upper and lower control chart limits are:

$$UCL_{\bar{x}} = \bar{\bar{x}} + A_2 \bar{R}$$
$$= 12 + (.577)(.25)$$
$$= 12 + .144$$
$$= 12.144 \text{ ounces}$$
$$LCL_{\bar{x}} = \bar{\bar{x}} - A_2 \bar{R}$$
$$= 12 - .144$$
$$= 11.856 \text{ ounces}$$

Insight: The advantage of using this range approach, instead of the standard deviation, is that it is easy to apply and may be less confusing.

Learning exercise: If the sample size was $n = 4$ and the average range = .20 ounces, what are the revised $UCL_{\bar{x}}$ and $LCL_{\bar{x}}$? [Answer: 12.146, 11.854.]

Related problems: 3a, 5, 6, 7, 9, 10b,c,d 11, 34

EXAMPLE 2

Setting mean limits using table values

Excel OM Data File
Ch06SExS2.xls

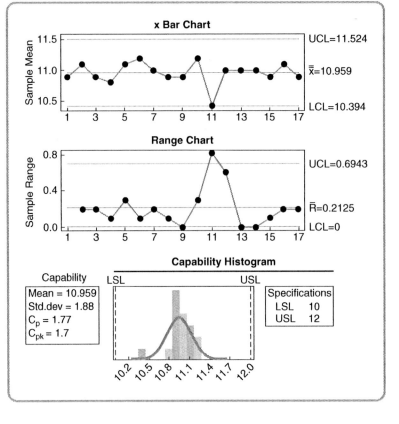

Salmon filets are monitored by Darden Restaurant's SPC software, which includes C_p, C_{pk}, $\bar{x}$-, and R-charts and a process capability histogram. The video case study "Farm to Fork," at the end of this supplement, asks you to interpret these figures.

Video S6.2

Farm to Fork: Quality of Darden Restaurants

Setting Range Chart Limits (R-Charts)

In Examples 1 and 2, we determined the upper and lower control limits for the process *average*. In addition to being concerned with the process average, operations managers are interested in the process *dispersion*, or *range*. Even though the process average is under control, the dispersion of the process may not be. For example, something may have worked itself loose in a piece of equipment that fills boxes of Oat Flakes. As a result, the average of the samples may remain the same, but the variation within the samples could be entirely too large. For this reason, operations managers use control charts for ranges to monitor the process variability, as well as control charts for averages, which monitor the process central tendency. The theory behind the control charts for ranges is the same as that for process average control charts. Limits are established that contain ±3 standard deviations of the distribution for the average range $\bar{R}$. We can use the following equations to set the upper and lower control limits for ranges:

> When determining the UCL_R and LCL_R, use the average range, $\bar{R}$. But when plotting points once the R-chart is developed, use the individual range values for each sample.

$$UCL_R = D_4\bar{R} \tag{7}$$

$$LCL_R = D_3\bar{R} \tag{8}$$

where
UCL_R = upper control chart limit for the range
LCL_R = lower control chart limit for the range
D_4 and D_3 = values from Table 1

Example 3 shows how to set control limits for sample ranges using Table 1 and the average range.

EXAMPLE 3

Setting range limits using table values

The average *range* of a product at Clinton Manufacturing is 5.3 pounds. With a sample size of 5, owner Roy Clinton wants to determine the upper and lower control chart limits.

Approach: Looking in Table 1 for a sample size of 5, he finds that $D_4 = 2.115$ and $D_3 = 0$.

Solution: The range control limits are:

$$UCL_R = D_4\bar{R} = (2.115)(5.3\text{ pounds}) = 11.2\text{ pounds}$$

$$LCL_R = D_3\bar{R} = (0)(5.3\text{ pounds}) = 0$$

Insight: Computing ranges with Table 1 is straightforward and an easy way to evaluate dispersion.

Learning exercise: Clinton decides to increase the sample size to $n = 7$. What are the new UCL_R and LCL_R values? [Answer: 10.197, 0.40.]

Related problems: 3b, 5, 6, 7, 9, 10c, 11, 12, 34

Using Mean and Range Charts

The normal distribution is defined by two parameters, the *mean* and *standard deviation*. The $\bar{x}$ (mean)-chart and the R-chart mimic these two parameters. The $\bar{x}$-chart is sensitive to shifts in the process mean, whereas the R-chart is sensitive to shifts in the process standard deviation. Consequently, by using both charts we can track changes in the process distribution.

For instance, the samples and the resulting $\bar{x}$-chart in Figure 5(a) show the shift in the process mean, but because the dispersion is constant, no change is detected by the R-chart. Conversely, the samples and the $\bar{x}$-chart in Figure 5(b) detect no shift (because none is present), but the R-chart does detect the shift in the dispersion. Both charts are required to track the process accurately.

Steps to Follow When Using Control Charts There are five steps that are generally followed in using $\bar{x}$- and R-charts:

1. Collect 20 to 25 samples, often of $n = 4$ or $n = 5$ observations each, from a stable process and compute the mean and range of each.
2. Compute the overall means ($\bar{\bar{x}}$ and $\bar{R}$), set appropriate control limits, usually at the 99.73% level, and calculate the preliminary upper and lower control limits. Refer to Table 2 for other control limits. *If the process is not currently stable,* use the desired mean, μ, instead of $\bar{\bar{x}}$ to calculate limits.

Table 2
Common z Values

Desired Control Limit (%)	z-Value (standard deviation required for desired level of confidence)
90.0	1.65
95.0	1.96
95.45	2.00
99.0	2.58
99.73	3.00

Learning Objective

4. List the five steps involved in building control charts

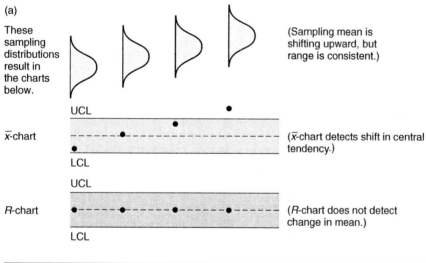

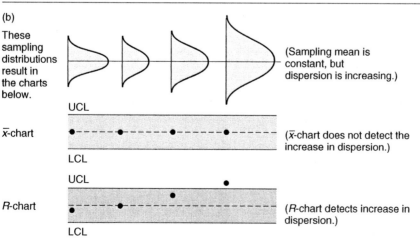

The two parameters are:
Mean → measure of central tendency.
Range → measure of dispersion.

Figure 5
Mean and Range Charts Complement Each Other by Showing the Mean and Dispersion of the Normal Distribution

OM in Action Frito-Lay Uses SPC to Keep Its Ruffles Tasty

No one wants to bite into a potato chip that is too salty—nor one that has no taste at all. Frito-Lay's Ruffles brand potato chips have to have just the right salt content, crispiness, and thickness.

Frito-Lay uses $\bar{x}$ charts and SPC to control its production at critical points in the process—instead of its old system of inspecting chips at the end of the process. Every 15 minutes, three batches of chips are taken from the conveyor, ground up, weighed, dissolved in distilled water, and filtered into a beaker. The salt content of the batches is analyzed electronically and averaged to get a mean for that sample. The sample mean is then plotted on an $\bar{x}$ chart whose target value is 1.6%. The lower and upper control limits are 1.12% and 2.08%, respectively;

Donna McWilliam, AP Wide World Photos

so if a batch is out of control, the process can be corrected before a huge number of defective Ruffles are produced. With SPC, variability among bags of chips has decreased by 50%.

Sources: Knight Ridder Tribune Business News (October 24, 2004): 1; COMAP, Annenberg/CPB Project (Needham Heights, MA: Allyn & Bacon); and Strategic Direction (February 2002): 8–11.

3. Graph the sample means and ranges on their respective control charts and determine whether they fall outside the acceptable limits.

4. Investigate points or patterns that indicate the process is out of control. Try to assign causes for the variation, address the causes, and then resume the process.

5. Collect additional samples and, if necessary, revalidate the control limits using the new data.

Applications of control charts appear in examples in this supplement, as well as in the *OM in Action* box "Frito-Lay Uses SPC to Keep Its Ruffles Tasty."

Control Charts for Attributes

Learning Objective

5. Build *p*-charts and *c*-charts

Control charts for $\bar{x}$ and R do not apply when we are sampling *attributes*, which are typically classified as *defective* or *nondefective*. Measuring defectives involves counting them (for example, number of bad lightbulbs in a given lot, or number of letters or data entry records typed with errors), whereas *variables* are usually measured for length or weight. There are two kinds of attribute control charts: (1) those that measure the *percent* defective in a sample—called *p*-charts—and (2) those that count the *number* of defects—called *c*-charts.

p-chart
A quality control chart that is used to control attributes.

p-Charts   Using **p-charts** is the chief way to control attributes. Although attributes that are either good or bad follow the binomial distribution, the normal distribution can be used to calculate *p*-chart limits when sample sizes are large. The procedure resembles the $\bar{x}$-chart approach, which is also based on the central limit theorem.

▶ *Although SPC charts can be generated by computer, this one is being prepared by hand. This chart is updated each hour and reflects a week of workshifts.*

Richard Pasley Photography

The formulas for *p*-chart upper and lower control limits follow:

$$UCL_p = \bar{p} + z\sigma_{\hat{p}} \tag{9}$$

$$LCL_p = \bar{p} - z\sigma_{\hat{p}} \tag{10}$$

where $\bar{p}$ = mean fraction defective in the sample
    z = number of standard deviations ($z = 2$ for 95.45% limits; $z = 3$ for 99.73% limits)
    $\sigma_{\hat{p}}$ = standard deviation of the sampling distribution

$\sigma_{\hat{p}}$ is estimated by the formula

$$\sigma_{\hat{p}} = \sqrt{\frac{\bar{p}(1 - \bar{p})}{n}} \tag{11}$$

where n = number of observations in *each* sample

Example S4 shows how to set control limits for *p*-charts for these standard deviations.

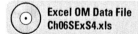

EXAMPLE 4

Setting control limits for percent defective

Clerks at Mosier Data Systems key in thousands of insurance records each day for a variety of client firms. CEO Donna Mosier wants to set control limits to include 99.73% of the random variation in the data entry process when it is in control.

Approach: Samples of the work of 20 clerks are gathered (and shown in the table). Mosier carefully examines 100 records entered by each clerk and counts the number of errors. She also computes the fraction defective in each sample. Equations (9), (10), and (11) are then used to set the control limits.

Excel OM Data File
Ch06SExS4.xls

Sample Number	Number of Errors	Fraction Defective	Sample Number	Number of Errors	Fraction Defective
1	6	.06	11	6	.06
2	5	.05	12	1	.01
3	0	.00	13	8	.08
4	1	.01	14	7	.07
5	4	.04	15	5	.05
6	2	.02	16	4	.04
7	5	.05	17	11	.11
8	3	.03	18	3	.03
9	3	.03	19	0	.00
10	2	.02	20	4	.04
				80	

Solution: $\bar{p} = \dfrac{\text{Total number of errors}}{\text{Total number of records examined}} = \dfrac{80}{(100)(20)} = .04$

$\sigma_{\hat{p}} = \sqrt{\dfrac{(.04)(1 - .04)}{100}} = .02$ (rounded up from .0196)

(Note: 100 is the size of *each* sample = *n*.)

$$UCL_p = \bar{p} + z\sigma_{\hat{p}} = .04 + 3(.02) = .10$$
$$LCL_p = \bar{p} - z\sigma_{\hat{p}} = .04 - 3(.02) = 0$$

(because we cannot have a negative percent defective)

Insight: When we plot the control limits and the sample fraction defectives, we find that only one data-entry clerk (number 17) is out of control. The firm may wish to examine that individual's work a bit more closely to see if a serious problem exists (see Figure 6).

 Active Model S6.1

Example 4 is further illustrated in Active Model S6.1 on the CD-ROM.

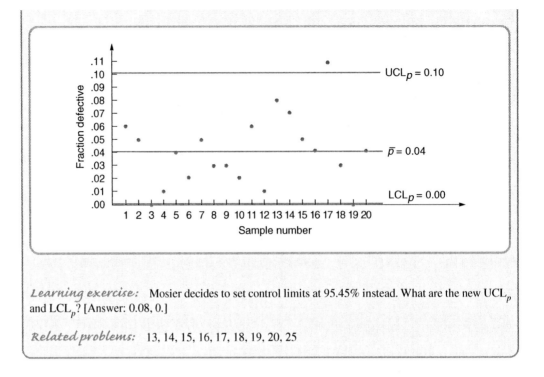

Learning exercise: Mosier decides to set control limits at 95.45% instead. What are the new UCL_p and LCL_p? [Answer: 0.08, 0.]

Related problems: 13, 14, 15, 16, 17, 18, 19, 20, 25

The *OM in Action* box "Unisys Corp.'s Costly Experiment in Health Care Services" provides a real-world follow-up to Example 4.

c-Charts   In Example 4, we counted the number of defective records entered. A defective record was one that was not exactly correct because it contained at least one defect. However, a bad record may contain more than one defect. We use **c-charts** to control the *number* of defects per unit of output (or per insurance record, in the preceding case).

c-chart

A quality control chart used to control the number of defects per unit of output.

Control charts for defects are helpful for monitoring processes in which a large number of potential errors can occur, but the actual number that do occur is relatively small. Defects may be errors in newspaper words, bad circuits in a microchip, blemishes on a table, or missing pickles on a fast-food hamburger.

OM in Action   Unisys Corp.'s Costly Experiment in Health Care Services

When Unisys Corp. expanded into the computerized health care service business things looked rosy. It had just beat out Blue Cross/Blue Shield of Florida for an $86 million contract to serve Florida's state employee health-insurance services. Its job was to handle the 215,000 Florida employees' claims processing—a seemingly simple and lucrative growth area for an old-line computer company like Unisys.

But 1 year later the contract was not only torn up, Unisys was fined more than $500,000 for not meeting quality standards. Here are two of the measures of quality, both attributes (that is, either "defective" or "not defective") on which the firm was out of control:

1. *Percent of claims processed with errors:* An audit over a 3-month period, by Coopers & Lybrand, found that Unisys made errors in 8.5% of claims processed. The industry standard is 3.5% "defectives."

2. *Percent of claims processed within 30 days:* For this attribute measure, a "defect" is a processing time longer than the contract's time allowance. In one month's sample, 13% of the claims exceeded the 30-day limit, far above the 5% allowed by the State of Florida.

The Florida contract was a migraine for Unisys, which underestimated the labor-intensiveness of health claims. CEO James Unruh pulled the plug on future ambitions in health care. Meanwhile, the State of Florida's Ron Poppel says, "We really need somebody that's in the insurance business."

Sources: Knight Ridder Tribune Business News (October 20, 2004): 1 and (February 7, 2002): 1; and *Business Week* (June 16, 1997): 6.

Charles O'Rear, CORBIS—NY

Sampling wine from these wooden barrels, to make sure it is aging properly, uses both SPC (for alcohol content and acidity) and subjective measures (for taste).

The Poisson probability distribution,[3] which has a variance equal to its mean, is the basis for c-charts. Because $\bar{c}$ is the mean number of defects per unit, the standard deviation is equal to $\sqrt{\bar{c}}$. To compute 99.73% control limits for $\bar{c}$, we use the formula:

$$\text{Control limits} = \bar{c} \pm 3\sqrt{\bar{c}} \tag{12}$$

Example 5 shows how to set control limits for a $\bar{c}$-chart.

EXAMPLE 5

Setting control limits for number defective

Red Top Cab Company receives several complaints per day about the behavior of its drivers. Over a 9-day period (where days are the units of measure), the owner, Gordon Hoft, received the following numbers of calls from irate passengers: 3, 0, 8, 9, 6, 7, 4, 9, 8, for a total of 54 complaints. Hoft wants to compute 99.73% control limits.

Approach: He applies Equation (12).

Solution: $\bar{c} = \dfrac{54}{9} = 6$ complaints per day

Thus:

$$\text{UCL}_c = \bar{c} + 3\sqrt{\bar{c}} = 6 + 3\sqrt{6} = 6 + 3(2.45) = 13.35, \text{ or } 13$$

$$\text{LCL}_c = \bar{c} - 3\sqrt{\bar{c}} = 6 - 3\sqrt{6} = 6 - 3(2.45) = 0 \leftarrow (\text{since it cannot be negative})$$

Insight: After Hoft plotted a control chart summarizing these data and posted it prominently in the drivers' locker room, the number of calls received dropped to an average of three per day. Can you explain why this occurred?

Learning exercise: Hoft collects 3 more days' worth of complaints (10, 12, and 8 complaints) and wants to combine them with the original 9 days to compute updated control limits. What are the revised UCL_c and LCL_c? [Answer: 14.94, 0.]

Related problems: 21, 22, 23, 24

Excel OM Data File Ch06SExS5.xls

Managerial Issues and Control Charts

In an ideal world, there is no need for control charts. Quality is uniform and so high that employees need not waste time and money sampling and monitoring variables and attributes. But because most processes have not reached perfection, managers must make three major decisions regarding control charts.

---

[3]A Poisson probability distribution is a discrete distribution commonly used when the items of interest (in this case, defects) are infrequent and/or occur in time and space.

▶ **Table 3**

Helping You Decide Which Control Chart to Use

Variable Data

Using an $\bar{x}$-Chart and an R-Chart

1. Observations are *variables*, which are usually products measured for size or weight. Examples are the width or length of a wire being cut and the weight of a can of Campbell's soup.
2. Collect 20 to 25 samples, usually of $n = 4$, $n = 5$, or more, each from a stable process, and compute the mean for an $\bar{x}$-chart and the range for an R-chart.
3. We track samples of n observations each, as in Example 1.

Attribute Data

Using a p-Chart

1. Observations are *attributes* that can be categorized as good or bad (or pass–fail, or functional–broken), that is, in two states.
2. We deal with fraction, proportion, or percent defectives.
3. There are several samples, with many observations in each. For example, 20 samples of $n = 100$ observations in each, as in Example 4.

Using a c-Chart

1. Observations are *attributes* whose defects per unit of output can be counted.
2. We deal with the number counted, which is a small part of the possible occurrences.
3. Defects may be: number of blemishes on a desk; complaints in a day; crimes in a year; broken seats in a stadium; typos in a chapter of this text; or flaws in a bolt of cloth, as is shown in Example 5.

First, managers must select the points in their process that need SPC. They may ask "Which parts of the job are critical to success?" or "Which parts of the job have a tendency to become out of control?"

Second, managers need to decide if variable charts (i.e., $\bar{x}$ and R) or attribute charts (i.e., p and c) are appropriate. Variable charts monitor weights or dimensions. Attribute charts are more of a "yes–no" or "go–no go" gauge and tend to be less costly to implement. Table 3 can help you understand when to use each of these types of control charts.

Third, the company must set clear and specific SPC policies for employees to follow. For example, should the data-entry process be halted if a trend is appearing in percent defective records being keyed? Should an assembly line be stopped if the average length of five successive samples is above the centerline? Figure 7 illustrates some of the patterns to look for over time in a process.

A tool called a **run test** is available to help identify the kind of abnormalities in a process that we see in Figure 7. In general, a run of 5 points above or below the target or centerline may suggest that an assignable, or nonrandom, variation is present. When this occurs, even though all the points may

Run test

A test used to examine the points in a control chart to see if nonrandom variation is present.

▶ **Figure 7**

Patterns to Look for on Control Charts

Source: Adapted from Bertrand L. Hansen, *Quality Control: Theory and Applications* (1991): 65. Reprinted by permission of Prentice Hall, Upper Saddle River, New Jersey.

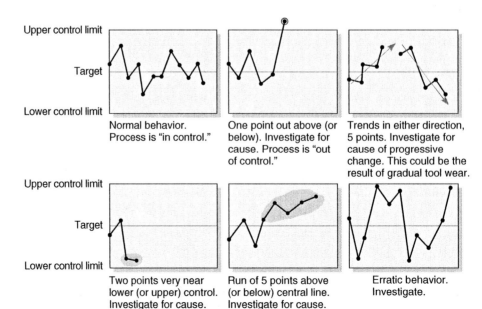

Normal behavior. Process is "in control."

One point out above (or below). Investigate for cause. Process is "out of control."

Trends in either direction, 5 points. Investigate for cause of progressive change. This could be the result of gradual tool wear.

Two points very near lower (or upper) control. Investigate for cause.

Run of 5 points above (or below) central line. Investigate for cause.

Erratic behavior. Investigate.

fall inside the control limits, a flag has been raised. This means the process may not be statistically in control. A variety of run tests are described in books on the subject of quality methods.[4]

PROCESS CAPABILITY

Statistical process control means keeping a process in control. This means that the natural variation of the process must be stable. But a process that is in statistical control may not yield goods or services that meet their *design specifications* (tolerances). The ability of a process to meet design specifications, which are set by engineering design or customer requirements, is called **process capability**. Even though that process may be statistically in control (stable), the output of that process may not conform to specifications.

For example, let's say the time a customer expects to wait for the completion of a lube job at Quik Lube is 12 minutes, with an acceptable tolerance of ±2 minutes. This tolerance gives an upper specification of 14 minutes and a lower specification of 10 minutes. The lube process has to be capable of operating within these design specifications—if not, some customers will not have their requirements met. As a manufacturing example, the tolerances for Harley-Davidson cam gears are extremely low, only 0.0005 inch—and a process must be designed that is capable of achieving this tolerance.

There are two popular measures for quantitatively determining if a process is capable: process capability ratio (C_p) and process capability index (C_{pk}).

Process Capability Ratio (C_p)

For a process to be capable, its values must fall within upper and lower specifications. This typically means the process capability is within ±3 standard deviations from the process mean. Since this range of values is 6 standard deviations, a capable process tolerance, which is the difference between the upper and lower specifications, must be greater than or equal to 6.

The process capability ratio, C_p, is computed as:

$$C_p = \frac{\text{Upper specification} - \text{Lower specification}}{6\sigma}$$ (13)

Example 6 shows the computation of C_p.

> **Process capability**
> The ability to meet design specifications.

> **Learning Objective**
> 6. Explain process capability and compute C_p and C_{pk}

> **C_p**
> A ratio for determining whether a process meets design specifications; a ratio of the specification to the process variation.

> **EXAMPLE 6**
>
> Process capability ratio (C_p)

In a GE insurance claims process, $\bar{x} = 210.0$ minutes, and $\sigma = .516$ minutes.

The design specification to meet customer expectations is 210 ± 3 minutes. So the Upper Specification is 213 minutes and the lower specification is 207 minutes. The OM manager wants to compute the process capability ratio.

Approach: GE applies Equation (13).

Solution: $C_p = \dfrac{\text{Upper specification} - \text{Lower specification}}{6\sigma} = \dfrac{213 - 207}{6(.516)} = 1.938$

Insight: Since a ratio of 1.00 means that 99.73% of a process's outputs are within specifications, this ratio suggests a very capable process, with nonconformance of less than 4 claims per million.

Learning exercise: If $\sigma = .60$ (instead of .516), what is the new C_p? [Answer: 1.667, a very capable process still.]

Related problems: 26, 27

Active Model S6.2

Example 6 is further illustrated in Active Model S6.2 on the CD-ROM.

A capable process has a C_p of at least 1.0. If the C_p is less than 1.0, the process yields products or services that are outside their allowable tolerance. With a C_p of 1.0, 2.7 parts in 1,000 can be expected to be "out of spec."[5] The higher the process capability ratio, the greater the likelihood

---

[4]See Gerald Smith, *Statistical Process Control and Process Improvement*, 6th ed. (Upper Saddle River, NJ: Prentice Hall, 2007).

[5]This is because a C_p of 1.0 has 99.73% of outputs within specifications. So 1.00 − .9973 = .0027; with 1,000 parts, there are .0027 × 1,000 = 2.7 defects.

For a C_p of 2.0, 99.99966% of outputs are "within spec." So 1.00 − .9999966 = .0000034; with 1 million parts, there are 3.4 defects.

the process will be within design specifications. Many firms have chosen a C_p of 1.33 (a 4-sigma standard) as a target for reducing process variability. This means that only 64 parts per million can be expected to be out of specification.

The concept of *Six Sigma* quality is championed by GE and Motorola. This standard equates to a C_p of 2.0, with only 3.4 defective parts per million (very close to zero defects) instead of the 2.7 parts per 1,000 with 3-sigma limits.

Although C_p relates to the spread (dispersion) of the process output relative to its tolerance, it does not look at how well the process average is centered on the target value.

Process Capability Index (C_{pk})

C_{pk}
A proportion of variation (3σ) between the center of the process and the nearest specification limit.

The process capability index, **C_{pk}**, measures the difference between the desired and actual dimensions of goods or services produced.

The formula for C_{pk} is:

$$C_{pk} = \text{Minimum of} \left[\frac{\text{Upper specification limit} - \bar{X}}{3\sigma}, \frac{\bar{X} - \text{Lower specification limit}}{3\sigma} \right] \quad (14)$$

where $\bar{X}$ = process mean
σ = standard deviation of the process population

When the C_{pk} index for both the upper and lower specification limits equals 1.0, the process variation is centered and the process is capable of producing within ±3 standard deviations (fewer than 2,700 defects per million). A C_{pk} of 2.0 means the process is capable of producing fewer than 3.4 defects per million. For C_{pk} to exceed 1, σ must be less than $\frac{1}{3}$ of the difference between the specification and the process mean ($\bar{X}$). Figure 8 shows the meaning of various measures of C_{pk}, and Example 7 shows an application of C_{pk}.

EXAMPLE 7

Process capability index (C_{pk})

You are the process improvement manager and have developed a new machine to cut insoles for the company's top-of-the-line running shoes. You are excited because the company's goal is no more than 3.4 defects per million and this machine may be the innovation you need. The insoles cannot be more than ±.001 of an inch from the required thickness of .250″. You want to know if you should replace the existing machine, which has a C_{pk} of 1.0.

Approach: You decide to determine the C_{pk}, using Equation (14), for the new machine and make a decision on that basis.

Solution:
Upper specification limit = .251 inch
Lower specification limit = .249 inch

Mean of the new process $\bar{X}$ = .250 inch.
Estimated standard deviation of the new process = σ = .0005 inch.

$$C_{pk} = \text{Minimum of} \left[\frac{\text{Upper specification limit} - \bar{X}}{3\sigma}, \frac{\bar{X} - \text{Lower specification limit}}{3\sigma} \right]$$

$$C_{pk} = \text{Minimum of} \left[\frac{(.251) - .250}{(3).0005}, \frac{.250 - (.249)}{(3).0005} \right]$$

Both calculations result in: $\frac{.001}{.0015} = .67$.

Insight: Because the new machine has a C_{pk} of only 0.67, the new machine should *not* replace the existing machine.

Learning exercise: If the insoles can be ±.002″ (instead of .001″) from the required .250″, what is the new C_{pk}? [Answer: 1.33 and the new machine *should* replace the existing one.]

Related problems: 27, 28, 29, 30, 31

Note that C_p and C_{pk} will be the same when the process is centered. However, if the mean of the process is not centered on the desired (specified) mean, then the smaller numerator in Equation (14) is used (the minimum of the difference between the upper specification limit and the mean or the lower specification limit and the mean). This application of C_{pk} is shown in Solved Problem 4. C_{pk} is the standard criterion used to express process performance.

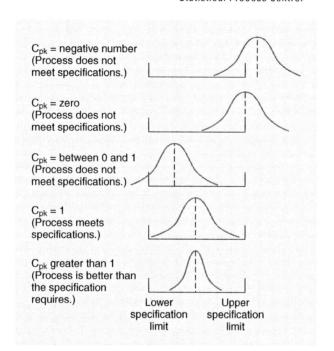

◀ **Figure 8**

Meanings of C_{pk} Measures

A C_{pk} index of 1.0 for both the upper and lower control limits indicates that the process variation is within the upper and lower control limits. As the C_{pk} index goes above 1.0, the process becomes increasingly target-oriented with fewer defects. If the C_{pk} is less than 1.0, the process will not produce within the specified tolerance. Because a process may not be centered, or may "drift," a C_{pk} above 1 is desired.

ACCEPTANCE SAMPLING[6]

Acceptance sampling is a form of testing that involves taking random samples of "lots," or batches, of finished products and measuring them against predetermined standards. Sampling is more economical than 100% inspection. The quality of the sample is used to judge the quality of all items in the lot. Although both attributes and variables can be inspected by acceptance sampling, attribute inspection is more commonly used, as illustrated in this section.

Acceptance sampling can be applied either when materials arrive at a plant or at final inspection, but it is usually used to control incoming lots of purchased products. A lot of items rejected, based on an unacceptable level of defects found in the sample, can (1) be returned to the supplier or (2) be 100% inspected to cull out all defects, with the cost of this screening usually billed to the supplier. However, acceptance sampling is not a substitute for adequate process controls. In fact, the current approach is to build statistical quality controls at suppliers so that acceptance sampling can be eliminated.

Acceptance sampling
A method of measuring random samples of lots or batches of products against predetermined standards.

Learning Objective

7. Explain acceptance sampling

Georgia Institute of Technology

◀ *Flowers Bakery in Villa Rica, Georgia, uses a digital camera to inspect just-baked sandwich buns as they move along the production line. Items that don't measure up in terms of color, shape, seed distribution, or size are identified and removed automatically from the conveyor.*

[6]**Refer to Tutorial 2 on your CD-ROM for an extended discussion of Acceptance Sampling.**

Operating Characteristic Curve

Operating characteristic (OC) curve

A graph that describes how well an acceptance plan discriminates between good and bad lots.

Producer's risk

The mistake of having a producer's good lot rejected through sampling.

Consumer's risk

The mistake of a customer's acceptance of a bad lot overlooked through sampling.

Acceptable quality level (AQL)

The quality level of a lot considered good.

Lot tolerance percent defective (LTPD)

The quality level of a lot considered bad.

The **operating characteristic (OC) curve** describes how well an acceptance plan discriminates between good and bad lots. A curve pertains to a specific plan—that is, to a combination of *n* (sample size) and *c* (acceptance level). It is intended to show the probability that the plan will accept lots of various quality levels.

With acceptance sampling, two parties are usually involved: the producer of the product and the consumer of the product. In specifying a sampling plan, each party wants to avoid costly mistakes in accepting or rejecting a lot. The producer usually has the responsibility of replacing all defects in the rejected lot or of paying for a new lot to be shipped to the customer. The producer, therefore, wants to avoid the mistake of having a good lot rejected (**producer's risk**). On the other hand, the customer or consumer wants to avoid the mistake of accepting a bad lot because defects found in a lot that has already been accepted are usually the responsibility of the customer (**consumer's risk**). The OC curve shows the features of a particular sampling plan, including the risks of making a wrong decision.[7]

Figure 9 can be used to illustrate one sampling plan in more detail. Four concepts are illustrated in this figure.

The **acceptable quality level (AQL)** is the poorest level of quality that we are willing to accept. In other words, we wish to accept lots that have this or a better level of quality, but no lower. If an acceptable quality level is 20 defects in a lot of 1,000 items or parts, then AQL is 20/1,000 = 2% defectives.

The **lot tolerance percent defective (LTPD)** is the quality level of a lot that we consider bad. We wish to reject lots that have this or a poorer level of quality. If it is agreed that an unacceptable quality level is 70 defects in a lot of 1,000, then the LTPD is 70/1,000 = 7% defective.

To derive a sampling plan, producer and consumer must define not only "good lots" and "bad lots" through the AQL and LTPD, but they must also specify risk levels.

Producer's risk (α) is the probability that a "good" lot will be rejected. This is the risk that a random sample might result in a much higher proportion of defects than the population of all items. A lot with an acceptable quality level of AQL still has an α chance of being rejected. Sampling plans are often designed to have the producer's risk set at $\alpha = .05$, or 5%.

▶ **Figure 9**

An Operating Characteristic (OC) Curve Showing Producer's and Consumer's Risks

A good lot for this particular acceptance plan has less than or equal to 2% defectives. A bad lot has 7% or more defectives.

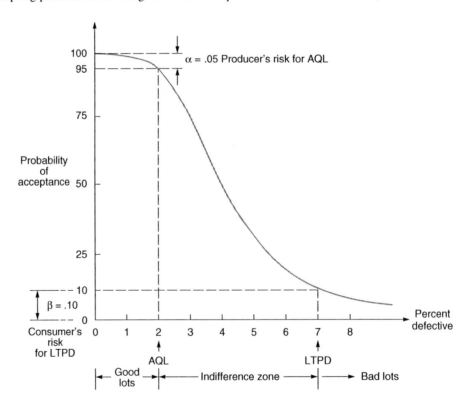

Active Model S6.3

Figure 9 is further illustrated in Active Model S6.3 on the CD.

[7]Note that sampling always runs the danger of leading to an erroneous conclusion. Let us say in one company that the total population under scrutiny is a load of 1,000 computer chips, of which in reality only 30 (or 3%) are defective. This means that we would want to accept the shipment of chips, because for this particular firm 4% is the allowable defect rate. However, if a random sample of *n* = 50 chips was drawn, we could conceivably end up with 0 defects and accept that shipment (that is, it is okay), or we could find all 30 defects in the sample. If the latter happened, we could wrongly conclude that the whole population was 60% defective and reject them all.

Roger Tully, Getty Images Inc.-Stone Allstock

◁ *This laser tracking device, by Faro Technologies, enables quality control personnel to measure and inspect parts and tools during production. The tracker can measure objects from 100 feet away and takes up to 1,000 readings per second.*

Consumer's risk (β) is the probability that a "bad" lot will be accepted. This is the risk that a random sample may result in a lower proportion of defects than the overall population of items. A common value for consumer's risk in sampling plans is β = .10, or 10%.

The probability of rejecting a good lot is called a **type I error**. The probability of accepting a bad lot is a **type II error**.

Sampling plans and OC curves may be developed by computer (as seen in the software available with this text), by published tables, or by calculation, using binomial or Poisson distributions.

Average Outgoing Quality

In most sampling plans, when a lot is rejected, the entire lot is inspected and all defective items replaced. Use of this replacement technique improves the average outgoing quality in terms of percent defective. In fact, given (1) any sampling plan that replaces all defective items encountered and (2) the true incoming percent defective for the lot, it is possible to determine the **average outgoing quality (AOQ)** in percent defective. The equation for AOQ is:

$$\text{AOQ} = \frac{(P_d)(P_a)(N - n)}{N} \tag{15}$$

where
P_d = true percent defective of the lot
P_a = probability of accepting the lot for a given sample size and quantity defective
N = number of items in the lot
n = number of items in the sample

The maximum value of AOQ corresponds to the highest average percent defective or the lowest average quality for the sampling plan. It is called the *average outgoing quality limit (AOQL)*.

Acceptance sampling is useful for screening incoming lots. When the defective parts are replaced with good parts, acceptance sampling helps to increase the quality of the lots by reducing the outgoing percent defective.

Figure 10 compares acceptance sampling, SPC, and C_{pk}. As Figure 10 shows, (a) acceptance sampling by definition accepts some bad units, (b) control charts try to keep the process in control, but (c) the C_{pk} index places the focus on improving the process. As operations managers, that is what we want to do—improve the process.

Type I error
Statistically, the probability of rejecting a good lot.

Type II error
Statistically, the probability of accepting a bad lot.

Average outgoing quality (AOQ)
The percent defective in an average lot of goods inspected through acceptance sampling.

Learning Objective

8. Compute the AOQ

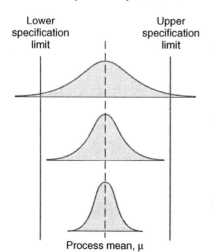

Lower specification limit

Upper specification limit

(a) Acceptance sampling (Some bad units accepted; the "lot" is good or bad.)

(b) Statistical process control (Keep the process "in control.")

(c) $C_{pk} > 1$ (Design a process that is in control.)

Process mean, μ

◁ **Figure 10**

The Application of Statistical Process Techniques Contributes to the Identification and Systematic Reduction of Process Variability

Summary

Statistical process control is a major statistical tool of quality control. Control charts for SPC help operations managers distinguish between natural and assignable variations. The $\bar{x}$-chart and the R-chart are used for variable sampling, and the p-chart and the c-chart for attribute sampling. The C_{pk} index is a way to express process capability. Operating characteristic (OC) curves facilitate acceptance sampling and provide the manager with tools to evaluate the quality of a production run or shipment.

Key Terms

Statistical process control (SPC)
Control chart
Natural variations
Assignable variation
$\bar{x}$-chart
R-chart
Central limit theorem
p-chart

c-chart
Run test
Process capability
C_p
C_p
Acceptance sampling
Operating characteristic (OC) curve
Producer's risk

Consumer's risk
Acceptable quality level (AQL)
Lot tolerance percent defective (LTPD)
Type I error
Type II error
Average outgoing quality (AOQ)

Using Software for

Excel, Excel OM, and POM for Windows may be used to develop control charts for most of the problems in this chapter.

Creating Excel Spreadsheets to Determine Control Limits for a c-Chart

Excel and other spreadsheets are extensively used in industry to maintain control charts. Program 1 is an example of how to use Excel to determine the control limits for a c-chart. C-charts are used when the number of defects per unit of output is known. The data from Example 5 are used. In this example, 54 complaints occurred over 9 days. Excel also contains a built-in graphing ability with Chart Wizard.

▶ **Program 1**

An Excel Spreadsheet for Creating a c-Chart for Example 5

	A	B	C	D	E	F	G	H
1	Red Top Cab Company							
2								
3	Number of samples	9						
4								
5		Complaints		Results				
6	Day 1	3		Total Defects	54			
7	Day 2	0		Defect rate, λ	6			
8	Day 3	8		Standard deviation	2.45			
9	Day 4	9		z value	3			99.73%
10	Day 5	6						
11	Day 6	7		Upper Control Limit	13.348469			
12	Day 7	4		Center Line	6			
13	Day 8	9		Lower Control Limit	0			
14	Day 9	8						

Value	Cell	Excel Formula
Total Defects	E6	=SUM(B6:B14)
Defect rate, λ	E7	=E6/B3
Standard deviation	E8	=SQRT(E7)
Upper Control Limit	E11	=E7+E9*E8
Center Line	E12	=E7
Lower Control Limit	E13	=IF(E7-E9*E8>0,E7-E9*E8,0)

Using Excel OM

Excel OM's Quality Control module has the ability to develop $\bar{x}$-charts, p-charts, and c-charts. It also handles OC curves, acceptance sampling, and process capability. Program 2 illustrates Excel OM's spreadsheet approach to computing the $\bar{x}$ control limits for the Oat Flakes company in Example 1.

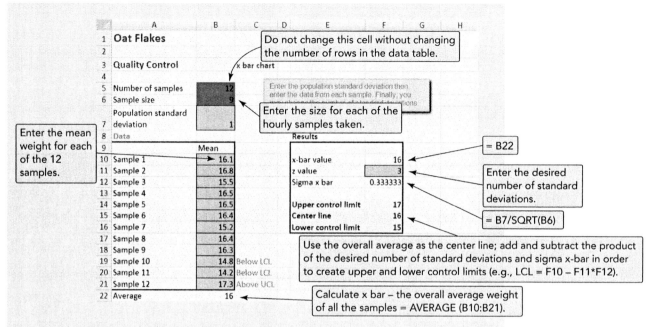

		A	B	C	D	E	F	G	H
1	Oat Flakes								
2									
3	Quality Control		x bar chart						
4									
5	Number of samples		12						
6	Sample size		9						
7	Population standard deviation		1						
8	Data					Results			
9		Mean							
10	Sample 1	16.1				x-bar value	16		
11	Sample 2	16.8				z value	3		
12	Sample 3	15.5				Sigma x bar	0.333333		
13	Sample 4	16.5							
14	Sample 5	16.5				Upper control limit	17		
15	Sample 6	16.4				Center line	16		
16	Sample 7	15.2				Lower control limit	15		
17	Sample 8	16.4							
18	Sample 9	16.3							
19	Sample 10	14.8	Below LCL						
20	Sample 11	14.2	Below LCL						
21	Sample 12	17.3	Above UCL						
22	Average	16							

Callouts: "Do not change this cell without changing the number of rows in the data table." — "Enter the population standard deviation then enter the data from each sample. Finally, you ..." — "Enter the size for each of the hourly samples taken." — "Enter the mean weight for each of the 12 samples." — "= B22" — "Enter the desired number of standard deviations." — "= B7/SQRT(B6)" — "Use the overall average as the center line; add and subtract the product of the desired number of standard deviations and sigma x-bar in order to create upper and lower control limits (e.g., LCL = F10 – F11*F12)." — "Calculate x bar – the overall average weight of all the samples = AVERAGE (B10:B21)."

▲ **Program 2**   **Excel OM Input and Selected Formulas for the Oat Flakes Example 1**

P Using POM for Windows

The POM for Windows Quality Control module has the ability to compute all the SPC control charts we introduced in this supplement, as well as OC curves, acceptance sampling, and process capability. See Appendix: Using Excel OM and POM for Windows for further details.

Solved Problems

 Virtual Office Hours help is available on Student DVD.

Solved Problem 1

A manufacturer of precision machine parts produces round shafts for use in the construction of drill presses. The average diameter of a shaft is .56 inch. Inspection samples contain 6 shafts each. The average range of these samples is .006 inch. Determine the upper and lower $\bar{x}$ control chart limits.

Solution

The mean factor A_2 from Table 1 where the sample size is 6, is seen to be .483. With this factor, you can obtain the upper and lower control limits:

$$\text{UCL}_{\bar{x}} = .56 + (.483)(.006)$$
$$= .56 + .0029$$
$$= .5629 \text{ inch}$$
$$\text{LCL}_{\bar{x}} = .56 - .0029$$
$$= .5571 \text{ inch}$$

Solved Problem 2

Nocaf Drinks, Inc., a producer of decaffeinated coffee, bottles Nocaf. Each bottle should have a net weight of 4 ounces. The machine that fills the bottles with coffee is new, and the operations manager wants to make sure that it is properly adjusted. Bonnie Crutcher, the operations manager, randomly selects and weighs $n = 8$ bottles and records the average and range in ounces for each sample. The data for several samples is given in the following table. Note that every sample consists of 8 bottles.

Sample	Sample Range	Sample Average	Sample	Sample Range	Sample Average
A	.41	4.00	E	.56	4.17
B	.55	4.16	F	.62	3.93
C	.44	3.99	G	.54	3.98
D	.48	4.00	H	.44	4.01

Is the machine properly adjusted and in control?

225

Solution

We first find that $\bar{\bar{x}} = 4.03$ and $\bar{R} = .505$. Then, using Table 1, we find:

$$\text{UCL}_{\bar{x}} = \bar{\bar{x}} + A_2\bar{R} = 4.03 + (.373)(.505) = 4.22$$

$$\text{LCL}_{\bar{x}} = \bar{\bar{x}} - A_2\bar{R} = 4.03 - (.373)(.505) = 3.84$$

$$\text{UCL}_R = D_4\bar{R} = (1.864)(.505) = .94$$

$$\text{LCL}_R = D_3\bar{R} = (.136)(.505) = .07$$

It appears that the process average and range are both in statistical control.

The operations manager needs to determine if a process with a mean (4.03) slightly above the desired mean of 4.00 is satisfactory; if it is not, the process will need to be changed.

Solved Problem 3

Altman Distributors, Inc., fills catalog orders. Samples of size $n = 100$ orders have been taken each day over the past six weeks. The average defect rate was .05. Determine the upper and lower limits for this process for 99.73% confidence.

Solution

$z = 3$, $\bar{p} = .05$. Using Equations 9, 10, and 11,

$$\text{UCL}_p = \bar{p} + 3\sqrt{\frac{\bar{p}(1-\bar{p})}{n}} = .05 + 3\sqrt{\frac{(.05)(1-.05)}{100}}$$

$$= .05 + 3(0.0218) = .1154$$

$$\text{LCL}_p = \bar{p} - 3\sqrt{\frac{\bar{p}(1-\bar{p})}{n}} = .05 - 3(.0218)$$

$$= .05 - .0654 = 0 \text{ (because percent defective cannot be negative)}$$

Solved Problem 4

Ettlie Engineering has a new catalyst injection system for your countertop production line. Your process engineering department has conducted experiments and determined that the mean is 8.01 grams with a standard deviation of .03. Your specifications are:

$\mu = 8.0$ and $\sigma = .04$, which means an upper specification limit of 8.12 [= 8.0 + 3(.04)] and a lower specification limit of 7.88 [= 8.0 − 3(.04)].

What is the C_{pk} performance of the injection system?

Solution

Using Equation (14):

$$C_{pk} = \text{Minimum of} \left[\frac{\text{Upper specification limit} - \bar{X}}{3\sigma}, \frac{\bar{X} - \text{Lower specification limit}}{3\sigma} \right]$$

where
$\bar{X}$ = process mean
σ = standard deviation of the process population

$$C_{pk} = \text{minimum of} \left[\frac{8.12 - 8.01}{(3)(.03)}, \frac{8.01 - 7.88}{(3)(.03)} \right]$$

$$\left[\frac{.11}{.09} = 1.22, \frac{.13}{.09} = 1.44 \right]$$

The minimum is 1.22, so the C_{pk} of 1.22 is within specifications and has an implied error rate of less than 2,700 defects per million.

Active Model Exercise

This Active Model, as well as Active Models S6.2 and S6.3, appears on your CD. Active Model S6.1 allows you to evaluate important elements in the *p*-charts.

Questions

1. Has the process been in control?

2. Suppose we use a 95 percent *p*-chart. What are the upper and lower control limits? Has the process gotten more out of control?

p-Chart

Reset Data	Questions

Number of samples	20
Sample size	100
z value	3.0000
Confidence	99.73%

Total Sample Size	2000	Upper Control Limit	0.10
Total Defects	80	Center Line	0.04
Percentage defects	0.04	Lower Control Limit	0.00
Std dev of p-bar	0.019596		

	# Defects	Fraction Defective
Sample 1	6	0.06
Sample 2	5	0.05
Sample 3	0	0.00
Sample 4	1	0.01
Sample 5	4	0.04
Sample 6	2	0.02
Sample 7	5	0.05
Sample 8	3	0.03
Sample 9	3	0.03
Sample 10	2	0.02
Sample 11	6	0.06
Sample 12	1	0.01
Sample 13	8	0.08
Sample 14	7	0.07
Sample 15	5	0.05
Sample 16	4	0.04
Sample 17	11	0.11 Above UCL
Sample 18	3	0.03
Sample 19	0	0.00
Sample 20	4	0.04

◄ Active Model S6.1

p-Chart for the Mosier Data Systems in Example 4.

3. Suppose that the sample size used was actually 120 instead of the 100 that it was supposed to be. How would this affect the chart?

4. What happens to the chart as we reduce the *z*-value?

5. What happens to the chart as we reduce the percentage defects?

Self-Test

- ***Before taking the self-test,*** *refer to the learning objectives listed at the beginning of the selection and the key terms listed at the end of the supplement.*
- *Use the key at the back of the text to* ***correct*** *your answers.*
- ***Restudy*** *pages that correspond to any questions you answered incorrectly or material you feel uncertain about.*

1. The type of chart used to control the central tendency of variables with continuous dimensions is:
   a) $\bar{x}$-bar chart
   b) *R*-chart
   c) *p*-chart
   d) *c*-chart
   e) none of the above

2. Control charts for attributes are:
   a) *p*-charts
   b) *c*-charts
   c) *R*-charts
   d) $\bar{x}$-charts
   e) all of the above

3. If parts in a sample are measured and the mean of the sample measurement is outside the tolerance limits:
   a) the process is out of control, and the cause should be established
   b) the process is in control, but not capable of producing within the established control limits
   c) the process is within the established control limits with only natural causes of variation
   d) all of the above are true

4. If *parts* in a sample are measured and the mean of the sample measurement is in the middle of the tolerance limits but some parts measure outside the control limits:
   a) the process is in control, with only assignable causes of variation
   b) the process is not producing within the established control limits
   c) the process is within the established control limits with only natural causes of variation
   d) the process has both natural and assignable causes of variation

5. If a 95.45% level of confidence is desired, the $\bar{x}$-chart limits will be set plus or minus _____.

6. The two techniques discussed to find and resolve assignable variations in process control are the _____ and the _____.

7. The _____ risk is the probability that a lot will be rejected despite the quality level exceeding or meeting the _____.

8. The ability of a process to meet design specifications is called:
   a) Taguchi
   b) process capability
   c) capability index
   d) acceptance sampling
   e) average outgoing quality

Internet and Student CD-ROM/DVD Exercises

Visit our Companion Web site or use your student CD-ROM/DVD to help with material in this supplement.

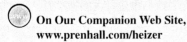 **On Our Companion Web Site,**
www.prenhall.com/heizer
- Self-Study Quizzes
- Practice Problems
- Virtual Company Tour
- Internet Case Study
- PowerPoint Lecture

On Your Student CD-ROM
- Practice Problems
- Active Model Exercises
- Excel OM Software
- Excel OM Data Files
- POM for Windows

On Your Student DVD
- Video Clips and Video Case Study
- Virtual Office Hours for Solved Problems

Discussion Questions

1. List Shewhart's two types of variation. What are they also called?
2. Define "in statistical control."
3. Explain briefly what an $\bar{x}$-chart and an R-chart do.
4. What might cause a process to be out of control?
5. List five steps in developing and using $\bar{x}$-charts and R-charts.
6. List some possible causes of assignable variation.
7. Explain how a person using 2-sigma control charts will more easily find samples "out of bounds" than 3-sigma control charts. What are some possible consequences of this fact?
8. When is the desired mean, μ, used in establishing the centerline of a control chart instead of $\bar{\bar{x}}$?
9. Can a production process be labeled as "out of control" because it is too good? Explain.

10. In a control chart, what would be the effect on the control limits if the sample size varied from one sample to the next?
11. Define C_{pk} and explain what a C_{pk} of 1.0 means. What is C_p?
12. What does a run of 5 points above or below the centerline in a control chart imply?
13. What are the acceptable quality level (AQL) and the lot tolerance percent defective (LTPD)? How are they used?
14. What is a run test and when is it used?
15. Discuss the managerial issues regarding the use of control charts.
16. What is an OC curve?
17. What is the purpose of acceptance sampling?
18. What two risks are present when acceptance sampling is used?
19. Is a *capable* process a *perfect* process? That is, does a capable process generate only output that meets specifications? Explain.

Problems*

• 1 Boxes of Organic Flakes are produced to contain 14 ounces, with a standard deviation of .1 ounce. Set up the 3-sigma $\bar{x}$-chart for a sample size of 36 boxes. **P✕**

• 2 The overall average on a process you are attempting to monitor is 50 units. The process standard deviation is 1.72. Determine the upper and lower control limits for a mean chart, if you choose to use a sample size of 5. Set $z = 3$. **P✕**

• 3 Thirty-five samples of size 7 each were taken from a fertilizer-bag-filling machine. The results were: Overall mean = 57.75 lb; Average range = 1.78 lb.
a) Determine the upper and lower control limits of the $\bar{x}$-chart, where $\sigma = 3$.
b) Determine the upper and lower control limits of the R-chart, where $\sigma = 3$. **P✕**

• 4 Pioneer Chicken advertises "lite" chicken with 30% fewer calories than standard chicken. When the process for "lite" chicken breast production is in control, the average chicken breast contains 420 calories, and the standard deviation in caloric content of the chicken breast population is 25 calories.

Pioneer wants to design an $\bar{x}$-chart to monitor the caloric content of chicken breasts, where 25 chicken breasts would be chosen at random to form each sample. What are the lower and upper con-

trol limits for this chart if these limits are chosen to be *four* standard deviations from the target? **P✕**

• 5 Cordelia Barrera is attempting to monitor a filling process that has an overall average of 705 cc. The average range is 6 cc. If you use a sample size of 10, what are the upper and lower control limits for the mean and range? **P✕**

•• 6 Sampling 4 pieces of precision-cut wire (to be used in computer assembly) every hour for the past 24 hours has produced the following results:

Hour	$\bar{x}$	R	Hour	$\bar{x}$	R
1	3.25"	.71"	13	3.11"	.85"
2	3.10	1.18	14	2.83	1.31
3	3.22	1.43	15	3.12	1.06
4	3.39	1.26	16	2.84	.50
5	3.07	1.17	17	2.86	1.43
6	2.86	.32	18	2.74	1.29
7	3.05	.53	19	3.41	1.61
8	2.65	1.13	20	2.89	1.09
9	3.02	.71	21	2.65	1.08
10	2.85	1.33	22	3.28	.46
11	2.83	1.17	23	2.94	1.58
12	2.97	.40	24	2.64	.97

Develop appropriate control charts and determine whether there is any cause for concern in the cutting process. Plot the information and look for patterns. **P✕**

Note: **P✕** means the problem may be solved with POM for Windows and/or Excel OM/Excel.

•• 7 Auto pistons at Yongpin Zhou's plant in Shanghai are produced in a forging process, and the diameter is a critical factor that must be controlled. From sample sizes of 10 pistons produced each day, the mean and the range of this diameter have been as follows:

Day	Mean (mm)	Range (mm)
1	156.9	4.2
2	153.2	4.6
3	153.6	4.1
4	155.5	5.0
5	156.6	4.5

Construct the 3-sigma $\bar{x}$-chart and the 3-sigma R-chart for this dimension, using the data observed in the table above. **P**✕

•• 8 Bill Kime's bowling ball factory makes bowling balls of adult size and weight only. The standard deviation in the weight of a bowling ball produced at the factory is known to be 0.12 pounds. Each day for 24 days, the average weight, in pounds, of nine of the bowling balls produced that day has been assessed as follows:

Day	Average (lb)	Day	Average (lb)
1	16.3	13	16.3
2	15.9	14	15.9
3	15.8	15	16.3
4	15.5	16	16.2
5	16.3	17	16.1
6	16.2	18	15.9
7	16.0	19	16.2
8	16.1	20	15.9
9	15.9	21	15.9
10	16.2	22	16.0
11	15.9	23	15.5
12	15.9	24	15.8

Establish a control chart for monitoring the average weights of the bowling balls in which the upper and lower control limits are each two standard deviations from the mean. What are the values of the control limits? **P**✕

•• 9 Whole Grains LLC uses statistical process control to ensure that its health-conscious, low-fat, multigrain sandwich loaves have the proper weight. Based on a previously stable and in-control process, the control limits of the $\bar{x}$- and R-charts are: $UCL_{\bar{x}} = 6.56$, $LCL_{\bar{x}} = 5.84$, $UCL_R = 1.141$, $LCL_R = 0$. Over the past few days, they have taken five random samples of four loaves each and have found the following:

	Net Weight			
Sample	Loaf #1	Loaf #2	Loaf #3	Loaf #4
1	6.3	6.0	5.9	5.9
2	6.0	6.0	6.3	5.9
3	6.3	4.8	5.6	5.2
4	6.2	6.0	6.2	5.9
5	6.5	6.6	6.5	6.9

Is the process still in control? **P**✕

••• 10 A process that is considered to be in control measures an ingredient in ounces. Below are the last 10 samples (each of size $n = 5$) taken. The population standard deviation is 1.36.

	Samples									
1	**2**	**3**	**4**	**5**	**6**	**7**	**8**	**9**	**10**
10	9	13	10	12	10	10	13	8	10
9	9	9	10	10	10	11	10	8	12
10	11	10	11	9	8	10	8	12	9
9	11	10	10	11	12	8	10	12	8
12	10	9	10	10	9	9	8	9	12

a) What is the process standard deviation σ? What is $\sigma_{\bar{x}}$?
b) If $z = 3$, what are the control limits for the mean chart?
c) What are the control limits for the range chart?
d) Is the process in control? **P**✕

••• 11 Twelve samples, each containing five parts, were taken from a process that produces steel rods. The length of each rod in the samples was determined. The results were tabulated and sample means and ranges were computed. The results were:

Sample	Sample Mean (in.)	Range (in.)
1	10.002	0.011
2	10.002	0.014
3	9.991	0.007
4	10.006	0.022
5	9.997	0.013
6	9.999	0.012
7	10.001	0.008
8	10.005	0.013
9	9.995	0.004
10	10.001	0.011
11	10.001	0.014
12	10.006	0.009

Determine the upper and lower control limits and the overall means for $\bar{x}$-charts and R-charts. Draw the chart and plot the values of the sample means and ranges. Do the data indicate a process that is in control? Why or why not? **P**✕

•• 12 Eagletrons are all-electric automobiles produced by Mogul Motors, Inc. One of the concerns of Mogul Motors is that the Eagletrons be capable of achieving appropriate maximum speeds. To monitor this, Mogul executives take samples of eight Eagletrons at a time. For each sample, they determine the average maximum speed and the range of the maximum speeds within the sample. They repeat this with 35 samples to obtain 35 sample means and 35 ranges. They find that the average sample mean is 88.50 miles per hour, and the average range is 3.25 miles per hour. Using these results, the executives decide to establish an R chart. They would like this chart to be established so that when it shows that the range of a sample is not within the control limits, there is only approximately a 0.0027 probability that this is due to natural variation. What will be the upper control limit (UCL) and the lower control limit (LCL) in this chart? **P**✕

• 13 The defect rate for data entry of insurance claims has historically been about 1.5%. What are the upper and lower control chart limits if you wish to use a sample size of 100 and 3-sigma limits? **P**✕

•• 14 You are attempting to develop a quality monitoring system for some parts purchased from Charles Sox Manufacturing Co. These parts are either good or defective. You have decided to take a sample of 100 units. Develop a table of the appropriate upper and lower control chart limits for various values of the average fraction defective in the samples taken. The values for $\bar{p}$ in this table should range from 0.02 to 0.10 in increments of 0.02. Develop the upper and lower control limits for a 99.73% confidence level.

n = 100		
$\bar{p}$	UCL	LCL
0.02		
0.04		
0.06		
0.08		
0.10		

•• 15 The results of inspection of DNA samples taken over the past 10 days are given below. Sample size is 100.

Day	1	2	3	4	5	6	7	8	9	10
Defectives	7	6	6	9	5	6	0	8	9	1

a) Construct a 3-sigma p-chart using this information.
b) If the number of defectives on the next three days are 12, 5, and 13, is the process in control?

• 16 In the past, the defect rate for your product has been 1.5%. What are the upper and lower control chart limits if you wish to use a sample size of 500 and $z = 3$?

• 17 Refer to Problem 16. If the defect rate was 3.5% instead of 1.5%, what would be the control limits ($z = 3$)?

•• 18 Five data entry operators work at the data processing department of the Georgia Bank. Each day for 30 days, the number of defective records in a sample of 250 records typed by these operators has been noted, as follows:

Sample No.	No. Defective	Sample No.	No. Defective	Sample No.	No. Defective
1	7	11	18	21	17
2	5	12	5	22	12
3	19	13	16	23	6
4	10	14	4	24	7
5	11	15	11	25	13
6	8	16	8	26	10
7	12	17	12	27	14
8	9	18	4	28	6
9	6	19	6	29	12
10	13	20	16	30	3

Establish 3σ upper and lower control limits.

•• 19 Detroit Central Hospital is trying to improve its image by providing a positive experience for its patients and their relatives. Part of the "image" program involves providing tasty, inviting patient meals that are also healthful. A questionnaire accompanies each meal served, asking the patient, among other things, whether he or she is satisfied or unsatisfied with the meal. A 100-patient sample of the survey results over the past 7 days yielded the following data:

Day	No. of Unsatisfied Patients	Sample Size
1	24	100
2	22	100
3	8	100
4	15	100
5	10	100
6	26	100
7	17	100

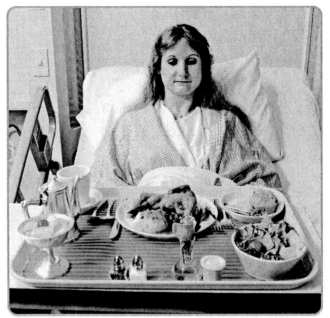

Corbis Digital Stock

Construct a p-chart that plots the percentage of patients unsatisfied with their meals. Set the control limits to include 99.73% of the random variation in meal satisfaction. Comment on your results.

•• 20 Chicago Supply Company manufactures paper clips and other office products. Although inexpensive, paper clips have provided the firm with a high margin of profitability. Samples of 200 are taken. Results are given for the last 10 samples. Establish upper and lower control limits for the control chart and graph the data. Is the process in control?

Sample	1	2	3	4	5	6	7	8	9	10
Defectives	5	7	4	4	6	3	5	6	2	8

• 21 Peter Ittig's department store, Ittig Brothers, is Amherst's largest independent clothier. The store receives an average of six returns per day. Using $z = 3$, would nine returns in a day warrant action?

•• 22 An ad agency tracks the complaints, by week received, about the billboards in its city:

Week	No. of Complaints
1	4
2	5
3	4
4	11
5	3
6	9

a) What type of control chart would you use to monitor this process and why?
b) What are the 3-sigma control limits for this process? Assume that the historical complaint rate is unknown.
c) Is the process mean in control, according to the control limits? Why or why not?
d) Assume now that the historical complaint rate has been 4 calls a week. What would the 3-sigma control limits for this process be now? Is the process in control according to the control limits?

230

• • 23 The school board is trying to evaluate a new math program introduced to second-graders in five elementary schools across the county this year. A sample of the student scores on standardized math tests in each elementary school yielded the following data:

School	No. of Test Errors
A	52
B	27
C	35
D	44
E	55

Construct a c-chart for test errors, and set the control limits to contain 99.73% of the random variation in test scores. What does the chart tell you? Has the new math program been effective? **P✗**

• • 24 Telephone inquiries of 100 IRS "customers" are monitored daily at random. Incidents of incorrect information or other nonconformities (such as impoliteness to customers) are recorded. The data for last week follow:

Day	No. of Nonconformities
1	5
2	10
3	23
4	20
5	15

Construct a 3-standard deviation c-chart of nonconformities. What does the control chart tell you about the IRS telephone operators? **P✗**

• • • 25 The accounts receivable department at Rick Wing Manufacturing has been having difficulty getting customers to pay the full amount of their bills. Many customers complain that the bills are not correct and do not reflect the materials that arrived at their receiving docks. The department has decided to implement SPC in its billing process. To set up control charts, 10 samples of 50 bills each were taken over a month's time and the items on the bills checked against the bill of lading sent by the company's shipping department to determine the number of bills that were not correct. The results were:

Sample No.	No. of Incorrect Bills	Sample No.	No. of Incorrect Bills
1	6	6	5
2	5	7	3
3	11	8	4
4	4	9	7
5	0	10	2

a) Determine the value of p-bar, the mean fraction defective. Then determine the control limits for the p-chart using a 99.73% confidence level (3 standard deviations). Is this process in control? If not, which sample(s) were out of control?
b) How might you use the quality tools discussed in Chapter 6 to determine the source of the billing defects and where you might start your improvement efforts to eliminate the causes? **P✗**

• 26 The difference between the upper specification and the lower specification for a process is 0.6″. The standard deviation is 0.1″. What is the process capability ratio, C_p? Interpret this number. **P✗**

• • 27 Meena Chavan Corp.'s computer chip production process yields DRAM chips with an average life of 1,800 hours and $\sigma = 100$ hours. The tolerance upper and lower specification limits are 2,400 hours and 1,600 hours, respectively. Is this process capable of producing DRAM chips to specification? **P✗**

• • 28 Blackburn, Inc., an equipment manufacturer in Nashville, has submitted a sample cutoff valve to improve your manufacturing process. Your process engineering department has conducted experiments and found that the valve has a mean (μ) of 8.00 and a standard deviation (σ) of .04. Your desired performance is $\mu = 8.0$ and $\sigma = .045$. What is the C_{pk} of the Blackburn valve? **P✗**

• • 29 The specifications for a plastic liner for concrete highway projects calls for a thickness of 3.0 mm ±.1 mm. The standard deviation of the process is estimated to be .02 mm. What are the upper and lower specification limits for this product? The process is known to operate at a mean thickness of 3.0 mm. What is the C_{pk} for this process? About what percentage of all units of this liner will meet specifications? **P✗**

• • 30 The manager of a food processing plant desires a quality specification with a mean of 16 ounces, an upper specification limit of 16.5, and a lower specification limit of 15.5. The process has a mean of 16 ounces and a standard deviation of 1 ounce. Determine the C_{pk} of the process. **P✗**

• • 31 A process filling small bottles with baby formula has a target of 3 ounces ±0.150 ounce. Two hundred bottles from the process were sampled. The results showed the average amount of formula placed in the bottles to be 3.042 ounces. The standard deviation of the amounts was 0.034 ounce. Determine the value of C_{pk}. Roughly what proportion of bottles meet the specifications? **P✗**

• • • 32 As the supervisor in charge of shipping and receiving, you need to determine *the average outgoing quality* in a plant where the known incoming lots from your assembly line have an average defective rate of 3%. Your plan is to sample 80 units of every 1,000 in a lot. The number of defects in the sample is not to exceed 3. Such a plan provides you with a probability of acceptance of each lot of .79 (79%). What is your average outgoing quality? **P✗**

• • • 33 An acceptance sampling plan has lots of 500 pieces and a sample size of 60. The number of defects in the sample may not exceed 2. This plan, based on an OC curve, has a probability of .57 of accepting lots when the incoming lots have a defective rate of 4%, which is the historical average for this process. What do you tell your customer the average outgoing quality is? **P✗**

• • • • 34 West Battery Corp. has recently been receiving complaints from retailers that its 9-volt batteries are not lasting as long as other name brands. James West, head of the TQM program at West's Austin plant, believes there is no problem because his batteries have had an average life of 50 hours, about 10% longer than competitors' models. To raise the lifetime above this level would require a new level of technology not available to West. Nevertheless, he is concerned enough to set up hourly assembly line checks. Previously, after ensuring that the process was running properly, West took size-5 samples of 9-volt batteries for each of 25 hours to establish the standards for control chart limits. Those 25 samples are shown in the following table:

West Battery Data—Battery Lifetimes (in hours)

Hour	Sample 1	2	3	4	5	$\bar{x}$	R
1	51	50	49	50	50	50.0	2
2	45	47	70	46	36	48.8	34
3	50	35	48	39	47	43.8	15
4	55	70	50	30	51	51.2	40
5	49	38	64	36	47	46.8	28
6	59	62	40	54	64	55.8	24
7	36	33	49	48	56	44.4	23
8	50	67	53	43	40	50.6	27
9	44	52	46	47	44	46.6	8
10	70	45	50	47	41	50.6	29
11	57	54	62	45	36	50.8	26
12	56	54	47	42	62	52.2	20
13	40	70	58	45	44	51.4	30
14	52	58	40	52	46	49.6	18
15	57	42	52	58	59	53.6	17
16	62	49	42	33	55	48.2	29
17	40	39	49	59	48	47.0	20
18	64	50	42	57	50	52.6	22
19	58	53	52	48	50	52.2	10

Hour	Sample 1	2	3	4	5	$\bar{x}$	R
20	60	50	41	41	50	48.4	19
21	52	47	48	58	40	49.0	18
22	55	40	56	49	45	49.0	16
23	47	48	50	50	48	48.6	3
24	50	50	49	51	51	50.2	2
25	51	50	51	51	62	53.0	12

With these limits established, West now takes 5 more hours of data, which are shown in the following table:

Hour	Sample 1	2	3	4	5
26	48	52	39	57	61
27	45	53	48	46	66
28	63	49	50	45	53
29	57	70	45	52	61
30	45	38	46	54	52

a) Determine means and the upper and lower control limits for $\bar{x}$ and R (using the first 25 hours only).
b) Is the manufacturing process in control?
c) Comment on the lifetimes observed. **Px**

Case Studies

Bayfield Mud Company

In November 2007, John Wells, a customer service representative of Bayfield Mud Company, was summoned to the Houston warehouse of Wet-Land Drilling, Inc., to inspect three boxcars of mud-treating agents that Bayfield had shipped to the Houston firm. (Bayfield's corporate offices and its largest plant are located in Orange, Texas, which is just west of the Louisiana–Texas border.) Wet-Land had filed a complaint that the 50-pound bags of treating agents just received from Bayfield were short-weight by approximately 5%.

The short-weight bags were initially detected by one of Wet-Land's receiving clerks, who noticed that the railroad scale tickets indicated that net weights were significantly less on all three boxcars than those of identical shipments received on October 25, 2007. Bayfield's traffic department was called to determine if lighter-weight pallets were used on the shipments. (This might explain the lighter net weights.) Bayfield indicated, however, that no changes had been made in loading or palletizing procedures. Thus, Wet-Land engineers randomly checked 50 bags and discovered that the average net weight was 47.51 pounds. They noted from past shipments that the process yielded bag net weights averaging exactly 50.0 pounds, with an acceptable standard deviation σ of 1.2 pounds. Consequently, they concluded that the sample indicated a significant short-weight. (The reader may wish to verify this conclusion.) Bayfield was then contacted, and Wells was sent to investigate the complaint. Upon arrival, Wells verified the complaint and issued a 5% credit to Wet-Land.

Wet-Land management, however, was not completely satisfied with the issuance of credit. The charts followed by their mud engineers on the drilling platforms were based on 50-pound bags of

treating agents. Lighter-weight bags might result in poor chemical control during the drilling operation and thus adversely affect drilling efficiency. (Mud-treating agents are used to control the pH and other chemical properties of the core during drilling operation.) This defect could cause severe economic consequences because of the extremely high cost of oil and natural gas well-drilling operations. Consequently, special-use instructions had to accompany the delivery of these shipments to the drilling platforms. Moreover, the short-weight shipments had to be isolated in Wet-Land's warehouse, causing extra handling and poor space utilization. Thus, Wells was informed that Wet-Land might seek a new supplier of mud-treating agents if, in the future, it received bags that deviated significantly from 50 pounds.

The quality control department at Bayfield suspected that the lightweight bags might have resulted from "growing pains" at the Orange plant. Because of the earlier energy crisis, oil and natural gas exploration activity had greatly increased. In turn, this increased activity created increased demand for products produced by related industries, including drilling muds. Consequently, Bayfield had to expand from a one-shift (6:00 A.M. to 2:00 P.M.) to a two-shift (2:00 P.M. to 10:00 P.M.) operation in mid-2005, and finally to a three-shift operation (24 hours per day) in the fall of 2007.

The additional night-shift bagging crew was staffed entirely by new employees. The most experienced foremen were temporarily assigned to supervise the night-shift employees. Most emphasis was placed on increasing the output of bags to meet ever-increasing demand. It was suspected that only occasional reminders were made to double-check the bag weight-feeder. (A double-check is per-

Time	Average Weight (pounds)	Range Smallest	Range Largest	Time	Average Weight (pounds)	Range Smallest	Range Largest
6:00 A.M.	49.6	48.7	50.7	6:00	46.8	41.0	51.2
7:00	50.2	49.1	51.2	7:00	50.0	46.2	51.7
8:00	50.6	49.6	51.4	8:00	47.4	44.0	48.7
9:00	50.8	50.2	51.8	9:00	47.0	44.2	48.9
10:00	49.9	49.2	52.3	10:00	47.2	46.6	50.2
11:00	50.3	48.6	51.7	11:00	48.6	47.0	50.0
12 Noon	48.6	46.2	50.4	12 Midnight	49.8	48.2	50.4
1:00 P.M.	49.0	46.4	50.0	1:00 A.M.	49.6	48.4	51.7
2:00	49.0	46.0	50.6	2:00	50.0	49.0	52.2
3:00	49.8	48.2	50.8	3:00	50.0	49.2	50.0
4:00	50.3	49.2	52.7	4:00	47.2	46.3	50.5
5:00	51.4	50.0	55.3	5:00	47.0	44.1	49.7
6:00	51.6	49.2	54.7	6:00	48.4	45.0	49.0
7:00	51.8	50.0	55.6	7:00	48.8	44.8	49.7
8:00	51.0	48.6	53.2	8:00	49.6	48.0	51.8
9:00	50.5	49.4	52.4	9:00	50.0	48.1	52.7
10:00	49.2	46.1	50.7	10:00	51.0	48.1	55.2
11:00	49.0	46.3	50.8	11:00	50.4	49.5	54.1
12 Midnight	48.4	45.4	50.2	12 Noon	50.0	48.7	50.9
1:00 A.M.	47.6	44.3	49.7	1:00 P.M.	48.9	47.6	51.2
2:00	47.4	44.1	49.6	2:00	49.8	48.4	51.0
3:00	48.2	45.2	49.0	3:00	49.8	48.8	50.8
4:00	48.0	45.5	49.1	4:00	50.0	49.1	50.6
5:00	48.4	47.1	49.6	5:00	47.8	45.2	51.2
6:00	48.6	47.4	52.0	6:00	46.4	44.0	49.7
7:00	50.0	49.2	52.2	7:00	46.4	44.4	50.0
8:00	49.8	49.0	52.4	8:00	47.2	46.6	48.9
9:00	50.3	49.4	51.7	9:00	48.4	47.2	49.5
10:00	50.2	49.6	51.8	10:00	49.2	48.1	50.7
11:00	50.0	49.0	52.3	11:00	48.4	47.0	50.8
12 Noon	50.0	48.8	52.4	12 Midnight	47.2	46.4	49.2
1:00 P.M.	50.1	49.4	53.6	1:00 A.M.	47.4	46.8	49.0
2:00	49.7	48.6	51.0	2:00	48.8	47.2	51.4
3:00	48.4	47.2	51.7	3:00	49.6	49.0	50.6
4:00	47.2	45.3	50.9	4:00	51.0	50.5	51.5
5:00	46.8	44.1	49.0	5:00	50.5	50.0	51.9

formed by systematically weighing a bag on a scale to determine if the proper weight is being loaded by the weight-feeder. If there is significant deviation from 50 pounds, corrective adjustments are made to the weight-release mechanism.)

To verify this expectation, the quality control staff randomly sampled the bag output and prepared the chart above. Six bags were sampled and weighed each hour.

Discussion Questions

1. What is your analysis of the bag-weight problem?
2. What procedures would you recommend to maintain proper quality control?

Source: Professor Jerry Kinard, Western Carolina University.

Alabama Airlines's On-Time Schedule

Alabama Airlines opened its doors in December 2001 as a commuter service with its headquarters and only hub located in Birmingham. A product of airline deregulation, Alabama Air joined the growing number of short-haul, point-to-point airlines, including Lone Star, Comair, Atlantic Southeast, and Skywest.

Alabama Air was started and managed by two former pilots, David Douglas (who had been with now-defunct Midway Airlines) and Michael Hanna (formerly with Continental). It acquired a fleet of 12 used prop-jet planes and the airport gates vacated by Delta Airlines in 2001 when it curtailed flights due to the terrorist attacks of 9/11.

One of Alabama Air's top competitive priorities is on-time arrivals. The airline defines "on-time" to mean any arrival that is within 20 minutes of the scheduled time.

Mike Hanna decided to personally monitor Alabama Air's performance. Each week for the past 30 weeks, Hanna checked a random sample of 100 flight arrivals for on-time performance. The table that follows contains the number of flights that did not meet Alabama Air's definition of on time:

Sample (week)	Late Flights	Sample (week)	Late Flights
1	2	16	2
2	4	17	3
3	10	18	7
4	4	19	3
5	1	20	2
6	1	21	3
7	13	22	7
8	9	23	4
9	11	24	3
10	0	25	2
11	3	26	2
12	4	27	0
13	2	28	1
14	2	29	3
15	8	30	4

Discussion Questions

1. Using a 95% confidence level, plot the overall percentage of late flights (p) and the upper and lower control limits on a control chart.
2. Assume that the airline industry's upper and lower control limits for flights that are not on time are .1000 and .0400, respectively. Draw them on your control chart.
3. Plot the percentage of late flights in each sample. Do all samples fall within Alabama Airlines's control limits? When one falls outside the control limits, what should be done?
4. What can Mike Hanna report about the quality of service?

Farm to Fork: Quality at Darden Restaurants

Video Case

Darden Restaurants, the $5.2 billion owner of such popular brands as Olive Garden, Red Lobster, Seasons 52, and Bahama Breeze, serves more than 300 million meals annually in its 1,450 restaurants across the U.S. and Canada. Before any one of these meals is placed before a guest, the ingredients for each recipe must pass quality control inspections from the source, ranging from measurement and weighing, to tasting, touching, or lab testing. Darden has differentiated itself from its restaurant peers by developing the gold standard in continuous improvement.

To assure both customers and the company that quality expectations are met, Darden uses a rigorous inspection process, employing statistical process control (SPC) as part of its "Farm to Fork" program. More than 50 food scientists, microbiologists, and public health professionals report to Ana Hooper, director of quality assurance.

As part of Darden's Point Source program, Hooper's team, based in Southeast Asia (in China, Thailand, and Singapore) and Latin America (in Equador, Honduras, and Chile), approves and inspects—and works with Darden buyers to purchase—more than 50 million pounds of seafood each year for restaurant use. Darden used to build quality in at the end by inspecting shipments as they reached U.S. distribution centers. Now, thanks to coaching and partnering with vendors abroad, Darden needs but a few domestic inspection labs to verify compliance to its exacting standards. Food vendors in source countries know that when supplying Darden, they are subject to regular audits that are stricter than U.S. Food & Drug Administration (FDA) standards.

Two Quality Success Stories
Quality specialists' jobs include raising the bar and improving quality and safety at all plants in their geographic area. The Thai quality representative, for example, worked closely with several of Darden's largest shrimp vendors to convert them to a production-line-integrated quality assurance program. The vendors were able to improve the quality of shrimp supplied and reduce the percentage of defects by 19%.

Likewise, when the Darden quality teams visited fields of growers/shippers in Mexico recently, it identified challenges such as low employee hygiene standards, field food safety problems, lack of portable toilets, child labor, and poor working conditions. Darden addressed these concerns and hired third party independent food safety verification firms to ensure continued compliance to standards.

SPC Charts
SPC charts, such as the one shown in this supplement, are particularly important. These charts document precooked food weights; meat, seafood and poultry temperatures; blemishes on produce; and bacteria counts on shrimp—just to name a few. Quality assurance is part of a much bigger process that is key to Darden's success—its supply chain. That's because quality comes from the source and flows through distribution to the restaurant and guests.

Discussion Questions*

1. How does Darden build quality into the supply chain?
2. Select two potential problems—one in the Darden supply chain and one in a restaurant—that can be analyzed with a fish-bone chart. Draw a complete chart to deal with each problem.
3. Darden applies SPC in many product attributes. Identify where these are probably used.
4. The SPC chart illustrates Darden's use of control charts to monitor the weight of salmon filets. Given these data, what conclusion do you, as a Darden quality control inspector, draw? What report do you issue to your supervisor? How do you respond to the salmon vendor?

*You might want to watch this video case on your DVD before answering these questions.

Additional Case Studies

Internet Case Study: Visit our Companion Web site at www.prenhall.com/heizer for this free case study:

- **Green River Chemical Company:** Involves a company that needs to set up a control chart to monitor sulfate content because of customer complaints.

Harvard has selected these Harvard Business School cases to accompany this supplement:

harvardbusinessonline.hbsp.harvard.edu

- **Deutsche Allgemeinversicherung** (#696-084): A German insurance company tries to adopt *p*-charts to a variety of services it performs.
- **Process Control at Polaroid (A)** (#696-047): This film-production plant moves from traditional QC inspection to worker-based SPC charts.

Bibliography

Bakir, S. T. "A Quality Control Chart for Work Performance Appraisal." *Quality Engineering* 17, no. 3 (2005): 429.

Burr, J. T. *Elementary Statistical Quality Control.* Boca Raton, FL: CRC Press, 2005.

Goetsch, David L., and Stanley B. Davis. *Quality Management*, 5th ed. Upper Saddle River, NJ: Prentice Hall, 2006.

Gryna, F. M., R. C. H. Chua, and J. A. DeFeo. *Juran's Quality Planning and Analysis*, 5th ed. New York: McGraw-Hill, 2007.

Johnson, K. "Six Sigma Delivers On-Time Service." *Quality Progress* 38, no. 12 (December 2005): 57–60.

Lin, H., and G. Sheen. "Practical Implementation of the Capability Index C_{pk} Based on Control Chart Data." *Quality Engineering* 17, no. 3 (2005): 371.

Montgomery, D. C. *Introduction to Statistical Quality Control*, 5th ed. New York: Wiley, 2004.

Roth, H. P. "How SPC Can Help Cut Costs." *Journal of Corporate Accounting and Finance* 16, no. 3 (March–April 2005): 21–30.

Smith, Gerald. *Statistical Process Control and Process Improvement.* 6th ed. Upper Saddle River, NJ: Prentice Hall, 2007.

Summers, Donna. *Quality*, 4th ed. Upper Saddle River, NJ: Prentice Hall, 2006.

Spigener, J. B., and P. J. Angelo. "What Would Deming Say?" *Quality Progress* 34, no. 3 (March 2001): 61–65.

Sumukadas, N., J. W. Fairfield-Sonn, and S. Morgan. "Ready-to-Use Simulation: Demystifying Statistical Process Control." *Simulation & Gaming* 36, no. 1 (March 2005): 134.

Internet Resources

American Society for Quality: **www.asq.org**
American Statistical Association: **www.amstat.org**
Associated Quality Consultants: **www.quality.org**
Business Process Improvement: **spcforexcel.com**
Institute of Statistics and Decision Science at Duke University: **www.isds.duke.edu**

Statistical Engineering Division of the Department of Commerce: **www.itl.nist.gov/div898/**
Total Quality Engineering: **www.tqe.com**

Solutions to Even Numbered Problems

2 $UCL_{\bar{x}} = 52.31$
$LCL_{\bar{x}} = 47.69$

4 $UCL_{\bar{x}} = 440$ calories
$LCL_{\bar{x}} = 400$ calories

6 $UCL_{\bar{x}} = 3.728$
$LCL_{\bar{x}} = 2.236$
$UCL_R = 2.336$
$LCL_R = 0.0$
The process is in control.

8 (a) $UCL_{\bar{x}} = 16.08$
$LCL_{\bar{x}} = 15.92$

10 (a) 1.36, 0.61
(b) Using $\sigma_{\bar{x}}$, $UCL_{\bar{x}} = 11.83$, and $LCL_{\bar{x}} = 8.17$.
Using A_2, $UCL_{\bar{x}} = 11.90$, and $LCL_{\bar{x}} = 8.10$.
(c) $UCL_R = 6.98$; $LCL_R = 0$
(d) Yes

12 $UCL_R = 6.058$; $LCL_R = 0.442$
Averages are increasing.

14

UCL	LCL
.062	0
.099	0
.132	0
.161	0
.190	.01

16 $UCL_p = .0313$; $LCL_p = 0$

18 $UCL_p = 0.077$; $LCL_p = 0.003$

20 (a) $UCL_p = .0581$
$LCL_p = 0$

22 (a) c-chart
(b) $UCL_c = 13.3$
$LCL_c = 0$

(c) in control

(d) not in control

24 $UCL_c = 26.063$

$LCL_c = 3.137$

26 $C_p = 1.0$. The process is barely capable.

28 $C_{pk} = 1.125$. Process *is* centered and will produce within tolerance.

30 $C_{pk} = .166$

32 $AOQ = 2.2\%$

34 (a) $UCL_{\bar{x}} = 61.131$, $LCL_{\bar{x}} = 38.421$, $UCL_R = 41.62$, $LCL_R = 0$

(b) Yes, the process is in control for both $\bar{x}$- and R-charts.

(c) They support West's claim. But variance from the mean needs to be reduced and controlled.

Solutions to Self Test

1. a; **2.** a; **3.** a; **4.** b; **5.** 2 std. dev.; **6.** $\bar{x}$-chart and R-chart; **7.** producer's risk, AQL; **8.** b.

Supplement 7

Capacity Planning

Capacity Planning

Outline

Learning Objectives

When you complete this selection you should be able to

1. Define capacity
2. Determine design capacity, effective capacity, and utilization
3. Compute break-even
4. Apply decision trees to capacity decisions
5. Compute net present value

From *Operations Management*, 9/e. Jay Heizer. Barry Render. Copyright © 2008 by Pearson Education. All rights reserved.

▷ *When designing a concert hall, management hopes that the forecasted capacity (the product mix—opera, symphony, and special events—and the technology needed for these events) is accurate and adequate for operation above the break-even point. However, in many concert halls, even when operating at full capacity, break-even is not achieved, and supplemental funding must be obtained.*

John Garrett, Getty Images, Inc.—Stone Allstock

CAPACITY

How many concertgoers should a facility seat? How many customers per day should an Olive Garden or a Hard Rock Cafe be able to service? How many computers should Dell's Nashville plant be able to produce in an 8-hour shift? And how should we build facilities to meet these uncertain demands?

Capacity

The "throughput" or number of units a facility can hold, receive, store, or produce in a period of time.

After selection of a production process, we need to determine capacity. **Capacity** is the "throughput," or the number of units a facility can hold, receive, store, or produce in a period of time. The capacity often determines capital requirements and therefore a large portion of fixed cost. Capacity also determines if demand will be satisfied or if facilities will be idle. If the facility is too large, portions of it will sit idle and add cost to existing production. If the facility is too small, customers and perhaps entire markets are lost. So determining facility size, with an objective of achieving high levels of utilization and a high return on investment, is critical.

Capacity planning can be viewed in three time horizons. In Figure 1 we note that long-range capacity (greater than 1 year) is a function of adding facilities and equipment that have a long lead time. In the intermediate range (3 to 18 months), we can add equipment, personnel, and shifts; we can subcontract; and we can build or use inventory. This is the aggregate planning task. In the short run (usually up to 3 months), we are primarily concerned with scheduling jobs and people, and allocating machinery. It is difficult to modify capacity in the short run; we are using capacity that already exists.

Learning Objective

1. Define capacity

▷ **Figure 1**

Types of Planning over a Time Horizon

	Modify capacity	Use capacity
Long-range planning	Add facilities. Add long lead time equipment.	*
Intermediate-range planning (aggregate planning)	Subcontract. Add equipment. Add shifts.	Add personnel. Build or use inventory.
Short-range planning (scheduling)	*	Schedule jobs. Schedule personnel. Allocate machinery.

* Limited options exist

Design and Effective Capacity

Design capacity

The theoretical maximum output of a system in a given period under ideal conditions.

Design capacity is the maximum theoretical output of a system in a given period under ideal conditions. It is normally expressed as a rate, such as the number of tons of steel that can be produced per week, per month, or per year. For many companies, measuring capacity can be straightforward: It is the maximum number of units produced in a specific time. However, for some organizations, determining capacity can be more difficult. Capacity can be measured in terms of beds (a hospital), active members (a church), or classroom size (a school). Other organizations use total work time available as a measure of overall capacity.

Most organizations operate their facilities at a rate less than the design capacity. They do so because they have found that they can operate more efficiently when their resources are not stretched to the limit. Instead, they expect to operate at perhaps 82% of design capacity. This concept is called effective capacity.

Effective capacity

The capacity a firm can expect to achieve, given its product mix, methods of scheduling, maintenance, and standards of quality.

Effective capacity is the capacity a firm *expects* to achieve given the current operating constraints. Effective capacity is often lower than design capacity because the facility may have been designed for an earlier version of the product or a different product mix than is currently being produced.

Utilization

Actual output as a percent of design capacity.

Efficiency

Actual output as a percent of effective capacity.

Two measures of system performance are particularly useful: utilization and efficiency. **Utilization** is simply the percent of *design capacity* actually achieved. **Efficiency** is the percent of *effective capacity* actually achieved. Depending on how facilities are used and managed, it may be difficult or impossible to reach 100% efficiency. Operations managers tend to be evaluated on efficiency. The key to improving efficiency is often found in correcting quality problems and in effective scheduling, training, and maintenance. Utilization and efficiency are computed below:

$$\text{Utilization} = \text{Actual output/Design capacity} \tag{1}$$

$$\text{Efficiency} = \text{Actual output/Effective capacity} \tag{2}$$

In Example 1 we determine these values.

EXAMPLE 1

Determining capacity utilization and efficiency

 Active Model S7.1

Example 1 is further illustrated in Active Model S7.1 on your CD-ROM.

Sara James Bakery has a plant for processing *Deluxe* breakfast rolls and wants to better understand its capability. Determine the design capacity, utilization, and efficiency for this plant when producing this *Deluxe* roll.

Approach: Last week the facility produced 148,000 rolls. The effective capacity is 175,000 rolls. The production line operates 7 days per week, with three 8-hour shifts per day. The line was designed to process the nut-filled, cinnamon-flavored *Deluxe* roll at a rate of 1,200 per hour. The firm first computes the design capacity and then uses Equation (1) to determine utilization and Equation (2) to determine efficiency.

Solution: Design capacity = (7 days × 3 shifts × 8 hours) × (1,200 rolls per hour) = 201,600 rolls

Utilization = Actual output/Design capacity = 148,000/201,600 = 73.4%

Efficiency = Actual output/Effective capacity = 148,000/175,000 = 84.6%

Insight: The bakery now has the information necessary to evaluate efficiency.

Learning exercise: If the actual output is 150,000, what is the efficiency? [Answer: 85.7%.]

Related problems: 1, 2, 4, 5, 11

Design capacity, utilization, and efficiency are all important measures for an operations manager. But managers often need to know the expected output of a facility or process. To do this, we solve for actual (or in this case, future or expected) output as shown in Equation (3):

$$\text{Actual (or Expected) output} = (\text{Effective capacity})(\text{Efficiency}) \tag{3}$$

Expected output is sometimes referred to as *rated capacity*. With a knowledge of effective capacity and efficiency, a manager can find the expected output of a facility. We do so in Example 2.

Learning Objective

2. Determine design capacity, effective capacity, and utilization

EXAMPLE 2

Determining expected output

The manager of Sara James Bakery (see Example 1) now needs to increase production of the increasingly popular *Deluxe* roll. To meet this demand, she will be adding a second production line.

Approach: The manager must determine the expected output of this second line for the sales department. Effective capacity on the second line is the same as on the first line, which is 175,000 *Deluxe* rolls. The first line is operating at an efficiency of 84.6%, as computed in Example 1. But output on the second line will be less than the first line because the crew will be primarily new hires; so the efficiency can be expected to be no more than 75%. What is the expected output?

Solution: Use Equation (3) to determine the expected output:

Expected output = (Effective capacity)(Efficiency) = (175,000)(.75) = 131,250 rolls

Insight: The sales department can now be told the expected output is 131,250 *Deluxe* rolls.

Learning exercise: After 1 month of training, the crew on the second production line is expected to perform at 80% efficiency. What is the revised expected output of *Deluxe* rolls? [Answer: 140,000.]

Related problems: 3, 6, 7, 8, 10

If the expected output is inadequate, additional capacity may be needed. Much of the remainder of this supplement addresses how to effectively and efficiently add that capacity.

Capacity and Strategy

Sustained profits come from building competitive advantage, not just from a good financial return on a specific process. Capacity decisions must be integrated into the organization's mission and strategy. Investments are not to be made as isolated expenditures, but as part of a coordinated plan that will place the firm in an advantageous position.[1] The questions to be asked are, Will these investments eventually win customers? and What competitive advantage (such as process flexibility, speed of delivery, improved quality, and so on) do we obtain?

All 10 decisions of operations management we discuss in this text, as well as other organizational elements such as marketing and finance, are affected by changes in capacity. Change in capacity will have sales and cash flow implications, just as capacity changes have quality, supply chain, human resource, and maintenance implications. All must be considered.

Capacity Considerations

In addition to tight integration of strategy and investments, there are four special considerations for a good capacity decision:

1. *Forecast demand accurately:* An accurate forecast is paramount to the capacity decision. The new product may be Olive Garden's veal scampi, a dish that places added demands on the restaurant's food service, or the product may be a new maternity capability at Arnold Palmer Hospital, or the new hybrid Lexus. Whatever the new product, its prospects and the life cycle of existing products, must be determined. Management must know which products are being added and which are being dropped, as well as their expected volumes.

2. *Understand the technology and capacity increments:* The number of initial alternatives may be large, but once the volume is determined, technology decisions may be aided by analysis of cost, human resources required, quality, and reliability. Such a review often reduces the number of alternatives to a few. The technology may dictate the capacity increment. Meeting added demand with a few extra tables in an Olive Garden may not be difficult, but meeting increased demand for a new automobile by adding a new assembly line at BMW may be very difficult—and expensive. The operations manager is held responsible for the technology and the correct capacity increment.

3. *Find the optimum operating level (volume):* Technology and capacity increments often dictate an optimal size for a facility. A roadside motel may require 50 rooms to be viable. If

[1]For an excellent discussion on investments that support competitive advantage, see Terry Hill, *Operations Management*, 2nd ed. (New York: Palgrave Macmillan, 2005).

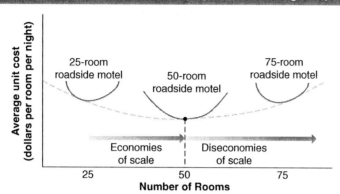

Chitose Suzuki, AP Wide World Photos

smaller, the fixed cost is too burdensome; if larger, the facility becomes more than one manager can supervise. A hypothetical optimum for the motel is shown in Figure 2. This issue is known as *economies and diseconomies of scale*. GM at one time believed that the optimum auto plant was one with 600 employees. As the Krispy Kreme photo suggests, most businesses have an optimal size—at least until someone comes along with a new business model. For decades, very large integrated steel mills were considered optimal. Then along came Nucor, CMC, and other minimills with a new process and a new business model that changed the optimum size of a steel mill.

4. *Build for change:* In our fast-paced world, change is inevitable. So operations managers build flexibility into the facility and equipment (see Figure 3. They evaluate the sensitivity of the decision by testing several revenue projections on both the upside and downside for potential risks. Buildings can often be built in phases; and buildings and equipment can be designed with modifications in mind to accommodate future changes in product, product mix, and processes.

Rather than strategically manage capacity, managers may tactically manage demand.

Managing Demand

Even with good forecasting and facilities built to that forecast, there may be a poor match between the actual demand that occurs and available capacity. A poor match may mean demand exceeds capacity or capacity exceeds demand. However, in both cases, firms have options.

Chitose Suzuki, AP Wide World Photos

◁ *Krispy Kreme originally had 8,000-square-foot stores but found them too large and too expensive for many markets. Then they tried tiny 1,300-square-foot stores, which required less investment, but such stores were too small to provide the mystique of seeing and smelling Krispy Kreme donuts being made. Krispy Kreme finally got it right with a 2,600-foot-store. This one includes a huge glass window to view doughnut production.*

▷ Figure 3 **Percent of North American Vehicles Made on Flexible Assembly Lines***

A large and growing percent of cars are made on flexible assembly lines. Chrysler, for example, discovered several years ago that its underutilized Belvidere, Illinois, plant was not flexible enough to paint a PT Cruiser (which was 1″ too tall). The company learned its lesson and is now a leader in investing in design flexibility.

*2007 estimate, *The Wall Street Journal* (April 11, 2006): A1 and (January 14–15, 2006): B14.

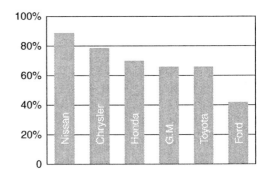

Demand Exceeds Capacity When *demand exceeds capacity*, the firm may be able to curtail demand simply by raising prices, scheduling long lead times (which may be inevitable), and discouraging marginally profitable business. However, because inadequate facilities reduce revenue below what is possible, the long-term solution is usually to increase capacity (as we see in the *OM in Action* box "Too Little Capacity at Dalrymple Bay").

Capacity Exceeds Demand When *capacity exceeds demand*, the firm may want to stimulate demand through price reductions or aggressive marketing, or it may accommodate the market through product changes. When decreasing customer demand is combined with old and inflexible processes, layoffs and plant closings may be necessary to bring capacity in line with demand. The *OM in Action* box "Too Much Capacity at G.M. and Ford" indicates how difficult adjusting capacity to declining demand can be.

Adjusting to Seasonal Demands A seasonal or cyclical pattern of demand is another capacity challenge. In such cases, management may find it helpful to offer products with complementary demand patterns—that is, products for which the demand is high for one when low for the other. For example, in Figure 4 the firm is adding a line of snowmobile motors to its line of jet skis to smooth demand. With appropriate complementing of products, perhaps the utilization of facility, equipment, and personnel can be smoothed.

OM in Action **Too Little Capacity at Dalrymple Bay**

Nearly 20 ships were anchored in the Coral Sea on a recent morning. They were waiting to be loaded with coal to fuel Asia's voracious steel mills. Australia has some of the most prolific coal mines in the world, but its key port of Dalrymple Bay, just outside Queensland, isn't big enough to meet demand. So the ships sit idle for days. Capacity at the port is far below what is needed for the current worldwide demand. This makes Dalrymple Bay one of the key choke points.

The process is rather simple but expensive. Trains are loaded with coal at the mines, travel several hours to the port, and dump their coal into piles that are sprayed with water to prevent black coal dust from blowing onto homes and beaches. Eventually, the coal is loaded onto a conveyor belt that moves 2.5 miles out into the Coral Sea, to be loaded onto ships.

The current plan is to invest $610 million to expand port capacity to 85 million metric tons of coal in the next 3 years. But this is still less than the estimated demand requirement of 107 million metric tons needed. As a result, coal companies, even after the expansion is completed, may still find access to shipping rationed.

The demand must exist, the port must expand, and the mines must enlarge. Without that assurance, the risk remains high and the necessary ROI (return on investment) is not there. Managers are not going to put significant money into expanding port capacity until they are comfortable that both the demand and coal supply support a larger port. To justify investment in capacity, each phase of the chain must support that investment.

Source: Australasian Business Intelligence (June 22, 2006); and *The Wall Street Journal* (July 7, 2005): C1, C4.

OM in Action Too Much Capacity at G.M. and Ford

For decades G.M. and Ford added capacity. The auto and truck market expanded, and they expanded along with it. They were the world's greatest automobile companies. They built specialized product-focused plants with little flexibility. And they grew capacity to millions of cars per year. G.M. alone produced over half of the cars sold in the U.S. But the world changed. Cars now arrive in the U.S. from every corner of the world. Germany, Italy, Japan, Korea, and now even Mexico and Brazil are making inroads into the U.S. market—with China on the horizon. And G.M. now makes fewer than one-fourth of the cars sold in the U.S.

Toyota, VW, Honda, BMW, Mercedes, and others are stealing sales. They are stealing sales with imports, and they are stealing sales with domestic production. Recently Toyota's U.S. plants were operating at 111% of expected output compared with 87% for G.M. and 79% for Ford.

G.M. and Ford are not sitting still. In an effort to drive down costs, both companies are increasing productivity and flexibility. For instance, in the past 6 years, the total labor-hours per vehicle necessary for stamping, assembly, and engine production have dropped by 26%, from 46.5 hours to 34.3 hours. The number of stamping machines necessary to make the fenders, hoods, doors, and so on have dropped from 330 to 241. This potent combination of lower sales and increased productivity means G.M. and Ford must cut capacity. By 2010, employment at the two automakers will drop by 50,000 people. Capacity adjustments, particularly on the down side, can be painful.

Source: The Wall Street Journal (January 21–22, 2006): A2; *The Economist* (January 7, 2006): 61; and *Knight Ridder Tribune Business News* (January 4, 2006): 1.

Tactics for Matching Capacity to Demand Various tactics for matching capacity to demand exist. Options for adjusting capacity include:

1. Making staffing changes (increasing or decreasing the number of employees or shifts)
2. Adjusting equipment (purchasing additional machinery or selling or leasing out existing equipment)
3. Improving processes to increase throughput
4. Redesigning products to facilitate more throughput
5. Adding process flexibility to better meet changing product preferences
6. Closing facilities

The foregoing tactics can be used to adjust demand to existing facilities. The strategic issue is, of course, how to have a facility of the correct size.

Demand and Capacity Management in the Service Sector

In the service sector, scheduling customers is *demand management*, and scheduling the workforce is *capacity management*.

Demand Management When demand and capacity are fairly well matched, demand management can often be handled with appointments, reservations, or a first-come, first-served rule. In some businesses, such as doctors' and lawyers' offices, an *appointment system* is the schedule and is adequate. *Reservations systems* work well in rental car agencies, hotels, and some restaurants as

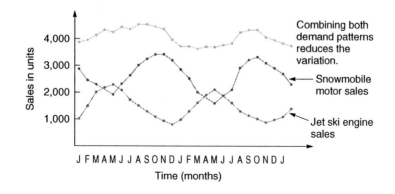

◀ **Figure 4**

By Combining Products That Have Complementary Seasonal Patterns, Capacity Can Be Better Utilized

A smoother sales demand contributes to improved scheduling and better human resource strategies.

> Many U.S. hospitals use services abroad to manage capacity for radiologists during night shifts. Night Hawk, an Idaho-based service with 50 radiologists in Zurich and Sydney, contracts with 900 facilities (20% of all U.S. hospitals). These trained experts, wide awake and alert in their daylight hours, usually return a diagnosis in 10 to 20 minutes, with a guarantee of 30 minutes.

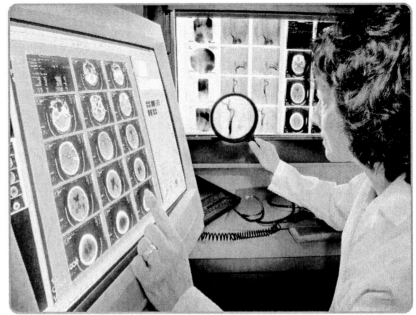

Lester Lefkowitz, Corbis—NY

a means of minimizing customer waiting time and avoiding disappointment over unfilled service. In retail shops, a post office, or a fast-food restaurant, a *first-come, first-served* rule for serving customers may suffice. Each industry develops its own approaches to matching demand and capacity. Other more aggressive approaches to demand management include many variations of discounts: "early bird" specials in restaurants, discounts for matinee performances or for seats at odd hours on an airline, and cheap weekend phone calls.

Capacity Management   When managing demand is not feasible, then managing capacity through changes in full-time, temporary, or part-time staff may be an option. This is the approach in many services. For instance, hospitals may find capacity limited by a shortage of board-certified radiologists willing to cover the graveyard shifts. Getting fast and reliable radiology readings can be the difference between life and death for an emergency room patient. As the photo above illustrates, when an overnight reading is required (and 40% of CT scans are done between 8 P.M. and 8 A.M.), the image can be sent by e-mail to a doctor in Europe or Australia for immediate analysis.

> FedEx's huge aircraft fleet is used to near capacity for nighttime delivery of packages but is 100% idle during the daytime. In an attempt to better utilize capacity (and leverage assets), FedEx considered two services with opposite or countercyclical demand patterns to its nighttime service—commuter passenger service and passenger charter service. However, after a thorough analysis, the 12% to 13% return on investment was judged insufficient for the risks involved. Facing the same issues, though, UPS decided to begin a charter airline that operates on weekends.

Charles Thatcher, C. Thatcher, Inc.

CAPACITY PLANNING

Setting future capacity requirements can be a complicated procedure, one based in large part on future demand. When demand for goods and services can be forecast with a reasonable degree of precision, determining capacity requirements can be straightforward. Determining capacity normally requires two phases. During the first phase, future demand is forecast with traditional models. During the second phase, this forecast is used to determine capacity requirements and the incremental size of each addition to capacity.[2] Interestingly, demand growth is typically gradual in small units, while capacity additions are typically instantaneous in large units. This contradiction often makes capacity expansion difficult.

Figure 5 reveals four approaches to new capacity. As we see in Figure 5(a), new capacity is acquired at the beginning of year 1. This capacity will handle increased demand until the beginning of year 2. At the beginning of year 2, new capacity is again acquired, which will allow the organization to stay ahead of demand until the beginning of year 3. This process can be continued indefinitely into the future.

The capacity plan shown in Figure 5(a) is only one of an almost limitless number of plans to satisfy future demand. In this figure, new capacity was acquired *incrementally*—at the beginning of year 1 *and* at the beginning of year 2. In Figure 5(b), a large increase in capacity is acquired at the beginning of year 1 to satisfy expected demand until the beginning of year 3.

The excess capacity provided by plans Figure 5(a) and Figure 5(b) gives operations managers flexibility. For instance, in the hotel industry, added capacity in the form of rooms can allow a

Video S7.1

Capacity Planning at
Arnold Palmer Hospital

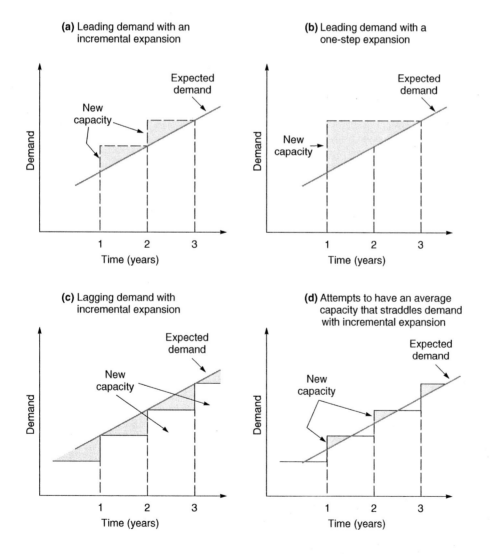

◀ **Figure 5**

Approaches to Capacity Expansion

---

[2]At this point, we make the assumption that management knows the technology and the *type* of facilities to be employed to satisfy future demand requirements—not a minor issue, but beyond the scope of this text.

wider variety of room options and perhaps flexibility in room cleanup schedules. In manufacturing, the excess capacity can be used to do more setups to shorten production runs, driving down inventory. The added capacity may also allow management to build excess inventory and thus delay the capital expenditure and disruption that come with adding additional new capacity.[3]

Alternatives Figure 5(a) and Figure 5(b) *lead* capacity—that is, acquire capacity to stay ahead of demand—but Figure 5(c) shows an option that *lags* capacity, perhaps using overtime or subcontracting to accommodate excess demand. Figure 5(d) straddles demand by building capacity that is "average," sometimes lagging demand and sometimes leading it.

In some cases, deciding between alternatives can be relatively easy. The total cost of each alternative can be computed, and the alternative with the least total cost can be selected. In other cases, determining the capacity and how to achieve it can be much more complicated. In most cases, numerous subjective factors are difficult to quantify and measure. These factors include technological options; competitor strategies; building restrictions; cost of capital; human resource options; and local, state, and federal laws and regulations.

BREAK-EVEN ANALYSIS

Learning Objective

3. Compute break-even

Break-even analysis
A means of finding the point, in dollars and units, at which costs equal revenues.

Fixed costs
Costs that continue even if no units are produced.

Variable costs
Costs that vary with the volume of units produced.

Contribution
The difference between selling price and variable costs.

Revenue function
The function that increases by the selling price of each unit.

Break-even analysis is a critical tool for determining the capacity a facility must have to achieve profitability. The objective of **break-even analysis** is to find the point, in dollars and units, at which costs equal revenue. This point is the break-even point. Firms must operate above this level to achieve profitability. As shown in Figure 6, break-even analysis requires an estimation of fixed costs, variable costs, and revenue.

Fixed costs are costs that continue even if no units are produced. Examples include depreciation, taxes, debt, and mortgage payments. **Variable costs** are those that vary with the volume of units produced. The major components of variable costs are labor and materials. However, other costs, such as the portion of the utilities that varies with volume, are also variable costs. The difference between selling price and variable cost is **contribution**. Only when total contribution exceeds total fixed cost will there be profit.

Another element in break-even analysis is the **revenue function**. In Figure 6, revenue begins at the origin and proceeds upward to the right, increasing by the selling price of each unit. Where the revenue function crosses the total cost line (the sum of fixed and variable costs), is the break-even point, with a profit corridor to the right and a loss corridor to the left.

Assumptions A number of assumptions underlie the basic break-even model. Notably, costs and revenue are shown as straight lines. They are shown to increase linearly—that is, in direct proportion to the volume of units being produced. However, neither fixed costs nor variable costs (nor, for that

▶ Figure 6

Basic Break-Even Point

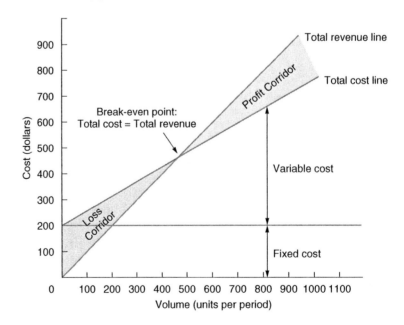

[3]See related discussion in S. Rajagopalan and J. M. Swaminathan, "Coordinated Production Planning Model with Capacity Expansion and Inventory Management," *Management Science* 47, no. 11, (November 2001): 1562–1580.

matter, the revenue function) need be a straight line. For example, fixed costs change as more capital equipment or warehouse space is used; labor costs change with overtime or as marginally skilled workers are employed; the revenue function may change with such factors as volume discounts.

Graphic Approach The first step in the graphic approach to break-even analysis is to define those costs that are fixed and sum them. The fixed costs are drawn as a horizontal line beginning at that dollar amount on the vertical axis. The variable costs are then estimated by an analysis of labor, materials, and other costs connected with the production of each unit. The variable costs are shown as an incrementally increasing cost, originating at the intersection of the fixed cost on the vertical axis and increasing with each change in volume as we move to the right on the volume (or horizontal) axis. Both fixed- and variable-cost information is usually available from a firm's cost accounting department, although an industrial engineering department may also maintain cost information.

> *Fixed costs do not remain constant over all volume; new warehouses and new overhead charges result in step functions in fixed cost.*

Algebraic Approach The respective formulas for the break-even point in units and dollars are shown below. Let:

BEP_x = break-even point in units
$BEP_\$$ = break-even point in dollars
P = price per unit (after all discounts)
x = number of units produced

TR = total revenue = Px
F = fixed costs
V = variable costs per unit
TC = total costs = $F + Vx$

The break-even point occurs where total revenue equals total costs. Therefore:

$$TR = TC \quad \text{or} \quad Px = F + Vx$$

Solving for x, we get

$$BEP_x = \frac{F}{P - V}$$

and:

$$BEP_\$ = BEP_x P = \frac{F}{P - V} P = \frac{F}{(P - V)/P}$$

$$= \frac{F}{1 - V/P}$$

$$\text{Profit} = TR - TC$$
$$= Px - (F + Vx) = Px - F - Vx$$
$$= (P - V)x - F$$

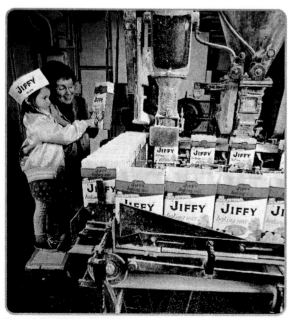

James Schnepf Photography, Inc.

◁ *Some companies adjust for a capacity change by modifying machinery or using older equipment—even though it may not be the most efficient. For instance, managers at the family-owned maker of Jiffy brand mixes decided that their OM strategy did not support additional capital investment in new equipment. Consequently, when making repairs, modifying equipment, or adjusting for peak loads, they draw on spare, often old, equipment.*

Using these equations, we can solve directly for break-even point and profitability. The two break-even formulas of particular interest are:

$$\text{Break-even in units} = \frac{\text{Total fixed cost}}{\text{Price} - \text{Variable cost}} \qquad (4)$$

$$\text{Break-even in dollars} = \frac{\text{Total fixed cost}}{1 - \dfrac{\text{Variable cost}}{\text{Selling price}}} \qquad (5)$$

Single-Product Case

In Example 3, we determine the break-even point in dollars and units for one product.

EXAMPLE 3

Single product break-even analysis

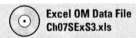

Excel OM Data File
Ch07SExS3.xls

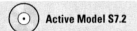

Active Model S7.2

Example 3 is further illustrated in Active Model S7.2 on the CD-ROM.

Stephens, Inc., wants to determine the minimum dollar volume and unit volume needed at its new facility to break even.

Approach: The firm first determines that it has fixed costs of $10,000 this period. Direct labor is $1.50 per unit, and material is $.75 per unit. The selling price is $4.00 per unit.

Solution: The break-even point in dollars is computed as follows:

$$BEP_\$ = \frac{F}{1 - (V/P)} = \frac{\$10,000}{1 - [(1.50 + .75)/(4.00)]} = \frac{\$10,000}{.4375} = \$22,857.14$$

The break-even point in units is:

$$BEP_x = \frac{F}{P - V} = \frac{\$10,000}{4.00 - (1.50 + .75)} = 5,714$$

Note that we use total variable costs (that is, both labor and material).

Insight: The management of Stevens, Inc., now has an estimate in both units and dollars of the volume necessary for the new facility.

Learning exercise: If Stevens finds that fixed cost will increase to $12,000, what happens to the break-even in units and dollars? [Answer: The break-even in units increases to 6,857, and break-even in dollars increases to $27,428.57.]

Related problems: 9, 12, 13, 14, 15, 16, 17, 18, 19, 20, 21, 22, 23

Multiproduct Case

Most firms, from manufacturers to restaurants (even fast-food restaurants), have a variety of offerings. Each offering may have a different selling price and variable cost. Utilizing break-even analysis, we modify Equation (5) to reflect the proportion of sales for each product. We do this by "weighting" each product's contribution by its proportion of sales. The formula is then:

$$BEP_\$ = \frac{F}{\sum\left[\left(1 - \dfrac{V_i}{P_i}\right) \times (W_i)\right]} \qquad (6)$$

where V = variable cost per unit
         P = price per unit
         F = fixed cost
         W = percent each product is of total dollar sales
         i = each product

Example 4 shows how to determine the break-even point for the multiproduct case at the Le Bistro restaurant.

◁ Paper machines such as the one shown here, at International Paper, require a high capital investment. This investment results in a high fixed cost but allows production of paper at a very low variable cost. The production manager's job is to maintain utilization above the break-even point to achieve profitability.

Jack Kenner, International Paper Company

EXAMPLE 4

Multiproduct break-even analysis

Le Bistro makes more than one product and would like to know its break-even point in dollars.

Approach: Information for Le Bistro follows. Fixed costs are $3,500 per month.

Item	Price	Cost	Annual Forecasted Sales Units
Sandwich	$2.95	$1.25	7,000
Soft drink	.80	.30	7,000
Baked potato	1.55	.47	5,000
Tea	.75	.25	5,000
Salad bar	2.85	1.00	3,000

With a variety of offerings, we proceed with break-even analysis just as in a single-product case, except that we weight each of the products by its proportion of total sales using Equation (6).

Solution: Multiproduct Break-Even: Determining Contribution

1	2	3	4	5	6	7	8
Item (i)	Selling Price (P)	Variable Cost (V)	(V/P)	$1 - (V/P)$	Annual Forecasted Sales $	% of Sales	Weighted Contribution (col. 5 × col. 7)
Sandwich	$2.95	$1.25	.42	.58	$20,650	.446	.259
Soft drink	.80	.30	.38	.62	5,600	.121	.075
Baked potato	1.55	.47	.30	.70	7,750	.167	.117
Tea	.75	.25	.33	.67	3,750	.081	.054
Salad bar	2.85	1.00	.35	.65	8,550	.185	.120
					$46,300	1.000	.625

Note: Revenue for sandwiches is $20,650 (2.95 × 7,000), which is 44.6% of the total revenue of $46,300. Therefore, the contribution for sandwiches is "weighted" by .446. The weighted contribution is .446 × .58 = .259. In this manner, its *relative* contribution is properly reflected.

Using this approach for each product, we find that the total weighted contribution is .625 for each dollar of sales, and the break-even point in dollars is $67,200:

$$BEP_\$ = \frac{F}{\sum\left[\left(1 - \frac{V_i}{P_i}\right) \times (W_i)\right]} = \frac{\$3,500 \times 12}{.625} = \frac{\$42,000}{.625} = \$67,200$$

The information given in this example implies total daily sales (52 weeks at 6 days each) of:

$$\frac{\$67,200}{312 \text{ days}} = \$215.38$$

Insight: The management of Le Bistro now knows that it must generate average sales of $215.38 each day to break even. Management also knows that if the forecasted sales of $46,300 are correct, Le Bistro will lose money, as break-even is $67,200.

Learning exercise: If the manager of Le Bistro wants to make an additional $2,000 per month and considers this a fixed cost, what is the new break-even point in average sales per day? [Answer: $338.46.]

Related problems: 24a, 25, 26a

Break-even figures by product provide the manager with added insight as to the realism of his or her sales forecast. They indicate exactly what must be sold each day, as we illustrate in Example 5.

EXAMPLE 5

Unit sales at break-even

Le Bistro also wants to know the break-even for the number of sandwiches that must be sold every day.

Approach: Using the data in Example 4, we take the forecast sandwich sales of 44.6% times the daily break-even of $215.38 divided by the selling price of each sandwich ($2.95).

Solution: At break-even, sandwich sales must then be:

$$\frac{.446 \times \$215.38}{\$2.95} = \text{Number of sandwiches} = 32.6 \approx 33 \text{ sandwiches each day}$$

Insight: With knowledge of individual product sales, the manager has a basis for determining material and labor requirements.

Learning exercise: At a dollar break-even of $338.46 per day, how many sandwiches must Le Bistro sell each day? [Answer: 51.]

Related problems: 24b, 26b, 35

Once break-even analysis has been prepared, analyzed, and judged to be reasonable, decisions can be made about the type and capacity of equipment needed. Indeed, a better judgment of the likelihood of success of the enterprise can now be made.

When capacity requirements are subject to significant unknowns, "probabilistic" models may be appropriate. One technique for making successful capacity planning decisions with an uncertain demand is decision theory, including the use of decision trees.

APPLYING DECISION TREES TO CAPACITY DECISIONS

Learning Objective

4. Apply decision trees to capacity decisions

Decision trees require specifying alternatives and various states of nature. For capacity planning situations, the state of nature usually is future demand or market favorability. By assigning probability values to the various states of nature, we can make decisions that maximize the expected value of the alternatives. Example 6 shows how to apply decision trees to a capacity decision.

EXAMPLE 6

Decision tree applied to capacity decision

Southern Hospital Supplies, a company that makes hospital gowns, is considering capacity expansion.

Approach: Southern's major alternatives are to do nothing, build a small plant, build a medium plant, or build a large plant. The new facility would produce a new type of gown, and currently the potential or marketability for this product is unknown. If a large plant is built and a favorable market exists, a profit of $100,000 could be realized. An unfavorable market would yield a $90,000 loss.

However, a medium plant would earn a $60,000 profit with a favorable market. A $10,000 loss would result from an unfavorable market. A small plant, on the other hand, would return $40,000 with favorable market conditions and lose only $5,000 in an unfavorable market. Of course, there is always the option of doing nothing.

Recent market research indicates that there is a .4 probability of a favorable market, which means that there is also a .6 probability of an unfavorable market. With this information, the alternative that will result in the highest expected monetary value (EMV) can be selected.

Solution: Prepare a decision tree and compute the EMV for each branch:

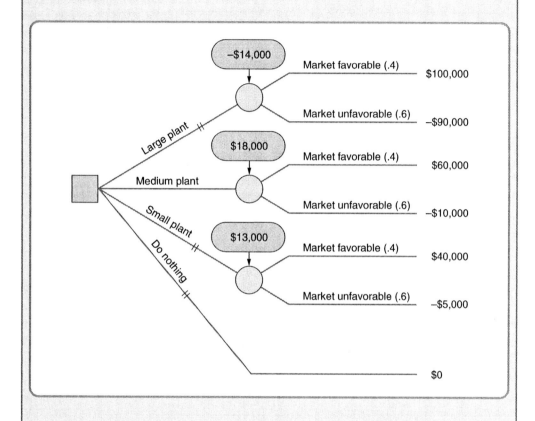

$$\text{EMV (large plant)} = (.4)(\$100,000) + (.6)(-\$90,000) = -\$14,000$$
$$\text{EMV (medium plant)} = (.4)(\$60,000) + (.6)(-\$10,000) = +\$18,000$$
$$\text{EMV (small plant)} = (.4)(\$40,000) + (.6)(-\$5,000) = +\$13,000$$
$$\text{EMV (do nothing)} = \$0$$

Based on EMV criteria, Southern should build a medium plant.

Insight: If Southern makes many decisions like this, then determining the EMV for each branch and selecting the highest EMV is a good decision criterion.

Learning exercise: If a new estimate of the loss from a medium plant in an unfavorable market increases to −$20,000 what is the new EMV for this branch? [Answer: $12,000, which changes the decision because the small plant EMV is now higher.]

Related problems: 27, 28.

APPLYING INVESTMENT ANALYSIS TO STRATEGY-DRIVEN INVESTMENTS

Once the strategy implications of potential investments have been considered, traditional investment analysis is appropriate. We introduce the investment aspects of capacity next.

An operations manager may be the one held responsible for return on investment (ROI).

Investment, Variable Cost, and Cash Flow

Capital investment requires cash flow as well as an evaluation of return on investments.

Because capacity and process alternatives exist, so do options regarding capital investment and variable cost. Managers must choose from among different financial options as well as capacity and process alternatives. Analysis should show the capital investment, variable cost, and cash flows as well as net present value for each alternative.

Net Present Value

Net present value

A means of determining the discounted value of a series of future cash receipts.

Determining the discount value of a series of future cash receipts is known as the **net present value** technique. By way of introduction, let us consider the time value of money. Say you invest $100.00 in a bank at 5% for 1 year. Your investment will be worth $100.00 + ($100.00)(.05) = $105.00. If you invest the $105.00 for a second year, it will be worth $105.00 + ($105.00)(.05) = $110.25 at the end of the second year. Of course, we could calculate the future value of $100.00 at 5% for as many years as we wanted by simply extending this analysis. However, there is an easier way to express this relationship mathematically. For the first year:

$$\$105 = \$100(1 + .05)$$

For the second year:

$$\$110.25 = \$105(1 + .05) = \$100(1 + .05)^2$$

In general:

$$F = P(1 + i)^N \tag{7}$$

where F = future value (such as $110.25 or $105)
P = present value (such as $100.00)
i = interest rate (such as .05)
N = number of years (such as 1 year or 2 years)

Learning Objective

5. Compute net present value

In most investment decisions, however, we are interested in calculating the present value of a series of future cash receipts. Solving for P, we get:

$$P = \frac{F}{(1+i)^N} \tag{8}$$

When the number of years is not too large, the preceding equation is effective. However, when the number of years, N, is large, the formula is cumbersome. For 20 years, you would have to compute $(1 + i)^{20}$. Without a sophisticated calculator, this computation would be difficult.

▲ *Matching capacity and demand can be a challenge. When market share is declining and facilities are old and inflexible, as is the case at this General Motors plant, the mismatch between demand and capacity means empty plants and laying off employees (left photo). On the other hand, when demand exceeds capacity, as at this opening of the Apple store on the outskirts of Rome, Italy, the mismatch may mean frustrated customers and lost revenue (right photo).*

Table 1

Present Value of $1

Year	5%	6%	7%	8%	9%	10%	12%	14%
1	.952	.943	.935	.926	.917	.909	.893	.877
2	.907	.890	.873	.857	.842	.826	.797	.769
3	.864	.840	.816	.794	.772	.751	.712	.675
4	.823	.792	.763	.735	.708	.683	.636	.592
5	.784	.747	.713	.681	.650	.621	.567	.519
6	.746	.705	.666	.630	.596	.564	.507	.456
7	.711	.665	.623	.583	.547	.513	.452	.400
8	.677	.627	.582	.540	.502	.467	.404	.351
9	.645	.592	.544	.500	.460	.424	.361	.308
10	.614	.558	.508	.463	.422	.386	.322	.270
15	.481	.417	.362	.315	.275	.239	.183	.140
20	.377	.312	.258	.215	.178	.149	.104	.073

Interest-rate tables, such as Table 1, alleviate this situation. First, let us restate the present value equation:

$$P = \frac{F}{(1+i)^N} = FX \qquad (9)$$

where X = a factor from Table 1 defined as = $1/(1 + i)^N$ and F = future value

Thus, all we have to do is find the factor X and multiply it by F to calculate the present value, P. The factors, of course, are a function of the interest rate, i, and the number of years, N. Table 1 lists some of these factors.

Equations (8) and (9) are used to determine the present value of one future cash amount, but there are situations in which an investment generates a series of uniform and equal cash amounts. This type of investment is called an *annuity*. For example, an investment might yield $300 per year for 3 years. Of course, you could use Equation (8) three times, for 1, 2, and 3 years, but there is a shorter method. Although there is a formula that can be used to solve for the present value of an annual series of uniform and equal cash flows (an annuity), an easy-to-use table has been developed for this purpose. Like the customary present value computations, this calculation involves a factor. The factors for annuities are in Table 2. The basic relationship is

$$S = RX$$

where X = factor from Table 2
S = present value of a series of uniform annual receipts
R = receipts that are received every year for the life of the investment (the annuity)

The present value of a uniform annual series of amounts is an extension of the present value of a single amount, and thus Table 2 can be directly developed from Table 1. The factors for any given interest rate in Table 2 are nothing more than the cumulative sum of the values in Table 1.

Table 2

Present Value of an
Annuity of $1

Year	5%	6%	7%	8%	9%	10%	12%	14%
1	.952	.943	.935	.926	.917	.909	.893	.877
2	1.859	1.833	1.808	1.783	1.759	1.736	1.690	1.647
3	2.723	2.673	2.624	2.577	2.531	2.487	2.402	2.322
4	3.546	3.465	3.387	3.312	3.240	3.170	3.037	2.914
5	4.329	4.212	4.100	3.993	3.890	3.791	3.605	3.433
6	5.076	4.917	4.766	4.623	4.486	4.355	4.111	3.889
7	5.786	5.582	5.389	5.206	5.033	4.868	4.564	4.288
8	6.463	6.210	5.971	5.747	5.535	5.335	4.968	4.639
9	7.108	6.802	6.515	6.247	5.985	5.759	5.328	4.946
10	7.722	7.360	7.024	6.710	6.418	6.145	5.650	5.216
15	10.380	9.712	9.108	8.559	8.060	7.606	6.811	6.142
20	12.462	11.470	10.594	9.818	9.128	8.514	7.469	6.623

In Table 1, for example, .952, .907, and .864 are the factors for years 1, 2, and 3 when the interest rate is 5%. The cumulative sum of these factors is 2.723 = .952 + .907 + .864. Now look at the point in Table 2 where the interest rate is 5% and the number of years is 3. The factor for the present value of an annuity is 2.723, as you would expect. Table 2 can be very helpful in reducing the computations necessary to make financial decisions. (Note, however, that there may be minor rounding differences between the tables.)

Example 7 shows how to determine the present value of an annuity.

EXAMPLE 7 Determining net present value of future receipts of equal value	River Road Medical Clinic is thinking of investing in a sophisticated new piece of medical equipment. It will generate $7,000 per year in receipts for 5 years. *Approach:* Determine the present value of this cash flow; assume an interest rate of 6%. *Solution:* The factor from Table 2 (4.212) is obtained by finding that value when the interest rate is 6% and the number of years is 5: $$S = RX = \$7,000(4.212) = \$29,484$$ *Insight:* There is another way of looking at this example. If you went to a bank and took a loan for $29,484 today, your payments would be $7,000 per year for 5 years if the bank used an interest rate of 6% compounded yearly. Thus, $29,484 is the present value. *Learning exercise:* If the interest rate is 8%, what is the present value? [Answer: $27,951.] *Related problems:* 29, 30, 31

The net present value method is one of the best methods of ranking investment alternatives. The procedure is straightforward: You simply compute the present value of all cash flows for each investment alternative. When deciding among investment alternatives, you pick the investment with the highest net present value. Similarly, when making several investments, those with higher net present values are preferable to investments with lower net present values.

Example 8 shows how to use the net present value to choose between investment alternatives.

EXAMPLE 8

Determining net present value of future receipts of different value

Quality Plastics, Inc., is considering two different investment alternatives.

Approach: To find the net present value of each investment, Quality first needs to determine the initial investment, cash flows, and interest rate. Investment A has an initial cost of $25,000, and investment B has an initial cost of $26,000. Both investments have a useful life of 4 years. The cash flows for these investments follow. The cost of capital or the interest rate (i) is 8%. (Factors come from Table 1).

Investment A's Cash Flow	Investment B's Cash Flow	Year	Present Value Factor at 8%
$10,000	$9,000	1	.926
9,000	9,000	2	.857
8,000	9,000	3	.794
7,000	9,000	4	.735

Solution: To find the present value of the cash flows for each investment, we multiply the present value factor by the cash flow for each investment for each year. The sum of these present value calculations minus the initial investment is the net present value of each investment. The computations appear in the following table:

Year	Investment A's Present Values	Investment B's Present Values
1	$ 9,260 = (.926)($10,000)	$ 8,334 = (.926)($9,000)
2	7,713 = (.857)($9,000)	7,713 = (.857)($9,000)
3	6,352 = (.794)($8,000)	7,146 = (.794)($9,000)
4	5,145 = (.735)($7,000)	6,615 = (.735)($9,000)
Totals	$28,470	$29,808
Minus initial investment	−25,000	−26,000
Net present value	$ 3,470	$ 3,808

Insight: The net present value criterion shows investment B to be more attractive than investment A because it has a higher present value.

Learning exercise: If the interest rate is 10%, does this change the decision? [Answer: no, but the difference between the two investments does narrow. NPV of investment A = $2,243; B = $2,500.]

Related problems: 32, 33, 34, 36

In Example 8, it was not necessary to make all those present value computations for investment B. Because the cash flows are uniform, Table 2, the annuity table, gives the present value factor. Of course, we would expect to get the same answer. As you recall, Table 2 gives factors for the present value of an annuity. In this example, for payments of $9,000, cost of capital is 8% and the number of years is 4. Looking at Table 2 under 8% and 4 years, we find a factor of 3.312. Thus, the present value of this annuity is (3.312)($9,000) = $29,808, the same value as in Example 8.

Although net present value is one of the best approaches to evaluating investment alternatives, it does have its faults. Limitations of the net present value approach include the following:

1. Investments with the same net present value may have significantly different projected lives and different salvage values.
2. Investments with the same net present value may have different cash flows. Different cash flows may make substantial differences in the company's ability to pay its bills.
3. The assumption is that we know future interest rates, which we do not.
4. Payments are always made at the end of the period (week, month, or year), which is not always the case.

Summary

Managers tie equipment selection and capacity decisions to the organization's missions and strategy. They design their equipment and processes to have capabilities beyond the tolerance required by their customers while ensuring the flexibility needed for adjustments in technology, features, and volumes.

Good forecasting, break-even analysis, decision trees, cash flow, and net present value (NPV) techniques are particularly useful to operations managers when making capacity decisions.

Capacity investments are made effective by ensuring that the investments support a long-term strategy. The criteria for investment decisions are contributions to the overall strategic plan and winning profitable orders, not just return on investment. Efficient firms select the correct process and the correct capacity that contributes to their long-term strategy.

Key Terms

Capacity
Design capacity
Effective capacity
Utilization

Efficiency
Break-even analysis
Fixed costs
Variable costs

Contribution
Revenue function
Net present value

Using Software for Break-Even Analysis

Excel, Excel OM, and POM for Windows all handle break-even and cost–volume analysis problems.

Using Excel

It is a straightforward task to develop the formulas to do a break-even analysis in Excel. Although we do not demonstrate the basics here, you can see most of the spreadsheet analysis in the Excel OM preprogrammed software that accompanies this text.

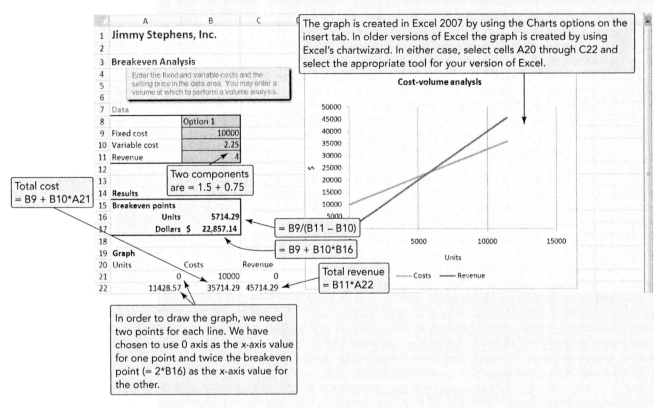

The graph is created in Excel 2007 by using the Charts options on the insert tab. In older versions of Excel the graph is created by using Excel's chartwizard. In either case, select cells A20 through C22 and select the appropriate tool for your version of Excel.

Enter the fixed and variable costs and the selling price in the data area. You may enter a volume at which to perform a volume analysis.

Two components are = 1.5 + 0.75

Total cost = B9 + B10*A21

= B9/(B11 – B10)

= B9 + B10*B16

Total revenue = B11*A22

In order to draw the graph, we need two points for each line. We have chosen to use 0 axis as the x-axis value for one point and twice the breakeven point (= 2*B16) as the x-axis value for the other.

▲ **Program 1** Excel OM's Break-Even Analysis, Using Example 3 Data

Using Excel OM

Excel OM's Break-Even Analysis module is illustrated in Program 1. Using the Stephens, Inc., information in Example 3, Program 1 shows input data, the Excel formulas used to compute the break-even points, and the solution and graphical output.

Using POM for Windows

Similar to Excel OM, POM for Windows also contains a break-even/cost–volume analysis module.

Solved Problems

Virtual Office Hours help is available on Student DVD.

Solved Problem 1

Sara James Bakery, described earlier in Examples 1 and 2, has decided to increase its facilities by adding one additional process line. The firm will have two process lines, each working 7 days a week, 3 shifts per day, 8 hours per shift. Effective capacity is now 300,000 rolls. This addition, however, will reduce overall system efficiency to 85%. Compute the expected production with this new effective capacity.

Solution

Expected production = (Effective capacity)(Efficiency)

= 300,000(.85)

= 255,000 rolls per week

Solved Problem 2

Marty McDonald has a business packaging software in Wisconsin. His annual fixed cost is $10,000, direct labor is $3.50 per package, and material is $4.50 per package. The selling price will be $12.50 per package. What is the break-even point in dollars? What is break-even in units?

Solution

$$BEP_\$ = \frac{F}{1 - (V/P)} = \frac{\$10,000}{1 - (\$8.00 / \$12.50)} = \frac{\$10,000}{.36} = \$27,777$$

$$BEP_x = \frac{F}{P - V} = \frac{\$10,000}{\$12.50 - \$8.00} = \frac{\$10,000}{\$4.50} = 2,222 \text{ units}$$

Solved Problem 3

John has been asked to determine whether the $22.50 cost of tickets for the community dinner theater will allow the group to achieve break-even and whether the 175 seating capacity is adequate. The cost for each performance of a 10-performance run is $2,500. The facility rental cost for the entire 10 performances is $10,000. Drinks and parking are extra charges and have their own price and variable costs, as shown below:

1	2	3	4	5	6	7	8	9
	Selling Price (P)	Variable Cost (V)	Percent Variable Cost (V/P)	Contribution 1 − (V/P)	Estimated Quantity of Sales Units (sales)	Dollar Sales (Sales × P)	Percent of Sales	Contribution Weighted by Percent Sales (col. 5 × col. 8)
Tickets with Dinner	$22.50	$10.50	0.467	0.533	175	$3,938	0.741	0.395
Drinks	$ 5.00	$ 1.75	0.350	0.650	175	$ 875	0.165	0.107
Parking	$ 5.00	$ 2.00	0.400	0.600	100	$ 500	0.094	0.056
					450	$5,313	1.000	0.558

solution

$$BEP_\$ = \frac{F}{\sum\left[\left(1-\frac{V_i}{P_i}\right)\times(W_i)\right]} = \frac{\$(10\times2,500)+\$10,000}{0.558} = \frac{\$35,000}{0.558} = \$62,724$$

Revenue for each day (from column 7) = $5,313
Total forecasted revenue for the 10 performances = (10 × $5,313) = $53,130
Forecasted revenue with this mix of sales shows a breakeven of $62,724

　　Thus, given this mix of costs, sales, and capacity John determines that the theatre will not break even.

Solved Problem 4

Your boss has told you to evaluate the cost of two machines. After some questioning, you are assured that they have the costs shown at the right. Assume:
a)　The life of each machine is 3 years, and
b)　The company thinks it knows how to make 14% on investments no riskier than this one.
Determine via the present value method which machine to purchase.

	Machine A	Machine B
Original cost	$13,000	$20,000
Labor cost per year	2,000	3,000
Floor space per year	500	600
Energy (electricity) per year	1,000	900
Maintenance per year	2,500	500
Total annual cost	$ 6,000	$ 5,000
Salvage value	$ 2,000	$ 7,000

solution

		Machine A			Machine B		
		Column 1	Column 2	Column 3	Column 4	Column 5	Column 6
Now	Expense	1.000	$13,000	$13,000	1.000	$20,000	$20,000
1 yr.	Expense	.877	6,000	5,262	.877	5,000	4,385
2 yr.	Expense	.769	6,000	4,614	.769	5,000	3,845
3 yr.	Expense	.675	6,000	4,050	.675	5,000	3,375
				$26,926			$31,605
3 yr.	Salvage Revenue	.675	$ 2,000	−1,350	.675	$ 7,000	−4,725
				$25,576			$26,880

We use 1.0 for payments with no discount applied against them (that is, when payments are made now, there is no need for a discount). The other values in columns 1 and 4 are from the 14% column and the respective year in Table 1 (for example, the intersection of 14% and 1 year is .877, etc.). Columns 3 and 6 are the products of the present value figures times the combined costs. This computation is made for each year and for the salvage value.

The calculation for machine A for the first year is:

$$.877 \times (\$2,000 + \$500 + \$1,000 + \$2,500) = \$5,262$$

The salvage value of the product is *subtracted* from the summed costs, because it is a receipt of cash. Since the sum of the net costs for machine B is larger than the sum of the net costs for machine A, machine A is the low-cost purchase, and your boss should be so informed.

259

Self-Test

- *Before taking the self-test*, refer to the learning objectives listed at the beginning of the supplement and the key terms listed at the end of the supplement.
- Use the key at the back of the text to **correct** your answers.
- *Restudy* pages that correspond to any questions you answered incorrectly or material you feel uncertain about.

1. Capacity decisions should be made on the basis of:
   a) building sustained competitive advantage
   b) good financial returns
   c) a coordinated plan
   d) integration into the company's strategy
   e) all of the above

2. Assumptions of the standard break-even model are:
   a) fixed and variable costs are linear and revenue is exponential
   b) fixed cost is linear and variable and revenue are exponential
   c) fixed cost, variable cost and revenue are linear
   d) break-even is computed in dollars only
   e) break-even is computed in units only

3. Effective capacity is:
   a) the capacity a firm expects to achieve given the current operating constraints
   b) percent of design capacity actually achieved
   c) the percent of capacity actually achieved
   d) actual output
   e) efficiency

4. Utilization is:
   a) the capacity a firm expects to achieve given the current operating constraints
   b) percent of design capacity actually achieved
   c) the percent of capacity actually achieved
   d) actual output
   e) efficiency

5. Efficiency is:
   a) the capacity a firm expects to achieve given the current operating constraints
   b) percent of design capacity actually achieved
   c) the percent of effective capacity actually achieved
   d) actual output
   e) design capacity

6. Capacity adjustments are accomplished through:
   a) making staffing changes
   b) adjusting equipment
   c) improving processes
   d) product redesign
   e) all of the above

7. The break-even point is:
   a) adding processes to meet the point of changing product demands
   b) improving processes to increase throughput point
   c) the point in dollars or units at which cost equals revenue
   d) adding or removing capacity to meet demand
   e) the total cost of a process alternative

8. Contribution is
   a) cost that continues even if no units are produced
   b) the difference between selling price and the variable costs
   c) the revenue that is directly in proportion to the units sold
   d) those cost that vary with the units sold
   e) all of the above

Internet and Student CD-ROM/DVD Exercises

Visit our Companion Web site or use your student CD-ROM/DVD to help with material in this supplement.

 On Our Companion Web Site,
   www.prenhall.com/heizer
- Self-Study Quizzes
- Practice Problems
- Virtual Company Tour
- Internet Cases
- PowerPoint Lecture

⊙ **On Your Student CD-ROM**
- Practice Problems
- Active Model Exercises
- Excel OM
- Excel OM Data Files
- POM for Windows

⊙ **On Your Student DVD**
- Video Clips and Video Case
- Virtual Office Hours for Solved Problems

Discussion Questions

1. Distinguish between design capacity and effective capacity.
2. What are the assumptions of break-even analysis?
3. Where does the manager obtain data for break-even analysis?
4. What keeps plotted revenue data from falling on a straight line in a break-even analysis?
5. Under what conditions would a firm want its capacity to lag demand? to lead demand?
6. Explain how net present value is an appropriate tool for comparing investments.
7. What is effective capacity?
8. What is efficiency?
9. How is actual, or expected, output computed?

Problems*

• 1   If a plant was designed to produce 7,000 hammers per day but is limited to making 6,000 hammers per day because of the time needed to change equipment between styles of hammers, what is the utilization?

• 2   For the past month, the plant in Problem 1, which has an effective capacity of 6,500, has made only 4,500 hammers per day because of material delay, employee absences, and other problems. What is its efficiency?

• 3   If a plant has an effective capacity of 6,500 and an efficiency of 88%, what is the actual (planned) output?

• 4   A plant has an effective capacity of 900 units per day and produces 800 units per day with its product mix; what is its efficiency?

• 5   Material delays have routinely limited production of household sinks to 400 units per day. If the plant efficiency is 80%, what is the effective capacity?

•• 6   What is the expected output for a plant with a design capacity of 108 chairs per day, if its effective capacity is 90 chairs and its efficiency is 90%?

• 7   A work center containing 4 machines of equal capability operates 2 shifts per day 5 days per week (8 hours per shift). This is the effective capacity. If the work center has a system efficiency of 95%, what is the expected output in hours per week?

• 8   The effective capacity and efficiency for the next quarter at MMU Mfg. in Waco, Texas, for each of three departments are shown:

Department	Effective Capacity	Recent Efficiency
Design	93,600	.95
Fabrication	156,000	1.03
Finishing	62,400	1.05

Compute the expected production for next quarter for each department.

• 9   Smithson Cutting is opening a new line of scissors for supermarket distribution. It estimates its fixed cost to be $500.00 and its variable cost to be $0.50 per unit. Selling price is expected to average $0.75 per unit.
a) What is Smithson's break-even point in units?
b) What is the break-even point in dollars?

•• 10   Under ideal conditions, a service bay at a Fast Lube can serve 6 cars per hour. The effective capacity and efficiency of a Fast Lube service bay are known to be 5.5 and 0.880, respectively. What is the minimum number of service bays Fast Lube needs to achieve an anticipated production of 200 cars per 8-hour day?

•• 11   Southeastern Oklahoma State University's business program has the facilities and faculty to handle an enrollment of 2,000 new students per semester. However, in an effort to limit class sizes to a "reasonable" level (under 200, generally), Southeastern's dean, Tom Choi, placed a ceiling on enrollment of 1,500 new students. Although there was ample demand for business courses last semester, conflicting schedules allowed only 1,450 new students to take business courses. What are the utilization and efficiency of this system?

*Note: ▶✗ means the problem may be solved with POM for Windows and/or Excel OM.

•• 12   Markland Manufacturing intends to increase capacity by overcoming a bottleneck operation by adding new equipment. Two vendors have presented proposals. The fixed costs for proposal A are $50,000, and for proposal B, $70,000. The variable cost for A is $12.00, and for B, $10.00. The revenue generated by each unit is $20.00.
a) What is the break-even point in units for proposal A?
b) What is the break-even point in units for proposal B? ▶✗

• 13   Using the data in Problem 12:
a) What is the break-even point in dollars for proposal A if you add $10,000 installation to the fixed cost?
b) What is the break-even point in dollars for proposal B if you add $10,000 installation to the fixed cost? ▶✗

• 14   Given the data in Problem 12, at what volume (units) of output would the two alternatives yield the same profit? ▶✗

•• 15   Janelle Heinke, the owner of Ha'Peppas!, is considering a new oven in which to bake the firm's signature dish, vegetarian pizza. Oven type A can handle 20 pizzas an hour. The fixed costs associated with oven A are $20,000 and the variable costs are $2.00 per pizza. Oven B is larger and can handle 40 pizzas an hour. The fixed costs associated with oven B are $30,000 and the variable costs are $1.25 per pizza. The pizzas sell for $14 each.
a) What is the break-even point for each oven?
b) If the owner expects to sell 9,000 pizzas, which oven should she purchase?
c) If the owner expects to sell 12,000 pizzas, which oven should she purchase?
d) At what volume should Janelle switch ovens? ▶✗

Corbis Digital Stock

• 16   Given the following data, calculate: a) BEP(x); b) BEP($); and c) the profit at 100,000 units:

$$P = \$8/\text{unit} \quad V = \$4/\text{unit} \quad F = \$50,000 \quad ▶✗$$

•• 17   You are considering opening a copy service in the student union. You estimate your fixed cost at $15,000 and the variable cost of each copy sold at $.01. You expect the selling price to average $.05.
a) What is the break-even point in dollars?
b) What is the break-even point in units? ▶✗

•• 18   Dr. Aleda Roth, a prolific author, is considering starting her own publishing company. She will call it DSI Publishing, Inc. DSI's estimated costs are:

Fixed	$250,000.00
Variable cost per book	$20.00
Selling price per book	$30.00

How many books must DSI sell to break even? What is its break-even point in dollars? **P**✕

•• 19   In addition to the costs in Problem 18, Dr. Roth wants to pay herself a salary of $75,000 per year.
a) Now what is her break-even point in units?
b) What is her break-even point in dollars? **P**✕

•• 20   An electronics firm is currently manufacturing an item that has a variable cost of $.50 per unit and a selling price of $1.00 per unit. Fixed costs are $14,000. Current volume is 30,000 units. The firm can substantially improve the product quality by adding a new piece of equipment at an additional fixed cost of $6,000. Variable cost would increase to $.60, but volume should jump to 50,000 units due to a higher-quality product. Should the company buy the new equipment? **P**✕

•• 21   The electronics firm in Problem 20 is now considering the new equipment and increasing the selling price to $1.10 per unit. With the higher-quality product, the new volume is expected to be 45,000 units. Under these circumstances, should the company purchase the new equipment and increase the selling price? **P**✕

•••• 22   Zan Azlett and Angela Zesiger have joined forces to start A&Z Lettuce Products, a processor of packaged shredded lettuce for institutional use. Zan has years of food processing experience, and Angela has extensive commercial food preparation experience. The process will consist of opening crates of lettuce and then sorting, washing, slicing, preserving, and finally packaging the prepared lettuce. Together, with help from vendors, they feel they can adequately estimate demand, fixed costs, revenues, and variable cost per 5-pound bag of lettuce. They think a largely manual process will have monthly fixed costs of $37,500 and variable costs of $1.75 per bag. A more mechanized process will have fixed costs of $75,000 per month with variable costs of $1.25 per 5-pound bag. They expect to sell the shredded lettuce for $2.50 per 5-pound bag.
a) What is the break-even quantity for the manual process?
b) What is the revenue at the break-even quantity for the manual process?
c) What is the break-even quantity for the mechanized process?
d) What is the revenue at the break-even quantity for the mechanized process?
e) What is the monthly profit or loss of the *manual* process if they expect to sell 60,000 bags of lettuce per month?
f) What is the monthly profit or loss of the *mechanized* process if they expect to sell 60,000 bags of lettuce per month?
g) At what quantity would Zan and Angela be indifferent to the process selected?
h) Over what range of demand would the *manual* process be preferred over the mechanized process? Over what range of demand would the *mechanized* process be preferred over the manual process? **P**✕

•• 23   Carter Manufacturing is currently producing a tape holder that has a variable cost of $0.75 per unit and a selling price of $2.00 per unit. Fixed costs are $20,000. Current volume is 40,000

units. The firm can produce a better product by adding a new piece of equipment to the process line. This equipment represents an increase of $5,000 in fixed cost. The variable cost would decrease $0.25 per unit. Volume for the new and improved product should rise to 50,000 units.
a) Should the company invest in the new equipment?
b) At what volume does the equipment choice change?
c) At a volume of 15,000 units, which process should be used?

••• 24   As a prospective owner of a club known as the Red Rose, you are interested in determining the volume of sales dollars necessary for the coming year to reach the break-even point. You have decided to break down the sales for the club into four categories, the first category being beer. Your estimate of the beer sales is that 30,000 drinks will be served. The selling price for each unit will average $1.50; the cost is $.75. The second major category is meals, which you expect to be 10,000 units with an average price of $10.00 and a cost of $5.00. The third major category is desserts and wine, of which you also expect to sell 10,000 units, but with an average price of $2.50 per unit sold and a cost of $1.00 per unit. The final category is lunches and inexpensive sandwiches, which you expect to total 20,000 units at an average price of $6.25 with a food cost of $3.25. Your fixed cost (that is, rent, utilities, and so on) is $1,800 per month plus $2,000 per month for entertainment.
a) What is your break-even point in dollars per month?
b) What is the expected number of meals each day if you are open 30 days a month?

••• 25   Using the data in Problem 24, make the problem more realistic by adding labor cost (as a variable cost) at one-third the total cost of meals and sandwiches. Also add variable expenses (kitchen supplies, tablecloths, napkins, etc.) at 10% of the food cost for each category.
a) What is your break-even point?
b) If you expect to make an annual profit of $35,000 (before taxes) for your 12-hour days, what must your total sales be?

••• 26   As manager of the St. Cloud Theatre Company, you have decided that concession sales will support themselves. The following table provides the information you have been able to put together thus far:

Item	Selling Price	Variable Cost	% of Revenue
Soft drink	$1.00	$ .65	25
Wine	1.75	.95	25
Coffee	1.00	.30	30
Candy	1.00	.30	20

Last year's manager, Jim Freeland, has advised you to be sure to add 10% of variable cost as a waste allowance for all categories.

You estimate labor cost to be $250.00 (5 booths with 3 people each). Even if nothing is sold, your labor cost will be $250.00, so you decide to consider this a fixed cost. Booth rental, which is a contractual cost at $50.00 for *each* booth per night, is also a fixed cost.
a) What is break-even volume per evening performance?
b) How much wine would you expect to sell at the break-even point?

•• 27   James Lawson's Bed and Breakfast, in a small historic Mississippi town, must decide how to subdivide (remodel) the large old home that will become its inn. There are three alternatives: Option A would modernize all baths and combine rooms, leaving the inn with four suites, each suitable for two to four adults.

Option B would modernize only the second floor; the results would be six suites, four for two to four adults, two for two adults only. Option C (the status quo option) leaves all walls intact. In this case, there are eight rooms available, but only two are suitable for four adults, and four rooms will not have private baths. Below are the details of profit and demand patterns that will accompany each option:

Alternatives	Annual Profit under Various Demand Patterns			
	High	p	Average	p
A (modernize all)	$90,000	.5	$25,000	.5
B (modernize 2nd)	$80,000	.4	$70,000	.6
C (status quo)	$60,000	.3	$55,000	.7

a) Draw the decision tree for Lawson.
b) Which option has the highest expected value? **P**✕

••• 28   As operations manager of Holz Furniture, you must make a decision about adding a line of rustic furniture. In discussing the possibilities with your sales manager, Steve Gilbert, you decide that there will definitely be a market and that your firm should enter that market. However, because rustic furniture has a different finish than your standard offering, you decide you need another process line. There is no doubt in your mind about the decision, and you are sure that you should have a second process. But you do question how large to make it. A large process line is going to cost $400,000; a small process line will cost $300,000. The question, therefore, is the demand for rustic furniture. After extensive discussion with Mr. Gilbert and Tim Ireland of Ireland Market Research, Inc., you determine that the best estimate you can make is that there is a two-out-of-three chance of profit from sales as large as $600,000 and a one-out-of-three chance as low as $300,000.

With a large process line, you could handle the high figure of $600,000. However, with a small process line you could not and would be forced to expand (at a cost of $150,000), after which time your profit from sales would be $500,000 rather than the $600,000 because of the lost time in expanding the process. If you do not expand the small process, your profit from sales would be held to $400,000. If you build a small process and the demand is low, you can handle all of the demand.

Should you open a large or small process line?

•• 29   What is the net present value of an investment that costs $75,000 and has a salvage value of $45,000? The annual profit from the investment is $15,000 each year for 5 years. The cost of capital at this risk level is 12%. **P**✕

• 30   The initial cost of an investment is $65,000 and the cost of capital is 10%. The return is $16,000 per year for 8 years. What is the net present value? **P**✕

• 31   An investment will produce $2,000 three years from now. What is the amount worth today? That is, what is the present value if the interest rate is 9%? **P**✕

• 32   What is the present value of $5,600 when the interest rate is 8% and the return of $5,600 will not be received for 15 years? **P**✕

•• 33   Tim Smunt has been asked to evaluate two machines. After some investigation, he determines that they have the costs shown in the following table. He is told to assume that:
a) the life of each machine is 3 years, and
b) the company thinks it knows how to make 12% on investments no more risky than this one.

	Machine A	Machine B
Original cost	$10,000	$20,000
Labor per year	2,000	4,000
Maintenance per year	4,000	1,000
Salvage value	2,000	7,000

Determine, via the present value method, which machine Tim should recommend.

•• 34   Your boss has told you to evaluate two ovens for Tink-the-Tinkers, a gourmet sandwich shop. After some questioning of vendors and receipt of specifications, you are assured that the ovens have the attributes and costs shown in the following table. The following two assumptions are appropriate:
1) The life of each machine is 5 years.
2) The company thinks it knows how to make 14% on investments no more risky than this one.

	Three Small Ovens at $1,250 Each	Two Large Ovens at $2,500 Each
Original cost	$3,750	$5,000
Labor per year in excess of larger models	$ 750 (total)	
Cleaning/ maintenance	$ 750 ($250 each)	$ 400 ($200 each)
Salvage value	$ 750 ($250 each)	$1,000 ($500 each)

a) Determine via the present value method which machine to tell your boss to purchase.
b) What assumption are you making about the ovens?
c) What assumptions are you making in your methodology?

•••• 35   Andre is investigating setting up a crepe stand on campus. He could rent space in the student union (which costs $300/month in rent and overhead). His materials and labor costs are $1 per crepe, and the sale price is $4 per crepe.
a) What is the break-even quantity for this option (i.e., how many crepes per month will Andre have to sell before making a profit)?
b) Andre could use a portable crepe maker from a friend and set up a booth outside the student union. He'd have no rent or other general overhead costs (i.e., no fixed costs), but his friend would demand $1.50 per crepe sold. What is the break-even quantity for this option?
c) Assume that an informal survey shows that Andre could expect 350 crepes to be sold per month. Which capacity option should he elect: student union stand or portable crepe maker?
d) What would his total monthly profit be on the better option?
e) By how much (and in what direction) would the demand have to be different before he would consider switching to the other capacity option?

•••• 36   Bold's Gym, a health club chain, is considering expanding into a new location: the initial investment would be $1 million in equipment, renovation, and a 6-year lease, and its annual upkeep and expenses would be $75,000. Its planning horizon is 6 years out, and at the end, it can sell the equipment for $50,000. Club capacity is 500 members who would pay an annual fee of $600. Bold's expects to have no problems filling membership slots. Assume that the interest rate is 10%. (See Table 1)
a) What is the present value profit/loss of the deal?
b) The club is considering offering a special deal to the members in the first year. For $3,000 upfront they get a full 6-year membership (i.e., 1 year free). Would it make financial sense to offer this deal?

Case Study

Capacity Planning at Arnold Palmer Hospital

Since opening day in 1989, the Arnold Palmer Hospital has experienced an explosive growth in demand for its services. One of only six hospitals in the U.S. to specialize in health care for women and children, Arnold Palmer Hospital has cared for over 1,500,000 patients who came to the Orlando facility from all 50 states and more than 100 countries. With patient satisfaction scores in the top 10% of U.S. hospitals surveyed (over 95% of patients would recommend the hospital to others), one of Arnold Palmer Hospital's main focuses is delivery of babies. Originally built with 281 beds and a capacity for 6,500 births per year, the hospital steadily approached and then passed 10,000 births. Looking at Table 3, Executive Director Kathy Swanson knew an expansion was necessary.

Table 3 Births at Arnold Palmer Hospital

Year	Births
1995	6,144
1996	6,230
1997	6,432
1998	6,950
1999	7,377
2000	8,655
2001	9,536
2002	9,825
2003	10,253
2004	10,555
2005	12,316
2006	13,070
2007 (est.)	13,600

With continuing population growth in its market area serving 18 central Florida counties, Arnold Palmer Hospital was delivering the equivalent of a kindergarten class of babies every day and still not meeting demand. Supported with substantial additional demographic analysis, the hospital was ready to move ahead with a capacity expansion plan and a new 11-story hospital building across the street from the existing facility.

Thirty-five planning teams were established to study such issues as (1) their specific forecasts, (2) services that would transfer to the new facility, (3) services that would remain in the existing facility, (4) staffing needs, (5) capital equipment, (6) pro forma accounting data, and (7) regulatory requirements. Ultimately, Arnold Palmer Hospital was ready to move ahead with a budget of $100 million and a commitment to an additional 150 beds. But given the growth of the central Florida region, Swanson decided to expand the hospital in stages: the top two floors would be empty interiors ("shell") to be completed at a later date, and the fourth-floor operating room could be doubled in size when needed. "With the new facility in place, we are now able to handle up to 16,000 births per year," says Swanson.

Discussion Questions*

1. Given the capacity planning discussion in the text (see Figure 5) what approach is being taken by Arnold Palmer Hospital toward matching capacity to demand?
2. What kind of major changes could take place in Arnold Palmer Hospital's demand forecast that would leave the hospital with an underutilized facility (namely, what are the risks connected with this capacity decision)?
3. Use regression analysis to forecast the point at which Swanson needs to "build out" the top two floors of the new building, namely, when demand will exceed 16,000 births.

*You may wish to view this video case on your DVD before addressing these questions.

Additional Case Studies

Internet case study: Visit our Companion Web site at www.prenhall.com/heizer for this free case study:

- **Southwestern University D:** Requires the development of a multiproduct break-even solution.

Harvard has selected these Harvard Business School cases to accompany this supplement:

harvardbusinessonline.hbsp.harvard.edu

- **National Cranberry Cooperative** (#688-122): Requires the student to analyze process, bottlenecks, and capacity.
- **Lenzing AG: Expanding in Indonesia** (#796-099): Considers how expansion affects the company's competitive position.
- **Chaparral Steel** (#687-045): Examines a major capacity expansion proposal of Chaparral Steel, a steel minimill.
- **Align Technology, Inc., Matching Manufacturing Capacity to Sales Demand** (#603-058): Analyzing and planning production capacity.
- **Samsung Heavy Industries: The Koje Shipyard** (#695-032): Explores manufacturing improvement but falling performance after major capital expansion.

Bibliography

Atamturk, A., and D. S. Hochbaum. "Capacity Acquisition, Subcontracting, and Lot-Sizing." *Management Science* 47, no. 8 (August 2001): 1081–1100.

Bowers, John, et al. "Modelling Outpatient Capacity for a Diagnosis and Treatment Center." *Health Care Management Science* 8, no. 3 (August 2005): 205.

Cheng, H. K., K. Dogan, R. A. Einicki. "Pricing and Capacity Decisions for Non-Profit Internet Service Providers." *Information Technology and Management* 7, no. 2 (April, 2006): 91.

Goodale, John C., Rohit Verma, and Madeleine E. Pullman. "A Market Utility-Based Model for Capacity Scheduling in Mass Services." *Production and Operations Management* 12, no. 2 (summer 2003): 165–185.

Hanfield, Robert B., and Kevin McCormack. "What You Need to Know About Sourcing from China." *Supply Chain Management Review* 9, no. 6 (September 2005): 28–37.

Jack, Eric P., and Amitabh S. Raturi. "Measuring and Comparing Volume Flexibility in the Capital Goods Industry." *Production and Operations Management* 12, no. 4 (winter 2003): 480–501.

Jonsson, Patrik, and Stig-Arne Mattsson. "Use and Applicability of Capacity Planning Methods." *Production and Inventory Management Journal* (3rd/4th quarter 2002): 89–95.

Kekre, Sunder, et al. "Reconfiguring a Remanufacturing Line at Visteon, Mexico." *Interfaces* 33, no. 6 (November–December 2003): 30–43.

Koste, L. L., M. K. Malhotra, and S. Sharma. "Measuring Dimensions of Manufacturing Flexibility." *Journal of Operations Management* 22, no. 2 (April 2004): 171–196.

Lovejoy, William S., and Ying Li. "Hospital Operating Room Expansion." *Management Science* 48, no. 11 (November 2002): 1369–1387.

Wacker, J. G., and C. Sheu. "Effectiveness of Manufacturing Planning and Central Systems on Manufacturing Competitiveness." *International Journal of Production Research* 44, no. 5 (March 2006): 1015.

Internet Resources

American Council of Engineering Companies: **www.acec.org**
Association for Manufacturing Excellence: **www.ame.org**

DARPA: U.S. Defense Dept., Innovative Prototype Systems: **www.DARPA.mil**

Solutions to Even Numbered Problems

2 69.2%

4 88.9%

6 81 chairs

8 Design = 88,920
Fabrication = 160,680
Finishing = 65,520

10 5.17 (or 6) bays

12 (a) 6,250 units
(b) 7,000 units

14 $x = 10,000$

16 (a) 12,500 units
(b) $100,000
(c) $350,000

18 $BEP_x = 25,000$

20 Present equipment = $1,000 profit
New equipment = 0 profit

22 (a) 50,000 bags
(b) $125,000
(c) 60,000 bags
(d) $150,000

(e) $7,500

(f) 0.0

(g) Indifferent at 75,000.

(h) Manual process below 75,000.
Mechanized process above 75,000.

24 $BEP_\$$ = $7,584.83 per mo.
Daily meals = 9

26 (a) $986.19
(b) 140.9 servings

28 Large line payoff = $100,000
Small line payoff = $66,666

30 NPV = $20,360

32 NPV = $1,764

34 (a) Purchase two large ovens.
(b) Equal quality, equal capacity.
(c) Payments are made at end of each time period. And future interest rates are known.

36 (a) $77,750
(b) Yes, NPV = $2,274

Solutions to Self Test

1. e; **2.** c; **3.** a; **4.** b; **5.** c; **6.** e; **7.** c; **8.** b.

Chapter 12

Inventory Management

Inventory Management

Outline

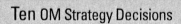

Ten OM Strategy Decisions

Design of Goods and Services

Managing Quality

Process Strategy

Location Strategies

Layout Strategies

Human Resources

Supply Chain Management

Inventory Management

    Independent Demand

    Dependent Demand

    JIT & Lean Operations

Scheduling

Maintenance

Learning Objectives

When you complete this selection you should be able to

1. Conduct an ABC analysis
2. Explain and use cycle counting
3. Explain and use the EOQ model for independent inventory demand
4. Compute a reorder point and explain safety stock
5. Apply the production order quantity model
6. Explain and use the quantity discount model
7. Understand service levels and probabilistic inventory models

From *Operations Management*, 9/e. Jay Heizer. Barry Render. Copyright © 2008 by Pearson Education. All rights reserved.

Inventory Management Provides Competitive Advantage at Amazon.com

When Jeff Bezos opened his revolutionary business in 1995, Amazon.com was intended to be a "virtual" retailer—no inventory, no warehouses, no overhead—just a bunch of computers taking orders and authorizing others to fill them. Things clearly didn't work out that way. Now, Amazon stocks millions of items of inventory, amid hundreds of thousands of bins on metal shelves, in warehouses (seven around the U.S. and three in Europe) that have twice the floor space of the Empire State Building.

Precisely managing this massive inventory has forced Amazon into becoming a world-class leader in warehouse management and automation, with annual sales of over $8 billion. This profile shows what goes on behind the scenes.

When you place an order at Amazon.com, not only are you doing business with an Internet company, you are doing business with a company that obtains competitive advantage through inventory management.

▶ **1. You order three items, and a computer in Seattle takes charge.** *A computer assigns your order—a book, a game, and a digital camera—to one of Amazon's massive U.S. distribution centers, such as the 750,000-square-foot facility in Coffeyville, Kansas.*

2. The "flow meister" in Coffeyville receives your order. *She determines which workers go where to fill your order.*

Marilyn Newton

David Burnett, Contact Press Images, Inc.

◀ **3. Rows of red lights show which products are ordered.** *Workers move from bulb to bulb, retrieving an item from the shelf above and pressing a button that resets the light. This is known as a "pick-to-light" system. This system doubles the picking speed of manual operators and drops the error rate to nearly zero.*

▼ **4. Your items are put into crates on moving belts.** *Each item goes into a large green crate that contains many customers' orders. When full, the crates ride a series of conveyor belts that wind more than 10 miles through the plant at a constant speed of 2.9 feet per second. The bar code on each item is scanned 15 times, by machines and by many of the 600 workers. The goal is to reduce errors to zero—returns are very expensive.*

David Burnett, Contact Press Images, Inc.

▶ 5. **All three items converge in a chute and then inside a box.** All the crates arrive at a central point where bar codes are matched with order numbers to determine who gets what. Your three items end up in a 3-foot-wide chute—one of several thousand—and are placed into a cardboard box with a new bar code that identifies your order. Picking is sequenced to reduce operator travel.

6. **Any gifts you've chosen are wrapped by hand.** Amazon trains an elite group of gift wrappers, each of whom processes 30 packages an hour.

David Burnett, Contact Press Images, Inc.

Contact Press Images, Inc.

◀ 7. **The box is packed, taped, weighed, and labeled before leaving the warehouse in a truck.** The Coffeyville plant was designed to ship as many as 200,000 pieces a day. About 60% of orders are shipped via the U.S. Postal Service; nearly everything else goes through United Parcel Service.

8. **Your order arrives at your doorstep.** Within a week, your order is delivered.

As Amazon.com well knows, inventory is one of the most expensive assets of many companies, representing as much as 50% of total invested capital. Operations managers around the globe have long recognized that good inventory management is crucial. On the one hand, a firm can reduce costs by reducing inventory. On the other hand, production may stop and customers become dissatisfied when an item is out of stock. *The objective of inventory management is to strike a balance between inventory investment and customer service.* You can never achieve a low-cost strategy without good inventory management.

All organizations have some type of inventory planning and control system. A bank has methods to control its inventory of cash. A hospital has methods to control blood supplies and pharmaceuticals. Government agencies, schools, and, of course, virtually every manufacturing and production organization are concerned with inventory planning and control.

In cases of physical products, the organization must determine whether to produce goods or to purchase them. Once this decision has been made, the next step is to forecast demand. Then operations managers determine the inventory necessary to service that demand. In this chapter, we discuss the functions, types, and management of inventory. We then address two basic inventory issues: how much to order and when to order.

Inventory investment: your company's largest asset.

FUNCTIONS OF INVENTORY

Inventory can serve several functions that add flexibility to a firm's operations. The four functions of inventory are:

1. To *"decouple" or separate various parts of the production process.* For example, if a firm's supplies fluctuate, extra inventory may be necessary to decouple the production process from suppliers.
2. To *decouple the firm from fluctuations in demand* and *provide a stock of goods that will provide a selection for customers.* Such inventories are typical in retail establishments.
3. To *take advantage of quantity discounts,* because purchases in larger quantities may reduce the cost of goods or their delivery.
4. To *hedge against inflation* and upward price changes.

Types of Inventory

To accommodate the functions of inventory, firms maintain four types of inventories: (1) raw material inventory, (2) work-in-process inventory, (3) maintenance/repair/operating supply (MRO) inventory, and (4) finished-goods inventory.

Raw material inventory has been purchased but not processed. This inventory can be used to decouple (i.e., separate) suppliers from the production process. However, the preferred approach is to eliminate supplier variability in quality, quantity, or delivery time so that separation is not needed. **Work-in-process (WIP) inventory** is components or raw material that have undergone some change but are not completed. WIP exists because of the time it takes for a product to be made (called *cycle time*). Reducing cycle time reduces inventory. Often this task is not difficult: During most of the time a product is "being made," it is in fact sitting idle. As Figure 1

Raw material inventory
Materials that are usually purchased but have yet to enter the manufacturing process.

Work-in-process (WIP) inventory
Products or components that are no longer raw materials but have yet to become finished products.

▼ **Figure 1** The Material Flow Cycle

Most of the time that work is in-process (95% of the cycle time) is not productive time.

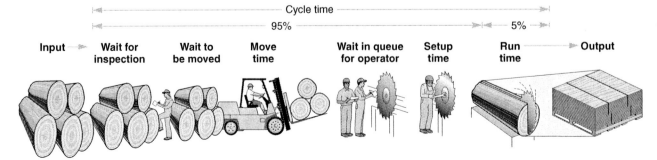

Input · Wait for inspection · Wait to be moved · Move time · Wait in queue for operator · Setup time · Run time · Output shows, actual work time, or "run" time, is a small portion of the material flow time, perhaps as low as 5%.

MROs are inventories devoted to **maintenance/repair/operating** supplies necessary to keep machinery and processes productive. They exist because the need and timing for maintenance and repair of some equipment are unknown. Although the demand for MRO inventory is often a function of maintenance schedules, other unscheduled MRO demands must be anticipated. **Finished-goods inventory** is completed product awaiting shipment. Finished goods may be inventoried because future customer demands are unknown.

MRO
Maintenance, repair, and operating materials.

Finished-goods inventory
An end item ready to be sold, but still an asset on the company's books.

INVENTORY MANAGEMENT

Operations managers establish systems for managing inventory. In this section, we briefly examine two ingredients of such systems: (1) how inventory items can be classified (called *ABC analysis*) and (2) how accurate inventory records can be maintained. We will then look at inventory control in the service sector.

ABC Analysis

ABC analysis divides on-hand inventory into three classifications on the basis of annual dollar volume. ABC analysis is an inventory application of what is known as the *Pareto principle*. The Pareto principle states that there are a "critical few and trivial many."[1] The idea is to establish inventory policies that focus resources on the *few critical* inventory parts and not the many trivial ones. It is not realistic to monitor inexpensive items with the same intensity as very expensive items.

ABC analysis
A method for dividing on-hand inventory into three classifications based on annual dollar volume.

To determine annual dollar volume for ABC analysis, we measure the *annual demand* of each inventory item times the *cost per unit*. *Class A* items are those on which the annual dollar volume is high. Although such items may represent only about 15% of the total inventory items, they represent 70% to 80% of the total dollar usage. *Class B* items are those inventory items of medium annual dollar volume. These items may represent about 30% of inventory items and 15% to 25% of the total value. Those with low annual dollar volume are *Class C*, which may represent only 5% of the annual dollar volume but about 55% of the total inventory items.

Learning Objective

1. Conduct an ABC analysis

Graphically, the inventory of many organizations would appear as presented in Figure 2. An example of the use of ABC analysis is shown in Example 1.

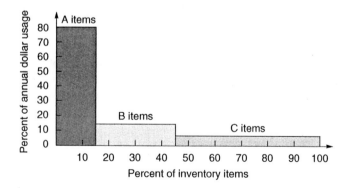

◁ **Figure 2**

Graphic Representation of ABC Analysis

Silicon Chips, Inc., maker of superfast DRAM chips, wants to categorize its 10 major inventory items using ABC analysis.

Approach: ABC analysis organizes the items on an annual dollar-volume basis. Shown on the following page (in columns 1–4) are the 10 items (identified by stock numbers), their annual demands, and unit costs.

Solution: Annual dollar volume is computed in column 5, along with the percent of the total represented by each item in column 6. Column 7 groups the 10 items into A, B, and C categories.

EXAMPLE 1

ABC analysis for a chip manufacturer

---

[1]After Vilfredo Pareto, 19th-century Italian economist.

Excel OM Data
FileCh12Ex1.xls

ABC Calculation

(1) Item Stock Number	(2) Percent of Number of Items Stocked	(3) Annual Volume (units)	× Unit Cost	= (5) Annual Dollar Volume	(6) Percent of Annual Dollar Volume		(7) Class
#10286	20%	1,000	$ 90.00	$ 90,000	38.8%	72%	A
#11526		500	154.00	77,000	33.2%		A
#12760		1,550	17.00	26,350	11.3%		B
#10867	30%	350	42.86	15,001	6.4%	23%	B
#10500		1,000	12.50	12,500	5.4%		B
#12572		600	14.17	8,502	3.7%		C
#14075		2,000	.60	1,200	.5%		C
#01036	50%	100	8.50	850	.4%	5%	C
#01307		1,200	.42	504	.2%		C
#10572		250	.60	150	.1%		C
		8,550		$232,057	100.0%		

Insight: The breakdown into A, B, and C categories is not hard and fast. The objective is to try to separate the "important" from the "unimportant."

Learning exercise: The unit cost for Item #10286 has increased from $90.00 to $120.00. How does this impact the ABC analysis? [Answer: The total annual dollar volume increases by $30,000, to $262,057, and the two A items now comprise 75% of that amount.]

Related problems: 1, 2, 3

Most automated inventory management systems include ABC analysis.

Criteria other than annual dollar volume can determine item classification. For instance, anticipated engineering changes, delivery problems, quality problems, or high unit cost may dictate upgrading items to a higher classification. The advantage of dividing inventory items into classes allows policies and controls to be established for each class.

Policies that may be based on ABC analysis include the following:

1. Purchasing resources expended on supplier development should be much higher for individual A items than for C items.
2. A items, as opposed to B and C items, should have tighter physical inventory control; perhaps they belong in a more secure area, and perhaps the accuracy of inventory records for A items should be verified more frequently.
3. Forecasting A items may warrant more care than forecasting other items.

Better forecasting, physical control, supplier reliability, and an ultimate reduction in safety stock can all result from appropriate inventory management policies. ABC analysis guides the development of those policies.

Record Accuracy

Video 12.1

Inventory Control at
Wheeled Coach Ambulance

Good inventory policies are meaningless if management does not know what inventory is on hand. Accuracy of records is a critical ingredient in production and inventory systems. Record accuracy allows organizations to focus on those items that are needed, rather than settling for being sure that "some of everything" is in inventory. Only when an organization can determine accurately what it has on hand can it make precise decisions about ordering, scheduling, and shipping.

To ensure accuracy, incoming and outgoing record keeping must be good, as must be stockroom security. A well-organized stockroom will have limited access, good housekeeping, and storage areas that hold fixed amounts of inventory. Bins, shelf space, and parts will be labeled accurately. The U.S. Marines' approach to improved inventory record accuracy is discussed in the *OM in Action* box "What the Marines Learned about Inventory from Wal-Mart."

OM in Action What the Marines Learned about Inventory from Wal-Mart

The U.S. Marine Corps knew it had inventory problems. A few years ago, when a soldier at Camp Pendleton, near San Diego, put in an order for a spare part, it took him a week to get it—from the other side of the base. Worse, the Corps had 207 computer systems worldwide. Called the "Rats' Nest" by Marine techies, most systems didn't even talk to each other.

To execute a victory over uncontrolled supplies, the Corps studied Wal-Mart, Caterpillar, Inc., and UPS. "We're in the middle of a revolution," says General Gary McKissock. McKissock aims to reduce inventory for the Corps by half, saving $200 million, and to shift 2,000 Marines from inventory detail to the battlefield.

By replacing inventory with information, the Corps won't have to stockpile tons of supplies near the battle-field, like it did during the Gulf War, only to find it couldn't keep track of what was in containers. Then there was the Marine policy requiring a 60-day supply of everything. McKissock figured out there was no need to overstock commodity items, like office supplies, that can be obtained anywhere. And with advice from the private sector, the Marines have been upgrading warehouses, adding wireless scanners for real-time inventory place-ment and tracking. Now, if containers need to be sent into a war zone, they will have radio frequency transpon-ders that, when scanned, will link to a database detailing what's inside.

Sources: Modern Materials Handling (August 2005): 24–25; and *Business Week* (December 24, 2001): 24.

Cycle Counting

Even though an organization may have made substantial efforts to record inventory accurately, these records must be verified through a continuing audit. Such audits are known as **cycle counting**. Historically, many firms performed annual physical inventories. This practice often meant shutting down the facility and having inexperienced people count parts and material. Inventory records should instead be verified via cycle counting. Cycle counting uses inventory clas-sifications developed through ABC analysis. With cycle counting procedures, items are counted, records are verified, and inaccuracies are periodically documented. The cause of inaccuracies is then traced and appropriate remedial action taken to ensure integrity of the inventory system. A items will be counted frequently, perhaps once a month; B items will be counted less frequently, perhaps once a quarter; and C items will be counted perhaps once every 6 months. Example 2 illus-trates how to compute the number of items of each classification to be counted each day.

Cycle counting
A continuing reconciliation of inventory with inventory records.

Learning Objective
2. Explain and use cycle counting

◄ *At John Deere, two workers fill orders for 3,000 parts from a six-stand carousel system, using a sophisticated computer system. The computer saves time searching for parts and speeds orders in the miles of warehouse shelving. While a worker pulls a part from one carousel, the computer sends the next request to the adjacent carousel.*

Deere & Company

Cole's Trucks, Inc., a builder of high-quality refuse trucks, has about 5,000 items in its inventory. It wants to determine how many items to cycle count each day.

Approach: After hiring Matt Clark, a bright young OM student, for the summer, the firm deter-mined that it has 500 A items, 1,750 B items, and 2,750 C items. Company policy is to count all A items every month (every 20 working days), all B items every quarter (every 60 working days), and all C items every 6 months (every 120 working days). The firm then allocates some items to be counted each day.

EXAMPLE 2

Cycle counting at a truck manufacturer

Solution:

Item Class	Quantity	Cycle Counting Policy	Number of Items Counted per Day
A	500	Each month (20 working days)	500/20 = 25/day
B	1,750	Each quarter (60 working days)	1,750/60 ≅ 29/day
C	2,750	Every 6 months (120 working days)	2,750/120 = 23/day
			77/day

Seventy-seven items are counted each day.

Insight: This daily audit of 77 items is much more efficient and accurate than conducting a massive inventory count once a year.

Learning exercise: Cole's reclassifies some B and C items so there are now 1,500 B items and 3,000 C items. How does this change the cycle count? [Answer: B and C both change to 25 items each per day, for a total of 75 items per day.]

Related problem: 4

In Example 2, the particular items to be cycle counted can be sequentially or randomly selected each day. Another option is to cycle count items when they are reordered.

Cycle counting also has the following advantages:

1. Eliminates the shutdown and interruption of production necessary for annual physical inventories.
2. Eliminates annual inventory adjustments.
3. Trained personnel audit the accuracy of inventory.
4. Allows the cause of the errors to be identified and remedial action to be taken.
5. Maintains accurate inventory records.

Control of Service Inventories

Management of service inventories deserves special consideration. Although we may think of the service sector of our economy as not having inventory, that is not always the case. For instance, extensive inventory is held in wholesale and retail businesses, making inventory management crucial and often a factor in a manager's advancement. In the food-service business, for example, control of inventory can make the difference between success and failure. Moreover, inventory that is in transit or idle in a warehouse is lost value. Similarly, inventory damaged or stolen prior to sale is a loss. In retailing, inventory that is unaccounted for between receipt and time of sale is known as **shrinkage**. Shrinkage occurs from damage and theft as well as from sloppy paperwork. Inventory theft is also known as **pilferage**. Retail inventory loss of 1% of sales is consid-

Shrinkage
Retail inventory that is unaccounted for between receipt and sale.

Pilferage
A small amount of theft.

▶ *Pharmaceutical distributor McKesson Corp., which is one of Arnold Palmer Hospital's main suppliers of surgical materials, makes heavy use of bar-code readers to automate inventory control. The device on the warehouse worker's arm combines a scanner, a computer, and a two-way radio to check orders. With rapid and accurate data, items are easily verified, improving inventory and shipment accuracy.*

McKesson Corporation

ered good, with losses in many stores exceeding 3%. Because the impact on profitability is substantial, inventory accuracy and control are critical. Applicable techniques include the following:

1. *Good personnel selection, training, and discipline:* These are never easy but very necessary in food-service, wholesale, and retail operations, where employees have access to directly consumable merchandise.

2. *Tight control of incoming shipments:* This task is being addressed by many firms through the use of bar-code and radio frequency ID (RFID) systems that read every incoming shipment and automatically check tallies against purchase orders. When properly designed, these systems are very hard to defeat. Each item has its own unique stock keeping unit (SKU; pronounced "skew").

3. *Effective control of all goods leaving the facility:* This job is accomplished with bar codes on items being shipped, magnetic strips on merchandise, or via direct observation. Direct observation can be personnel stationed at exits (as at Costco and Sam's Club wholesale stores) and in potentially high-loss areas or can take the form of one-way mirrors and video surveillance.

Handheld reader can scan RFID tags, aiding control of both incoming and outgoing shipments.

Successful retail operations require very good store-level control with accurate inventory in its proper location. One recent study found that consumers and clerks could not find 16% of the items at one of the U.S.'s largest retailers—not because the items were out of stock but because they were misplaced (in a backroom, a storage area, or on the wrong aisle). By the researcher's estimates, major retailers lose 10% to 25% of overall profits due to poor or inaccurate inventory records.[2]

INVENTORY MODELS

We now examine a variety of inventory models and the costs associated with them.

Independent vs. Dependent Demand

Inventory control models assume that demand for an item is either independent of or dependent on the demand for other items. For example, the demand for refrigerators is *independent* of the demand for toaster ovens. However, the demand for toaster oven components is *dependent* on the requirements of toaster ovens.

This selection focuses on managing inventory where demand is *independent*.

Jens Meyer, AP Wide World Photos

◁ *Even for a firm that manages its inventory better than most, Amazon was overwhelmed with the warehousing costs of the latest Harry Potter book. With popular products and seasonality causing surges in demand, retailers and suppliers often rely on large inventories. Full warehouses in November, in preparation for the holiday season, can mean huge holding costs.*

[2]See E. Malykhina, "Retailers Take Stock," *Information Week* (February 7, 2005): 20–22 and A. Raman, N. DeHoratius, and Z. Ton, "Execution: The Missing Link in Retail Operations," *California Management Review* 43, no. 3 (spring 2001): 136–141.

▶ **Table 1**

Determining Inventory
Holding Costs

Category	Cost (and range) as a Percent of Inventory Value
Housing costs (building rent or depreciation, operating cost, taxes, insurance)	6% (3–10%)
Material handling costs (equipment lease or depreciation, power, operating cost)	3% (1–3.5%)
Labor cost (receiving, warehousing, security)	3% (3–5%)
Investment costs (borrowing costs, taxes, and insurance on inventory)	11% (6–24%)
Pilferage, scrap, and obsolescence (much higher in rapid-change industries like PCs and cell phones)	3% (2–5%)
Overall carrying cost	**26%**

Note: All numbers are approximate, as they vary substantially depending on the nature of the business, location, and current interest rates. Any inventory holding cost of less than 15% is suspect, but annual inventory holding costs often approach 40% of the value of inventory and even more in high tech and fashion industries.

Holding, Ordering, and Setup Costs

Holding cost

The cost to keep or carry inventory in stock.

Holding costs are the costs associated with holding or "carrying" inventory over time. Therefore, holding costs also include obsolescence and costs related to storage, such as insurance, extra staffing, and interest payments. Table 1 shows the kinds of costs that need to be evaluated to determine holding costs. Many firms fail to include all the inventory holding costs. Consequently, inventory holding costs are often understated.

Ordering cost

The cost of the ordering process.

Setup cost

The cost to prepare a machine or process for production.

Setup time

The time required to prepare a machine or process for production.

Ordering cost includes costs of supplies, forms, order processing, purchasing, clerical support, and so forth. When orders are being manufactured, ordering costs also exist, but they are a part of what is called setup costs. **Setup cost** is the cost to prepare a machine or process for manufacturing an order. This includes time and labor to clean and change tools or holders. Operations managers can lower ordering costs by reducing setup costs and by using such efficient procedures as electronic ordering and payment.

In many environments, setup cost is highly correlated with **setup time**. Setups usually require a substantial amount of work before a setup is actually performed at the work center. With proper planning much of the preparation required by a setup can be done prior to shutting down the machine or process. Setup times can thus be reduced substantially. Machines and processes that traditionally have taken hours to set up are now being set up in less than a minute by the more imaginative world-class manufacturers. As we shall see later in this chapter, reducing setup times is an excellent way to reduce inventory investment and to improve productivity.

INVENTORY MODELS FOR INDEPENDENT DEMAND

In this section, we introduce three inventory models that address two important questions: *when to order* and *how much to order*. These *independent* demand models are:

1. Basic economic order quantity (EOQ) model
2. Production order quantity model
3. Quantity discount model

The Basic Economic Order Quantity (EOQ) Model

Economic order quantity (EOQ) model

An inventory-control technique that minimizes the total of ordering and holding costs.

The **economic order quantity (EOQ) model** is one of the oldest and most commonly known inventory-control techniques.[3] This technique is relatively easy to use but is based on several assumptions:

1. Demand is known, constant, and independent.
2. Lead time—that is, the time between placement and receipt of the order—is known and constant.
3. Receipt of inventory is instantaneous and complete. In other words, the inventory from an order arrives in one batch at one time.
4. Quantity discounts are not possible.

[3]The research on EOQ dates to 1915; see Ford W. Harris, *Operations and Cost* (Chicago: A. W. Shaw, 1915).

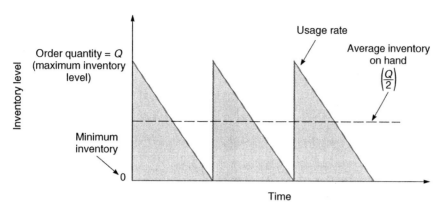

Figure 3

Inventory Usage over Time

5. The only variable costs are the cost of setting up or placing an order (setup cost) and the cost of holding or storing inventory over time (holding or carrying cost). These costs were discussed in the previous section.

6. Stockouts (shortages) can be completely avoided if orders are placed at the right time.

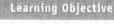
Learning Objective

3. Explain and use the EOQ model for independent inventory demand

With these assumptions, the graph of inventory usage over time has a sawtooth shape, as in Figure 3. In Figure 3, Q represents the amount that is ordered. If this amount is 500 dresses, all 500 dresses arrive at one time (when an order is received). Thus, the inventory level jumps from 0 to 500 dresses. In general, an inventory level increases from 0 to Q units when an order arrives.

Because demand is constant over time, inventory drops at a uniform rate over time. (Refer to the sloped lines in Figure 3.) Each time the inventory level reaches 0, the new order is placed and received, and the inventory level again jumps to Q units (represented by the vertical lines). This process continues indefinitely over time.

Minimizing Costs

The objective of most inventory models is to minimize total costs. With the assumptions just given, significant costs are setup (or ordering) cost and holding (or carrying) cost. All other costs, such as the cost of the inventory itself, are constant. Thus, if we minimize the sum of setup and holding costs, we will also be minimizing total costs. To help you visualize this, in Figure 4 we graph total costs as a function of the order quantity, Q. The optimal order size, Q^*, will be the quantity that minimizes the total costs. As the quantity ordered increases, the total number of orders placed per year will decrease. Thus, as the quantity ordered increases, the annual setup or ordering cost will decrease. But as the order quantity increases, the holding cost will increase due to the larger average inventories that are maintained.

As we can see in Figure 4, a reduction in either holding or setup cost will reduce the total cost curve. A reduction in setup cost curve also reduces the optimal order quantity (lot size). In addi-

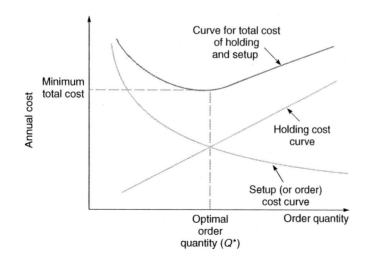

Figure 4

Total Cost as a Function of Order Quantity

279

tion, smaller lot sizes have a positive impact on quality and production flexibility. At Toshiba, the $40 billion Japanese conglomerate, workers can make as few as 10 laptop computers before changing models. This lot-size flexibility has allowed Toshiba to move toward a "build-to-order" mass customization system, an important ability in an industry that has product life cycles measured in months, not years.

You should note that in Figure 4, the optimal order quantity occurs at the point where the ordering-cost curve and the carrying-cost curve intersect. This was not by chance. With the EOQ model, the optimal order quantity will occur at a point where the total setup cost is equal to the total holding cost.[4] We use this fact to develop equations that solve directly for Q^*. The necessary steps are:

1. Develop an expression for setup or ordering cost.
2. Develop an expression for holding cost.
3. Set setup cost equal to holding cost.
4. Solve the equation for the optimal order quantity.

Using the following variables, we can determine setup and holding costs and solve for Q^*:

$$Q = \text{Number of units per order}$$
$$Q^* = \text{Optimum number of units per order (EOQ)}$$
$$D = \text{Annual demand in units for the inventory item}$$
$$S = \text{Setup or ordering cost for each order}$$
$$H = \text{Holding or carrying cost per unit per year}$$

1. Annual set up cost = (Number of orders placed per year) × (Setup or order cost per order)

$$= \left(\frac{\text{Annual demand}}{\text{Number of units in each order}} \right) (\text{Setup or order cost per order})$$

$$= \left(\frac{D}{Q} \right)(S) = \frac{D}{Q} S$$

2. Annual holding cost = (Average inventory level) × (Holding cost per unit per year)

$$= \left(\frac{\text{Order quantity}}{2} \right) (\text{Holding cost per unit per year})$$

$$= \left(\frac{Q}{2} \right)(H) = \frac{Q}{2} H$$

3. Optimal order quantity is found when annual setup cost equals annual holding cost, namely:

$$\frac{D}{Q} S = \frac{Q}{2} H$$

4. To solve for Q^*, simply cross-multiply terms and isolate Q on the left of the equal sign:

$$2DS = Q^2 H$$
$$Q^2 = \frac{2DS}{H}$$
$$Q^* = \sqrt{\frac{2DS}{H}} \tag{1}$$

Now that we have derived the equation for the optimal order quantity, Q^*, it is possible to solve inventory problems directly, as in Example 3.

---

[4]This is the case when holding costs are linear and begin at the origin—that is, when inventory costs do not decline (or they increase) as inventory volume increases and all holding costs are in small increments. Additionally, there is probably some learning each time a setup (or order) is executed—a fact that lowers subsequent setup costs. Consequently, the EOQ model is probably a special case. However, we abide by the conventional wisdom that this model is a reasonable approximation.

EXAMPLE 3

Finding the optimal
order size at
Sharp, Inc.

Sharp, Inc., a company that markets painless hypodermic needles to hospitals, would like to reduce its inventory cost by determining the optimal number of hypodermic needles to obtain per order.

Approach: The annual demand is 1,000 units; the setup or ordering cost is $10 per order; and the holding cost per unit per year is $.50.

Solution: Using these figures, we can calculate the optimal number of units per order:

$$Q^* = \sqrt{\frac{2DS}{H}}$$

$$Q^* = \sqrt{\frac{2(1,000)(10)}{0.50}} = \sqrt{40,000} = 200 \text{ units}$$

Insight: Sharp, Inc., now knows how many needles to order per order. The firm also has a basis for determining ordering and holding costs for this item, as well as the number of orders to be processed by the receiving and inventory departments.

Learning exercise: If D increases to 1,200 units, what is the new Q^*? [Answer: $Q^* = 219$ units.]

Related problems: 5, 6, 7, 8, 9, 12, 13, 15, 36, 38

Excel OM Data File Ch12Ex3.xls

We can also determine the expected number of orders placed during the year (N) and the expected time between orders (T), as follows:

$$\text{Expected number of orders} = N = \frac{\text{Demand}}{\text{Order quantity}} = \frac{D}{Q^*} \qquad (2)$$

$$\text{Expected time between orders} = T = \frac{\text{Number of working days per year}}{N} \qquad (3)$$

Example 4 illustrates this concept.

EXAMPLE 4

Computing number
of orders and time
between orders at
Sharp, Inc.

Sharp, Inc. (in Example 3), has a 250-day working year and wants to find the number of orders (N) and the expected time between orders (T).

Approach: Using Equations (2) and (3), Sharp enters the data given in Example 3.

Solution:

$$N = \frac{\text{Demand}}{\text{Order quantity}}$$

$$= \frac{1,000}{200} = 5 \text{ orders per year}$$

$$T = \frac{\text{Number of working days per year}}{\text{Expected number of orders}}$$

$$= \frac{250 \text{ working days per year}}{5 \text{ orders}} = 50 \text{ days between orders}$$

Insight: The company now knows not only how many needles to order per order but that the time between orders is 50 days and that there are five orders per year.

Learning exercise: If D = 1,200 units instead of 1,000, find N and T. [Answer: $N \cong 5.48$, $T = 45.62$.]

Related problems: 12, 13, 15

As mentioned earlier in this section, the total annual variable inventory cost is the sum of setup and holding costs:

$$\text{Total annual cost} = \text{Setup (order) cost} + \text{Holding cost} \qquad (4)$$

In terms of the variables in the model, we can express the total cost TC as:

$$TC = \frac{D}{Q}S + \frac{Q}{2}H \qquad (5)$$

Example 5 shows how to use this formula.

Active Model 12.1

Examples 3, 4, and 5 are further illustrated in Active Model 12.1 on your CD-ROM.

> This store takes 4 weeks to get an order for Levis 501 jeans filled by the manufacturer. If the store sells 10 pairs of size 30–32 Levis a week, the store manager could set up two containers, keep 40 pairs of jeans in the second container, and place an order whenever the first container is empty. This would be a fixed-quantity reordering system. It is also called a "two-bin" system and is an example of a very elementary, but effective, approach to inventory management

AP Wide World Photos

EXAMPLE 5

Computing combined cost of ordering and holding

Sharp, Inc. (from Examples 3 and 4), wants to determine the combined annual ordering and holding costs.

Approach: Apply Equation (5), using the data in Example 3.

Solution:

$$TC = \frac{D}{Q}S + \frac{Q}{2}H$$

$$= \frac{1,000}{200}(\$10) + \frac{200}{2}(\$.50)$$

$$= (5)(\$10) + (100)(\$.50)$$

$$= \$50 + \$50 = \$100$$

Insight: These are the annual setup and holding costs. The $100 total does not include the actual cost of goods. Notice that in the EOQ model, holding costs always equal setup (order) costs.

Learning exercise: Find the total annual cost if $D = 1,200$ units in Example 3. [Answer: $109.54.]

Related problems: 9, 12, 13, 14, 38b,c

Inventory costs may also be expressed to include the actual cost of the material purchased. If we assume that the annual demand and the price per hypodermic needle are known values (e.g., 1,000 hypodermics per year at $P = \$10$) and total annual cost should include purchase cost, then Equation (5) becomes:

$$TC = \frac{D}{Q}S + \frac{Q}{2}H + PD$$

Because material cost does not depend on the particular order policy, we still incur an annual material cost of $D \times P = (1,000)(\$10) = \$10,000$. (Later in this chapter we will discuss the case in which this may not be true—namely, when a quantity discount is available.)[5]

---

[5]The formula for the economic order quantity (Q^*) can also be determined by finding where the total cost curve is at a minimum (i.e., where the slope of the total cost curve is zero). Using calculus, we set the derivative of the total cost with respect to Q^* equal to 0.

The calculations for finding the minimum of $TC = \frac{D}{Q}S + \frac{Q}{2}H + PD$

are Expected number of ord

Thus, $Q^* = \sqrt{\frac{2DS}{H}}$.

Robust Model A benefit of the EOQ model is that it is robust. By **robust** we mean that it gives satisfactory answers even with substantial variation in its parameters. As we have observed, determining accurate ordering costs and holding costs for inventory is often difficult. Consequently, a robust model is advantageous. Total cost of the EOQ changes little in the neighborhood of the minimum. The curve is very shallow. This means that variations in setup costs, holding costs, demand, or even EOQ make relatively modest differences in total cost. Example 6 shows the robustness of EOQ.

Robust

Giving satisfactory answers even with substantial variation in the parameters.

EXAMPLE 6

EOQ is a robust model

Management in the Sharp, Inc., examples underestimates total annual demand by 50% (say demand is actually 1,500 needles rather than 1,000 needles) while using the same Q. How will the annual inventory cost be impacted?

Approach: We will solve for annual costs twice. First, we will apply the wrong EOQ; then we will recompute costs with the correct EOQ.

Solution: The annual inventory cost increases only $25 ($100 vs. $125), or 25%. Here is why: If demand in Example 5 is actually 1,500 needles rather than 1,000, but management uses an order quantity of $Q = 200$ (when it should be $Q = 244.9$ based on $D = 1,500$), the sum of holding and ordering cost increases 25%:

$$\text{Annual cost} = \frac{D}{Q}S + \frac{Q}{2}H$$
$$= \frac{1,500}{200}(\$10) + \frac{200}{2}(\$.50)$$
$$= \$75 + \$50 = \$125$$

However, had we known that the demand was for 1,500 with an EOQ of 244.9 units, we would have spent $122.47, as shown:

$$\text{Annual cost} = \frac{1,500}{244.9}(\$10) + \frac{244.9}{2}(\$.50)$$
$$= 6.125(\$10) + 122.45(\$.50)$$
$$= \$61.25 + \$61.22 = \$122.47$$

Insight: Note that the expenditure of $125.00, made with an estimate of demand that was substantially wrong, is only 2% ($2.52/$122.47) higher than we would have paid had we known the actual demand and ordered accordingly. Note also, that were if not due to rounding, the annual holding costs and ordering costs would be exactly equal.

Learning exercise: Demand at Sharp remains at 1,000, H is still $.50, and we order 200 needles at a time (as in Example 5). But if the true order cost = S = $15 (rather than $10), what is the annual cost? [Answer: Annual order cost increases to $75, and annual holding cost stays at $50. So the total cost = $125.]

Related problems: 8b, 14

We may conclude that the EOQ is indeed robust and that significant errors do not cost us very much. This attribute of the EOQ model is most convenient because our ability to accurately forecast demand, holding cost, and ordering cost is limited.

Reorder Points

Now that we have decided *how much* to order, we will look at the second inventory question, *when* to order. Simple inventory models assume that receipt of an order is instantaneous. In other words, they assume (1) that a firm will place an order when the inventory level for that particular item reaches zero and (2) that it will receive the ordered items immediately. However, the time between placement and receipt of an order, called **lead time**, or delivery time, can be as short as a few

Lead time

In purchasing systems, the time between placing an order and receiving it; in production systems, the wait, move, queue, setup, and run times for each component produced.

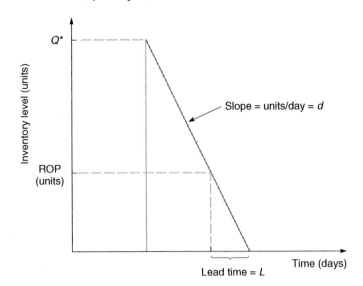

Figure 5

The Reorder Point (ROP)

Q^* is the optimum order quantity, and lead time represents the time between placing and receiving an order.

Reorder point (ROP)

The inventory level (point) at which action is taken to replenish the stocked item.

Safety stock

Extra stock to allow for uneven demand; a buffer.

hours or as long as months. Thus, the when-to-order decision is usually expressed in terms of a **reorder point (ROP)**—the inventory level at which an order should be placed (see Figure 5).

The reorder point (ROP) is given as:

$$\text{ROP} = (\text{Demand per day}) \times (\text{Lead time for a new order in days})$$
$$= d \times L \tag{6}$$

This equation for ROP *assumes that demand during lead time and lead time itself are constant.* When this is not the case, extra stock, often called **safety stock**, should be added.

The demand per day, d, is found by dividing the annual demand, D, by the number of working days in a year:

$$d = \frac{D}{\text{Number of working days in a year}}$$

Computing the reorder point is demonstrated in Example 7.

EXAMPLE 7

Computing reorder points (ROP) for iPods

An Apple distributor has a demand for 8,000 iPods per year. The firm operates a 250-day working year. On average, delivery of an order takes 3 working days. It wants to calculate the reorder point.

Approach: Compute the daily demand and then apply Equation (6).

Solution:
$$d = \frac{D}{\text{Number of working days in a year}} = \frac{8,000}{250}$$
$$= 32 \text{ units}$$
$$\text{ROP} = \text{Reorder point} = d \times L = 32 \text{ units per day} \times 3 \text{ days}$$
$$= 96 \text{ units}$$

Insight: Thus, when iPod inventory stock drops to 96 units, an order should be placed. The order will arrive 3 days later, just as the distributor's stock is depleted.

Learning exercise: If there are only 200 working days per year, what is the correct ROP? [Answer: 120 iPods.]

Related problems: 9d, 10, 11, 13f

Learning Objective

4. Compute a reorder point and explain safety stock

Safety stock is especially important in firms whose raw material deliveries may be uniquely unreliable. For example, San Miguel Corp. in the Philippines uses cheese curd imported from Europe. Because the normal mode of delivery is lengthy and variable, safety stock may be substantial.

284

Production Order Quantity Model

In the previous inventory model, we assumed that the entire inventory order was received at one time. There are times, however, when the firm may receive its inventory over a period of time. Such cases require a different model, one that does not require the instantaneous-receipt assumption. This model is applicable under two situations: (1) when inventory continuously flows or builds up over a period of time after an order has been placed or (2) when units are produced and sold simultaneously. Under these circumstances, we take into account daily production (or inventory-flow) rate and daily demand rate. Figure 6 shows inventory levels as a function of time.

Because this model is especially suitable for the production environment, it is commonly called the **production order quantity model**. It is useful when inventory continuously builds up over time, and traditional economic order quantity assumptions are valid. We derive this model by setting ordering or setup costs equal to holding costs and solving for optimal order size, Q^*. Using the following symbols, we can determine the expression for annual inventory holding cost for the production order quantity model:

Learning Objective

5. Apply the production order quantity model

Production order quantity model
An economic order quantity technique applied to production orders.

$$Q = \text{Number of units per order}$$
$$H = \text{Holding cost per unit per year}$$
$$p = \text{Daily production rate}$$
$$d = \text{Daily demand rate, or usage rate}$$
$$t = \text{Length of the production run in days}$$

1. $\left(\begin{array}{c}\text{Annual inventory} \\ \text{holding cost}\end{array}\right) = (\text{Average inventory level}) \times \left(\begin{array}{c}\text{Holding cost} \\ \text{per unit per year}\end{array}\right)$

2. $\left(\begin{array}{c}\text{Average inventory} \\ \text{level}\end{array}\right) = (\text{Maximum inventory level})/2$

3. $\left(\begin{array}{c}\text{Maximum} \\ \text{inventory level}\end{array}\right) = \left(\begin{array}{c}\text{Total production during} \\ \text{the production run}\end{array}\right) - \left(\begin{array}{c}\text{Total used during} \\ \text{the production run}\end{array}\right)$
$$= pt - dt$$

However, $Q = \text{total produced} = pt$, and thus $t = Q/p$. Therefore:

$$\text{Maximum inventory level} = p\left(\frac{Q}{p}\right) - d\left(\frac{Q}{p}\right) = Q - \frac{d}{p}Q$$
$$= Q\left(1 - \frac{d}{p}\right)$$

4. Annual inventory holding cost (or simply holding cost) =

$$\frac{\text{Maximum inventory level}}{2}(H) = \frac{Q}{2}\left[1 - \left(\frac{d}{p}\right)\right]H$$

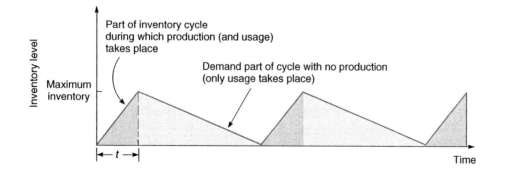

Part of inventory cycle during which production (and usage) takes place

Demand part of cycle with no production (only usage takes place)

Inventory level

Maximum inventory

Time

t

◁ **Figure 6**

Change in Inventory Levels over Time for the Production Model

▶ *Each order may require a change in the way a machine or process is set up. Reducing setup time usually means a reduction in setup cost; and reductions in setup costs make smaller batches (lots) economical to produce. Increasingly, set up (and operation) is performed by computer-controlled machines, such as this one, operating from previously written programs.*

Using this expression for holding cost and the expression for setup cost developed in the basic EOQ model, we solve for the optimal number of pieces per order by equating setup cost and holding cost:

$$\text{Setup cost} = (D/Q)S$$

$$\text{Holding cost} = \tfrac{1}{2}HQ[1-(d/p)]$$

Set ordering cost equal to holding cost to obtain Q_p^*:

$$\frac{D}{Q}S = \tfrac{1}{2}HQ[1-(d/p)]$$

$$Q^2 = \frac{2DS}{H[1-(d/p)]}$$

$$Q_p^* = \sqrt{\frac{2DS}{H[1-(d/p)]}} \tag{7}$$

In Example 8, we use the above equation, Q_p^*, to solve for the optimum order or production quantity when inventory is consumed as it is produced.

EXAMPLE 8

A production order quantity model

Excel Data OM File Ch12Ex8.xls

Nathan Manufacturing, Inc., makes and sells specialty hubcaps for the retail automobile aftermarket. Nathan's forecast for its wire-wheel hubcap is 1,000 units next year, with an average daily demand of 4 units. However, the production process is most efficient at 8 units per day. So the company produces 8 per day but uses only 4 per day. The company wants to solve for the optimum number of units per order. (*Note:* This plant schedules production of this hubcap only as needed, during the 250 days per year the shop operates.)

Approach: Gather the cost data and apply Equation (7):

$$\text{Annual demand} = D = 1{,}000 \text{ units}$$
$$\text{Setup costs} = S = \$10$$
$$\text{Holding cost} = H = \$0.50 \text{ per unit per year}$$
$$\text{Daily production rate} = p = 8 \text{ units daily}$$
$$\text{Daily demand rate} = d = 4 \text{ units daily}$$

Solution:

$$Q_p^* = \sqrt{\frac{2DS}{H[1-(d/p)]}}$$

$$Q_p^* = \sqrt{\frac{2(1,000)(10)}{0.50[1-(4/8)]}}$$

$$= \sqrt{\frac{20,000}{0.50(1/2)}} = \sqrt{80,000}$$

$$= 282.8 \text{ hubcaps, or } 283 \text{ hubcaps}$$

Active Model 12.2

Example 8 is further illustrated in Active Model 12.2 on the CD-ROM.

Insight: The difference between the production order quantity model and the basic EOQ model is the annual holding cost, which is reduced in the production order quantity model.

Learning exercise: If Nathan can increase its daily production rate from 8 to 10, how does TC change? [Answer: $Q_p^* = 258$.]

Related problems: 16, 17, 18, 37

You may want to compare this solution with the answer in Example 3, which had identical D, S, and H values. Eliminating the instantaneous-receipt assumption, where $p = 8$ and $d = 4$, resulted in an increase in Q^* from 200 in Example 3 to 283 in Example 8. This increase in Q^* occurred because holding cost dropped from \$.50 to (\$.50 $\times \frac{1}{2}$), making a larger order quantity optimal. Also note that:

$$d = 4 = \frac{D}{\text{Number of days the plant is in operation}} = \frac{1,000}{250}$$

We can also calculate Q_p^* when *annual* data are available. When annual data are used, we can express Q_p^* as:

$$Q_p^* = \sqrt{\frac{2DS}{H\left(1-\dfrac{\text{Annual demand rate}}{\text{Annual production rate}}\right)}} \tag{8}$$

OM in Action Inventory Accuracy at Milton Bradley

Milton Bradley, a division of Hasbro, Inc., has been manufacturing toys for more than 100 years. Founded by Milton Bradley in 1860, the company started by making a lithograph of Abraham Lincoln. Using his printing skills, Bradley developed games, including the Game of Life, Chutes and Ladders, Candy Land, Scrabble, and Lite Brite. Today, the company produces hundreds of games, requiring billions of plastic parts.

Once Milton Bradley has determined the optimal quantities for each production run, it must make them and assemble them as a part of the proper game. Some games require literally hundreds of plastic parts, including spinners, hotels, people, animals, cars, and so on. According to Gary Brennan, director of manufacturing, getting the right number of pieces to the right toys and production lines is the most important issue for the credibility of the company. Some orders can require 20,000 or more perfectly assembled games delivered to their warehouses in a matter of days.

Games with the incorrect number of parts and pieces can result in some very unhappy customers. It is also

Anthony Labbe Photography

time-consuming and expensive for Milton Bradley to supply the extra parts or to have toys or games returned. When shortages are found during the assembly stage, the entire production run is stopped until the problem is corrected. Counting parts by hand or machine is not always accurate. As a result, Milton Bradley now weighs pieces and completed games to determine if the correct number of parts have been included. If the weight is not exact, there is a problem that is resolved before shipment. Using highly accurate digital scales, Milton Bradley is now able to get the right parts in the right game at the right time. Without this simple innovation, the most sophisticated production schedule is meaningless.

Sources: The Wall Street Journal (April 15, 1999): B1; *Plastics World* (March 1997): 22–26; and *Modern Materials Handling* (September 1997): 55–57.

Quantity Discount Models

Quantity discount
A reduced price for items purchased in large quantities.

To increase sales, many companies offer quantity discounts to their customers. A **quantity discount** is simply a reduced price (P) for an item when it is purchased in larger quantities. Discount schedules with several discounts for large orders are common. A typical quantity discount schedule appears in Table 2. As can be seen in the table, the normal price of the item is $5. When 1,000 to 1,999 units are ordered at one time, the price per unit drops to $4.80; when the quantity ordered at one time is 2,000 units or more, the price is $4.75 per unit. As always, management must decide when and how much to order. However, with an opportunity to save money on quantity discounts, how does the operations manager make these decisions?

As with other inventory models discussed so far, the overall objective is to minimize total cost. Because the unit cost for the third discount in Table 2 is the lowest, you may be tempted to order 2,000 units or more merely to take advantage of the lower product cost. Placing an order for that quantity, however, even with the greatest discount price, may not minimize total inventory cost. Granted, as discount quantity goes up, the product cost goes down. However, holding cost increases because orders are larger. Thus the major trade-off when considering quantity discounts is between *reduced product cost* and *increased holding cost*. When we include the cost of the product, the equation for the total annual inventory cost can be calculated as follows:

Total cost = Setup cost + Holding cost + Product cost

Learning Objective

6. Explain and use the quarterly discount model

or

$$TC = \frac{D}{Q}S + \frac{Q}{2}H + PD \qquad (9)$$

where
Q = Quantity ordered
D = Annual demand in units
S = Ordering or setup cost per order or per setup
P = Price per unit
H = Holding cost per unit per year

Now, we have to determine the quantity that will minimize the total annual inventory cost. Because there are several discounts, this process involves four steps:

Step 1: For each discount, calculate a value for optimal order size Q^*, using the following equation:

$$Q^* = \sqrt{\frac{2DS}{IP}} \qquad (10)$$

Note that the holding cost is IP instead of H. Because the price of the item is a factor in annual holding cost, we cannot assume that the holding cost is a constant when the price per unit changes for each quantity discount. Thus, it is common to express the holding cost as a percent (I) of unit price (P) instead of as a constant cost per unit per year, H.

Don't forget to adjust order quantity upward if the quantity is too low to qualify for the discount.

Step 2: For any discount, if the order quantity is too low to qualify for the discount, adjust the order quantity upward to the *lowest* quantity that will qualify for the discount. For example, if Q^* for discount 2 in Table 2 were 500 units, you would adjust this value up to 1,000 units. Look at the second discount in Table 2. Order quantities between 1,000 and 1,999 will qualify for the 4% discount. Thus, if Q^* is below 1,000 units, we will adjust the order quantity up to 1,000 units.

▶ **Table 2**

A Quantity Discount Schedule

Discount Number	Discount Quantity	Discount (%)	Discount Price (P)
1	0 to 999	no discount	$5.00
2	1,000 to 1,999	4	$4.80
3	2,000 and over	5	$4.75

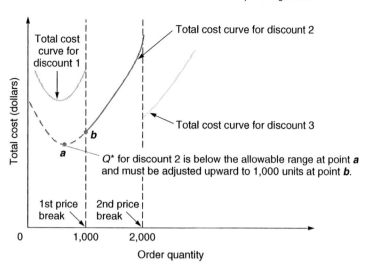

Total cost (dollars) vs Order quantity graph

Total cost curve for discount 1

Total cost curve for discount 2

Total cost curve for discount 3

b

a

Q^* for discount 2 is below the allowable range at point **a** and must be adjusted upward to 1,000 units at point **b**.

1st price break

2nd price break

0   1,000   2,000

Order quantity

Figure 7 label

Figure 7

Total Cost Curve for the Quantity Discount Model

The reasoning for step 2 may not be obvious. If the order quantity, Q^*, is below the range that will qualify for a discount, a quantity within this range may still result in the lowest total cost.

As shown in Figure 7, the total cost curve is broken into three different total cost curves. There is a total cost curve for the first ($0 \leq Q \leq 999$), second ($1,000 \leq Q \leq 1,999$), and third ($Q \geq 2,000$) discount. Look at the total cost (*TC*) curve for discount 2. Q^* for discount 2 is less than the allowable discount range, which is from 1,000 to 1,999 units. As the figure shows, the lowest allowable quantity in this range, which is 1,000 units, is the quantity that minimizes total cost. Thus, the second step is needed to ensure that we do not discard an order quantity that may indeed produce the minimum cost. Note that an order quantity computed in step 1 that is *greater* than the range that would qualify it for a discount may be discarded.

Step 3: Using the preceding total cost equation, compute a total cost for every Q^* determined in steps 1 and 2. If you had to adjust Q^* upward because it was below the allowable quantity range, be sure to use the adjusted value for Q^*.

Step 4: Select the Q^* that has the lowest total cost, as computed in step 3. It will be the quantity that will minimize the total inventory cost.

Let us see how this procedure can be applied with an example.

EXAMPLE 9

Quantity discount model

Excel OM Data File
Ch12Ex9.xls

Wohl's Discount Store stocks toy race cars. Recently, the store has been given a quantity discount schedule for these cars. This quantity schedule was shown in Table 2. Thus, the normal cost for the toy race cars is $5.00. For orders between 1,000 and 1,999 units, the unit cost drops to $4.80; for orders of 2,000 or more units, the unit cost is only $4.75. Furthermore, ordering cost is $49.00 per order, annual demand is 5,000 race cars, and inventory carrying charge, as a percent of cost, *I*, is 20%, or .2. What order quantity will minimize the total inventory cost?

Approach: We will follow the four steps just outlined for a quantity discount model.

Solution: The first step is to compute Q^* for every discount in Table 2. This is done as follows:

$$Q_1^* = \sqrt{\frac{2(5,000)(49)}{(.2)(5.00)}} = 700 \text{ cars per order}$$

$$Q_2^* = \sqrt{\frac{2(5,000)(49)}{(.2)(4.80)}} = 714 \text{ cars per order}$$

$$Q_3^* = \sqrt{\frac{2(5,000)(49)}{(.2)(4.75)}} = 718 \text{ cars per order}$$

The second step is to adjust upward those values of Q^* that are below the allowable discount range. Since Q_1^* is between 0 and 999, it need not be adjusted. Because Q_2^* is below the allowable range of 1,000 to 1,999, it must be adjusted to 1,000 units. The same is true for Q_3^*: It must be adjusted to 2,000 units. After this step, the following order quantities must be tested in the total cost equation:

$$Q_1^* = 700$$

$$Q_2^* = 1,000\text{—adjusted}$$

$$Q_3^* = 2,000\text{—adjusted}$$

The third step is to use the total cost equation (9) and compute a total cost for each order quantity. This step is taken with the aid of Table 3, which presents the computations for each level of discount introduced in Table 2.

▷ **Table 3**

Total Cost Computations for Wohl's Discount Store

Discount Number	Unit Price	Order Quantity	Annual Product Cost	Annual Ordering Cost	Annual Holding Cost	Total
1	$5.00	700	$25,000	$350	$350	$25,700
2	$4.80	1,000	$24,000	$245	$480	$24,725
3	$4.75	2,000	$23,750	$122.50	$950	$24,822.50

The fourth step is to select that order quantity with the lowest total cost. Looking at Table 3, you can see that an order quantity of 1,000 toy race cars will minimize the total cost. You should see, however, that the total cost for ordering 2,000 cars is only slightly greater than the total cost for ordering 1,000 cars. Thus, if the third discount cost is lowered to $4.65, for example, then this quantity might be the one that minimizes total inventory cost.

Insight: The quantity discount model's third cost factor, annual product cost, is now a major variable with impact on the final cost and decision. It takes substantial increases in order and holding costs to compensate for a large quantity price break.

Learning exercise: Wohl's has just been offered a third price break. If it orders 2,500 or more cars at a time, the unit cost drops to $4.60. What is the optimal order quantity now? [Answer: $Q_4^* = 2,500$, for a total cost of $24,248.]

Related problems: 19, 20, 21, 22, 23, 24, 25

PROBABILISTIC MODELS AND SAFETY STOCK

All the inventory models we have discussed so far make the assumption that demand for a product is constant and certain. We now relax this assumption. The following inventory models apply when product demand is not known but can be specified by means of a probability distribution. These types of models are called **probabilistic models**.

An important concern of management is maintaining an adequate service level in the face of uncertain demand. The **service level** is the *complement* of the probability of a stockout. For instance, if the probability of a stockout is 0.05, then the service level is .95. Uncertain demand raises the possibility of a stockout. One method of reducing stockouts is to hold extra units in inventory. As we noted, such inventory is usually referred to as safety stock. It involves adding a number of units as a buffer to the reorder point. As you recall from our previous discussion:

$$\text{Reorder point} = \text{ROP} = d \times L$$

where d = Daily demand

L = Order lead time, or number of working days it takes to deliver an order

The inclusion of safety stock (*ss*) changes the expression to:

$$\text{ROP} = d \times L + ss \tag{11}$$

Probabilistic model

A statistical model applicable when product demand or any other variable is not known but can be specified by means of a probability distribution.

Service level

The complement of the probability of a stockout.

The amount of safety stock maintained depends on the cost of incurring a stockout and the cost of holding the extra inventory. Annual stockout cost is computed as follows:

$$\text{Annual stockout costs} = \text{The sum of the units short for each demand level}$$
$$\times \text{ The probability of that demand level} \times \text{The stockout cost/unit}$$
$$\times \text{ The number of orders per year} \qquad (12)$$

Example 10 illustrates this concept.

EXAMPLE 10

Determining safety stock with probabilistic demand and constant lead time

David Rivera Optical has determined that its reorder point for eyeglass frames is 50 ($d \times L$) units. Its carrying cost per frame per year is $5, and stockout (or lost sale) cost is $40 per frame. The store has experienced the following probability distribution for inventory demand during the reorder period. The optimum number of orders per year is six.

	Number of Units	Probability
	30	.2
	40	.2
ROP →	50	.3
	60	.2
	70	.1
		1.0

How much safety stock should David Rivera keep on hand?

Approach: The objective is to find the amount of safety stock that minimizes the sum of the additional inventory holding costs and stockout costs. The annual holding cost is simply the holding cost per unit multiplied by the units added to the ROP. For example, a safety stock of 20 frames, which implies that the new ROP, with safety stock, is 70 (= 50 + 20), raises the annual carrying cost by $5(20) = $100.

However, computing annual stockout cost is more interesting. For any level of safety stock, stockout cost is the expected cost of stocking out. We can compute it, as in Equation (12), by multiplying the number of frames short (Demand – ROP) by the probability of demand at that level, by the stockout cost, by the number of times per year the stockout can occur (which in our case is the number of orders per year). Then we add stockout costs for each possible stockout level for a given ROP.

Solution: We begin by looking at zero safety stock. For this safety stock, a shortage of 10 frames will occur if demand is 60, and a shortage of 20 frames will occur if the demand is 70. Thus the stockout costs for zero safety stock are:

(10 frames short) (.2) ($40 per stockout) (6 possible stockouts per year)
+ (20 frames short) (.1) ($40) (6) = $960

The following table summarizes the total costs for each of the three alternatives:

Safety Stock	Additional Holding Cost	Stockout Cost		Total Cost
20	(20) ($5) = $100		$ 0	$100
10	(10) ($5) = $ 50	(10) (.1) ($40) (6)	= $240	$290
0	$ 0	(10) (.2) ($40) (6) + (20) (.1) ($40) (6) = $960		$960

The safety stock with the lowest total cost is 20 frames. Therefore, this safety stock changes the reorder point to 50 + 20 = 70 frames.

Insight: The optical company now knows that a safety stock of 20 frames will be the most economical decision.

Learning exercise: David Rivera's holding cost per frame is now estimated to be $20, while the stockout cost is $30 per frame. Does the reorder point change? [Answer: Safety stock = 10 now, with a total cost of $380, which is the lowest of the three. ROP = 60 frames.]

Related problems: 29, 30, 31

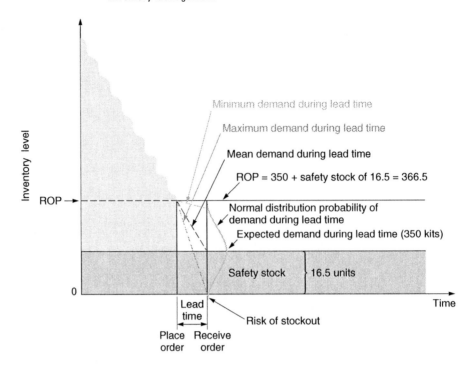

> **Figure 8**

Probabilistic Demand for a Hospital Item

Expected number of kits needed during lead time is 350, but for a 95% service level, the reorder point should be raised to 366.5.

When it is difficult or impossible to determine the cost of being out of stock, a manager may decide to follow a policy of keeping enough safety stock on hand to meet a prescribed customer service level. For instance, Figure 8 shows the use of safety stock when demand (for hospital resuscitation kits) is probabilistic. We see that the safety stock in Figure 8 is 16.5 units, and the reorder point is also increased by 16.5.

The manager may want to define the service level as meeting 95% of the demand (or, conversely, having stockouts only 5% of the time). Assuming that demand during lead time (the reorder period) follows a normal curve, only the mean and standard deviation are needed to define the inventory requirements for any given service level. Sales data are usually adequate for computing the mean and standard deviation. In the following example we use a normal curve with a known mean (μ) and standard deviation (σ) to determine the reorder point and safety stock necessary for a 95% service level. We use the following formula:

$$\text{ROP} = \text{Expected demand during lead time} + Z\sigma_{dLT} \qquad (13)$$

where $\quad Z = $ Number of standard deviations

$\qquad \sigma_{dLT} = $ Standard deviation of demand during lead time

---

EXAMPLE 11

Safety stock with probabilistic demand

Memphis Regional Hospital stocks a "code blue" resuscitation kit that has a normally distributed demand during the reorder period. The mean (average) demand during the reorder period is 350 kits, and the standard deviation is 10 kits. The hospital administrator wants to follow a policy that results in stockouts only 5% of the time.

(a) What is the appropriate value of Z? (b) How much safety stock should the hospital maintain? (c) What reorder point should be used?

Approach: The hospital determines how much inventory is needed to meet the demand 95% of the time. The figure in this example may help you visualize the approach. The data are as follows:

$\mu = $ Mean demand $= 350$ kits

$\sigma_{dLT} = $ Standard deviation of demand during lead time $= 10$ kits

$Z = $ Number of standard normal deviations

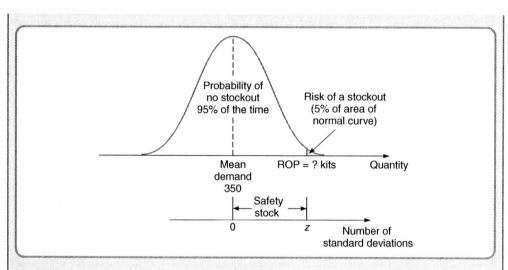

solution:

a. We use the properties of a standardized normal curve to get a Z-value for an area under the normal curve of .95 (or 1 − .05). Using a normal table (see Appendix I), we find a Z-value of 1.65 standard deviations from the mean.

b. Because: Safety stock = $x - \mu$

And: $$Z = \frac{x - \mu}{\sigma_{dLT}}$$

Then: Safety stock = $Z\sigma_{dLT}$ (14)

Solving for safety stock, as in Equation (14), gives:

Safety stock = 1.65(10) = 16.5 kits

This is the situation illustrated in Figure 8.

c. The reorder point is:

ROP = Expected demand during lead time + Safety stock

= 350 kits + 16.5 kits of safety stock = 366.5, or 367 kits

Insight: The cost of the inventory policy increases dramatically (exponentially) with an increase in service levels.

Learning exercise: What policy results in stockouts 10% of the time? [Answer: $Z = 1.28$; safety stock = 12.8; ROP = 363 kits.]

Related problems: 27, 28, 38

Other Probabilistic Models

Equations (13) and (14) assume that both an estimate of expected demand during lead times and its standard deviation are available. When data on lead time demand are *not* at hand, these formulas cannot be applied. However, three other models are available. We need to determine which model to use for three situations:

1. Demand is variable and lead time is constant
2. Lead time is variable, and demand is constant
3. Both demand and lead time are variable

All three models assume that demand and lead time are independent variables. Note that our examples use days, but weeks can also be used. Let us examine these three situations separately, because a different formula for the ROP is needed for each.

Learning Objective

7. Understand service levels and probabilistic inventory models

Demand Is Variable and Lead Time Is Constant When *only the demand is variable*, then:

$$ROP = (Average \text{ daily demand} \times \text{Lead time in days}) + Z\sigma_{dLT}$$ (15)

where σ_{dLT} = Standard deviation of demand during lead time = $\sigma_d \sqrt{\text{Lead time}}$

and σ_d = Standard deviation of demand per day

EXAMPLE 12

ROP for variable demand and constant lead time

The *average* daily demand for Apple iPods at a Circuit Town store is 15, with a standard deviation of 5 units. The lead time is constant at 2 days. Find the reorder point if management wants a 90% service level (i.e., risk stockouts only 10% of the time). How much of this is safety stock?

Approach: Apply Equation (15) to the following data:

Average daily demand (normally distributed) = 15
Lead time in days (constant) = 2
Standard deviation of daily demand = σ_d = 5
Service level = 90%

Solution: From the normal table (Appendix I), we derive a Z-value for 90% of 1.28. Then:

$$ROP = (15 \text{ units} \times 2 \text{ days}) + Z\sigma_d \sqrt{\text{Lead time}}$$
$$= 30 + 1.28(5)(\sqrt{2})$$
$$= 30 + 1.28(5)(1.41) = 30 + 9.02 = 39.02 \cong 39$$

Thus, safety stock is about 9 iPods.

Insight: The value of Z depends on the manager's stockout risk level. The smaller the risk, the higher the Z.

Learning exercise: If the Circuit Town manager wants a 95% service level, what is the new ROP? [Answer: ROP = 41.63, or 42.]

Related problem: 32

Lead Time Is Variable and Demand is Constant When the demand is constant and *only the lead time is variable*, then:

$$ROP = (\text{Daily demand} \times Average \text{ lead time in days}) + Z (\text{Daily demand}) \times \sigma_{LT} \quad (16)$$

where σ_{LT} = Standard deviation of lead time in days

EXAMPLE 13

ROP for constant demand and variable lead time

The Circuit Town store in Example 12 sells about 10 digital cameras a day (almost a constant quantity). Lead time for camera delivery is normally distributed with a mean time of 6 days and a standard deviation of 3 days. A 98% service level is set. Find the ROP.

Aproach: Apply Equation (16) to the following data:

Daily demand = 10
Average lead time = 6 days
Standard deviation of lead time = σ_{LT} = 3 days
Service level = 98%, so Z (from Appendix I) = 2.055

Solution: From the equation we get:

$$ROP = (10 \text{ units} \times 6 \text{ days}) + 2.055(10 \text{ units})(3)$$
$$= 60 + 61.65 = 121.65$$

The reorder point is about 122 cameras.

Insight: Note how the very high service level of 98% drives the ROP up.

Learning exercise: If a 90% service level is applied, what does the ROP drop to? [Answer: ROP = 60 + (1.28)(10)(3) = 60 + 38.4 = 98.4, since the Z-value is only 1.28.]

Related problem: 33

Both Demand and Lead Time Are Variable When both the demand and lead time are variable, the formula for reorder point becomes more complex[6]:

$$ROP = (\text{Average daily demand} \times \text{Average lead time}) + Z\sigma_{dLT} \quad (17)$$

where σ_d = Standard deviation of demand per day

σ_{LT} = Standard deviation of lead time in days

and $\sigma_{dLT} = \sqrt{(\text{Average lead time} \times \sigma_d^2) + (\text{Average daily demand})^2 \sigma_{LT}^2}$

[6]Refer to S. Narasimhan, D. W. McLeavey, and P. Billington, *Production Planning and Inventory Control*, 2nd ed. (Upper Saddle River, NJ: Prentice Hall, 1995), Chap. 6, for details. Note that Equation (17) can also be expressed as
ROP = Average daily demand × Average lead time + $Z\sqrt{(\text{Average lead time} \times \sigma_d^2) + \bar{d}^2\sigma_{LT}^2}$

EXAMPLE 14

ROP for variable demand and variable lead time

The Circuit Town store's most popular item is six-packs of 9-volt batteries. About 150 packs are sold per day, following a normal distribution with a standard deviation of 16 packs. Batteries are ordered from an out-of-state distributor; lead time is normally distributed with an average of 5 days and a standard deviation of 1 day. To maintain a 95% service level, what ROP is appropriate?

Approach: Determine a quantity at which to reorder by applying Equation (17) to the following data:

Average daily demand = 150 packs
Standard deviation of demand = σ_d = 16 packs
Average lead time = 5 days
Standard deviation of lead time = σ_{LT} = 1 day
Service level = 95%, so Z = 1.65 (from Appendix I)

Solution: From the equation we compute:

$$\text{ROP} = (150 \text{ packs} \times 5 \text{ days}) + 1.65\,\sigma_{dLT}$$

where

$$\sigma_{dLT} = \sqrt{(5 \text{ days} \times 16^2) + (150^2 \times 1^2)}$$
$$= \sqrt{(5 \times 256) + (22{,}500 \times 1)}$$
$$= \sqrt{1{,}280 + 22{,}500} = \sqrt{23{,}780} \cong 154$$

So ROP = $(150 \times 5) + 1.65(154) \cong 750 + 254 = 1{,}004$ packs

Insight: When both demand and lead time are variable, the formula looks quite complex. But it is just the result of squaring the standard deviations in Equations (15) and (16) to get their variances, then summing them, and finally taking the square root.

Learning exercise: For an 80% service level, what is the ROP? [Answer: Z = .84 and ROP = 879 packs.]

Related problem: 34

FIXED-PERIOD (P) SYSTEMS

The inventory models that we have considered so far are **fixed-quantity**, or **Q**, **systems**. That is, the same fixed amount is added to inventory every time an order for an item is placed. We saw that orders are event triggered. When inventory decreases to the reorder point (ROP), a new order for Q units is placed.

To use the fixed-quantity model, inventory must be continuously monitored. This is called a **perpetual inventory system**. Every time an item is added to or withdrawn from inventory, records must be updated to make sure the ROP has not been reached.

In a **fixed-period**, or **P**, **system**, on the other hand, inventory is ordered at the end of a given period. Then, and only then, is on-hand inventory counted. Only the amount necessary to bring total inventory up to a prespecified target level is ordered. Figure 9 illustrates this concept.

Fixed-quantity (Q) system
An EOQ ordering system with the same order amount each time.

Perpetual inventory system
A system that keeps track of each withdrawal or addition to inventory continuously, so records are always current.

Fixed-period (P) system
A system in which inventory orders are made at regular time intervals.

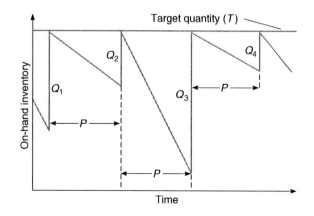

◀ **Figure 9**

Inventory Level in a Fixed-Period (P) System

Various amounts (Q_1, Q_2, Q_3, etc.) are ordered at regular time intervals (P) based on the quantity necessary to bring inventory up to the target quantity (T).

Fixed-period systems have several of the same assumptions as the basic EOQ fixed-quantity system:

- The only relevant costs are the ordering and holding costs.
- Lead times are known and constant.
- Items are independent of one another.

The downward-sloped line in Figure 9 again represents on-hand inventory. But now, when the time between orders (P) passes, we place an order to raise inventory up to the target quantity (T). The amount ordered during the first period may be Q_1, the second period Q_2, and so on. The Q_i value is the difference between current on-hand inventory and the target inventory level. Example 15 illustrates how much to reorder in a simple P system.

EXAMPLE 15

P-system ordering

Hard Rock London has a back order for three leather bomber jackets in its retail shop. There are no jackets in stock, none are expected from earlier orders, and it is time to place an order. The target value is 50 jackets. How many bomber jackets should be ordered?

Approach: Consider the four variables: the target quantity, on-hand inventory, earlier orders en route, and back orders.

Solution: Order amount (Q) = Target quantity (T) – On-hand inventory – Earlier orders not yet received + Back orders = 50 – 0 – 0 + 3 = 53 jackets

Insight: Because demand in a P system is variable, some orders will be larger than the EOQ and some will be smaller.

Learning exercise: Hard Rock has a back order of 5 London T-shirts, no on-hand inventory, a target quantity of 400, and no orders not yet received. What is Q? [Answer: 405 T-shirts.]

Related problem: 35

The advantage of the fixed-period system is that there is no physical count of inventory items after an item is withdrawn—this occurs only when the time for the next review comes up. This procedure is also convenient administratively, especially if inventory control is only one of several duties of an employee.

A fixed-period system is appropriate when vendors make routine (i.e., at fixed-time interval) visits to customers to take fresh orders or when purchasers want to combine orders to save ordering and transportation costs (therefore, they will have the same review period for similar inventory items). For example, a vending machine company may come to refill its machines every Tuesday. This is also the case at Anheuser-Busch, whose sales reps may visit a store every 5 days (see the *OM in Action* box "66,207,896 Bottles of Beer on the Wall").

OM in Action 66,207,89X Bottles of Beer on the Wall

When Dereck Gurden pulls up at one of his customers' stores—7-Eleven, Buy N Save, or one of dozens of liquor marts and restaurants in the 800-square-mile territory he covers in California's Central Valley—managers usually stop what they're doing and grab a note pad. This is because, as Gurden claims, "I know more about these guys' businesses than they do . . . at least in the beer section."

What makes Gurden and other sales reps for Anheuser-Busch distributors so smart? It's BudNet, the King of Beer's top-secret crown jewel—a nationwide data network through which drivers and reps report, in excruciating detail, on sales, shelf space, inventory, and displays at thousands of stores. How does it work? As Gurden walks a store, he inputs what he sees to his handheld PC, then plugs into a cell phone and fires off new orders, along with

the data he has gathered. Anheuser has made a deadly accurate science of finding out what beer lovers are buying, as well as when, where, and why.

Matching these data with U.S. census figures of neighborhoods, Anheuser mines data down to the sales at individual stores. The company can pinpoint age, ethnicity, education, political, and sexual orientation of customers at your local 7-Eleven. BudNet is the primary reason Anheuser's share of the $75 billion U.S. beer market continues to increase, and the company has posted double-digit profit gains for 20 straight quarters while its competitors have flat-lined.

Sources: Business 2.0 (January/February 2001): 47–49; *Beverage Industry* (May 2004): 20–23; and *The Wall Street Journal* (March 23, 2004): C3.

The disadvantage of the *P* system is that because there is no tally of inventory during the review period, there is the possibility of a stockout during this time. This scenario is possible if a large order draws the inventory level down to zero right after an order is placed. Therefore, a higher level of safety stock (as compared to a fixed-quantity system) needs to be maintained to provide protection against stockout during both the time between reviews and the lead time.

Summary

Inventory represents a major investment for many firms. This investment is often larger than it should be because firms find it easier to have "just-in-case" inventory rather than "just-in-time" inventory. Inventories are of four types:

1. Raw material and purchased components
2. Work-in-process
3. Maintenance, repair, and operating (MRO)
4. Finished goods

In this chapter, we discussed independent inventory, ABC analysis, record accuracy, cycle counting, and inventory models used to control independent demands. The EOQ model, production order quantity model, and quantity discount model can all be solved using Excel, Excel OM, or POM for Windows software. A summary of the inventory models presented in this chapter is shown in Table 4.

◀ **Table 4**

Models for Independent Demand Summarized

Q = Number of units per order	P = Price
EOQ = Optimum order quantity ($Q*$)	I = Annual inventory carrying cost as a percent
D = Annual demand in units	μ = Mean demand
S = Setup or ordering cost for each order	σ_{dLT} = Standard deviation of demand during lead-time
H = Holding or carrying cost per unit per year in dollars	σ_{LT} = Standard deviation of lead time
p = Daily production rate	Z = Standardized value under the normal curve
d = Daily demand rate	

EOQ:

$$Q* = \sqrt{\frac{2DS}{H}} \tag{1}$$

EOQ production order quantity model:

$$Q_p^* = \sqrt{\frac{2DS}{H[1-(d/p)]}} \tag{7}$$

Total cost for the EOQ and quantity discount EOQ models:

$$TC = \text{Total cost}$$
$$= \text{Setup cost} + \text{Holding cost} + \text{Product cost}$$
$$= \frac{D}{Q}S + \frac{Q}{2}H + PD \tag{9}$$

Quantity discount EOQ model:

$$Q* = \sqrt{\frac{2DS}{IP}} \tag{10}$$

Probability model with expected lead time demand known:

$$\text{ROP} = \text{Expected demand during lead time} + Z\sigma_{dLT} \tag{13}$$

$$\text{Safety stock} = Z\sigma_{dLT} \tag{14}$$

Probability model with variable demand and constant lead time:

$$\text{ROP} = (\text{Average daily demand} \times \text{Lead time in days}) + Z\sigma_{dLT} \tag{15}$$

Probability model with constant demand and variable lead time:

$$\text{ROP} = (\text{Daily demand} \times \text{Average lead time in days}) + Z(\text{Daily demand}) \sigma_{LT} \tag{16}$$

Probability model with both demand and lead time variable:

$$\text{ROP} = (\text{Average daily demand} \times \text{Average lead time in days}) + Z\sigma_{dLT} \tag{17}$$

Key Terms

Raw material inventory
Work-in-process (WIP) inventory
MRO
Finished-goods inventory
ABC analysis
Cycle counting
Shrinkage
Pilferage
Holding cost

Ordering cost
Setup cost
Setup time
Economic order quantity (EOQ) model
Robust
Lead time
Reorder point (ROP)
Safety stock
Production order quantity model

Quantity discount
Probabilistic model
Service level
Fixed-quantity (Q) system
Perpetual inventory system
Fixed-period (P) system

Using Software to Solve Inventory Problems

This section presents three ways to solve inventory problems with computer software. First, you can create your own Excel spreadsheets. Second, you can use the Excel OM software that comes with this text and is found on the student CD. Third, POM for Windows, also on your CD, can solve all problems marked with a **P**.

Creating Your Own Excel Spreadsheets

Program 1 illustrates how you can make an Excel model to solve Example 8. This is a production order quantity model. Below Program 1 is a listing of the formulas needed to create the spreadsheet.

▶ **Program 1**

Using Excel for a Production Model, with Data from Example 8

	A	B
1	**Nathan Manufacturing, Inc.**	
2		
3	Demand rate, D	1000
4	Setup cost, S	$ 10.00
5	Holding cost, H	$ 0.50
6	Daily production rate, p	8
7	Daily demand rate, d	4
8	Days per year	250
9	Unit price, P	$ 200.00
10		
11		
12	Optimal production quantity, Q*	282.84
13	Maximum Inventory	141.42
14	Average Inventory	70.71
15	Number of Setups	3.54
16	Time (days) between production runs	70.71
17		
18	Holding cost	$ 35.36
19	Setup cost	$ 35.36
20		
21	Unit costs	$ 200,000
22		
23	Total cost, Tc	$ 200,071
24		

Computations

Value	Cell	Excel Formula
Optimal production quantity, Q*	B12	=SQRT(2*B3*B4/B5)*SQRT(B6/(B6-B7))
Maximum Inventory	B13	=B12*(B6-B7)/B6
Average Inventory	B14	=B13/2
Number of Setups	B15	=B3/B12
Time (days) between production runs	B16	=B8/B15
Holding cost	B18	=B14*B5
Setup cost	B19	=B15*B4
Unit costs	B21	=B9*B3
Total cost, Tc	B22	=B18+B19+B21

Using Excel OM

Excel OM allows us to easily model inventory problems ranging from ABC analysis, to the basic EOQ model, to the production model, to quantity discount situations.

Program 2 shows the input data, selected formulas, and results for an ABC analysis, using data from Example 1. After the data are entered, we use the *Data* and *Sort* Excel commands to rank the items from largest to smallest dollar volumes.

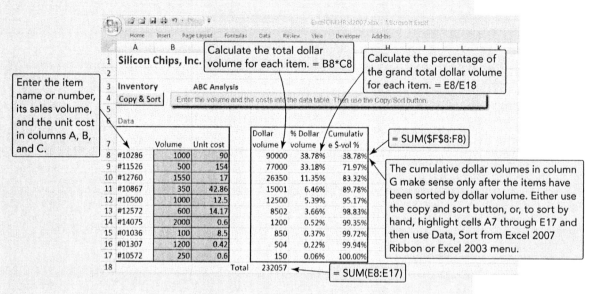

▲ **Program 2** Using Excel OM for an ABC Analysis, with Data from Example 1

Using POM for Windows

The POM for Windows Inventory module can also solve the entire EOQ family of problems.

Solved Problems

Virtual Office help is available on Student DVD.

Solved Problem 1

David Alexander has compiled the following table of six items in inventory at Angelo Products, along with the unit cost and the annual demand in units:

Identification Code	Unit Cost ($)	Annual Demand (units)
XX1	5.84	1,200
B66	5.40	1,110
3CPO	1.12	896
33CP	74.54	1,104
R2D2	2.00	1,110
RMS	2.08	961

Use ABC analysis to determine which item(s) should be carefully controlled using a quantitative inventory technique and which item(s) should not be closely controlled.

Solution

The item that needs strict control is 33CP, so it is an A item. Items that do not need to be strictly controlled are 3CPO, R2D2, and RMS; these are C items. The B items will be XX1 and B66.

Code	Annual dollar volume = Unit Cost × Demand
XX1	$ 7,008.00
B66	$ 5,994.00
3CPO	$ 1,003.52
33CP	$82,292.16
R2D2	$ 2,220.00
RMS	$ 1,998.88

Total cost = $100,516.56

70% of total cost = $70,347.92

Solved Problem 2

The Warren W. Fisher Computer Corporation purchases 8,000 transistors each year as components in minicomputers. The unit cost of each transistor is $10, and the cost of carrying one transistor in inventory for a year is $3. Ordering cost is $30 per order.

What are (a) the optimal order quantity, (b) the expected number of orders placed each year, and (c) the expected time between orders? Assume that Fisher operates on a 200-day working year.

Solution

(a) $Q^* = \sqrt{\dfrac{2DS}{H}} = \sqrt{\dfrac{2(8,000)(30)}{3}} = 400$ units

(b) $N = \dfrac{D}{Q^*} = \dfrac{8,000}{400} = 20$ orders

(c) Time between orders $= T = \dfrac{\text{Number of working days}}{N} = \dfrac{200}{20} = 10$ working days

With 20 orders placed each year, an order for 400 transistors is placed every 10 working days.

Solved Problem 3

Annual demand for notebook binders at Meyer's Stationery Shop is 10,000 units. Brad Meyer operates his business 300 days per year and finds that deliveries from his supplier generally take 5 working days. Calculate the reorder point for the notebook binders.

Solution

$$L = 5 \text{ days}$$

$$d = \frac{10,000}{300} = 33.3 \text{ units per day}$$

$$ROP = d \times L = (33.3 \text{ units per day})(5 \text{ days})$$
$$= 166.7 \text{ units}$$

Thus, Brad should reorder when his stock reaches 167 units.

Solved Problem 4

Leonard Presby, Inc., has an annual demand rate of 1,000 units but can produce at an average production rate of 2,000 units. Setup cost is $10; carrying cost is $1. What is the optimal number of units to be produced each time?

Solution

$$Q_p^* = \sqrt{\dfrac{2DS}{H\left(1 - \dfrac{\text{Annual demand rate}}{\text{Annual production rate}}\right)}} = \sqrt{\dfrac{2(1,000)(10)}{1[1 - (1,000/2,000)]}}$$

$$= \sqrt{\dfrac{20,000}{1/2}} = \sqrt{40,000} = 200 \text{ units}$$

Solved Problem 5

Whole Nature Foods sells a gluten-free product for which the annual demand is 5,000 boxes. At the moment it is paying $6.40 for each box; carrying cost is 25% of the unit cost; ordering costs are $25. A new supplier has offered to sell the same item for $6.00 if Whole Nature Foods buys at least 3,000 boxes per order. Should the firm stick with the old supplier, or take advantage of the new quantity discount?

Solution

Under present price of $6.40 per box:

Economic order quantity, using Equation (10):

$$Q^* = \sqrt{\frac{2DS}{IP}}$$

$$Q^* = \sqrt{\frac{2(5,000)(25)}{(0.25)(6.40)}}$$

$$= 395.3, \text{ or } 395 \text{ boxes}$$

where D = period demand
S = order cost
P = price per box
I = holding cost as percent
H = holding cost = IP

Total cost = Order cost + Holding cost + Purchase cost

$$= \frac{DS}{Q} + \frac{Q}{2}H + PD$$

$$= \frac{(5,000)(25)}{395} + \frac{(395)(0.25)(6.40)}{2} + (6.40)(6,000)$$

$$= 316 + 316 + 32,000$$

$$= \$32,632$$

Note: Order and carrying costs are rounded.

Under the quantity discount price of $6.00 per box:

Total cost = Order cost + Holding cost + Purchase cost

$$= \frac{DS}{Q} + \frac{Q}{2}H + PD$$

$$= \frac{(5,000)(25)}{3000} + \frac{(5,000)(0.25)(6.00)}{2} + (6.00)(5,000)$$

$$= 42 + 3,750 + 30,000$$

$$= \$33,792$$

Therefore, the old supplier with whom Whole Nature Foods would incur a total cost of $32,632 is preferable.

Solved Problem 6

Children's art sets are ordered once each year by Ashok Kumar, Inc., and the reorder point, without safety stock (dL) is 100 art sets. Inventory carrying cost is $10 per set per year, and the cost of a stockout is $50 per set per year. Given the following demand probabilities during the reorder period, how much safety stock should be carried?

Demand during Reorder Period	Probability
0	.1
50	.2
ROP → 100	.4
150	.2
200	.1
	1.0

Solution

Safety Stock	Carrying Cost	Incremental Costs Stockout Cost	Total Cost
0	0	50 × (50 × 0.2 + 100 × 0.1) = 1,000	$1,000
50	50 × 10 = 500	50 × (0.1 × 50) = 250	750
100	100 × 10 = 1,000	0	1,000

The safety stock that minimizes total incremental cost is 50 sets. The reorder point then becomes 100 sets + 50 sets, or 150 sets.

Solved Problem 7

What safety stock should Ron Satterfield Corporation maintain if mean sales are 80 during the reorder period, the standard deviation is 7, and Ron can tolerate stockouts 10% of the time?

solution

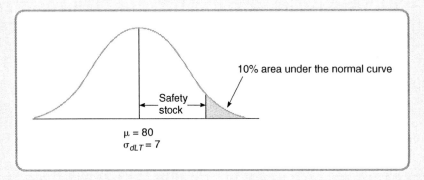

From Appendix I, Z at an area of .9 (or $1 - .10$) = 1.28, and Equation (14):

$$\text{Safety stock} = Z\sigma_{dLT}$$
$$= 1.28(7) = 8.96 \text{ units, or 9 units}$$

Solved Problem 8

The daily demand for 52″ plasma TVs at Sarah's Discount Emporium is normally distributed, with an average of 5 and a standard deviation of 2 units. The lead time for receiving a shipment of new TVs is 10 days and is fairly constant. Determine the reorder point and safety stock for a 95% service level.

solution

The ROP for this variable demand and constant lead time model uses Equation (15):

$$\text{ROP} = (\text{Average daily demand} \times \text{Lead time in days}) + Z\sigma_{dLT}$$

where $\sigma_{dLT} = \sigma_d\sqrt{\text{Lead time}}$

So, with $Z = 1.65$,

$$\text{ROP} = (5 \times 10) + 1.65(2)\sqrt{10}$$
$$= 50 + 10.4 = 60.4 \cong 60 \text{ TVs}$$

The safety stock is 10.4, or about 10 TVs.

Solved Problem 9

The demand at Arnold Palmer Hospital for a specialized surgery pack is 60 per week, virtually every week. The lead time from McKesson, its main supplier, is normally distributed, with a mean of 6 weeks for this product and a standard deviation of 2 weeks. A 90% weekly service level is desired. Find the ROP.

solution

Here the demand is constant and lead time is variable, with data given in weeks, not days. We apply Equation (16):

$$\text{ROP} = (\text{Weekly demand} \times \text{Average lead time in weeks}) + Z (\text{Weekly demand}) \sigma_{LT}$$

where σ_{LT} = standard deviation of lead time in weeks = 2

So, with $Z = 1.28$, for a 90% service level:

$$\text{ROP} = (60 \times 6) + 1.28(60)(2)$$
$$= 360 + 153.6 = 513.6 \cong 514 \text{ surgery packs}$$

Self-Test

- **Before taking the self-test,** refer to the learning objectives listed at the beginning of the selection and the key terms listed at the end of the selection.
- Use the key at the back of the selection to **correct** your answers.
- **Restudy** pages that correspond to any questions you answered incorrectly or material you feel uncertain about.

1. ABC analysis divides on-hand inventory into three classes based upon:
   a) unit price
   b) the number of units on hand
   c) annual demand
   d) annual dollar values

2. Cycle counting:
   a) provides a measure of inventory turnover
   b) assumes that all inventory records must be verified with the same frequency
   c) is a process by which inventory records are periodically verified
   d) all of the above

3. The service industry is improving inventory management through a number of methods. These include:
   a) shrinkage and pilferage
   b) good personnel selection
   c) bar coding of incoming and outgoing merchandise
   d) a and b above
   e) b and c above

4. Annual holding costs are usually:
   a) under 6% of inventory value
   b) 6% to 9% of inventory value
   c) 9% to 12% of inventory value
   d) 12% to 15% of inventory value
   e) over 15% of inventory value

5. The difference(s) between the basic EOQ model and the production order quantity model is(are) that:
   a) the production order quantity model does not require the assumption of known, constant demand
   b) the EOQ model does not require the assumption of negligible lead time
   c) the production order quantity model does not require the assumption of instantaneous delivery
   d) all of the above

6. Extra units held in inventory to reduce stockouts are called:
   a) reorder point
   b) safety stock
   c) just-in-time inventory
   d) all of the above

7. The two most important inventory-based questions answered by the typical inventory model are:
   a) when to place an order and the cost of the order
   b) when to place an order and how much of an item to order
   c) how much of an item to order and the cost of the order
   d) how much of an item to order and with whom the order should be placed

8. The appropriate level of safety stock is typically determined by:
   a) minimizing an expected stockout cost
   b) choosing the level of safety stock that assures a given service level
   c) carrying sufficient safety stock so as to eliminate all stockouts

9. Inventory record accuracy can be improved through:
   a) cycle counting
   b) reorder points
   c) ABC analysis
   d) all of the above

Active Model Exercise

This active model explores the basics of a typical inventory decision and the sensitivity of the model to changes in demand and costs. It uses the data from Examples 3, 4, and 5.

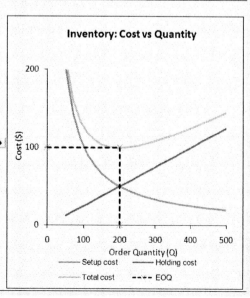

Economic Order Quantity (EOQ) Model

Reset Data   Questions

Demand rate, D	1000	
Setup cost, S	10	
Holding cost, H	0.5	
Unit Price, P	0	

	Optimal	Other
Order Quantity, Q*	200.00	200.00
Maximum Inventory	200.00	200.00
Average Inventory	100.00	100.00
Number of orders, N	5.00	5.00
Holding cost	$ 50.00	$50.00
Setup cost	$ 50.00	$50.00
Unit costs	$ -	$0.00
Total cost, TCmin	$ 100.00	$100.00
	Difference	$0.00
	% Difference	0.00%

◄ **Active Model 12.1**

An EOQ Analysis of the Data in Examples 3, 4, and 5 for Sharp, Inc.

Questions

1. What is the EOQ and what is the lowest total cost?

2. What is the annual cost of *carrying* inventory at the EOQ and the annual cost of *ordering* inventory at the EOQ of 200 units?

3. From the graph, what can you conclude about the relationship between the lowest total cost and the costs of ordering and carrying inventory?

4. How much does the total cost increase if the store manager orders 50 more hypodermics than the EOQ? 50 fewer hypodermics?

5. What happens to the EOQ and total cost when demand is doubled? When carrying cost is doubled?

6. Scroll through lower setup cost values and describe the changes to the graph. What happens to the EOQ?

7. Comment on the sensitivity of the EOQ model to errors in demand or cost estimates.

Internet and Student CD-ROM Exercises

Visit our Companion Web site or use your student CD-ROM/DVD to help with material in this chapter.

 On Our Companion Web Site,
www.prenhall.com/heizer
- Self-Study Quizzes
- Practice Problems
- Virtual Company Tour
- Internet Cases
- PowerPoint Lecture

 On Your Student CD-ROM
- Practice Problems
- Active Model Exercises
- Excel OM
- Excel OM Example Data Files
- POM for Windows

 On Your Student DVD
- Video Clip and Video Case
- Virtual Office Hours for Solved Problems

Discussion Questions

1. Describe the four types of inventory.
2. With the advent of low-cost computing, do you see alternatives to the popular ABC classifications?
3. What is the purpose of the ABC classification system?
4. Identify and explain the types of costs that are involved in an inventory system.
5. Explain the major assumptions of the basic EOQ model.
6. What is the relationship of the economic order quantity to demand? To the holding cost? To the setup cost?
7. Explain why it is not necessary to include product cost (price or price times quantity) in the EOQ model, but the quantity discount model requires this information.
8. What are the advantages of cycle counting?
9. What impact does a decrease in setup time have on EOQ?
10. When quantity discounts are offered, why is it not necessary to check discount points that are below the EOQ or points above the EOQ that are not discount points?

11. What is meant by *service level*?
12. Explain the following: All things being equal, the production inventory quantity will be larger than the economic order quantity.
13. Describe the difference between a fixed-quantity (Q) and a fixed-period (P) inventory system.
14. Explain what is meant by the expression "robust model." Specifically, what would you tell a manager who exclaimed, "Uh-oh, we're in trouble! The calculated EOQ is wrong, Actual demand is 10% greater than estimated."
15. What is "safety stock"? What does safety stock provide safety against?
16. When demand is not constant, the reorder point is a function of what four parameters?
17. How are inventory levels monitored in retail stores?
18. State a major advantage, and a major disadvantage, of a fixed-period (P) system.

Ethical Dilemma

Wayne Hills Hospital in tiny Wayne, Nebraska, faces a problem common to large, urban hospitals as well as to small, remote ones like itself. That problem is deciding how much of each type of whole blood to keep in stock. Because blood is expensive and has a limited shelf life (up to 5 weeks under 1–6°C refrigeration), Wayne Hills naturally wants to keep its stock as low as possible. Unfortunately, past disasters such as a major tornado and a train wreck demonstrated that lives would be lost when not enough blood was available to handle massive needs. The hospital administrator wants to set an 85% service level based on demand over the past decade. Discuss the implications of this decision. What is the hospital's responsibility with regard to stocking lifesaving medicines with short shelf lives? How would you set the inventory level for a commodity such as blood?

Problems*

•• 1 L. Houts Plastics is a large manufacturer of injection-molded plastics in North Carolina. An investigation of the company's manufacturing facility in Charlotte yields the information presented in the table below. How would the plant classify these items according to an ABC classification system?

L. Houts Plastics Charlotte Inventory Levels

Item Code #	Average Inventory (units)	Value ($/unit)
1289	400	3.75
2347	300	4.00
2349	120	2.50
2363	75	1.50
2394	60	1.75
2395	30	2.00
6782	20	1.15
7844	12	2.05
8210	8	1.80
8310	7	2.00
9111	6	3.00 P✗

• 2 Boreki Enterprise has the following 10 items in inventory. Theodore Boreki asks you, a recent OM graduate, to divide these items into ABC classifications. What do you report back?

Item	Annual Demand	Cost/Unit
A2	3,000	$ 50
B8	4,000	12
C7	1,500	45
D1	6,000	10
E9	1,000	20
F3	500	500
G2	300	1,500
H2	600	20
I5	1,750	10
J8	2,500	5 P✗

•• 3 Jean-Marie Bourjolly's restaurant has the following inventory items that it orders on a weekly basis:

Inventory Item	$ Value/Case	# Ordered/Week
Rib eye steak	135	3
Lobster tail	245	3
Pasta	23	12
Salt	3	2
Napkins	12	2
Tomato sauce	23	11
French fries	43	32
Pepper	3	3
Garlic powder	11	3
Trash can liners	12	3
Table cloths	32	5
Fish filets	143	10
Prime rib roasts	166	6
Oil	28	2

Inventory Item	$ Value/Case	# Ordered/Week
Lettuce (case)	35	24
Chickens	75	14
Order pads	12	2
Eggs (case)	22	7
Bacon	56	5
Sugar	4	2

a) Which is the most expensive item, using annual dollar volume?
b) Which are C items?
c) What is the annual dollar volume for all 20 items? P✗

• 4 Howard Electronics, a small manufacturer of electronic research equipment, has approximately 7,000 items in its inventory and has hired Joan Blasco-Paul to manage its inventory. Joan has determined that 10% of the items in inventory are A items, 35% are B items, and 55% are C items. She would like to set up a system in which all A items are counted monthly (every 20 working days), all B items are counted quarterly (every 60 working days), and all C items are counted semiannually (every 120 working days). How many items need to be counted each day?

• 5 William Beville's computer training school, in Richmond, stocks workbooks with the following characteristics:

$$\text{Demand } D = 19{,}500 \text{ units/year}$$
$$\text{Ordering cost } S = \$25/\text{order}$$
$$\text{Holding cost } H = \$4/\text{unit/year}$$

a) Calculate the EOQ for the workbooks.
b) What are the annual holding costs for the workbooks?
c) What are the annual ordering costs? P✗

• 6 If $D = 8,000$ per month, $S = \$45$ per order, and $H = \$2$ per unit per month, what is the economic order quantity? P✗

•• 7 Henry Crouch's law office has traditionally ordered ink refills 60 units at a time. The firm estimates that carrying cost is 40% of the $10 unit cost and that annual demand is about 240 units per year. The assumptions of the basic EOQ model are thought to apply. For what value of ordering cost would its action be optimal?

• 8 Madeline Thimmes's Dream Store sells water beds and assorted supplies. Her best-selling bed has an annual demand of 400 units. Ordering cost is $40; holding cost is $5 per unit per year.

a) To minimize the total cost, how many units should be ordered each time an order is placed?
b) If the holding cost per unit was $6 instead of $5, what would the optimal order quantity be? P✗

• 9 Southeastern Bell stocks a certain switch connector at its central warehouse for supplying field service offices. The yearly demand for these connectors is 15,000 units. Southeastern estimates its annual holding cost for this item to be $25 per unit. The cost to place and process an order from the supplier is $75. The company operates 300 days per year, and the lead time to receive an order from the supplier is 2 working days.

a) Find the economic order quantity.
b) Find the annual holding costs.
c) Find the annual ordering costs.
d) What is the reorder point? P✗

*Note: P✗ means the problem may be solved with POM for Windows and/or Excel OM.

• **10** Lead time for one of your fastest-moving products is 21 days. Demand during this period averages 100 units per day. What would be an appropriate reorder point?

• **11** Annual demand for the notebook binders at Duncan's Stationery Shop is 10,000 units. Dana Duncan operates her business 300 days per year and finds that deliveries from her supplier generally take 5 working days. Calculate the reorder point for the notebook binders that she stocks.

•• **12** Thomas Kratzer is the purchasing manager for the headquarters of a large insurance company chain with a central inventory operation. Thomas's fastest-moving inventory item has a demand of 6,000 units per year. The cost of each unit is $100, and the inventory carrying cost is $10 per unit per year. The average ordering cost is $30 per order. It takes about 5 days for an order to arrive, and the demand for 1 week is 120 units. (This is a corporate operation, and there are 250 working days per year.)
a) What is the EOQ?
b) What is the average inventory if the EOQ is used?
c) What is the optimal number of orders per year?
d) What is the optimal number of days in between any two orders?
e) What is the annual cost of ordering and holding inventory?
f) What is the total annual inventory cost, including cost of the 6,000 units? **P✕**

•• **13** Joe Henry's machine shop uses 2,500 brackets during the course of a year. These brackets are purchased from a supplier 90 miles away. The following information is known about the brackets:

Annual demand:	2,500
Holding cost per bracket per year:	$1.50
Order cost per order:	$18.75
Lead time:	2 days
Working days per year:	250

a) Given the above information, what would be the economic order quantity (EOQ)?
b) Given the EOQ, what would be the average inventory? What would be the annual inventory holding cost?
c) Given the EOQ, how many orders would be made each year? What would be the annual order cost?
d) Given the EOQ, what is the total annual cost of managing the inventory?
e) What is the time between orders?
f) What is the reorder point (ROP)? **P✕**

•• **14** Myriah Fitzgibbon, of L.A. Plumbing, uses 1,200 of a certain spare part that costs $25 for each order, with an annual holding cost of $24.
a) Calculate the total cost for order sizes of 25, 40, 50, 60, and 100.
b) Identify the economic order quantity and consider the implications for making an error in calculating economic order quantity. **P✕**

••• **15** M. Cotteleer Electronics supplies microcomputer circuitry to a company that incorporates microprocessors into refrigerators and other home appliances. One of the components has an annual demand of 250 units, and this is constant throughout the year. Carrying cost is estimated to be $1 per unit per year, and the ordering cost is $20 per order.
a) To minimize cost, how many units should be ordered each time an order is placed?
b) How many orders per year are needed with the optimal policy?

c) What is the average inventory if costs are minimized?
d) Suppose that the ordering cost is not $20, and Cotteleer has been ordering 150 units each time an order is placed. For this order policy (of $Q = 150$) to be optimal, determine what the ordering cost would have to be. **P✕**

•• **16** Race One Motors is an Indonesian car manufacturer. At its largest manufacturing facility, in Jakarta, the company produces subcomponents at a rate of 300 per day, and it uses these subcomponents at a rate of 12,500 per year (of 250 working days). Holding costs are $2 per item per year, and ordering costs are $30 per order.
a) What is the economic production quantity?
b) How many production runs per year will be made?
c) What will be the maximum inventory level?
d) What percentage of time will the facility be producing components?
e) What is the annual cost of ordering and holding inventory? **P✕**

•• **17** Radovilsky Manufacturing Company, in Hayward, California, makes flashing lights for toys. The company operates its production facility 300 days per year. It has orders for about 12,000 flashing lights per year and has the capability of producing 100 per day. Setting up the light production costs $50. The cost of each light is $1. The holding cost is $0.10 per light per year.
a) What is the optimal size of the production run?
b) What is the average holding cost per year?
c) What is the average setup cost per year?
d) What is the total cost per year, including the cost of the lights? **P✕**

•• **18** Arthur Meiners is the production manager of Wheel-Rite, a small producer of metal parts. Wheel-Rite supplies Cal-Tex, a larger assembly company, with 10,000 wheel bearings each year. This order has been stable for some time. Setup cost for Wheel-Rite is $40, and holding cost is $.60 per wheel bearing per year. Wheel-Rite can produce 500 wheel bearings per day. Cal-Tex is a just-in-time manufacturer and requires that 50 bearings be shipped to it each business day.
a) What is the optimum production quantity?
b) What is the maximum number of wheel bearings that will be in inventory at Wheel-Rite?
c) How many production runs of wheel bearings will Wheel-Rite have in a year?
d) What is the total setup + holding cost for Wheel-Rite? **P✕**

•• **19** Cesar Rogo Computers, a Mississippi chain of computer hardware and software retail outlets, supplies both educational and commercial customers with memory and storage devices. It currently faces the following ordering decision relating to purchases of CD-ROMs:

$$D = 36{,}000 \text{ disks}$$
$$S = \$25$$
$$H = \$0.45$$
$$\text{Purchase price} = \$0.85$$
$$\text{Discount price} = \$0.82$$
$$\text{Quantity needed to qualify for the discount} = 6{,}000 \text{ disks}$$

Should the discount be taken? **P✕**

•• **20** Bell Computers purchases integrated chips at $350 per chip. The holding cost is $35 per unit per year, the ordering cost is $120 per order, and sales are steady, at 400 per month. The com-

306

pany's supplier, Rich Blue Chip Manufacturing, Inc., decides to offer price concessions in order to attract larger orders. The price structure is shown below.

a) What is the optimal order quantity and the minimum cost for Bell Computers to order, purchase, and hold these integrated chips?

Rich Blue Chip's Price Structure

Quantity Purchased	Price/Unit
1–99 units	$350
100–199 units	$325
200 or more units	$300

b) Bell Computers wishes to use a 10% holding cost rather than the fixed $35 holding cost in part a. What is the optimal order quantity, and what is the optimal cost? **P**×

•• **21** Wang Distributors has an annual demand for an airport metal detector of 1,400 units. The cost of a typical detector to Wang is $400. Carrying cost is estimated to be 20% of the unit cost, and the ordering cost is $25 per order. If Ping Wang, the owner, orders in quantities of 300 or more, he can get a 5% discount on the cost of the detectors. Should Wang take the quantity discount? **P**×

•• **22** The catering manager of LaVista Hotel, Lisa Ferguson, is disturbed by the amount of silverware she is losing every week. Last Friday night, when her crew tried to set up for a banquet for 500 people, they did not have enough knives. She decides she needs to order some more silverware, but wants to take advantage of any quantity discounts her vendor will offer.

For a small order (2,000 pieces or less) her vendor quotes a price of $1.80/piece.

If she orders 2,001–5,000 pieces, the price drops to $1.60/piece. 5,001–10,000 pieces brings the price to $1.40/piece, and 10,001 and above reduces the price to $1.25.

Lisa's order costs are $200 per order, her annual holding costs are 5%, and the annual demand is 45,000 pieces. For the best option:
a) What is the optimal order quantity?
b) What is the annual holding cost?
c) What is the annual ordering (setup) cost?
d) What are the annual costs of the silverware itself with an optimal order quantity?
e) What is the total annual cost, including ordering, holding, and purchasing the silverware? **P**×

•• **23** Rocky Mountain Tire Center sells 20,000 go-cart tires per year. The ordering cost for each order is $40, and the holding cost is 20% of the purchase price of the tires per year. The purchase price is $20 per tire if fewer than 500 tires are ordered, $18 per tire if 500 or more—but fewer than 1,000—tires are ordered, and $17 per tire if 1,000 or more tires are ordered. How many tires should Rocky Mountain order each time it places an order? **P**×

•• **24** M. P. VanOyen Manufacturing has gone out on bid for a regulator component. Expected demand is 700 units per month. The item can be purchased from either Allen Manufacturing or Baker Manufacturing. Their price lists are shown in the table. Ordering cost is $50, and annual holding cost per unit is $5.

Allen Mfg.		Baker Mfg.	
Quantity	Unit Price	Quantity	Unit Price
1–499	$16.00	1–399	$16.10
500–999	15.50	400–799	15.60
1,000+	15.00	800+	15.10

a) What is the economic order quantity?
b) Which supplier should be used? Why?
c) What is the optimal order quantity and total annual cost of ordering, purchasing, and holding the component? **P**×

••• **25** Chris Sandvig Irrigation, Inc., has summarized the price list from four potential suppliers of an underground control valve. See the table below. Annual usage is 2,400 valves; order cost is $10 per order; and annual inventory holding costs are $3.33 per unit.

Which vendor should be selected and what order quantity is best if Sandvig Irrigation wants to minimize total cost?

Vendor A		Vendor B	
Quantity	Price	Quantity	Price
1–49	$35.00	1–74	$34.75
50–74	34.75	75–149	34.00
75–149	33.55	150–299	32.80
150–299	32.35	300–499	31.60
300–499	31.15	500+	30.50
500+	30.75		

Vendor C		Vendor D	
Quantity	Price	Quantity	Price
1–99	$34.50	1–199	$34.25
100–199	33.75	200–399	33.00
200–399	32.50	400+	31.00
400+	31.10		**P**×

••• **26** Emery Pharmaceutical uses an unstable chemical compound that must be kept in an environment where both temperature and humidity can be controlled. Emery uses 800 pounds per month of the chemical, estimates the holding cost to be 50% of the purchase price (because of spoilage), and estimates order costs to be $50 per order. The cost schedules of two suppliers are as follows:

Vendor 1		Vendor 2	
Quantity	Price/lb	Quantity	Price/lb
1–499	$17.00	1–399	$17.10
500–999	16.75	400–799	16.85
1,000+	16.50	800–1,199	16.60
		1,200+	16.25

a) What is the economic order quantity for both suppliers?
b) What quantity should be ordered and which supplier should be used?
c) What is the total cost for the most economic order size?
d) What factor(s) should be considered besides total cost? **P**×

•• **27** Barbara Flynn is in charge of maintaining hospital supplies at General Hospital. During the past year, the mean lead time demand for bandage BX-5 was 60 (and was normally distributed). Furthermore, the standard deviation for BX-5 was 7. Ms. Flynn would like to maintain a 90% service level.
a) What safety stock level do you recommend for BX-5?
b) What is the appropriate reorder point? **P**×

•• **28** Based on available information, lead time demand for PC jump drives averages 50 units (normally distributed), with a standard deviation of 5 drives. Management wants a 97% service level.
a) What value of Z should be applied?
b) How many drives should be carried as safety stock?
c) What is the appropriate reorder point? **P**×

••• 29 Authentic Thai rattan chairs (shown in the photo) are delivered to Gary Schwartz's chain of retail stores, called The Kathmandu Shop, once a year. The reorder point, without safety stock, is 200 chairs. Carrying cost is $30 per unit per year, and the cost of a stockout is $70 per chair per year. Given the following demand probabilities during the reorder period, how much safety stock should be carried?

Demand during Reorder Period	Probability
0	0.2
100	0.2
200	0.2
300	0.2
400	0.2

•• 30 Tobacco is shipped from North Carolina to a cigarette manufacturer in Cambodia once a year. The reorder point, without safety stock, is 200 kilos. The carrying cost is $15 per kilo per year, and the cost of a stockout is $70 per kilo per year. Given the following demand probabilities during the reorder period, how much safety stock should be carried?

Demand During Reorder Period (kilos)	Probability
0	0.1
100	0.1
200	0.2
300	0.4
400	0.2

••• 31 Mr. Beautiful, an organization that sells weight training sets, has an ordering cost of $40 for the BB-1 set. (BB-1 stands for Body Beautiful Number 1.) The carrying cost for BB-1 is $5 per set per year. To meet demand, Mr. Beautiful orders large quantities of BB-1 seven times a year. The stockout cost for BB-1 is estimated to be $50 per set. Over the past several years, Mr. Beautiful has observed the following demand during the lead time for BB-1:

Demand during Lead Time	Probability
40	.1
50	.2
60	.2
70	.2
80	.2
90	.1
	1.0

The reorder point for BB-1 is 60 sets. What level of safety stock should be maintained for BB-1?

•• 32 Chicago's Hard Rock Hotel distributes a mean of 1,000 bath towels per day to guests at the pool and in their rooms. This demand is normally distributed with a standard deviation of 100 towels per day, based on occupancy. The laundry firm that has the linen contract requires a 2-day lead time. The hotel expects a 98% service level to satisfy high guest expectations.
a) What is the ROP?
b) What is the safety stock?

•• 33 First Printing has contracts with legal firms in San Francisco to copy their court documents. Daily demand is almost constant at 12,500 pages of documents. The lead time for paper delivery is normally distributed with a mean of 4 days and a standard deviation of 1 day. A 97% service level is expected. Compute First's ROP.

••• 34 Gainesville Cigar stocks Cuban cigars that have variable lead times because of the difficulty in importing the product: Lead time is normally distributed with an average of 6 weeks and a standard deviation of 2 weeks. Demand is also a variable and normally distributed with a mean of 200 cigars per week and a standard deviation of 25 cigars. For a 90% service level, what is the ROP?

• 35 Louisiana Power and Light orders utility poles on the first business day of each month from its supplier in Oregon. The target value is 40 poles in this fixed-period system (P-system). It is time to order and there are 5 poles on hand. Because of a delayed shipment last month, 18 poles ordered earlier should arrive shortly. How many poles should be ordered now?

••• 36 Kim Clark has asked you to help him determine the best ordering policy for a new product. The demand for the new product has been forecasted to be about 1,000 units annually. To help you get a handle on the carrying and ordering costs, Kim has given you the list of last year's costs. He thought that these costs might be appropriate for the new product.

Cost Factor	Cost ($)	Cost Factor	Cost ($)
Taxes for the warehouse	2,000	Warehouse supplies	280
Receiving and incoming inspection	1,500	Research and development	2,750
New product development	2,500	Purchasing salaries & wages	30,000
Acct. Dept. costs to pay invoices	500	Warehouse salaries & wages	12,800
Inventory insurance	600	Pilferage of inventory	800
Product advertising	800	Purchase order supplies	500
Spoilage	750	Inventory obsolescence	300
Sending purchasing orders	800	Purchasing Dept. overhead	1,000

He also told you that these data were compiled for 10,000 inventory items that were carried or held during the year. You have also determined that 200 orders were placed last year. Your job as a new operations management graduate is to help Kim determine the economic order quantity for the new product.

• • • • 37 Emarpy Appliance is a company that produces all kinds of major appliances. Bud Banis, the president of Emarpy, is concerned about the production policy for the company's best-selling refrigerator. The annual demand for this has been about 8,000 units each year, and this demand has been constant throughout the year. The production capacity is 200 units per day. Each time production starts, it costs the company $120 to move materials into place, reset the assembly line, and clean the equipment. The holding cost of a refrigerator is $50 per year. The current production plan calls for 400 refrigerators to be produced in each production run. Assume there are 250 working days per year.

a) What is the daily demand of this product?
b) If the company were to continue to produce 400 units each time production starts, how many days would production continue?
c) Under the current policy, how many production runs per year would be required? What would the annual setup cost be?
d) If the current policy continues, how many refrigerators would be in inventory when production stops? What would the average inventory level be?
e) If the company produces 400 refrigerators at a time, what would the total annual setup cost and holding cost be?

f) If Bud Banis wants to minimize the total annual inventory cost, how many refrigerators should be produced in each production run? How much would this save the company in inventory costs compared to the current policy of producing 400 in each production run? **P**X

• • • • 38 A gourmet coffee shop in downtown San Francisco is open 200 days a year and sells an average of 75 pounds of Kona coffee beans a day. (Demand can be assumed to be distributed normally with a standard deviation of 15 pounds per day). After ordering (fixed cost = $16 per order), beans are always shipped from Hawaii within exactly 4 days. Per-pound annual holding costs for the beans are $3.

a) What is the economic order quantity (EOQ) for Kona coffee beans?
b) What are the total annual holding costs of stock for Kona coffee beans?
c) What are the total annual ordering costs for Kona coffee beans?
d) Assume that management has specified that no more than a 1% risk during stockout is acceptable. What should the reorder point (ROP) be?
e) What is the safety stock needed to attain a 1% risk of stockout during lead time?
f) What is the annual holding cost of maintaining the level of safety stock needed to support a 1% risk?
g) If management specified that a 2% risk of stockout during lead time would be acceptable, would the safety stock holding costs decrease or increase?

Case Studies

Zhou Bicycle Company

Zhou Bicycle Company (ZBC), located in Seattle, is a wholesale distributor of bicycles and bicycle parts. Formed in 1981, by University of Washington Professor Yong-Pin Zhou, the firm's primary retail outlets are located within a 400-mile radius of the distribution center. These retail outlets receive the order from ZBC within 2 days after notifying the distribution center, provided that the stock is available. However, if an order is not fulfilled by the company, no backorder is placed; the retailers arrange to get their shipment from other distributors, and ZBC loses that amount of business.

The company distributes a wide variety of bicycles. The most popular model, and the major source of revenue to the company, is the AirWing. ZBC receives all the models from a single manufacturer in China, and shipment takes as long as 4 weeks from the time an order is placed. With the cost of communication, paperwork, and customs clearance included, ZBC estimates that each time an order is placed, it incurs a cost of $65. The purchase price paid by ZBC, per bicycle, is roughly 60% of the suggested retail price for all the styles available, and the inventory carrying cost is 1% per month (12% per year) of the purchase price paid by ZBC. The retail price (paid by the customers) for the AirWing is $170 per bicycle.

ZBC is interested in making an inventory plan for 2008. The firm wants to maintain a 95% service level with its customers to minimize the losses on the lost orders. The data collected for the past 2 years are summarized in the following table. A forecast for AirWing model sales in 2008 has been developed and will be used to make an inventory plan for ZBC.

Demands for AirWing Model

Month	2006	2007	Forecast for 2008
January	6	7	8
February	12	14	15
March	24	27	31
April	46	53	59
May	75	86	97
June	47	54	60
July	30	34	39
August	18	21	24
September	13	15	16
October	12	13	15
November	22	25	28
December	38	42	47
Total	343	391	439

Discussion Questions

1. Develop an inventory plan to help ZBC.
2. Discuss ROPs and total costs.
3. How can you address demand that is not at the level of the planning horizon?

Source: Professor Kala Chand Seal, Loyola Marymount University.

Sturdivant Sound Systems

Sturdivant Sound Systems manufactures and sells sound systems for both home and auto. All parts of the sound systems, with the exception of DVD players, are produced in the Rochester, New York, plant. DVD players used in the assembly of Sturdivant systems are purchased from Morris Electronics of Concord, New Hampshire.

Sturdivant purchasing agent Mary Kim submits a purchase requisition for DVD players once every 4 weeks. The company's annual requirements total 5,000 units (20 per working day), and the cost per unit is $60. (Sturdivant does not purchase in greater quantities because Morris Electronics does not offer quantity discounts.) Because Morris promises delivery within 1 week following receipt of a purchase requisition, rarely is there a shortage of DVD players. (Total time between date of order and date of receipt is 5 days.)

Associated with the purchase of each shipment are procurement costs. These costs, which amount to $20 per order, include the costs of preparing the requisition, inspecting and storing the delivered goods, updating inventory records, and issuing a voucher and a check for payment. In addition to procurement costs, Sturdivant incurs inventory carrying costs that include insurance, storage, handling, taxes, and so forth. These costs equal $6 per unit per year.

Beginning in August of this year, Sturdivant management will embark on a companywide cost-control program in an attempt to improve its profits. One area to be closely scrutinized for possible cost savings is inventory procurement.

Discussion Questions

1. Compute the optimal order quantity of DVD players.
2. Determine the appropriate reorder point (in units).
3. Compute the cost savings that the company will realize if it implements the optimal inventory procurement decision.
4. Should procurement costs be considered a linear function of the number of orders?

Source: Reprinted by permission of Professor Jerry Kinard, Western Carolina University.

Inventory Control at Wheeled Coach

Video Case

Controlling inventory is one of Wheeled Coach's toughest problems. Operating according to a strategy of mass customization and responsiveness, management knows that success is dependent on tight inventory control. Anything else results in an inability to deliver promptly, chaos on the assembly line, and a huge inventory investment. Wheeled Coach finds that almost 50% of the $40,000 to $100,000 cost of every ambulance it manufactures is purchased materials. A large proportion of that 50% is in chassis (purchased from Ford), aluminum (from Reynolds Metal), and plywood used for flooring and cabinetry construction (from local suppliers). Wheeled Coach tracks these A inventory items quite carefully, maintaining tight security/control and ordering carefully so as to maximize quantity discounts while minimizing on-hand stock. Because of long lead times and scheduling needs at Reynolds, aluminum must actually be ordered as much as 8 months in advance.

In a crowded ambulance industry in which it is the only giant, its 45 competitors don't have the purchasing power to draw the same discounts as Wheeled Coach. But this competitive cost advantage cannot be taken lightly, according to President Bob Collins.

"Cycle counting in our stockrooms is critical. No part can leave the locked stockrooms without appearing on a bill of materials."

Accurate bills of material (BOM) are a requirement if products are going to be built on time. Additionally, because of the custom nature of each vehicle, most orders are won only after a bidding process. Accurate BOMs are critical to cost estimation and the resulting bid. For these reasons, Collins was emphatic that Wheeled Coach maintain outstanding inventory control. The *Global Company Profile* featuring Wheeled Coach provides further details about the ambulance inventory control and production process.

Discussion Questions*

1. Explain how Wheeled Coach implements ABC analysis.
2. If you were to take over as inventory control manager at Wheeled Coach, what additional policies and techniques would you initiate to ensure accurate inventory records?
3. How would you go about implementing these suggestions?

*You may wish to view this case on your DVD before answering these questions.

Additional Case Studies

Internet case studies: Visit our Companion Web site at www.prenhall.com/heizer for these free case studies:

- **Southwestern University F:** The university must decide how many football day programs to order, and from whom.
- **LaPlace Power and Light:** This utility company is evaluating its current inventory policies.

Harvard has selected these Harvard Business School cases to accompany this chapter:

harvardbusinessonline.hbsp.harvard.edu

- **Pioneer Hi-Bred International, Inc.** (#898-238): Deals with the challenges in managing inventory in a large, complex agribusiness firm.
- **L.L. Bean, Inc.: Item Forecasting and Inventory** (#893-003): The firm must balance costs of understocking and overstocking when demand for catalog items is uncertain.
- **Blanchard Importing and Distribution Co., Inc.** (#673-033): Illustrates two main types of errors resulting from the use of EOQ models.

Bibliography

Abernathy, Frederick H., et al. "Control Your Inventory in a World of Lean Retailing." *Harvard Business Review* 78, no. 6 (November–December 2000): 169–176.

Arnold, David. "Seven Rules of International Distribution." *Harvard Business Review* 78, no. 6 (November–December 2000): 131–137.

Arnold, J. R., and S. Chapman. *Introduction to Materials Management*, 5th ed. Upper Saddle River, NJ: Prentice Hall (2004).

Balakrishnan, R., B. Render, and R. M. Stair. *Managerial Decision Modeling with Spreadsheets*, 2nd ed. Upper Saddle River, NJ: Prentice Hall (2007).

Bradley, James R., and Richard W. Conway. "Managing Cyclic Inventories." *Production and Operations Management* 12, no. 4 (winter 2003): 464–479.

Cannon, Alan R., and Richard E. Crandall, "The Way Things Never Were." *APICS—The Performance Advantage* (January 2004): 32–35.

Chapmas, Stephen. *Fundamentals of Production Planning and Control*. Upper Saddle River, NJ: Prentice Hall (2006).

Chopra, Sunil, Gilles Reinhardt, and Maqbool Dada. "The Effect of Lead Time Uncertainty on Safety Stocks." *Decision Sciences* 35, no. 1 (winter 2004): 1–24.

Coleman, B. Jay. "Determining the Correct Service Level Target." *Production and Inventory Management Journal* 41, no. 1 (1st quarter 2000): 19–23.

Corsten, Daniel, and Nirmalya Kumar. "Profits in the Pie of the Beholder." *Harvard Business Review* (May 2003): 22–23.

Landvater, D. V. *World Class Production and Inventory Management*. Newburg, NH: Oliver Wight Publications (1997).

Noblitt, James M. "The Economic Order Quantity Model: Panacea or Plague?" *APICS—The Performance Advantage* (February 2001): 53–57.

Robison, James A. "Inventory Profile Analysis." *Production and Inventory Management Journal* 42, no. 2 (2nd quarter 2001): 8–13.

Rubin, Paul A., and W. C. Benton. "A Generalized Framework for Quantity Discount Pricing Schedules." *Decision Sciences* 34, no. 1 (winter 2003): 173–188.

Sell, William H. "Recovering Value from I.O.\$." *APICS—The Performance Advantage* (November/December 2003): 50–53.

Vollmann, T. E., W. L. Berry, D. C. Whybark, and F. R. Jacobs. *Manufacturing Planning and Control for Supply Chain Management*, 5th ed. Burr Ridge, IL: Irwin/McGraw (2005).

Witt, Clyde E. "Mobile Warehouse Supplies U.S. Marines in Iraq." *Material Handling Management* 60, no. 8 (August 2005): 24–25.

Zipkin, Paul. *Foundations of Inventory Management*. New York: Irwin/McGraw-Hill (2000).

Internet Resources

APICS: The Educational Society for Resource Management: **www.apics.org**
Center for Inventory Management: **www.inventorymanagement.com**

Institute of Industrial Engineers: **www.iienet.org**
Inventory Control Forum: **www.cris.com/~kthill/sites.htm**

Solutions to Even Numbered Problems

2 A items are G2 and F3; B items are A2, C7, and D1; all others are C.

4 108 items

6 600 units

8 (a) 80 units
 (b) 73 units

10 2,100 units

12 (a) 189.74 units
 (b) 94.87
 (c) 31.62
 (d) 7.91
 (e) $1,897.30
 (f) $601,897

14 (a) Order quantity variations have limited impact on total cost.
 (b) EOQ = 50

16 (a) 671 units
 (b) 18.63
 (c) 559 = max. inventory
 (d) 16.7%
 (e) $1,117.90

18 (a) 1,217 units
 (b) 1,095 = max. inventory
 (c) 8.22 production runs
 (d) $657.30

20 (a) EOQ = 200, total cost = $1,446,380
 (b) EOQ = 200, total cost = $1,445,880

22 (a) 16,971 units
 (b) $530.33
 (c) $530.33
 (d) $56,250
 (e) $57,310.66

24 (a) EOQ = 410
 (b) Vendor Allen has slightly lower cost.
 (c) Optimal order quantity = 1,000 @ total cost of $128,920

26 (a) EOQ (1) = 336; EOQ (2) = 335
 (b) Order 1,200 from Vendor 2.
 (c) At 1,200 lb., total cost = $161,275.
 (d) Storage space and perishability.

28 **(a)** Z = 1.88

(b) Safety stock = Zσ = 1.88(5) = 9.4 drives

(c) ROP = 59.4 drives

30 100 kilos of safety stock

32 **(a)** 2,291 towels

(b) 291 towels

34 ROP = 1,718 cigars

36 EOQ = 442

38 **(a)** Q = 400 lbs

(b) $600

(c) $600

(d) ROP = 369.99

(e) 69.99

(f) $209.97

(g) Safety stock = 61.61

Solutions to Self Test

1. d; **2.** c; **3.** e; **4.** e; **5.** c; **6.** b; **7.** b; **8.** b; **9.** d.

Chapter 14

Material Requirements Planning (MRP) and ERP

Material Requirements Planning (MRP) and ERP

Outline

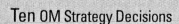

Ten OM Strategy Decisions

Design of Goods and Services

Managing Quality

Process Strategy

Location Strategies

Layout Strategies

Human Resources

Supply Chain Management

Inventory Management
- Independent Demand
- Dependent Demand
- JIT and Lean Operations

Scheduling
- Aggregate
- Short-Term

Maintenance

Learning Objectives

When you complete this selection you should be able to

1. Develop a product structure
2. Build a gross requirements plan
3. Build a net requirements plan
4. Determine lot sizes for lot-for-lot, EOQ, and PPB
5. Describe MRP II
6. Describe closed-loop MRP
7. Describe ERP

From *Operations Management*, 9/e. Jay Heizer. Barry Render. Copyright © 2008 by Pearson Education. All rights reserved.

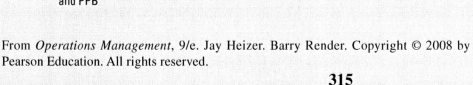

MRP Provides a Competitive Advantage for Wheeled Coach

Wheeled Coach, headquartered in Winter Park, Florida, is the largest manufacturer of ambulances in the world. The $200 million firm is an international competitor that sells more than 25% of its vehicles to markets outside the U.S. Twelve major ambulance designs are produced on assembly lines (i.e., a repetitive process) at the Florida plant, using 18,000 different inventory items, of which 6,000 are manufactured and 12,000 purchased. Most of the product line is custom designed and

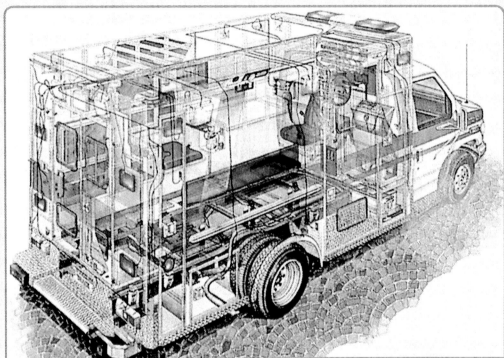

Collins Industries, Inc.

◄ *This cutaway of one ambulance interior indicates the complexity of the product, which for some rural locations may be the equivalent of a hospital emergency room in miniature. To complicate production, virtually every ambulance is custom-ordered. This customization necessitates precise orders, excellent bills of materials, exceptional inventory control from supplier to assembly, and an MRP system that works.*

▶ *Wheeled Coach uses work cells to feed the assembly line. It maintains a complete carpentry shop (to provide interior cabinetry), a paint shop (to prepare, paint, and detail each vehicle), an electrical shop (to provide for the complex electronics in a modern ambulance), an upholstery shop (to make interior seats and benches), and as shown here, a metal fabrication shop (to construct the shell of the ambulance).*

Wheeled Coach Industries, Incorporated

assembled to meet the specific and often unique requirements demanded by the ambulance's application and customer preferences.

This variety of products and the nature of the process demand good material requirements planning. Effective use of an MRP system requires accurate bills of material and inventory records. The Wheeled Coach system, which uses MAPICS DB software, provides daily updates and has reduced inventory by more than 30% in just 2 years.

Wheeled Coach insists that four key tasks be performed properly. First, the material plan must meet both the requirements of the master schedule and the capabilities of the production facility.

Second, the plan must be executed as designed. Third, inventory investment must be minimized through effective "time-phased" material deliveries, consignment inventories, and a constant review of purchase methods. Finally, excellent record integrity must be maintained. Record accuracy is recognized as a fundamental ingredient of Wheeled Coach's successful MRP program. Its cycle counters are charged with material audits that not only correct errors but also investigate and correct problems.

Wheeled Coach Industries uses MRP as the catalyst for low inventory, high quality, tight schedules, and accurate records. Wheeled Coach has found competitive advantage via MRP.

Wheeled Coach Industries, Incorporated

◀ *On six parallel lines, ambulances move forward each day to the next workstation. The MRP system makes certain that just the materials needed at each station arrive overnight for assembly the next day.*

 Video 14.1

MRP at Wheeled Coach Ambulances

▶ *Here an employee is installing the wiring for an ambulance. There are an average of 15 miles of wire in a Wheeled Coach vehicle. This compares to 17 miles of wire in a sophisticated F-16 fighter jet.*

Collins Industries, Inc.

Wheeled Coach and many other firms have found important benefits in MRP. These benefits include (1) better response to customer orders as the result of improved adherence to schedules, (2) faster response to market changes, (3) improved utilization of facilities and labor, and (4) reduced inventory levels. Better response to customer orders and to the market wins orders and market share. Better utilization of facilities and labor yields higher productivity and return on investment. Less inventory frees up capital and floor space for other uses. These benefits are the result of a strategic decision to use a *dependent* inventory scheduling system. Demand for every component of an ambulance is dependent.

DEPENDENT DEMAND

Dependent demand means that the demand for one item is related to the demand for another item. Consider a Ford F-150 truck. Ford's demand for tires and radiators depends on the production of F-150's. Five tires and one radiator go into each finished F-150 truck. Demand for items is *dependent* when the relationship between the items can be determined. Therefore, once management receives an order or makes a forecast of the demand for the final product, quantities required for all components can be computed, because all components are dependent items. The Boeing Aircraft operations manager who schedules production of one plane per week, for example, knows the requirements down to the last rivet. For any product, all components of that product are dependent demand items. *More generally, for any item for which a schedule can be established, dependent techniques should be used.*

When the requirements of MRP are met, dependent models are preferable to the EOQ models.[1] Dependency exists for all component parts, subassemblies, and supplies once a master schedule is known. Dependent models are better not only for manufacturers and distributors but also for a wide variety of firms from restaurants to hospitals. The dependent technique used in a production environment is called **material requirements planning (MRP)**.

Material requirements planning (MRP)

A dependent demand technique that uses a bill-of-material, inventory, expected receipts, and a master production schedule to determine material requirements.

Because MRP provides such a clean structure for dependent demand, it has evolved as the basis for Enterprise Resource Planning (ERP). ERP is an information system for identifying and planning the enterprise-wide resources needed to take, make, ship, and account for customer orders. We will discuss ERP in the latter part of this selection.

DEPENDENT INVENTORY MODEL REQUIREMENTS

Effective use of dependent inventory models requires that the operations manager know the following:

1. Master production schedule (what is to be made and when)
2. Specifications or bill of material (materials and parts required to make the product)
3. Inventory availability (what is in stock)
4. Purchase orders outstanding (what is on order, also called expected receipts)
5. Lead times (how long it takes to get various components)

We now discuss each of these requirements in the context of material requirements planning (MRP).

Master Production Schedule

Master production schedule (MPS)

A timetable that specifies what is to be made and when.

A **master production schedule (MPS)** specifies what is to be made (i.e., the number of finished products or items) and when. The schedule must be in accordance with a production plan. The production plan sets the overall level of output in broad terms (e.g., product families, standard hours, or dollar volume). The plan also includes a variety of inputs, including financial plans, customer demand, engineering capabilities, labor availability, inventory fluctuations, supplier performance, and other considerations. Each of these inputs contributes in its own way to the production plan, as shown in Figure 1.

As the planning process moves from the production plan to execution, each of the lower-level plans must be feasible. When one is not, feedback to the next higher level is used to make the

---

[1]The inventory models (EOQ) assume that the demand for one item is independent of the demand for another item. For example, EOQ assumes the demand for refrigerator parts is *independent* of the demand for refrigerators and that demand for parts is constant.

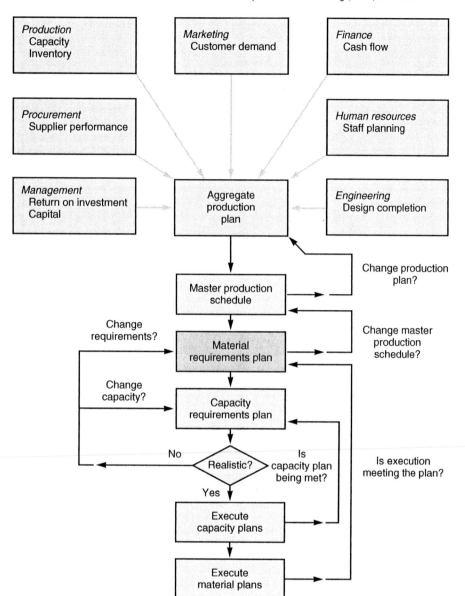

Figure 1

The Planning Process

Regardless of the complexity of the planning process, the aggregate production plan and its derivative, the master production schedule, must be developed.

necessary adjustment. One of the major strengths of MRP is its ability to determine precisely the feasibility of a schedule within aggregate capacity constraints. This planning process can yield excellent results. The production plan sets the upper and lower bounds on the master production schedule. The result of this production planning process is the master production schedule.

The master production schedule tells us what is required to satisfy demand and meet the production plan. This schedule establishes what items to make and when: It *disaggregates* the aggregate production plan. While the *aggregate production plan* (as discussed in previous chapter) is established in gross terms such as families of products or tons of steel, the *master production schedule* is established in terms of specific products. Figure 2 shows the master production schedules for three stereo models that flow from the aggregate production plan for a family of stereo amplifiers.

The master production schedule is derived from the aggregate schedule.

Managers must adhere to the schedule for a reasonable length of time (usually a major portion of the production cycle—the time it takes to produce a product). Many organizations establish a master production schedule and establish a policy of not changing ("fixing") the near-term portion of the plan. This near-term portion of the plan is then referred to as the "fixed," "firm," or "frozen" schedule. Wheeled Coach, the subject of the *Global Company Profile* for this chapter, fixes the last 14 days of its schedule. Only changes farther out, beyond the fixed schedule are permitted. The master production schedule is a "rolling" production schedule. For example, a fixed 7-week plan has an additional week added to it as each week is completed, so a 7-week fixed schedule is

▶ **Figure 2**

The Aggregate Production Plan Provides the Basis for Development of the Detailed Master Production Schedule

Months	January				February			
Aggregate Production Plan (Shows the total quantity of amplifiers)	1,500				1,200			
Weeks	1	2	3	4	5	6	7	8
Master Production Schedule (Shows the specific type and quantity of amplifier to be produced)								
240-watt amplifier	100		100		100		100	
150-watt amplifier		500		500		450		450
75-watt amplifier			300				100	

maintained. Note that the master production schedule is a statement of *what is to be produced*, not a forecast of demand. The master schedule can be expressed in any of the following terms:

1. A *customer order in a job shop* (make-to-order) company
2. *Modules in a repetitive* (assemble-to-order or forecast) company
3. An *end item in a continuous* (stock-to-forecast) company

This relationship of the master production schedule to the processes is shown in Figure 3.

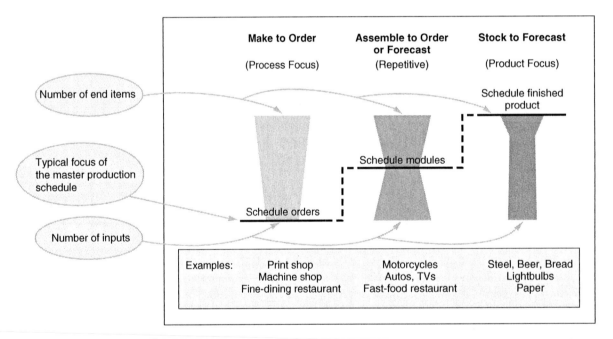

▲ **Figure 3** **Typical Focus of the Master Production Schedule in Three Process Strategies**

A master production schedule for two of Nancy's Specialty Foods' products, crabmeat quiche and spinach quiche, might look like Table 1.

▶ **Table 1**

Master Production Schedule for Crabmeat Quiche and Spinach Quiche at Nancy's Specialty Foods

Gross Requirements for Crabmeat Quiche										
Day	6	7	8	9	10	11	12	13	14	and so on
Amount	50		100	47	60		110	75		
Gross Requirements for Spinach Quiche										
Day	7	8	9	10	11	12	13	14	15	16	and so on
Amount	100	200	150			60	75		100		

Bills of Material

Defining what goes into a product may seem simple, but it can be difficult in practice. To aid this process, manufactured items are defined via a bill of material. A **bill of material (BOM)** is a list of quantities of components, ingredients, and materials required to make a product. Individual drawings describe not only physical dimensions but also any special processing as well as the raw material from which each part is made. Nancy's Specialty Foods has a recipe for quiche, specifying ingredients and quantities, just as Wheeled Coach has a full set of drawings for an ambulance. Both are bills of material (although we call one a recipe, and they do vary somewhat in scope).

Because there is often a rush to get a new product to market, however, drawings and bills of material may be incomplete or even nonexistent. Moreover, complete drawings and BOMs (as well as other forms of specifications) often contain errors in dimensions, quantities, or countless other areas. When errors are identified, engineering change notices (ECNs) are created, further complicating the process. An *engineering change notice* is a change or correction to an engineering drawing or bill of material.

One way a bill of material defines a product is by providing a product structure. Example 1 shows how to develop the product structure and "explode" it to reveal the requirements for each component. A bill of material for item A in Example 1 consists of items B and C. Items above any level are called *parents*; items below any level are called *components* or *children*. By convention, the top level in a BOM is the 0 level.

Bill of material (BOM)
A listing of the components, their description, and the quantity of each required to make one unit of a product.

Speaker Kits, Inc., packages high-fidelity components for mail order. Components for the top-of-the-line speaker kit, "Awesome" (A), include 2 standard 12-inch speaker kits (Bs) and 3 speaker kits with amp-boosters (Cs).

Each B consists of 2 speakers (Ds) and 2 shipping boxes each with an installation kit (E). Each of the three 300-watt speaker kits (Cs) has 2 speaker boosters (Fs) and 2 installation kits (Es). Each speaker booster (F) includes 2 speakers (Ds) and 1 amp-booster (G). The total for each Awesome is 4 standard 12-inch speakers and twelve 12-inch speakers with the amp-booster. (Most purchasers require hearing aids within 3 years, and at least one court case is pending because of structural damage to a men's dormitory.) As we can see, the demand for B, C, D, E, F, and G is completely dependent on the master production schedule for A—the Awesome speaker kits.

Approach: Given the above information, we construct a product structure and "explode" the requirements.

Solution: This structure has four levels: 0, 1, 2, and 3. There are four parents: A, B, C, and F. Each parent item has at least one level below it. Items B, C, D, E, F, and G are components because each item has at least one level above it. In this structure, B, C, and F are both parents and components. The number in parentheses indicates how many units of that particular item are needed to make the item immediately above it. Thus, $B_{(2)}$ means that it takes two units of B for every unit of A, and $F_{(2)}$ means that it takes two units of F for every unit of C.

EXAMPLE 1

Developing a product structure and gross requirements

Learning Objective

1. Develop a product structure

Excel Om Data File
Ch14Ex1.xls

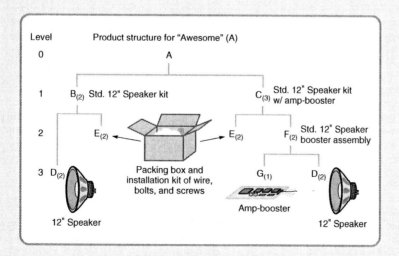

Once we have developed the product structure, we can determine the number of units of each item required to satisfy demand for a new order of 50 Awesome speaker kits. We "explode" the requirements as shown:

Part B:	$2 \times$ number of As $=$	$(2)(50) =$	100
Part C:	$3 \times$ number of As $=$	$(3)(50) =$	150
Part D:	$2 \times$ number of Bs $+ 2 \times$ number of Fs $=$	$(2)(100) + (2)(300) =$	800
Part E:	$2 \times$ number of Bs $+ 2 \times$ number of Cs $=$	$(2)(100) + (2)(150) =$	500
Part F:	$2 \times$ number of Cs $=$	$(2)(150) =$	300
Part G:	$1 \times$ number of Fs $=$	$(1)(300) =$	300

Insight: We now have a visual picture of the Awesome speaker kit requirements and knowledge of the quantities required. Thus, for 50 units of A, we will need 100 units of B, 150 units of C, 800 units of D, 500 units of E, 300 units of F, and 300 units of G.

Learning exercise: If there are 100 Fs in stock, how many Ds do you need? [Answer: 600.]

Related problems: 1, 3a, 13a, 25a

Bills of material not only specify requirements but also are useful for costing, and they can serve as a list of items to be issued to production or assembly personnel. When bills of material are used in this way, they are usually called *pick lists*.

Modular Bills Bills of material may be organized around product modules (see previous chapter). *Modules* are not final products to be sold but are components that can be produced and assembled into units. They are often major components of the final product or product options. Bills of material for modules are called **modular bills**. Bills of material are sometimes organized as modules (rather than as part of a final product) because production scheduling and production are often facilitated by organizing around relatively few modules rather than a multitude of final assemblies. For instance, a firm may make 138,000 different final products but may have only 40 modules that are mixed and matched to produce those 138,000 final products. The firm builds an aggregate production plan and prepares its master production schedule for the 40 modules, not the 138,000 configurations of the final product. This approach allows the MPS to be prepared for a reasonable number of items (the narrow portion of the middle graphic in Figure 3) and to postpone assembly. The 40 modules can then be configured for specific orders at final assembly.

Modular bills

Bills of material organized by major subassemblies or by product options.

Planning Bills and Phantom Bills Two other special kinds of bills of material are planning bills and phantom bills. **Planning bills** are created in order to assign an artificial parent to the bill of material. Such bills are used (1) when we want to group subassemblies so the number of items to be scheduled is reduced and (2) when we want to issue "kits" to the production department. For instance, it may not be efficient to issue inexpensive items such as washers and cotter pins with each of numerous subassemblies, so we call this a *kit* and generate a planning bill. The planning bill specifies the *kit* to be issued. Consequently, a planning bill may also be known as **kitted material**, or **kit**. **Phantom bills of material** are bills of material for components, usually subassemblies, that exist only temporarily. These components go directly into another assembly and are never inventoried. Therefore, components of phantom bills of material are coded to receive special treatment; lead times are zero, and they are handled as an integral part of their parent item. An example is a transmission shaft with gears and bearings assembly that is placed directly into a transmission.

Planning bills (or kits)

A material grouping created in order to assign an artificial parent to a bill of material; also called "pseudo" bills.

Phantom bills of material

Bills of material for components, usually assemblies, that exist only temporarily; they are never inventoried.

Low-level coding

A number that identifies items at the lowest level at which they occur.

Low-Level Coding Low-level coding of an item in a BOM is necessary when identical items exist at various levels in the BOM. **Low-level coding** means that the item is coded at the lowest level at which it occurs. For example, item D in Example 1 is coded at the lowest level at which

◄ *For manufacturers like Harley-Davidson, which produces a large number of end products from a relatively small number of options, modular bills of material provide an effective solution.*

Dave Bartruff, Stock Boston

it is used. Item D could be coded as part of B and occur at level 2. However, because D is also part of F, and F is level 2, item D becomes a level-3 item. Low-level coding is a convention to allow easy computing of the requirements of an item. When the BOM has thousands of items or when requirements are frequently recomputed, the ease and speed of computation become a major concern.

Low-level coding ensures that an item is always at the lowest level of usage.

Accurate Inventory Records

Knowledge of what is in stock is the result of good inventory management. Good inventory management is an absolute necessity for an MRP system to work. If the firm has not achieved at least 99% record accuracy, then material requirements planning will not work.[2]

Purchase Orders Outstanding

Knowledge of outstanding orders should exist as a by-product of well-managed purchasing and inventory-control departments. When purchase orders are executed, records of those orders and their scheduled delivery dates must be available to production personnel. Only with good purchasing data can managers prepare good production plans and effectively execute an MRP system.

Lead Times for Components

Once managers determine when products are needed, they determine when to acquire them. The time required to acquire (that is, purchase, produce, or assemble) an item is known as **lead time**. Lead time for a manufactured item consists of *move*, *setup*, and *assembly* or *run times* for each component. For a purchased item, the lead time includes the time between recognition of need for an order and when it is available for production.

When the bill of material for Awesome speaker kits (As), in Example 1, is turned on its side and modified by adding lead times for each component (see Table 2), we then have a *time-phased product structure*. Time in this structure is shown on the horizontal axis of Figure 4 with item A due for completion in week 8. Each component is then offset to accommodate lead times.

Lead time

In purchasing systems, the time between recognition of the need for an order and receiving it; in production systems, it is the order, wait, move, queue, setup, and run times for each component.

---

[2]Record accuracy of 99% may sound good, but note that even when each component has an availability of 99% and a product has only seven components, the likelihood of a product being completed is only .932 (since $.99^7 = .932$).

Figure 4

Time-Phased Product Structure

> **Figure 4**

Time-Phased Product Structure

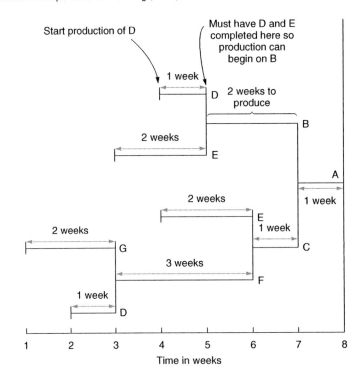

▼ **Table 2**

Lead Times for Awesome Speaker Kits (As)

Component	Lead Time
A	1 week
B	2 weeks
C	1 week
D	1 week
E	2 weeks
F	3 weeks
G	2 weeks

MRP STRUCTURE

Although most MRP systems are computerized, the MRP procedure is straightforward and can be done by hand. A master production schedule, a bill of material, inventory and purchase records, and lead times for each item are the ingredients of a material requirements planning system (see Figure 5).

Once these ingredients are available and accurate, the next step is to construct a gross material requirements plan. The **gross material requirements plan** is a schedule, as shown in Example 2. It combines a master production schedule (that requires one unit of A in week 8) and the time-phased schedule (Figure 4). It shows when an item must be ordered from suppliers if there is no inventory on hand or when the production of an item must be started to satisfy demand for the finished product by a particular date.

Gross material requirements plan

A schedule that shows the total demand for an item (prior to subtraction of on-hand inventory and scheduled receipts) and (1) when it must be ordered from suppliers, or (2) when production must be started to meet its demand by a particular date.

> **Figure 5**

Structure of the MRP System

MRP software programs are popular because many organizations face dependent demand situations.

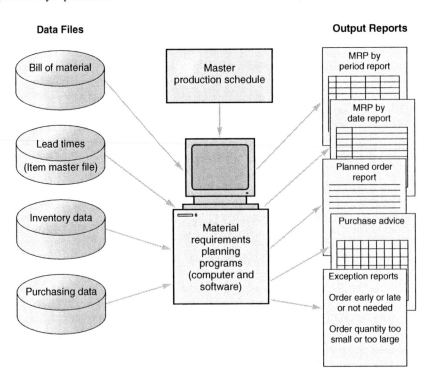

EXAMPLE 2

Building a gross
requirements plan

Each Awesome speaker kit (item A of Example 1) requires all the items in the product structure for A. Lead times are shown in Table 2.

Approach: Using the information in Example 1 and Table 2, we construct the gross material requirements plan with a production schedule that will satisfy the demand of 50 units of A by week 8.

Solution: We prepare a schedule as shown in Table 3.

◀ **Table 3**

Gross Material Requirements Plan for 50 Awesome Speaker Kits (As)

	Week								
	1	2	3	4	5	6	7	8	Lead Time
A. Required date								50	
Order release date							50		1 week
B. Required date							100		
Order release date					100				2 weeks
C. Required date							150		
Order release date						150			1 week
E. Required date					200	300			
Order release date			200	300					2 weeks
F. Required date						300			
Order release date			300						3 weeks
D. Required date			600		200				
Order release date		600		200					1 week
G. Required date			300						
Order release date	300								2 weeks

You can interpret the gross material requirements shown in Table 3 as follows: If you want 50 units of A at week 8, you must start assembling A in week 7. Thus, in week 7, you will need 100 units of B and 150 units of C. These two items take 2 weeks and 1 week, respectively, to produce. Production of B, therefore, should start in week 5, and production of C should start in week 6 (lead time subtracted from the required date for these items). Working backward, we can perform the same computations for all of the other items. Because D and E are used in two different places in Awesome speaker kits, there are two entries in each data record.

Insight: The gross material requirements plan shows when production of each item should begin and end in order to have 50 units of A at week 8. Management now has an initial plan.

Learning exercise: If the lead time for G decreases from 2 weeks to 1 week, what is the new order release date for G? [Answer: 300 in week 2.]

Related problems: 2, 4, 6, 8b, 9, 10a, 11a, 13b, 25b

So far, we have considered *gross material requirements*, which assumes that there is no inventory on hand. When there is inventory on hand, we prepare a **net requirements plan**. When considering on-hand inventory, we must realize that many items in inventory contain subassemblies or parts. If the gross requirement for Awesome speaker kits (As) is 100 and there are 20 of those speakers on hand, the net requirement for Awesome speaker kits (As) is 80 (that is, 100 − 20). However, each Awesome speaker kit on hand contains 2 Bs. As a result, the requirement for Bs drops by 40 Bs (20 A kits on hand × 2 Bs per A). Therefore, if inventory is on hand for a parent item, the requirements for the parent item and all its components decrease because each Awesome kit contains the components for lower-level items. Example 3 shows how to create a net requirements plan.

Net material requirements
The result of adjusting gross requirements for inventory on hand and scheduled receipts.

EXAMPLE 3

Determining net requirements

Speaker Kits, Inc., developed a product structure from a bill of material in Example 1. Example 2 developed a gross requirements plan. Given the following on-hand inventory, Speaker Kits, Inc., now wants to construct a net requirements plan.

Active Model 14.1

Examples 1–3 are further illustrated in Active Model 14.1 on the CD-ROM.

Item	On Hand	Item	On Hand
A	10	E	10
B	15	F	5
C	20	G	0
D	10		

Approach: A net material requirements plan includes gross requirements, on-hand inventory, net requirements, planned order receipt, and planned order release for each item. We begin with A and work backward through the components.

Solution: Shown in the chart below is the net material requirements plan for product A.

Lot Size	Lead Time (weeks)	On Hand	Safety Stock	Allo-cated	Low-Level Code	Item Identi-fication		Week 1	2	3	4	5	6	7	8
Lot-for-Lot	1	10	—	—	0	A	Gross Requirements								50
							Scheduled Receipts								
							Projected On Hand 10	10	10	10	10	10	10	10	10
							Net Requirements								40
							Planned Order Receipts								40
							Planned Order Releases							40	
Lot-for-Lot	2	15	—	—	1	B	Gross Requirements							80[A]	
							Scheduled Receipts								
							Projected On Hand 15	15	15	15	15	15	15	15	
							Net Requirements							65	
							Planned Order Receipts							65	
							Planned Order Releases						65		
Lot-for-Lot	1	20	—	—	1	C	Gross Requirements							120[A]	
							Scheduled Receipts								
							Projected On Hand 20	20	20	20	20	20	20	20	
							Net Requirements							100	
							Planned Order Receipts							100	
							Planned Order Releases						100		
Lot-for-Lot	2	10	—	—	2	E	Gross Requirements					130[B]	200[C]		
							Scheduled Receipts								
							Projected On Hand 10	10	10	10	10	10			
							Net Requirements					120	200		
							Planned Order Receipts					120	200		
							Planned Order Releases			120	200				
Lot-for-Lot	3	5	—	—	2	F	Gross Requirements						200[C]		
							Scheduled Receipts								
							Projected On Hand 5	5	5	5	5	5	5		
							Net Requirements						195		
							Planned Order Receipts						195		
							Planned Order Releases			195					
Lot-for-Lot	1	10	—	—	3	D	Gross Requirements			390[F]		130[B]			
							Scheduled Receipts								
							Projected On Hand 10	10	10	10					
							Net Requirements			380		130			
							Planned Order Receipts			380		130			
							Planned Order Releases		380		130				
Lot-for-Lot	2	0	—	—	3	G	Gross Requirements			195[F]					
							Scheduled Receipts								
							Projected On Hand			0					
							Net Requirements			195					
							Planned Order Receipts			195					
							Planned Order Releases	195							

Net Material Requirements Plan for Product A   *Note that the superscript is the source of the demand.*

Constructing a net requirements plan is similar to constructing a gross requirements plan. Starting with item A, we work backward to determine net requirements for all items. To do these computations, we refer to the product structure, on-hand inventory, and lead times. The gross requirement for A is 50 units in week 8. Ten items are on hand; therefore, the net requirements and the scheduled **planned order receipt** are both 40 items in week 8. Because of the 1-week lead time, the **planned order release** is 40 items in week 7 (see the arrow connecting the order receipt and order release). Referring to week 7 and the product structure in Example 1, we can see that 80 (2×40) items of B and 120 (3×40) items of C are required in week 7 to have a total for 50 items of A in week 8. The letter superscripted A to the right of the gross figure for items B and C was generated as a result of the demand for the parent, A. Performing the same type of analysis for B and C yields the net requirements for D, E, F, and G. Note the on-hand inventory in row E in week 6 is zero. It is zero because the on-hand inventory (10 units) was used to make B in week 5. By the same token, the inventory for D was used to make F in week 3.

Insight: Once a net requirement plan is completed, management knows the quantities needed, an ordering schedule, and a production schedule for each component.

Learning exercise: If the on-hand inventory quantity of component F is 95 rather than 5, how many units of G will need to be ordered in week 1? [Answer: 105 units.]

Related problems: 5, 7, 8c, 10b, 11b, 12, 13c, 14, 15, 16a, 25, 27

Planned order receipt
The quantity planned to be received at a future date.

Planned order release
The scheduled date for an order to be released.

Examples 2 and 3 considered only product A, the Awesome speaker kit, and its completion only in week 8. Fifty units of A were required in week 8. Normally, however, there is a demand for many products over time. For each product, management must prepare a master production schedule (as we saw earlier in Table 1). Scheduled production of each product is added to the master schedule and ultimately to the net material requirements plan. Figure 6 shows how several product schedules, including requirements for components sold directly, can contribute to one gross material requirements plan.

Most inventory systems also note the number of units in inventory that have been assigned to specific future production but not yet used or issued from the stockroom. Such items are often referred to as *allocated* items. Allocated items increase requirements and may then be included in an MRP planning sheet, as shown in Figure 7.

The allocated quantity has the effect of increasing the requirements (or, alternatively, reducing the quantity on hand). The logic, then, of a net requirements MRP is:

Learning Objective

3. Build a net requirements plan

$$\underbrace{\left[\binom{\text{Gross}}{\text{requirements}} + \left(\text{Allocations}\right)\right]}_{\text{Total requirements}} - \underbrace{\left[\binom{\text{On}}{\text{hand}} + \binom{\text{Scheduled}}{\text{receipts}}\right]}_{\text{Available inventory}} = \frac{\text{Net}}{\text{requirements}}$$

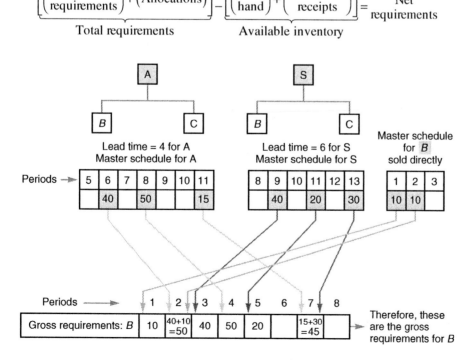

◀ Figure 6

Several Schedules Contributing to a Gross Requirements Schedule for B

One B is in each A, and one B is in each S; additionally, 10 Bs sold directly are scheduled in week 1, and 10 more that are sold directly are scheduled in week 2.

Lot Size	Lead Time	On Hand	Safety Stock	Allocated	Low-Level Code	Item ID		Period							
								1	2	3	4	5	6	7	8
Lot FoR Lot	1	0	0	10	0	Z	Gross Requirements								80 90
							Scheduled Receipts								0
							Projected On Hand 0	0	0	0	0	0	0	0	0
							Net Requirements								90
							Planned Order Receipts								90
							Planned Order Releases							90	

▲ **Figure 7** Sample MRP Planning Sheet for Item Z

Safety Stock   The continuing task of operations managers is to remove variability. This is the case in MRP systems as in other operations systems. Realistically, however, managers need to realize that bills of material and inventory records, like purchase and production quantities, as well as lead times, may not be perfect. This means that some consideration of safety stock may be prudent. Because of the significant domino effect of any change in requirements, safety stock should be minimized, with a goal of ultimate elimination. When safety stock is deemed absolutely necessary, the usual policy is to build it into the projected on-hand inventory of the MRP logic. Distortion can be minimized when safety stock is held at the finished goods level and at the purchased component or raw material level.

MRP MANAGEMENT

The material requirements plan is not static. And since MRP systems increasingly are integrated with just-in-time (JIT) techniques, we now discuss these two issues.

MRP Dynamics

Bills of material and material requirements plans are altered as changes in design, schedules, and production processes occur. Additionally, changes occur in material requirements whenever the master production schedule is modified. Regardless of the cause of any changes, the MRP model can be manipulated to reflect them. In this manner, an up-to-date requirements schedule is possible.

Due to the changes that occur in MRP data, it is not uncommon to recompute MRP requirements about once a week. Conveniently, a central strength of MRP is its timely and accurate *replanning* capability. However, many firms find they do not want to respond to minor scheduling or quantity changes even if they are aware of them. These frequent changes generate what is called **system nervousness** and can create havoc in purchasing and production departments if implemented. Consequently, OM personnel reduce such nervousness by evaluating the need and impact of changes prior to disseminating requests to other departments. Two tools are particularly helpful when trying to reduce MRP system nervousness.

The first is time fences. **Time fences** allow a segment of the master schedule to be designated as "not to be rescheduled." This segment of the master schedule is therefore not changed during the periodic regeneration of schedules. The second tool is pegging. **Pegging** means tracing upward in the BOM from the component to the parent item. By pegging upward, the production planner can determine the cause for the requirement and make a judgment about the necessity for a change in the schedule.

With MRP, the operations manager *can* react to the dynamics of the real world. How frequently the manager wishes to impose those changes on the firm requires professional judgment. Moreover, if the nervousness is caused by legitimate changes, then the proper response may be to investigate the production environment—not adjust via MRP.

MRP and JIT

MRP does not do detailed scheduling—it plans. MRP will tell you that a job needs to be completed on a certain week or day but does not tell you that Job X needs to run on Machine A at 10:30 A.M. and be completed by 11:30 A.M. so that Job X can then run on machine B. MRP is also

System nervousness
Frequent changes in an MRP system.

Time fences
A means for allowing a segment of the master schedule to be designated as "not to be rescheduled."

Pegging
In material requirements planning systems, tracing upward in the bill of material from the component to the parent item.

a planning technique with *fixed* lead times. Fixed lead times can be a limitation. For instance, the lead time to produce 50 units may vary substantially from the lead time to produce 5 units. These limitations complicate the marriage of MRP and just-in-time (JIT). What is needed is a way to make MRP more responsive to moving material rapidly in small batches. An MRP system combined with JIT can provide the best of both worlds. MRP provides the plan and an accurate picture of requirements; then JIT rapidly moves material in small batches, reducing work-in-process inventory. Let's look at four approaches for integrating MRP and JIT: finite capacity scheduling, small buckets, balanced flow, and supermarkets.

Finite Capacity Scheduling (FCS)

Most MRP software loads work into infinite size "buckets." The **buckets** are time units, usually one week. Traditionally, when work is to be done in a given week, MRP puts the work there without regard to capacity. Consequently, MRP is considered an *infinite* scheduling technique. Frequently, as you might suspect, this is not realistic. Finite capacity scheduling (FCS) considers department and machine capacity, which is *finite*, hence the name. FCS provides the precise scheduling needed for rapid material movement. We are now witnessing a convergence of FCS and MRP. Sophisticated FCS systems modify the output from MRP systems to provide a finite schedule.

Buckets
Time units in a material requirements planning system.

Small Bucket Approach

MRP is an excellent tool for resource and scheduling management in process-focused facilities, that is, in job shops. Such facilities include machine shops, hospitals, and restaurants, where lead times are relatively stable and poor balance between work centers is expected. Schedules are often driven by work orders, and lot sizes are the exploded bill-of-material size. In these enterprises, MRP can be integrated with JIT through the following steps.

Step 1: Reduce MRP "buckets" from weekly to daily to perhaps hourly. Buckets are time units in an MRP system. Although the examples in this chapter have used weekly *time buckets*, many firms now use daily or even fraction-of-a-day time buckets. Some systems use a **bucketless system** in which all time-phased data have dates attached rather than defined time periods or buckets.

Bucketless system
Time-phased data are referenced using dated records rather than defined time periods, or buckets.

Step 2: The planned receipts that are part of a firm's planned orders in an MRP system are communicated to the work areas for production purposes and used to sequence production.

Step 3: Inventory is moved through the plant on a JIT basis.

Step 4: As products are completed, they are moved into inventory (typically finished-goods inventory) in the normal way. Receipt of these products into inventory reduces the quantities required for subsequent planned orders in the MRP system.

Step 5: A system known as *back flush* is used to reduce inventory balances. **Back flushing** uses the bill of material to deduct component quantities from inventory as each unit is completed.

Back flush
A system to reduce inventory balances by deducting everything in the bill of material on completion of the unit.

The focus in these facilities becomes one of maintaining schedules. Nissan achieves success with this approach by computer communication links to suppliers. These schedules are confirmed, updated, or changed every 15 to 20 minutes. Suppliers provide deliveries 4 to 16 times per day. Master schedule performance is 99% on time, as measured every hour. On-time delivery from suppliers is 99.9% and for manufactured piece parts, 99.5%.

Balanced Flow Approach

MRP supports the planning and scheduling necessary for repetitive operations, such as the assembly lines at Harley-Davidson, Whirlpool, and a thousand other places. In these environments, the planning portion of MRP is combined with JIT execution. The JIT portion uses kanbans, visual signals, and reliable suppliers to pull the material through the facility. In these systems, execution is achieved by maintaining a carefully balanced flow of material to assembly areas with small lot sizes.

Supermarket

Another technique that joins MRP and JIT is the use of a "supermarket." In many firms, subassemblies, their components, and hardware items are common to a variety of products. In such cases, releasing orders for these common items with traditional lead-time offset, as is done in an MRP system, is not necessary. The subassemblies, components, and hardware items can be maintained in a common area, sometimes called a **supermarket**, adjacent to the production areas where they are used. Items in the supermarket are replenished by a JIT/kanban system.

Supermarket
An inventory area that holds common items that are replenished by a kanban system.

LOT-SIZING TECHNIQUES

An MRP system is an excellent way to determine production schedules and net requirements. However, whenever we have a net requirement, a decision must be made about *how much* to order. This decision is called a **lot-sizing decision**. There are a variety of ways to determine lot sizes in an MRP system; commercial MRP software usually includes the choice of several lot-sizing techniques. We now review a few of them.

Lot-sizing decision

The process of, or techniques used in, determining lot size.

Lot-for-lot

A lot-sizing technique that generates exactly what is required to meet the plan.

Lot-for-Lot In Example 3, we used a lot-sizing technique known as **lot-for-lot**, which produced exactly what was required. This decision is consistent with the objective of an MRP system, which is to meet the requirements of *dependent* demand. Thus, an MRP system should produce units only as needed, with no safety stock and no anticipation of further orders. When frequent orders are economical and just-in-time inventory techniques implemented, lot-for-lot can be very efficient. However, when setup costs are significant or management has been unable to implement JIT, lot-for-lot can be expensive. Example 4 uses the lot-for-lot criteria and determines cost for 10 weeks of demand.

EXAMPLE 4

Lot sizing with lot-for-lot

Learning Objective

4. Determine lot sizes for lot-for-lot, EOQ, and PPB

Speaker Kits, Inc., wants to compute its ordering and carrying cost of inventory on lot-for-lot criteria.

Approach: With lot-for-lot, we order material only as it is needed. Once we have the cost of ordering (setting up), the cost of holding each unit for a given time period, and the production schedule, we can assign orders to our net requirements plan.

Solution: Speaker Kits has determined that, for the 12-inch speaker unit, setup cost is $100 and holding cost is $1 per period. The production schedule, as reflected in net requirements for assemblies, is as follows:

MRP Lot Sizing: Lot-for-Lot Technique*

		1	2	3	4	5	6	7	8	9	10
Gross requirements		35	30	40	0	10	40	30	0	30	55
Scheduled receipts											
Projected on hand	35	35	0	0	0	0	0	0	0	0	0
Net requirements		0	30	40	0	10	40	30	0	30	55
Planned order receipts			30	40		10	40	30		30	55
Planned order releases		30	40		10	40	30		30	55	

*Holding costs = $1/unit/week; setup cost = $100; gross requirements average per week = 27; lead time = 1 week.

The lot-sizing solution using the lot-for-lot technique is shown in the table. The holding cost is zero as there is never any inventory; but seven separate setups (one associated with each order) yield a total cost of $700.

Insight: When supply is reliable and frequent orders are inexpensive, but holding cost or obsolescence is high, lot-for-lot ordering can be very efficient.

Learning exercise: What is the impact on total cost if holding cost is $2 per period rather than $1? [Answer: Total holding cost remains zero, as no units are held from one period to the next with lot-for-lot.]

Related problems: 17, 20, 21, 22

MRP is preferable when demand is dependent. Statistical techniques such as EOQ may be preferable when demand is independent.

Economic Order Quantity EOQ can be used as a lot-sizing technique. But as we indicated there, EOQ is preferable when *relatively constant* independent demand exists, not when we *know* the demand. EOQ is a statistical technique using averages (such as average demand for a year), whereas the MRP procedure assumes *known* (dependent) demand reflected in a master production schedule. Operations managers should take advantage of demand information when it is known, rather than assuming a constant demand. EOQ is examined in Example 5.

John Russell, AP Wide World Photos

◄ This Nissan line in Smyrna, Tennessee, has little inventory because Nissan schedules to a razor's edge. At Nissan, MRP helps reduce inventory to world-class standards. World-class automobile assembly requires that purchased parts have a turnover of slightly more than once a day and that overall turnover approaches 150 times per year.

per week of $1, Speaker Kits, Inc., wants to examine its cost with lot sizes based on an EOQ criteria.

Approach: Using the same cost and production schedule as in Example 4, we determine net requirements and EOQ lot sizes.

Solution: Ten-week usage equals a gross requirement of 270 units; therefore, weekly usage equals 27, and 52 weeks (annual usage) equals 1,404 units. The EOQ model is:

$$Q^* = \sqrt{\frac{2DS}{H}}$$

where
D = annual usage = 1,404
S = setup cost = $100
H = holding (carrying) cost, on an annual basis per unit
= $1 × 52 weeks = $52

$$Q^* = 73 \text{ units}$$

MRP Lot Sizing: EOQ Technique*

		1	2	3	4	5	6	7	8	9	10
Gross requirements		35	30	40	0	10	40	30	0	30	55
Scheduled receipts											
Projected on hand	35	35	0	43	3	3	66	26	69	69	39
Net requirements		0	30	0	0	7	0	4	0	0	16
Planned order receipts			73			73		73			73
Planned order releases		73			73		73		73		

*Holding costs = $1/unit/week; setup cost = $100; gross requirements average per week = 27; lead time = 1 week.

Setups = 1,404/73 = 19 per year

Setup cost = 19 × $100 = $1,900

Holding cost = $\frac{73}{2}$ × ($1 × 52 weeks) = $1,898

Setup cost + Holding cost = $1,900 + 1,898 = $3,798

The EOQ solution yields a computed 10-week cost of $730 [$3,798 × (10 weeks/52 weeks) = $730].

With a setup cost of $100 and a holding cost

Insight: EOQ can be an effective lot-sizing technique when demand is relatively constant. However, notice that actual holding cost will vary from the computed $730, depending on the rate of actual usage. From the preceding table, we can see that in our 10-week example, costs really are $400 for four setups, plus a holding cost of 318 units at $1 per week for a total of $718. Because usage was not constant, the actual computed cost was in fact less than the theoretical EOQ ($730), but more than the lot-for-lot rule ($700). If any stockouts had occurred, these costs too would need to be added to our actual EOQ cost of $718.

Learning exercise: What is the impact on total cost if holding cost is $2 per period rather than $1? [Answer: The EOQ quantity becomes 52, the theoretical annual total cost becomes $5,404, and the 10-week cost is $1,039 ($5,404 × (10/52).]

Related problems: 18, 20, 21, 22

Part period balancing (PPB)
An inventory ordering technique that balances setup and holding costs by changing the lot size to reflect requirements of the next lot size in the future.

Economic part period (EPP)
A period of time when the ratio of setup cost to holding cost is equal.

Part Period Balancing **Part period balancing (PPB)** is a more dynamic approach to balance setup and holding cost.[3] PPB uses additional information by changing the lot size to reflect requirements of the next lot size in the future. PPB attempts to balance setup and holding cost for known demands. Part period balancing develops an **economic part period (EPP)**, which is the ratio of setup cost to holding cost. For our Speaker Kits example, EPP = $100/$1 = 100 units. Therefore, holding 100 units for one period would cost $100, exactly the cost of one setup. Similarly, holding 50 units for two periods also costs $100 (2 periods × $1 × 50 units). PPB merely adds requirements until the number of part periods approximates the EPP—in this case, 100. Example 6 shows the application of part period balancing.

EXAMPLE 6

Lot sizing with part period balancing

Speaker Kits, Inc., wants to compute the costs associated with lot sizing using part period balancing. It will use a setup cost of $100 and a $1 holding cost.

Approach: Using the same costs and production schedule as Examples 3 and 4, we develop a format that helps us compute the PPB quantity and apply that to our net requirements plan.

Solution: The procedure for computing the order releases of 80, 100, and 55 is shown in the following PPB calculation. In the second table, we apply the PPB order quantities to the net requirements plan.

PPB Calculations

Periods Combined	Trial Lot Size (cumulative net requirements)	Part Periods	Costs Setup	Holding	Total
2	30	0		40 units held for 1 period = $40	
2, 3	70	40 = 40 × 1		10 units held for 3 periods = $30	
2, 3, 4	70	40			
2, 3, 4, 5	80	70 = 40 × 1 + 10 × 3	100 +	70	= 170
2, 3, 4, 5, 6	120	230 = 40 × 1 + 10 × 3 + 40 × 4			
(Therefore, combine periods 2 through 5: 70 is as close to our EPP of 100 as we are going to get.)					
6	40	0			
6, 7	70	30 = 30 × 1			
6, 7, 8	70	30 = 30 × 1 + 0 × 2			
6, 7, 8, 9	100	120 = 30 × 1 + 30 × 3	100 +	120	= 220
(Therefore, combine periods 6 through 9: 120 is as close to our EPP of 100 as we are going to get.)					
10	55	0	100 +	0	= 100
			300 +	190	= 490

---

[3]J. J. DeMatteis, "An Economic Lot-Sizing Technique: The Part-Period Algorithms," *IBM Systems Journal* 7 (1968): 30–38.

MRP Lot Sizing: PPB Technique*

		1	2	3	4	5	6	7	8	9	10
Gross requirements		35	30	40	0	10	40	30	0	30	55
Scheduled receipts											
Projected on hand	35	35	0	50	10	10	0	60	30	30	0
Net requirements		0	30	0	0	0	40	0	0	0	55
Planned order receipts			80				100				55
Planned order releases		80				100				55	

*Holding costs = $1/unit/week; setup cost = $100; gross requirements average per week = 27; lead time = 1 week.

EPP is 100 (setup cost divided by holding cost = $100/$1). The first lot is to cover periods 1, 2, 3, 4, and 5 and is 80.

The total costs are $490, with setup costs totaling $300 and holding costs totaling $190.

Insight: Both the EOQ and PPB approaches to lot sizing balance holding cost and ordering cost. But PPB places an order each time holding cost equals ordering cost, while EOQ takes a longer averaging approach.

Learning exercise: What is the impact on total cost if holding cost is $2 per period rather than $1? [Answer: With higher holding costs, reorder points become more frequent, with orders now being placed for 70 units in period 1, 50 in period 4, 60 in period 6, and 55 in period 9.]

Related problems: 19, 20, 21, 22

Wagner-Whitin Algorithm The **Wagner-Whitin procedure** is a dynamic programming model that adds some complexity to the lot-size computation. It assumes a finite time horizon beyond which there are no additional net requirements. It does, however, provide good results.[4]

Wagner-Whitin procedure
A technique for lot-size computation that assumes a finite time horizon beyond which there are no additional net requirements to arrive at an ordering strategy.

Lot-Sizing Summary In the three Speaker Kits lot-sizing examples, we found the following costs:

Lot-for-lot	$700
EOQ	$730
Part period balancing	$490

These examples should not, however, lead operations personnel to hasty conclusions about the preferred lot-sizing technique. In theory, new lot sizes should be computed whenever there is a schedule or lot-size change anywhere in the MRP hierarchy. However, in practice, such changes cause the instability and system nervousness referred to earlier in this chapter. Consequently, such frequent changes are not made. This means that all lot sizes are wrong because the production system cannot respond to frequent changes.

In general, the lot-for-lot approach should be used whenever low-cost deliveries can be achieved. Lot-for-lot is the goal. Lots can be modified as necessary for scrap allowances, process constraints (for example, a heat-treating process may require a lot of a given size), or raw material purchase lots (for example, a truckload of chemicals may be available in only one lot size). However, caution should be exercised prior to any modification of lot size because the modification can cause substantial distortion of actual requirements at lower levels in the MRP hierarchy. When setup costs are significant and demand is reasonably smooth, part period balancing (PPB), Wagner-Whitin, or even EOQ should provide satisfactory results. Too much concern with lot sizing yields false accuracy because of MRP dynamics. A correct lot size can be determined only after the fact, based on what actually happened in terms of requirements.

---

[4]We leave discussion of the algorithm to mathematical programming texts. The Wagner-Whitin algorithm yields a cost of $455 for the data in Examples 4, 5, and 6.

User Solutions, Inc.

Many MRP programs, such as Resource Manager for Excel *and* DB, *are commercially available.* Resource Manager's *initial menu screen is shown here.*

A demo program is available for student use at **www.usersolutions.com**.

EXTENSIONS OF MRP

In this section, we review three extensions of MRP.

Material Requirements Planning II (MRP II)

Material requirements planning II is an extremely powerful technique. Once a firm has MRP in place, inventory data can be augmented by labor-hours, by material cost (rather than material quantity), by capital cost, or by virtually any other resource. When MRP is used this way, it is usually referred to as **MRP II**, and *resource* is usually substituted for *requirements*. MRP then stands for material *resource* planning.

For instance, so far in our discussion of MRP, we have scheduled units (quantities). However, each of these units requires resources in addition to its components. Those additional resources include labor-hours, machine-hours, and accounts payable (cash). Each of these resources can be used in an MRP format just as we used quantities. Table 4 shows how to determine the labor-hours, machine-hours, and cash that a sample master production schedule will require in each period. These requirements are then compared with the respective capacity (that is, labor-hours, machine-hours, cash, etc.), so operations managers can make schedules that will work.

To aid the functioning of MRP II, most MRP II computer programs are tied into other computer files that provide data to the MRP system or receive data from the MRP system. Purchasing, production scheduling, capacity planning, and warehouse management are a few examples of this data integration.

Material requirements planning II (MRP II)

A system that allows, with MRP in place, inventory data to be augmented by other resource variables; in this case, MRP becomes *material resource planning*.

Learning Objective

5. Describe MRP II

▶ **Table 4**

Material Resource Planning (MRP II)

By utilizing the logic of MRP, resources such as labor, machine-hours, and cost can be accurately determined and scheduled. Weekly demand for labor, machine-hours, and payables for 100 units are shown.

	Week			
	5	**6**	**7**	**8**
A. Units (lead time 1 week)				100
Labor: 10 hours each				1,000
Machine: 2 hours each				200
Payable: $0 each				$ 0
B. Units (lead time 2 weeks, 2 each required)			200	
Labor: 10 hours each			2,000	
Machine: 2 hours each			400	
Payable: Raw material at $5 each			$1,000	
C. Units (lead time 4 weeks, 3 each required)	300			
Labor: 2 hours each	600			
Machine: 1 hour each	300			
Payable: Raw material at $10 each	$3,000			

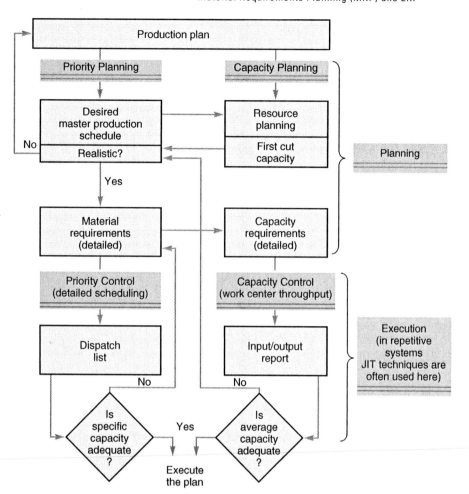

◄ **Figure 8**

Closed-Loop Material Requirements Planning

Source: Adapted from *Capacity Planning and Control Study Guide* (Alexandria, VA: American Production and Inventory Control Society). Reprinted by permission.

Learning Objective

6. Describe closed-loop MRP

Closed-Loop MRP

Closed-loop material requirements planning implies an MRP system that provides feedback to scheduling from the inventory control system. Specifically, a **closed-loop MRP system** provides information to the capacity plan, master production schedule, and ultimately to the production plan (as shown in Figure 8). Virtually all commercial MRP systems are closed-loop.

Capacity Planning

In keeping with the definition of closed-loop MRP, feedback about workload is obtained from each work center. **Load reports** show the resource requirements in a work center for all work currently assigned to the work center, all work planned, and expected orders. Figure 9(a) shows that the initial load in the milling center exceeds capacity in weeks 4 and 6. Closed-loop MRP systems allow production planners to move the work between time periods to smooth the load or at least bring it within capacity. (This is the "capacity planning" side of Figure 8.) The closed-loop MRP system can then reschedule all items in the net requirements plan (see Figure 9[b]).

Tactics for smoothing the load and minimizing the impact of changed lead time include the following:

1. *Overlapping,* which reduces the lead time, sends pieces to the second operation before the entire lot is completed on the first operation.
2. *Operations splitting* sends the lot to two different machines for the same operation. This involves an additional setup, but results in shorter throughput times, because only part of the lot is processed on each machine.
3. *Order,* or, *lot splitting* involves breaking up the order and running part of it ahead of schedule.

Example 7 shows a brief detailed capacity scheduling example using order splitting to improve utilization.

Closed-loop MRP system

A system that provides feedback to the capacity plan, master production schedule, and production plan so planning can be kept valid at all times.

Load report

A report for showing the resource requirements in a work center for all work currently assigned there as well as all planned and expected orders.

▶ Figure 9

(a) Initial Resource
Requirements Profile
for a Milling Center
(b) Smoothed Resource
Requirements Profile
for a Milling Center

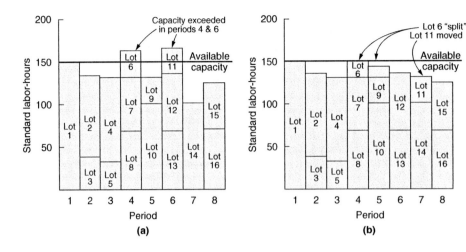

EXAMPLE 7

Order splitting

Kevin Watson, the production planner at Wiz Products, needs to develop a capacity plan for the direct numeric control (DNC) work cell. He has the production orders shown below for the next 5 days and 440 minutes available in the work center each day. The parts being produced require 20 minutes each.

Day	1	2	3	4	5
Orders	20	24	23	20	24

Approach: Compute the time available in the work center and the time necessary to complete the production requirements.

Solution:

Day	Units Ordered	Capacity Required (minutes)	Capacity Available (minutes)	Utilization: Over/ (Under) (minutes)	Production Planner's Action	New Production Schedule
1	20	400	440	(40)		22
2	24	480	440	40	Split order: move 2 units to day 1	22
3	23	460	440	20	Split order: move 1 unit to day 4	22
4	20	400	440	(40)		22
5	24	480	440	40	Split order: move 1 unit to day 4 and 1 unit to day 6 or request overtime.	22
	111					

Insight: By splitting the order, the production planner is able to utilize capacity more effectively and still meet the order requirements.

Learning exercise: If the units ordered for day 5 increase to 26, what are the production planner's options? [Answer: In addition to moving 1 unit to day 4, move the 3 units of production to day 6, or request overtime.]

Related problems: 23, 24

When the workload consistently exceeds work-center capacity, the tactics just discussed are not adequate. This may mean adding capacity. Options include adding capacity via personnel, machinery, overtime, or subcontracting.

MRP IN SERVICES

The demand for many services or service items is classified as dependent demand when it is directly related to or derived from the demand for other services. Such services often require product-structure trees, bills-of-material and labor, and scheduling. MRP can make a major contribution to operational performance in such services. Examples from restaurants, hospitals, and hotels follow.

Restaurants In restaurants, ingredients and side dishes (bread, vegetables, and condiments) are typically meal components. These components are dependent on the demand for meals. The meal is an end item in the master schedule. Figure 10 shows (a) a product-structure tree and (b) a bill of material for veal picante, a top-selling entrée in a New Orleans restaurant. Note that the various components of veal picante (that is, veal, sauce, and linguini) are prepared by different kitchen personnel (see part [a] of Figure 10). These preparations also require different amounts of time to complete. Figure 10(c) shows a bill-of-labor for the veal dish. It lists the operations to be performed, the order of operations, and the labor requirements for each operation (types of labor and labor-hours).

Hospitals MRP is also applied in hospitals, especially when dealing with surgeries that require known equipment, materials, and supplies. Houston's Park Plaza Hospital and many hospital suppliers, for example, use the technique to improve the scheduling and management of expensive surgical inventory.

Hotels Marriott develops a bill-of-material (BOM) and a bill-of-labor when it renovates each of its hotel rooms. Marriott managers explode the BOM to compute requirements for materials, furniture, and decorations. MRP then provides net requirements and a schedule for use by purchasing and contractors.

Distribution Resource Planning (DRP)

When dependent techniques are used in the supply chain, they are called distribution resource planning (DRP). **Distribution resource planning (DRP)** is a time-phased stock-replenishment plan for all levels of the supply chain.

Distribution resource planning (DRP)
A time-phased stock-replenishment plan for all levels of a distribution network.

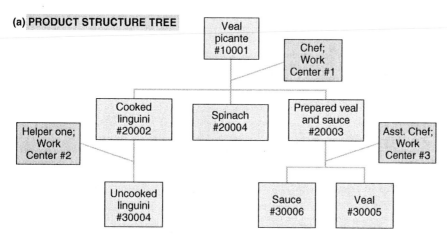

(a) PRODUCT STRUCTURE TREE

(b) BILL OF MATERIALS

Part Number	Description	Quantity	Unit of Measure	Unit Cost
10001	Veal picante	1	Serving	—
20002	Cooked linguini	1	Serving	—
20003	Prepared veal and sauce	1	Serving	—
20004	Spinach	0.1	Bag	0.94
30004	Uncooked linguini	0.5	Pound	—
30005	Veal	1	Serving	2.15
30006	Sauce	1	Serving	0.80

(c) BILL OF LABOR FOR VEAL PICANTE

Work Center	Operation	Labor Type	Labor-Hours Setup Time	Run Time
1	Assemble dish	Chef	.0069	.0041
2	Cook linguini	Helper one	.0005	.0022
3	Cook veal and sauce	Assistant chef	.0125	.0500

◀ **Figure 10**

Product Structure Tree, Bill-of-Material, and Bill-of-Labor for Veal Picante

Source: Adapted from John G. Wacker, "Effective Planning and Cost Control for Restaurants," *Production and Inventory Management* (1st quarter 1985): 60. Reprinted by permission of American Production and Inventory Control Society.

DRP procedures and logic are analogous to MRP. With DRP, expected demand becomes gross requirements. Net requirements are determined by allocating available inventory to gross requirements. The DRP procedure starts with the forecast at the retail level (or the most distant point of the distribution network being supplied). All other levels are computed. As is the case with MRP, inventory is then reviewed with an aim to satisfying demand. So that stock will arrive when it is needed, net requirements are offset by the necessary lead time. A planned order release quantity becomes the gross requirement at the next level down the distribution chain.

DRP *pulls* inventory through the system. Pulls are initiated when the top or retail level orders more stock. Allocations are made to the top level from available inventory and production after being adjusted to obtain shipping economies. Effective use of DRP requires an integrated information system to rapidly convey planned order releases from one level to the next. The goal of the DRP system is small and frequent replenishment within the bounds of economical ordering and shipping.

ENTERPRISE RESOURCE PLANNING (ERP)

Enterprise resource planning (ERP)
An information system for identifying and planning the enterprise-wide resources needed to take, make, ship, and account for customer orders.

Advances in MRP II systems that tie customers and suppliers to MRP II have led to the development of enterprise resource planning (ERP) systems. **Enterprise resource planning (ERP)** is software that allows companies to (1) automate and integrate many of their business processes, (2) share a common database and business practices throughout the enterprise, and (3) produce information in real time. A schematic showing some of these relationships for a manufacturing firm appears in Figure 11.

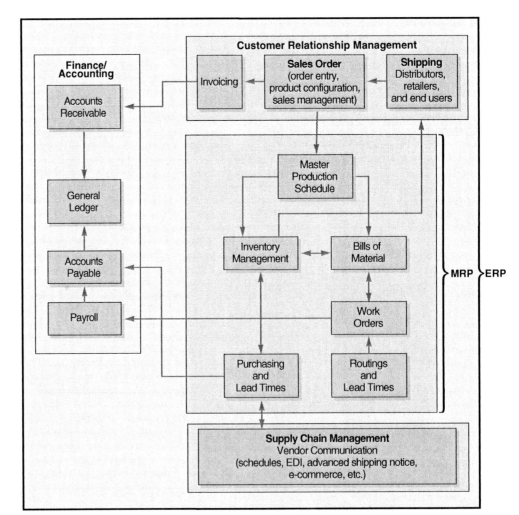

▶ **Figure 11**

MRP and ERP Information Flows, Showing Customer Relationship Management (CRM), Supply Chain Management (SCM), and Finance/Accounting

Other functions such as human resources are often also included in ERP systems.

The objective of an ERP system is to coordinate a firm's whole business, from supplier evaluation to customer invoicing. This objective is seldom achieved, but ERP systems are evolving as umbrella systems that tie together a variety of specialized systems. This is accomplished by using a centralized database to assist the flow of information among business functions. Exactly what is tied together, and how, varies on a case-by-case basis. In addition to the traditional components of MRP, ERP systems usually provide financial and human resource (HR) management information. ERP systems also include:

- *Supply chain management (SCM)* software to support sophisticated vendor communication, e-commerce, and those activities necessary for efficient warehousing and logistics. The idea is to tie operations (MRP) to procurement, to materials management, and to suppliers, providing the tools necessary for effective management of all four areas.
- *Customer relationship management (CRM)* software for the incoming side of the business. CRM is designed to aid analysis of sales, target the most profitable customers, and manage the sales force.

Learning Objective

7. Describe ERP

Besides these five modules (MRP, finance, HR, SCM, and CRM), many other options are usually available from vendors of ERP software. These vendors have built modules to provide a variety of "solution" packages that are mixed and matched to individual company needs. Indeed, the trick to these large database and integrated ERP systems is to develop interfaces that allow file access to the databases. SAP, a large ERP vendor, has developed about a thousand *business application-programming interfaces* (BAPIs) to access its database. Similarly, other ERP vendors have designed the systems to facilitate integration with third-party software. The demand for interfaces to ERP systems is so large that a new software industry has developed to write the interfaces. This new category of programs is sometimes called *middleware* or *enterprise application integration* (EAI) software. These interfaces allow the expansion of ERP systems so they can integrate with other systems, such as warehouse management, logistics exchanges, electronic catalogs, quality management, and product life cycle management. It is this potential for integration with other systems, including the rich supply of third-party software offerings, that makes ERP so enticing.

In addition to data integration, ERP software promises reduced transaction costs and fast, accurate information. A strategic emphasis on just-in-time systems and supply chain integration drives the desire for enterprise-wide software. The *OM in Action* box "Managing Benetton with ERP Software," provides an example of how ERP software helps integrate company operations.

OM in Action   Managing Benetton with ERP Software

Thanks to ERP, the Italian sportswear company Benetton can probably claim to have the world's fastest factory and the most efficient distribution in the garment industry. Located in Ponzano, Italy, Benetton makes and ships 50 million pieces of clothing each year. That is 30,000 boxes every day—boxes that must be filled with exactly the items ordered going to the correct store of the 5,000 Benetton outlets in 60 countries. This highly automated distribution center uses only 19 people. Without ERP, hundreds of people would be needed.

Here is how ERP software works:

1. *Ordering:* A salesperson in the south Boston store finds that she is running out of a best-selling blue sweater. Using a laptop PC, her local Benetton sales agent taps into the ERP sales module.
2. *Availability:* ERP's inventory software simultaneously forwards the order to the mainframe in Italy and finds that half the order can be filled immediately from the Italian warehouse. The rest will be manufactured and shipped in 4 weeks.

3. *Production:* Because the blue sweater was originally created by computer-aided design (CAD), ERP manufacturing software passes the specifications to a knitting machine. The knitting machine makes the sweaters.
4. *Warehousing:* The blue sweaters are boxed with a radio frequency ID (RFID) tag addressed to the Boston store and placed in one of the 300,000 slots in the Italian warehouse. A robot flies by, reading RFID tags, picks out any and all boxes ready for the Boston store, and loads them for shipment.
5. *Order tracking:* The Boston salesperson logs onto the ERP system through the Internet and sees that the sweater (and other items) are completed and being shipped.
6. *Planning:* Based on data from ERP's forecasting and financial modules, Benetton's chief buyer decides that blue sweaters are in high demand and quite profitable. She decides to add three new hues.

Sources: The Wall Street Journal (April 10, 2007): B1; *Frontline Solutions* (April 2003): 54; and *MIT Sloan Management Review* (fall 2001): 46–53.

In an ERP system, data are entered only once into a common, complete, and consistent database shared by all applications. For example, when a Nike salesperson enters an order into his ERP system for 20,000 pairs of sneakers for Foot Locker, the data are instantly available on the manufacturing floor. Production crews start filling the order if it is not in stock, accounting prints Foot Locker's invoice, and shipping notifies the Foot Locker of the future delivery date. The salesperson, or even the customer, can check the progress of the order at any point. This is all accomplished using the same data and common applications. To reach this consistency, however, the data fields must be defined identically across the entire enterprise. In Nike's case, this means integrating operations at production sites from Vietnam to China to Mexico, at business units across the globe, in many currencies, and with reports in a variety of languages.

Each ERP vendor produces unique products. The major vendors, SAP AG (a German firm), BEA (Canada), SSAGlobal, American Software, PeopleSoft/Oracle, CMS Software (all of the U.S.), sell software or modules designed for specific industries (a set of SAP's modules is shown in Figure 12). However, companies must determine if their way of doing business will fit the standard ERP module. If they determine that the product will not fit the standard ERP product, they can change the way they do business to accommodate the software. But such a change can have an adverse impact on their business process, reducing a competitive advantage. Alternatively, ERP software can be customized to meet their specific process requirements. Although the vendors build the software to keep the customization process simple, many companies spend up to five times the cost of the software to customize it. In addition to the expense, the major downside of customization is that when ERP vendors provide an upgrade or enhancement to the software, the customized part of the code must be rewritten to fit into the new version. ERP programs cost from a minimum of $300,000 for a small company to hundreds of millions of dollars for global giants like General Motors and Coca-Cola. It is easy to see, then, that ERP systems

▼ **Figure 12** SAP's Modules for ERP

Cash to Cash
Covers all financial related activity:

| Accounts receivable | General ledger | Cash management |
| Accounts payable | Treasury | Asset management |

Promote to Deliver
Covers front-end customer-oriented activities:

Marketing

Quote and order processing

Transportation

Documentation and labeling

After sales service

Warranty and guarantees

Design to Manufacture
Covers internal production activities:

Design engineering	Shop floor reporting
Production engineering	Contract/project management
Plant maintenance	
	Subcontractor management

Recruit to Retire
Covers all HR- and payroll-oriented activity:

| Time and attendance | Payroll |
| Travel and expenses | |

Procure to Pay
Covers sourcing activities:

Vendor sourcing

Purchase requisitioning

Purchase ordering

Purchase contracts

Inbound logistics

Supplier invoicing/matching

Supplier payment/settlement

Supplier performance

Dock to Dispatch
Covers internal inventory management:

| Warehousing | Forecasting | Physical inventory |
| Distribution planning | Replenishment planning | Material handling |

Source: www.sap.com.

OM in Action — There Is Nothing Easy about ERP

In 2000, the Switzerland-based consumer food giant Nestlé SA signed a $200 million contract with SAP for an ERP system. To this $200 million, Nestlé added $80 million for consulting and maintenance. And this was in addition to $500 million for hardware and software as part of a data center overhaul. Jeri Dunn, CIO of Nestlé USA, counsels that successful implementation is dependent on changing business processes and achieving universal "buy-in." Then, and only then, can an organization focus on installing the software. With many autonomous divisions and 200 operating companies and subsidiaries in 80 countries, the challenge of changing the processes and obtaining buy-in was substantial.

Standardizing processes is difficult, fraught with dead ends and costly mistakes. Nestlé had 28 points of customer order entry, multiple purchasing systems, and no idea how much volume was being done with a particular vendor; every factory did purchasing on its own with its own specifications. Nestlé USA was paying 29 different prices for vanilla—to the same vendor!

The newly established common databases and business processes led to consistent data and more trustworthy demand forecasts for the many Nestlé products. Nestlé now forecasts down to the level of the distribution center. This improved forecasting allows the company to reduce inventory and the related transportation expenses that occur when too much of a product is sent to one place while there is a shortage in another. The supply chain improvements accounted for much of Nestlé's $325 million in savings.

ERP projects are notorious for taking a long time and a lot of money, and this one was no exception, but after 3 years, the last modules of Nestlé's system were installed—and Nestlé thinks this installation is a success.

Sources: Materials Management and Distribution (March 2003): 27; Businessline (March 12, 2004): 1; and CIO (May 15, 2002): 62–70.

---

are expensive, full of hidden issues, and time consuming to install. As the *OM in Action* box "There Is Nothing Easy about ERP" notes, Nestlé, too, found nothing easy about ERP.

Advantages and Disadvantages of ERP Systems

We have alluded to some of the pluses and minuses of ERP. Here is a more complete list of both.

Advantages:
1. Provides integration of the supply chain, production, and administrative process.
2. Creates commonality of databases.
3. Can incorporate improved, reengineered, "best processes."
4. Increases communication and collaboration among business units and sites.
5. Has a software database that is off-the-shelf coding.
6. May provide a strategic advantage over competitors.

Disadvantages:
1. Is very expensive to purchase, and even more costly to customize.
2. Implementation may require major changes in the company and its processes.
3. Is so complex that many companies cannot adjust to it.
4. Involves an ongoing process for implementation, which may never be completed.
5. Expertise in ERP is limited, with staffing an ongoing problem.

ERP in the Service Sector

ERP vendors have developed a series of service modules for such markets as health care, government, retail stores, and financial services. Springer-Miller Systems, for example, has created an ERP package for the hotel market with software that handles all front- and back-office functions. This system integrates tasks such as maintaining guest histories, booking room and dinner reservations, scheduling golf tee times, and managing multiple properties in a chain. PeopleSoft/Oracle combines ERP with supply chain management to coordinate airline meal preparation. In the grocery industry, these supply chain systems are known as *efficient consumer response* (ECR) systems. As is the case in manufacturing, **efficient consumer response** systems tie sales to buying, to inventory, to logistics, and to production.

Efficient consumer response (ECR)
Supply chain management systems in the grocery industry that tie sales to buying, to inventory, to logistics, and to production.

Summary

Material requirements planning (MRP) is the preferred way to schedule production and inventory when demand is dependent. For MRP to work, management must have a master schedule, precise requirements for all components, accurate inventory and purchasing records, and accurate lead times.

Production should often be lot-for-lot in an MRP system. When properly implemented, MRP can contribute in a major way to reduction in inventory while improving customer-service levels. MRP techniques allow the operations manager to schedule and replenish stock on a "need-to-order" basis rather than simply a "time-to-order" basis.

The continuing development of MRP systems has led to the integration of production data with a variety of other activities, including the supply chain and sales. As a result, we now have integrated database-oriented enterprise resource planning (ERP) systems. These expensive and difficult-to-install ERP systems, when successful, support strategies of differentiation, response, and cost leadership.

Key Terms

Material requirements planning (MRP)	Planned order receipt	Lot-for-lot
Master production schedule (MPS)	Planned order release	Part period balancing (PPB)
Bill of material (BOM)	System nervousness	Economic part period (EPP)
Modular bills	Time fences	Wagner-Whitin procedure
Planning bills (or kits)	Pegging	Material requirements planning II (MRP II)
Phantom bills of material	Buckets	Closed-loop MRP system
Low-level coding	Bucketless system	Load report
Lead time	Back flush	Distribution resource planning (DRP)
Gross material requirements plan	Supermarket	Enterprise resource planning (ERP)
Net material requirements	Lot-sizing decision	Efficient consumer response (ECR)

Using Software to Solve MRP Problems

There are many commercial MRP software packages, for companies of all sizes. MRP software for small and medium-size companies includes User Solutions, Inc., a demo of which is available at **www.usersolutions.com**, and MAX, from Exact Software North America, Inc. Software for larger systems is available from SAP, CMS, BEA, Oracle, i2 Technologies, and many others. The Excel OM software that accompanies this text includes an MRP module, as does POM for Windows. The use of both is explained in the following sections.

Using Excel OM

Using Excel OM's MRP module requires the careful entry of several pieces of data. The initial MRP screen is where we enter (1) the total number of occurrences of items in the BOM (including the top item), (2) what we want the BOM items to be called (i.e., Item no., Part), (3) total number of periods to be scheduled, and (4) what we want the periods called (i.e., days, weeks).

Excel OM's second MRP screen provides the data entry for an indented bill of material. Here we enter (1) the name of each item in the BOM, (2) the quantity of that item in the assembly, and (3) the correct indent (i.e., parent/child relationship) for each item. The indentations are critical as they provide the logic for the BOM explosion. The indentations should follow the logic of the product structure tree with indents for each assembly item in that assembly.

Excel OM's third MRP screen repeats the indented BOM and provides the standard MRP tableau for entries. This is shown in Program 1 using the data from Examples 1, 2, and 3.

Using POM for Windows

The POM for Windows MRP module can also solve Examples 1 to 3. Up to 18 periods can be analyzed. Here are the inputs required:

1. *Item names:* The item names are entered in the left column. The same item name will appear in more than one row if the item is used by two parent items. Each item must follow its parents.
2. *Item level:* The level in the indented BOM must be given here. The item *cannot* be placed at a level more than one below the item immediately above.
3. *Lead-time:* The lead time for an item is entered here. The default is 1 week.
4. *Number per parent:* The number of units of this subassembly needed for its parent is entered here. The default is 1.
5. *On hand:* List current inventory on hand once, even if the subassembly is listed twice.

The data in columns A, B, C, D (down to row 15) are entered on the second screen and automatically transferred here.

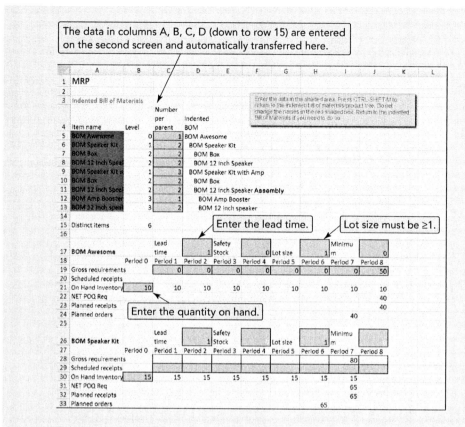

◀ **Program 1**

**Using Excel OM's
MRP Module to Solve
Examples 1, 2, and 3**

6. *Lot size:* The lot size can be specified here. A 0 or 1 will perform lot-for-lot ordering. If another number is placed here, then all orders for that item will be in integer multiples of that number.

7. *Demands:* The demands are entered in the end item row in the period in which the items are demanded.

8. *Scheduled receipts:* If units are scheduled to be received in the future, they should be listed in the appropriate time period (column) and item (row). (An entry here in level 1 is a demand; all other levels are receipts.)

Solved Problems

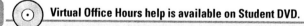 **Virtual Office Hours help is available on Student DVD.**

Solved Problem 1

Determine the low-level coding and the quantity of each component necessary to produce 10 units of an assembly we will call Alpha. The product structure and quantities of each component needed for each assembly are noted in parenthesis.

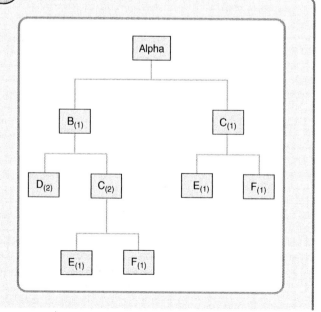

solution

Redraw the product structure with low-level coding. Then multiply down the structure until the requirements of each branch are determined. Then add across the structure until the total for each is determined.

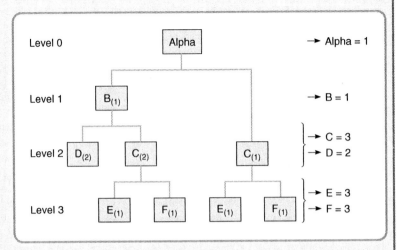

Es required for left branch:

$$(1_{\text{alpha}} \times 1_B \times 2_C \times 1_E) = 2$$

and Es required for right branch:

$$(1_{\text{alpha}} \times 1_C \times 1_E) = \frac{1}{3} \text{ Es required in total}$$

Then "explode" the requirement by multiplying each by 10, as shown in the following table:

Level	Item	Quantity per Unit	Total Requirements for 10 Alpha
0	Alpha	1	10
1	B	1	10
2	C	3	30
2	D	2	20
3	E	3	30
3	F	3	30

Solved Problem 2

Using the product structure for Alpha in Solved Problem 1, and the following lead times, quantity on hand, and master production schedule, prepare a net MRP table for Alphas.

Item	Lead Time	Qty On Hand
Alpha	1	10
B	2	20
C	3	0
D	1	100
E	1	10
F	1	50

Master Production Schedule for Alpha

Period	6	7	8	9	10	11	12	13
Gross requirements			50			50		100

solution

See the chart on the next page.

Net Material Requirements Planning Sheet for Alpha

The letter in parentheses (A) is the source of the demand.

Lot Size	Lead Time (# of Periods)	On Hand	Safety Stock	Allocated	Low-Level Code	Item ID		1	2	3	4	5	6	7	8	9	10	11	12	13
Lot-for-Lot	1	10	—	—	0	Alpha (A)	Gross Requirements								50			50		100
							Scheduled Receipts													
							Projected On Hand 10													
							Net Requirements								40			50		100
							Planned Order Receipts								40			50		100
							Planned Order Releases							40			50		100	
Lot-for-Lot	2	20	—	—	1	B	Gross Requirements							40(A)			50(A)		100(A)	
							Scheduled Receipts													
							Projected On Hand 20													
							Net Requirements							20			50		100	
							Planned Order Receipts							20			50		100	
							Planned Order Releases					20			50		100			
Lot-for-Lot	3	0	—	—	2	C	Gross Requirements					40(B)		40(A)	100(B)		200(B) + 50(A)		100(A)	
							Scheduled Receipts													
							Projected On Hand 0													
							Net Requirements					40		40	100		250		100	
							Planned Order Receipts					40		40	100		250		100	
							Planned Order Releases		40		40	100		250		100				
Lot-for-Lot	1	100	—	—	2	D	Gross Requirements					40(B)			100(B)		200(B)			
							Scheduled Receipts													
							Projected On Hand 100					60			0					
							Net Requirements					0			40		200			
							Planned Order Receipts								40		200			
							Planned Order Releases							40		200				
Lot-for-Lot	1	10	—	—	3	E	Gross Requirements		40(C)		40(C)	100(C)		250(C)		100(C)				
							Scheduled Receipts													
							Projected On Hand 10		0											
							Net Requirements		30		40	100		250		100				
							Planned Order Receipts		30		40	100		250		100				
							Planned Order Releases	30		40	100		250		100					
Lot-for-Lot	1	50	—	—	3	F	Gross Requirements		40(C)		40(C)	100(C)		250(C)		100(C)				
							Scheduled Receipts													
							Projected On Hand 50		10		0									
							Net Requirements		0		30	100		250		100				
							Planned Order Receipts				30	100		250		100				
							Planned Order Releases			30	100		250		100					

Self-Test

- **Before taking the self-test**, refer to the learning objectives listed at the beginning of the selection and the key terms listed at the end of the selection.
- Use the key at the back of the text to **correct** your answers.
- **Restudy** pages that correspond to any questions you answered incorrectly or material you feel uncertain about.

1. The list of quantities of components, ingredients, and materials required to produce a product is the:
   a) bill-of-material
   b) engineering change notice
   c) purchase order
   d) all of the above

2. _____ allows a segment of the master schedule to be designated as "not to be rescheduled."
   a) Regenerative MRP
   b) System nervousness
   c) Pegging
   d) DRP
   e) None of the above

3. A lot-sizing procedure that assumes a finite time horizon beyond which there are no additional net requirements is:
   a) Wagner-Whitin algorithm
   b) part period balancing
   c) economic order quantity
   d) all of the above

4. Breaking up the order and running part of it ahead of schedule is known as:
   a) overlapping
   b) operations splitting
   c) order, or lot, splitting
   d) pegging

5. In a product structure diagram:
   a) parents are found only at the top level of the diagram
   b) parents are found at every level in the diagram
   c) children are found at every level of the diagram except the top level
   d) all items in the diagrams are both parents and children
   e) all of the above are true

6. The difference between a gross material requirements plan (gross MRP) and a net materials requirements plan (net MRP) is:
   a) the gross MRP may not be computerized, but the net MRP must be computerized
   b) the gross MRP includes consideration of the inventory on hand, whereas the net MRP doesn't include the inventory consideration
   c) the net MRP includes consideration of the inventory on hand, whereas the gross MRP doesn't include the inventory consideration
   d) the gross MRP doesn't take taxes into account, whereas the net MRP includes the tax considerations
   e) the net MRP is only an estimate, whereas the gross MRP is used for actual production scheduling

7. To effectively use dependent inventory models, the operations manager needs to know:
   a) the master production schedule (which tells what is to be made and when)
   b) the specifications or bill-of-material (which tells how to make the product)
   c) the purchase orders outstanding (which tell what is on order)
   d) the lead times (or how long it takes to get various components)
   e) all of the above

8. A phantom bill-of-material is a bill-of-material developed for:
   a) a final product for which production is to be discontinued
   b) a subassembly that exists only temporarily
   c) a module that is a major component of a final product
   d) the purpose of grouping subassemblies when we wish to issue "kits" for later use

9. When a bill-of-material is used in order to assign an artificial parent to a bill-of-material, it is usually called a:
   a) modular bill-of-material
   b) pick list
   c) phantom bill-of-material
   d) planning bill-of-material

Active Model Exercise

We use Active Model 14.1 to demonstrate the effects of lot sizes (multiples) and minimum lot sizes.

Questions

1. Suppose that item B must be ordered in multiples of dozens. Which items are affected by this change?

2. Suppose that the minimum order quantity for item C is 200 units. Which items are affected by this change?

Order Releases

Reset Data   Questions

Master Production Schedule

	Week 1	2	3	4	5	6	7	8
Item A	0	0	0	0	0	0	0	50

Item Master File

	Lead time	On hand	Lot size multiple	Minimum lot size
A	1	10	1	0
B	2	15	1	0
C	1	20	1	0
D	1	10	1	0
E	2	10	1	0
F	3	5	1	0
G	2	0	1	0

Planned Order Releases

	Week 1	2	3	4	5	6	7	8
A							40	
B					65			
C						100		
D		380		130				
E			120	200				
F			195					
G	195							

◄ **Active Model 14.1**

An Analysis of the MRP Model Used by Speaker Kits, Inc., in Examples 1–3

Internet and Student CD-ROM/DVD Exercises

Visit our Companion Web site or use your student CD-ROM/DVD to help with material in this chapter.

On Our Companion Web Site, www.prenhall.com/heizer
- Self-Study Quizzes
- Practice Problems
- Virtual Company Tour
- Internet Cases
- PowerPoint Lecture

On Your Student CD-ROM
- Practice Problems
- Active Model Exercise
- Excel OM
- Excel OM Example Data File
- POM for Windows

On Your Student DVD
- Video Clip and Video Case
- Virtual Office Hours for Solved Problems

Discussion Questions

1. What is the difference between a *gross* requirements plan and a *net* requirements plan?
2. Once a material requirements plan (MRP) has been established, what other managerial applications might be found for the technique?
3. What are the similarities between MRP and DRP?
4. How does MRP II differ from MRP?
5. Which is the best lot-sizing policy for manufacturing organizations?
6. What impact does ignoring carrying cost in the allocation of stock in a DRP system have on lot sizes?
7. MRP is more than an inventory system; what additional capabilities does MRP possess?
8. What are the options for the production planner who has: (a) scheduled more than capacity in a work center next week? (b) a consistent lack of capacity in that work center?
9. Master schedules are expressed in three different ways depending on whether the process is continuous, a job shop, or repetitive. What are these three ways?
10. What functions of the firm affect an MRP system? How?
11. What is the rationale for (a) a phantom bill of material, (b) a planning bill of material, and (c) a pseudo bill of material?

12. Identify five specific requirements of an effective MRP system.
13. What are the typical benefits of ERP?
14. What are the distinctions between MRP, DRP, and ERP?
15. What are the disadvantages of ERP?
16. Use the Web or other sources to:
    (a) Find stories that highlight the advantages of an ERP system.
    (b) Find stories that highlight the difficulties of purchasing, installing, or failure of an ERP system.
17. Use the Web or other sources to identify what an ERP vendor (SAP, PeopleSoft/Oracle, American Software, etc.) includes in these software modules:
    (a) Customer relationship management.
    (b) Supply chain management.
    (c) Product life cycle management.
18. The very structure of MRP systems suggests fixed lead times. However, many firms have moved toward JIT and kanban techniques. What are the techniques, issues, and impact of adding JIT inventory and purchasing techniques to an organization that has MRP?

Ethical Dilemma

For many months your prospective ERP customer has been analyzing the hundreds of assumptions built into the $800,000 ERP software you are selling. So far, you have knocked yourself out to try to make this sale. If the sale goes through, you will reach your yearly quota and get a nice bonus. On the other hand, loss of this sale may mean you start looking for other employment.

The accounting, human resource, supply chain, and marketing teams put together by the client have reviewed the specifications and finally recommended purchase of the software. However, as you looked over their shoulders and helped them through the evaluation process, you began to realize that their purchasing procedures—with much of the purchasing being done at hundreds of regional stores—were not a good fit for the software. At the very least, the customizing will add $250,000 to the implementation and training cost. The team is not aware of the issue, and you know that the necessary $250,000 is not in the budget.

What do you do?

Problems*

• 1 You have developed the following simple product structure of items needed for your gift bag for a rush party for prospective pledges in your organization. You forecast 200 attendees. Assume that there is no inventory on hand of any of the items. Explode the bill of material. (Subscripts indicate the number of units required.)

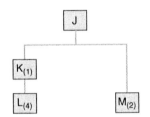

•• 2 You are expected to have the gift bags in Problem 1 ready at 5 P.M.. However, you need to personalize the items (monogrammed pens, note pads, literature from the printer, etc.). The lead time is 1 hour to assemble 200 Js once the other items are prepared. The other items will take a while as well. Given the volunteers you have, the other time estimates are item K (2 hours), item L (1 hour), and item M (4 hours). Develop a time-phased assembly plan to prepare the gift bags.

•• 3 The demand for subassembly S is 100 units in week 7. Each unit of S requires 1 unit of T and 2 units of U. Each unit of T requires 1 unit of V, 2 units of W, and 1 unit of X. Finally, each unit of U requires 2 units of Y and 3 units of Z. One firm manufactures all items. It takes 2 weeks to make S, 1 week to make T, 2 weeks to make U, 2 weeks to make V, 3 weeks to make W, 1 week to make X, 2 weeks to make Y, and 1 week to make Z.
a) Construct a product structure. Identify all levels, parents, and components.
b) Prepare a time-phased product structure.

•• 4 Using the information in Problem 3, construct a gross material requirements plan. Px

•• 5 Using the information in Problem 3, construct a net material requirements plan using the following on-hand inventory.

Item	On-Hand Inventory	Item	On-Hand Inventory
S	20	W	30
T	20	X	25
U	40	Y	240
V	30	Z	40 Px

•• 6 Refer again to Problems 3 and 4. In addition to 100 units of S, there is also a demand for 20 units of U, which is a component of S. The 20 units of U are needed for maintenance purposes. These units are needed in week 6. Modify the *gross material requirements plan* to reflect this change. Px

•• 7 Refer again to Problems 3 and 5. In addition to 100 units of S, there is also a demand for 20 units of U, which is a component of S. The 20 units of U are needed for maintenance purposes. These units are needed in week 6. Modify the *net material requirements plan* to reflect this change. Px

•• 8 As the production planner for Adams-Ebert Products, Inc., you have been given a bill of material for a bracket that is made up of a base, two springs, and four clamps. The base is assembled from one clamp and two housings. Each clamp has one handle and one casting. Each housing has two bearings and one shaft. There is no inventory on hand.
a) Design a product structure noting the quantities for each item and show the low-level coding.
b) Determine the gross quantities needed of each item if you are to assemble 50 brackets.
c) Compute the net quantities needed if there are 25 of the base and 100 of the clamp in stock. Px

•• 9 Your boss at Adams-Ebert Products, Inc., has just provided you with the schedule and lead times for the bracket in Problem 8. The unit is to be prepared in week 10. The lead times for the components are bracket (1 week), base (1 week), spring (1 week), clamp (1 week), housing (2 weeks), handle (1 week), casting (3 weeks), bearing (1 week), and shaft (1 week).
a) Prepare the time-phased product structure for the bracket.
b) In what week do you need to start the castings? Px

••• 10 a) Given the product structure and master production schedule (Figure 14 on the next page), develop a gross requirements plan for all items.
b) Given the preceding product structure, master production schedule, and inventory status (Figure 14), develop a net materials requirements (planned order release) for all items. Px

*Note: Px means the problem may be solved with POM for Windows and/or Excel OM. Many of the exercises in this selection (1 through 16 and 23 through 27) can be done on *Resource Manager for Excel*, a commercial system made available by User Solutions, Inc. Access to a trial version of the software and a set of notes for the user is available at **www.usersolutions.com**.

Lot Size	Lead Time (# of periods)	On Hand	Safety Stock	Allocated	Low-Level Code	Item ID		Period (week, day)							
								1	2	3	4	5	6	7	8
							Gross Requirements								
							Scheduled Receipts								
							Projected On Hand								
							Net Requirements								
							Planned Order Receipts								
							Planned Order Releases								
							Gross Requirements								
							Scheduled Receipts								
							Projected On Hand								
							Net Requirements								
							Planned Order Receipts								
							Planned Order Releases								
							Gross Requirements								
							Scheduled Receipts								
							Projected On Hand								
							Net Requirements								
							Planned Order Receipts								
							Planned Order Releases								
							Gross Requirements								
							Scheduled Receipts								
							Projected On Hand								
							Net Requirements								
							Planned Order Receipts								
							Planned Order Releases								
							Gross Requirements								
							Scheduled Receipts								
							Projected On Hand								
							Net Requirements								
							Planned Order Receipts								
							Planned Order Releases								

▲ **Figure 13** **MRP Form for Homework Problems in this chapter**

For several problems in this chapter, a copy of this form may be helpful.

••• **11** Given the following product structure, master production schedule, and inventory status (Figure 15) and assuming the requirements for each BOM item is 1: (a) develop a gross requirements plan for Item C; (b) develop a net requirements plan for Item C. P✗

•••• **12** Based on the following data (see Figure 15), complete a net material requirements schedule for:

a) All items (10 schedules in all), assuming the requirement for each BOM item is 1.

b) All 10 items, assuming the requirement for all items is 1, except B, C, and F, which require *2 each*. P✗

••• **13** Electro Fans has just received an order for one thousand 20-inch fans due week 7. Each fan consists of a housing assembly, two grills, a fan assembly, and an electrical unit. The housing assembly consists of a frame, two supports, and a handle. The fan assembly consists of a hub and five blades. The electrical unit consists of a motor, a switch, and a knob. The

---

▼ **Figure 14** **Information for Problem 10**

Master Production Schedule for X1

PERIOD	7	8	9	10	11	12
Gross requirements		50		20		100

ITEM	LEAD TIME	ON HAND		ITEM	LEAD TIME	ON HAND
X1	1	50		C	1	0
B1	2	20		D	1	0
B2	2	20		E	3	10
A1	1	5				

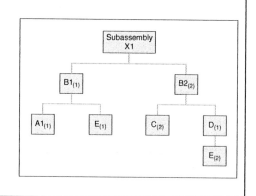

▶ **Figure 15**

Information for Problems 11 and 12

PERIOD	8	9	10	11	12
Gross requirements: A	100		50		150
Gross requirements: H		100		50	

ITEM	ON HAND	LEAD TIME	ITEM	ON HAND	LEAD TIME
A	0	1	F	75	2
B	100	2	G	75	1
C	50	2	H	0	1
D	50	1	J	100	2
E	75	2	K	100	2

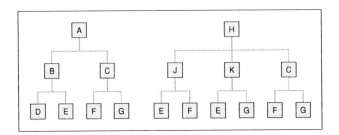

following table gives lead times, on-hand inventory, and scheduled receipts.
a) Construct a product structure.
b) Construct a time-phased product structure.
c) Prepare a net material requirements plan. **P**X

Data Table for Problem 13

Component	Lead Time	On Hand Inventory	Lot Size	Scheduled Receipt
20″ Fan	1	100	—	
Housing	1	100	—	
Frame	2	—	—	
Supports (2)	1	50	100	
Handle	1	400	500	
Grills (2)	2	200	500	
Fan Assembly	3	150	—	
Hub	1	—	—	
Blades (5)	2	—	100	
Electrical Unit	1	—	—	
Motor	1	—	—	
Switch	1	20	12	
Knob	1	—	25	200 knobs in week 2

••• 14   A part structure, lead time (weeks), and on-hand quantities for product A are shown in Figure 16. From the information shown, generate
a) An indented bill of material for product A.
b) Net requirements for each part to produce 10 As in week 8 using lot-for-lot. **P**X

••• 15   You are product planner for product A (in Problem 14 and Figure 16). The field service manager, Al Trostel, has just called and told you that the requirements for B and F should each be increased by 10 units for his repair requirements in the field.
a) Prepare a list showing the quantity of each part required to produce the requirements for the service manager *and* the production request of 10.
b) Prepare a net requirement plan by date for the new requirements (for both production and field service), assuming that the field service manager wants his 10 units of B and F in week 6 and the 10 production units in week 8. **P**X

••• 16   You have just been notified via fax that the lead time for component G of product A (Problem 15 and Figure 16) has been increased to 4 weeks.
a) Which items have changed and why?

▶ **Figure 16**

Information for Problems 14, 15 and 16

PART	INVENTORY ON HAND
A	0
B	2
C	10
D	5
E	4
F	5
G	1
H	10

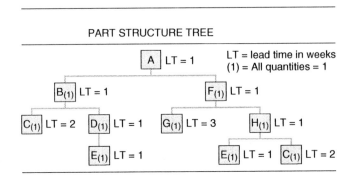

b) What are the implications for the production plan?

c) As production planner, what can you do? **P**✗

Data Table for Problems 17 through 19*

Period	1	2	3	4	5	6	7	8	9	10	11	12
Gross requirements	30		40		30	70	20		10	80		50

*Holding cost = $2.50/unit/week; setup cost = $150; lead time = 1 week; beginning inventory = 40.

••• 17   Develop a lot-for-lot solution and calculate total relevant costs for the data in the preceding table. **P**✗

••• 18   Develop an EOQ solution and calculate total relevant costs for the data in the preceding table. Stockout costs equal $10 per unit. **P**✗

••• 19   Develop a PPB solution and calculate total relevant costs for the data in the preceding table. **P**✗

••• 20   Using the gross requirements schedule in Examples 4, 5, and 6 in the text, prepare an alternative ordering system that always orders 100 units the week prior to a shortage (a fixed order quantity of 100) with the same costs as in the example (setup at $100 each, holding at $1 per unit per period). What is the cost of this ordering system? **P**✗

••• 21   Using the gross requirements schedule in Examples 4, 5, and 6 in the text, prepare an alternative ordering system that orders every 3 weeks for 3 weeks ahead (a periodic order quantity). Use the same costs as in the example (setup at $100 each, holding at $1 per unit per period). What is the cost of this ordering system? **P**✗

••• 22   Using the gross requirements schedule in Examples 4, 5, and 6 in the text, prepare an alternative ordering system of your own design that uses the same cost as in the example (setup at $100 each, holding at $1 per unit per period). Can you do better than the costs shown in the text? What is the cost of your ordering system? **P**✗

••• 23   Katherine Hepburn, Inc., has received the following orders:

Period	1	2	3	4	5	6	7	8	9	10
Order size	0	40	30	40	10	70	40	10	30	60

The entire fabrication for these units is scheduled on one machine. There are 2,250 usable minutes in a week, and each unit will take 65 minutes to complete. Develop a capacity plan, using lot splitting, for the 10-week time period.

••• 24   David Jurman, Ltd., has received the following orders:

Period	1	2	3	4	5	6	7	8	9	10
Order size	60	30	10	40	70	10	40	30	40	0

The entire fabrication for these units is scheduled on one machine. There are 2,250 usable minutes in a week, and each unit will take 65 minutes to complete. Develop a capacity plan, using lot splitting, for the 10-week time period.

•• 25   Heather Adams, production manager for a Colorado exercise equipment manufacturer, needs to schedule an order for 50 UltimaSteppers, which are to be shipped in week 8. Subscripts indicate quantity required for each parent. Assume lot-for-lot ordering. Below is information about the steppers:

Item	Lead Time	On-Hand Inventory	Components
Stepper	2	20	$A_{(1)}, B_{(3)}, C_{(2)}$
A	1	10	$D_{(1)}, F_{(2)}$
B	2	30	$E_{(1)}, F_{(3)}$
C	3	10	$D_{(2)}, E_{(3)}$
D	1	15	
E	2	5	
F	2	20	

a) Develop a product structure for Heather.

b) Develop a time-phased structure.

c) Develop a net material requirements plan for F. **P**✗

•••• 26   You are scheduling production of your popular Rustic Coffee Table. The table requires a top, four legs, $\frac{1}{8}$ gallon of stain, $\frac{1}{16}$ gallon of glue, 2 short braces between the legs and 2 long braces between the legs, and a brass cap that goes on the bottom of each leg. You have 100 gallons of glue in inventory, but none of the other components. All items except the brass caps, stain, and glue are ordered on a lot-for-lot basis. The caps are purchased in quantities of 1,000, stain and glue by the gallon. Lead time is 1 day for each item. Schedule the order releases necessary to produce 640 coffee tables on days 5 and 6, and 128 on days 7 and 8. **P**✗

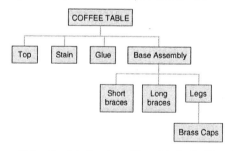

•••• 27   Using the data for the coffee table in Problem 26, build a labor schedule when the labor standard for each top is 2 labor hours; each leg including brass cap installation requires $\frac{1}{4}$ hour, as does each cross brace. Base assembly requires 1 labor-hour, and final assembly requires 2 labor-hours. What is the total number of labor-hours required each day, and how many employees are needed each day at 8 hours per day?

Case Studies

Ikon's Attempt at ERP

Ikon Office Solutions is the world's largest independent office technology company, with revenues approaching $5 billion and operations in the U.S., Canada, Mexico, the United Kingdom, France, Germany, and Denmark. Ikon is pursing a growth strategy to move from what was more than 80 individually operating copier dealers to an integrated solutions company. Its goal is to provide total office technology solutions, ranging from copiers, digital printers, and document management services to systems integration, training, and other network technology services. The company has rapidly expanded its service capability with an aggressive acquisition effort that has included technology services and document management companies.

Given these objectives, the company seemed to need ERP software. A few years ago, it began a pilot project in the Northern California district to assess the possibility of using SAP's enterprise software applications companywide. Chief Information Officer David Gadra, who joined Ikon about a month after the pilot system was turned on, however, decided not to roll it out. Ikon will take a $25 million write-off on the cost of the pilot.

"There were a number of factors that made us decide this project was more challenging than beneficial for us," says Gadra. "When we added everything up—human factors, functionality gaps, and costs incurred—we decided our environment is ill defined for SAP." Instead, Ikon is bringing all 13 of its regional operations onto a home-grown application system.

"I don't blame the consultants or SAP," he says. "We made errors on our side in estimating the amount of business change we'd have to make as part of this implementation."

The vast majority of the $25 million loss represents consultant fees; less than 10% went to pay for the software itself. At any given point in the project, Ikon was paying 40 to 50 outside consultants $300 an hour.

Ikon budgeted $12 million to get the system running. That cost came in at over $14 million, including $8 million paid to IBM for consulting.

A major reason the company decided to drop SAP was its conclusion that the software didn't sufficiently address the needs of a service company like Ikon, as opposed to those of manufacturers. For example, SAP didn't have an adequate feature for tracking service calls. Ikon also had great difficulty assembling an internal team of SAP experts. Ikon's costs were high because the firm relied heavily on consultants.

"I am extremely disappointed by Ikon's announcement," says SAP America president Jeremy Coote, describing Ikon's earlier pilot as on time and "extremely successful." Coote calls Ikon's decision to scrap the project "an example of what happens when you don't sell at the corporate level" as well as the divisional level. A newer version of SAP is to include a service management module.

Discussion Questions

1. What are the information needs at Ikon and what alternatives does Ikon have to meet these needs?
2. What are the advantages and disadvantages of ERP software in meeting these needs?
3. What risks did the company take in selecting SAP software for evaluation?
4. Why did Ikon cancel the SAP project?

Sources: Ikon Annual Reports; *Information Week* (April 1997): 25; and J. R. Gordon and S. R. Gordon, *Information Systems: A Management Approach*, 3rd ed. (New York: Wiley, 2003).

MRP at Wheeled Coach

Video Case

Wheeled Coach, the world's largest manufacturer of ambulances, builds thousands of different and constantly changing configurations of its products. The custom nature of its business means lots of options and special designs—and a potential scheduling and inventory nightmare. Wheeled Coach addressed such problems, and succeeded in solving a lot of them, with an MRP system (described in the *Global Company Profile* that opens this chapter). As with most MRP installations, however, solving one set of problems uncovers a new set.

One of the new issues that had to be addressed by plant manager Lynn Whalen was newly discovered excess inventory. Managers discovered a substantial amount of inventory that was not called for in any finished products. Excess inventory was evident because of the new level of inventory accuracy required by the MRP system. The other reason was a new series of inventory reports generated by the IBM MAPICS MRP system purchased by Wheeled Coach. One of those reports indicates where items are used and is known as the "Where Used" report. Interestingly, many inventory items were not called out on bills-of-material (BOMs) for any current products. In some cases, the reason some parts were in the stockroom remained a mystery.

The discovery of this excess inventory led to renewed efforts to ensure that the BOMs were accurate. With substantial work, BOM accuracy increased and the number of engineering change notices

(ECNs) decreased. Similarly, purchase-order accuracy, with regard to both part numbers and quantities ordered, was improved. Additionally, receiving department and stockroom accuracy went up, all helping to maintain schedule, costs, and ultimately, shipping dates and quality.

Eventually, Lynn Whalen concluded that the residual amounts of excess inventory were the result, at least in part, of rapid changes in ambulance design and technology. Another source was customer changes made after specifications had been determined and materials ordered. This latter excess occurs because, even though Wheeled Coach's own throughput time is only 17 days, many of the items that it purchases require much longer lead times.

Discussion Questions*

1. Why is accurate inventory such an important issue at Wheeled Coach?
2. Why does Wheeled Coach have excess inventory, and what kind of a plan would you suggest for dealing with it?
3. Be specific in your suggestions for reducing inventory and how to implement them.

*You may wish to view this case on your DVD before answering the questions.

Additional Case Studies

Internet Case Study: Visit our Companion Web site at www.prenhall.com/heizer *for this free case study:*

- **Auto Parts, Inc.:** Distributor of automobile replacement parts has major MRP problems.

Harvard has selected these Harvard Business School cases to accompany this chapter:

harvardbusinessonline.hbsp.harvard.edu

- **Digital Equipment Corp.: The Endpoint Model** (#688-059): Describes implementation of an MRP II system to reduce cycle time of orders.
- **Tektronix, Inc.: Global ERP Implementation** (#699-043): Examines Tektronix's implementation of an ERP system in its three global business divisions.
- **Vardelay Industries, Inc.** (#697-037): Discusses ERP and related issues of process reengineering, standardization, and change management.
- **Moore Medical Corp.** (#601-142): Examines Moore's ERP investment and further investment in additional modules.

Bibliography

Anussornnitisarn, P., and S. F. Nof. "e-Work: The Challenge of the Next Generation ERP Systems." *Production Planning & Control* 14, no. 8 (December 2003): 753–765.

Bell, Steve. "Time Fence Secrets." *APICS* 16, no. 4 (April 2006): 44–48.

Bolander, Steven F., and Sam G. Taylor. "Scheduling Techniques: A Comparison of Logic." *Production and Inventory Management Journal* 41, no. 1 (1st quarter 2000): 1–5.

Crandall, Richard E. "The Epic Life of ERP." *APICS* 16, no. 2 (February 2006): 17–19.

Gattiker, Thomas F. "Anatomy of an ERP Implementation Gone Awry." *Production and Inventory Management* 43, nos. 3–4 (3rd/4th quarter 2002): 96–105.

Kanet, J., and V. Sridharan. "The Value of Using Scheduling Information in Planning Material Requirements." *Decision Sciences* 29, no. 2 (spring 1998): 479–498.

Koh, S. C. L., and S. M. Saad. "Managing Uncertainty in ERP-controlled Manufacturing Environments." *International Journal of Production Economics* 101, no. 1 (May 2006): 109.

Krupp, James A. G. "Integrating Kanban and MRP to Reduce Lead Time." *Production and Inventory Management Journal* 43, nos. 3–4 (3rd/4th quarter 2002): 78–82.

Lawrence, Barry F., Daniel F. Jennings, and Brian E. Reynolds. *ERP in Distribution.* Florence, KY: Thomson South-Western, (2005).

Moncrief, Stephen. "Push and Pull." *APICS—The Performance Advantage* (June 2003): 46–51.

Norris, G. *E-Business & ERP.* New York: Wiley (2005).

Olson, D. L. *Managerial Issues of Enterprise Resource Planning.* New York: McGraw-Hill (2004).

Segerstedt, A. "Master Production Scheduling and a Comparison of MRP and Cover-Time Planning." *International Journal of Production Research* 44, no. 18–19 (September 2006): 3585.

Summer, M. *Enterprise Resource Planning.* Upper Saddle River, NJ: Prentice Hall (2005).

Wacker, John G., and Malcolm Miller. "Configure-to-Order Planning Bills of Material: Simplifying a Complex Product Structure for Manufacturing Planning and Control." *Production and Inventory Management Journal* 41, no. 2 (2nd quarter 2000): 21–26.

Wagner, H. M., and T. M. Whitin. "Dynamic Version of the Economic Lot Size Model." *Management Science* 5, no. 1 (1958): 89–96.

Internet Resources

American Software: **www.amsoftware.com**

APICS magazine online edition:
www.apics.org/resources/magazine

Armstrong Management Group: **www.armstrongmg.com**

Business Research in Information and Technology: **www.brint.com**

CMS Software, Inc.: **www.cmssoftware.com**

i2 Technologies: **www.i2.com**

Intelligent Enterprise Software: **www.iqms.com**

Oracle/Peoplesoft: **www.oracle.com**

SAP America: **www.sap.com**

Software evaluation: **www.technologyevaluation.com**

SSA Global: **www.ssaglobal.com**

2 The time-phased plan for the gift bags is:

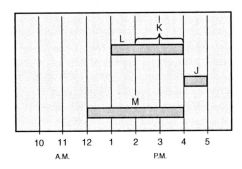

10 11 12 1 2 3 4 5
A.M.   P.M.

Someone should start on item M by noon.

4 Gross material requirements plan:

Item		Week								Lead Time (wk.)
		1	2	3	4	5	6	7	8	
S	Gross req.							100		
	Order release					100				2
T	Gross req.							100		
	Order release				100					1
U	Gross req.						200			
	Order release			200						2
V	Gross req.					100				
	Order release		100							2
W	Gross req.					200				
	Order release	200								3
X	Gross req.					100				
	Order release			100						1
Y	Gross req.				400					
	Order release		400							2
Z	Gross req.			600						
	Order release		600							1

6 Gross material requirements plan, modified to include the 20 units of U required for maintenance purposes:

Item		Week								Lead Time (wk.)
		1	2	3	4	5	6	7	8	
S	Gross req.							100		
	Order release					100				2
T	Gross req.						100			
	Order release					100				1
U	Gross req.					200	20			
	Order release			200	20					2
V	Gross req.					100				
	Order release		100							2
W	Gross req.					200				
	Order release	200								3
X	Gross req.					100				
	Order release			100						1
Y	Gross req.				400	40				
	Order release	400	40							2
Z	Gross req.			600	60					
	Order release	600	60							1

8 (a)

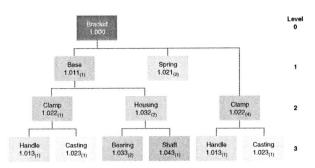

(b) For 50 brackets, the gross requirements are for 50 bases, 100 springs, 250 clamps, 250 handles, 250 castings, 100 housings, 200 bearings, and 100 shafts.

(c) For 50 brackets, net requirements are 25 bases, 100 springs, 125 clamps, 125 handles, 125 castings, 50 housings, 100 bearings, and 50 shafts.

10 (a) Gross material requirements plan for the first three items:

Item		Week											
		1	2	3	4	5	6	7	8	9	10	11	12
X1	Gross req.							50		20			100
	Order release						50		20		100		
B1	Gross req.							50		20			100
	Order release					50		20		100			
B2	Gross req.							100		40			200
	Order release				100		40		200				

(b) The net materials requirement plan for the first two items:

Level: 0 Item: X1	Parent: Lead Time:	Quantity: Lot Size: L4L										
Week No.	1	2	3	4	5	6	7	8	9	10	11	12
Gross Requirement							50		20			100
Scheduled Receipt												
On-Hand Inventory							50		0			0
Net Requirement							0		20			100
Planned Order Receipt									20			100
Planned Order Release								20		100		

Level: 1 Item: B1	Parent: X1 Lead Time: 2	Quantity: 1X Lot Size: L4L										
Week No.	1	2	3	4	5	6	7	8	9	10	11	12
Gross Requirement									20			100
Scheduled Receipt												
On-Hand Inventory									20			0
Net Requirement									0			100
Planned Order Receipt												100
Planned Order Release									100			

12 (a) Net material requirements schedule (only items A and H are shown):

	Week											
	1 2 3 4	5	6	7	8	9	10	11	12
A Gross required					100		50		150
On hand					0		0		0
Net required					100		50		150
Order receipt					100		50		150
Order release				100		50		150	
H Gross required					100		50		
On hand					0		0		
Net required					100		50		
Order receipt					100		50		
Order release				100		50			

(b) Net material requirements schedule (only items B and C are shown; schedule for items A and H remains the same as in part a.)

	Week												
	1 2 3 4	5	6	7	8	9	10	11	12	13
B Gross Requirements					200		100		300	
Scheduled Receipts										
Projected On Hand	100				100		0		0	
Net Requirements					100		100		300	
Planned Order Receipts					100		100		300	
Planned Order Releases			100		100		300			
C Gross Requirements				200	200	100	100	300		
Scheduled Receipts										
Projected On Hand	50			50						
Net Requirements				150	200	100	100	300		
Planned Order Receipts				150	200	100	100	300		
Planned Order Releases			150	200	100	100	300			

14 (a)

Level	Description	Qty
0	A	1
1	B	1
2	C	1
2	D	1
3	E	1
1	F	1
2	G	1
2	H	1
3	E	1
3	C	1

Note: with low-level coding, "C" would be a level-3 code.

(b) Solution for Items A, B, F (on next page):

14 (b)

Lot Size	Lead Time	On Hand	Safety Stock	Allo-cated	Low-Level Code	Item ID		Period (week) 1	2	3	4	5	6	7	8
Lot	1	0	—	—	1	A	Gross Requirement								10
for							Scheduled Receipt								
Lot							Projected On Hand								0
							Net Requirement								10
							Planned Receipt								10
							Planned Release							10	
Lot	1	2	—	—	1	B	Gross Requirement							10	
for							Scheduled Receipt								
Lot							Projected On Hand	2	2	2	2	2	2	2	0
							Net Requirement							8	
							Planned Receipt							8	
							Planned Release						8		
Lot	1	5	—	—	1	F	Gross Requirement							10	
for							Scheduled Receipt								
Lot							Projected On Hand	5	5	5	5	5	5	5	0
							Net Requirement							5	
							Planned Receipt							5	
							Planned Release						5		

16 (a) Only item G changes.

(b) Component F and 4 units of A will be delayed one week.

(c) Options include: delaying 4 units of A for 1 week; asking supplier of G to expedite production.

18 EOQ = 57; Total cost = $1,630

20 $650

22 $455

24 Selection for first 5 weeks:

Week	Units	Capacity Required (time)	Capacity Available (time)	Over/ (Under)	Production Scheduler's Action
1	60	3,900	2,250	1650	Lot split. Move 300 minutes (4.3 units) to week 2 and 1,350 minutes to week 3.
2	30	1,950	2,250	(300)	
3	10	650	2,250	(1,600)	
4	40	2,600	2,250	350	Lot split. Move 250 minutes to week 3. Operations split. Move 100 minutes to another machine, overtime, or subcontract.
5	70	4,550	2,250	2,300	Lot split. Move 1,600 minutes to week 6. Overlap operations to get product out door. Operations split. Move 700 minutes to another machine, overtime, or subcontract.

26 Here are the order releases for the table and the top:

Lot Size	Lead Time (# of periods)	On Hand	Safety Stock	Allo- cated	Low- Level Code	Item ID		Period (day)							
								1	2	3	4	5	6	7	8
Lot for Lot	1	—	—	—	0	Table	Gross Requirements					640	640	128	128
							Scheduled Receipts								
							Projected on Hand								
							Net Requirements					640	640	128	128
							Planned Order Receipts					640	640	128	128
							Planned Order Releases				640	640	128	128	
Lot for Lot	1	—	—	—	1	Top	Gross Requirements					640	640	128	128
							Scheduled Receipts								
							Projected on Hand								
							Net Requirements					640	640	128	128
							Planned Order Receipts					640	640	128	128
							Planned Order Releases				640	640	128	128	

Solutions to Self Test

1. a; **2.** e; **3.** a; **4.** c; **5.** c; **6.** c; **7.** e; **8.** b; **9.** d.

Chapter 16

JIT and Lean Operations

JIT and Lean Operations

Outline

Ten OM Strategy Decisions

Design of Goods and Services

Managing Quality

Process Strategy

Location Strategies

Layout Strategies

Human Resources

Supply Chain Management

Inventory Management

   Independent Demand

   Dependent Demand

   JIT and Lean Operations

Scheduling

Maintenance

Learning Objectives

When you complete this selection you should be able to

1. Define just-in-time, TPS, and lean operations
2. Define the seven wastes and the 5Ss
3. Explain JIT partnerships
4. Determine optimal setup time
5. Define kanban
6. Compute the required number of kanbans
7. Explain the principles of the Toyota Production System

From *Operations Management*, 9/e. Jay Heizer. Barry Render. Copyright © 2008 by Pearson Education. All rights reserved.

Achieving Competitive Advantage with Lean Operations at Toyota Motor Corporation

Toyota Motor Corporation, with annual sales of over 9 million cars and trucks, is the largest vehicle manufacturer in the world. Two techniques, just-in-time (JIT) and the Toyota Production System (TPS), have been instrumental in this post-WWII growth. Toyota, with a wide range of vehicles, competes head-to-head with successful long-established companies in Europe and the U.S. Taiichi Ohno, a former vice president of Toyota, created the basic framework for the world's most discussed systems for improving productivity, JIT and TPS. These two concepts provide much of the foundation for lean operations:

- Central to JIT is a philosophy of continued problem solving. In practice, JIT means making only what is needed, when it is needed. JIT provides an excellent vehicle for finding and eliminating problems because problems are easy to find in a system that has no slack. When excess inventory is eliminated, quality, layout, scheduling, and supplier issues become immediately evident—as does excess production.

- Central to TPS is a continuing effort to create and produce products under ideal conditions. Ideal conditions exist only when facilities, machines, and people are brought together, adding value without waste. Waste undermines productivity by diverting resources to excess inventory, unnecessary processing, and poor quality. Respect for people, extensive training, cross-training, and standard work practices of empowered employees focusing on driving out waste are fundamental to TPS.

Toyota's latest implementation of TPS and JIT are present at its new San Antonio plant,

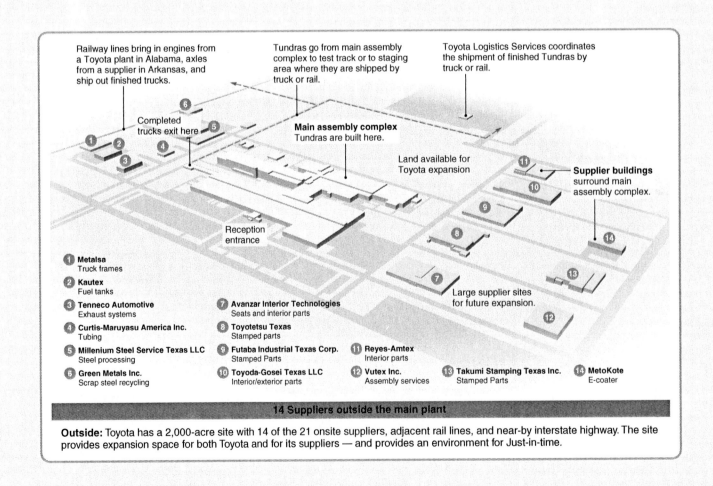

Railway lines bring in engines from a Toyota plant in Alabama, axles from a supplier in Arkansas, and ship out finished trucks.

Tundras go from main assembly complex to test track or to staging area where they are shipped by truck or rail.

Toyota Logistics Services coordinates the shipment of finished Tundras by truck or rail.

Completed trucks exit here

Main assembly complex
Tundras are built here.

Land available for Toyota expansion

Supplier buildings surround main assembly complex.

Reception entrance

Large supplier sites for future expansion.

1. **Metalsa** Truck frames
2. **Kautex** Fuel tanks
3. **Tenneco Automotive** Exhaust systems
4. **Curtis-Maruyasu America Inc.** Tubing
5. **Millenium Steel Service Texas LLC** Steel processing
6. **Green Metals Inc.** Scrap steel recycling
7. **Avanzar Interior Technologies** Seats and interior parts
8. **Toyotetsu Texas** Stamped parts
9. **Futaba Industrial Texas Corp.** Stamped Parts
10. **Toyoda-Gosei Texas LLC** Interior/exterior parts
11. **Reyes-Amtex** Interior parts
12. **Vutex Inc.** Assembly services
13. **Takumi Stamping Texas Inc.** Stamped Parts
14. **MetoKote** E-coater

14 Suppliers outside the main plant

Outside: Toyota has a 2,000-acre site with 14 of the 21 onsite suppliers, adjacent rail lines, and near-by interstate highway. The site provides expansion space for both Toyota and for its suppliers — and provides an environment for Just-in-time.

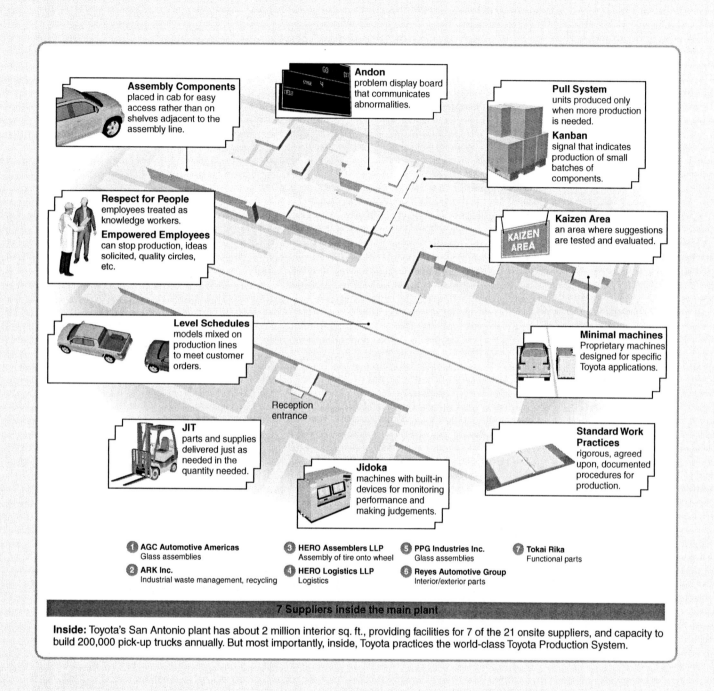

Assembly Components placed in cab for easy access rather than on shelves adjacent to the assembly line.

Andon problem display board that communicates abnormalities.

Pull System units produced only when more production is needed.

Kanban signal that indicates production of small batches of components.

Respect for People employees treated as knowledge workers.

Empowered Employees can stop production, ideas solicited, quality circles, etc.

Kaizen Area an area where suggestions are tested and evaluated.

KAIZEN AREA

Level Schedules models mixed on production lines to meet customer orders.

Minimal machines Proprietary machines designed for specific Toyota applications.

Reception entrance

JIT parts and supplies delivered just as needed in the quantity needed.

Jidoka machines with built-in devices for monitoring performance and making judgements.

Standard Work Practices rigorous, agreed upon, documented procedures for production.

① **AGC Automotive Americas** Glass assemblies

② **ARK Inc.** Industrial waste management, recycling

③ **HERO Assemblers LLP** Assembly of tire onto wheel

④ **HERO Logistics LLP** Logistics

⑤ **PPG Industries Inc.** Glass assemblies

⑥ **Reyes Automotive Group** Interior/exterior parts

⑦ **Tokai Rika** Functional parts

7 Suppliers inside the main plant

Inside: Toyota's San Antonio plant has about 2 million interior sq. ft., providing facilities for 7 of the 21 onsite suppliers, and capacity to build 200,000 pick-up trucks annually. But most importantly, inside, Toyota practices the world-class Toyota Production System.

the largest Toyota land site for an automobile assembly plant in the U.S. Interestingly, despite its annual production of 200,000 Tundra pick-up trucks, the building itself is one of the smallest in the industry. Modern automobiles have 30,000 parts, but at Toyota, independent suppliers combine many of these parts into sub-assemblies. Twenty-one of these suppliers are on site at the San Antonio facility and transfer components to the assembly line on a JIT basis.

Operations such as these taking place in the new San Antonio plant are why Toyota continues to perform near the top in quality and maintain the lowest labor-hour assembly time in the industry. JIT, TPS, and lean operations work—and they provide a competitive advantage at Toyota Motor Corporation.

As shown in the *Global Company Profile*, the Toyota Production System (TPS) contributes to a world-class operation at Toyota Motor Corporation. In this chapter, we discuss JIT, TPS, and lean operations as approaches to continuing improvement that drive out waste and lead to world-class organizations.

JUST-IN-TIME, THE TOYOTA PRODUCTION SYSTEM, AND LEAN OPERATIONS

Learning Objective

1. Define just-in-time, TPS, and lean operations

Just-in-time (JIT)
Continuous and forced problem solving via a focus on throughput and reduced inventory.

Toyota Production System (TPS)
Focus on continuous improvement, respect for people, and standard work practices.

Lean operations
Eliminates waste through a focus on exactly what the customer wants.

Just-in-time (JIT) is an approach of continuous and forced problem solving via a focus on throughput and reduced inventory. The **Toyota Production System (TPS)**, with its emphasis on continuous improvement, respect for people, and standard work practices, is particularly suited for assembly lines. **Lean operations** supplies the customer with exactly what the customer wants when the customer wants it, without waste, through continuous improvement. Lean operations are driven by workflow initiated by the "pull" of the customer's order. When implemented as a comprehensive manufacturing strategy, JIT, TPS, and lean systems sustain competitive advantage and result in increased overall returns.[1]

If there is any distinction between JIT, TPS, and lean operations, it is that:

- JIT emphasizes forced problem solving.
- TPS emphasizes employee learning and empowerment in an assembly-line environment.
- Lean operations emphasize understanding the customer.

However, in practice, there is little difference, and the terms are often used interchangeably. Leading organizations use the approaches and techniques that make sense for them. In this chapter, we use the term *lean operations* to encompass all of the related approaches and techniques.

Regardless of the label put on operations improvement, good production systems require that managers address three issues that are pervasive and fundamental to operations management: eliminate waste, remove variability, and speed throughput. We first introduce these three issues and then discuss the major attributes of JIT, TPS, and lean operations. Finally, we look at lean operations applied to services.

Eliminate Waste

Learning Objective

2. Define the seven wastes and the 5Ss

Seven wastes
Overproduction
Queues
Transportation
Inventory
Motion
Overprocessing
Defective product

Traditional producers have limited goals—accepting, for instance, the production of some defective parts and inventory. Lean producers set their sights on perfection: no bad parts, no inventory, only value-added activities, and no waste. Any activity that does not add value in the eyes of the customer is a waste. The customer defines product value. If the customer does not want to pay for it, it is a waste. Taiichi Ohno, noted for his work on the Toyota Production System, identified seven categories of waste. These categories have become popular in lean organizations and cover many of the ways organizations waste or lose money. Ohno's **seven wastes** are:

- *Overproduction:* Producing more than the customer orders or producing early (before it is demanded) is waste. Inventory of any kind is usually a waste.
- *Queues:* Idle time, storage, and waiting are wastes (they add no value).
- *Transportation:* Moving material between plants or between work centers and handling more than once is waste.
- *Inventory:* Unnecessary raw material, work-in-process (WIP), finished goods, and excess operating supplies add no value and are wastes.
- *Motion:* Movement of equipment or people that adds no value is waste.
- *Overprocessing:* Work performed on the product that adds no value is waste.
- *Defective product:* Returns, warranty claims, rework, and scrap are a waste.

A broader perspective—one that goes beyond immediate production—suggests that other resources, such as energy, water, and air, are often wasted but should not be. Efficient, ethical, socially responsible production minimizes inputs and maximizes outputs, wasting nothing.

---

[1]Research suggests that the more JIT is comprehensive in breadth and depth, the greater overall returns will be. See Rosemary R. Fullerton and Cheryl S. McWatters, "The Production Performance Benefits from JIT Implementation," *Journal of Operations Management* 19, no. 1 (January 2001): 81–96.

For over a century, managers have used "housekeeping" for a neat, orderly, and efficient workplace and as a means of reducing waste. Operations managers have embellished "housekeeping" to include a checklist—now known as the 5Ss.[2] The Japanese developed the initial 5Ss. Not only are the 5Ss a good checklist for lean operations, they also provide an easy vehicle with which to assist the culture change that is often necessary to bring about lean operations. The **5Ss** follow:

5Ss
A lean production checklist:
Sort
Simplify
Shine
Standardize
Sustain

- *Sort/segregate:* Keep what is needed and remove everything else from the work area; when in doubt, throw it out. Identify non-value items and remove them. Getting rid of these items makes space available and usually improves work flow.
- *Simplify/straighten:* Arrange and use methods analysis tools to improve work flow and reduce wasted motion. Consider long-run and short-run ergonomic issues. Label and display for easy use only what is needed in the immediate work area.
- *Shine/sweep:* Clean daily; eliminate all forms of dirt, contamination, and clutter from the work area.
- *Standardize:* Remove variations from the process by developing standard operating procedures and checklists; good standards make the abnormal obvious. Standardize equipment and tooling so that cross-training time and cost are reduced. Train and retrain the work team so that when deviations occur, they are readily apparent to all.
- *Sustain/self-discipline:* Review periodically to recognize efforts and to motivate to sustain progress. Use visuals wherever possible to communicate and sustain progress.

U.S. managers often add two additional Ss that contribute to establishing and maintaining a lean workplace:

- *Safety:* Build good safety practices into the above five activities.
- *Support/maintenance:* Reduce variability, unplanned downtime, and costs. Integrate daily shine tasks with preventive maintenance.

The Ss provide a vehicle for continuous improvement with which all employees can identify. Operations managers need think only of the examples set by a well-run hospital emergency room or the spit-and-polish of a fire department for a benchmark. Offices and retail stores, as well as manufacturers, have also successfully used the 5Ss in their respective efforts to eliminate waste and move to lean operations.[3] Operations managers reduce waste any way possible so assets are released for other, more productive, purposes.

Remove Variability

Managers seek to remove variability caused by both internal and external factors. **Variability** is any deviation from the optimum process that delivers perfect product on time, every time. Variability is a polite word for problems. The less variability in a system, the less waste in the system. Most variability is caused by tolerating waste or by poor management. Among the many sources of variability are:

Variability
Any deviation from the optimum process that delivers perfect product on time, every time.

- Incomplete or inaccurate drawings or specifications
- Poor production processes that allow employees and suppliers to produce improper quantities or late or non-conforming units
- Unknown customer demands

Both JIT and inventory reduction are effective tools for identifying causes of variability. The precise timing of JIT makes variability evident, just as inventory hides variability. The removal of variability allows managers to move good materials on schedule and add value at each step of the production process.

---

[2]The term 5S comes from the Japanese words seiri (*sort* and clear out), seiton (*straighten* and configure), seiso (*scrub* and cleanup), seiketsu (maintain *sanitation* and cleanliness of self and workplace), and shitsuke (*self-discipline and standardization* of these practices).

[3]Jeff Arnold and Christy Bures, "Revisiting a Retail Challenge," *Industrial Engineer* 35, no. 12 (December 2003): 38–41; and Lea A. P. Tonkin, "Elgin Sweeper Company Employees Clear a Path Toward Lean Operations with Their Lean Enterprise System," *Target* 20, no. 2 (2004): 46–52.

Improve Throughput

Throughput
The time required to move orders through the production process, from receipt to delivery.

Manufacturing cycle time
The time between the arrival of raw materials and the shipping of finished products.

Pull system
A concept that results in material being produced only when requested and moved to where it is needed just as it is needed.

Throughput is a measure (in units or time) that it takes to move an order from receipt to delivery. Each minute products remain on the books, costs accumulate and competitive advantage is lost. The time that an order is in the shop is called **manufacturing cycle time**. This is the time between the arrival of raw materials and the shipping of finished product. For example, phone-system manufacturer Northern Telecom now has materials pulled directly from qualified suppliers to the assembly line. This effort has reduced a segment of Northern's manufacturing cycle time from 3 weeks to just 4 hours, the incoming inspection staff from 47 to 24, and problems on the shop floor caused by defective materials by 97%. Driving down manufacturing cycle time can make a major improvement in throughput.

A technique for increasing throughput is a pull system. A **pull system** *pulls a* unit to where it is needed just as it is needed. Pull systems are a standard tool of JIT systems. Pull systems use signals to request production and delivery from supplying stations to stations that have production capacity available. The pull concept is used both within the immediate production process and with suppliers. By *pulling* material through the system in very small lots—just as it is needed—waste and inventory are removed. As inventory is removed, problems become evident, and continuous improvement is emphasized. Removing the cushion of inventory also reduces both investment in inventory and manufacturing cycle time. A push system dumps orders on the next downstream workstation, regardless of timeliness and resource availability. Push systems are the antithesis of JIT. Pulling material through a production process as it is needed rather than in a "push" mode typically lowers cost and improves schedule performance, enhancing customer satisfaction.

JUST-IN-TIME (JIT)

With its forced problem solving via a focus on rapid throughput and reduced inventory, JIT provides a powerful strategy for improving operations. With JIT, materials arrive *where* they are needed only *when* they are needed. When good units do not arrive just as needed, a "problem" has been identified. By driving out waste and delay in this manner, JIT reduces costs associated with excess inventory, cuts variability and waste, and improves throughput. JIT is a key ingredient of lean operations and is particularly helpful in supporting strategies of rapid response and low cost. Every moment material is held, an activity that adds value should be occurring. Consequently, as Figure 1 suggests, JIT often yields a competitive advantage.

Effective JIT requires a meaningful buyer–supplier partnership.

▶ *Many services have adopted JIT techniques as a normal part of their business. Restaurants like Olive Garden and Red Lobster expect and receive JIT deliveries. Both buyer and supplier expect fresh, high-quality produce delivered without fail just when it is needed. The system doesn't work any other way.*

Culinary Institute of America

JIT TECHNIQUES:

Suppliers:	Few vendors; Supportive supplier relationships; Quality deliveries on time, directly to work areas.
Layout:	Work-cells; Group technology; Flexible machinery; Organized workplace; Reduced space for inventory.
Inventory:	Small lot sizes; Low setup time; Specialized parts bins
Scheduling:	Zero deviation from schedules; Level schedules; Suppliers informed of schedules; Kanban techniques
Preventive maintenance:	Scheduled; Daily routine; Operator involvement
Quality production:	Statistical process control; Quality suppliers; Quality within the firm
Employee empowerment:	Empowered and cross-trained employees; Training support; Few job classifications to ensure flexibility of employees
Commitment:	Support of management, employees, and suppliers

◀ **Figure 1**

JIT Contributes to Competitive Advantage

WHICH RESULTS IN:

Rapid throughput frees assets

Quality improvement reduces waste

Cost reduction adds pricing flexibility

Variability reduction

Rework reduction

WHICH WINS ORDERS BY:

Faster response to the customer at lower cost and higher quality—

A Competitive Advantage

JIT Partnerships

A **JIT partnership** exists when a supplier and a purchaser work together with open communication and a goal of removing waste and driving down costs. Close relationships and trust are critical to the success of JIT. Figure 2 shows the characteristics of JIT partnerships. Some specific goals of JIT partnerships are:

- *Removal of unnecessary activities*, such as receiving, incoming inspection, and paperwork related to bidding, invoicing, and payment.
- *Removal of in-plant inventory* by delivery in small lots directly to the using department as needed.
- *Removal of in-transit inventory* by encouraging suppliers to locate nearby and provide frequent small shipments. The shorter the flow of material in the resource pipeline, the less inventory. Inventory can also be reduced through a technique known as *consignment*. **Consignment inventory** (see the *OM in Action* box "Lean Production at Cessna Aircraft"), a variation of vendor-managed inventory, means the supplier maintains the title to the inventory until it is used. For instance, an assembly plant may find a hardware supplier that is willing to locate its warehouse where the user currently has its stockroom. In this manner, when hardware is needed, it is no farther than the stockroom, and the supplier can ship to other, perhaps smaller, purchasers from the "stockroom."
- *Obtain improved quality and reliability* through long-term commitments, communication, and cooperation.

Leading organizations view suppliers as extensions of their own organizations and expect suppliers to be fully committed to improvement. Such relationships require a high degree of respect by both supplier and purchaser. Supplier concerns can be significant; Harley-Davidson, for example, initially had difficulty implementing JIT because supplier issues outweighed the perceived benefits.

JIT partnerships

Partnerships of suppliers and purchasers that remove waste and drive down costs for mutual benefits.

Consignment inventory

An arrangement in which the supplier maintains title to the inventory until it is used.

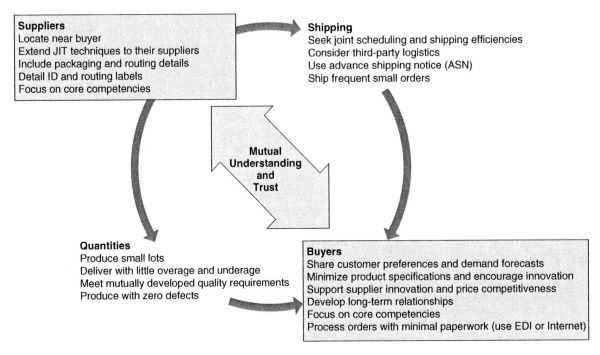

Suppliers
Locate near buyer
Extend JIT techniques to their suppliers
Include packaging and routing details
Detail ID and routing labels
Focus on core competencies

Shipping
Seek joint scheduling and shipping efficiencies
Consider third-party logistics
Use advance shipping notice (ASN)
Ship frequent small orders

Mutual Understanding and Trust

Quantities
Produce small lots
Deliver with little overage and underage
Meet mutually developed quality requirements
Produce with zero defects

Buyers
Share customer preferences and demand forecasts
Minimize product specifications and encourage innovation
Support supplier innovation and price competitiveness
Develop long-term relationships
Focus on core competencies
Process orders with minimal paperwork (use EDI or Internet)

▲ **Figure 2** Characteristics of JIT Partnerships

Concerns of Suppliers

Learning Objective

3. Explain JIT partnerships

Successful JIT partnerships require that supplier concerns be addressed. These concerns include:

1. *Diversification:* Suppliers may not want to tie themselves to long-term contracts with one customer. The suppliers' perception is that they reduce their risk if they have a variety of customers.
2. *Scheduling:* Many suppliers have little faith in the purchaser's ability to produce orders to a smooth, coordinated schedule.
3. *Changes:* Engineering or specification changes can play havoc with JIT because of inadequate lead time for suppliers to implement the necessary changes.
4. *Quality:* Capital budgets, processes, or technology may limit quality.
5. *Lot sizes:* Suppliers may see frequent delivery in small lots as a way to transfer buyer's holding costs to suppliers.

OM in Action Lean Production at Cessna Aircraft

When Cessna Aircraft opened its new plant in Independence, Kansas, it saw the opportunity to switch from a craftwork mentality producing small single-engine planes to a lean manufacturing system. In doing so, Cessna adopted three lean practices.

First, Cessna set up consignment- and vendor-managed inventories with several of its suppliers. Blanket purchase orders allow Honeywell, for example, to maintain a 30-day supply of avionic parts onsite. Other vendors were encouraged to use a nearby warehouse to keep parts that could then be delivered daily to the production line.

Second, Cessna managers committed to cross-training, in which team members learn the duties of other team members and can shift across assembly lines as needed. To develop these technical skills, Cessna brought in 60 retired assembly-line workers to mentor and teach new employees. Employees were taught to work as a team and to assume responsibility for their team's quality.

Cessna Aircraft Company

Third, the company used group technology and manufacturing cells to move away from a batch process that resulted in large inventories and unsold planes. Now, Cessna pulls product through its plant only when a specific order is placed.

These commitments to manufacturing efficiency are part of the lean operations that has made Cessna the world's largest manufacturer of single-engine aircraft.

Sources: **www.cessna.com** (2007); *Strategic Finance* (November 2002): 32; *Purchasing* (September 4, 2003): 25–30; and *Fortune* (May 1, 2000): 1222B.

JIT LAYOUT

JIT layouts reduce another kind of waste—movement. The movement of material on a factory floor (or paper in an office) does not add value. Consequently, managers want flexible layouts that reduce the movement of both people and material. JIT layouts place material directly in the location where needed. For instance, an assembly line should be designed with delivery points next to the line so material need not be delivered first to a receiving department and then moved again. This is what VF Corporation's Wrangler Division in Greensboro, North Carolina, did; denim is now delivered directly to the line. Toyota has gone one step farther and places hardware and components in the chassis of each vehicle moving down the assembly line. This is not only convenient, but it allows Toyota to save space and opens areas adjacent to the assembly line previously occupied by shelves. When a layout reduces distance, firms often save labor and space and may have the added bonus of eliminating potential areas for accumulation of unwanted inventory. Table 1 provides a list of layout tactics.

Distance Reduction

Reducing distance is a major contribution of work cells, work centers, and focused factories. The days of long production lines and huge economic lots, with goods passing through monumental, single-operation machines, are gone. Now firms use work cells, often arranged in a U shape, containing several machines performing different operations. These work cells are often based on group technology codes. Group technology codes help identify components with similar characteristics so we can group them into families. Once families are identified, work cells are built for them. The result can be thought of as a small product-oriented facility where the "product" is actually a group of similar products—a family of products. The cells produce one good unit at a time, and ideally they produce the units *only* after a customer orders them.

Increased Flexibility

Modern work cells are designed so they can be easily rearranged to adapt to changes in volume, product improvements, or even new designs. Almost nothing in these new departments is bolted down. This same concept of layout flexibility applies to office environments. Not only is most office furniture and equipment movable, but so are office walls, computer connections, and telecommunications. Equipment is modular. Layout flexibility aids the changes that result from product *and* process improvements that are inevitable with a philosophy of continuous improvement.

Impact on Employees

Employees working together are cross trained so they can bring flexibility and efficiency to the work cell. JIT layouts allow employees to work together so they can tell each other about problems and opportunities for improvement. When layouts provide for sequential operations, feedback can be immediate. Defects are waste. When workers produce units one at a time, they test each product or component at each subsequent production stage. Machines in work cells with self-testing poka-yoke functions detect defects and stop automatically when they occur. Before JIT, defective products were replaced from inventory. Because surplus inventory is not kept in JIT facilities, there are no such buffers. Getting it right the first time is critical.

Reduced Space and Inventory

Because JIT layouts reduce travel distance, they also reduce inventory by removing space for inventory. When there is little space, inventory must be moved in very small lots or even single units. Units are always moving because there is no storage. For instance, each month Security Pacific Corporation's focused facility sorts 7 million checks, processes 5 million statements, and mails 190,000 customer statements. With a JIT layout, mail processing time has been reduced by 33%, salary costs by tens of thousands of dollars per year, floor space by 50%, and in-process waiting lines by 75% to 90%. Storage, including shelves and drawers, has been removed.

▼ **Table 1**

JIT Layout Tactics

Build work cells for families of products
Include a large number of operations in a small area
Minimize distance
Design little space for inventory
Improve employee communication
Use poka-yoke devices
Build flexible or movable equipment
Cross-train workers to add flexibility

In a JIT system, each worker inspects the arriving part, knowing that the part must be good before it goes on to the next "customer."

Just-in-time tactics are being incorporated in manufacturing to improve quality, drive down inventory investment, and reduce other costs. However, JIT is also established practice in restaurants, where customers expect it, and a necessity in the produce business, where there is little choice. Pacific Pre-Cut Produce, a $14 million fruit and vegetable processing company in Tracy, California, holds inventory to zero. Buyers are in action in the wee hours of the morning. At 6 A.M., produce production crews show up. Orders for very specific cuts and mixtures of fruit and vegetable salads and stir-fry ingredients for supermarkets, restaurants, and institutional kitchens pour in from 8 A.M. until 4 P.M. Shipping begins at 10 P.M. and continues until the last order is filled and loaded at 5 A.M. the next morning. Inventories are once again zero, and things are relatively quiet for an hour or so; then the routine starts

again. Pacific Pre-Cut Produce has accomplished a complete cycle of purchase, manufacture, and shipping in about 24 hours.

VP Bob Borzone calls the process the ultimate in mass customization. "We buy everything as a bulk commodity, then slice and dice it to fit the exact requirements of the end user. There are 20 different stir-fry mixes. Some customers want the snow peas clipped on both ends, some just on one. Some want only red bell peppers in the mix, some only yellow. You tailor the product to the customer's requirements. You're trying to satisfy the need of a lot of end users, and each restaurant and retailer wants to look different."

Sources: Supermarket News (September 27, 2004): 31; *Inbound Logistics* (August 1997): 26–32; and *Progressive Grocer* (January 1998): 51–56.

JIT INVENTORY

Inventories in production and distribution systems often exist "just in case" something goes wrong. That is, they are used just in case some variation from the production plan occurs. The "extra" inventory is then used to cover variations or problems. Effective inventory tactics require "just in time," not "just in case." **Just-in-time inventory** is the minimum inventory necessary to keep a perfect system running. With just-in-time inventory, the exact amount of goods arrives at the moment it is needed, not a minute before or a minute after. The *OM in Action* box "Let's Try Zero Inventory" suggests that it can be done. Some useful JIT inventory tactics are shown in Table 2 and discussed in more detail in the following sections.

Just-in-time inventory

The minimum inventory necessary to keep a perfect system running.

Reduce Variability

The idea behind JIT is to eliminate inventory that hides variability in the production system. This concept is illustrated in Figure 3, which shows a lake full of rocks. The water in the lake represents inventory flow, and the rocks represent problems such as late deliveries, machine breakdowns, and poor personnel performance. The water level in the lake hides variability and problems. Because inventory hides problems, they are hard to find.

▶ **Figure 3**

Inventory Has Two Costs, One for Holding the Inventory and One for the Problems It Hides— Just as Water in a Lake Hides the Rocks

Video 16.1

Sailing through the Problems of Excess Inventory

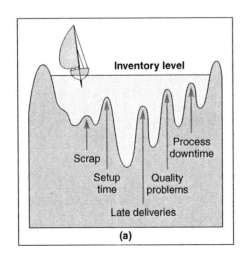
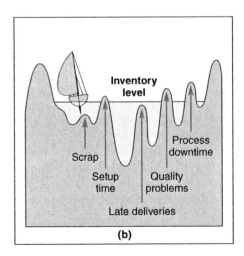

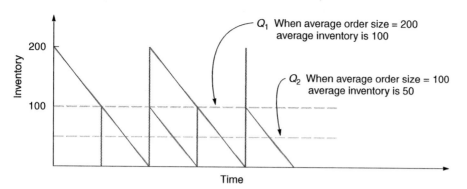

Q_1 When average order size = 200 average inventory is 100

Q_2 When average order size = 100 average inventory is 50

◀ **Figure 4**

Frequent Orders Reduce Average Inventory

A lower order size increases the number of orders and total ordering cost but reduces average inventory and total holding cost.

Reduce Inventory

Operations managers move toward JIT by first removing inventory. Reducing inventory uncovers the "rocks" in Figure 3(a) that represent the variability and problems currently being tolerated. With reduced inventory, management chips away at the exposed problems until the lake is clear. After the lake is clear, managers make additional cuts in inventory and continue to chip away at the next level of exposed problems (see Figure 3[b]). Ultimately, there will be virtually no inventory and no problems (variability).

Dell estimates that the rapid changes in technology costs $\frac{1}{2}\%$ to 2% of its inventory's value *each week*. Shigeo Shingo, co-developer of the Toyota JIT system, says, "Inventory is evil." He is not far from the truth. If inventory itself is not evil, it hides evil at great cost.

"Inventory is evil."
Shigeo Shingo

Reduce Lot Sizes

Just-in-time has also come to mean elimination of waste by reducing investment in inventory. The key to JIT is producing good product in small lot sizes. Reducing the size of batches can be a major help in reducing inventory and inventory costs. When inventory usage is constant, the average inventory level is the sum of the maximum inventory plus the minimum inventory divided by 2. Figure 4 shows that lowering the order size increases the number of orders but drops inventory levels.

Ideally, in a JIT environment, order size is one and single units are being pulled from one adjacent process to another. More realistically, analysis of the process, transportation time, and containers used for transport are considered when determining lot size. Such analysis typically results in a small lot size but a lot size larger than one. Once a lot size has been determined, the EOQ production order quantity model can be modified to determine the desired setup time. The production order quantity model takes the form:

$$Q^* = \sqrt{\frac{2DS}{H[1-(d/p)]}} \qquad (1)$$

where D = Annual demand
S = Setup cost
H = Holding cost
d = Daily demand
p = Daily production

Example 1 shows how to determine the desired setup time.

▼ **Table 2**

JIT Inventory Tactics

Use a pull system to move inventory
Reduce lot size
Develop just-in-time delivery systems with suppliers
Deliver directly to the point of use
Perform to schedule
Reduce setup time
Use group technology

Crate Furniture, Inc., a firm that produces rustic furniture, desires to move toward a reduced lot size. Crate Furniture's production analyst, Aleda Roth, determined that a 2-hour production cycle would be acceptable between two departments. Further, she concluded that a setup time that would accommodate the 2-hour cycle time should be achieved.

EXAMPLE 1

Determining optimal setup time

Approach: Roth developed the following data and procedure to determine optimum setup time analytically:

D = Annual demand = 400,000 units

d = Daily demand = 400,000 per 250 days = 1,600 units per day

p = Daily production rate = 4,000 units per day

Q = EOQ desired = 400 (which is the 2-hour demand; that is, 1,600 per day per four 2-hour periods)

H = Holding cost = $20 per unit per year

S = Setup cost (to be determined)

Solution: Roth determines that the cost, on an hourly basis, of setting up equipment is $30. Further, she computes that the setup cost per setup should be:

$$Q = \sqrt{\frac{2DS}{H(1-d/p)}}$$

$$Q^2 = \frac{2DS}{H(1-d/p)}$$

$$S = \frac{(Q^2)(H)(1-d/p)}{2D}$$

$$S = \frac{(400)^2(20)(1-1,600/4,000)}{2(400,000)}$$

$$= \frac{(3,200,000)(0.6)}{800,000} = \$2.40$$

Setup time = $2.40/(hourly labor rate)

= $2.40/($30 per hour)

= 0.08 hour, or 4.8 minutes

Learning Objective

4. Determine optimal set-up time

Insight: Now, rather than produce components in large lots, Crate Furniture can produce in a 2-hour cycle with the advantage of an inventory turnover of four *per day*.

Learning exercise: If labor cost goes to $40 per hour, what should be the setup time? [Answer: .06 hour, or 3.6 minutes.]

Related problems: 8, 9, 10

Only two changes need to be made for small-lot material flow to work. First, material handling and work flow need to be improved. With short production cycles, there can be very little wait time. Improving material handling is usually easy and straightforward. The second change is more challenging, and that is a radical reduction in setup times. We discuss setup reduction next.

Reduce Setup Costs

Both inventory and the cost of holding it go down as the inventory-reorder quantity and the maximum inventory level drop. However, because inventory requires incurring an ordering or setup cost that must be applied to the units produced, managers tend to purchase (or produce) large orders. With large orders, each unit purchased or ordered absorbs only a small part of the setup cost. Consequently, the way to drive down lot sizes *and* reduce average inventory is to reduce setup cost, which in turn lowers the optimum order size.

Reduced lot sizes must be accompanied by reduced setup times; otherwise, the setup cost is assigned to fewer units.

The effect of reduced setup costs on total cost and lot size is shown in Figure 5. Moreover, smaller lot sizes hide fewer problems. In many environments, setup cost is highly correlated with setup time. In a manufacturing facility, setups usually require a substantial amount of preparation. Much of the preparation required by a setup can be done prior to shutting down the machine or process. Setup times can be reduced substantially, as shown in Figure 6. For instance, in Kodak's Guadalajara, Mexico, plant a team reduced the setup time to change a bearing from 12 hours to 6 minutes![4] This is the kind of progress that is typical of world-class manufacturers.

[4]Frank Carguello and Marty Levin, "Excellence at Work in Guadalajara, Mexico, Operation," *Target* 15, no. 3 (3rd quarter 1999): 51–53.

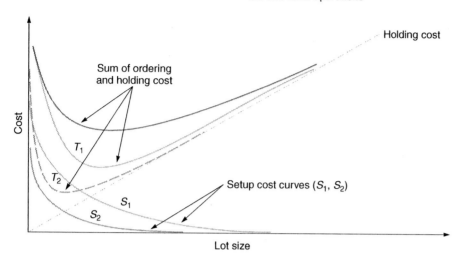

Holding cost

Figure 5

Lower Setup Costs Will Lower Total Cost

More frequent orders require reducing setup costs; otherwise, inventory costs will rise. As the setup costs are lowered (from S_1 to S_2), inventory costs also fall (from T_1 to T_2).

Just as setup costs can be reduced at a machine in a factory, setup time can also be reduced during the process of getting the order ready. It does little good to drive down factory setup time from hours to minutes if orders are going to take 2 weeks to process or "set up" in the office. This is exactly what happens in organizations that forget that JIT concepts have applications in offices as well as in the factory. Reducing setup time (and cost) is an excellent way to reduce inventory investment and to improve productivity.

JIT SCHEDULING

Effective schedules, communicated both within the organization and to outside suppliers, support JIT. Better scheduling also improves the ability to meet customer orders, drives down inventory by allowing smaller lot sizes, and reduces work-in-process. For instance, Ford Motor Company now ties some suppliers to its final assembly schedule. Ford communicates its schedules to bumper manufacturer Polycon Industries from the Ford Oakville production control system. The scheduling system describes the style and color of the bumper needed for each vehicle moving down the final assembly line. The scheduling system transmits the information to portable terminals carried by Polycon warehouse personnel who load the bumpers onto conveyors leading to the loading dock. The bumpers are then trucked 50 miles to the Ford plant. Total time is 4 hours. Table 3 suggests several items that can contribute to achieving these goals, but two techniques (in addition to communicating schedules) are paramount. They are *level schedules* and *kanban*.

Table 3

JIT Scheduling Tactics

Communicate schedules to suppliers
Make level schedules
Freeze part of the schedule
Perform to schedule
Seek one-piece-make and one-piece-move
Eliminate waste
Produce in small lots
Use kanbans
Make each operation produce a perfect part

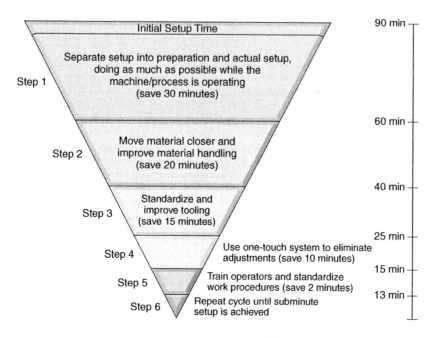

Figure 6

Steps for Reducing Setup Times

Reduced setup times are a major JIT component.

JIT Level Material-Use Approach

AA BBB C AA BBB C AA BBB C AA BBB C AA BBB C AA BBB C AA BBB C AA BBB C

Large-Lot Approach

AAAAAA BBBBBBBBB CCC AAAAAA BBBBBBBBB CCC AAAAAA BBBBBBBBB CCC

Time

▲ **Figure 7**　Scheduling Small Lots of Parts A, B, and C Increases Flexibility to Meet Customer Demand and Reduces Inventory

The JIT approach to scheduling produces just as many of each model per time period as the large-lot approach, provided that setup times are lowered.

Level Schedules

Level schedules

Scheduling products so that each day's production meets the demand for that day.

Level schedules process frequent small batches rather than a few large batches. Because this technique schedules many small lots that are always changing, it has on occasion been called "jelly bean" scheduling. Figure 7 contrasts a traditional large-lot approach using large batches with a JIT level schedule using many small batches. The operations manager's task is to make and move small lots so the level schedule is economical. This requires success with the issues discussed in this chapter that allow small lots. As lots get smaller, the constraints may change and become increasingly challenging. At some point, processing a unit or two may not be feasible. The constraint may be the way units are sold and shipped (four to a carton), or an expensive paint changeover (on an automobile assembly line), or the proper number of units in a sterilizer (for a food-canning line).

The scheduler may find that *freezing* the portion of the schedule closest to due dates allows the production system to function and the schedule to be met. Freezing means not allowing changes to be part of the schedule. Operations managers expect the schedule to be achieved with no deviations from the schedule.

Kanban

One way to achieve small lot sizes is to move inventory through the shop only as needed rather than *pushing* it on to the next workstation whether or not the personnel there are ready for it. As noted earlier, when inventory is moved only as needed, it is referred to as a *pull* system, and the ideal lot size is one. The Japanese call this system *kanban*. Kanbans allow arrivals at a work center to match (or nearly match) the processing time.

Kanban

The Japanese word for *card*, which has come to mean "signal"; a kanban system moves parts through production via a "pull" from a signal.

Kanban is a Japanese word for *card*. In their effort to reduce inventory, the Japanese use systems that "pull" inventory through work centers. They often use a "card" to signal the need for another container of material—hence the name *kanban*. *The card is the authorization for the next container of material to be produced.* Typically, a kanban signal exists for each container of items

▶ *A kanban need not be as formal as signal lights or empty carts. The cook in a fast-food restaurant knows that when six cars are in line, eight meat patties and six orders of french fries should be cooking.*

Donna Shader

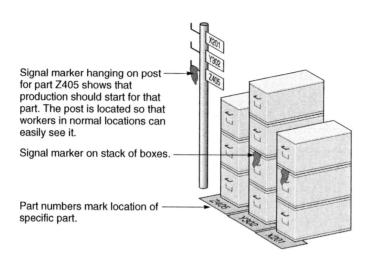

◀ **Figure 8**

Diagram of Outbound Stockpoint with Warning-Signal Marker

Signal marker hanging on post for part Z405 shows that production should start for that part. The post is located so that workers in normal locations can easily see it.

Signal marker on stack of boxes.

Part numbers mark location of specific part.

to be obtained. An order for the container is then initiated by each kanban and "pulled" from the producing department or supplier. A sequence of kanbans "pulls" the material through the plant.

The system has been modified in many facilities so that even though it is called a *kanban*, the card itself does not exist. In some cases, an empty position on the floor is sufficient indication that the next container is needed. In other cases, some sort of signal, such as a flag or rag (Figure 8) alerts that it is time for the next container.

When there is visual contact between producer and user, the process works like this:

Learning Objective

5. Define kanban

1. The user removes a standard-size container of parts from a small storage area, as shown in Figure 8.
2. The signal at the storage area is seen by the producing department as authorization to replenish the using department or storage area. Because there is an optimum lot size, the producing department may make several containers at a time.

Figure 9 shows how a kanban works, pulling units as needed from production. This system is similar to the resupply that occurs in your neighborhood supermarket: The customer buys; the stock clerk observes the shelf or receives notice from the end-of-day sales list and restocks. When the limited supply, if any, in the store's storage is depleted, a "pull" signal is sent to the warehouse, distributor, or manufacturer for resupply, usually that night. The complicating factor in a manufacturing firm is the time needed for actual manufacturing (production) to take place.

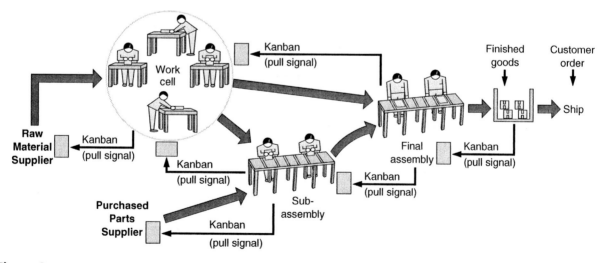

▲ **Figure 9**   Kanban Signals "Pull" Material Through the Production Process

As a customer "pulls" an order from finished goods, a signal (card) is sent to the final assembly area. The final assembly area produces and resupplies finished goods. When final assembly needs components, it sends a signal to its suppliers, a subassembly area and a work cell. These areas supply final assembly. The work cell, in turn, sends a signal to the raw material supplier, and the subassembly area notifies the work cell and purchased parts supplier of a requirement.

Kanban containers at Harley-Davidson are specially made for individual parts, and many feature padding to protect the finish. These containers serve an important role in inventory reduction: Because they are the only place inventory is stored, they serve as a signal to supply new parts to the line. After all the pieces have been removed, the container is returned to its originating cell, signaling the worker there to build more.

Video 16.2

JIT at Harley-Davidson

Several additional points regarding kanbans may be helpful:

- When the producer and user are not in visual contact, a card can be used; otherwise, a light or flag or empty spot on the floor may be adequate.
- Because a pull station may require several resupply components, several kanban pull techniques can be used for different products at the same pull station.
- Usually, each card controls a specific quantity or parts, although multiple card systems are used if the producing work cell produces several components or if the lot size is different from the move size.
- In an MRP system, the schedule can be thought of as a "build" authorization and the kanban as a type of "pull" system that initiates the actual production.
- The kanban cards provide a direct control (limit) on the amount of work-in-process between cells.
- If there is an immediate storage area, a two-card system may be used—one card circulates between user and storage area, and the other circulates between the storage area and the producing area.

Determining the Number of Kanban Cards or Containers The number of kanban cards, or containers, in a JIT system sets the amount of authorized inventory. To determine the number of containers moving back and forth between the using area and the producing areas, management first sets the size of each container. This is done by computing the lot size, using a model such as the production order quantity model (shown in Equation 11). Setting the number of containers involves knowing (1) lead time needed to produce a container of parts and (2) the amount of safety stock needed to account for variability or uncertainty in the system. The number of kanban cards is computed as follows:

$$\text{Number of kanbans (containers)} = \frac{\text{Demand during lead time} + \text{Safety stock}}{\text{Size of container}}$$

Example 2 illustrates how to calculate the number of kanbans needed.

EXAMPLE 2

Determining the number of kanban containers

Hobbs Bakery produces short runs of cakes that are shipped to grocery stores. The owner, Ken Hobbs, wants to try to reduce inventory by changing to a kanban system. He has developed the following data and asked you to finish the project.

Daily demand = 500 cakes

Production lead time = Wait time + Material handling time + Processing time = 2 days

Safety stock = $\frac{1}{2}$ day

Container size (determined on a production order size EOQ basis) = 250 cakes

Approach: Having determined that the EOQ size is 250, we then determine the number of kanbans (containers) needed.

Learning Objective

6. Compute the required number of kanbans

Solution: Demand during lead time (= Lead time × Daily demand = 2 days × 500 cakes =) 1,000

Safety stock = 250

$$\text{Number of kanbans (containers) needed} = \frac{\text{Demand during lead time} + \text{Safety stock}}{\text{Container size}} = \frac{1,000 + 250}{250} = 5$$

Insight: Once the reorder point is hit, five containers should be released.

Learning exercise: If lead time drops to 1 day, how many containers are needed? [Answer: 3.]

Related problems: 1, 2, 3, 4, 5, 6

Advantages of Kanban   Containers are typically very small, usually a matter of a few hours' worth of production. Such a system requires tight schedules. Small quantities must be produced several times a day. The process must run smoothly with little variability in quality of lead time because any shortage has an almost immediate impact on the entire system. Kanban places added emphasis on meeting schedules, reducing the time and cost required by setups, and economical material handling.

Whether it is called kanban or something else, the advantages of small inventory and *pulling* material through the plant only when needed are significant. For instance, small batches allow only a very limited amount of faulty or delayed material. Problems are immediately evident. Numerous aspects of inventory are bad; only one aspect—availability—is good. Among the bad aspects are poor quality, obsolescence, damage, occupied space, committed assets, increased insurance, increased material handling, and increased accidents. Kanban systems put downward pressure on all these negative aspects of inventory.

The manufacturing inventory to sales ratio continues to drop, thanks in large part to JIT.

In-plant kanban systems often use standardized, reusable containers that protect the specific quantities to be moved. Such containers are also desirable in the supply chain. Standardized containers reduce weight and disposal costs, generate less wasted space in trailers, and require less labor to pack, unpack, and prepare items.

JIT QUALITY

The relationship between JIT and quality is a strong one. They are related in three ways. First, JIT cuts the cost of obtaining good quality. This saving occurs because scrap, rework, inventory investment, and damage costs are buried in inventory. JIT forces down inventory; therefore, fewer bad units are produced and fewer units must be reworked. In short, whereas inventory *hides* bad quality, JIT immediately *exposes* it.

New United Motor Manufacturing, Inc. (NUMMI)

◀ *The New United Motor Manufacturing (NUMMI) plant in Fremont, California, is a joint venture between Toyota and General Motors and builds cars for both companies. The plant was, of course, designed as a Toyota Production System (TPS), using just-in-time (JIT). Management even moved a water tower to ensure that new loading docks would facilitate JIT arrivals and JIT movement of parts within the plant. This plant, like most JIT facilities, also empowers employees so they can stop the entire production line by pulling the overhead cord if any quality problems are spotted.*

▼ **Table 4**

JIT Quality Tactics

Use statistical process
control
Empower employees
Build fail-safe methods
(poka-yoke,
checklists, etc.)
Expose poor quality
with small lot JIT
Provide immediate
feedback

Second, JIT improves quality. As JIT shrinks queues and lead time, it keeps evidence of errors fresh and limits the number of potential sources of error. In effect, JIT creates an early warning system for quality problems so that fewer bad units are produced and feedback is immediate. This advantage can accrue both within the firm and with goods received from outside vendors.

Finally, better quality means fewer buffers are needed and, therefore, a better, easier-to-employ JIT system can exist. Often the purpose of keeping inventory is to protect against unreliable quality. If consistent quality exists, JIT allows firms to reduce all costs associated with inventory. Table 4 suggests some requirements for quality in a JIT environment.

TOYOTA PRODUCTION SYSTEM

Learning Objective

7. Explain the principles of
the Toyota Production System

Toyota Motor's Eiji Toyoda and Taiichi Ohno are given credit for the Toyota Production System (TPS) (see the *Global Company Profile* that opens this chapter). Three core components of TPS are continuous improvement, respect for people, and standard work practice.

Continuous Improvement

Continuous improvement under TPS means building an organizational culture and instilling in its people a value system stressing that processes can be improved—indeed, that improvement is an integral part of every employee's job. Instilling these values begins at recruiting and continues through extensive and continuing training. One of the reasons continuous improvement works at Toyota, we should note, is because of another core value at Toyota, Toyota's respect for people.

Respect for People

At Toyota, people are recruited, trained, and treated as knowledge workers. Aided by aggressive cross-training and few job classifications, TPS engages the mental as well as physical capacities of employees in the challenging task of improving operations. Employees are empowered. They are empowered to make improvements. They are empowered to stop machines and processes when quality problems exist. Indeed, empowered employees are a necessary part of TPS. This means that those tasks that have traditionally been assigned to staff are moved to employees. Toyota recognizes that employees know more about their jobs than anyone else. TPS respects employees by giving them the opportunity to enrich both their jobs and their lives.

Standard Work Practice

Standard work practice at Toyota includes these underlying principles:

- Work is completely specified as to content, sequence, timing, and outcome.
- Internal and external customer–supplier connections are direct, specifying personnel, methods, timing, and quantity.
- Product and service flows are to be simple and direct. Goods and services are directed to a specific person or machine.
- Improvements in the system must be made in accordance with the "scientific method," at the lowest possible level in the organization.[5]

TPS requires that activities, connections, and flows include built-in tests to automatically signal problems. Any gap between what is expected and what occurs becomes immediately evident. The education and training of Toyota's employees and the responsiveness of the system to problems make the seemingly rigid system flexible and adaptable to changing circumstances. The result is ongoing improvements in reliability, flexibility, safety, and efficiency.

[5]Adopted from Steven J. Spear, "Learning to Lead at Toyota," *Harvard Business Review* 82, no. 5 (May 2004): 78–86; Steven Spear and H. Kent Bowen, "Decoding the DNA of the Toyota Production System," *Harvard Business Review* 77, no. 5 (September–October 1999): 97–106.

LEAN OPERATIONS

Lean production can be thought of as the end result of a well-run OM function. While JIT and TPS tend to have an *internal* focus, lean production begins *externally* with a focus on the customer. Understanding what the customer wants and ensuring customer input and feedback are starting points for lean production. Lean operations means identifying customer value by analyzing all the activities required to produce the product and then optimizing the entire process from the customer's perspective. The manager identifies what creates value for the customer and what does not.

Building a Lean Organization

The transition to lean production is difficult. Building an organizational culture where learning, empowerment, and continuous improvement are the norm is a challenge. However, organizations that focus on JIT, quality, and employee empowerment are often lean producers. Such firms drive out activities that do not add value in the eyes of the customer: they include leaders like United Parcel Service, Harley-Davidson, and, of course, Toyota. Even traditionally craft-oriented organizations such as Louis Vuitton (see the *OM in Action* box) find improved productivity with lean operations. Lean operations adopt a philosophy of minimizing waste by striving for perfection through continuous learning, creativity, and teamwork. They tend to share the following attributes:

- *Use JIT techniques* to eliminate virtually all inventory.
- *Build systems that help employees* produce a perfect part every time.
- *Reduce space requirements* by minimizing travel distance.
- *Develop partnerships with suppliers*, helping them to understand the needs of the ultimate customer.
- *Educate suppliers* to accept responsibility for satisfying end customer needs.
- *Eliminate all but value-added activities.* Material handling, inspection, inventory, and rework are the likely targets because these do not add value to the product.
- *Develop employees* by constantly improving job design, training, employee commitment, teamwork, and empowerment.
- *Make jobs challenging*, pushing responsibility to the lowest level possible.
- *Build worker flexibility* through cross-training and reducing job classifications.

Success requires the full commitment and involvement of managers, employees, and suppliers. The rewards that lean producers reap are spectacular. Lean producers often become benchmark performers.

OM in Action — Going Lean at Louis Vuitton

LVMH Moet Hennessy Louis Vuitton is the world's largest luxury-goods company. Its Louis Vuitton unit, responsible for half of the company's profit, makes very upscale handbags and enjoys a rich markup on sales of about $5 billion. The return-on-investment is excellent, but sales could be even better: the firm often can't match production with the sales pace of a successful new product. In the high fashion business that is all about speed-to-market, this is bad news; a massive overhaul was in order.

Changes on the factory floor were key to the overhaul. The traditional approach to manufacturing at Louis Vuitton was batch production: craftsmen, working on partially completed handbags, performed specialized tasks such as cutting, gluing, sewing, and assembly. Carts moved batches of semi-finished handbags on to the next workstation. It took 20 to 30 workers 8 days to make a handbag. And defects were high. Lean manufacturing looked like the way to go.

Craftsmen were retrained to do multiple tasks in small U-shaped work cells. Each work cell now contains 6 to 12

Colin Young-Wolff, PhotoEdit Inc.

cross-trained workers and the necessary sewing machines and work tables. Consistent with one-piece flow, the work is passed through the cell from worker to worker. The system reduces inventory and allows workers to detect flaws earlier. Rework under the old system was sometimes as high as 50% and internal losses as high as 4%. Returns are down by two-thirds. The system has not only improved productivity and quality, it also allows Louis Vuitton to respond to the market faster—with daily scheduling as opposed to weekly scheduling.

Sources: The Wall Street Journal (October 9, 2006): A1, A15 and (January 31, 2006): A1, A13.

LEAN OPERATIONS IN SERVICES

The features of lean operations apply to services just as they do in other sectors. Here are some examples applied to suppliers, layout, inventory, and scheduling in the service sector.

Suppliers   As we have noted, virtually every restaurant deals with its suppliers on a JIT basis. Those that do not are usually unsuccessful. The waste is too evident—food spoils and customers complain or get sick.

Lean hospitals have suppliers bring ready-to-use supplies directly to storage areas, nurses' stations, and operating rooms. Only a 24-hour reserve is maintained.

Layouts   Lean layouts are required in restaurant kitchens, where cold food must be served cold and hot food hot. McDonald's, for example, has reconfigured its kitchen layout at great expense to drive seconds out of the production process, thereby speeding delivery to customers. With the new process, McDonald's can produce made-to-order hamburgers in 45 seconds. Layouts also make a difference in airline baggage claim, where customers expect their bags just-in-time.

Inventory   Stockbrokers drive inventory down to nearly zero every day. Most sell and buy orders occur on an immediate basis because an unexecuted sell or buy order is not acceptable to most clients. A broker may be in serious trouble if left holding an unexecuted trade. Similarly, McDonald's reduces inventory waste by maintaining a finished-goods inventory of only 10 minutes; after that, it is thrown away. Hospitals, such as Arnold Palmer (described in this chapter's Video Case Study), manage JIT inventory and low safety stocks for many items. Even critical supplies such as pharmaceuticals may be held to low levels by developing community networks as backup systems. In this manner, if one pharmacy runs out of a needed drug, another member of the network can supply it until the next day's shipment arrives.

Video 16.3

JIT at Arnold Palmer Hospital

Scheduling   At airline ticket counters, the focus of the system is customer demand, but rather than being satisfied by inventory availability, demand is satisfied by personnel. Through elaborate scheduling, ticket counter personnel show up just-in-time to cover peaks in customer demand. In other words, rather than "things" inventoried, personnel are scheduled. At a salon, the focus is only slightly different: the *customer* is scheduled to assure prompt service. At McDonald's and Wal-Mart, scheduling of personnel is down to 15-minute increments, based on precise forecasting of demand. Additionally, at McDonald's, production is done in small lots to ensure that fresh, hot hamburgers are delivered just-in-time. In short, both personnel and production are scheduled to meet specific demand. Notice that in all three of these lean organizations—the airline ticket counter, the salon, and McDonald's—scheduling is a key ingredient. Excellent forecasts drive those schedules. Those forecasts may be very elaborate, with seasonal, daily, and even hourly components in the case of the airline ticket counter (holiday sales, flight time, etc.), seasonal and weekly components at the salon (holidays and Fridays create special problems), or down to a few minutes at McDonald's.

▶ *Lean operations take on an unusual form in an operating room. McKesson-General, Baxter International, and many other hospital suppliers provide surgical supplies for hospitals on a JIT basis. (1) They deliver prepackaged surgical supplies based on hospital operating schedules, and (2) the surgical packages themselves are prepared so supplies are available in the sequence in which they will be used during surgery.*

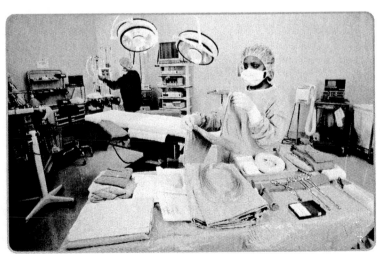

Cardinal Health, Medical Products & Services

To deliver goods and services to customers under continuously changing demand, suppliers need to be reliable, inventories lean, cycle times short, and schedules nimble. A lean focus engages and empowers employees to create and deliver the customer's perception of value, eliminating whatever does not contribute to this goal. Lean operations are currently being developed with great success in many firms, regardless of their products. Lean techniques are widely used in both goods-producing and service-producing firms; they just look different.

Summary

JIT, TPS, and lean operations are philosophies of continuous improvement. Lean operations focus on customer desires, TPS focuses on respect for people and standard work practices, and JIT focuses on driving out waste by reducing inventory. But all three approaches reduce waste in the production process. And because waste is found in anything that does not add value, organizations that implement these techniques are adding value more efficiently than other firms. The expectation of these systems is that empowered employees work with committed management to build systems that respond to customers with ever-lower cost and higher quality.

Key Terms

Just-in-time (JIT)
Toyota Production System (TPS)
Lean operations
Seven wastes
5Ss

Variability
Throughput
Manufacturing cycle time
Pull system
JIT partnerships

Consignment inventory
Just-in-time inventory
Level schedules
Kanban

Solved Problem

 Virtual Office Hours help is available on Student DVD.

Solved Problem 1

Krupp Refrigeration, Inc., is trying to reduce inventory and wants you to install a kanban system for compressors on one of its assembly lines. Determine the size of the kanban and the number of kanbans (containers) needed.

Setup cost = \$10

Annual holding cost per compressor = \$100

Daily production = 200 compressors

Annual usage = 25,000 (50 weeks × 5 days each
× daily usage of 100 compressors)

Lead time = 3 days

Safety stock = $\frac{1}{2}$ day's production of compressors

solution

First, we must determine kanban container size. To do this, we determine the production order quantity (see Equation [1]), which determines the kanban size:

$$Q_p = \sqrt{\frac{2DS}{H\left(1-\dfrac{d}{p}\right)}} = \sqrt{\frac{2(25,000)(10)}{H\left(1-\dfrac{d}{p}\right)}} = \sqrt{\frac{500,000}{100\left(1-\dfrac{100}{200}\right)}} = \sqrt{\frac{500,000}{50}}$$

$= \sqrt{10,000} = 100$ compressors. So the production order size and the size of the kanban container = 100.

Then we determine the number of kanbans:

Demand during lead time = 300 (= 3 days × daily usage of 100)

Safety stock = 100 (= $\frac{1}{2}$ day's production × 200)

$$\text{Number of kanbans} = \frac{\text{Demand during lead time} + \text{Safety stock}}{\text{Size of container}}$$

$$= \frac{300+100}{100} = \frac{400}{100} = 4 \text{ containers}$$

Self-Test

- *Before taking the self-test*, refer to the learning objectives listed at the beginning of the selection and the key terms listed at the end of the selection.
- Use the key at the back of the text to **correct** your answers.
- **Restudy** pages that correspond to any questions you answered incorrectly or material you feel uncertain about.

1. Continuous improvement and forced problem solving is a reasonable definition of:
   a) lean operations
   b) expedited management
   c) the 5Ss of housekeeping
   d) just-in-time
   e) Toyota Production System

2. Supplying the customer needs without waste best describes:
   a) lean operations
   b) expedited management
   c) the 5Ss of housekeeping
   d) just-in-time
   e) Toyota Production System

3. Employee empowerment and standard work practices best describes:
   a) lean operations
   b) expedited management
   c) the 5Ss of housekeeping
   d) just-in-time
   e) Toyota Production System

4. Taiichi Ohno's seven wastes are _____, _____, _____, _____, _____, _____, and _____.

5. The 5Ss for lean production are _____, _____, _____, _____, and _____.

6. A "pull" system:
   a) dumps orders on the next downstream workstation
   b) defines the time between arrival and shipping
   c) is the time it takes to move an order from receipt to delivery
   d) produces material only when requested
   e) all of the above

7. Concerns of suppliers when moving to JIT include:
   a) small lots may seem economically prohibitive
   b) realistic quality demands
   c) changes without adequate lead time
   d) erratic schedules
   e) all of the above

8. TPS's standard work practices include:
   a) completely specified work
   b) "pull" systems
   c) level scheduling
   d) kanbans
   e) JIT techniques

9. Lean producers remove waste by:
   a) focusing on inventory reduction
   b) using JIT techniques
   c) reducing space requirements
   d) developing partnerships with suppliers
   e) all of the above

10. Manufacturing cycle time is:
    a) time to push an order through a facility
    b) time from order receipt to delivery
    c) time between arrival of raw material and shipping of finished product
    d) time between placing an order with a supplier and receipt

Internet and Student CD-ROM/DVD Exercises

Visit our Companion Web site or use your student CD-ROM/DVD to help with material in this chapter.

 On Our Companion Web Site,
   www.prenhall.com/heizer
- Self-Study Quizzes
- Practice Problems
- Virtual Company Tour
- PowerPoint Lecture

 On Your Student CD-ROM
- Practice Problems
- Excel OM
- POM for Windows

 On Your Student DVD
- Video Clips and Video Case
- Virtual Office Hours for Solved Problem

Discussion Questions

1. What is JIT?
2. What is a lean producer?
3. What is TPS?
4. What is level scheduling?
5. JIT attempts to remove delays, which do not add value. How then does JIT cope with weather and its impact on crop harvest and transportation times?

6. What are three ways in which JIT and quality are related?
7. How does TPS contribute to competitive advantage?
8. What are the characteristics of just-in-time partnerships with respect to suppliers?
9. Discuss how the Japanese word for *card* has application in the study of JIT.

10. Standardized, reusable containers have fairly obvious benefits for shipping. What is the purpose of these devices within the plant?

11. Does lean production work in the service sector? Provide an illustration.

12. Which lean techniques work in both the manufacturing *and* service sectors?

Ethical Dilemma

In this lean operations world, in an effort to lower handling costs, speed delivery, and reduce inventory, retailers are forcing their suppliers to do more and more in the way of preparing their merchandise for their cross-docking warehouses, shipment to specific stores, and shelf presentation. Your company, a small manufacturer of aquarium decorations, is in a tough position. First, Mega-Mart wanted you to develop bar-code technology, then special packaging, then small individual shipments bar coded for each store (this way when the merchandise hits the warehouse it is cross-docked immediately to the correct truck and store and is ready for shelf placement). And now Mega-Mart wants you to develop RFID—immediately. Mega-Mart has made it clear that suppliers that cannot keep up with the technology will be dropped.

Earlier, when you didn't have the expertise for bar codes, you had to borrow money and hire an outside firm to do the development, purchase the technology, and train your shipping clerk. Then, meeting the special packaging requirement drove you into negative income for several months, resulting in a loss for last year. Now it appears that the RFID request is impossible. Your business, under the best of conditions, is marginally profitable, and the bank may not be willing to bail you out again. Over the years, Mega-Mart has slowly become your major customer and without them, you are probably out of business. What are the ethical issues and what do you do?

Problems*

• 1 Leblanc Electronics, Inc., in Nashville, produces short runs of custom airwave scanners for the defense industry. You have been asked by the owner, Larry Leblanc, to reduce inventory by introducing a kanban system. After several hours of analysis, you develop the following data for scanner connectors used in one work cell. How many kanbans do you need for this connector?

Daily demand	1,000 connectors
Lead time	2 days
Safety stock	$\frac{1}{2}$ day
Kanban size	500 connectors

• 2 Chip Gillikin's company wants to establish kanbans to feed a newly established work cell. The following data have been provided. How many kanbans are needed?

Daily demand	250 units
Production lead time	$\frac{1}{2}$ day
Safety stock	$\frac{1}{4}$ day
Kanban size	50 units

•• 3 Chris Millikan Manufacturing, Inc., is moving to kanbans to support its telephone switching-board assembly lines. Determine the size of the kanban for subassemblies and the number of kanbans needed.

Setup cost = $30

Annual holding
        cost = $120 per subassembly

Daily production = 20 subassemblies

Annual usage = 2,500 (50 weeks × 5 days each
             × daily usage of 10 subassemblies)

Lead time = 16 days

Safety stock = 4 days' production of subassemblies. Px

•• 4 Maggie Moylan Motorcycle Corp. uses kanbans to support its transmission assembly line. Determine the size of the kanban for the mainshaft assembly and the number of kanbans needed.

Setup cost = $20

Annual holding cost
of mainshaft assembly = $250 per unit

Daily production = 300 mainshafts

Annual usage = 20,000 (= 50 weeks × 5 days each
             × daily usage of 80 mainshafts)

Lead time = 3 days

Safety stock = $\frac{1}{2}$ day's production of mainshafts Px

Green Gear Cycling, Inc.

*Note: Px means the problem may be solved with POM for Windows and/or Excel OM.

383

• 5 Discount-Mart, a major East Coast retailer, wants to determine the economic order quantity for its halogen lamps. It currently buys all halogen lamps from Specialty Lighting Manufacturers, in Atlanta. Annual demand is 2,000 lamps, ordering cost per order is $30, carrying cost per lamp is $12.

a) What is the EOQ?

b) What are the total annual costs of holding and ordering (managing) this inventory?

c) How many orders should Discount-Mart place with Specialty Lighting per year? **P**x

••• 6 Discount-Mart (see Problem 5), as part of its new JIT program, has signed a long-term contract with Specialty Lighting and will place orders electronically for its halogen lamps. Ordering costs will drop to $.50 per order, but Discount-Mart also reassessed its carrying costs and raised them to $20 per lamp.

a) What is the new economic order quantity?

b) How many orders will now be placed?

c) What is the total annual cost of managing the inventory with this policy? **P**x

•• 7 How do your answers to Problems 5 and 6 provide insight into a JIT purchasing strategy?

••• 8 Bill Penny has a repetitive manufacturing plant producing trailer hitches in Arlington, Texas. The plant has an average inventory turnover of only 12 times per year. He has therefore determined that he will reduce his component lot sizes. He has developed the following data for one component, the safety chain clip:

$$\text{Annual demand} = 31,200 \text{ units}$$

$$\text{Daily demand} = 120 \text{ units}$$

$$\text{Daily production (in 8 hours)} = 960 \text{ units}$$

$$\text{Desired lot size (1 hour of production)} = 120 \text{ units}$$

$$\text{Holding cost per unit per year} = \$12$$

$$\text{Setup labor cost per hour} = \$20$$

How many minutes of setup time should he have his plant manager aim for regarding this component?

••• 9 Given the following information about a product, at Phyllis Simon's firm, what is the appropriate setup time?

$$\text{Annual demand} = 39,000 \text{ units}$$

$$\text{Daily demand} = 150 \text{ units}$$

$$\text{Daily production} = 1,000 \text{ units}$$

$$\text{Desired lot size} = 150 \text{ units}$$

$$\text{Holding cost per unit per year} = \$10$$

$$\text{Setup labor cost per hour} = \$40$$

••• 10 Rick Wing has a repetitive manufacturing plant producing automobile steering wheels. Use the following data to prepare for a reduced lot size. The firm uses a work year of 305 days.

Annual demand for steering wheels	30,500
Daily demand	100
Daily production (8 hours)	800
Desired lot size (2 hours of production)	200
Holding cost per unit per year	$10

a) What is the setup cost, based on the desired lot size?

b) What is the setup time, based on $40 per hour setup labor?

Case Studies

Mutual Insurance Company of Iowa

Mutual Insurance Company of Iowa (MICI) has a major insurance office facility located in Des Moines, Iowa. The Des Moines office is responsible for processing all of MICI's insurance claims for the entire nation. The company's sales have experienced rapid growth during the last year, and as expected, record levels in claims followed. Over 2,500 forms for claims a day are now flowing into the office for processing. Unfortunately, fewer than 2,500 forms a day are flowing out. The total time to process a claim, from the time it arrives to the time a check is mailed, has increased from 10 days to 10 weeks. As a result, some customers are threatening legal action. Sally Cook, the manager of Claims Processing, is particularly distressed, as she knows that a claim seldom requires more than 3 hours of actual work. Under the current administrative procedures, human resources limitations, and facility constraints, there appear to be no easy fixes for the problem. But clearly, something must be done, as the workload has overwhelmed the existing system.

MICI management wants aggressive, but economical, action taken to fix the problem. Ms. Cook has decided to try a JIT approach to claim processing. With support from her bosses, and as a temporary fix, Cook has brought in part-time personnel from MICI sales divisions across the country to help. They are to work down the claims backlog while a new JIT system is installed.

Meanwhile, Claims Processing managers and employees are to be trained in JIT principles. With JIT principles firmly in mind, managers will redesign jobs to move responsibilities for quality control activities to each employee, holding them responsible for quality work and any necessary corrections. Cook will also initiate worker-training programs that explain the entire claim processing flow, as well as provide comprehensive training on each step in the process. Data-entry skills will also be taught to both employees and managers in an effort to fix responsibility for data accuracy on the processor rather than on data entry clerks. Additionally, cross training will be emphasized to enable workers within departments to process a variety of customer claim applications in their entirety.

Cook and her supervisors are also reexamining the insurance and claim forms currently in use. They want to see if standardization of forms will cut processing time, reduce data-entry time, and cut work-in-process.

They hope the changes will also save training time. Making changes in work methods and worker skills leads logically to a need for change in the layout of the Claims Processing Department. This potential change represents a major move from the departmental layout of the past, and will be a costly step. To help ensure the successful implementation of this phase of the changeover, Cook estab-

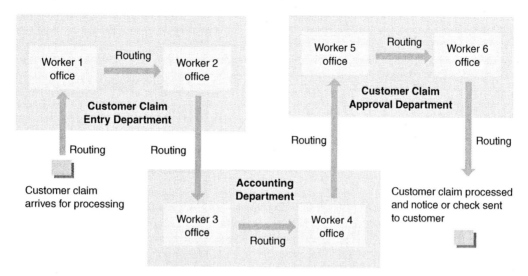

▲ **Figure 10** Claims Processing Department Layout

lished a team made up of supervisors, employees, and an outside office layout consultant. She also had the team visit the Kawasaki motorcycle plant in Lincoln, Nebraska, to observe their use of work cells to aid JIT.

The team concluded that a change in the office facilities was necessary to successfully implement and integrate JIT concepts at MICI. The team believes it should revise the layout of the operation and work methods to bring them in line with "group technology cell" layouts. An example of the current departmental layout and claim processing flow pattern is presented in Figure 10. As can be seen in this figure, customer claims arrive for processing at the facility and flow through a series of offices and departments to eventually complete the claim process. Although the arrangement of the offices and workers in Figure 10 is typical, the entire facility actually operates 20 additional flows, each consisting of the same three departments. However, not all of the 20 flows are configured the same. The number of employees, for example, varies depending on the claim form requirements (larger claims have to be approved by more people). So while all forms must pass through the same three departments (Customer Claim Entry,

Accounting, and Customer Claim Approval), the number of workers for each claim may vary from two to four. For this reason, the MICI facility currently maintains a staff of over 180 office workers just to process and route claims. All these people work for Ms. Cook.

Discussion Questions

1. Identify the attributes you would expect the Claims Processing Department at MICI to have once the new JIT system is in place.
2. What will the restructured cell layout for claim processing in Figure 10 look like? Draw it.
3. What assumptions are you making about personnel and equipment in the new group technology cell layout?
4. How will the new JIT oriented system benefit the MICI operation? Explain.

Source: Adapted from Marc J. Schniederjans, *Topics in Just-in-Time Management*, pp. 283–285. Reprinted by permission of Prentice Hall, Inc., Upper Saddle River, NJ.

JIT after the Fire

World-renowned Toyota Motor Corporation has a worldwide presence, with Toyota's investment in North America alone exceeding $13 billion in 11 manufacturing plants. Toyota is at the forefront of lean firms and a showcase of JIT. Executives from all over the world make the journey to Toyota to see how JIT works.

But early one Saturday morning in February, a fire roared through the huge Aisin Seiki plant in Kariya, Japan. The fire incinerated the main source of crucial brake valves that Toyota buys from Aisin and uses in most of its cars. Aisin has long been a supplier of the critical brake-fluid-proportioning valves (P-valves), supplying 99% of Toyota's requirement for the valve. About 80% of Aisin's total output goes to Toyota. As the smoke cleared, the extent of the disaster was clear—most of the 506 special machines used to manufacture the P-valves were useless. A few might be repaired in 2 weeks, but most would need to be replaced—and the

lead time was 6 weeks. Both Aisin and Toyota had been operating at full capacity.

Consistent with JIT practices, Toyota maintained only a 4-hour supply of the valve. And there were few of the valves in the closely knit network that constituted Toyota's supply chain. Depending on a single source and holding little inventory is a risk, but it also keeps Toyota lean and its costs low. The Toyota plants in Japan build 14,000 cars a day. Without that valve, production would come to a rapid halt. Moreover, Toyota production managers were dismayed to find they needed 200 variations of the P-valve.

Consistent with the *keiretsu* networks that are typical of Japan's manufacturing sector, Toyota holds 23% of Aisin's stock, and Aisin's president is Kanshiro Toyoda of the Toyoda family that founded the automaker. Kosuke Ikebuchi, a Toyota senior managing director, was tracked down at 8 A.M. at a golf course clubhouse and given the bad news.

Discussion Questions

1. If you are Mr. Ikebuchi, what do you do?
2. What does this experience tell you (and Aisin and Toyota) about just-in-time?

3. If you had been in charge of Chrysler's JIT supplies the morning of September 11, 2001, what actions would you have taken?

Sources: Case is based on material in: *The Wall Street Journal* (July 20, 2007): B1, (May 8, 1997): A1, A5 and (September 24, 2001): B1, B4; and *Harvard Business Review* (September–October 1999): 97–106.

JIT at Arnold Palmer Hospital

Video Case

Orlando's Arnold Palmer Hospital, founded in 1989, specializes in treatment of women and children and is renowned for its high-quality rankings (top 10% of 2000 benchmarked hospitals), its labor and delivery volume (more than 13,000 births per year, and growing), and its neonatal intensive care unit (one of the highest survival rates in the nation). But quality medical practices and high patient satisfaction require costly inventory—some $30 million per year and thousands of SKUs.* With pressure on medical care to manage and reduce costs, Arnold Palmer Hospital has turned toward controlling its inventory with just-in-time (JIT) techniques.

Within the hospital, for example, drugs are now distributed at nursing workstations via dispensing machines (almost like vending machines) that electronically track patient usage and post the related charge to each patient. The dispensing stations are refilled each night, based on patient demand and prescriptions written by doctors.

To address JIT issues externally, Arnold Palmer Hospital turned toward a major distribution partner, McKesson General Medical, which as a first-tier supplier provides the hospital with about one quarter of all its medical/surgical inventory. McKesson supplies sponges, basins, towels, mayo stand covers, syringes, and hundreds of other medical/surgical items. To ensure coordinated daily delivery of inventory purchased from McKesson, an account executive has been assigned to the hospital on a full-time basis, as well as two other individuals who address customer service and product issues. The result has been a drop in Central Supply average daily inventory from $400,000 to $114,000 since JIT.

JIT success has also been achieved in the area of *custom surgical packs*. Custom surgical packs are the sterile coverings, disposable plastic trays, gauze, and the like, specialized to each type of surgical procedure. Arnold Palmer Hospital uses 10 different custom packs for various surgical procedures. "Over 50,000 packs are used each year, for a total cost of about $1.5 million," says George DeLong, head of Supply Chain Management.

The packs are not only delivered in a JIT manner but packed that way as well. That is, they are packed in the reverse order they are used so each item comes out of the pack in the sequence it is needed. The packs are bulky, expensive, and must remain sterile. Reducing

the inventory and handling while maintaining an assured sterile supply for scheduled surgeries presents a challenge to hospitals.

Here is how the supply chain works: Custom packs are *assembled* by a packing company with *components supplied* primarily from manufacturers selected by the hospital, and *delivered* by McKesson from its local warehouse. Arnold Palmer Hospital works with its own surgical staff (through the Medical Economics Outcome Committee) to identify and standardize the custom packs to reduce the number of custom pack SKUs. With this integrated system, pack safety stock inventory has been cut to one day.

The procedure to drive the custom surgical pack JIT system begins with a "pull" from the doctor's daily surgical schedule. Then, Arnold Palmer Hospital initiates an electronic order to McKesson between 1:00 and 2:00 P.M. daily. At 4:00 A.M. the next morning McKesson delivers the packs. Hospital personnel arrive at 7:00 A.M. and stock the shelves for scheduled surgeries. McKesson then reorders from the packing company, which in turn "pulls" necessary inventory for the quantity of packs needed from the manufacturers.

Arnold Palmer Hospital's JIT system reduces inventory investment, expensive traditional ordering, and bulky storage, and supports quality with a sterile delivery.

Discussion Questions**

1. What do you recommend be done when an error is found in a pack as it is opened for an operation?
2. How might the procedure for custom surgical packs described here be improved?
3. When discussing JIT in services, the text notes that suppliers, layout, inventory, and scheduling are all used. Provide an example of each of these at Arnold Palmer Hospital.
4. When a doctor proposes a new surgical procedure, how do you recommend the SKU for a new custom pack be entered into the hospital's supply chain system?

*SKU = stock keeping unit

**You may wish to view this video case on your student DVD before answering these questions.

Additional Case Studies

Harvard has selected these Harvard Business School cases to accompany this text:

harvardbusinessonline.hbsp.harvard.edu

- **Johnson Controls Automotive Systems Group: The Georgetown, Kentucky, Plant** (#693-086): Examines the challenge of JIT with growing variation and a change from JIT delivery to JIT assembly.
- **Injex Industries** (#697-003): Examines supplier concerns as Injex provides components to a single, demanding customer on a JIT basis.

Bibliography

Ahls, Bill. "Advanced Memory and Lean Change," *IIE Solutions* 33, no. 1 (January 2001): 40–42.

Bacheldor, Beth, and Laurie Sullivan. "Never Too Lean." *Information Week* 985 (April 19, 2004): 36–42.

Bruun, Peter, and Robert N. Mefford. "Lean Production and the Internet." *International Journal of Production Economics* 89, no. 3 (June 18, 2004): 247.

Burke, Robert, and Gregg Messel. "From Simulation to Implementation: Cardinal Health's Lean Journey." *Target: Innovation at Work* 19, no. 2 (2nd quarter 2003): 27–32.

Hall, Robert W. "'Lean' and the Toyota Production System." *Target* 20, no. 3 (3rd issue 2004): 22–27.

Keyte, Beau, and Drew Locher. *The Complete Lean Enterprise.* University Park, IL: Productivity Press, 2004.

King, Andrew A., and Michael J. Lenox. "Lean and Green? An Empirical Examination of the Relationship Between Lean Production and Environmental Performance." *Production and Operations Management* 10, no. 3 (fall 2001): 244–256.

Klassen, Robert D. "Just-in-Time Manufacturing and Pollution Prevention Generate Mutual Benefits in the Furniture Industry." *Interfaces* 30, no. 3 (May–June 2000): 95–106.

Morgan, James M., and Jeffrey K. Liker. *The Toyota Product Development System.* New York: Productivity Press, 2007.

Parks, Charles M. "The Bare Necessities of Lean." *Industrial Engineer* 35, no. 8 (August 2003): 39.

Schonberger, Richard J. "Lean Extended." *Industrial Engineer* (December 2005): 26–31.

van Veen-Dirks, Paula. "Management Control and the Production Environment." *International Journal of Production Economics* 93 (January 8, 2005): 263.

Womack, James P., and Daniel T. Jones. "Lean Consumption." *Harvard Business Review* (March 2005): 58–68.

Womack, James P., and Daniel T. Jones. *Lean Solutions: How Companies and Customers Can Create Value and Wealth Together.* New York: The Free Press, 2005.

Internet Resources

Business Open Learning Archive: **www.bola.biz/index.html**
Gemba Research: **www.gemba.com**
Kanban—and the environment:
www.epa.gov/lean/thinking/kanban.htm
Kanban—explanation:
www.graphicproducts.com/tutorials/kanban/

Manufacturing Engineering: **www.mfgeng.com**
Mid-America Manufacturing Technology Center:
www.mamtc.com
Toyota Motor Corp.:
www.toyota.co.jp/en/vision/production_system

Solutions to Even Numbered Problems

2 3.75, or 4 kanbans
4 Size of kanban = 66; number of kanbans = 5.9, or 6
6 (a) EOQ = 10 lamps
   (b) 200 orders/yr.
   (c) $200

8 7.26 min.
10 (a) Setup cost = $5.74
   (b) Setup time = 8.61 min.

Solutions to Self test

1. d; **2.** a; **3.** e; **4.** overproduction, queues, transportation, inventory, motion, overprocessing, defective product; **5.** sort; simplify; shine; standardize; sustain; **6.** d; **7.** e; **8.** a; **9.** e; **10.** c.

Module A

Decision Making Tools

Decision-Making Tools

Outline

Learning Objectives

When you complete this selection you should be able to

1. Create a simple decision tree
2. Build a decision table
3. Explain when to use each of the three types of decision-making environments
4. Calculate an expected monetary value (EMV)
5. Compute the expected value of perfect information (EVPI)
6. Evaluate the nodes in a decision tree
7. Create a decision tree with sequential decisions

From *Operations Management*, 9/e. Jay Heizer. Barry Render. Copyright © 2008 by Pearson Education. All rights reserved.

EyeWire Collection, Getty Images—Photodisc

▲ *The wildcatter's decision was a tough one. Which of his new Kentucky lease areas—Blair East or Blair West—should he drill for oil? A wrong decision in this type of wildcat oil drilling could mean the difference between success and bankruptcy. Talk about decision making under uncertainty and pressure! But using a decision tree, Tomco Oil President Thomas E. Blair identified 74 different options, each with its own potential net profit. What had begun as an overwhelming number of geological, engineering, economic, and political factors now became much clearer. Says Blair, "Decision tree analysis provided us with a systematic way of planning these decisions and clearer insight into the numerous and varied financial outcomes that are possible."[1]*

"The business executive is by profession a decision maker. Uncertainty is his opponent. Overcoming it is his mission."

John McDonald

Operations managers are decision makers. To achieve the goals of their organizations, managers must understand how decisions are made and know which decision-making tools to use. To a great extent, the success or failure of both people and companies depends on the quality of their decisions. Bill Gates, who developed the DOS and Windows operating systems, became chairman of the most powerful software firm in the world (Microsoft) and a billionaire. In contrast, the Firestone manager who headed the team that designed the flawed tires that caused so many accidents with Ford Explorers in the late 1990s is not working there anymore.

THE DECISION PROCESS IN OPERATIONS

What makes the difference between a good decision and a bad decision? A "good" decision—one that uses analytic decision making—is based on logic and considers all available data and possible alternatives. It also follows these six steps:

1. Clearly define the problem and the factors that influence it.
2. Develop specific and measurable objectives.
3. Develop a model—that is, a relationship between objectives and variables (which are measurable quantities).
4. Evaluate each alternative solution based on its merits and drawbacks.
5. Select the best alternative.
6. Implement the decision and set a timetable for completion.

Throughout this book, we have introduced a broad range of mathematical models and tools to help operations managers make better decisions. Effective operations depend on careful decision making. Fortunately, there are a whole variety of analytic tools to help make these decisions.

---

[1]J. Hosseini, "Decision Analysis and Its Application in the Choice between Two Wildcat Ventures," *Interfaces* 16, no. 2. Reprinted by permission, INFORMS, 901 Elkridge Landing Road, Suite 400, Linthicum, Maryland 21090 USA.

This module introduces two of them—decision tables and decision trees. They are used in a wide number of OM situations, ranging from new-product analysis, to capacity planning, to location planning, to scheduling, and to maintenance planning.

FUNDAMENTALS OF DECISION MAKING

Regardless of the complexity of a decision or the sophistication of the technique used to analyze it, all decision makers are faced with alternatives and "states of nature." The following notation will be used in this module:

1. Terms:
   a. *Alternative*—A course of action or strategy that may be chosen by a decision maker (e.g., not carrying an umbrella tomorrow).
   b. *State of nature*—An occurrence or a situation over which the decision maker has little or no control (e.g., tomorrow's weather).
2. Symbols used in a decision tree:
   a. □—decision node from which one of several alternatives may be selected.
   b. ○—a state-of-nature node out of which one state of nature will occur.

To present a manager's decision alternatives, we can develop *decision trees* using the above symbols. When constructing a decision tree, we must be sure that all alternatives and states of nature are in their correct and logical places and that we include *all* possible alternatives and states of nature.

> "*Management means, in the last analysis, the substitution of thought for brawn and muscle, of knowledge for folklore and tradition, and of cooperation for force.*"
>
> *Peter Drucker*

EXAMPLE 1

A simple decision tree

Getz Products Company is investigating the possibility of producing and marketing backyard storage sheds. Undertaking this project would require the construction of either a large or a small manufacturing plant. The market for the product produced—storage sheds—could be either favorable or unfavorable. Getz, of course, has the option of not developing the new product line at all.

Approach: Getz decides to build a decision tree.

Solution: Figure 1 illustrates Getz's decision tree.

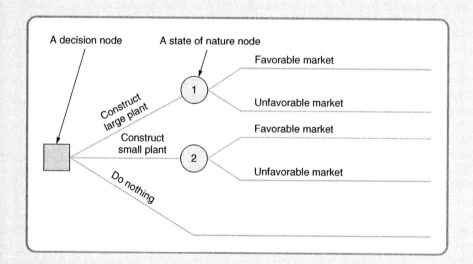

◁ **Figure 1**
Getz Products Decision Tree

Learning Objective

1. Create a simple decision tree

Insight: We never want to overlook the option of "doing nothing" in a decision tree as that is usually a possible decision.

Learning exercise: Getz now considers constructing a medium-sized plant as a fourth option. Redraw the tree in Figure 1 to accommodate this. [Answer: Your tree will have a new node and branches between "Construct large plant" and "Construct small plant."]

Related problems: 2e, 8b, 14a, 15a, 17a, 18

DECISION TABLES

Decision table

A tabular means of analyzing decision alternatives and states of nature.

We may also develop a decision or payoff table to help Getz Products define its alternatives. For any alternative and a particular state of nature, there is a *consequence* or *outcome*, which is usually expressed as a monetary value. This is called a *conditional value*. Note that all of the alternatives in Example 2 are listed down the left side of the table, that states of nature (outcomes) are listed across the top, and that conditional values (payoffs) are in the body of the **decision table**.

EXAMPLE 2

A decision table

Learning Objective

2. Build a decision table

Getz Products now wishes to organize the following information into a table. With a favorable market, a large facility will give Getz Products a net profit of $200,000. If the market is unfavorable, a $180,000 net loss will occur. A small plant will result in a net profit of $100,000 in a favorable market, but a net loss of $20,000 will be encountered if the market is unfavorable.

Approach: These numbers become conditional values in the decision table. We list alternatives in the left column and states of nature across the top of the table.

Solution: The completed table is shown in Table 1.

▶ **Table 1**

Decision Table with Conditional Values for Getz Products

	States of Nature	
Alternatives	**Favorable Market**	**Unfavorable Market**
Construct large plant	$200,000	−$180,000
Construct small plant	$100,000	−$ 20,000
Do nothing	$ 0	$ 0

Insight: The toughest part of decision tables is getting the data to analyze.

Learning exercise: In Examples 3 and 4, we see how to use tables to make decisions.

TYPES OF DECISION-MAKING ENVIRONMENTS

Learning Objective

3. Explain when to use each of the three types of decision-making environments

The types of decisions people make depend on how much knowledge or information they have about the situation. There are three decision-making environments:

- Decision making under uncertainty
- Decision making under risk
- Decision making under certainty

Decision Making Under Uncertainty

When there is complete *uncertainty* as to which state of nature in a decision environment may occur (that is, when we cannot even assess probabilities for each possible outcome), we rely on three decision methods:

Maximax

A criterion that finds an alternative that maximizes the maximum outcome.

Maximin

A criterion that finds an alternative that maximizes the minimum outcome.

Equally likely

A criterion that assigns equal probability to each state of nature.

1. **Maximax:** This method finds an alternative that *maximizes* the *maximum* outcome for every alternative. First, we find the maximum outcome within every alternative, and then we pick the alternative with the maximum number. Because this decision criterion locates the alternative with the *highest* possible *gain*, it has been called an "optimistic" decision criterion.

2. **Maximin:** This method finds the alternative that *maximizes* the *minimum* outcome for every alternative. First, we find the minimum outcome within every alternative, and then we pick the alternative with the maximum number. Because this decision criterion locates the alternative that has the *least* possible *loss*, it has been called a "pessimistic" decision criterion.

3. **Equally likely:** This method finds the alternative with the highest average outcome. First, we calculate the average outcome for every alternative, which is the sum of all outcomes divided by the number of outcomes. We then pick the alternative with the maximum number. The equally likely approach assumes that each state of nature is equally likely to occur.

EXAMPLE 3

A decision table analysis under uncertainty

Getz Products Company would like to apply each of these three approaches now.

Approach: Given Getz's decision table of Example 2, he determines the maximax, maximin, and equally likely decision criteria.

Solution: Table 2 provides the solution.

◄ Table 2

Decision Table for Decision Making under Uncertainty

	States of Nature				
Alternatives	**Favorable Market**	**Unfavorable Market**	**Maximum in Row**	**Minimum in Row**	**Row Average**
Construct large plant	$200,000	−$180,000	$200,000 ◄	−$180,000	$10,000
Construct small plant	$100,000	−$ 20,000	$100,000	−$ 20,000	$40,000 ◄
Do nothing	$ 0	$ 0	$ 0	$ 0 ◄	$ 0
			Maximax ─┘	Maximin ─┘	Equally ─┘ likely

1. The maximax choice is to construct a large plant. This is the *maximum* of the *maximum* number within each row, or alternative.
2. The maximin choice is to do nothing. This is the *maximum* of the *min*imum number within each row, or alternative.
3. The equally likely choice is to construct a small plant. This is the maximum of the average outcome of each alternative. This approach assumes that all outcomes for any alternative are *equally likely.*

Insight: There are optimistic decision makers ("maximax") and pessimistic ones ("maximin"). Maximax and maximin present best case–worst case planning scenarios.

Learning exercise: Getz reestimates the outcome for constructing a large plant when the market is favorable and raises it to $250,000. What numbers change in Table 2? Do the decisions change? [Answer: The maximax is now $250,000, and the row average is $35,000 for large plant. No decision changes.]

Related problems: 1, 2b–d, 4, 6

Decision Making Under Risk

Decision making under risk, a more common occurrence, relies on probabilities. Several possible states of nature may occur, each with an assumed probability. The states of nature must be mutually exclusive and collectively exhaustive and their probabilities must sum to 1.[2] Given a decision table with conditional values and probability assessments for all states of nature, we can determine the **expected monetary value (EMV)** for each alternative. This figure represents the expected value or *mean* return for each alternative *if we could repeat the decision a large number of times.*

The EMV for an alternative is the sum of all possible payoffs from the alternative, each weighted by the probability of that payoff occurring:

$$\text{EMV (Alternative } i) = \text{(Payoff of 1st state of nature)}$$
$$\times \text{(Probability of 1st state of nature)}$$
$$+ \text{(Payoff of 2nd state of nature)}$$
$$\times \text{(Probability of 2nd state of nature)}$$
$$+ \cdots + \text{(Payoff of last state of nature)}$$
$$\times \text{(Probability of last state of nature)}$$

Example 4 illustrates how to compute the maximum EMV.

Expected monetary value (EMV)

The expected payout or value of a variable that has different possible states of nature, each with an associated probability.

Learning Objective

4. Calculate an expected monetary value (EMV)

[2]To review these and other statistical terms, refer to the CD-ROM Tutorial 1, "Statistical Review for Managers."

EXAMPLE 4

Expected monetary value

▶ **Table 3**

Decision Table for Getz Products

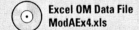

Excel OM Data File ModAEx4.xls

Getz would like to find the EMV for each alternative.

Approach: Getz Products' operations manager believes that the probability of a favorable market is exactly the same as that of an unfavorable market; that is, each state of nature has a .50 chance of occurring. He can now determine the EMV for each alternative (see Table 3):

	States of Nature	
Alternatives	**Favorable Market**	**Unfavorable Market**
Construct large plant (A_1)	$200,000	−$180,000
Construct small plant (A_2)	$100,000	−$ 20,000
Do nothing (A_3)	$ 0	$ 0
Probabilities	.50	.50

Solution:

1. EMV(A_1) = (.5)($200,000) + (.5)(−$180,000) = $10,000
2. EMV(A_2) = (.5)($100,000) + (.5)(−$20,000) = $40,000
3. EMV(A_3) = (.5)($0) + (.5)($0) = $0

Insight: The maximum EMV is seen in alternative A_2. Thus, according to the EMV decision criterion, Getz would build the small facility.

Learning exercise: What happens to the three EMVs if Getz increases the conditional value on the "large plant/favorable market" result to $250,000? [Answer: EMV($A_1$) = $35,000. No change in decision.]

Related problems: 2e, 3a, 5a, 7a, 8, 9a, 10, 11, 12, 14a,b, 16a, 22

Decision Making Under Certainty

Now suppose that the Getz operations manager has been approached by a marketing research firm that proposes to help him make the decision about whether to build the plant to produce storage sheds. The marketing researchers claim that their technical analysis will tell Getz with certainty whether the market is favorable for the proposed product. In other words, it will change Getz's environment from one of decision making *under risk* to one of decision making *under certainty*. This information could prevent Getz from making a very expensive mistake. The marketing research firm would charge Getz $65,000 for the information. What would you recommend? Should the operations manager hire the firm to make the study? Even if the information from the study is perfectly accurate, is it worth $65,000? What might it be worth? Although some of these questions are difficult to answer, determining the value of such *perfect information* can be very useful. It places an upper bound on what you would be willing to spend on information, such as that being sold by a marketing consultant. This is the concept of the expected value of perfect information (EVPI), which we now introduce.

EVPI places an upper limit on what you should pay for information.

Expected Value of Perfect Information (EVPI)

If a manager were able to determine which state of nature would occur, then he or she would know which decision to make. Once a manager knows which decision to make, the payoff increases because the payoff is now a certainty, not a probability. Because the payoff will increase with knowledge of which state of nature will occur, this knowledge has value. Therefore, we now look at how to determine the value of this information. We call this difference between the payoff under perfect information and the payoff under risk the **expected value of perfect information (EVPI)**.

Expected value of perfect information (EVPI)

The difference between the payoff under perfect information and the payoff under risk.

Expected value with perfect information (EVwPI)

The expected (average) return if perfect information is available.

EVPI = Expected value with perfect information − Maximum EMV

To find the EVPI, we must first compute the **expected value *with* perfect information (EVwPI)**, which is the expected (average) return if we have perfect information before a decision has to be made. To calculate this value, we choose the best alternative for each state of nature and multiply its payoff times the probability of occurrence of that state of nature:

Expected value with
perfect information (EVwPI) = (Best outcome or consequence for 1st state of nature)
　　　　　　　　　　× (Probability of 1st state of nature)
　　　　　　　　+ (Best outcome for 2nd state of nature)
　　　　　　　　　　× (Probability of 2nd state of nature)
　　　　　　　　+ ··· + (Best outcome for last state of nature)
　　　　　　　　　　× (Probability of last state of nature)

Learning Objective

5. Compute the expected value of perfect information (EVPI)

In Example 5 we use the data and decision table from Example 4 to examine the expected value of perfect information.

EXAMPLE 5

Expected value of perfect information

The Getz operations manager would like to calculate the maximum that he would pay for information—that is, the expected value of perfect information, or EVPI.

Approach: Referring back to Table 3, he follows a two-stage process. First, the expected value *with* perfect information (EVwPI) is computed. Then, using this information, EVPI is calculated.

Solution:

1. The best outcome for the state of nature "favorable market" is "build a large facility" with a payoff of $200,000. The best outcome for the state of nature "unfavorable market" is "do nothing" with a payoff of $0. Expected value *with* perfect information = ($200,000)(0.50) + ($0)(0.50) = $100,000. Thus, if we had perfect information, we would expect (on the average) $100,000 if the decision could be repeated many times.

2. The maximum EMV is $40,000 for A_2, which is the expected outcome without perfect information. Thus:

$$EVPI = EVwPI - Maximum\ EMV$$
$$= \$100,000 - \$40,000 = \$60,000$$

Insight: The *most* Getz should be willing to pay for perfect information is $60,000. This conclusion, of course, is again based on the assumption that the probability of each state of nature is 0.50.

Learning exercise: How does the EVPI change if the "large plant/favorable market" conditional value is $250,000? [Answer: EVPI = $85,000.]

Related problems: 3b, 5b, 7, 9, 14, 16

DECISION TREES

Decisions that lend themselves to display in a decision table also lend themselves to display in a decision tree. We will therefore analyze some decisions using decision trees. Although the use of a decision table is convenient in problems having one set of decisions and one set of states of nature, many problems include *sequential* decisions and states of nature. When there are two or more sequential decisions, and later decisions are based on the outcome of prior ones, the decision tree approach becomes appropriate. A **decision tree** is a graphic display of the decision process that indicates decision alternatives, states of nature and their respective probabilities, and payoffs for each combination of decision alternative and state of nature.

Expected monetary value (EMV) is the most commonly used criterion for decision tree analysis. One of the first steps in such analysis is to graph the decision tree and to specify the monetary consequences of all outcomes for a particular problem.

Analyzing problems with *decision trees* involves five steps:

Decision tree

A graphical means of analyzing decision alternatives and states of nature.

1. Define the problem.
2. Structure or draw the decision tree.
3. Assign probabilities to the states of nature.
4. Estimate payoffs for each possible combination of decision alternatives and states of nature.
5. Solve the problem by computing the expected monetary values (EMV) for each state-of-nature node. This is done by working *backward*—that is, by starting at the right of the tree and working back to decision nodes on the left.

Decision tree software permits users to solve decision-analysis problems with flexibility, power, and ease. Programs such as DPL, Tree Plan, and Supertree allow decision problems to be analyzed with less effort and in greater depth than ever before. Full-color presentations of the options open to managers always have impact. In this photo, wildcat drilling options are explored with DPL software.

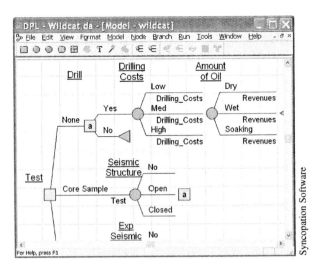

EXAMPLE 6

Solving a tree for EMV

Getz wants to develop a completed and solved decision tree.

Approach: The payoffs are placed at the right-hand side of each of the tree's branches (see Figure 2). The probabilities (first used by Getz in Example A4) are placed in parentheses next to each state of nature. The expected monetary values for each state-of-nature node are then calculated and placed by their respective nodes. The EMV of the first node is $10,000. This represents the branch from the decision node to "construct a large plant." The EMV for node 2, to "construct a small plant," is $40,000. The option of "doing nothing" has, of course, a payoff of $0.

Solution: The branch leaving the decision node leading to the state-of-nature node with the highest EMV will be chosen. In Getz's case, a small plant should be built.

▶ **Figure 2**

Completed and Solved Decision Tree for Getz Products

Learning Objective

6. Evaluate the nodes in a decision tree

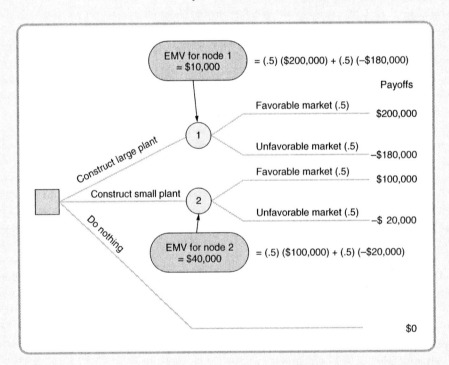

Insight: This graphical approach is an excellent way for managers to understand all the options in making a major decision. Visual models are often preferred over tables.

Learning exercise: Correct Figure 2 to reflect a $250,000 payoff for "construct large plant/favorable market." [Answer: Change one payoff and recompute the EMV for node 1.]

Related problems: 2e, 8b, 14a,b, 17, 18

A More Complex Decision Tree

When a *sequence* of decisions must be made, decision trees are much more powerful tools than are decision tables. Let's say that Getz Products has two decisions to make, with the second decision dependent on the outcome of the first. Before deciding about building a new plant, Getz has the option of conducting its own marketing research survey, at a cost of $10,000. The information from this survey could help it decide whether to build a large plant, to build a small plant, or not to build at all. Getz recognizes that although such a survey will not provide it with *perfect* information, it may be extremely helpful.

Getz's new decision tree is represented in Figure 3 of Example 7. Take a careful look at this more complex tree. Note that *all possible outcomes and alternatives* are included in their logical sequence. This procedure is one of the strengths of using decision trees. The manager is forced to examine all possible outcomes, including unfavorable ones. He or she is also forced to make decisions in a logical, sequential manner.

> *There is a widespread use of decision trees beyond just OM decision making.*

Getz Products wishes to develop the new tree for this sequential decision.

Approach: Examining the tree in Figure 3, we see that Getz's first decision point is whether to conduct the $10,000 market survey. If it chooses not to do the study (the lower part of the tree), it can either build a large plant, a small plant, or no plant. This is Getz's second decision point. If the decision is to build, the market will be either favorable (.50 probability) or unfavorable (also .50 probability). The payoffs for each of the possible consequences are listed along the right-hand side. As a matter of fact, this lower portion of Getz's tree is *identical* to the simpler decision tree shown in Figure 2.

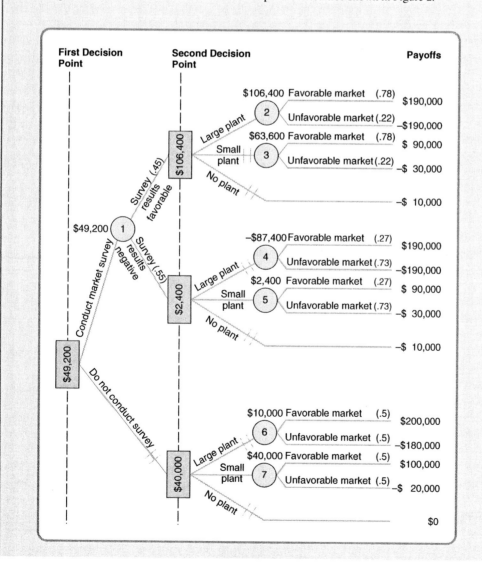

EXAMPLE 7

A decision tree with sequential decisions

◄ **Figure 3**

Getz Products Decision Tree with Probabilities and EMVs Shown

The short parallel lines mean "prune" that branch, as it is less favorable than another available option and may be dropped.

Learning Objective

7. Create a decision tree with sequential decisions

Solution: The upper part of Figure 3 reflects the decision to conduct the market survey. State-of-nature node number 1 has 2 branches coming out of it. Let us say there is a 45% chance that the survey results will indicate a favorable market for the storage sheds. We also note that the probability is .55 that the survey results will be negative.

The rest of the probabilities shown in parentheses in Figure 3 are all *conditional* probabilities. For example, .78 is the probability of a favorable market for the sheds given a favorable result from the market survey. Of course, you would expect to find a high probability of a favorable market given that the research indicated that the market was good. Don't forget, though: There is a chance that Getz's $10,000 market survey did not result in perfect or even reliable information. Any market research study is subject to error. In this case, there remains a 22% chance that the market for sheds will be unfavorable given positive survey results.

Likewise, we note that there is a 27% chance that the market for sheds will be favorable given negative survey results. The probability is much higher, .73, that the market will actually be unfavorable given a negative survey.

Finally, when we look to the payoff column in Figure 3, we see that $10,000—the cost of the marketing study—has been subtracted from each of the top 10 tree branches. Thus, a large plant constructed in a favorable market would normally net a $200,000 profit. Yet because the market study was conducted, this figure is reduced by $10,000. In the unfavorable case, the loss of $180,000 would increase to $190,000. Similarly, conducting the survey and building *no plant* now results in a –$10,000 payoff.

With all probabilities and payoffs specified, we can start calculating the expected monetary value of each branch. We begin at the end or right-hand side of the decision tree and work back toward the origin. When we finish, the best decision will be known.

1. Given favorable survey results:

$$\text{EMV (node 2)} = (.78)(\$190,000) + (.22)(-\$190,000) = \$106,400$$

$$\text{EMV (node 3)} = (.78)(\$90,000) + (.22)(-\$30,000) = \$63,600$$

The EMV of no plant in this case is –$10,000. Thus, if the survey results are favorable, a large plant should be built.

2. Given negative survey results:

$$\text{EMV (node 4)} = (.27)(\$190,000) + (.73)(-\$190,000) = -\$87,400$$

$$\text{EMV (node 5)} = (.27)(\$90,000) + (.73)(-\$30,000) = \$2,400$$

The EMV of no plant is again –$10,000 for this branch. Thus, given a negative survey result, Getz should build a small plant with an expected value of $2,400.

3. Continuing on the upper part of the tree and moving backward, we compute the expected value of conducting the market survey:

$$\text{EMV(node 1)} = (.45)(\$106,400) + (.55)(\$2,400) = \$49,200$$

4. If the market survey is *not* conducted:

$$\text{EMV (node 6)} = (.50)(\$200,000) + (.50)(-\$180,000) = \$10,000$$

$$\text{EMV (node 7)} = (.50)(\$100,000) + (.50)(-\$20,000) = \$40,000$$

The EMV of no plant is $0. Thus, building a small plant is the best choice, given the marketing research is not performed.

5. Because the expected monetary value of conducting the survey is $49,200—versus an EMV of $40,000 for not conducting the study—the best choice is to *seek marketing information*. If the survey results are favorable, Getz Products should build the large plant; if they are unfavorable, it should build the small plant.

Insight: You can reduce complexity in a large decision tree by viewing and solving a number of smaller trees—start at the end branches of a large one. Take one decision at a time.

Learning exercise: Getz estimates that if he conducts a market survey, there is really only a 35% chance the results will indicate a favorable market for the sheds. How does the tree change? [Answer: The EMV of conducting the survey = $38,800, so Getz should not do it now.]

Related problems: 13, 18, 19, 20, 21, 23

Using Decision Trees in Ethical Decision Making

Decision trees can also be a useful tool to aid ethical corporate decision making. The decision tree illustrated in Example A8, developed by Harvard Professor Constance Bagley, provides guidance as to how managers can both maximize shareholder value and behave ethically. The tree can be applied to any action a company contemplates, whether it is expanding operations in a developing country or reducing a workforce at home.

Smithson Corp. is opening a plant in Malaysia, a country with much less stringent environmental laws than the U.S., its home nation. Smithson can save $18 million in building the manufacturing facility—and boost its profits—if it does not install pollution-control equipment that is mandated in the U.S. but not in Malaysia. But Smithson also calculates that pollutants emitted from the plant, if unscrubbed, could damage the local fishing industry. This could cause a loss of millions of dollars in income as well as create health problems for local inhabitants.

Approach: Smithson decides to build a decision tree to model the problem.

Solution: Figure 4 outlines the choices management can consider. For example, if in management's best judgment the harm to the Malaysian community by building the plant will be greater than the loss in company returns, the response to the question "Is it ethical?" will be no.

Now, say Smithson proposes building a somewhat different plant, one *with* pollution controls, despite a negative impact on company returns. That decision takes us to the branch "Is it ethical *not* to take action?" If the answer (for whatever reason) is no, the decision tree suggests proceeding with the plant but notifying the Smithson Board, shareholders, and others about its impact.

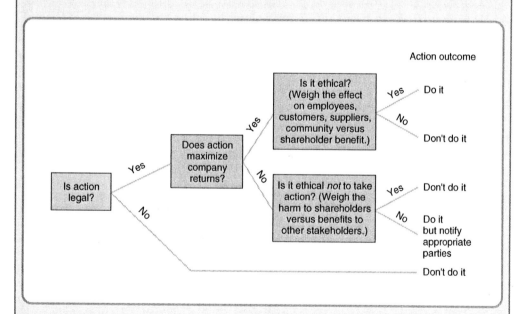

Insight: This tree allows managers to view the options graphically. This is a good way to start the process.

EXAMPLE 8

Ethical decision making

◀ **Figure 4**

Smithson's Decision Tree for Ethical Dilemma

Source: Modified from Constance E. Bagley, "The Ethical Leader's Decision Tree," *Harvard Business Review* (January–February 2003): 18–19.

Ethical decisions can be quite complex: What happens, for example, if a company builds a polluting plant overseas, but this allows the company to sell a life-saving drug at a lower cost around the world? Does a decision tree deal with all possible ethical dilemmas? No—but it does provide managers with a framework for examining those choices.

Summary

This module examines two of the most widely used decision techniques—decision tables and decision trees. These techniques are especially useful for making decisions under risk. Many decisions in research and development, plant and equipment, and even new buildings and structures can be ana- lyzed with these decision models. Problems in inventory con- trol, aggregate planning, maintenance, scheduling, and pro- duction control are just a few other decision table and deci- sion tree applications.

Key Terms

Decision table
Maximax
Maximin
Equally likely

Expected monetary value (EMV)
Expected value of perfect information
 (EVPI)

Expected value with perfect information
 (EVwPI)
Decision tree

Using Software for Decision Models

Analyzing decision tables is straightforward with Excel, Excel OM, and POM for Windows. When deci- sion trees are involved, Excel OM or commercial packages such as DPL, Tree Plan, and Supertree pro- vide flexibility, power, and ease. POM for Windows will also analyze trees but does not have graphic capabilities.

✗ Using Excel OM

Excel OM allows decision makers to evaluate decisions quickly and to perform sensitivity analysis on the results. Program 1 uses the Getz data to illustrate input, output, and selected formulas needed to compute the EMV and EVPI values.

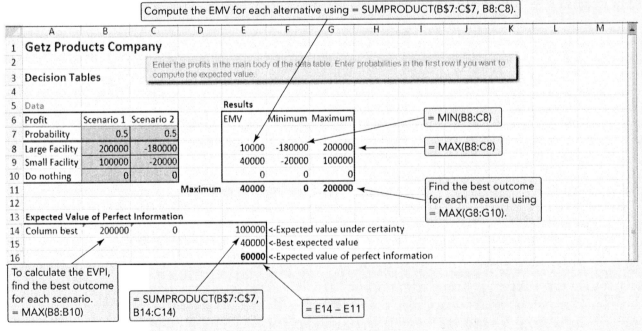

▲ **Program 1**   **Using Excel OM to Compute EMV and Other Measures for Getz**

Program 2 uses Excel OM to create the decision tree for Getz Products shown earlier in Example 6. The tool to create the tree is seen in the window on the right.

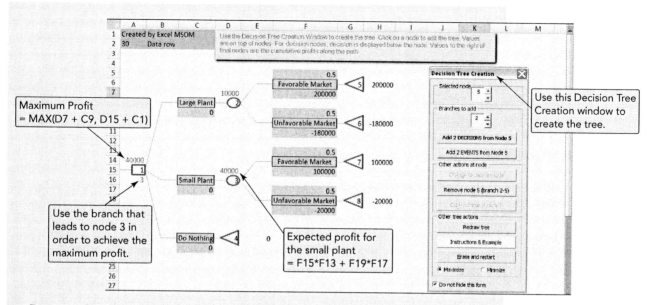

▲ **Program 2** **Getz Products' Decision Tree Using Excel OM**

Ⓟ Using POM for Windows

POM for Windows can be used to calculate all of the information described in the decision tables and decision trees in this module. For details on how to use this software, please refer to Appendix IV.

Self-Test

- *Before taking the self-test, refer to the learning objectives at the beginning of the selection, the notes in the margins, and the glossary at the end of the selection.*
- *Use the key at the back of the book to* ***correct*** *your answers.*
- ***Restudy*** *pages that correspond to any questions you answered incorrectly or material you feel uncertain about.*

1. In decision theory terminology, a course of action or a strategy that may be chosen by a decision maker is called a(n):
   a) payoff
   b) alternative
   c) state of nature
   d) all of the above

2. In decision theory, probabilities are associated with:
   a) payoffs
   b) alternatives
   c) states of nature
   d) all of the above

3. If probabilities are available to the decision maker, then the decision-making environment is called:
   a) certainty
   b) uncertainty
   c) risk
   d) none of the above

4. Which of the following is a decision-making criterion that is used for decision making under risk?
   a) expected monetary value criterion
   b) pessimistic (maximin) criterion
   c) optimistic (maximax) criterion
   d) equally likely criterion

5. The most that a person should pay for perfect information is:
   a) the EVPI
   b) the maximum EMV minus the minimum EMV
   c) the minimum EMV
   d) the maximum EMV

6. A decision tree is preferable to a decision table when:
   a) a number of sequential decisions are to be made
   b) probabilities are available
   c) the maximax criterion is used
   d) the objective is to maximize regret

7. On a decision tree, at each state-of-nature node:
   a) the alternative with the greatest EMV is selected
   b) an EMV is calculated
   c) all probabilities are added together
   d) the branch with the highest probability is selected

8. On a decision tree, once the tree has been drawn and the payoffs and probabilities have been placed on the tree, the analysis (computing EMVs and selecting the best alternative):
   a) is done by working backward (starting on the right and moving to the left)
   b) is done by working forward (starting on the left and moving to the right)
   c) is done by starting at the top of the tree and moving down
   d) is done by starting at the bottom of the tree and moving up

Solved Problem 1

Stella Yan Hua is considering the possibility of opening a small dress shop on Fairbanks Avenue, a few blocks from the university. She has located a good mall that attracts students. Her options are to open a small shop, a medium-sized shop, or no shop at all. The market for a dress shop can be good, average, or bad. The probabilities for these three possibilities are .2 for a good market, .5 for an average market, and .3 for a bad market. The net profit or loss for the medium-sized or small shops for the various market conditions are given in the following table. Building no shop at all yields no loss and no gain. What do you recommend?

| | States of Nature | | |
Alternatives	Good Market ($)	Average Market ($)	Bad Market ($)
Small shop	75,000	25,000	-40,000
Medium-sized shop	100,000	35,000	-60,000
No shop	0	0	0
Probabilities	.20	.50	.30

solution

The problem can be solved by computing the expected monetary value (EMV) for each alternative:

$$EMV \text{ (Small shop)} = (.2)(\$75,000) + (.5)(\$25,000) + (.3)(-\$40,000) = \$15,500$$
$$EMV \text{ (Medium-sized shop)} = (.2)(\$100,000) + (.5)(\$35,000) + (.3)(-\$60,000) = \$19,500$$
$$EMV \text{ (No shop)} = (.2)(\$0) + (.5)(\$0) + (.3)(\$0) = \$0$$

As you can see, the best decision is to build the medium-sized shop. The EMV for this alternative is $19,500.

Solved Problem 2

T.S. Amer's Ski Shop in Nevada has a 100-day season. T.S. has established the probability of various store traffic, based on historical records of skiing condition, as indicated in the table to the right. T.S. has four merchandising plans, each focusing on a popular name brand. Each plan yields a daily net profit as noted in the table. He also has a meteorologist friend, who for a small fee, will accurately tell tomorrow's weather so T.S. can implement one of his four merchandising plans.

a) What is the expected monetary value (EMV) under risk?
b) What is the expected value with perfect information (EVwPI)?
c) What is the expected value of perfect information (EVPI)?

Decision Alternatives (merchandising plan focusing on:)	Traffic in Store Because of Ski Conditions (states of nature)			
	1	2	3	4
Patagonia	$40	92	20	48
North Face	50	84	10	52
Cloud Veil	35	80	40	64
Columbia	45	72	10	60
Probabilities	.20	.25	.30	.25

solution

a) The highest expected monetary value under risk is:

$$EMV \text{ (Patagonia)} = .20(40) + .25(92) + .30(20) + .25(48) = \$49$$
$$EMV \text{ (North Face)} = .20(50) + .25(84) + .30(10) + .25(52) = \$47$$
$$EMV \text{ (Cloud Veil)} = .20(35) + .25(80) + .30(40) + .25(64) = \$55$$
$$EMV \text{ (Columbia)} = .20(45) + .25(72) + .30(10) + .25(60) = \$45$$

So the maximum EMV = $55

b) The expected value with perfect information is:

$$EVwPI = .20(50) + .25(92) + .30(40) + .25(64)$$
$$= 10 + 23 + 12 + 16 = \$61$$

c) The expected value of perfect information is:

$$EVPI = EVwPI - \text{Maximum EMV} = 61 - 55 = \$6$$

Solved Problem 3

Daily demand for cases of Tidy Bowl cleaner at Ravinder Nath's Supermarket has always been 5, 6, or 7 cases. Develop a decision tree that illustrates her decision alternatives as to whether to stock 5, 6, or 7 cases.

Solution

The decision tree is shown in Figure 5.

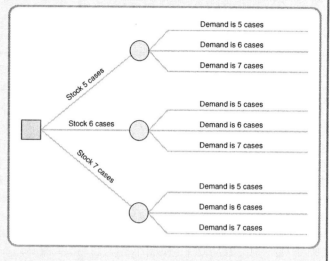

▲ **Figure 5** **Demand at Ravinder Nath's Supermarket**

Internet and Student CD-ROM/DVD Exercises

Visit our Companion Web site or use your student CD-ROM/DVD to help with this material in this module.

On Our Companion Web Site, www.prenhall.com/heizer
- Self-Study Quizzes
- Practice Problems
- Internet Case
- PowerPoint Lecture

On Your Student CD-ROM
- Practice Problems
- Excel OM
- Excel OM Example Data File
- POM for Windows

On Your Student DVD
- Virtual Office Hours for Solved Problems

Discussion Questions

1. Identify the six steps in the decision process.
2. Give an example of a good decision you made that resulted in a bad outcome. Also give an example of a bad decision you made that had a good outcome. Why was each decision good or bad?
3. What is the *equally likely* decision model?
4. Discuss the differences between decision making under certainty, under risk, and under uncertainty.
5. What is a decision tree?
6. Explain how decision trees might be used in several of the 10 OM decisions.
7. What is the expected value of perfect information?
8. What is the expected value *with* perfect information?
9. Identify the five steps in analyzing a problem using a decision tree.
10. Why are the maximax and maximin strategies considered to be optimistic and pessimistic, respectively?
11. The expected value criterion is considered to be the rational criterion on which to base a decision. Is this true? Is it rational to consider risk?
12. When are decision trees most useful?

Problems*

- 1 Given the following conditional value table, determine the appropriate decision under uncertainty using:
a) Maximax.
b) Maximin.
c) Equally likely.

*Note: means the problem may be solved with POM for Windows and/or Excel OM.

	States of Nature		
Alternatives	**Very Favorable Market**	**Average Market**	**Unfavorable Market**
Build new plant	$350,000	$240,000	−$300,000
Subcontract	$180,000	$90,000	−$20,000
Overtime	$110,000	$60,000	−$10,000
Do nothing	$0	$0	$0

405

• • 2   Even though independent gasoline stations have been having a difficult time, Susan Helms has been thinking about starting her own independent gasoline station. Susan's problem is to decide how large her station should be. The annual returns will depend on both the size of her station and a number of marketing factors related to the oil industry and demand for gasoline. After a careful analysis, Susan developed the following table:

Size of First Station	Good Market ($)	Fair Market ($)	Poor Market ($)
Small	50,000	20,000	–10,000
Medium	80,000	30,000	–20,000
Large	100,000	30,000	–40,000
Very large	300,000	25,000	–160,000

For example, if Susan constructs a small station and the market is good, she will realize a profit of $50,000.

a) Develop a decision table for this decision, like the one illustrated in Table A.2 earlier.
b) What is the maximax decision?
c) What is the maximin decision?
d) What is the equally likely decision?
e) Develop a decision tree. Assume each outcome is equally likely, then find the highest EMV. **PX**

• 3   Clay Whybark, a soft-drink vendor at Hard Rock Cafe's annual Rockfest, created a table of conditional values for the various alternatives (stocking decision) and states of nature (size of crowd):

| Alternatives | States of Nature (demand) | | |
	Big	Average	Small
Large stock	$22,000	$12,000	–$2,000
Average stock	$14,000	$10,000	$6,000
Small stock	$ 9,000	$ 8,000	$4,000

The probabilities associated with the states of nature are 0.3 for a big demand, 0.5 for an average demand, and 0.2 for a small demand.

a) Determine the alternative that provides Clay Whybark the greatest expected monetary value (EMV).
b) Compute the expected value of perfect information (EVPI). **PX**

• • 4   Raymond Jacobs owns a health and fitness center, the Muscle-Up, in Ashland. He is considering adding more floor space to meet increasing demand. He will either add no floor space (N), a moderate area of floor space (M), a large area of floor space (L), or an area of floor space that doubles the size of the facility (D). Demand will either stay fixed, increase slightly, or increase greatly. The following are the changes in Muscle-Up's annual profits under each combination of expansion level and demand change level:

| Demand Change | Expansion Level | | | |
	N	M	L	D
Fixed	$ 0	–$4,000	–$10,000	–$50,000
Slight Increase	$2,000	$8,000	$ 6,000	$ 4,000
Major Increase	$3,000	$9,000	$20,000	$40,000

Raymond is risk averse and wishes to use the maximin criterion.

a) What are his decision alternatives and what are the states of nature?
b) What should he do? **PX**

• 5   Howard Weiss, Inc., is considering building a sensitive new airport scanning device. His managers believe that there is a probability of 0.4 that the ATR Co. will come out with a competitive product. If Weiss adds an assembly line for the product and ATR Co.

does not follow with a competitive product, Weiss's expected profit is $40,000; if Weiss adds an assembly line and ATR follows suit, Weiss still expects $10,000 profit. If Weiss adds a new plant addition and ATR does not produce a competitive product, Weiss expects a profit of $600,000; if ATR does compete for this market, Weiss expects a loss of $100,000.

a) Determine the EMV of each decision.
b) Compute the expected value of perfect information. **PX**

• • 6   Deborah Watson's factory is considering three approaches for meeting an expected increase in demand. These three approaches are increasing capacity, using overtime, and buying more equipment. Demand will increase either slightly (S), moderately (M), or greatly (G). The profits for each approach under each possible scenario are as follows:

| Approach | Demand Scenario | | |
	S	M	G
Increasing Capacity	$700,000	$700,000	$ 700,000
Using Overtime	$500,000	$600,000	$1,000,000
Buying Equipment	$600,000	$800,000	$ 800,000

Since the goal is to maximize, and Deborah is risk-neutral, she decides to use the *equally likely* decision criterion to make the decision as to which approach to use. According to this criterion, which approach should be used?

• 7   The following payoff table provides profits based on various possible decision alternatives and various levels of demand at Amber Gardner's software firm:

| | Demand | |
	Low	High
Alternative 1	$10,000	$30,000
Alternative 2	$ 5,000	$40,000
Alternative 3	–$ 2,000	$50,000

The probability of low demand is 0.4, whereas the probability of high demand is 0.6.

a) What is the highest possible expected monetary value?
b) What is the expected value *with* perfect information (EVwPI)?
c) Calculate the expected value of perfect information for this situation. **PX**

• 8   Leah Johnson, director of Legal Services of Brookline, wants to increase capacity to provide free legal advice but must decide whether to do so by hiring another full-time lawyer or by using part-time lawyers. The table below shows the expected *costs* of the two options for three possible demand levels:

| Alternatives | States of Nature | | |
	Low Demand	Medium Demand	High Demand
Hire full-time	$300	$500	$ 700
Hire part-time	$ 0	$350	$1,000
Probabilities	.2	.5	.3

a) Using expected value, what should Ms. Johnson do?
b) Draw an appropriate decision tree showing payoffs and probabilities. **PX**

• • 9   Chung Manufacturing is considering the introduction of a family of new products. Long-term demand for the product group is somewhat predictable, so the manufacturer must be concerned with the risk of choosing a process that is inappropriate. Chen Chung is VP of operations. He can choose among batch manufacturing or custom manufacturing, or he can invest in group technology. Chen won't be able to forecast demand accurately until after he makes the process choice. Demand will be classified into four compartments: poor, fair, good, and excellent. The table below indicates the payoffs (profits) associated with each process/demand combination, as well as the probabilities of each long-term demand level:

	Poor	Fair	Good	Excellent
Probability	.1	.4	.3	.2
Batch	-$ 200,000	$1,000,000	$1,200,000	$1,300,000
Custom	$ 100,000	$ 300,000	$ 700,000	$ 800,000
Group technology	-$1,000,000	-$ 500,000	$ 500,000	$2,000,000

a) Based on expected value, what choice offers the greatest gain?
b) What would Chen Chung be willing to pay for a forecast that would accurately determine the level of demand in the future? **P**✗

•• 10   Consider the following decision table, which Dinesh Dave has developed for Appalacian Enterprises:

Decision Alternatives	Probability:	States of Nature		
		.40 Low	.20 Medium	.40 High
A		$40	$100	$60
B		$85	$ 60	$70
C		$60	$ 70	$70
D		$65	$ 75	$70
E		$70	$ 65	$80

Which decision alternative maximizes the expected value of the payoff? **P**✗

•• 11   The University of Dallas bookstore stocks textbooks in preparation for sales each semester. It normally relies on departmental forecasts and preregistration records to determine how many copies of a text are needed. Preregistration shows 90 operations management students enrolled, but bookstore manager Curtis Ketterman has second thoughts, based on his intuition and some historical evidence. Curtis believes that the distribution of sales may range from 70 to 90 units, according to the following probability model:

Demand	70	75	80	85	90
Probability	.15	.30	.30	.20	.05

This textbook costs the bookstore $82 and sells for $112. Any unsold copies can be returned to the publisher, less a restocking fee and shipping, for a net refund of $36.
a) Construct the table of conditional profits.
b) How many copies should the bookstore stock to achieve highest expected value? **P**✗

•• 12   Palmer Cheese Company is a small manufacturer of several different cheese products. One product is a cheese spread sold to retail outlets. Susan Palmer must decide how many cases of cheese spread to manufacture each month. The probability that demand will be 6 cases is .1, for 7 cases it is .3, for 8 cases it is .5, and for 9 cases it is .1. The cost of every case is $45, and the price Susan gets for each case is $95. Unfortunately, any cases not sold by the end of the month are of no value as a result of spoilage. How many cases should Susan manufacture each month? **P**✗

••• 13   Ronald Lau, chief engineer at South Dakota Electronics, has to decide whether to build a new state-of-the-art processing facility. If the new facility works, the company could realize a profit of $200,000. If it fails, South Dakota Electronics could lose $180,000. At this time, Lau estimates a 60% chance that the new process will fail.

The other option is to build a pilot plant and then decide whether to build a complete facility. The pilot plant would cost $10,000 to build. Lau estimates a 50-50 chance that the pilot plant will work. If the pilot plant works, there is a 90% probability that the complete plant, if it is built, will also work. If the pilot plant does not work, there is only a 20% chance that the complete project (if it is constructed) will work. Lau faces a dilemma. Should he build the plant? Should he build the pilot project and then make a decision? Help Lau by analyzing this problem. **P**✗

•• 14   Karen Villagomez, president of Wright Industries, is considering whether to build a manufacturing plant in the Ozarks. Her decision is summarized in the following table:

Alternatives	Favorable Market	Unfavorable Market
Build large plant	$400,000	-$300,000
Build small plant	$ 80,000	-$ 10,000
Don't build	$ 0	$ 0
Market probabilities	0.4	0.6

a) Construct a decision tree.
b) Determine the best strategy using expected monetary value (EMV).
c) What is the expected value of perfect information (EVPI)? **P**✗

•• 15   Deborah Kellogg buys Breathalyzer test sets for the Denver Police Department. The quality of the test sets from her two suppliers is indicated in the following table:

Percent Defective	Probability for Loomba Technology	Probability for Stewart-Douglas Enterprises
1	.70	.30
3	.20	.30
5	.10	.40

For example, the probability of getting a batch of tests that are 1% defective from Loomba Technology is .70. Because Kellogg orders 10,000 tests per order, this would mean that there is a .7 probability of getting 100 defective tests out of the 10,000 tests if Loomba

Jim Varney, Photo Researchers, Inc.

Technology is used to fill the order. A defective Breathalyzer test set can be repaired for $0.50. Although the quality of the test sets of the second supplier, Stewart-Douglas Enterprises, is lower, it will sell an order of 10,000 test sets for $37 less than Loomba.
a) Develop a decision tree.
b) Which supplier should Kellogg use? **Px**

•• 16 Deborah Hollwager, a concessionaire for the Des Moines ballpark, has developed a table of conditional values for the various alternatives (stocking decision) and states of nature (size of crowd):

Alternatives	States of Nature (size of crowd)		
	Large	Average	Small
Large inventory	$20,000	$10,000	−$2,000
Average inventory	$15,000	$12,000	$6,000
Small inventory	$ 9,000	$ 6,000	$5,000

If the probabilities associated with the states of nature are 0.3 for a large crowd, 0.5 for an average crowd, and 0.2 for a small crowd, determine:
a) The alternative that provides the greatest expected monetary value (EMV).
b) The expected value of perfect information (EVPI). **Px**

• 17 Joseph Biggs owns his own sno-cone business and lives 30 miles from a California beach resort. The sale of sno-cones is highly dependent on his location and on the weather. At the resort, his profit will be $120 per day in fair weather, $10 per day in bad weather. At home, his profit will be $70 in fair weather and $55 in bad weather. Assume that on any particular day, the weather service suggests a 40% chance of foul weather.
a) Construct Joseph's decision tree.
b) What decision is recommended by the expected value criterion? **Px**

•• 18 Kenneth Boyer is considering opening a bicycle shop in north Chicago. Boyer enjoys biking, but this is to be a business endeavor from which he expects to make a living. He can open a small shop, a large shop, or no shop at all. Because there will be a 5-year lease on the building that Boyer is thinking about using, he wants to make sure he makes the correct decision. Boyer is also thinking about hiring his old marketing professor to conduct a marketing research study to see if there is a market for his services. The results of such a study could be either favorable or unfavorable. Develop a decision tree for Boyer. **Px**

••• 19 F. J. Brewerton Retailers, Inc., must decide whether to build a small or a large facility at a new location in south Texas. Demand at the location will either be low or high, with probabilities 0.4 and 0.6, respectively. If Brewerton builds a small facility and demand proves to be high, he then has the option of expanding the facility. If a small facility is built and demand proves to be high, and then the retailer expands the facility, the payoff is $270,000. If a small facility is built and demand proves to be high, but Brewerton then decides not to expand the facility, the payoff is $223,000.
If a small facility is built and demand proves to be low, then there is no option to expand and the payoff is $200,000. If a large facility is built and demand proves to be low, Brewerton then has the option of stimulating demand through local advertising. If he does not exercise this option, then the payoff is $40,000. If he does exercise the advertising option, then the response to advertising will either be modest or sizable, with probabilities of 0.3 and 0.7, respectively. If the response is modest, the payoff is $20,000. If it is sizable, the pay-

off is $220,000. Finally, if a large facility is built and demand proves to be high, then no advertising is needed and the payoff is $800,000.
a) What should Brewerton do to maximize his expected payoff?
b) What is the value of this expected payoff?

••• 20 Dick Holliday is not sure what he should do. He can build either a large video rental section or a small one in his drugstore. He can also gather additional information or simply do nothing. If he gathers additional information, the results could suggest either a favorable or an unfavorable market, but it would cost him $3,000 to gather the information. Holliday believes that there is a 50–50 chance that the information will be favorable. If the rental market is favorable, Holliday will earn $15,000 with a large section or $5,000 with a small. With an unfavorable video-rental market, however, Holliday could lose $20,000 with a large section or $10,000 with a small section. Without gathering additional information, Holliday estimates that the probability of a favorable rental market is .7. A favorable report from the study would increase the probability of a favorable rental market to .9. Furthermore, an unfavorable report from the additional information would decrease the probability of a favorable rental market to .4. Of course, Holliday could ignore these numbers and do nothing. What is your advice to Holliday?

••••21 Jeff Kaufmann's machine shop sells a variety of machines for job shops. A customer wants to purchase a model XPO2 drilling machine from Jeff's store. The model XPO2 sells for $180,000, but Jeff is out of XPO2s. The customer says he will wait for Jeff to get a model XPO2 in stock. Jeff knows that there is a wholesale market for XPO2s from which he can purchase an XPO2. Jeff can buy an XPO2 today for $150,000, or he can wait a day and buy an XPO2 (if one is available) tomorrow for $125,000. If at least one XPO2 is still available tomorrow, Jeff can wait until the day after tomorrow and buy an XPO2 (if one is still available) for $110,000.
There is an 0.40 probability that there will be no model XPO2s available tomorrow. If there are model XPO2s available tomorrow, there is a 0.70 probability that by the day after tomorrow, there will be no model XPO2s available in the wholesale market. Three days from now, it is certain that no model XPO2s will be available on the wholesale market. What is the maximum expected profit that Jeff can achieve? What should Jeff do?

••••22 The city of Segovia is contemplating building a second airport to relieve congestion at the main airport and is considering two potential sites, X and Y. Hard Rock Hotels would like to purchase land to build a hotel at the new airport. The value of land has been rising in anticipation and is expected to skyrocket once the city decides between sites X and Y. Consequently, Hard Rock would like to purchase land now. Hard Rock will sell the land if the city chooses not to locate the airport nearby. Hard Rock has four choices: (1) buy land at X, (2) buy land at Y, (3) buy land at both X and Y, or (4) do nothing. Hard Rock has collected the following data (which are in millions of euros):

	Site X	Site Y
Current purchase price	27	15
Profits if airport and hotel built at this site	45	30
Sale price if airport not built at this site	9	6

Hard Rock determines there is a 45% chance the airport will be built at X (hence, a 55% chance it will be built at Y).
a) Set up the decision table.
b) What should Hard Rock decide to do to maximize total net profit? **Px**

••••23 Louisiana is busy designing new lottery scratch-off games. In the latest game, Bayou Boondoggle, the player is instructed to scratch off one spot: A, B, or C. A can reveal "Loser, " "Win $1," or "Win $50." B can reveal "Loser" or "Take a Second Chance." C can reveal "Loser" or "Win $500." On the second chance, the player is instructed to scratch off D or E. D can reveal "Loser" or "Win $1." E can reveal "Loser" or "Win $10." The probabilities at A are .9, .09, and .01. The probabilities at B are .8 and .2. The probabilities at C are .999 and .001. The probabilities at D are .5 and .5. Finally, the probabilities at E are .95 and .05. Draw the decision tree that represents this scenario. Use proper symbols and label all branches clearly. Calculate the expected value of this game. **PX**

Case Studies

Tom Tucker's Liver Transplant

Tom Tucker, a robust 50-year-old executive living in the northern suburbs of St. Paul, has been diagnosed by a University of Minnesota internist as having a decaying liver. Although he is otherwise healthy, Tucker's liver problem could prove fatal if left untreated.

Firm research data are not yet available to predict the likelihood of survival for a man of Tucker's age and condition without surgery. However, based on her own experience and recent medical journal articles, the internist tells him that if he elects to avoid surgical treatment of the liver problem, chances of survival will be approximately as follows: only a 60% chance of living 1 year, a 20% chance of surviving for 2 years, a 10% chance for 5 years, and

a 10% chance of living to age 58. She places his probability of survival beyond age 58 without a liver transplant to be extremely low.

The transplant operation, however, is a serious surgical procedure. Five percent of patients die during the operation or its recovery stage, with an additional 45% dying during the first year. Twenty percent survive for 5 years, 13% survive for 10 years, and 8%, 5%, and 4% survive, respectively, for 15, 20, and 25 years.

Discussion Questions

1. Do you think that Tucker should select the transplant operation?
2. What other factors might be considered?

Ski Right Corp.

After retiring as a physician, Bob Guthrie became an avid downhill skier on the steep slopes of the Utah Rocky Mountains. As an amateur inventor, Bob was always looking for something new. With the recent deaths of several celebrity skiers, Bob knew he could use his creative mind to make skiing safer and his bank account larger. He knew that many deaths on the slopes were caused by head injuries. Although ski helmets have been on the market for some time, most skiers consider them boring and basically ugly. As a physician, Bob knew that some type of new ski helmet was the answer.

Bob's biggest challenge was to invent a helmet that was attractive, safe, and fun to wear. Multiple colors and using the latest fashion designs would be musts. After years of skiing, Bob knew that many skiers believe that how you look on the slopes is more important than how you ski. His helmets would have to look good and fit in with current fashion trends. But attractive helmets were not enough. Bob had to make the helmets fun and useful. The name of the new ski helmet, Ski Right, was sure to be a winner. If Bob could come up with a good idea, he believed that there was a 20% chance that the market for the Ski Right helmet would be excellent. The chance of a good market should be 40%. Bob also knew that the market for his helmet could be only average (30% chance) or even poor (10% chance).

The idea of how to make ski helmets fun and useful came to Bob on a gondola ride to the top of a mountain. A busy executive on the gondola ride was on his cell phone trying to complete a complicated merger. When the executive got off the gondola, he dropped the phone and it was crushed by the gondola mechanism. Bob decided that his new ski helmet would have a built-in cell phone and an AM/FM stereo radio. All the electronics could be operated by a control pad worn on a skier's arm or leg.

Bob decided to try a small pilot project for Ski Right. He enjoyed being retired and didn't want a failure to cause him to go back to work. After some research, Bob found Progressive Products (PP). The company was willing to be a partner in developing the Ski Right and sharing any profits. If the market was excellent, Bob would net $5,000 per month. With a good market, Bob would net $2,000. An average market would result in a loss of $2,000, and a poor market would mean Bob would be out $5,000 per month.

Another option for Bob was to have Leadville Barts (LB) make the helmet. The company had extensive experience in making bicycle helmets. Progressive would then take the helmets made by Leadville Barts and do the rest. Bob had a greater risk. He estimated that he could lose $10,000 per month in a poor market or $4,000 in an average market. A good market for Ski Right would result in $6,000 profit for Bob, and an excellent market would mean a $12,000 profit per month.

A third option for Bob was to use TalRad (TR), a radio company in Tallahassee, Florida. TalRad had extensive experience in making military radios. TalRad could also make the helmets, and Progressive Products could do the rest of production and distribution. Again, Bob would be taking on greater risk. A poor market would mean a $15,000 loss per month, and an average market would mean a $10,000 loss. A good market would result in a net profit of $7,000 for Bob. An excellent market would return $13,000 per month.

Bob could also have Celestial Cellular (CC) develop the cell phones. Thus, another option was to have Celestial make the phones and have Progressive do the rest of the production and distribution. Because the cell phone was the most expensive component of the helmet, Bob could lose $30,000 per month in a poor market. He could lose $20,000 in an average market. If the market was good or excellent, Bob would see a net profit of $10,000 or $30,000 per month, respectively.

Bob's final option was to forget about Progressive Products entirely. He could use Leadville Barts to make the helmets, Celestial Cellular to make the phones, and TalRad to make the AM/FM stereo radios. Bob could then hire some friends to assemble everything and market the finished Ski Right helmets. With this final alternative, Bob could realize a net profit of $55,000 a month in an excellent market. Even if the market was just good, Bob would net $20,000. An average market, however, would mean a loss of $35,000. If the market was poor Bob would lose $60,000 per month.

Discussion Questions

1. What do you recommend?
2. Compute the expected value of perfect information.
3. Was Bob completely logical in how he approached this decision problem?

Source: B. Render, R. M. Stair, and M. Hanna, *Quantitative Analysis for Management*, 10th ed. Upper Saddle River, N.J.: Prentice Hall (2009). Reprinted by permission of Prentice Hall, Inc.

Additional Case Study

See our Companion Web site at **www.prenhall.com/heizer** *for this additional free case study:*

- **Arctic, Inc.:** A refrigeration company has several major options with regard to capacity and expansion.

Bibliography

Balakrishnan, R., B. Render, and R. M. Stair, Jr. *Managerial Decision Modeling with Spreadsheets*, 2nd ed. Upper Saddle River, NJ: Prentice Hall (2007).

Collin, Ian. "Scale Management and Risk Assessment for Deepwater Developments." *World Oil* 224, no. 5 (May 2003): 62.

Hammond, J. S., R. L. Kenney, and H. Raiffa. "The Hidden Traps in Decision Making." 76, no. 5 *Harvard Business Review* (September–October 1998): 47–60.

Keefer, Donald L. "Balancing Drug Safety and Efficacy for a Go/No-Go Decision." *Interfaces* 34, no. 2 (March–April 2004): 113–116.

Lin, H. "Decision Theory and Analysis." *Futurics* 28, no. 1–2 (2004): 27–47.

Miller, C. C., and R. D. Ireland. "Intuition in Strategic Decision Making." *Academy of Management Executive* 19, no. 1 (February 2005): 19.

Raiffa, H., and R. Schlaifer. *Applied Statistical Decision Theory.* New York: Wiley (2000).

Render, B., R. M. Stair Jr., and M. Hanna. *Quantitative Analysis for Management*, 10th ed. Upper Saddle River, NJ: Prentice Hall (2009).

Solutions to Even Numbered Problems

2 (a)

Size of First Station	Good Market ($)	Fair Market ($)	Poor Market ($)	EV Under Equally Likely
Small	50,000	20,000	−10,000	20,000
Medium	80,000	30,000	−20,000	30,000
Large	100,000	30,000	−40,000	30,000
Very large	300,000	25,000	−160,000	55,000

(b) Maximax: Build a very large station.
(c) Maximin: Build a small station.
(d) Equally likely: Build a very large station.

(e)

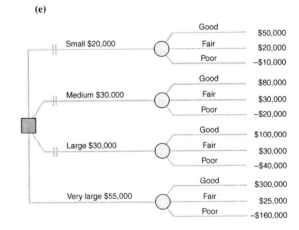

4 (a) Alternatives: N, M, L, D. States of nature: Fixed, Slight Increase, Major Increase

   (b) Use maximin criterion. No floor space (*N*).

6 Buying equipment at $733,333

8 (a) E(cost full-time) = $520

      E(cost part-timers) = $475

10 Alternative B; 74

12 8 cases; EMV = $352.50

14 (a)

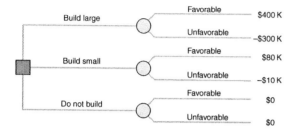

   (b) Small plant with EMV = $26,000

   (c) EVPI = $134,000

16 (a) Max EMV = $11,700

   (b) EVPI = $13,200 − $11,700 = $1,500

18

20 No information and build large; $4,500.

22 (b) EMV(Y) = 4.2, which is best

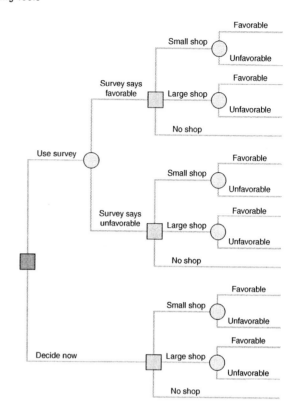

Solutions to Self Test

1. b; 2. c; 3. c; 4. a; 5. a; 6. a; 7. b; 8. a.

Module B

Linear Programming

Linear Programming

Outline

Learning Objectives

When you complete this selection you should be able to

1. Formulate linear programming models, including an objective function and constraints
2. Graphically solve an LP problem with the iso-profit line method
3. Graphically solve an LP problem with the corner-point method
4. Interpret sensitivity analysis and shadow prices
5. Construct and solve a minimization problem
6. Formulate production-mix, diet, and labor scheduling problems

From *Operations Management*, 9/e. Jay Heizer. Barry Render. Copyright © 2008 by Pearson Education. All rights reserved.

The storm front closed in quickly on Chicago's O'Hare Airport, shutting it down without warning. The heavy thunderstorms, lightning, and poor visibility sent American Airlines passengers and ground crew scurrying. Because American Airlines uses linear programming (LP) to schedule flights, hotels, crews, and refueling, LP has a direct impact on profitability. If American gets a major weather disruption at one of its hubs, a lot of flights may get canceled, which means a lot of crews and airplanes in the wrong places. LP is the tool that helps airlines such as American unsnarl and cope with this weather mess.

Harry M. Walker

Many operations management decisions involve trying to make the most effective use of an organization's resources. Resources typically include machinery (such as planes, in the case of an airline), labor (such as pilots), money, time, and raw materials (such as jet fuel). These resources may be used to produce products (such as machines, furniture, food, or clothing) or services (such as airline schedules, advertising policies, or investment decisions). **Linear programming (LP)** is a widely used mathematical technique designed to help operations managers plan and make the decisions necessary to allocate resources.

A few examples of problems in which LP has been successfully applied in operations management are:

1. Scheduling school buses to *minimize* the total distance traveled when carrying students
2. Allocating police patrol units to high crime areas to *minimize* response time to 911 calls
3. Scheduling tellers at banks so that needs are met during each hour of the day while *minimizing* the total cost of labor
4. Selecting the product mix in a factory to make best use of machine- and labor-hours available while *maximizing* the firm's profit
5. Picking blends of raw materials in feed mills to produce finished feed combinations at *minimum* cost
6. Determining the distribution system that will *minimize* total shipping cost from several warehouses to various market locations
7. Developing a production schedule that will satisfy future demands for a firm's product and at the same time *minimize* total production and inventory costs
8. Allocating space for a tenant mix in a new shopping mall so as to *maximize* revenues to the leasing company (see the *OM in Action* box "Using LP to Select Tenants in a Shopping Mall").

REQUIREMENTS OF A LINEAR PROGRAMMING PROBLEM

Linear programming (LP)
A mathematical technique designed to help operations managers plan and make decisions relative to the trade-offs necessary to allocate resources.

All LP problems have four properties in common:

Objective function
A mathematical expression in linear programming that maximizes or minimizes some quantity (often profit or cost, but any goal may be used).

1. LP problems seek to *maximize* or *minimize* some quantity (usually profit or cost). We refer to this property as the **objective function** of an LP problem. The major objective of a typical firm is to maximize dollar profits in the long run. In the case of a trucking or airline distribution system, the objective might be to minimize shipping costs.

Constraints
Restrictions that limit the degree to which a manager can pursue an objective.

2. The presence of restrictions, or **constraints**, limits the degree to which we can pursue our objective. For example, deciding how many units of each product in a firm's product line to manufacture is restricted by available labor and machinery. We want, therefore, to maximize or minimize a quantity (the objective function) subject to limited resources (the constraints).

OM in Action **Using LP to Select Tenants in a Shopping Mall**

Homart Development Company is one of the largest shopping-center developers in the U.S. When starting a new center, Homart produces a tentative floor plan, or "footprint," for the mall. This plan outlines sizes, shapes, and spaces for large department stores. Leasing agreements are reached with the two or three major department stores that will become anchor stores in the mall. The anchor stores are able to negotiate highly favorable occupancy agreements. Homart's profits come primarily from the rent paid by the nonanchor tenants—the smaller stores that lease space along the aisles of the mall. The decision as to allocating space to potential tenants is, therefore, crucial to the success of the investment.

The tenant mix describes the desired stores in the mall by their size, general location, and type of merchandise or service provided. For example, the mix might specify two small jewelry stores in a central section of the mall and a medium-size shoe store and a large restau-rant in one of the side aisles. In the past, Homart devel-oped a plan for tenant mix using "rules of thumb" devel-oped over years of experience in mall development.

Now, to improve its bottom line in an increasingly competitive marketplace, Homart treats the tenant-mix problem as an LP model. First, the model assumes that tenants can be classified into categories according to the type of merchandise or service they provide. Second, the model assumes that for each store type, store sizes can be estimated by distinct category. For example, a small jewelry store is said to contain about 700 square feet and a large one about 2,200 square feet. The tenant-mix model is a powerful tool for enhancing Homart's mall planning and leasing activities.

Sources: Chain Store Age (March 2000): 191–192; *Business World* (March 18, 2002): 1; and *Interfaces* (March–April 1988): 1–9.

3. There must be *alternative courses of action* to choose from. For example, if a company pro-duces three different products, management may use LP to decide how to allocate among them its limited production resources (of labor, machinery, and so on). If there were no alter-natives to select from, we would not need LP.

4. The objective and constraints in linear programming problems must be expressed in terms of *linear equations* or inequalities.

FORMULATING LINEAR PROGRAMMING PROBLEMS

One of the most common linear programming applications is the *product-mix problem.* Two or more products are usually produced using limited resources. The company would like to deter-mine how many units of each product it should produce to maximize overall profit given its lim-ited resources. Let's look at an example.

Shader Electronics Example

The Shader Electronics Company produces two products: (1) the Shader x-pod, a portable music player, and (2) the Shader BlueBerry, an internet-connected color telephone. The production process for each product is similar in that both require a certain number of hours of electronic work and a certain number of labor-hours in the assembly department. Each x-pod takes 4 hours of electronic work and 2 hours in the assembly shop. Each BlueBerry requires 3 hours in elec-tronics and 1 hour in assembly. During the current production period, 240 hours of electronic time are available, and 100 hours of assembly department time are available. Each x-pod sold yields a profit of $7; each BlueBerry produced may be sold for a $5 profit.

Shader's problem is to determine the best possible combination of x-pods and BlueBerrys to manufacture to reach the maximum profit. This product-mix situation can be formulated as a lin-ear programming problem.

We begin by summarizing the information needed to formulate and solve this problem (see Table 1). Further, let's introduce some simple notation for use in the objective function and con-straints. Let:

$$X_1 = \text{number of x-pods to be produced}$$
$$X_2 = \text{number of BlueBerrys to be produced}$$

 Active Model B.1

This example is further illustrated in Active Model B.1 on the CD-ROM.

We name the decision variables X_1 and X_2 here but point out that any notation (e.g., x-p and B) would be fine as well.

▶ **Table 1**

Shader Electronics Company Problem Data

	Hours Required to Produce One Unit		
Department	x-pods (X_1)	BlueBerrys (X_2)	Available Hours This Week
Electronic	4	3	240
Assembly	2	1	100
Profit per unit	$7	$5	

Now we can create the LP *objective function* in terms of X_1 and X_2:

$$\text{Maximize profit} = \$7X_1 + \$5X_2$$

Our next step is to develop mathematical relationships to describe the two constraints in this problem. One general relationship is that the amount of a resource used is to be less than or equal to ($\leq$) the amount of resource *available*.

First constraint: Electronic time used is $\leq$ Electronic time available.

$$4X_1 + 3X_2 \leq 240 \text{ (hours of electronic time)}$$

Second constraint: Assembly time used is $\leq$ Assembly time available.

$$2X_1 + 1X_2 \leq 100 \text{ (hours of assembly time)}$$

Both these constraints represent production capacity restrictions and, of course, affect the total profit. For example, Shader Electronics cannot produce 70 x-pods during the production period because if $X_1 = 70$, both constraints will be violated. It also cannot make $X_1 = 50$ x-pods and $X_2 = 10$ BlueBerrys. This constraint brings out another important aspect of linear programming; that is, certain interactions will exist between variables. The more units of one product that a firm produces, the fewer it can make of other products.

GRAPHICAL SOLUTION TO A LINEAR PROGRAMMING PROBLEM

The easiest way to solve a small LP problem such as that of the Shader Electronics Company is the **graphical solution approach**. The graphical procedure can be used only when there are two **decision variables** (such as number of x-pods to produce, X_1, and number of BlueBerrys to produce, X_2). When there are more than two variables, it is *not* possible to plot the solution on a two-dimensional graph; we then must turn to more complex approaches described later in this module.

Graphical Representation of Constraints

To find the optimal solution to a linear programming problem, we must first identify a set, or region, of feasible solutions. The first step in doing so is to plot the problem's constraints on a graph.

The variable X_1 (x-pods, in our example) is usually plotted as the horizontal axis of the graph, and the variable X_2 (BlueBerrys) is plotted as the vertical axis. The complete problem may be restated as:

$$\text{Maximize profit} = \$7X_1 + \$5X_2$$

Subject to the constraints:

$$4X_1 + 3X_2 \leq 240 \text{ (\emph{electronics constraint})}$$
$$2X_1 + 1X_2 \leq 100 \text{ (\emph{assembly constraint})}$$
$$X_1 \geq 0 \text{ (\emph{number of x-pods produced is greater than or equal to} 0)}$$
$$X_2 \geq 0 \text{ (\emph{number of BlueBerrys produced is greater than or equal to} 0)}$$

The first step in graphing the constraints of the problem is to convert the constraint *inequalities* into *equalities* (or equations).

$$\text{Constraint A:} \quad 4X_1 + 3X_2 = 240$$
$$\text{Constraint B:} \quad 2X_1 + 1X_2 = 100$$

The equation for constraint A is plotted in Figure 1 and for constraint B in Figure 2.

Learning Objective

1. Formulate linear programming models, including an objective function and constraints

Graphical solution approach
A means of plotting a solution to a two-variable problem on a graph.

Decision variables
Choices available to a decision maker.

These last two constraints are also called the nonnegativity constraints.

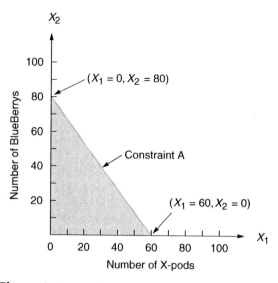

Figure 1 Constraint A

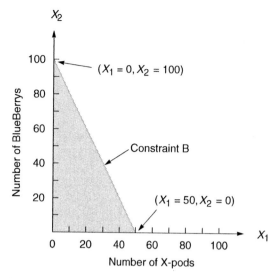

Figure 2 Constraint B

To plot the line in Figure 1, all we need to do is to find the points at which the line $4X_1 + 3X_2 = 240$ intersects the X_1 and X_2 axes. When $X_1 = 0$ (the location where the line touches the X_2 axis), it implies that $3X_2 = 240$ and that $X_2 = 80$. Likewise, when $X_2 = 0$, we see that $4X_1 = 240$ and that $X_1 = 60$. Thus, constraint A is bounded by the line running from ($X_1 = 0, X_2 = 80$) to ($X_1 = 60, X_2 = 0$). The shaded area represents all points that satisfy the original *inequality*.

Constraint B is illustrated similarly in Figure 2. When $X_1 = 0$, then $X_2 = 100$; and when $X_2 = 0$, then $X_1 = 50$. Constraint B, then, is bounded by the line between ($X_1 = 0$, $X_2 = 100$) and ($X_1 = 50$, $X_2 = 0$). The shaded area represents the original inequality.

Figure 3 shows both constraints together. The shaded region is the part that satisfies both restrictions. The shaded region in Figure 3 is called the *area of feasible solutions*, or simply the **feasible region**. This region must satisfy *all* conditions specified by the program's constraints and is thus the region where all constraints overlap. Any point in the region would be a *feasible solution* to the Shader Electronics Company problem. Any point outside the shaded area would represent an *infeasible solution*. Hence, it would be feasible to manufacture 30 x-pods and 20 BlueBerrys ($X_1 = 30$, $X_2 = 20$), but it would violate the constraints to produce 70 x-pods and 40 BlueBerrys. This can be seen by plotting these points on the graph of Figure 3.

Feasible region
The set of all feasible combinations of decision variables.

Iso-Profit Line Solution Method

Now that the feasible region has been graphed, we can proceed to find the *optimal* solution to the problem. The optimal solution is the point lying in the feasible region that produces the highest profit.

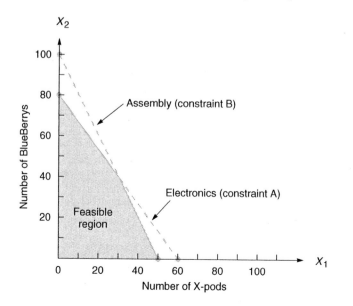

Figure 3

Feasible Solution Region for the Shader Electronics Company Problem

Iso-profit line method

An approach to solving a linear programming maximization problem graphically.

Once the feasible region has been established, several approaches can be taken in solving for the optimal solution. The speediest one to apply is called the **iso-profit line method**.[1]

We start by letting profits equal some arbitrary but small dollar amount. For the Shader Electronics problem, we may choose a profit of $210. This is a profit level that can easily be obtained without violating either of the two constraints. The objective function can be written as $210 = 7X_1 + 5X_2$.

This expression is just the equation of a line; we call it an *iso-profit line*. It represents all combinations (of X_1, X_2) that will yield a total profit of $210. To plot the profit line, we proceed exactly as we did to plot a constraint line. First, let $X_1 = 0$ and solve for the point at which the line crosses the X_2 axis:

$$\$210 = \$7(0) + \$5X_2$$
$$X_2 = 42 \text{ BlueBerrys}$$

Learning Objective

2. Graphically solve an LP problem with the iso-profit line method

Then let $X_2 = 0$ and solve for X_1:

$$\$210 = \$7X_1 + \$5(0)$$
$$X_1 = 30 \text{ x-pods}$$

We can now connect these two points with a straight line. This profit line is illustrated in Figure 4. All points on the line represent feasible solutions that produce a profit of $210.

We see, however, that the iso-profit line for $210 does not produce the highest possible profit to the firm. In Figure 5, we try graphing three more lines, each yielding a higher profit. The middle equation, $280 = 7X_1 + 5X_2$, was plotted in the same fashion as the lower line. When $X_1 = 0$:

$$\$280 = \$7(0) + 5X_2$$
$$X_2 = 56 \text{ BlueBerrys}$$

When $X_2 = 0$:

$$\$280 = \$7X_1 + \$5(0)$$
$$X_1 = 40 \text{ x-pods}$$

Again, any combination of x-pods (X_1) and BlueBerrys (X_2) on this iso-profit line will produce a total profit of $280.

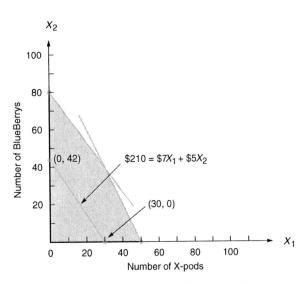

▲ **Figure 4** A Profit Line of $210 Plotted for the Shader Electronics Company

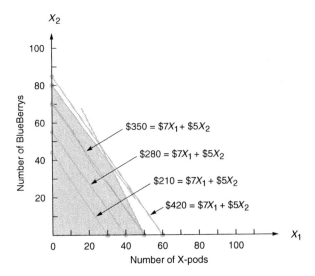

▲ **Figure 5** Four Iso-Profit Lines Plotted for the Shader Electronics Company

[1]*Iso* means "equal" or "similar." Thus, an iso-profit line represents a line with all profits the same, in this case $210.

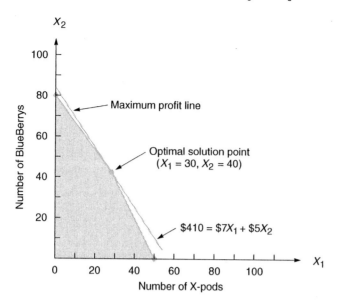

◁ **Figure 6**

**Optimal Solution for
the Shader Electronics
Problem**

Note that the third line generates a profit of $350, even more of an improvement. The farther we move from the 0 origin, the higher our profit will be. Another important point to note is that these iso-profit lines are parallel. We now have two clues as to how to find the optimal solution to the original problem. We can draw a series of parallel profit lines (by carefully moving our ruler in a plane parallel to the first profit line). The highest profit line that still touches some point of the feasible region will pinpoint the optimal solution. Notice that the fourth line ($420) is too high to count because it does not touch the feasible region.

The highest possible iso-profit line is illustrated in Figure 6. It touches the tip of the feasible region at the corner point ($X_1 = 30$, $X_2 = 40$) and yields a profit of $410.

Corner-Point Solution Method

A second approach to solving linear programming problems employs the **corner-point method**. This technique is simpler in concept than the iso-profit line approach, but it involves looking at the profit at every corner point of the feasible region.

The mathematical theory behind linear programming states that an optimal solution to any problem (that is, the values of X_1, X_2 that yield the maximum profit) will lie at a *corner point*, or *extreme point*, of the feasible region. Hence, it is necessary to find only the values of the variables at each corner; the maximum profit or optimal solution will lie at one (or more) of them.

Once again we can see (in Figure 7) that the feasible region for the Shader Electronics Company problem is a four-sided polygon with four corner, or extreme, points. These points are

Corner-point method

A method for solving graphical linear programming problems.

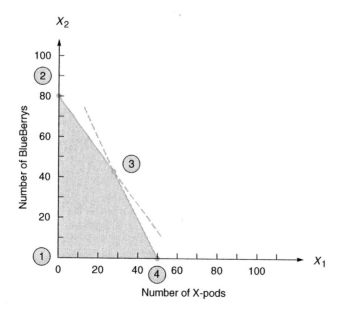

◁ **Figure 7**

**The Four Corner Points
of the Feasible Region**

Learning Objective

3. Graphically solve an LP problem with the corner-point method

labeled ①, ②, ③ and ④ on the graph. To find the (X_1, X_2) values producing the maximum profit, we find out what the coordinates of each corner point are, then determine and compare their profit levels:

Point ① $(X_1 = 0, X_2 = 0)$ Profit $\$7(0) + \$5(0) = \$0$

Point ② $(X_1 = 0, X_2 = 80)$ Profit $\$7(0) + \$5(80) = \$400$

Point ③ $(X_1 = 50, X_2 = 0)$ Profit $\$7(50) + \$5(0) = \$350$

We skipped corner point ③ momentarily because to find its coordinates *accurately*, we will have to solve for the intersection of the two constraint lines. As you may recall from algebra, we can apply the method of *simultaneous equations* to the two constraint equations:

$$4X_1 + 3X_2 = 240 \quad (electronics\ time)$$
$$2X_1 + 1X_2 = 100 \quad (assembly\ time)$$

To solve these equations simultaneously, we multiply the second equation by –2:

$$-2(2X_1 + 1X_2 = 100) = -4X_1 - 2X_2 = -200$$

and then add it to the first equation:

$$+4X_1 + 3X_2 = 240$$
$$-4X_1 - 2X_2 = -200$$
$$+ 1X_2 = 40$$

or:

$$X_2 = 40$$

Doing this has enabled us to eliminate one variable, X_1, and to solve for X_2. We can now substitute 40 for X_2 in either of the original equations and solve for X_1. Let us use the first equation. When $X_2 = 40$, then:

$$4X_1 + 3(40) = 240$$
$$4X_1 + 120 = 240$$

or:

$$4X_1 = 120$$
$$X_1 = 30$$

Although the values for X_1 and X_2 are integers for Shader Electronics, this will not always be the case.

Thus, point ③ has the coordinates $(X_1 = 30, X_2 = 40)$. We can compute its profit level to complete the analysis:

Point ③: $(X_1 = 30, X_2 = 40)$ Profit = $\$7(30) + \$5(40) = \$410$

Because point ③ produces the highest profit of any corner point, the product mix of $X_1 = 30$ x-pods and $X_2 = 40$ BlueBerrys is the optimal solution to the Shader Electronics problem. This solution will yield a profit of $410 per production period; it is the same solution we obtained using the iso-profit line method.

SENSITIVITY ANALYSIS

Parameter
Numerical value that is given in a model.

Sensitivity analysis
An analysis that projects how much a solution may change if there are changes in the variables or input data.

Operations managers are usually interested in more than the optimal solution to an LP problem. In addition to knowing the value of each decision variable (the X_is) and the value of the objective function, they want to know how sensitive these answers are to input **parameter** changes. For example, what happens if the coefficients of the objective function are not exact, or if they change by 10% or 15%? What happens if right-hand-side values of the constraints change? Because solutions are based on the assumption that input parameters are constant, the subject of sensitivity analysis comes into play. **Sensitivity analysis**, or postoptimality analysis, is the study of how sensitive solutions are to parameter changes.

► **Program 1**

Sensitivity Analysis for Shader Electronics Using Excel's Solver

There are two approaches to determining just how sensitive an optimal solution is to changes. The first is simply a trial-and-error approach. This approach usually involves resolving the entire problem, preferably by computer, each time one input data item or parameter is changed. It can take a long time to test a series of possible changes in this way.

The approach we prefer is the analytic postoptimality method. After an LP problem has been solved, we determine a range of changes in problem parameters that will not affect the optimal solution or change the variables in the solution. This is done without resolving the whole problem. LP software, such as Excel's Solver or POM for Windows, has this capability. Let us examine several scenarios relating to the Shader Electronics example.

Program 1 is part of the Excel Solver computer-generated output available to help a decision maker know whether a solution is relatively insensitive to reasonable changes in one or more of the parameters of the problem. (The complete computer run for these data, including input and full output, is illustrated in Programs 2 and 3 later in this module.)

Learning Objective

4. Interpret sensitivity analysis and shadow prices

Sensitivity Report

The Excel *Sensitivity Report* for the Shader Electronics example in Program 1 has two distinct components: (1) a table titled Adjustable Cells and (2) a table titled Constraints. These tables permit us to answer several what-if questions regarding the problem solution.

It is important to note that while using the information in the sensitivity report to answer what-if questions, we assume that we are considering a change to only a *single* input data value. That is, the sensitivity information does not always apply to simultaneous changes in several input data values.

The *Adjustable Cells* table presents information regarding the impact of changes to the objective function coefficients (i.e., the unit profits of $7 and $5) on the optimal solution. The *Constraints* table presents information related to the impact of changes in constraint right-hand-side (RHS) values (i.e., the 240 hours and 100 hours) on the optimal solution. Although different LP software packages may format and present these tables differently, the programs all provide essentially the same information.

The Sensitivity Report has two parts: Adjustable Cells and Constraints.

We are analyzing only one change at a time.

Changes in the Resources or Right-Hand-Side Values

The right-hand-side values of the constraints often represent resources available to the firm. The resources could be labor-hours or machine time or perhaps money or production materials available. In the Shader Electronics example, the two resources are hours available of electronics time and hours of assembly time. If additional hours were available, a higher total profit could be realized. How much should the company be willing to pay for additional hours? Is it profitable to

423

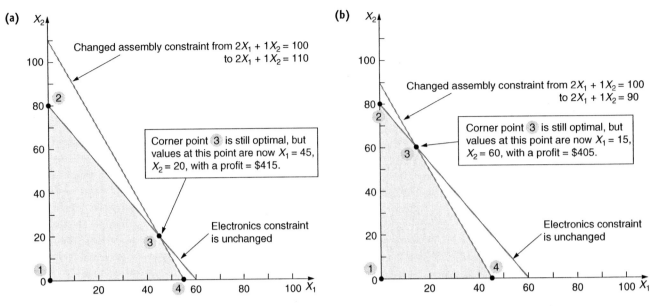

(a) *(Changed assembly constraint from $2X_1 + 1X_2 = 100$ to $2X_1 + 1X_2 = 110$)*

Corner point 3 is still optimal, but values at this point are now $X_1 = 45$, $X_2 = 20$, with a profit = $415.

Electronics constraint is unchanged

(b) *(Changed assembly constraint from $2X_1 + 1X_2 = 100$ to $2X_1 + 1X_2 = 90$)*

Corner point 3 is still optimal, but values at this point are now $X_1 = 15$, $X_2 = 60$, with a profit = $405.

Electronics constraint is unchanged

▲ **Figure 8**   Shader Electronics Sensitivity Analysis on Right-Hand-Side (RHS) Resources

---

If the size of the feasible region increases, the optimal objective function value could improve.

Shadow price (or dual)
The value of one additional unit of a scarce resource in LP.

The shadow price is valid only as long as the change in the RHS is within the Allowable Increase and Allowable Decrease values.

have some additional electronics hours? Should we be willing to pay for more assembly time? Sensitivity analysis about these resources will help us answer these questions.

If the right-hand side of a constraint is changed, the feasible region will change (unless the constraint is redundant), and often the optimal solution will change. In the Shader example, there were 100 hours of assembly time available each week and the maximum possible profit was $410. If the available assembly hours are *increased* to 110 hours, the new optimal solution seen in Figure 8(a) is (45,20) and the profit is $415. Thus, the extra 10 hours of time resulted in an increase in profit of $5 or $0.50 per hour. If the hours are *decreased* to 90 hours as shown in Figure 8(b), the new optimal solution is (15,60) and the profit is $405. Thus, reducing the hours by 10 results in a decrease in profit of $5 or $0.50 per hour. This $0.50 per hour change in profit that resulted from a change in the hours available is called the shadow price, or **dual** value. The **shadow price** for a constraint is the improvement in the objective function value that results from a one-unit increase in the right-hand side of the constraint.

Validity Range for the Shadow Price   Given that Shader Electronics' profit increases by $0.50 for each additional hour of assembly time, does it mean that Shader can do this indefinitely, essentially earning infinite profit? Clearly, this is illogical. How far can Shader increase its assembly time availability and still earn an extra $0.50 profit per hour? That is, for what level of increase in the RHS value of the assembly time constraint is the shadow price of $0.50 valid?

The shadow price of $0.50 is valid as long as the available assembly time stays in a range within which all current corner points continue to exist. The information to compute the upper and lower limits of this range is given by the entries labeled Allowable Increase and Allowable Decrease in the *Sensitivity Report* in Program 1. In Shader's case, these values show that the shadow price of $0.50 for assembly time availability is valid for an increase of up to 20 hours from the current value and a decrease of up to 20 hours. That is, the available assembly time can range from a low of 80 (= 100 − 20) to a high of 120 (= 100 +20) for the shadow price of $0.50 to be valid. Note that the allowable decrease implies that for each hour of assembly time that Shader loses (up to 20 hours), its profit decreases by $0.50.

Changes in the Objective Function Coefficient

Let us now focus on the information provided in Program B.1 titled Adjustable Cells. Each row in the Adjustable Cells table contains information regarding a decision variable (i.e., x-pods or BlueBerrys) in the LP model.

424

Allowable Ranges for Objective Function Coefficients As the unit profit contribution of either product changes, the slope of the iso-profit lines we saw earlier in Figure 5 changes. The size of the feasible region, however, remains the same. That is, the locations of the corner points do not change.

The limits to which the profit coefficient of x-pods or BlueBerrys can be changed without affecting the optimality of the current solution is revealed by the values in the Allowable Increase and Allowable Decrease columns of the *Sensitivity Report* in Program 1. The allowable increase in the objective function coefficient for BlueBerrys is only $0.25. In contrast, the allowable decrease is $1.50. Hence, if the unit profit of BlueBerrys drops to $4 (i.e., a decrease of $1 from the current value of $5), it is still optimal to produce 30 x-pods and 40 BlueBerrys. The total profit will drop to $370 (from $410) because each BlueBerry now yields less profit (of $1 per unit). However, if the unit profit drops below $3.50 per BlueBerry (i.e., a decrease of more than $1.50 from the current $5 profit), the current solution is no longer optimal. The LP problem will then have to be resolved using Solver, or other software, to find the new optimal corner point.

> *There is an allowable decrease and an allowable increase for each objective function coefficient over which the current optimal solution remains optimal.*

> *A new corner point becomes optimal if an objective function coefficient is decreased or increased too much.*

SOLVING MINIMIZATION PROBLEMS

Many linear programming problems involve *minimizing* an objective such as cost instead of maximizing a profit function. A restaurant, for example, may wish to develop a work schedule to meet staffing needs while minimizing the total number of employees. Also, a manufacturer may seek to distribute its products from several factories to its many regional warehouses in such a way as to minimize total shipping costs.

Minimization problems can be solved graphically by first setting up the feasible solution region and then using either the corner-point method or an **iso-cost** line approach (which is analogous to the iso-profit approach in maximization problems) to find the values of X_1 and X_2 that yield the minimum cost.

Example 1 shows how to solve a minimization problem.

> **Learning Objective**
>
> 5. Construct and solve a minimization problem

> **Iso-cost**
> An approach to solving a linear programming minimization problem graphically.

> **EXAMPLE 1**
>
> A minimization problem with two variables

Cohen Chemicals, Inc., produces two types of photo-developing fluids. The first, a black-and-white picture chemical, costs Cohen $2,500 per ton to produce. The second, a color photo chemical, costs $3,000 per ton.

Based on an analysis of current inventory levels and outstanding orders, Cohen's production manager has specified that at least 30 tons of the black-and-white chemical and at least 20 tons of the color chemical must be produced during the next month. In addition, the manager notes that an existing inventory of a highly perishable raw material needed in both chemicals must be used within 30 days. To avoid wasting the expensive raw material, Cohen must produce a total of at least 60 tons of the photo chemicals in the next month.

Approach: Formulate this information as a minimization LP problem.

Let:

X_1 = number of tons of black-and-white picture chemical produced

X_2 = number of tons of color picture chemical produced

Objective: Minimize cost = $2,500X_1 + $3,000X_2$

Subject to:

$$X_1 \geq 30 \text{ tons of black-and-white chemical}$$

$$X_2 \geq 20 \text{ tons of color chemical}$$

$$X_1 + X_2 \geq 60 \text{ tons total}$$

$$X_1, X_2 \geq 0 \text{ nonnegativity requirements}$$

Solution: To solve the Cohen Chemicals problem graphically, we construct the problem's feasible region, shown in Figure 9.

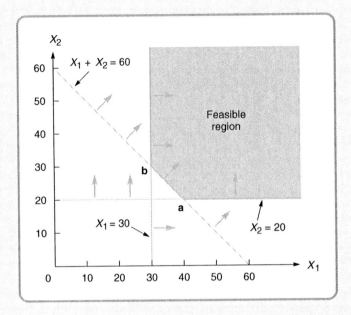

Minimization problems are often unbounded outward (that is, on the right side and on the top), but this characteristic causes no problem in solving them. As long as they are bounded inward (on the left side and the bottom), we can establish corner points. The optimal solution will lie at one of the corners.

In this case, there are only two corner points, **a** and **b**, in Figure 9. It is easy to determine that at point **a**, $X_1 = 40$ and $X_2 = 20$, and that at point **b**, $X_1 = 30$ and $X_2 = 30$. The optimal solution is found at the point yielding the lowest total cost.

Thus:

$$\text{Total cost at } \mathbf{a} = 2,500X_1 + 3,000X_2$$
$$= 2,500(40) + 3,000(20)$$
$$= \$160,000$$
$$\text{Total cost at } \mathbf{b} = 2,500X_1 + 3,000X_2$$
$$= 2,500(30) + 3,000(30)$$
$$= \$165,000$$

The lowest cost to Cohen Chemicals is at point **a**. Hence the operations manager should produce 40 tons of the black-and-white chemical and 20 tons of the color chemical.

Insight: The area is either not bounded to the right or above in a minimization problem (as it is in a maximization problem).

Learning exercise: Cohen's second constraint is recomputed and should be $X_2 \geq 15$. Does anything change in the answer? [Answer: Now $X_1 = 45$, $X_2 = 15$, and Total cost = \$157,500.]

Related problems: 3, 5, 6, 11, 12, 22, 24

LINEAR PROGRAMMING APPLICATIONS

The foregoing examples each contained just two variables (X_1 and X_2). Most real-world problems contain many more variables, however. Let's use the principles already developed to formulate a few more-complex problems. The practice you will get by "paraphrasing" the following LP situations should help develop your skills for applying linear programming to other common operations situations.

OM in Action **Continental and Delta Save $100s of Millions with LP**

It has been said that an airline seat is the most perishable commodity in the world. Each time an airliner takes off with an empty seat, a revenue opportunity is lost forever. For Continental, Delta, and other major airlines, which each fly thousands of flight legs per day on hundreds of planes, the schedule is their very heartbeat. These schedules, all developed with massive LP models (Delta's program has 40,000 constraints and 60,000 variables), assign aircraft to specific routes and assign pilots and flight attendants to each of these aircraft.

One flight leg for Continental might consist of a Boeing 777 assigned to fly at 7:05 A.M. from Houston to Chicago to arrive at 9:15 A.M. Continental's problem, like that of Delta and every other competitor, is to match planes such as 737s, 767s, or 777s to flight legs such as Houston–Chicago and to fill seats with paying passengers. And when schedule disruptions occur due to a hur-

ricane (like Katrina in 2005), mechanical problems, or crew unavailability, planes and people are often in the wrong place.

That is why Continental runs its *Crew Solver* and *OptSolver* systems and Delta runs its *ColdStart* model every day. These LP models include constraints such as aircraft availability, maintenance needs, crew training requirements, arrival/departure needs, and so on. The airlines' objectives are to minimize a combination of operating costs and lost passenger revenue, called "spill costs."

The savings from LP have been about $100 million per year at Continental and $300 million per year at the larger Delta Air Lines.

Sources: Interfaces (July–August 2004): 253–271, (January–February 2003): 5–22, and (September–October 1999): 123–131.

Production-Mix Example

Example 2 involves another *production-mix* decision. Limited resources must be allocated among various products that a firm produces. The firm's overall objective is to manufacture the selected products in such quantities as to maximize total profits.

EXAMPLE 2

A production mix problem

Failsafe Electronics Corporation primarily manufactures four highly technical products, which it supplies to aerospace firms that hold NASA contracts. Each of the products must pass through the following departments before they are shipped: wiring, drilling, assembly, and inspection. The time requirements in each department (in hours) for each unit produced and its corresponding profit value are summarized in this table:

	Department				
Product	**Wiring**	**Drilling**	**Assembly**	**Inspection**	**Unit Profit**
XJ201	.5	3	2	.5	$ 9
XM897	1.5	1	4	1.0	$12
TR29	1.5	2	1	.5	$15
BR788	1.0	3	2	.5	$11

The production time available in each department each month and the minimum monthly production requirement to fulfill contracts are as follows:

Department	Capacity (hours)	Product	Minimum Production Level
Wiring	1,500	XJ201	150
Drilling	2,350	XM897	100
Assembly	2,600	TR29	200
Inspection	1,200	BR788	400

Approach: Formulate this production-mix situation as an LP problem. The production manager first specifies production levels for each product for the coming month. He lets:

X_1 = number of units of XJ201 produced

X_2 = number of units of XM897 produced

X_3 = number of units of TR29 produced

X_4 = number of units of BR788 produced

Solution: The LP formulation is:

Objective: Maximize profit = $9X_1 + 12X_2 + 15X_3 + 11X_4$

subject to:

$$.5X_1 + 1.5X_2 + 1.5X_3 + 1X_4 \leq 1,500 \text{ hours of wiring available}$$
$$3X_1 + 1X_2 + 2X_3 + 3X_4 \leq 2,350 \text{ hours of drilling available}$$
$$2X_1 + 4X_2 + 1X_3 + 2X_4 \leq 2,600 \text{ hours of assembly available}$$
$$.5X_1 + 1X_2 + .5X_3 + .5X_4 \leq 1,200 \text{ hours of inspection}$$
$$X_1 \geq 150 \text{ units of XJ201}$$
$$X_2 \geq 100 \text{ units of XM897}$$
$$X_3 \geq 200 \text{ units of TR29}$$
$$X_4 \geq 400 \text{ units of BR788}$$
$$X_1, X_2, X_3, X_4 \geq 0$$

Insight: There can be numerous constraints in an LP problem. The constraint right-hand sides may be in different units, but the objective function uses one common unit—dollars of profit, in this case. Because there are more than two decision variables, this problem is not solved graphically.

Learning exercise: Solve this LP problem as formulated. What is the solution? [Answer: $X_1 = 150$, $X_2 = 300$, $X_3 = 200$, $X_4 = 400$.]

Related problems: 7, 8, 10, 19, 20, 21, 23, 28, 29

Diet Problem Example

Example B3 illustrates the *diet problem*, which was originally used by hospitals to determine the most economical diet for patients. Known in agricultural applications as the *feed-mix problem*, the diet problem involves specifying a food or feed ingredient combination that will satisfy stated nutritional requirements at a minimum cost level.

EXAMPLE 3

A diet problem

The Feed 'N Ship feedlot fattens cattle for local farmers and ships them to meat markets in Kansas City and Omaha. The owners of the feedlot seek to determine the amounts of cattle feed to buy to satisfy minimum nutritional standards and, at the same time, minimize total feed costs.

Each grain stock contains different amounts of four nutritional ingredients: A, B, C, and D. Here are the ingredient contents of each grain, in *ounces per pound of grain*:

	Feed		
Ingredient	Stock X	Stock Y	Stock Z
A	3 oz	2 oz	4 oz
B	2 oz	3 oz	1 oz
C	1 oz	0 oz	2 oz
D	6 oz	8 oz	4 oz

The cost per pound of grains X, Y, and Z is $0.02, $0.04, and $0.025, respectively. The minimum requirement per cow per month is 64 ounces of ingredient A, 80 ounces of ingredient B, 16 ounces of ingredient C, and 128 ounces of ingredient D.

The feedlot faces one additional restriction—it can obtain only 500 pounds of stock Z per month from the feed supplier, regardless of its need. Because there are usually 100 cows at the Feed 'N Ship feedlot at any given time, this constraint limits the amount of stock Z for use in the feed of each cow to no more than 5 pounds, or 80 ounces, per month.

Approach: Formulate this as a minimization LP problem.

Let: X_1 = number of pounds of stock X purchased per cow each month

X_2 = number of pounds of stock Y purchased per cow each month

X_3 = number of pounds of stock Z purchased per cow each month

Solution:

Objective: Minimize cost = $.02X_1 + .04X_2 + .025X_3$

subject to: Ingredient A requirement: $3X_1 + 2X_2 + 4X_3 \geq 64$

Ingredient B requirement: $2X_1 + 3X_2 + 1X_3 \geq 80$

Ingredient C requirement: $1X_1 + 0X_2 + 2X_3 \geq 16$

Ingredient D requirement: $6X_1 + 8X_2 + 4X_3 \geq 128$

Stock Z limitation: $X_3 \leq 80$

$X_1, X_2, X_3 \geq 0$

The cheapest solution is to purchase 40 pounds of grain X_1, at a cost of $0.80 per cow.

Insight: Because the cost per pound of stock X is so low, the optimal solution excludes grains Y and Z.

Learning exercise: The cost of a pound of stock X just increased by 50%. Does this affect the solution? [Answer: Yes, when the cost per pound of grain X is $0.03, $X_1 = 16$ pounds, $X_2 = 16$ pounds, $X_3 = 0$, and cost = $1.12 per cow.]

Related problems: 6, 30

Labor Scheduling Example

Labor scheduling problems address staffing needs over a specific time period. They are especially useful when managers have some flexibility in assigning workers to jobs that require overlapping or interchangeable talents. Large banks and hospitals frequently use LP to tackle their labor scheduling. Example 4 describes how one bank uses LP to schedule tellers.

EXAMPLE 4

Scheduling bank tellers

Arlington Bank of Commerce and Industry is a busy bank that has requirements for between 10 and 18 tellers depending on the time of day. Lunchtime, from noon to 2 P.M., is usually heaviest. The table below indicates the workers needed at various hours that the bank is open.

Time Period	Number of Tellers Required	Time Period	Number of Tellers Required
9 A.M.–10 A.M.	10	1 P.M.–2 P.M.	18
10 A.M.–11 A.M.	12	2 P.M.–3 P.M.	17
11 A.M.–Noon	14	3 P.M.–4 P.M.	15
Noon–1 P.M.	16	4 P.M.–5 P.M.	10

The bank now employs 12 full-time tellers, but many people are on its roster of available part-time employees. A part-time employee must put in exactly 4 hours per day but can start anytime between 9 A.M. and 1 P.M. Part-timers are a fairly inexpensive labor pool because no retirement or lunch benefits are provided them. Full-timers, on the other hand, work from 9 A.M. to 5 P.M. but are allowed 1 hour for lunch. (Half the full-timers eat at 11 A.M., the other half at noon.) Full-timers thus provide 35 hours per week of productive labor time.

By corporate policy, the bank limits part-time hours to a maximum of 50% of the day's total requirement.

Part-timers earn $6 per hour (or $24 per day) on average, whereas full-timers earn $75 per day in salary and benefits on average.

Approach: The bank would like to set a schedule, using LP, that would minimize its total manpower costs. It will release 1 or more of its full-time tellers if it is profitable to do so.

We can let:

F = full-time tellers

P_1 = part-timers starting at 9 A.M. (leaving at 1 P.M.)

P_2 = part-timers starting at 10 A.M. (leaving at 2 P.M.)

P_3 = part-timers starting at 11 A.M. (leaving at 3 P.M.)

P_4 = part-timers starting at noon (leaving at 4 P.M.)

P_5 = part-timers starting at 1 P.M. (leaving at 5 P.M.)

Solution: Objective function:

$$\text{Minimize total daily manpower cost} = \$75F + \$24(P_1 + P_2 + P_3 + P_4 + P_5)$$

Constraints: For each hour, the available labor-hours must be at least equal to the required labor-hours:

$$F + P_1 \geq 10 \quad \text{(9 A.M. to 10 A.M. needs)}$$
$$F + P_1 + P_2 \geq 12 \quad \text{(10 A.M. to 11 A.M. needs)}$$
$$\tfrac{1}{2}F + P_1 + P_2 + P_3 \geq 14 \quad \text{(11 A.M. to noon needs)}$$
$$\tfrac{1}{2}F + P_1 + P_2 + P_3 + P_4 \geq 16 \quad \text{(noon to 1 P.M. needs)}$$
$$F + P_2 + P_3 + P_4 + P_5 \geq 18 \quad \text{(1 P.M to 2 P.M. needs)}$$
$$F + P_3 + P_4 + P_5 \geq 17 \quad \text{(2 P.M to 3 P.M. needs)}$$
$$F + P_4 + P_5 \geq 15 \quad \text{(3 P.M to 4 P.M. needs)}$$
$$F + P_5 \geq 10 \quad \text{(4 P.M to 5 P.M. needs)}$$

Only 12 full-time tellers are available, so:

$$F \leq 12$$

Part-time worker-hours cannot exceed 50% of total hours required each day, which is the sum of the tellers needed each hour:

$$4(P_1 + P_2 + P_3 + P_4 + P_5) \leq .50(10 + 12 + 14 + 16 + 18 + 17 + 15 + 10)$$

or:

$$4P_1 + 4P_2 + 4P_3 + 4P_4 + 4P_5 \leq 0.50(112)$$
$$F, P_1, P_2, P_3, P_4, P_5 \geq 0$$

There are two alternative optimal schedules that Arlington Bank can follow. The first is to employ only 10 full-time tellers ($F = 10$) and to start 7 part-timers at 10 A.M. ($P_2 = 7$), 2 part-timers at 11 A.M. and noon ($P_3 = 2$ and $P_4 = 2$), and 3 part-timers at 1 P.M. ($P_5 = 3$). No part-timers would begin at 9 A.M.

The second solution also employs 10 full-time tellers, but starts 6 part-timers at 9 A.M. ($P_1 = 6$), 1 part-timer at 10 A.M. ($P_2 = 1$), 2 part-timers at 11 A.M. and noon ($P_3 = 2$ and $P_4 = 2$), and 3 part-timers at 1 P.M. ($P_5 = 3$). The cost of either of these two policies is \$1,086 per day.

Insight: It is not unusual for multiple optimal solutions to exist in large LP problems. In this case, it gives management the option of selecting, at the same cost, between schedules. To find an alternate optimal solution, you may have to enter the constraints in a different sequence.

Learning exercise: The bank decides to give part-time employees a raise to \$7 per hour. Does the solution change? [Answer: Yes, cost = \$1,142, $F = 10$, $P_1 = 6$, $P_2 = 1$, $P_3 = 2$, $P_4 = 5$, $P_5 = 0$.]

Related problem: 18

THE SIMPLEX METHOD OF LP

Simplex method

An algorithm for solving linear programming problems of all sizes.

Most real-world linear programming problems have more than two variables and thus are too complex for graphical solution. A procedure called the **simplex method** may be used to find the optimal solution to such problems. The simplex method is actually an algorithm (or a set of instructions) with which we examine corner points in a methodical fashion until we arrive at the best solution—highest profit or lowest cost. Computer programs (such as Excel OM and POM for Windows) and Excel spreadsheets are available to solve linear programming problems via the simplex method.

For details regarding the algebraic steps of the simplex algorithm, see Tutorial 3 on the CD-ROM that accompanies this book, or refer to a management science textbook.[2]

[2]See, for example, Barry Render, Ralph M. Stair, and Michael Hanna, *Quantitative Analysis for Management*, 9th ed. (Upper Saddle River, NJ: Prentice Hall, 2006): Chapters 7–9; or Raju Balakrishnan, Barry Render, and Ralph M. Stair, *Managerial Decision Modeling with Spreadsheets*, 2nd ed. (Upper Saddle River, NJ: Prentice Hall, 2007): Chapters 2–4.

Summary

This module introduces a special kind of model, linear programming. LP has proven to be especially useful when trying to make the most effective use of an organization's resources.

The first step in dealing with LP models is problem formulation, which involves identifying and creating an objective function and constraints. The second step is to solve the problem. If there are only two decision variables, the problem can be solved graphically, using the corner-point method or the iso-profit/iso-cost line method. With either approach, we first identify the feasible region, then find the corner point yielding the greatest profit or least cost. LP is used in a wide variety of business applications, as the examples and homework problems in this module reveal.

Key Terms

Linear programming (LP)
Objective function
Constraints
Graphical solution approach
Decision variables

Feasible region
Iso-profit line method
Corner-point method
Parameter
Sensitivity analysis

Shadow price (or dual)
Iso-cost
Simplex method

Using Software to Solve LP Problems

All LP problems can also be solved with the simplex method, using software such as Excel OM and POM for Windows or Excel. This approach produces valuable economic information such as the shadow price, or dual, and provides complete sensitivity analysis on other inputs to the problems. Excel uses Solver, which requires that you enter your own constraints. Excel OM and POM for Windows require only that demand data, supply data, and shipping costs be entered. In the following section we illustrate how to create an Excel spreadsheet for LP problems.

Using Excel Spreadsheets

Excel offers the ability to analyze linear programming problems using built-in problem-solving tools. Excel's tool is named Solver. Solver is limited to 200 changing cells (variables), each with 2 boundary constraints and up to 100 additional constraints. These capabilities make Solver suitable for the solution of complex, real-world problems.

We use Excel to set up the Shader Electronics problem in Program 2. The objective and constraints are repeated here:

Objective function: Maximize profit =
$$\$7(\text{No. of x-pods}) + \$5(\text{No. of BlueBerrys})$$
Subject to: $4(\text{x-pods}) + 3(\text{BlueBerrys}) \leq 240$
$$2(\text{x-pods}) + 1(\text{BlueBerry}) \leq 100$$

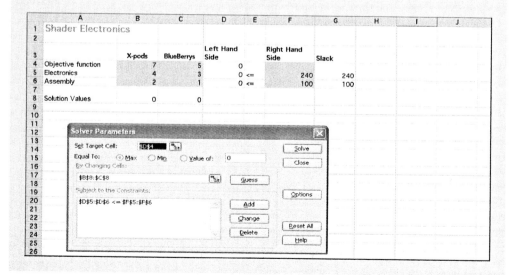

Program 2

Using Excel to Formulate the Shader Electronics Problem

		Computations	
Value	**Cell**	**Excel Formula**	**Action**
Left Hand Side	D4	=SUMPRODUCT($B$8:$C$8,B4:C4)	Copy to D5:D6
Slack	G5	=F5-D5	Copy to G6
			Select Tools, Solver
			Set Solver parameters as displayed
			Press Solve

The Excel screen in Program 3 shows Solver's solution to the Shader Electronics Company problem. Note that the optimal solution is now shown in the *changing cells* (cells B8 and C8, which served as the variables). The Reports selection performs more extensive analysis of the solution and its environment. Excel's sensitivity analysis capability was illustrated earlier in Program 1.

> **Program 3**

Excel Solution to Shader Electronics LP Problem

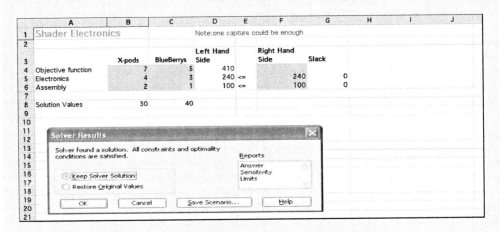

Using Excel OM and POM for Windows

Excel OM and POM for Windows can handle relatively large LP problems. As output, the software provides optimal values for the variables, optimal profit or cost, and sensitivity analysis. In addition, POM for Windows provides graphical output for problems with only two variables.

Solved Problems

Virtual Office Hours help is available on Student DVD.

Solved Problem 1

Smith's, a Niagara, New York clothing manufacturer that produces men's shirts and pajamas, has two primary resources available: sewing-machine time (in the sewing department) and cutting-machine time (in the cutting department). Over the next month, owner Barbara Smith can schedule up to 280 hours of work on sewing machines and up to 450 hours of work on cutting machines. Each shirt produced requires 1.00 hour of sewing time and 1.50 hours of cutting time. Producing each pair of pajamas requires .75 hour of sewing time and 2 hours of cutting time.

To express the LP constraints for this problem mathematically, we let:

$$X_1 = \text{number of shirts produced}$$
$$X_2 = \text{number of pajamas produced}$$

solution

First constraint: $1X_1 + .75X_2 \leq 280$ hours of sewing-machine time available—our first scarce resource

Second constraint: $1.5X_1 + 2X_2 \leq 450$ hours of cutting-machine time available—our second scarce resource

Note: This means that each pair of pajamas takes 2 hours of the cutting resource.

Smith's accounting department analyzes cost and sales figures and states that each shirt produced will yield a $4 contribution to profit and that each pair of pajamas will yield a $3 contribution to profit.

This information can be used to create the LP *objective function* for this problem:

Objective function: maximize total contribution to profit = $4X_1 + $3X_2$

Solved Problem 2

We want to solve the following LP problem for Kevin Caskey Wholesale Inc. using the corner-point method:

Objective: Maximize profit $= \$9X_1 + \$7X_2$

Constraints: $2X_1 + 1X_2 \leq 40$

$X_1 + 3X_2 \leq 30$

$X_1, X_2 \geq 0$

solution

Figure 10 illustrates these constraints:

Corner-point **a**: $(X_1 = 0, X_2 = 0)$ Profit $= 0$

Corner-point **b**: $(X_1 = 0, X_2 = 10)$ Profit $= 9(0) + 7(10) = \$70$

Corner-point **d**: $(X_1 = 20, X_2 = 0)$ Profit $= 9(20) + 7(0) = \$180$

Corner-point **c** is obtained by solving equations $2X_1 + 1X_2 = 40$ and $X_1 + 3X_2 = 30$ simultaneously. Multiply the second equation by -2 and add it to the first.

$$2X_1 + 1X_2 = 40$$
$$\underline{-2X_1 + 6X_2 = -60}$$
$$-5X_2 = -20$$

Thus $X_2 = 4$.

And $X_1 + 3(4) = 30$ or $X_1 + 12 = 30$ or $X_1 = 18$

Corner-point **c**: $(X_1 = 18, X_2 = 4)$ Profit $= 9(18) + 7(4) = \$190$

Hence the optimal solution is:

$(x_1 = 18, x_2 = 4)$ Profit $= \$190$

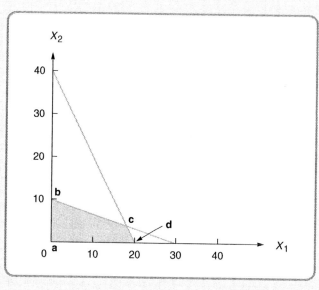

▲ **Figure 10**   K. Caskey Wholesale, Inc.'s Feasible Region

Solved Problem 3

Holiday Meal Turkey Ranch is considering buying two different types of turkey feed. Each feed contains, in varying proportions, some or all of the three nutritional ingredients essential for fattening turkeys. Brand Y feed costs the ranch $.02 per pound. Brand Z costs $.03 per pound. The rancher would like to determine the lowest-cost diet that meets the minimum monthly intake requirement for each nutritional ingredient.

The following table contains relevant information about the composition of brand Y and brand Z feeds, as well as the minimum monthly requirement for each nutritional ingredient per turkey.

	Composition of Each Pound of Feed		
Ingredient	**Brand Y Feed**	**Brand Z Feed**	**Minimum Monthly Requirement**
A	5 oz	10 oz	90 oz
B	4 oz	3 oz	48 oz
C	.5 oz	0	1.5 oz
Cost/lb	$.02	$.03	

solution

If we let:

X_1 = number of pounds of brand Y feed purchased

X_2 = number of pounds of brand Z feed purchased

then we may proceed to formulate this linear programming problem as follows:

Objective: Minimize cost (in cents) $= 2X_1 + 3X_2$

subject to these constraints:

$5X_1 + 10X_2 \geq 90$ oz   (*ingredient A constraint*)

$4X_1 + 3X_2 \geq 48$ oz   (*ingredient B constraint*)

$\frac{1}{2}X_1 \geq 1\frac{1}{2}$ oz   (*ingredient C constraint*)

Figure 11 illustrates these constraints.

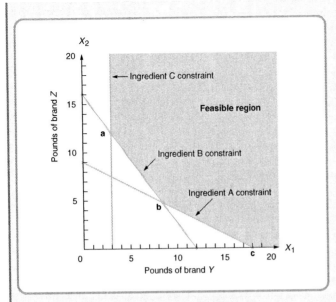

The iso-cost line approach may be used to solve LP minimization problems such as that of the Holiday Meal Turkey Ranch. As with iso-profit lines, we need not compute the cost at each corner point, but instead draw a series of parallel cost lines. The last cost point to touch the feasible region provides us with the optimal solution corner.

For example, we start in Figure 12 by drawing a 54¢ cost line, namely, $54 = 2X_1 + 3X_2$. Obviously, there are many points in the feasible region that would yield a lower total cost. We proceed to move our iso-cost line toward the lower left, in a plane parallel to the 54¢ solution line. The last point we touch while still in contact with the feasible region is the same as corner point **b** of Figure B.11. It has the coordinates ($X_1 = 8.4$, $X_2 = 4.8$) and an associated cost of 31.2 cents.

△ Figure 11 **Feasible Region for the Holiday Meal Turkey Ranch Problem**

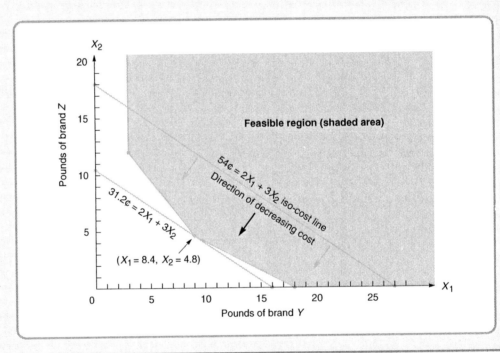

▷ Figure 12

Graphical Solution to the Holiday Meal Turkey Ranch Problem Using the Iso-Cost Line

Note that the last line parallel to the 54¢ iso-cost line that touches the feasible region indicates the optimal corner point.

Active Model Exercise

This Active Model describes the Shader Electronics example maximization problem, which has two less-than-or-equal-to constraints. You can use the scrollbars to change any of the eight numbers in the example or to move the iso-profit line.

Questions

1. By how much does the profit on x-pods need to rise to make it the only product manufactured?

2. By how much does the profit on x-pods need to fall to stop manufacturing it?

3. What happens to the profit as the number of assembly hours available increases by 1 hour at a time? For how many hours is this true?

4. What happens if we can reduce the electronics time for BlueBerrys to 2.5 hours?

LP Graph

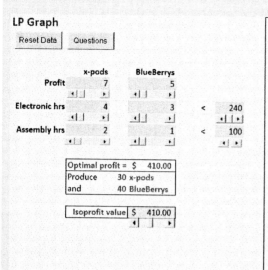

Reset Data   Questions

	x-pods	BlueBerrys		
Profit	7	5		
Electronic hrs	4	3	<	240
Assembly hrs	2	1	<	100

Optimal profit =	$	410.00
Produce	30	x-pods
and	40	BlueBerrys

| Isoprofit value | $ | 410.00 |

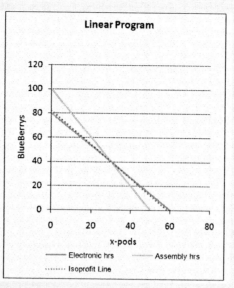

◀ **Active Model B.1**

Analysis of the Shader Electronics Example Data

Self-Test

- ***Before taking the self-test***, *refer to the learning objectives listed at the beginning of the selection and the key terms listed at the end of the selection.*
- *Use the key at the back of the text to **correct** your answers.*
- ***Restudy*** *pages that correspond to any questions you answered incorrectly or material you feel uncertain about.*

1. When using a graphical solution procedure, the region bounded by the set of constraints is called the:
   a) solution
   b) feasible region
   c) infeasible region
   d) maximum profit region
   e) iso region

2. Using the *graphical solution procedure* to solve a maximization problem requires that we:
   a) move the iso-profit line up until it no longer intersects with any constraint equation
   b) move the iso-profit line down until it no longer intersects with any constraint equation
   c) apply the method of simultaneous equations to solve for the intersections of constraints
   d) find the value of the objective function at the origin

3. Which of the following is *not* a property of all linear programming problems?
   a) the presence of restrictions
   b) optimization of some objective
   c) a computer program
   d) alternate courses of action to choose from
   e) usage of only linear equations and inequalities

4. A feasible solution to a linear programming problem:
   a) must satisfy all of the problem's constraints simultaneously
   b) need not satisfy all of the constraints, only some of them
   c) must be a corner point of the feasible region
   d) must give the maximum possible profit

5. Consider the following linear programming problem:

   Maximize $12X + 10Y$
   Subject to: $4X + 3Y \leq 480$
   $2X + 3Y \leq 360$
   $X, Y \geq 0$

   The maximum possible value for the objective function is:
   a) 1,600   d) 1,440
   b) 1,520   e) 0
   c) 1,800

6. Consider the following linear programming problem:

   Maximize $12X + 10Y$
   Subject to: $4X + 3Y \leq 480$
   $2X + 3Y \leq 360$
   $X, Y \geq 0$

   Which of the following points (*X, Y*) is *not* feasible?
   a) (0, 100)   d) (20, 90)
   b) (100, 10)   e) (0, 70)
   c) (70, 70)

7. Consider the following linear programming problem:

   Maximize $4X + 10Y$
   Subject to: $3X + 4Y \leq 480$
   $4X + 2Y \leq 360$
   $X, Y \geq 0$

   The feasible corner points are (48, 84), (0, 120), (0, 0), (90, 0). What is the maximum possible value for the objective function?
   a) 1,032   d) 1,600
   b) 1,200   e) 840
   c) 360

435

Visit our Companion Web site or use your student CD-ROM/DVD to help with material in this module.

 **On Our Companion Web Site,**
www.prenhall.com/heizer
- Self-Study Quizzes
- Practice Problems
- Internet Case
- PowerPoint Lecture

 On Your Student CD-ROM
- Practice Problems
- Active Model Exercise
- POM for Windows

 On Your Student DVD
- Virtual Office Hours for Solved Problems

Discussion Questions

1. List at least four applications of linear programming problems.
2. What is a "corner point"? Explain why solutions to linear programming problems focus on corner points.
3. Define the feasible region of a graphical LP problem. What is a feasible solution?
4. Each linear programming problem that has a feasible region has an infinite number of solutions. Explain.
5. Under what circumstances is the objective function more important than the constraints in a linear programming model?
6. Under what circumstances are the constraints more important than the objective function in a linear programming model?
7. Why is the diet problem, in practice, applicable for animals but not for people?
8. How many feasible solutions are there in a linear program? Which ones do we need to examine to find the optimal solution?

9. Define shadow price (or dual).
10. Explain how to use the iso-cost line in a graphical minimization problem.
11. Compare how the corner-point and iso-profit line methods work for solving graphical problems.
12. Where a constraint crosses the vertical or horizontal axis, the quantity is fairly obvious. How does one go about finding the quantity coordinates where two constraints cross, not at an axis?
13. Suppose a linear programming (maximation) problem has been solved and that the optimal value of the objective function is $300. Suppose an additonal constraint is added to this problem. Explain how this might affect each of the following:
    (a) The feasible region.
    (b) The optimal value of the objective function.

Problems*

• 1 Solve the following linear programming problem graphically:

$$\text{Maximize} \quad Z = 4X + 6Y$$
$$\text{Subject to:} \quad X + 2Y \le 8$$
$$5X + 4Y \le 20$$
$$X, Y \ge 0 \quad \text{PX}$$

2 Solve the following linear programming problem graphically:

$$\text{Maximize} \quad Z = X + 10Y$$
$$\text{Subject to:} \quad 4X + 3Y \le 36$$
$$2X + 4Y \le 40$$
$$Y \ge 3$$
$$X, Y \ge 0 \quad \text{PX}$$

• 3 Solve the following linear program graphically:

$$\text{Minimize} \quad Z = X_1 + X_2$$
$$8X_1 + 16X_2 \ge 64$$
$$X_1 \ge 0$$
$$X_2 \ge -2 \quad \text{PX}$$

*Note: PX means the problem may be solved with POM for Windows and/or Excel or Excel OM.

•• 4 Consider the following linear programming problem:

$$\text{Maximize} \quad Z = 30X_1 + 10X_2$$
$$\text{Subject to:} \quad 3X_1 + X_2 \le 300$$
$$X_1 + X_2 \le 200$$
$$X \le 100$$
$$X_2 \ge 50$$
$$X_1 - X_2 \le 0$$
$$X_1, X_2 \ge 0$$

a) Solve the problem graphically.
b) Is there more than one optimal solution? Explain. PX

• 5 Solve the following LP problem graphically:

$$\text{Minimize} \quad Z = 24X + 15Y$$
$$\text{Subject to:} \quad 7X + 11Y \ge 77$$
$$16X + 4Y \ge 80$$
$$X, Y \ge 0 \quad \text{PX}$$

•• 6 Ed Silver Dog Food Company wishes to introduce a new brand of dog biscuits composed of chicken- and liver-flavored biscuits that meet certain nutritional requirements. The liver-flavored biscuits contain 1 unit of nutrient A and 2 units of nutrient B; the chicken-flavored biscuits contain 1 unit of nutrient A and 4 units of nutrient B. According to federal requirements, there must be at least 40 units of nutrient A and 60 units of nutrient B in a package of the new mix. In addition, the company has decided that there can be no more than 15 liver-flavored biscuits in a package. If it costs 1¢ to make 1 liver-flavored biscuit and 2¢ to make 1 chicken-flavored, what is the optimal product mix for a package of the biscuits to minimize the firm's cost?

a) Formulate this as a linear programming problem.

b) Solve this problem graphically, giving the optimal values of all variables.

c) What is the total cost of a package of dog biscuits using the optimal mix? **P**✗

• 7 The Electrocomp Corporation manufactures two electrical products: air conditioners and large fans. The assembly process for each is similar in that both require a certain amount of wiring and drilling. Each air conditioner takes 3 hours of wiring and 2 hours of drilling. Each fan must go through 2 hours of wiring and 1 hour of drilling. During the next production period, 240 hours of wiring time are available and up to 140 hours of drilling time may be used. Each air conditioner sold yields a profit of $25. Each fan assembled may be sold for a $15 profit.

Formulate and solve this LP production-mix situation, and find the best combination of air conditioners and fans that yields the highest profit. **P**✗

• 8 The Lauren Shur Tub Company manufactures two lines of bathtubs, called model A and model B. Every tub requires blending a certain amount of steel and zinc; the company has available a total of 25,000 lb of steel and 6,000 lb of zinc. Each model A bathtub requires a mixture of 125 lb of steel and 20 lb of zinc, and each yields a profit of $90. Each model B tub requires 100 lb of steel and 30 lb of zinc and can be sold for a profit of $70.

Find by graphical linear programming the best production mix of bathtubs. **P**✗

•• 9 Spitzfire, Inc., manufactures specialty cars and trucks. It has just opened a new factory where the C1 car and the T1 truck can both be manufactured. To make either vehicle, processing in the assembly shop and in the paint shop are required. It takes 1/40 of a day and 1/60 of a day to paint a truck of type T1 and a car of type C1 in the paint shop, respectively. It takes 1/50 of a day to assemble either type of vehicle in the assembly shop.

A T1 truck and a C1 car yield profits of $300 and $220, respectively, per vehicle sold.

a) Define the objective function and constraint equations.

b) Graph the feasible region.

c) What is a maximum-profit daily production plan at the new factory?

d) How much profit will such a plan yield, assuming whatever is produced is sold. **P**✗

• 10 MSA Computer Corporation manufactures two models of minicomputers, the Alpha 4 and the Beta 5. The firm employs 5 technicians, working 160 hours each per month, on its assembly line. Management insists that full employment (that is, *all* 160 hours of time) be maintained for each worker during next month's operations. It requires 20 labor-hours to assemble each Alpha 4 computer and 25 labor-hours to assemble each Beta 5 model. MSA wants to see at least 10 Alpha 4s and at least 15 Beta 5s produced during the production period. Alpha 4s generate a $1,200 profit per unit, and Betas yield $1,800 each.

Determine the most profitable number of each model of minicomputer to produce during the coming month. **P**✗

• 11 The Sweet Smell Fertilizer Company markets bags of manure labeled "not less than 60 lb dry weight." The packaged manure is a combination of compost and sewage wastes. To provide good-quality fertilizer, each bag should contain at least 30 lb of compost but no more than 40 lb of sewage. Each pound of compost costs Sweet Smell 5¢ and each pound of sewage costs 4¢. Use a graphical LP method to determine the least-cost blend of compost and sewage in each bag. **P**✗

• 12 Consider Faud Shatara's following linear programming formulation:

$$\text{Minimize cost} = \$1X_1 + \$2X_2$$
$$\text{Subject to:} \quad X_1 + 3X_2 \geq 90$$
$$8X_1 + 2X_2 \geq 160$$
$$3X_1 + 2X_2 \geq 120$$
$$X_2 \leq 70$$

a) Graphically illustrate the feasible region to indicate to Faud which corner point produces the optimal solution.

b) What is the cost of this solution? **P**✗

• 13 The LP relationships that follow were formulated by Jeffrey Rummel at the Connecticut Chemical Company. Which ones are invalid for use in a linear programming problem, and why?

$$\text{Maximize} = 6X_1 + \tfrac{1}{2}X_1X_2 + 5X_3$$
$$\text{Subject to:} \quad 4X_1X_2 + 2X_3 \leq 70$$
$$7.9X_1 - 4X_2 \geq 15.6$$
$$3X_1 + 3X_2 + 3X_3 \geq 21$$
$$19X_2 - \tfrac{1}{3}X_3 = 17$$
$$-X_1 - X_2 + 4X_3 = 5$$
$$4X_1 + 2X_2 + 3\sqrt{X_3} \leq 80$$

•• 14 Kalyan Singhal Corp. makes three products, and it has three machines available as resources as given in the following LP problem:

$$\text{Maximize contribution} = 4X_1 + 4X_2 + 7X_3$$
$$\text{Subject to:} \quad 1X_1 + 7X_2 + 4X_3 \leq 100 \text{ (hours on machine 1)}$$
$$2X_1 + 1X_2 + 7X_3 \leq 110 \text{ (hours on machine 2)}$$
$$8X_1 + 4X_2 + 1X_3 \leq 100 \text{ (hours on machine 3)}$$

a) Determine the optimal solution using LP software.

b) Is there unused time available on any of the machines with the optimal solution?

c) What would it be worth to the firm to make an additional hour of time available on the third machine?

d) How much would the firm's profit increase if an extra 10 hours of time were made available on the second machine at no extra cost? **P**✗

•• 15 Consider the following LP problem developed at Jeff Spencer's San Antonio optical scanning firm:

$$\text{Maximize profit} = \$1X_1 + \$1X_2$$
$$\text{Subject to:} \quad 2X_1 + 1X_2 \leq 100$$
$$1X_1 + 2X_2 \leq 100$$

437

a) What is the optimal solution to this problem? Solve it graphically.

b) If a technical breakthrough occurred that raised the profit per unit of X_1 to $3, would this affect the optimal solution?

c) Instead of an increase in the profit coefficient X_1, to $3, suppose that profit was overestimated and should only have been $1.25. Does this change the optimal solution? **PX**

••• 16   The Arden County, Maryland, superintendent of education is responsible for assigning students to the three high schools in his county. He recognizes the need to bus a certain number of students, for several sectors, A–E, of the county are beyond walking distance to a school. The superintendent partitions the county into five geographic sectors as he attempts to establish a plan that will minimize the total number of student miles traveled by bus. He also recognizes that if a student happens to live in a certain sector and is assigned to the high school in that sector, there is no need to bus him because he can walk to school. The three schools are located in sectors B, C, and E.

Dennis MacDonald, PhotoEdit, Inc.

The accompanying table reflects the number of high-school-age students living in each sector and the distance in miles from each sector to each school:

| | Distance to School | | | |
Sector	School in Sector B	School in Sector C	School in Sector E	Number of Students
A	5	8	6	700
B	0	4	12	500
C	4	0	7	100
D	7	2	5	800
E	12	7	0	400
				2,500

Each high school has a capacity of 900 students.

a) Set up the objective function and constraints of this problem using linear programming so that the total number of student miles traveled by bus is minimized.

b) Solve the problem. **PX**

•• 17   The National Credit Union has $250,000 available to invest in a 12-month commitment. The money can be placed in Treasury notes yielding an 8% return or in municipal bonds at an average rate of return of 9%. Credit union regulations require diversification to the extent that at least 50% of the investment be placed in Treasury notes. Because of defaults in such municipalities as Cleveland and New York, it is decided that no more than 40% of the investment be placed in bonds. How much should the National

Credit Union invest in each security so as to maximize its return on investment? **PX**

•• 18   Boston's famous Limoges Restaurant is open 24 hours a day. Servers report for duty at 3 A.M., 7 A.M., 11 A.M., 3 P.M., 7 P.M., or 11 P.M., and each works an 8-hour shift. The following table shows the minimum number of workers needed during the 6 periods into which the day is divided:

Period	Time	Number of Servers Required
1	3 A.M.–7 A.M.	3
2	7 A.M.–11 A.M.	12
3	11 A.M.–3 P.M.	16
4	3 P.M.–7 P.M.	9
5	7 P.M.–11 P.M.	11
6	11 P.M.–3 A.M.	4

Owner Michelle Limoges' scheduling problem is to determine how many servers should report for work at the start of each time period in order to minimize the total staff required for one day's operation. (*Hint:* Let X_i equal the number of servers beginning work in time period i, where $i = 1, 2, 3, 4, 5, 6$.) **PX**

• 19   A craftsman named Chuck Synovec builds two kinds of birdhouses, one for wrens and a second for bluebirds. Each wren birdhouse takes 4 hours of labor and 4 units of lumber. Each bluebird house requires 2 hours of labor and 12 units of lumber. The craftsman has available 60 hours of labor and 120 units of lumber. Wren houses yield a profit of $6 each and bluebird houses yield a profit of $15 each.

a) Write out the objective and constraints.

b) Solve graphically. **PX**

•• 20   Each coffee table produced by Robert West Designers nets the firm a profit of $9. Each bookcase yields a $12 profit. West's firm is small and its resources limited. During any given production period (of 1 week), 10 gallons of varnish and 12 lengths of high-quality redwood are available. Each coffee table requires approximately 1 gallon of varnish and 1 length of redwood. Each bookcase takes 1 gallon of varnish and 2 lengths of wood.

Formulate West's production-mix decision as a linear programming problem, and solve. How many tables and bookcases should be produced each week? What will the maximum profit be? **PX**

•• 21   Par, Inc., produces a standard golf bag and a deluxe golf bag on a weekly basis. Each golf bag requires time for cutting and dyeing and time for sewing and finishing, as shown in the following table:

| | Hours Required per Bag | |
Product	Cutting and Dyeing	Sewing and Finishing
Standard Bag	1/2	1
Deluxe Bag	1	2/3

The profits per bag and weekly hours available for cutting and dyeing and for sewing and finishing are as follows:

Product	Profit per Unit ($)
Standard bag	10
Deluxe bag	8

Activity	Weekly Hours Available
Cutting and dyeing	300
Sewing and finishing	360

438

Par Inc., will sell whatever quantities it produces of these two products.

a) Find the mix of standard and deluxe golf bags to produce per week that maximizes weekly profit from these activities.

b) What is the value of the profit? **P**✗

• 22 Solve the following linear programming problem graphically:

$$\text{Minimize cost} = 4X_1 + 5X_2$$
$$\text{Subject to:} \quad X_1 + 2X_2 \geq 80$$
$$3X_1 + X_2 \geq 75$$
$$X_1, X_2 \geq 0 \quad \textbf{P}✗$$

•• 23 Thompson Distributors packages and distributes industrial supplies. A standard shipment can be packaged in a class A container, a class K container, or a class T container. A single class A container yields a profit of $9; a class K container, a profit of $7; and a class T container, a profit of $15. Each shipment prepared requires a certain amount of packing material and a certain amount of time.

Resources Needed per Standard Shipment

Class of Container	Packing Material (pounds)	Packing Time (hours)
A	2	2
K	1	6
T	3	4
Total amount of resource available each week	130 pounds	240 hours

Jason Thompson, head of the firm, must decide the optimal number of each class of container to pack each week. He is bound by the previously mentioned resource restrictions but also decides that he must keep his 6 full-time packers employed all 240 hours (6 workers × 40 hours) each week.

Formulate and solve this problem using LP software. **P**✗

•• 24 How many corner points are there in the feasible region of the following problem?

$$\text{Minimize } Z = X - Y$$
$$\text{Subject to:} \quad X \leq 4$$
$$-X \leq 2$$
$$X + 2Y \leq 6$$
$$-X + 2Y \leq 8$$
$$Y \geq 0$$

(*Note:* X values can be negative in this problem.)

•• 25 The Denver advertising agency promoting the new Breem dishwashing detergent wants to get the best exposure possible for the product within the $100,000 advertising budget ceiling placed on it. To do so, the agency needs to decide how much of the budget to spend on each of its two most effective media: (1) television spots during the afternoon hours and (2) large ads in the city's Sunday newspaper. Each television spot costs $3,000; each Sunday newspaper ad costs $1,250. The expected exposure, based on industry ratings, is 35,000 viewers for each TV commercial and 20,000 readers for each newspaper advertisement. The agency director, Deborah Kellogg, knows from experience that it is important to use both media in order to reach the broadest spectrum of potential Breem customers. She decides that at least 5 but no more than 25 television spots should be ordered, and that at least 10 newspaper ads should be contracted. How many times should each of the two media be used to obtain maximum exposure while staying within the budget? Use the graphical method to solve. **P**✗

••• 26 Libby Temple Manufacturing has three factories (1, 2, and 3) and three warehouses (A, B, and C). The following table shows the shipping costs between each factory and warehouse, the factory manufacturing capabilities (in thousands), and the warehouse capacities (in thousands). Management would like to keep the warehouses filled to capacity in order to generate demand.

a) Write the objective function and the constraint in equations. Let X_{1A} = 1,000s of units shipped from factory 1 to warehouse A, and so on.

b) Solve by computer.

To\From	Warehouse A	Warehouse B	Warehouse C	Production Capability
Factory 1	$ 6	$ 5	$ 3	6
Factory 2	$ 8	$10	$ 8	8
Factory 3	$11	$14	$18	10
Capacity	7	12	5	**P**✗

•••• 27 A fertilizer manufacturer has to fulfill supply contracts to its two main customers (650 tons to Customer A and 800 tons to Customer B). It can meet this demand by shipping existing inventory from any of its three warehouses. Warehouse 1 (W1) has 400 tons of inventory onhand, Warehouse 2 (W2) has 500 tons, and Warehouse 3 (W3) has 600 tons. The company would like to arrange the shipping for the lowest cost possible, where the per-ton transit costs are as follows:

	W1	W3	W3
Customer A	$7.50	$6.25	$6.50
Customer B	6.75	7.00	8.00

a) Explain what each of the six decision variables (V) is: (*Hint:* Look at the Solver report on the next page.)

V1: _____
V2: _____
V3: _____
V4: _____
V5: _____
V6: _____

b) Write out the objective function in terms of the variables (V1, V2, etc.) and the objective coefficients.

c) Aside from nonnegativity of the variables, what are the five constraints? Write a short description for each constraint, and write out the formula (and circle the type of equality/inequality).

Description	Variables and Coefficients	What Type?	RHS
C1: _____	Formula: _____	(=> | = | =<)	_____
C2: _____	Formula: _____	(=> | = | =<)	_____
C3: _____	Formula: _____	(=> | = | =<)	_____
C4: _____	Formula: _____	(=> | = | =<)	_____
C5: _____	Formula: _____	(=> | = | =<	_____

After you formulate and enter the linear program for Problem 27 in Excel, the Solver gives you the following sensitivity report:

Adjustable Cells

Cell	Name	Final Value	Reduced Cost	Objective Coefficient	Allowable Increase	Allowable Decrease
$B$6	V1	0	1.5	7.5	1E+30	1.5
$C$6	V2	100	0	6.25	0.25	0.75
$D$6	V3	550	0	6.5	0.75	0.25
$E$6	V4	400	0	6.75	0.5	1E+30
$F$6	V5	400	0	7	0.75	0.5
$G$6	V6	0	0.75	8	1E+30	0.75

Constraints

Cell	Name	Final Value	Shadow Price	Constraint R.H. Side	Allowable Increase	Allowable Decrease
$H$7	C1	650	6.5	650	50	550
$H$8	C2	800	7.25	800	50	400
$H$9	C3	400	–0.5	400	400	50
$H$10	C4	500	–0.25	500	550	50
$H$11	C5	550	0	600	1E+30	50

d) How many of the constraints are binding?

e) How much slack/surplus is there with the nonbinding constraint(s)?

f) What is the range of optimality on variable V3?

g) If we could ship 10 tons less to Customer A, how much money *might* we be able to save? If we could chose to short *either* Customer A or Customer B by 10 tons, which would we prefer to short? Why? ✗

•••• 28   New Orleans's Mt. Sinai Hospital is a large, private, 600-bed facility complete with laboratories, operating rooms, and X-ray equipment. In seeking to increase revenues, Mt. Sinai's administration has decided to make a 90-bed addition on a portion of adjacent land currently used for staff parking. The administrators feel that the labs, operating rooms, and X-ray department are not being fully utilized at present and do not need to be expanded to handle additional patients. The addition of 90 beds, however, involves deciding how many beds should be allocated to the medical staff (for medical patients) and how many to the surgical staff (for surgical patients).

The hospital's accounting and medical records departments have provided the following pertinent information. The average hospital stay for a medical patient is 8 days, and the average medical patient generates $2,280 in revenues. The average surgical patient is in the hospital 5 days and generates $1,515 in revenues. The laboratory is capable of handling 15,000 tests per year more than it *was* handling. The average medical patient requires 3.1 lab tests, the average surgical patient 2.6 lab tests. Furthermore, the average medical patient uses 1 X-ray, the average surgical patient 2 X-rays. If the hospital were expanded by 90 beds, the X-ray department could handle up to 7,000 X-rays without significant additional cost. Finally, the administration estimates that up to 2,800 additional operations could be performed in existing operating-room facilities. Medical patients, of course, require no surgery, whereas each surgical patient generally has one surgery performed.

Formulate this problem so as to determine how many medical beds and how many surgical beds should be added to maximize revenues. Assume that the hospital is open 365 days per year. Px

•••• 29   Charles Watts Electronics manufactures the following six peripheral devices used in computers especially designed for jet fighter planes: internal modems, external modems, graphics circuit boards, jump drives, hard disk drives, and memory expansion boards. Each of these technical products requires time, in minutes, on three types of electronic testing equipment as shown in the following table:

	Internal Modem	External Modem	Circuit Board	Jump Drives	Hard Drives	Memory Boards
Test device 1	7	3	12	6	18	17
Test device 2	2	5	3	2	15	17
Test device 3	5	1	3	2	9	2

The first two test devices are available 120 hours per week. The third (device 3) requires more preventive maintenance and may be used only 100 hours each week. The market for all six computer components is vast, and Watts Electronics believes that it can sell as many units of each product as it can manufacture. The table that follows summarizes the revenues and material costs for each product:

Device	Revenue per Unit Sold ($)	Material Cost per Unit ($)
Internal modem	200	35
External modem	120	25
Graphics circuit board	180	40
Jump drive	130	45
Hard disk drive	430	170
Memory expansion board	260	60

In addition, variable labor costs are $15 per hour for test device 1, $12 per hour for test device 2, and $18 per hour for test device 3. Watts Electronics wants to maximize its profits.

a) Formulate this problem as an LP model.

b) Solve the problem by computer. What is the best product mix?

c) What is the value of an additional minute of time per week on test device 1? test device 2? test device 3? Should Watts Electronics add more test device time? If so, on which equipment? Px

•••• 30   You have just been hired as a planner for the municipal school system, and your first assignment is to redesign the subsidized lunch program. In particular, you are to formulate the least expensive lunch menu that will still meet all state and federal nutritional guidelines.

The guidelines are as follows: A meal must be between 500 and 800 calories. It must contain at least 200 calories of protein, at least 200 calories of carbohydrates, and no more than 400 calories of fat. It also needs to have at least 200 calories of a food classified as a fruit or vegetable.

Here is the list of the foods you can consider as possible menu items, with contract-determined prices and nutritional information. Note that all percentages sum to 100% per food—as all calories are protein, carbohydrate, or fat calories. For example, a serving of applesauce has 100 calories, all of which are carbohydrate, and it counts as a fruit/veg food. You are allowed to use fractional servings, such as 2.25 servings of turkey breast and a 0.33 portion of salad. Cost and nutritional attributes scale likewise: e.g., a 0.33 portion of salad cost $.30 and has 33 calories.

Food	Cost/Serving	Calories/Serving	% protein	% carbs	% fat	Fruit/Veg
Applesauce	$0.30	100	0%	100%	0%	Y
Canned corn	$0.40	150	20%	80%	0%	Y
Fried chicken	$0.90	250	55%	5%	40%	N
French fries	$0.20	400	5%	35%	60%	N
Mac and cheese	$0.50	430	20%	30%	50%	N
Turkey breast	$1.50	300	67%	0%	33%	N
Garden salad	$0.90	100	15%	40%	45%	Y

Formulate and solve as a linear problem. Print out your formulation in Excel showing the objective function coefficients and constraint matrix in standard form.

- Display, on a separate page, the full *Answer Report* as generated by Excel Solver.

- Highlight *and label as* Z the objective value for the optimal solution on the Answer Report.
- Highlight the nonzero decision variables for the optimal solution on the Answer Report.
- Display, on a separate page, the full *Sensitivity Report* as generated by Excel Solver.

Case Study

Golding Landscaping and Plants, Inc.

Kenneth and Patricia Golding spent a career as a husband-and-wife real estate investment partnership in Washington, DC. When they finally retired to a 25-acre farm in northern Virginia's Fairfax County, they became ardent amateur gardeners. Kenneth planted shrubs and fruit trees, and Patricia spent her hours potting all sizes of plants. When the volume of shrubs and plants reached the point that the Goldings began to think of their hobby in a serious vein, they built a greenhouse adjacent to their home and installed heating and watering systems.

By 2005, the Goldings realized their retirement from real estate had really only led to a second career—in the plant and shrub business—and they filed for a Virginia business license. Within a matter of months, they asked their attorney to file incorporation documents and formed the firm Golding Landscaping and Plants, Inc.

Early in the new business's existence, Kenneth Golding recognized the need for a high-quality commercial fertilizer that he could blend himself, both for sale and for his own nursery. His goal was to keep his costs to a minimum while producing a top-notch product that was especially suited to the northern Virginia climate.

Working with chemists at George Mason University, Golding blended "Golding-Grow." It consists of four chemical compounds, C-30, C-92, D-21, and E-11. The cost per pound for each compound is indicated in the following table:

Chemical Compound	Cost per Pound
C-30	$.12
C-92	.09
D-21	.11
E-11	.04

The specifications for Golding-Grow are established as:

a. Chemical E-11 must constitute at least 15% of the blend.
b. C-92 and C-30 must together constitute at least 45% of the blend.
c. D-21 and C-92 can together constitute no more than 30% of the blend.
d. Golding-Grow is packaged and sold in 50-lb bags.

Discussion Questions

1. Formulate an LP problem to determine what blend of the four chemicals will allow Golding to minimize the cost of a 50-lb bag of the fertilizer.
2. Solve to find the best solution.

Additional Case Study

See our Companion Web site at www.prenhall.com/heizer *for this additional internet case study:*

- **Chase Manhattan Bank:** This scheduling case involves finding the optimal number of full-time versus part-time employees at a bank.

Bibliography

Bard, J. F. "Staff Scheduling in High Volume Services with Downgrading." *IIE Transactions* 36 (October 2004): 985.

Begley, S. "Did You Hear About the Salesman Who Travelled Better?" *OR/MS Today* 31 (January 2004): 20.

Brown, G., R. F. Dell, and A. M. Newman. "Optimizing Military Capital Planning." *Interfaces* 34, no. 6 (November–December 2004): 415–425.

Chakravarti, N. "Tea Company Steeped in OR." *OR/MS Today* 27 (April 2000): 32–34.

daSilva, C. G., et al. "An Interactive Decision Support System for an Aggregate Planning Production Model." *Omega* 34 (April 2006): 167.

Desroisers, Jacques. "Air Transat Uses ALTITUDE to Manage Its Aircraft Routing, Crew Pairing, and Work Assignment." *Interfaces* 30 (March–April 2000): 41–53.

Le Blanc, Larry J., et al. "Nu-Kote's Spreadsheet Linear Programming Models for Optimizing Transportation." *Interfaces* 34 (March–April 2004): 139–146.

Lyon, Peter, R. John Milne, Robert Orzell, and Robert Rice. "Matching Assets with Demand in Supply Chain Management at IBM Microelectronics." *Interfaces* 31 (January 2001): 108–124.

Martin, C. H. "Ohio University's College of Business Uses Integer Programming to Schedule Classes." *Interfaces* 34 (November–December 2004): 460–465.

Neureuther, B. D., G. G. Polak, and N. R. Sanders. "A Hierarchical Production Plan for a Make-to-order Steel Fabrication Plant." *Production Planning & Control* 15 (April 2004): 324.

Peeteis, M., and Z. Degraeve. "An LP Based Lower Bound for the Simple Assembly Line Balancing Problem." *European Journal of Operational Research* 168 (February 2006): 716.

Render, B., R. M. Stair, and Michael Hanna. *Quantitative Analysis for Management*, 9th ed. Upper Saddle River, NJ: Prentice Hall (2006).

Render, B., R. M. Stair, and R. Balakrishman. *Managerial Decision Modeling with Spreadsheets*, 2nd ed. Upper Saddle River, NJ: Prentice Hall (2007).

Sodhi, M. S., and S. Norri. "A Fast and Optimal Modeling Approach Applied to Crew Rostering at London Underground." *Annals of OR* 127 (March 2004): 259.

Taylor, Bernard. *Introduction to Management Science*, 9th ed. Upper Saddle River, NJ: Prentice Hall (2008).

van den Briel, M. H. L., et. al. "America West Airlines Develops Efficient Boarding Strategies." *Interfaces* 35, no. 3 (May–June 2005): 191–201.

Yu, G., et al. "Optimizing Pilot Planning and Training for Continental Airlines." *Interfaces* 34 (July–August 2004): 253–271.

Solutions to Even Numbered Problems

2 Profit = $100 at $X = 0$, $Y = 10$

4 **(b)** Yes; $P = \$3,000$ at (75, 75) and (50, 150)

6 **(a)** Min $X_1 + 2X_2$

$$X_1 + X_2 \geq 40$$
$$2X_1 + 4X_2 \geq 60$$
$$x_1 \leq 15$$

   (b) Cost = $.65 at (15, 25)

   (c) 65¢

8 $x_1 = 200$, $x_2 = 0$, profit = $18,000

10 10 Alpha 4s, 24 Beta 5s, profit = $55,200

12 **(a)** $x_1 = 25.71$, $x_2 = 21.43$

   (b) Cost = $68.57

14 **(a)** $x_1 = 7.95$, $x_2 = 5.95$, $x_3 = 12.6$, $P = \$143.76$

   (b) No unused time

   (c) 26¢

   (d) $7.86

16 **(a)** Let X_{ij} = number of students bused from sector i to school j.

   Objective: minimize total travel miles =

$$5X_{AB} + 8X_{AC} + 6X_{AE}$$
$$+ \; 0X_{BB} + 4X_{BC} + 12X_{BE}$$
$$+ \; 4X_{CB} + 0X_{CC} + 7X_{CE}$$
$$+ \; 7X_{DB} + 2X_{DC} + 5X_{DE}$$
$$+ 12X_{EB} + 7X_{EC} + 0X_{EE}$$

   Subject to:

$$X_{AB} + X_{AC} + X_{AE} = 700 \text{ (number of students in sector } A)$$

$$X_{BB} + X_{BC} + X_{BE} = 500 \text{ (number students in sector } B)$$
$$X_{CB} + X_{CC} + X_{CE} = 100 \text{ (number students in sector } C)$$
$$X_{DB} + X_{DC} + X_{DE} = 800 \text{ (number students in sector } D)$$
$$X_{EB} + X_{EC} + X_{EE} = 400 \text{ (number of students in sector } E)$$
$$X_{AB} + X_{BB} + X_{CB} + X_{DB} + X_{EB} \leq 900 \text{ (school } B \text{ capacity)}$$
$$X_{AC} + X_{BC} + X_{CC} + X_{DC} + X_{EC} \leq 900 \text{ (school } C \text{ capacity)}$$
$$X_{AE} + X_{BE} + X_{CE} + X_{DE} + X_{EE} \leq 900 \text{ (school } E \text{ capacity)}$$

   (b) Solution: $X_{AB} = 400$
   $X_{AE} = 300$
   $X_{BB} = 500$
   $X_{CC} = 100$
   $X_{DC} = 800$
   $X_{EE} = 400$

   Distance = 5,400 "student miles"

18 Hire 30 workers; three solutions are feasible; two of these are:

   16 begin at 7 A.M.

   9 begin at 3 P.M.

   2 begin at 7 P.M.

   3 begin at 11 P.M.

   An alternate optimum is:

   3 begin at 3 A.M.

   9 begin at 7 A.M.

   7 begin at 11 A.M.

   2 begin at 3 P.M.

   9 begin at 7 P.M.

   0 begin at 11 P.M.

20 Max $P = 9x_1 + 12x_2$
Subject to:
$x_1 + x_2 \leq 10$
$x_1 + 2x_2 \leq 12$
$x_1 = 8, x_2 = 2$; profit = $96

22 $x_1 = 14, x_2 = 33$, cost = 221

24 5 corner points

26 **(a)** Minimize = $6X_{1A} + 5X_{1B} + 3X_{1C} + 8X_{2A} + 10X_{2B} + 8X_{2C} + 11X_{3A} + 14X_{3B} + 18X_{3C}$
Subject to:
$X_{1A} + X_{2A} + X_{3A} = 7$
$X_{1B} + X_{2B} + X_{3B} = 12$

$X_{1C} + X_{2C} + X_{3C} = 5$
$X_{1A} + X_{1B} + X_{1C} \leq 6$
$X_{2A} + X_{2B} + X_{2C} \leq 8$
$X_{3A} + X_{3B} + X_{3C} \leq 10$
(b) Minimum cost = $219,000

28 One approach results in 2,790 medical patients and 2,104 surgical patients, with a revenue of $9,551,659 per year (which can change slightly with rounding). This yields 61 medical beds and 29 surgical beds.

30 Apple sauce = 0, Canned corn = 1.33, Fried chicken = 0.46, French fries = 0, Mac & Cheese = 1.13, Turkey = 0, Garden salad = 0, Cost = $1.51.

Solutions to Self Test

1. b; **2.** a; **3.** c; **4.** a; **5.** b; **6.** c; **7.** b.

Module D

Waiting-Line Models

Waiting-Line Models

Outline

Characteristics of a Waiting-Line
System
Arrival Characteristics
Waiting-Line Characteristics
Service Characteristics
Measuring a Queue's Performance

Queuing Costs

The Variety of Queuing Models
Model A (M/M/1): Single-Channel Queuing
Model with Poisson Arrivals and
Exponential Service Times
Model B (M/M/S): Multiple-Channel
Queuing Model
Model C (M/D/1): Constant-Service-Time
Model
Model D: Limited-Population Model

Other Queuing Approaches

Summary
Key Terms
Using Software to Solve Queuing Problems
Solved Problems
Self-Test
Active Model Exercise
Internet and Student CD-ROM/DVD
    Exercises
Discussion Questions
Problems
Case Studies: New England Foundry;
    The Winter Park Hotel
Additional Case Study
Bibliography

Learning Objectives

When you complete this selection you should be able to

1. Describe the characteristics
   of arrivals, waiting lines,
   and service systems
2. Apply the single-channel queuing
   model equations
3. Conduct a cost analysis
   for a waiting line

4. Apply the multiple-channel queuing
   model formulas
5. Apply the constant-service-time
   model equations
6. Perform a limited-population model
   analysis

From *Operations Management*, 9/e. Jay Heizer. Barry Render. Copyright © 2008 by
Pearson Education. All rights reserved.

Jeff Greenberg, PhotoEdit, Inc.

Paris's EuroDisney, Tokyo's Disney Japan, and the U.S.'s Disney World and Disneyland all have one feature in common—long lines and seemingly endless waits. However, Disney is one of the world's leading companies in the scientific analysis of queuing theory. It analyzes queuing behaviors and can predict which rides will draw what length crowds. To keep visitors happy, Disney makes lines appear to be constantly moving forward, entertains people while they wait, and posts signs telling visitors how many minutes until they reach each ride.

Queuing theory
A body of knowledge about waiting lines.

Waiting line (queue)
Items or people in a line awaiting service.

The body of knowledge about waiting lines, often called **queuing theory**, is an important part of operations and a valuable tool for the operations manager. **Waiting lines** are a common situation—they may, for example, take the form of cars waiting for repair at a Midas Muffler Shop, copying jobs waiting to be completed at a Kinko's print shop, or vacationers waiting to enter the Space Mountain ride at Disney. Table 1 lists just a few OM uses of waiting-line models.

Waiting-line models are useful in both manufacturing and service areas. Analysis of queues in terms of waiting-line length, average waiting time, and other factors helps us to understand service systems (such as bank teller stations), maintenance activities (that might repair broken machinery), and shop-floor control activities. Indeed, patients waiting in a doctor's office and broken drill presses waiting in a repair facility have a lot in common from an OM perspective. Both use human and equipment resources to restore valuable production assets (people and machines) to good condition.

CHARACTERISTICS OF A WAITING-LINE SYSTEM

In this section, we take a look at the three parts of a waiting-line, or queuing, system (as shown in Figure 1):

Learning Objective

1. Describe the characteristics of arrivals, waiting lines, and service systems.

1. *Arrivals or inputs to the system:* These have characteristics such as population size, behavior, and a statistical distribution.
2. *Queue discipline, or the waiting line itself:* Characteristics of the queue include whether it is limited or unlimited in length and the discipline of people or items in it.
3. *The service facility:* Its characteristics include its design and the statistical distribution of service times.

We now examine each of these three parts.

▶ **Table 1**

Common Queuing Situations

Situation	Arrivals in Queue	Service Process
Supermarket	Grocery shoppers	Checkout clerks at cash register
Highway toll booth	Automobiles	Collection of tolls at booth
Doctor's office	Patients	Treatment by doctors and nurses
Computer system	Programs to be run	Computer processes jobs
Telephone company	Callers	Switching equipment forwards calls
Bank	Customers	Transactions handled by teller
Machine maintenance	Broken machines	Repair people fix machines
Harbor	Ships and barges	Dock workers load and unload

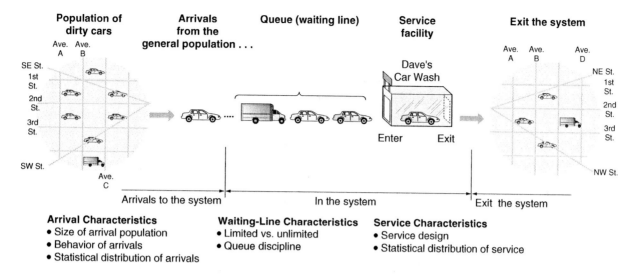

Arrival Characteristics
• Size of arrival population
• Behavior of arrivals
• Statistical distribution of arrivals

Waiting-Line Characteristics
• Limited vs. unlimited
• Queue discipline

Service Characteristics
• Service design
• Statistical distribution of service

▲ **Figure 1** Three Parts of a Waiting Line, or Queuing System, at Dave's Car Wash

Arrival Characteristics

The input source that generates arrivals or customers for a service system has three major characteristics:

1. *Size* of the arrival population
2. *Behavior* of arrivals
3. *Pattern* of arrivals (statistical distribution)

Size of the Arrival (Source) Population Population sizes are considered either unlimited (essentially infinite) or limited (finite). When the number of customers or arrivals on hand at any given moment is just a small portion of all potential arrivals, the arrival population is considered **unlimited**, or **infinite**. Examples of unlimited populations include cars arriving at a big-city car wash, shoppers arriving at a supermarket, and students arriving to register for classes at a large university. Most queuing models assume such an infinite arrival population. An example of a **limited**, or **finite**, population is found in a copying shop that has, say, eight copying machines. Each of the copiers is a potential "customer" that may break down and require service.

Pattern of Arrivals at the System Customers arrive at a service facility either according to some known schedule (for example, one patient every 15 minutes or one student every half hour) or else they arrive *randomly*. Arrivals are considered random when they are independent of one another and their occurrence cannot be predicted exactly. Frequently in queuing problems, the number of arrivals per unit of time can be estimated by a probability distribution known as the **Poisson distribution**.[1] For any given arrival time (such as 2 customers per hour or 4 trucks per minute), a discrete Poisson distribution can be established by using the formula:

$$P(x) = \frac{e^{-\lambda}\lambda^x}{x!} \quad \text{for } x = 0,1,2,3,4\ldots \tag{1}$$

where $P(x)$ = probability of x arrivals
x = number of arrivals per unit of time
λ = average arrival rate
e = 2.7183 (which is the base of the natural logarithms)

With the help of the table in the Appendix, which gives the value of $e^{-\lambda}$ for use in the Poisson distribution, these values are easy to compute. Figure 2 illustrates the Poisson distribution for $\lambda = 2$ and $\lambda = 4$. This means that if the average arrival rate is $\lambda = 2$ customers per hour, the probability of

Unlimited, or infinite, population
A queue in which a virtually unlimited number of people or items could request the services, or in which the number of customers or arrivals on hand at any given moment is a very small portion of potential arrivals.

Limited, or finite, population
A queue in which there are only a limited number of potential users of the service.

Poisson distribution
A discrete probability distribution that often describes the arrival rate in queuing theory.

[1] When the arrival rates follow a Poisson process with mean arrival rate, λ, the time between arrivals follows a negative exponential distribution with mean time between arrivals of $1/\lambda$. The negative exponential distribution, then, is also representative of a Poisson process but describes the time between arrivals and specifies that these time intervals are completely random.

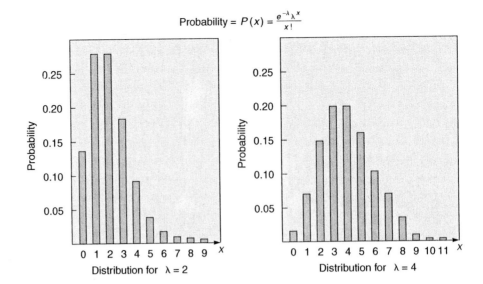

▶ Figure 2

Two Examples of the Poisson Distribution for Arrival Times

$$\text{Probability} = P(x) = \frac{e^{-\lambda}\lambda^x}{x!}$$

Distribution for $\lambda = 2$

Distribution for $\lambda = 4$

0 customers arriving in any random hour is about 13%, probability of 1 customer is about 27%, 2 customers about 27%, 3 customers about 18%, 4 customers about 9%, and so on. The chances that 9 or more will arrive are virtually nil. Arrivals, of course, are not always Poisson distributed (they may follow some other distribution). Patterns, therefore, should be examined to make certain that they are well approximated by Poisson before that distribution is applied.

Behavior of Arrivals Most queuing models assume that an arriving customer is a patient customer. Patient customers are people or machines that wait in the queue until they are served and do not switch between lines. Unfortunately, life is complicated by the fact that people have been known to balk or to renege. Customers who *balk* refuse to join the waiting line because it is too long to suit their needs or interests. *Reneging* customers are those who enter the queue but then become impatient and leave without completing their transaction. Actually, both of these situations just serve to highlight the need for queuing theory and waiting-line analysis.

Waiting-Line Characteristics

The waiting line itself is the second component of a queuing system. The length of a line can be either limited or unlimited. A queue is *limited* when it cannot, either by law or because of physical restrictions, increase to an infinite length. A small barbershop, for example, will have only a limited number of waiting chairs. Queuing models are treated in this module under an assumption of *unlimited* queue length. A queue is *unlimited* when its size is unrestricted, as in the case of the toll booth serving arriving automobiles.

A second waiting-line characteristic deals with *queue discipline*. This refers to the rule by which customers in the line are to receive service. Most systems use a queue discipline known as the **first-in, first-out (FIFO) rule**. In a hospital emergency room or an express checkout line at a supermarket, however, various assigned priorities may preempt FIFO. Patients who are critically injured will move ahead in treatment priority over patients with broken fingers or noses. Shoppers with fewer than 10 items may be allowed to enter the express checkout queue (but are *then* treated as first-come, first-served). Computer-programming runs also operate under priority scheduling. In most large companies, when computer-produced paychecks are due on a specific date, the payroll program gets highest priority.[2]

Service Characteristics

The third part of any queuing system are the service characteristics. Two basic properties are important: (1) design of the service system and (2) the distribution of service times.

"The other line always moves faster."
Etorre's Observation

"If you change lines, the one you just left will start to move faster than the one you are now in."
O'Brien's Variation

First-in, first-out (FIFO) rule
A queue discipline in which the first customers in line receive the first service.

---

[2]The term *FIFS* (first-in, first-served) is often used in place of FIFO. Another discipline, LIFS (last-in, first-served) also called last-in, first-out (LIFO), is common when material is stacked or piled so that the items on top are used first.

Basic Queuing System Designs Service systems are usually classified in terms of their number of channels (for example, number of servers) and number of phases (for example, number of service stops that must be made). A **single-channel queuing system**, with one server, is typified by the drive-in bank with only one open teller. If, on the other hand, the bank has several tellers on duty, with each customer waiting in one common line for the first available teller, then we would have a **multiple-channel queuing system**. Most banks today are multichannel service systems, as are most large barbershops, airline ticket counters, and post offices.

In a **single-phase system**, the customer receives service from only one station and then exits the system. A fast-food restaurant in which the person who takes your order also brings your food and takes your money is a single-phase system. So is a driver's license agency in which the person taking your application also grades your test and collects your license fee. However, say the restaurant requires you to place your order at one station, pay at a second, and pick up your food at a third. In this case, it is a **multiphase system**. Likewise, if the driver's license agency is large or busy, you will probably have to wait in one line to complete your application (the first service stop), queue again to have your test graded, and finally go to a third counter to pay your fee. To help you relate the concepts of channels and phases, Figure 3 presents four possible channel configurations.

Single-channel queuing system

A service system with one line and one server.

Multiple-channel queuing system

A service system with one waiting line but with several servers.

Single-phase system

A system in which the customer receives service from only one station and then exits the system.

Multiphase system

A system in which the customer receives services from several stations before exiting the system.

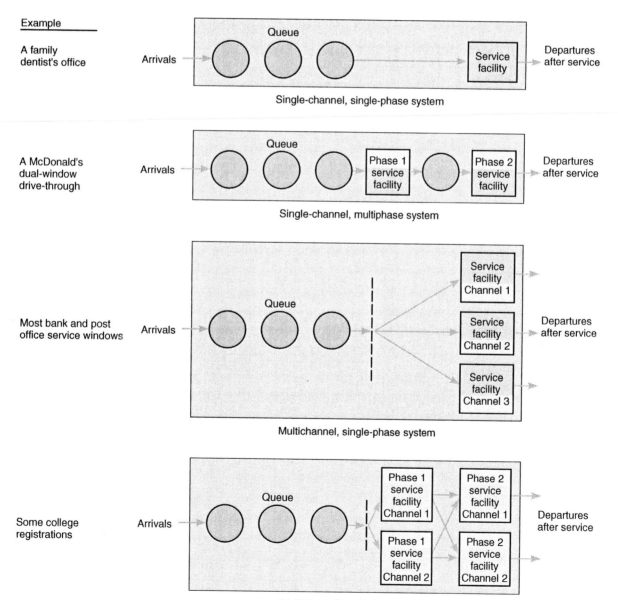

▲ **Figure 3** **Basic Queuing System Designs**

> **Figure 4**

Two Examples of the Negative Exponential Distribution for Service Times

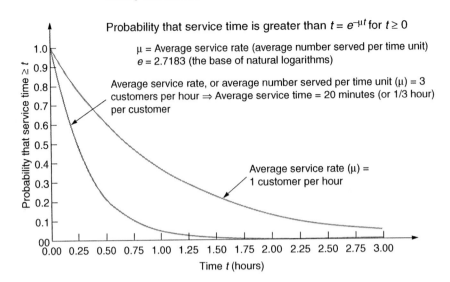

Probability that service time is greater than $t = e^{-\mu t}$ for $t \geq 0$

μ = Average service rate (average number served per time unit)
e = 2.7183 (the base of natural logarithms)

Average service rate, or average number served per time unit (μ) = 3 customers per hour $\Rightarrow$ Average service time = 20 minutes (or 1/3 hour) per customer

Average service rate (μ) = 1 customer per hour

(y-axis) Probability that service time $\geq t$

(x-axis) Time t (hours)

Although Poisson and exponential distributions are commonly used to describe arrival rates and service times, normal and Erlang distributions, or others, may be more valid in certain cases.

Negative exponential probability distribution

A continuous probability distribution often used to describe the service time in a queuing system.

Service Time Distribution   Service patterns are like arrival patterns in that they may be either constant or random. If service time is constant, it takes the same amount of time to take care of each customer. This is the case in a machine-performed service operation such as an automatic car wash. More often, service times are randomly distributed. In many cases, we can assume that random service times are described by the **negative exponential probability distribution**.

Figure 4 shows that if *service times* follow a negative exponential distribution, the probability of any very long service time is low. For example, when an average service time is 20 minutes (or three customers per hour), seldom if ever will a customer require more than 1.5 hours in the service facility. If the mean service time is 1 hour, the probability of spending more than 3 hours in service is quite low.

Measuring a Queue's Performance

Queuing models help managers make decisions that balance service costs with waiting-line costs. Queuing analysis can obtain many measures of a waiting-line system's performance, including the following:

1. Average time that each customer or object spends in the queue.
2. Average queue length.
3. Average time that each customer spends in the system (waiting time plus service time).
4. Average number of customers in the system.
5. Probability that the service facility will be idle.
6. Utilization factor for the system.
7. Probability of a specific number of customers in the system.

QUEUING COSTS

As described in the *OM in Action* box "Free Movie Tickets if You Aren't Seen in 30 Minutes at the ER," operations managers must recognize the trade-off that takes place between two costs: the cost of providing good service and the cost of customer or machine waiting time. Managers want queues that are short enough so that customers do not become unhappy and either leave without buying or buy but never return. However, managers may be willing to allow some waiting if it is balanced by a significant savings in service costs.

One means of evaluating a service facility is to look at total expected cost. Total cost is the sum of expected service costs plus expected waiting costs.

As you can see in Figure 5, service costs increase as a firm attempts to raise its level of service. Managers in *some* service centers can vary capacity by having standby personnel and machines that they can assign to specific service stations to prevent or shorten excessively long lines. In grocery stores, for example, managers and stock clerks can open extra checkout counters. In banks and airport check-in points, part-time workers may be called in to help. As the level of service improves (that is, speeds up), however, the cost of time spent waiting in lines decreases. (Refer again to Figure 5.) Waiting cost may reflect lost productivity of workers while

What does the long wait in the typical doctor's office tell you about the doctor's perception of your cost of waiting?

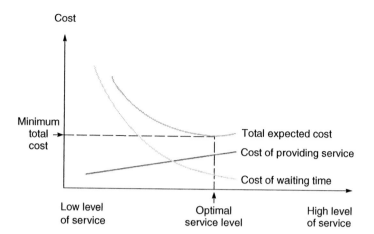

◁ **Figure 5**

The Trade-off between Waiting Costs and Service Costs

Different organizations place different values on their customers' time, don't they?

tools or machines await repairs or may simply be an estimate of the cost of customers lost because of poor service and long queues. In some service systems (for example, an emergency ambulance service), the cost of long waiting lines may be intolerably high.

THE VARIETY OF QUEUING MODELS

A wide variety of queuing models may be applied in operations management. We will introduce you to four of the most widely used models. These are outlined in Table 2, and examples of each follow in the next few sections. More complex models are described in queuing theory textbooks[3] or can be developed through the use of simulation (the topic of module F). Note that all four queuing models listed in Table 2 have three characteristics in common. They all assume:

Visit a bank or a drive-through restaurant and time arrivals to see what kind of distribution (Poisson or other) they might reflect.

1. Poisson distribution arrivals
2. FIFO discipline
3. A single-service phase

In addition, they all describe service systems that operate under steady, ongoing conditions. This means that arrival and service rates remain stable during the analysis.

OM in Action — Free Movie Tickets if You Aren't Seen in 30 Minutes at the ER

Other hospitals smirked when Dearborn, Michigan's Oakwood Healthcare rolled out an emergency room (ER) guarantee that promised a written apology and movie tickets to patients not seen by a doctor within 30 minutes. Even employees cringed at what sounded like a cheap marketing ploy.

But if you have visited an ER lately and watched some patients wait for hours on end—the *official* average wait is 47 minutes, according to a national hospital group—you can understand why Oakwood's patient satisfaction levels have soared. The 30-minute guarantee was a huge success, and all four of Oakwood Healthcare's hospitals have now rolled it out. Fewer than 1% of last year's 191,000 ER patients asked for free tickets.

"We're down to 17 minutes on average," says Corrine Victor, the ER administrator. Soon, she claims, "we'll start offering a 15-minute guarantee." Oakwood's CEO even extended the ER guarantee to on-time surgery, 45-minute meal service orders, and other custom room services. "Medicine is a service business," says Larry Alexander, the

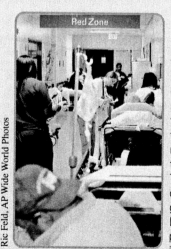

Ric Feld, AP Wide World Photos

head of an ER in Sanford, Florida. "And people are in the mindset of the fast-food industry."

How did Oakwood make good on its promise to shorten the ER queue? It first studied queuing theory, then reengineered its billing, records, and lab operations to drive down service time. Then, to improve service capability, Oakwood upgraded its technical staff. Finally, it replaced its ER physicians with a crew willing to work longer hours.

Sources: The Wall Street Journal (July 3, 2002); D1; and Crain's Detroit Business (March 4, 2002): 1.

---

[3]See, for example, N. U. Prabhu, *Foundations of Queuing Theory*, Kluwer Academic Publishers (1997).

▼ Table 2 Queuing Models Described in This Chapter

Model	Name (technical name in parentheses)	Example	Number of Channels	Number of Phases	Arrival Rate Pattern	Service Time Pattern	Population Size	Queue Discipline
A	Single-channel system (M/M/1)	Information counter at department store	Single	Single	Poisson	Exponential	Unlimited	FIFO
B	Multichannel (M/M/S)	Airline ticket counter	Multi-channel	Single	Poisson	Exponential	Unlimited	FIFO
C	Constant service (M/D/1)	Automated car wash	Single	Single	Poisson	Constant	Unlimited	FIFO
D	Limited population (finite population)	Shop with only a dozen machines that might break	Single	Single	Poisson	Exponential	Limited	FIFO

Model A (M/M/1): Single-Channel Queuing Model with Poisson Arrivals and Exponential Service Times

The most common case of queuing problems involves the *single-channel*, or single-server, waiting line. In this situation, arrivals form a single line to be serviced by a single station (see Figure 3). We assume that the following conditions exist in this type of system:

Learning Objective

2. Apply the single-channel queuing model equations

What is the impact of equal service and arrival rates?

1. Arrivals are served on a first-in, first-out (FIFO) basis, and every arrival waits to be served, regardless of the length of the line or queue.
2. Arrivals are independent of preceding arrivals, but the average number of arrivals (*arrival rate*) does not change over time.
3. Arrivals are described by a Poisson probability distribution and come from an infinite (or very, very large) population.
4. Service times vary from one customer to the next and are independent of one another, but their average rate is known.
5. Service times occur according to the negative exponential probability distribution.
6. The service rate is faster than the arrival rate.

When these conditions are met, the series of equations shown in Table 3 can be developed. Examples 1 and 2 illustrate how Model A (which in technical journals is known as the M/M/1 model) may be used.[4]

▶ *The giant Moscow McDonald's boosts 900 seats, 800 workers, and $80 million in annual sales (vs. less than $2 million in a U.S. outlet). Americans would balk at the average waiting time of 45 minutes, but Russians are used to such long lines. McDonald's represents good service in Moscow.*

Roy/EXPLORER, Photo Researchers, Inc.

[4]In queuing notation, the first letter refers to the arrivals (where M stands for Poisson distribution); the second letter refers to service (where M is again a Poisson distribution, which is the same as an exponential rate for service—and a D is a constant service rate); the third symbol refers to the number of servers. So an M/D/1 system (our Model C) has Poisson arrivals, constant service, and one server.

λ = mean number of arrivals per time period

μ = mean number of people or items served per time period

L_s = average number of units (customers) in the system (waiting and being served)

$$= \frac{\lambda}{\mu - \lambda}$$

W_s = average time a unit spends in the system (waiting time plus service time)

$$= \frac{1}{\mu - \lambda}$$

L_q = average number of units waiting in the queue

$$= \frac{\lambda^2}{\mu(\mu - \lambda)}$$

W_q = average time a unit spends waiting in the queue

$$= \frac{\lambda}{\mu(\mu - \lambda)} = \frac{L_q}{\lambda}$$

ρ = utilization factor for the system

$$= \frac{\lambda}{\mu}$$

P_0 = probability of 0 units in the system (that is, the service unit is idle)

$$= 1 - \frac{\lambda}{\mu}$$

$P_{n>k}$ = probability of more than k units in the system, where n is the number of units in the system

$$= \left(\frac{\lambda}{\mu}\right)^{k+1}$$

◀ **Table 3**

Queuing Formulas for Model A: Single-Channel System, Also Called M/M/1

Tom Jones, the mechanic at Golden Muffler Shop, is able to install new mufflers at an average rate of 3 per hour (or about 1 every 20 minutes), according to a negative exponential distribution. Customers seeking this service arrive at the shop on the average of 2 per hour, following a Poisson distribution. They are served on a first-in, first-out basis and come from a very large (almost infinite) population of possible buyers.

We would like to obtain the operating characteristics of Golden Muffler's queuing system.

Approach: This is a single-channel (M/M/1) system and we apply the formulas in Table 3.

Solution:

$$\lambda = 2 \text{ cars arriving per hour}$$

$$\mu = 3 \text{ cars serviced per hour}$$

$$L_s = \frac{\lambda}{\mu - \lambda} = \frac{2}{3-2} = \frac{2}{1}$$

$$= 2 \text{ cars in the system, on average}$$

$$W_s = \frac{1}{\mu - \lambda} = \frac{1}{3-2} = 1$$

$$= 1\text{-hour average time in the system}$$

$$L_q = \frac{\lambda^2}{\mu(\mu - \lambda)} = \frac{2^2}{3(3-2)} = \frac{4}{3(1)} = \frac{4}{3}$$

$$= 1.33 \text{ cars waiting in line, on average}$$

$$W_q = \frac{\lambda}{\mu(\mu - \lambda)} = \frac{2}{3(3-2)} = \frac{2}{3} \text{ hour}$$

$$= 40\text{-minute average waiting time per car}$$

$$\rho = \frac{\lambda}{\mu} = \frac{2}{3}$$

$$= 66.6\% \text{ of time mechanic is busy}$$

$$P_0 = 1 - \frac{\lambda}{\mu} = 1 - \frac{2}{3}$$

$$= .33 \text{ probability there are 0 cars in the system}$$

EXAMPLE 1

A single-channel queue

Excel OM Data File ModDExD1.xls

Active Model D.1

Example 1 is further illustrated in Active Model D.1 on your CD-ROM.

Probability of More Than k Cars in the System

k	$P_{n>k} = (2/3)^{k+1}$
0	.667 ← Note that this is equal to $1 - P_0 = 1 - .33 = .667$.
1	.444
2	.296
3	.198 ← Implies that there is a 19.8% chance that more than 3 cars are in the system.
4	.132
5	.088
6	.058
7	.039

Insight: Recognize that arrival and service times are converted to the same rate. For example, a service time of 20 minutes is stated as an average *rate* of 3 mufflers *per hour*. It's also important to differentiate between time in the *queue* and time in the *system*.

Learning exercise: If $\mu = 4$ cars/hour instead of the current 3 arrivals, what are the new values of L_s, W_s, L_q, W_q, ρ and P_0? [Answer: 1 car, 30 min., .5 cars, 15 min., 50%, .50.]

Related problems: 1, 2, 3, 4, 6, 7, 8, 9a–e, 10, 11a–c, 12a–d.

Once we have computed the operating characteristics of a queuing system, it is often important to do an economic analysis of their impact. Although the waiting-line model described above is valuable in predicting potential waiting times, queue lengths, idle times, and so on, it does not identify optimal decisions or consider cost factors. As we saw earlier, the solution to a queuing problem may require management to make a trade-off between the increased cost of providing better service and the decreased waiting costs derived from providing that service.

Example 2 examines the costs involved in Example 1.

EXAMPLE 2

Economic analysis of example 1

Learning Objective

3. Conduct a cost analysis for a waiting line

Golden Muffler Shop's owner is interested in cost factors as well as the queuing parameters computed in Example D1. He estimates that the cost of customer waiting time, in terms of customer dissatisfaction and lost goodwill, is $10 per hour spent *waiting* in line. Jones, the mechanic, is paid $7 per hour.

Approach: First compute the average daily customer waiting time, then the daily salary for Jones, and finally the total expected cost.

Solution: Because the average car has a $\frac{2}{3}$-hour wait (W_q) and because there are approximately 16 cars serviced per day (2 arrivals per hour times 8 working hours per day), the total number of hours that customers spend waiting each day for mufflers to be installed is:

$$\frac{2}{3}(16) = \frac{32}{3} = 10\frac{2}{3}\text{ hour}$$

Hence, in this case:

$$\text{Customer waiting-time cost} = \$10\left(10\frac{2}{3}\right) = \$106.67\text{ per day}$$

The only other major cost that Golden's owner can identify in the queuing situation is the salary of Jones, the mechanic, who earns $7 per hour, or $56 per day. Thus:

$$\text{Total expected costs} = \$106.67 + \$56$$
$$= \$162.67\text{ per day}$$

This approach will be useful in Solved Problem 2.

Insight: L_q and W_q are the two most important queuing parameters when it comes to cost analysis. Calculating customer wait times, we note, is based on average time waiting in the queue (W_q) times the number of arrivals per hour (λ) times the number of hours per day. This is because this example is set on a daily basis. This is the same as using L_q, since $L_q = W_q \lambda$.

Learning exercise: If the customer waiting time is actually $20 per hour and Jones gets a salary increase to $10 per hour, what are the total daily expected costs? [Answer: $293.34.]

Related problems: 12e–f, 13, 22, 23, 24

M = number of channels open

λ = average arrival rate

μ = average service rate at each channel

The probability that there are zero people or units in the system is:

$$P_0 = \frac{1}{\left[\displaystyle\sum_{n=0}^{M-1} \frac{1}{n!}\left(\frac{\lambda}{\mu}\right)^n\right] + \frac{1}{M!}\left(\frac{\lambda}{\mu}\right)^M \frac{M\mu}{M\mu - \lambda}} \quad \text{for } M\mu > \lambda$$

The average number of people or units in the system is:

$$L_s = \frac{\lambda\mu(\lambda/\mu)^M}{(M-1)!(M\mu - \lambda)^2} P_0 + \frac{\lambda}{\mu}$$

The average time a unit spends in the waiting line and being serviced (namely, in the system) is:

$$W_s = \frac{\mu(\lambda/\mu)^M}{(M-1)!(M\mu - \lambda)^2} P_0 + \frac{1}{\mu} = \frac{L_s}{\lambda}$$

The average number of people or units in line waiting for service is:

$$L_q = L_s - \frac{\lambda}{\mu}$$

The average time a person or unit spends in the queue waiting for service is:

$$W_q = W_s - \frac{1}{\mu} = \frac{L_q}{\lambda}$$

◄ **Table 4**

Queuing Formulas for Model B: Multichannel System, Also Called M/M/S

Model B (M/M/S): Multiple-Channel Queuing Model

Now let's turn to a multiple-channel queuing system in which two or more servers or channels are available to handle arriving customers. We still assume that customers awaiting service form one single line and then proceed to the first available server. Multichannel, single-phase waiting lines are found in many banks today: A common line is formed, and the customer at the head of the line proceeds to the first free teller. (Refer to Figure 3 for a typical multichannel configuration.)

The multiple-channel system presented in Example 3 again assumes that arrivals follow a Poisson probability distribution and that service times are exponentially distributed. Service is first-come, first-served, and all servers are assumed to perform at the same rate. Other assumptions listed earlier for the single-channel model also apply.

The queuing equations for Model B (which also has the technical name M/M/S) are shown in Table 4. These equations are obviously more complex than those used in the single-channel model; yet they are used in exactly the same fashion and provide the same type of information as the simpler model. (*Note:* The POM for Windows and Excel OM software described later in this chapter can prove very useful in solving multiple-channel, as well as other, queuing problems.)

Learning Objective

4. Apply the multiple-channel queuing model formulas

The Golden Muffler Shop has decided to open a second garage bay and hire a second mechanic to handle installations. Customers, who arrive at the rate of about $\lambda = 2$ per hour, will wait in a single line until 1 of the 2 mechanics is free. Each mechanic installs mufflers at the rate of about $\mu = 3$ per hour.

The company wants to find out how this system compares with the old single-channel waiting-line system.

Approach: Compute several operating characteristics for the $M = 2$ channel system, using the equations in Table 4, and compare the results with those found in Example 1.

EXAMPLE 3

A multiple-channel queue

⊙ **Excel OM Data File ModDExD3.xls**

solution:

$$P_0 = \cfrac{1}{\left[\displaystyle\sum_{n=0}^{1}\frac{1}{n!}\left(\frac{2}{3}\right)^n\right] + \frac{1}{2!}\left(\frac{2}{3}\right)^2 \frac{2(3)}{2(3)-2}}$$

$$= \cfrac{1}{1 + \frac{2}{3} + \frac{1}{2}\left(\frac{4}{9}\right)\left(\frac{6}{6-2}\right)} = \cfrac{1}{1 + \frac{2}{3} + \frac{1}{3}} = \frac{1}{2}$$

$$= .5 \text{ probability of zero cars in the system}$$

Then:

$$L_s = \frac{(2)(3)(2/3)^2}{1![2(3)-2]^2}\left(\frac{1}{2}\right) + \frac{2}{3} = \frac{8/3}{16}\left(\frac{1}{2}\right) + \frac{2}{3} = \frac{3}{4}$$

$$= .75 \text{ average number of cars in the system}$$

$$W_s = \frac{L_s}{\lambda} = \frac{3/4}{2} = \frac{3}{8} \text{ hour}$$

$$= 22.5 \text{ minutes average time a car spends in the system}$$

$$L_q = L_s - \frac{\lambda}{\mu} = \frac{3}{4} - \frac{2}{3} = \frac{9}{12} - \frac{8}{12} = \frac{1}{12}$$

$$= .083 \text{ average number of cars in the queue (waiting)}$$

$$W_q = \frac{L_q}{\lambda} = \frac{.083}{2} = .0415 \text{ hour}$$

$$= 2.5 \text{ minutes average time a car spends in the queue (waiting)}$$

Insight: It is very interesting to see the big differences in service performance when an additional server is added.

Learning exercise: If $\mu = 4$ per hour, instead of $\mu = 3$, what are the new values for P_0, L_s, W_s, L_q, and W_q? [Answers: 0.6, .53 cars, 16 min, .033 cars, 1 min.]

Related problems: 9f, 11d, 15, 20

Active Model D.2

Examples 2 and 3 are further illustrated in Active Model D.2 on the CD-ROM.

We can summarize the characteristics of the 2-channel model in Example 3 and compare them to those of the single-channel model in Example 1 as follows:

	Single Channel	Two Channels
P_0	.33	.5
L_s	2 cars	.75 car
W_s	60 minutes	22.5 minutes
L_q	1.33 cars	.083 car
W_q	40 minutes	2.5 minutes

The increased service has a dramatic effect on almost all characteristics. For instance, note that the time spent waiting in line drops from 40 minutes to only 2.5 minutes.

Use of Waiting Line Tables Imagine the work a manager would face in dealing with $M = 3$, 4, or 5 channel waiting line models if a computer was not readily available. The arithmetic becomes increasingly troublesome. Fortunately, much of the burden of manually examining multiple channel queues can be avoided by using Table 5. This table, the result of hundreds of computations, represents the relationship between three things: (1) a ratio we call ρ ([rho] which is simple to find—it's just λ/μ), (2) number of service channels open, and (3) the average number of customers in the queue, L_q (which is what we'd like to find). For any combination of utilization rate (ρ) and $M = 1, 2, 3, 4,$ or 5 open service channels, you can quickly look in the body of the table to read off the appropriate value for L_q.

Table 5

Values of L_q for M = 1–5 Service Channels and Selected Values of $\rho = \lambda/\mu$

Poisson Arrivals, Exponential Service Times

ρ	Number of Service Channels, M				
	1	2	3	4	5
.10	.0111				
.15	.0264	.0008			
.20	.0500	.0020			
.25	.0833	.0039			
.30	.1285	.0069			
.35	.1884	.0110			
.40	.2666	.0166			
.45	.3681	.0239	.0019		
.50	.5000	.0333	.0030		
.55	.6722	.0449	.0043		
.60	.9000	.0593	.0061		
.65	1.2071	.0767	.0084		
.70	1.6333	.0976	.0112		
.75	2.2500	.1227	.0147		
.80	3.2000	.1523	.0189		
.85	4.8166	.1873	.0239	.0031	
.90	8.1000	.2285	.0300	.0041	
.95	18.0500	.2767	.0371	.0053	
1.0		.3333	.0454	.0067	
1.2		.6748	.0904	.0158	
1.4		1.3449	.1778	.0324	.0059
1.6		2.8444	.3128	.0604	.0121
1.8		7.6734	.5320	.1051	.0227
2.0			.8888	.1739	.0398
2.2			1.4907	.2770	.0659
2.4			2.1261	.4305	.1047
2.6			4.9322	.6581	.1609
2.8			12.2724	1.0000	.2411
3.0				1.5282	.3541
3.2				2.3856	.5128
3.4				3.9060	.7365
3.6				7.0893	1.0550
3.8				16.9366	1.5184
4.0					2.2164
4.2					3.3269
4.4					5.2675
4.6					9.2885
4.8					21.6384

> "Queuing theory has shown that the death toll from a terrorist anthrax attack on Washington, D.C., could be cut by 90% by flying in 8,500 more doctors and nurses to reduce hospital waiting lines."
>
> *Fortune, September 4, 2006*

Example 4 illustrates the use of Table 5.

EXAMPLE 4

Use of waiting line tables

Alaska National Bank is trying to decide how many drive-in teller windows to open on a busy Saturday. CEO Ted Eschenbach estimates that customers arrive at a rate of about λ = 18 per hour, and that each teller can service about μ = 20 customers per hour.

Approach: Ted decides to use Table 5 to compute L_q and W_q.

Solution: The ratio is $\rho = \lambda/\mu = \frac{18}{20}$ = .90. Turning to the table, under ρ = .90, Ted sees that if only M = 1 service window is open, the average number of customers in line will be 8.1. If two windows are open, L_q drops to .2285 customers, to .03 for M = 3 tellers, and to .0041 for M = 4 tellers. Adding more open windows at this point will result in an average queue length of 0.

It is also a simple matter to compute the average waiting time in the queue, W_q, since $W_q = L_q/\lambda$. When one channel is open, W_q = 8.1 customers/(18 customers per hour) = .45 hours = 27 minutes waiting time; when two tellers are open, W_q = .2285 customers/(18 customers per hour) = .0127 hours $\cong \frac{3}{4}$ minute; and so on.

Insight: If a computer is not readily available, Table 5 makes it easy to find L_q and to then compute W_q. Table 5 is especially handy to compare L_q for different numbers of servers (M).

Learning exercise: The number of customers arriving on a Thursday afternoon at Alaska National is 15/hour. The service rate is still 20 customers/hour. How many people are in the queue if there are 1, 2, or 3 servers? [Answer: 2.25, .1227, .0147.]

Related problem: 5

▶ *Long check-in lines such as at Los Angeles International (LAX) are a common airport sight. This is an M/M/S model—passengers wait in a single queue for one of several agents. Based on arrival rates that differ by the fraction of an hour, the airlines staff the counters with fewer or more servers.*

David Young-Wolff, PhotoEdit, Inc.

You might also wish to check the calculations in Example 3 against tabled values just to practice the use of Table 5. You may need to interpolate if your exact ρ value is not found in the first column. Other common operating characteristics besides L_q are published in tabular form in queuing theory textbooks.

Model C (M/D/1): Constant-Service-Time Model

Learning Objective

5. Apply the constant-service-time model equations

Some service systems have constant, instead of exponentially distributed, service times. When customers or equipment are processed according to a fixed cycle, as in the case of an automatic car wash or an amusement park ride, constant service times are appropriate. Because constant rates are certain, the values for L_q, W_q, L_s, and W_s are always less than they would be in Model A, which has variable service rates. As a matter of fact, both the average queue length and the average waiting time in the queue are halved with Model C. Constant-service-model formulas are given in Table 6. Model C also has the technical name M/D/1 in the literature of queuing theory.

▶ **Table 6**

Queuing Formulas for Model C: Constant Service, Also Called M/D/1

Average length of queue: $L_q = \dfrac{\lambda^2}{2\mu(\mu - \lambda)}$

Average waiting time in queue: $W_q = \dfrac{\lambda}{2\mu(\mu - \lambda)}$

Average number of customers in system: $L_s = L_q + \dfrac{\lambda}{\mu}$

Average time in system: $W_s = W_q + \dfrac{1}{\mu}$

Example 5 gives a constant-service-time analysis.

Inman Recycling, Inc., collects and compacts aluminum cans and glass bottles in Reston, Louisiana. Its truck drivers currently wait an average of 15 minutes before emptying their loads for recycling. The cost of driver and truck time while they are in queues is valued at $60 per hour. A new automated compactor can be purchased to process truckloads at a *constant* rate of 12 trucks per hour (that is, 5 minutes per truck). Trucks arrive according to a Poisson distribution at an average rate of 8 per hour. If the new compactor is put in use, the cost will be amortized at a rate of $3 per truck unloaded.

Approach: CEO Tony Inman hires a summer college intern to conduct an analysis to evaluate the costs versus benefits of the purchase. The intern uses the equation for W_q in Table 6.

Solution: Current waiting cost/trip = (1/4 hr waiting now)($60/hr cost) = $15/trip

New system: $\lambda = 8$ trucks/hr arriving $\mu = 12$ trucks/hr served

Average waiting time in queue $= W_q = \dfrac{\lambda}{2\mu(\mu - \lambda)} = \dfrac{8}{2(12)(12 - 8)} = \dfrac{1}{12}$ hr

Waiting cost/trip with new compactor = (1/12 hr wait)($60/hr cost) = $5/trip

Savings with new equipment = $15(current system) − $5(new system) = $10/trip

Cost of new equipment amortized: = $3/trip

Net savings: $7/trip

Insight: Constant service times, usually attained through automation, help control the variability inherent in service systems. This can lower average queue length and average waiting time. Note the 2 in the denominator of the equations for L_q and W_q in Table 6.

Learning exercise: With the new constant-service-time system, what are the average waiting time in the queue, average number of trucks in the system, and average waiting time in the system? [Answer: 0.0833 hours, 1.33, 0.1667 hours.]

Related problems: 14, 16, 21

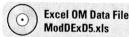

EXAMPLE 5

A constant-service model

Excel OM Data File
ModDExD5.xls

Active Model D.3

Example D5 is further illustrated in Active Model D.3 on your CD-ROM.

Model D: Limited-Population Model

When there is a limited population of potential customers for a service facility, we must consider a different queuing model. This model would be used, for example, if we were considering equipment repairs in a factory that has 5 machines, if we were in charge of maintenance for a fleet of 10 commuter airplanes, or if we ran a hospital ward that has 20 beds. The limited-population model allows any number of repair people (servers) to be considered.

This model differs from the three earlier queuing models because there is now a *dependent* relationship between the length of the queue and the arrival rate. Let's illustrate the extreme situation: If your factory had five machines and all were broken and awaiting repair, the arrival rate would drop to zero. In general, then, as the *waiting line* becomes longer in the limited population model, the *arrival rate* of customers or machines drops.

Table 7 displays the queuing formulas for the limited-population model. Note that they employ a different notation than Models A, B, and C. To simplify what can become time-consuming calculations, finite queuing tables have been developed that determine D and F. D represents the probability that a machine needing repair will have to wait in line. F is a waiting-time efficiency factor. D and F are needed to compute most of the other finite model formulas.

A small part of the published finite queuing tables is illustrated in this section. Table 8 provides data for a population of $N = 5$.[5]

Learning Objective

6. Perform a limited-population model analysis

---

[5]Limited, or finite, queuing tables are available to handle arrival populations of up to 250. Although there is no definite number that we can use as a dividing point between limited and unlimited populations, the general rule of thumb is this: If the number in the queue is a significant proportion of the arrival population, use a limited population queuing model. For a complete set of N-values, see L. G. Peck and R. N. Hazelwood, *Finite Queuing Tables* (New York: Wiley, 1958).

▶ **Table 7**

Queuing Formulas and Notation for Model D: Limited-Population Formulas

Service factor: $X = \dfrac{T}{T+U}$

Average number running: $J = NF(1 - X)$

Average number waiting: $L = N(1 - F)$

Average number being serviced: $H = FNX$

Average waiting time: $W = \dfrac{L(T+U)}{N-L} = \dfrac{T(1-F)}{XF}$

Number of population: $N = J + L + H$

Notation

D = probability that a unit will have to wait in queue
F = efficiency factor
H = average number of units being served
J = average number of units not in queue or in service bay
L = average number of units waiting for service
M = number of service channels

N = number of potential customers
T = average service time
U = average time between unit service requirements
W = average time a unit waits in line
X = service factor

Source: L. G. Peck and R. N. Hazelwood. *Finite Queuing Tables* (New York: Wiley, 1958).

To use Table 8, we follow four steps:

1. Compute X (the service factor), where $X = T/(T + U)$.
2. Find the value of X in the table and then find the line for M (where M is the number of service channels).
3. Note the corresponding values for D and F.
4. Compute L, W, J, H, or whichever are needed to measure the service system's performance.

Example 6 illustrates these steps.

EXAMPLE 6

A limited-population model

Excel OM Data File ModDExD6.xls

Past records indicate that each of the 5 laser computer printers at the U.S. Department of Energy, in Washington, DC, needs repair after about 20 hours of use. Breakdowns have been determined to be Poisson distributed. The one technician on duty can service a printer in an average of 2 hours, following an exponential distribution. Printer downtime costs $120 per hour. Technicians are paid $25 per hour. Should the DOE hire a second technician?

Approach: Assuming the second technician can also repair a printer in an average of 2 hours, we can use Table 8 (because there are $N = 5$ machines in this limited population) to compare the costs of 1 versus 2 technicians.

Solution:

1. First, we note that $T = 2$ hours and $U = 20$ hours.

2. Then, $X = \dfrac{T}{T+U} = \dfrac{2}{2+20} = \dfrac{2}{22} = .091$ (close to .090 [to use for determining D and F]).

3. For $M = 1$ server, $D = .350$ and $F = .960$.

4. For $M = 2$ servers, $D = .044$ and $F = .998$.

5. The average number of printers *working* is $J = NF(1 - X)$.
   For $M = 1$, this is $J = (5)(.960)(1 - .091) = 4.36$.
   For $M = 2$, it is $J = (5)(.998)(1 - .091) = 4.54$.

6. The cost analysis follows:

Number of Technicians	Average Number Printers Down $(N - J)$	Average Cost/Hr for Downtime $(N - J)(\$120/\text{hr})$	Cost/Hr. for Technicians (at $25/hr)	Total Cost/hr
1	.64	$76.80	$25.00	$101.80
2	.46	$55.20	$50.00	$105.20

Insight: This analysis suggests that having only one technician on duty will save a few dollars per hour ($105.20 − $101.80 = $3.40). This may seem like a small amount, but it adds up to over $7,000 per year.

Learning exercise: DOE has just replaced its printers with a new model that seems to break down after about 18 hours of use. Recompute the costs. [Answer: For $M = 1$, $F = .95$, $J = 4.275$, and total cost/hr = $112.00. For $M = 2$, $F = .997$, $J = 4.487$, and total cost/hr = $111.56.]

Related problems: 17, 18, 19

▼ Table 8   Finite Queuing Tables for a Population of $N = 5$*

X	M	D	F	X	M	D	F	X	M	D	F	X	M	D	F	X	M	D	F
.012	1	.048	.999		1	.404	.945		1	.689	.801	.330	4	.012	.999		3	.359	.927
.019	1	.076	.998	.110	2	.065	.996	.210	3	.032	.998		3	.112	.986	.520	2	.779	.728
.025	1	.100	.997		1	.421	.939		2	.211	.973		2	.442	.904		1	.988	.384
.030	1	.120	.996	.115	2	.071	.995		1	.713	.783		1	.902	.583	.540	4	.085	.989
.034	1	.135	.995		1	.439	.933	.220	3	.036	.997	.340	4	.013	.999		3	.392	.917
.036	1	.143	.994	.120	2	.076	.995		2	.229	.969		3	.121	.985		2	.806	.708
.040	1	.159	.993		1	.456	.927		1	.735	.765		2	.462	.896		1	.991	.370
.042	1	.167	.992	.125	2	.082	.994	.230	3	.041	.997		1	.911	.569	.560	4	.098	.986
.044	1	.175	.991		1	.473	.920		2	.247	.965	.360	4	.017	.998		3	.426	.906
.046	1	.183	.990	.130	2	.089	.933		1	.756	.747		3	.141	.981		2	.831	.689
.050	1	.198	.989		1	.489	.914	.240	3	.046	.996		2	.501	.880		1	.993	.357
.052	1	.206	.988	.135	2	.095	.993		2	.265	.960		1	.927	.542	.580	4	.113	.984
.054	1	.214	.987		1	.505	.907		1	.775	.730	.380	4	.021	.998		3	.461	.895
.056	2	.018	.999	.140	2	.102	.992	.250	3	.052	.995		3	.163	.976		2	.854	.670
	1	.222	.985		1	.521	.900		2	.284	.955		2	.540	.863		1	.994	.345
.058	2	.019	.999	.145	3	.011	.999		1	.794	.712		1	.941	.516	.600	4	.130	.981
	1	.229	.984		2	.109	.991	.260	3	.058	.994	.400	4	.026	.977		3	.497	.883
.060	2	.020	.999		1	.537	.892		2	.303	.950		3	.186	.972		2	.875	.652
	1	.237	.983	.150	3	.012	.999		1	.811	.695		2	.579	.845		1	.996	.333
.062	2	.022	.999		2	.115	.990	.270	3	.064	.994		1	.952	.493	.650	4	.179	.972
	1	.245	.982		1	.553	.885		2	.323	.944	.420	4	.031	.997		3	.588	.850
.064	2	.023	.999	.155	3	.013	.999		1	.827	.677		3	.211	.966		2	.918	.608
	1	.253	.981		2	.123	.989	.280	3	.071	.993		2	.616	.826		1	.998	.308
.066	2	.024	.999		1	.568	.877		2	.342	.938		1	.961	.471	.700	4	.240	.960
	1	.260	.979	.160	3	.015	.999		1	.842	.661	.440	4	.037	.996		3	.678	.815
.068	2	.026	.999		2	.130	.988	.290	4	.007	.999		3	.238	.960		2	.950	.568
	1	.268	.978		1	.582	.869		3	.079	.992		2	.652	.807		1	.999	.286
.070	2	.027	.999	.165	3	.016	.999		2	.362	.932		1	.969	.451	.750	4	.316	.944
	1	.275	.977		2	.137	.987		1	.856	.644	.460	4	.045	.995		3	.763	.777
.075	2	.031	.999		1	.597	.861	.300	4	.008	.999		3	.266	.953		2	.972	.532
	1	.294	.973	.170	3	.017	.999		3	.086	.990		2	.686	.787	.800	4	.410	.924
.080	2	.035	.998		2	.145	.985		2	.382	.926		1	.975	.432		3	.841	.739
	1	.313	.969		1	.611	.853		1	.869	.628	.480	4	.053	.994		2	.987	.500
.085	2	.040	.998	.180	3	.021	.999	.310	4	.009	.999		3	.296	.945	.850	4	.522	.900
	1	.332	.965		2	.161	.983		3	.094	.989		2	.719	.767		3	.907	.702
.090	2	.044	.998		1	.638	.836		2	.402	.919		1	.980	.415		2	.995	.470
	1	.350	.960	.190	3	.024	.998		1	.881	.613	.500	4	.063	.992	.900	4	.656	.871
.095	2	.049	.997		2	.117	.980	.320	4	.010	.999		3	.327	.936		3	.957	.666
	1	.368	.955		1	.665	.819		3	.103	.988		2	.750	.748		2	.998	.444
.100	2	.054	.997	.200	3	.028	.998		2	.422	.912		1	.985	.399	.950	4	.815	.838
	1	.386	.950	.200	2	.194	.976		1	.892	.597	.520	4	.073	.991		3	.989	.631
.105	2	.059	.997																

*See notation in Table 7.

▶ *This isn't Disney World, where waits are made tolerable—or even fun—via amusements and entertainment. This long line of frustrated customers is the Chicago office of the Consulate of Mexico, where immigrants apply for ID cards that are considered legal documents. How could the principles in this module be used to improve this queuing system?*

Stephen J. Carrera, AP Wide World Photos

OTHER QUEUING APPROACHES

Many practical waiting-line problems that occur in service systems have characteristics like those of the four mathematical models already described. Often, however, *variations* of these specific cases are present in an analysis. Service times in an automobile repair shop, for example, tend to follow the normal probability distribution instead of the exponential. A college registration system in which seniors have first choice of courses and hours over other students is an example of a first-come, first-served model with a preemptive priority queue discipline. A physical examination for military recruits is an example of a multiphase system, one that differs from the single-phase models discussed earlier in this module. A recruit first lines up to have blood drawn at one station, then waits for an eye exam at the next station, talks to a psychiatrist at the third, and is examined by a doctor for medical problems at the fourth. At each phase, the recruit must enter another queue and wait his or her turn. Many models, some very complex, have been developed to deal with situations such as these. One of these is described in the *OM in Action* box "L.L. Bean Turns to Queuing Theory."

OM in Action   L.L. Bean Turns to Queuing Theory

L.L. Bean faced severe problems. It was the peak selling season, and the service level for incoming calls was simply unacceptable. Widely known as a high-quality outdoor goods retailer, about 65% of L.L. Bean's sales volume is generated through telephone orders via its toll-free service centers located in Maine.

Here is how bad the situation was: During certain periods, 80% of the calls received a busy signal, and those who did not often had to wait up to 10 minutes before speaking with a sales agent. L.L. Bean estimated it lost $10 million in profit because of the way it allocated telemarketing resources. Keeping customers waiting "in line" (on the phone) was costing $25,000 per day. On exceptionally busy days, the total orders lost because of queuing problems approached $500,000 in gross revenues.

Developing queuing models similar to those presented here, L.L. Bean was able to set the number of phone lines and the number of agents to have on duty for each half hour of every day of the season. Within a year, use of the model resulted in 24% more calls answered, 17% more orders taken, and 16% more revenues. The new system also meant 81% fewer abandoned callers and an 84% faster answering time. The percent of callers spending less than 20 seconds in the queue increased from 25% to 77%. Needless to say, queuing theory changed the way L.L. Bean thought about telecommunications.

Sources: Human Resource Management International Digest (November–December 2002): 4–9; and *Interfaces* (January/February 1991): 75–91 and (March/April 1993): 14–20.

Summary

Queues are an important part of the world of operations management. In this module, we describe several common queuing systems and present mathematical models for analyzing them.

The most widely used queuing models include Model A, the basic single-channel, single-phase system with Poisson arrivals and exponential service times; Model B, the multi-channel equivalent of Model A; Model C, a constant-service-rate model; and Model D, a limited-population system. All four models allow for Poisson arrivals, first-in, first-out service, and a single-service phase. Typical operating characteristics we examine include average time spent waiting in the queue and system, average number of customers in the queue and system, idle time, and utilization rate.

A variety of queuing models exists for which all the assumptions of the traditional models need not be met. In these cases, we use more complex mathematical models or turn to a technique called *simulation*.

Key Terms

Queuing theory
Waiting line (queue)
Unlimited, or infinite, population
Limited, or finite, population

Poisson distribution
First-in, first-out (FIFO) rule
Single-channel queuing system
Multiple-channel queuing system

Single-phase system
Multiphase system
Negative exponential probability
 distribution

Using Software to Solve Queuing Problems

Both Excel OM and POM for Windows may be used to analyze all but the last two homework problems in this module.

✕ Using Excel OM

Excel OM's Waiting-Line program handles all four of the models developed in this module. Program 1 illustrates our first model, the M/M/1 system, using the data from Example 1.

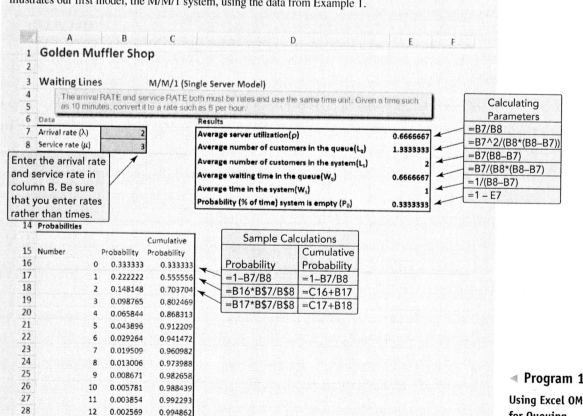

◀ **Program 1**

**Using Excel OM
for Queuing**

Example 1's (Golden Muffler Shop) data are illustrated in the M/M/1 model.

P Using POM For Windows

There are several POM for Windows queuing models from which to select in that program's Waiting-Line module. The program can include an economic analysis of cost data, and, as an option, you may display probabilities of various numbers of people/items in the system. See Appendix for further details.

Solved Problems

 Virtual Office Hours help is available on Student DVD.

Solved Problem 1

Sid Das Brick Distributors currently employs 1 worker whose job is to load bricks on outgoing company trucks. An average of 24 trucks per day, or 3 per hour, arrive at the loading platform, according to a Poisson distribution. The worker loads them at a rate of 4 trucks per hour, following approximately the exponential distribution in his service times.

Das believes that adding an additional brick loader will substantially improve the firm's productivity. He estimates that a two-person crew loading each truck will double the loading rate (μ) from 4 trucks per hour to 8 trucks per hour. Analyze the effect on the queue of such a change and compare the results to those achieved with one worker. What is the probability that there will be more than 3 trucks either being loaded or waiting?

Solution

	Number of Brick Loaders	
	1	2
Truck arrival rate (λ)	3/hr	3/hr
Loading rate (μ)	4/hr	8/hr
Average number in system (L_s)	3 trucks	.6 truck
Average time in system (W_s)	1 hr	.2 hr
Average number in queue (L_q)	2.25 trucks	.225 truck
Average time in queue (W_q)	.75 hr	.075 hr
Utilization rate (ρ)	.75	.375
Probability system empty (P_0)	.25	.625

Probability of More Than k Trucks in System

	Probability $n > k$	
k	One Loader	Two Loaders
0	.75	.375
1	.56	.141
2	.42	.053
3	.32	.020

These results indicate that when only one loader is employed, the average truck must wait three quarters of an hour before it is loaded. Furthermore, there is an average of 2.25 trucks waiting in line to be loaded. This situation may be unacceptable to management. Note also the decline in queue size after the addition of a second loader.

Solved Problem 2

Truck drivers working for Sid Das (see Solved Problem 1) earn an average of $10 per hour. Brick loaders receive about $6 per hour. Truck drivers waiting *in the queue or at the loading platform* are drawing a salary but are productively idle and unable to generate revenue during that time. What would be the *hourly* cost savings to the firm if it employed 2 loaders instead of 1?

Referring to the data in Solved Problem 1, we note that the average number of trucks *in the system* is 3 when there is only 1 loader and 6 when there are 2 loaders.

Solution

	Number of Loaders	
	1	2
Truck driver idle time costs [(Average number of trucks) × (Hourly rate)] = (3)($10) = $30		$ 6 = (.6)($10)
Loading costs	6	12 = (2)($6)
Total expected cost per hour	$36	$18

The firm will save $18 per hour by adding another loader.

Solved Problem 3

Sid Das is considering building a second platform or gate to speed the process of loading trucks. This system, he thinks, will be even more efficient than simply hiring another loader to help out on the first platform (as in Solved Problem 1).

Assume that the worker at each platform will be able to load 4 trucks per hour each and that trucks will continue to arrive at the rate of 3 per hour. Then apply the appropriate equations to find the waiting line's new operating conditions. Is this new approach indeed speedier than the other two that Das has considered?

solution

$$P_0 = \cfrac{1}{\left[\displaystyle\sum_{n=0}^{1} \frac{1}{n!}\left(\frac{3}{4}\right)^n\right] + \frac{1}{2!}\left(\frac{3}{4}\right)^2 \frac{2(4)}{2(4)-3}}$$

$$= \cfrac{1}{1 + \frac{3}{4} + \frac{1}{2}\left(\frac{3}{4}\right)^2\left(\frac{8}{8-3}\right)} = .4545$$

$$L_s = \frac{3(4)(3/4)^2}{(1)!(8-3)^2}(.4545) + \frac{3}{4} = .873$$

$$W_s = \frac{.873}{3} = .291 \text{ hr}$$

$$L_q = .873 - 3/4 = .123$$

$$W_q = \frac{.123}{3} = .041 \text{ hr}$$

Looking back at Solved Problem 1, we see that although length of the *queue* and average time in the queue are lowest when a second platform is open, the average number of trucks in the *system* and average time spent waiting in the system are smallest when two workers are employed at a *single* platform. Thus, we would probably recommend not building a second platform.

Solved Problem 4

St. Elsewhere Hospital's cardiac care unit (CCU) has 5 beds, which are virtually always occupied by patients who have just undergone major heart surgery. Two registered nurses are on duty in the CCU in each of the three 8-hour shifts. About every 2 hours (following a Poisson distribution), one of the patients requires a nurse's attention. The nurse will then spend an average of 30 minutes (exponen-

tially distributed) assisting the patient and updating medical records regarding the problem and care provided.

Because immediate service is critical to the 5 patients, two important questions are: What is the average number of patients being attended by the nurses? What is the average time that a patient spends waiting for one of the nurses to arrive?

solution

$$N = 5 \text{ patients}$$

$$M = 2 \text{ nurses}$$

$$T = 30 \text{ minutes}$$

$$U = 120 \text{ minutes}$$

$$X = \frac{T}{T+U} = \frac{30}{30+120} = .20$$

From Table 8 , with $X = .20$ and $M = 2$, we see that:

$$F = .976$$

$$H = \text{average number being attended to} = FNX$$

$$= (.976)(5)(.20) = .98 \approx 1 \text{ patient at any given time}$$

$$W = \text{average waiting time for a nurse} = \frac{T(1-F)}{XF}$$

$$= \frac{30(1-.976)}{(.20)(.976)} = 3.69 \text{ minutes}$$

Self-Test

- *Before taking the self-test*, refer to the learning objectives listed at the beginning of the selection and the key terms listed at the end of the selection.
- Use the key at the back of the text to **correct** your answers.
- *Restudy* pages that correspond to any questions you answered incorrectly or material you feel uncertain about.

1. Most systems use the queue discipline known as:
   a) last-in, first-out (LIFO)
   b) first-in, first-out (FIFO)
   c) balking customers first
   d) exponential smoothing
   e) self-serve

2. Which of the following is *not* an assumption in common queuing mathematical models?
   a) arrivals come from an infinite, or very large population
   b) arrivals are Poisson distributed
   c) arrivals are treated on a first-in, first-out basis and do not balk or renege
   d) service times follow the exponential distribution
   e) the average arrival rate is faster than the average service rate

3. Which of the following is *not* a key operating characteristic for a queuing system?
   a) utilization rate
   b) percent idle time
   c) average time spent waiting in the system and in the queue
   d) average number of customers in the system and in the queue
   e) average number of customers who renege

4. Three parts of a queuing system are:
   a) the inputs, the queue, and the service facility
   b) the calling population, the utilization, and the service facility
   c) the arrival system, the waiting line, and the service facility
   d) all of the above

5. A company has one computer technician who is responsible for repairs on the company's 20 computers. As a computer breaks, the technician is called to make the repair. If the repairperson is busy, the machine must wait to be repaired. This is an example of:
   a) a multichannel system
   b) a finite population system
   c) a constant service rate system
   d) a multiphase system
   e) all of the above

6. If everything else remains the same, including the mean arrival rate and service rate, except that the service time becomes constant instead of exponential:
   a) the average queue length will be halved
   b) the average waiting time will be doubled
   c) the average queue length will increase
   d) we cannot tell from the information provided

7. Customers enter the waiting line at a cafeteria's only cash register on a first-come, first-served basis. The arrival rate follows a Poisson distribution, while service times follow an exponential distribution. If the average number of arrivals is six per minute and the average service rate of a single server is ten per minute, what is the average number of customers in the system?
   a) 0.6
   b) 0.9
   c) 1.5
   d) .25
   e) 1.0

Active Model Exercise

In this active model example, we can examine the relationship between arrival and service rates, and costs and the number of servers. The first two inputs to the model are arrival and service rates in customers per hour. The average time between arrivals and service time is also displayed, but do not change these two numbers, which are shaded in pink.

Questions

1. What number of mechanics yields the lowest total daily cost? What is the minimum total daily cost?

2. Use the scrollbar on the arrival rate. What would the arrival rate need to be to require a third mechanic?

3. Use the scrollbar on the goodwill cost and determine the range of goodwill costs for which you would have exactly 1 mechanic. Two mechanics?

4. How high would the wage rate need to be to make 1 mechanic the least costly option?

5. If a second mechanic is added, is it less costly to have the 2 mechanics working separately or to have the 2 mechanics work as a single team with a service rate that is twice as fast?

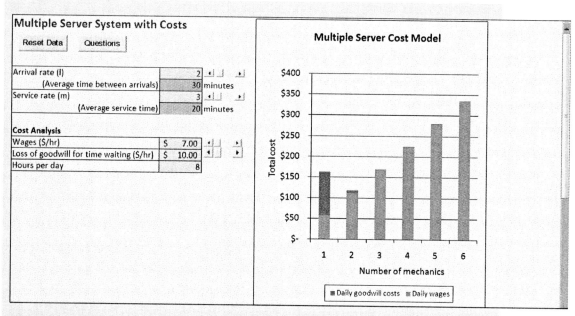

Multiple Server System with Costs

Reset Data   Questions

Arrival rate (l)	2	
(Average time between arrivals)	30	minutes
Service rate (m)	3	
(Average service time)	20	minutes

Cost Analysis

Wages (S/hr)	$ 7.00	
Loss of goodwill for time waiting (S/hr)	$ 10.00	
Hours per day	8	

Multiple Server Cost Model

(bar chart: Total cost vs. Number of mechanics (1–6), Daily goodwill costs, Daily wages)

▲ **Active Model D2** **An Analysis of the Golden Muffler Shop (Examples 2–3) with Cost as a Variable**

Internet and Student CD-ROM/DVD Exercises

Visit our Companion Web site or use your student CD-ROM/DVD to help with material in this selection.

On Our Companion Web Site,
www.prenhall.com/heizer
- Self-Study Quizzes
- Practice Problems
- Internet Case
- PowerPoint Lecture

On Your Student CD-ROM
- Practice Problems
- Active Model Exercises
- Excel OM
- Excel OM Example Data Files
- POM for Windows

On Your Student DVD
- Virtual Office Hours for Solved Problems

Discussion Questions

1. Name the three parts of a typical queuing system.
2. When designing a waiting line system, what "qualitative" concerns need to be considered?
3. Name the three factors that govern the structure of "arrivals" in a queuing system.
4. State the seven common measures of queuing system performance.
5. State the assumptions of the "basic" single-channel queuing model (Model A or M/M/1).
6. Is it good or bad to operate a supermarket bakery system on a strict first-come, first-served basis? Why?
7. Describe what is meant by the waiting-line terms *balk* and *renege*. Provide an example of each.
8. Which is larger, W_s or W_q? Explain.
9. Briefly describe three situations in which the first-in, first-out (FIFO) discipline rule is not applicable in queuing analysis.
10. Describe the behavior of a waiting line where $\lambda > \mu$. Use both analysis and intuition.
11. Discuss the likely outcome of a waiting line system where $\mu > \lambda$, but only by a tiny amount. (For example, $\mu = 4.1$, $\lambda = 4$).

12. Provide examples of four situations in which there is a limited, or finite, waiting line.
13. What are the components of the following queuing systems? Draw and explain the configuration of each.
    (a) Barbershop.
    (b) Car wash.
    (c) Laundromat.
    (d) Small grocery store.
14. Do doctors' offices generally have random arrival rates for patients? Are service times random? Under what circumstances might service times be constant?
15. What happens if two single-channel systems have the same mean arrival and service rates, but the service time is constant in one and exponential in the other?
16. What dollar value do you place on yourself per hour that you spend waiting in lines? What value do your classmates place on themselves? Why do the values differ?

Problems*

• 1 Customers arrive at Paul Harrold's Styling Shop at a rate of 3 per hour, distributed in a Poisson fashion. Paul can perform haircuts at a rate of 5 per hour, distributed exponentially.
a) Find the average number of customers waiting for haircuts.
b) Find the average number of customers in the shop.
c) Find the average time a customer waits until it is his or her turn.
d) Find the average time a customer spends in the shop.
e) Find the percentage of time that Paul is busy. **P**X

• 2 There is only one copying machine in the student lounge of the business school. Students arrive at the rate of $\lambda = 40$ per hour (according to a Poisson distribution). Copying takes an average of 40 seconds, or $\mu = 90$ per hour (according to an exponential distribution). Compute the following:
a) The percentage of time that the machine is used.
b) The average length of the queue.
c) The average number of students in the system.
d) The average time spent waiting in the queue.
e) The average time in the system. **P**X

• 3 Glen Schmidt owns and manages a chili-dog and soft-drink stand near the Georgeville campus. While Glen can service 30 customers per hour on the average (μ), he gets only 20 customers per hour (λ). Because Glen could wait on 50% more customers than actually visit his stand, it doesn't make sense to him that he should have any waiting lines.

Glen hires you to examine the situation and to determine some characteristics of his queue. After looking into the problem, you find it follows the six conditions for a single-channel waiting line (as seen in Model A). What are your findings? **P**X

• 4 Sam Certo, a Longwood vet, is running a rabies vaccination clinic for dogs at the local grade school. Sam can "shoot" a dog every 3 minutes. It is estimated that the dogs will arrive independently and randomly throughout the day at a rate of one dog every 6 minutes according to a Poisson distribution. Also assume that Sam's shooting times are exponentially distributed. Compute the following:
a) The probability that Sam is idle.
b) The proportion of the time that Sam is busy.
c) The average number of dogs being vaccinated and waiting to be vaccinated.
d) The average number of dogs waiting to be vaccinated.
e) The average time a dog waits before getting vaccinated.
f) The average amount of time a dog spends waiting in line and being vaccinated. **P**X

•• 5 The pharmacist at Arnold Palmer Hospital, Saad Alwan, receives 12 requests for prescriptions each hour, Poisson distributed. It takes him a mean time of 4 minutes to fill each, following a negative exponential distribution. Use the waiting line table, Table 5 and $W_q = \dfrac{L_q}{\lambda}$, to answer these questions.
a) What is the average number of prescriptions in the queue?
b) How long will the average prescription spend in the queue?
c) Alwan decides to hire a second pharmacist, Ajay Aggerwal, whom he went to school with and who operates at the same speed in filling prescriptions. How will the answers to parts a and b change? **P**X

• 6 Calls arrive at James Hamann's hotel switchboard at a rate of 2 per minute. The average time to handle each is 20 seconds. There is only one switchboard operator at the current time. The Poisson and exponential distributions appear to be relevant in this situation.
a) What is the probability that the operator is busy?
b) What is the average time that a caller must wait before reaching the operator?
c) What is the average number of calls waiting to be answered? **P**X

•• 7 Automobiles arrive at the drive-through window at the downtown Urbana, Illinois, post office at the rate of 4 every 10 minutes. The average service time is 2 minutes. The Poisson distribution is appropriate for the arrival rate and service times are exponentially distributed.
a) What is the average time a car is in the system?
b) What is the average number of cars in the system?
c) What is the average number of cars waiting to receive service?
d) What is the average time a car is in the queue?
e) What is the probability that there are no cars at the window?
f) What percentage of the time is the postal clerk busy?
g) What is the probability that there are exactly 2 cars in the system? **P**X

• 8 Missouri's Stephen Allen Electronics Corporation retains a service crew to repair machine breakdowns that occur on an average of $\lambda = 3$ per 8-hour workday (approximately Poisson in nature). The crew can service an average of $\mu = 8$ machines per workday, with a repair time distribution that resembles the exponential distribution.
a) What is the utilization rate of this service system?
b) What is the average downtime for a broken machine?
c) How many machines are waiting to be serviced at any given time?
d) What is the probability that more than one machine is in the system? the probability that more than two are broken and waiting to be repaired or being serviced? more than three? more than four? **P**X

•• 9 Zimmerman's Bank is the only bank in the small town of St. Thomas. On a typical Friday, an average of 10 customers per hour arrive at the bank to transact business. There is one teller at the bank, and the average time required to transact business is 4 minutes. It is assumed that service times may be described by the exponential distribution. A single line would be used, and the customer at the front of the line would go to the first available bank teller. If a single teller is used, find:
a) The average time in the line.
b) The average number in the line.
c) The average time in the system.
d) The average number in the system.
e) The probability that the bank is empty.
f) Zimmerman is considering adding a second teller (who would work at the same rate as the first) to reduce the waiting time for customers. She assumes that this will cut the waiting time in half. If a second teller is added, find the new answers to parts (a) to (e). **P**X

•• 10 Susan Slotnick manages a Cleveland, Ohio, movie theater complex called Cinema I, II, III, and IV. Each of the four auditoriums plays a different film; the schedule staggers starting times

*Note: **P**X means the problem may be solved with POM for Windows and/or Excel OM.

to avoid the large crowds that would occur if all four movies started at the same time. The theater has a single ticket booth and a cashier who can maintain an average service rate of 280 patrons per hour. Service times are assumed to follow an exponential distribution. Arrivals on a normally active day are Poisson distributed and average 210 per hour.

To determine the efficiency of the current ticket operation, Susan wishes to examine several queue-operating characteristics.

a) Find the average number of moviegoers waiting in line to purchase a ticket.

b) What percentage of the time is the cashier busy?

c) What is the average time that a customer spends in the system?

d) What is the average time spent waiting in line to get to the ticket window?

e) What is the probability that there are more than two people in the system? More than three people? More than four? **PX**

•• **11** Bill Youngdahl has been collecting data at the TU student grill. He has found that, between 5:00 P.M. and 7:00 P.M., students arrive at the grill at a rate of 25 per hour (Poisson distributed) and service time takes an average of 2 minutes (exponential distribution). There is only 1 server, who can work on only 1 order at a time.

a) What is the average number of students in line?

b) What is the average time a student is in the grill area?

c) Suppose that a second server can be added to team up with the first (and, in effect, act as one faster server). This would reduce the average service time to 90 seconds. How would this affect the average time a student is in the grill area?

d) Suppose a second server is added and the 2 servers act independently, with *each* taking an average of 2 minutes. What would be the average time a student is in the system? **PX**

••• **12** The wheat harvesting season in the American Midwest is short, and farmers deliver their truckloads of wheat to a giant central storage bin within a 2-week span. Because of this, wheat-filled trucks waiting to unload and return to the fields have been known to back up for a block at the receiving bin. The central bin is owned cooperatively, and it is to every farmer's benefit to make the unloading/storage process as efficient as possible. The cost of grain deterioration caused by unloading delays and the cost of truck rental and idle driver time are significant concerns to the cooperative members. Although farmers have difficulty quantify-

ing crop damage, it is easy to assign a waiting and unloading cost for truck and driver of $18 per hour. During the 2-week harvest season, the storage bin is open and operated 16 hours per day, 7 days per week, and can unload 35 trucks per hour according to an exponential distribution. Full trucks arrive all day long (during the hours the bin is open) at a rate of about 30 per hour, following a Poisson pattern.

To help the cooperative get a handle on the problem of lost time while trucks are waiting in line or unloading at the bin, find the following:

a) The average number of trucks in the unloading system.

b) The average time per truck in the system.

c) The utilization rate for the bin area.

d) The probability that there are more than three trucks in the system at any given time.

e) The total daily cost to the farmers of having their trucks tied up in the unloading process.

f) As mentioned, the cooperative uses the storage bin heavily only 2 weeks per year. Farmers estimate that enlarging the bin would cut unloading costs by 50% next year. It will cost $9,000 to do so during the off-season. Would it be worth the expense to enlarge the storage area? **PX**

••• **13** Radovilsky's Department Store in Haywood, California, maintains a successful catalog sales department in which a clerk takes orders by telephone. If the clerk is occupied on one line, incoming phone calls to the catalog department are answered automatically by a recording machine and asked to wait. As soon as the clerk is free, the party who has waited the longest is transferred and serviced first. Calls come in at a rate of about 12 per hour. The clerk can take an order in an average of 4 minutes. Calls tend to follow a Poisson distribution, and service times tend to be exponential.

The cost of the clerk is $10 per hour, but because of lost goodwill and sales, Radovilsky's loses about $25 per hour of customer time spent waiting for the clerk to take an order.

a) What is the average time that catalog customers must wait before their calls are transferred to the order clerk?

b) What is the average number of callers waiting to place an order?

c) Radovilsky's is considering adding a second clerk to take calls. The store's cost would be the same $10 per hour. Should it hire another clerk? Explain your decision. **PX**

• **14** Karen Brown's Coffee Shop decides to install an automatic coffee vending machine outside one of its stores to reduce the number of people standing in line inside. Karen charges $3.50 per cup. However, it takes too long for people to make change. The service time is a constant 3 minutes, and the arrival rate is 15 per hour (Poisson distributed).

a) What is the average wait in line?

b) What is the average number of people in line?

c) Karen raises the price to $5 per cup and takes 60 seconds off the service time. However, because the coffee is now so expensive, the arrival rate drops to 10 per hour. Now what are the average wait time and the average number of people in the queue (waiting)? **PX**

••• **15** The typical subway station in Washington, DC, has six turnstiles, each of which can be controlled by the station manager to be used for either entrance or exit control—but never for both. The manager must decide at different times of the day how many turnstiles to use for entering passengers and how many to use for exiting passengers.

Markus Matzel/das Fotoarchiv, Peter Arnold, Inc.

At the George Washington University (GWU) Station, passengers enter the station at a rate of about 84 per minute between the hours of 7 A.M. and 9 A.M. Passengers exiting trains at the stop reach the exit turnstile area at a rate of about 48 per minute during the same morning rush hours. Each turnstile can allow an average of 30 passengers per minute to enter or exit. Arrival and service times have been thought to follow Poisson and exponential distributions, respectively. Assume riders form a common queue at both entry and exit turnstile areas and proceed to the first empty turnstile.

The GWU station manager, Ernie Forman, does not want the average passenger at his station to have to wait in a turnstile line for more than 6 seconds, nor does he want more than 8 people in any queue at any average time.

a) How many turnstiles should be opened in each direction every morning?

b) Discuss the assumptions underlying the solution of this problem using queuing theory. **Px**

•• 16   Yvette Freeman's Car Wash takes a constant time of 4.5 minutes in its automated car wash cycle. Autos arrive following a Poisson distribution at the rate of 10 per hour. Yvette wants to know:

a) The average waiting time in line.

b) The average length of the line. **Px**

••• 17   Debra Bishop's cabinet-making shop, in Des Moines, has five tools that automate the drilling of holes for the installation of hinges. These machines need setting up for each order of cabinets. The orders appear to follow the Poisson distribution, averaging 3 per 8-hour day. There is a single technician for setting these machines. Her service times are exponential, averaging 2 hours each.

a) What is the service factor for this system?

b) What is the average number of these machines in service?

c) What impact on machines in service would there be if a second technician were available? **Px**

••• 18   Two technicians, working separately, monitor a group of 5 computers that run an automated manufacturing facility. It takes an average of 15 minutes (exponentially distributed) to adjust a computer that develops a problem. Computers run for an average of 85 minutes (Poisson distributed) without requiring adjustments. Determine the following:

a) The average number of computers waiting for adjustment.

b) The average number being adjusted.

c) The average number of computers not in working order. **Px**

••• 19   One mechanic services 5 drilling machines for a steel plate manufacturer. Machines break down on an average of once every 6 working days, and breakdowns tend to follow a Poisson distribution. The mechanic can handle an average of one repair job per day. Repairs follow an exponential distribution.

a) On the average, how many machines are waiting for service?

b) On the average, how many drills are in running order?

c) How much would waiting time be reduced if a second mechanic were hired? **Px**

••• 20   Richard Insinga, the administrator at an Onienta Hospital emergency room faces the problem of providing treatment for patients who arrive at different rates during the day. There are 4 doctors available to treat patients when needed. If not needed, they can be assigned other responsibilities (such as doing lab tests, reports, X-ray diagnoses) or else rescheduled to work at other hours.

It is important to provide quick and responsive treatment, and Rchard feels that, on the average, patients should not have to sit in the waiting area for more than 5 minutes before being seen by a doctor. Patients are treated on a first-come, first-served basis and see the first available doctor after waiting in the queue. The arrival pattern for a typical day is as follows:

Time	Arrival Rate
9 A.M.–3 P.M.	6 patients/hour
3 P.M.–8 P.M.	4 patients/hour
8 P.M.–midnight	12 patients/hour

Arrivals follow a Poisson distribution, and treatment times, 12 minutes on the average, follow the exponential pattern.

How many doctors should be on duty during each period to maintain the level of patient care expected? **Px**

••• 21   The Ponchatrain Bridge is a 16-mile toll bridge that crosses Lake Ponchatrain in New Orleans. Currently, there are 7 toll booths, each staffed by an employee. Since Hurricane Katrina, the Port Authority has been considering replacing the employees with machines. Many factors must be considered because the employees are unionized. However, one of the Port Authority's concerns is the effect that replacing the employees with machines will have on the times that drivers spend in the system. Customers arrive to any one toll booth at a rate of 10 per minute. In the exact change lanes with employees, the service time is essentially constant at 5 seconds for each driver. With machines, the average service time would still be 5 seconds, but it would be exponential rather than constant, because it takes time for the coins to rattle around in the machine. Contrast the two systems for a single lane. **Px**

••• 22   The registration area at a large convention of building contractors is taking place in Las Vegas. There are 200 people arriving per hour (Poisson distributed), and the cost of their waiting time in the queue is valued at $100 per person per hour. The Las Vegas Convention Bureau provides servers to register guests at a fee of $15 per person per hour. It takes about one minute to register an attendee (exponentially distributed). A single waiting line, with multiple servers, is set up.

a) What is the minimum number of servers for this system?

b) What is the optimal number of servers for this system?

c) What is the cost for the system, per hour, at the optimum number of servers?

d) What is the server utilization rate with the minimum number of servers? **Px**

•• 23   Refer to Problem 22. A new registration manager, Lisa Houts, is hired who initiates a program to entertain the people in line with a juggler whom she pays $15/hour. This reduces the waiting costs to $50 per hour.

a) What is the optimal number of servers?

b) What is the cost for the system, per hour, at the optimal service level?

•••• 24   The Chattanooga Furniture store gets an average of 50 customers per shift. Marilyn Helms, the manager, wants to calculate whether she should hire 1, 2, 3, or 4 salespeople. She has determined that average waiting times will be 7 minutes with one salesperson, 4 minutes with two salespeople, 3 minutes with three salespeople, and 2 minutes with four salespeople. She has estimated the cost per minute that customers wait at $1. The cost per salesperson per shift (including fringe benefits) is $70.

How many salespeople should be hired?

Case Studies

New England Foundry

For more than 75 years, New England Foundry, Inc. (NEFI), has manufactured wood stoves for home use. In recent years, with increasing energy prices, president George Mathison has seen sales triple. This dramatic increase has made it difficult for George to maintain quality in all his wood stoves and related products.

Unlike other companies manufacturing wood stoves, NEFI is in the business of making *only* stoves and stove-related products. Its major products are the Warmglo I, the Warmglo II, the Warmglo III, and the Warmglo IV. The Warmglo I is the smallest wood stove, with a heat output of 30,000 BTUs, and the Warmglo IV is the largest, with a heat output of 60,000 BTUs.

The Warmglo III outsold all other models by a wide margin. Its heat output and available accessories were ideal for the typical home. The Warmglo III also had a number of other outstanding features that made it one of the most attractive and heat-efficient stoves on the market. These features, along with the accessories, resulted in expanding sales and prompted George to build a new factory to manufacture the Warmglo III model. An overview diagram of the factory is shown in Figure 6.

The new foundry used the latest equipment, including a new Disamatic that helped in manufacturing stove parts. Regardless of new equipment or procedures, casting operations have remained basically unchanged for hundreds of years. To begin with, a wooden pattern is made for every cast-iron piece in the stove. The wooden pattern is an exact duplicate of the cast-iron piece that is to be manufactured. All NEFI patterns are made by Precision Patterns, Inc. and are stored in the pattern shop and maintenance room. Next, a specially formulated sand is molded around the wooden pattern. There can be two or more sand molds for each pattern. The sand is mixed and the molds are made in the molding room. When the wooden pattern is removed, the resulting sand molds form a negative image of the desired casting. Next, molds are transported to the casting room, where molten iron is poured into them and allowed to cool. When the iron has solidified, molds are moved into the cleaning, grinding, and preparation room, where they are dumped into large vibrators that shake most of the sand from the casting. The rough castings are then subjected to both sandblasting to remove the rest of the sand and grinding to finish some of their surfaces. Castings are then painted with a special heat-resistant paint, assembled into workable stoves, and inspected for manufacturing defects that may have gone undetected. Finally, finished stoves are moved

▲ **Figure 6** Overview of Factory

▲ **Figure 7** Overview of Factory after Changes

to storage and shipping, where they are packaged and transported to the appropriate locations.

At present, the pattern shop and the maintenance department are located in the same room. One large counter is used by both maintenance personnel, who store tools and parts (which are mainly used by the casting department); and sand molders, who need various patterns for the molding operation. Pete Nawler and Bob Dillman, who work behind the counter, can service a total of 10 people per hour (about 5 per hour each). On the average, 4 people from casting and 3 from molding arrive at the counter each hour. People from molding and casting departments arrive randomly, and to be served, they form a single line.

Pete and Bob have always had a policy of first come, first served. Because of the location of the pattern shop and maintenance department, it takes an average of 3 minutes for an individual from the casting department to walk to the pattern and maintenance room, and it takes about 1 minute for an individual to walk from the molding department to the pattern and maintenance room.

After observing the operation of the pattern shop and maintenance room for several weeks, George decided to make some changes to the factory layout. An overview of these changes appears in Figure 7.

Separating the maintenance shop from the pattern shop would have a number of advantages. It would take people from the casting department only 1 minute instead of 3 to get to the new maintenance room. The time from molding to the pattern shop would be unchanged. Using motion and time studies, George was also able to determine that improving the layout of the maintenance room would allow Bob to serve 6 people from the casting department per hour; improving the layout of the pattern department would allow Pete to serve 7 people from the molding shop per hour.

Discussion Questions

1. How much time would the new layout save?
2. If casting personnel were paid $9.50 per hour and molding personnel were paid $11.75 per hour, how much could be saved per hour with the new factory layout?
3. Should George have made the change in layout?

Source: From *Quantitative Analysis for Management*, 9th ed., by B. Render, R. Stair, and M. Hanna, pp. 602–604. Copyright © 2006. Reprinted by permission of Prentice Hall, Inc., Upper Saddle River, NJ.

The Winter Park Hotel

Donna Shader, manager of the Winter Park Hotel, is considering how to restructure the front desk to reach an optimum level of staff efficiency and guest service. At present, the hotel has five clerks on duty, each with a separate waiting line, during peak check-in time of 3:00 P.M. to 5:00 P.M. Observation of arrivals during this period shows that an average of 90 guests arrive each hour (although there is no upward limit on the number that could arrive at any given time). It takes an average of 3 minutes for the front-desk clerk to register each guest.

Ms. Shader is considering three plans for improving guest service by reducing the length of time that guests spend waiting in line. The first proposal would designate one employee as a quick-service clerk for guests registering under corporate accounts, a market segment that fills about 30% of all occupied rooms. Because corporate guests are preregistered, their registration takes just 2 minutes. With these guests separated from the rest of the clientele, the average time for registering a typical guest would climb to 3.4 minutes. Under this plan, noncorporate guests would choose any of the remaining four lines.

The second plan is to implement a single-line system. All guests could form a single waiting line to be served by whichever of five clerks became available. This option would require sufficient lobby space for what could be a substantial queue.

The use of an automatic teller machine (ATM) for check-ins is the basis of the third proposal. This ATM would provide about the same service rate as would a clerk. Because initial use of this technology might be minimal, Shader estimates that 20% of customers, primarily frequent guests, would be willing to use the machines. (This might be a conservative estimate if guests perceive direct benefits from using the ATM, as bank customers do. Citibank reports that some 95% of its Manhattan customers use its ATMs.) Ms. Shader would set up a single queue for customers who prefer human check-in clerks. This line would be served by the five clerks, although Shader is hopeful that the ATM will allow a reduction to four.

Discussion Questions

1. Determine the average amount of time that a guest spends checking in. How would this change under each of the stated options?
2. Which option do you recommend?

Source: From *Quantitative Analysis for Management*, 9th ed., by B. Render, R. Stair, and M. Hanna, p. 604. Copyright © 2006. Reprinted by permission of Prentice Hall, Inc., Upper Saddle River, NJ.

Additional Case Study

See our Companion Web site at **www.prenhall.com/heizer** *for this additional free internet case study:*

- **Pantry Shopper:** The case requires the redesign of a checkout system for a supermarket.

Bibliography

Cabral, F. B. "The Slow Server Problem for Uninformed Customers." *Queuing Systems* 50, no. 4 (August 2005): 353.

Dasgupta, Ani, and Ghosh, Madhubani. "Including Performance in a Queue via Prices: The Case of a Riverine Port." *Management Science* 46, no. 11 (November 2000): 1466–1484.

Joy, M., and S. Jones. "Transient Probabilities for Queues with Applications to Hospital Waiting Line Management." *Health Care Management Science* 8, no. 3 (August 2005): 231.

Prabhu, N. U. *Foundations of Queuing Theory.* Dordecht, Netherlands: Kluwer Academic Publishers (1997).

Ramaswami, V., et al. "Ensuring Access to Emergency Services in the Presence of Long Internet Dial-Up Calls." *Interfaces* 35, no. 5 (September–October 2005): 411–425.

Render, B., R. M. Stair, and R. Balakrishnan. *Managerial Decision Modeling with Spreadsheets*, 2nd ed. Upper Saddle River, NJ: Prentice Hall (2007).

Render, B., R. M. Stair, and M. Hanna. *Quantitative Analysis for Management*, 9th ed. Upper Saddle River, NJ: Prentice Hall (2006).

Ryan, Sarah M. "Stochastic Models in Queuing Theory Review." *Journal of the American Statistical Association* 100 (March 2005): 350.

Windmeijer, F., H. Gravelle, and P. Hoonhout. "Waiting Lists, Waiting Times and Admissions." *Health Economics* 14, no. 9 (September 2005): 971.

Solutions to Even Numbered Problems

2 (a) 44%
 (b) .36 people
 (c) .8 people
 (d) .53 min.
 (e) 1.2 min.
4 (a) .5
 (b) .5
 (c) 1
 (d) .5
 (e) .05 hr.
 (f) .1 hr.
6 (a) .667
 (b) .667 min.
 (c) 1.33

8 (a) .375
   (b) 1.6 hr. (or .2 days)
   (c) .225
   (d) 0.141, 0.053, 0.020, 0.007
10 (a) 2.25
   (b) .75
   (c) .857 min. (.014 hr.)
   (d) .64 min. (.011 hr.)
   (e) 42%, 32%, 24%
12 (a) 6 trucks
   (b) 12 min.
   (c) .857
   (d) .54
   (e) $1,728/day
   (f) Yes, save $3,096 in the first year.

14 (a) .075 hrs (4.5 min.)
   (b) 1.125 people
   (c) .0083 hrs (0.5 min.), 0.083 people
16 (a) .113 hr. = 6.8 min.
   (b) 1.13 cars
18 (a) .05
   (b) .743
   (c) .793
20 3, 2, 4 MDs, respectively
22 (a) 4 servers
   (b) 6 servers
   (c) $109
   (d) 83.33%
24 2 salespeople ($340)

Solutions to Self Test

1. b; **2.** e; **3.** e; **4.** c; **5.** b; **6.** a; **7.** d.

Appendix I

Normal Curve Areas

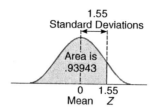

1.55
Standard Deviations

Area is
.93943

0   1.55
Mean Z

To find the area under the normal curve, you can apply either Table 1 or Table 2. In Table 1, you must know how many standard deviations that point is to the right of the mean. Then, the area under the normal curve can be read directly from the normal table. For example, the total area under the normal curve for a point that is 1.55 standard deviations to the right of the mean is .93943.

TABLE 1

z	.00	.01	.02	.03	.04	.05	.06	.07	.08	.09
.0	.50000	.50399	.50798	.51197	.51595	.51994	.52392	.52790	.53188	.53586
.1	.53983	.54380	.54776	.55172	.55567	.55962	.56356	.56749	.57142	.57535
.2	.57926	.58317	.58706	.59095	.59483	.59871	.60257	.60642	.61026	.61409
.3	.61791	.62172	.62552	.62930	.63307	.63683	.64058	.64431	.64803	.65173
.4	.65542	.65910	.66276	.66640	.67003	.67364	.67724	.68082	.68439	.68793
.5	.69146	.69497	.69847	.70194	.70540	.70884	.71226	.71566	.71904	.72240
.6	.72575	.72907	.73237	.73565	.73891	.74215	.74537	.74857	.75175	.75490
.7	.75804	.76115	.76424	.76730	.77035	.77337	.77637	.77935	.78230	.78524
.8	.78814	.79103	.79389	.79673	.79955	.80234	.80511	.80785	.81057	.81327
.9	.81594	.81859	.82121	.82381	.82639	.82894	.83147	.83398	.83646	.83891
1.0	.84134	.84375	.84614	.84849	.85083	.85314	.85543	.85769	.85993	.86214
1.1	.86433	.86650	.86864	.87076	.87286	.87493	.87698	.87900	.88100	.88298
1.2	.88493	.88686	.88877	.89065	.89251	.89435	.89617	.89796	.89973	.90147
1.3	.90320	.90490	.90658	.90824	.90988	.91149	.91309	.91466	.91621	.91774
1.4	.91924	.92073	.92220	.92364	.92507	.92647	.92785	.92922	.93056	.93189
1.5	.93319	.93448	.93574	.93699	.93822	.93943	.94062	.94179	.94295	.94408
1.6	.94520	.94630	.94738	.94845	.94950	.95053	.95154	.95254	.95352	.95449
1.7	.95543	.95637	.95728	.95818	.95907	.95994	.96080	.96164	.96246	.96327
1.8	.96407	.96485	.96562	.96638	.96712	.96784	.96856	.96926	.96995	.97062
1.9	.97128	.97193	.97257	.97320	.97381	.97441	.97500	.97558	.97615	.97670
2.0	.97725	.97784	.97831	.97882	.97932	.97982	.98030	.98077	.98124	.98169
2.1	.98214	.98257	.98300	.98341	.98382	.98422	.98461	.98500	.98537	.98574
2.2	.98610	.98645	.98679	.98713	.98745	.98778	.98809	.98840	.98870	.98899
2.3	.98928	.98956	.98983	.99010	.99036	.99061	.99086	.99111	.99134	.99158
2.4	.99180	.99202	.99224	.99245	.99266	.99286	.99305	.99324	.99343	.99361
2.5	.99379	.99396	.99413	.99430	.99446	.99461	.99477	.99492	.99506	.99520
2.6	.99534	.99547	.99560	.99573	.99585	.99598	.99609	.99621	.99632	.99643
2.7	.99653	.99664	.99674	.99683	.99693	.99702	.99711	.99720	.99728	.99736
2.8	.99744	.99752	.99760	.99767	.99774	.99781	.99788	.99795	.99801	.99807
2.9	.99813	.99819	.99825	.99831	.99836	.99841	.99846	.99851	.99856	.99861
3.0	.99865	.99869	.99874	.99878	.99882	.99886	.99899	.99893	.99896	.99900
3.1	.99903	.99906	.99910	.99913	.99916	.99918	.99921	.99924	.99926	.99929
3.2	.99931	.99934	.99936	.99938	.99940	.99942	.99944	.99946	.99948	.99950
3.3	.99952	.99953	.99955	.99957	.99958	.99960	.99961	.99962	.99964	.99965
3.4	.99966	.99968	.99969	.99970	.99971	.99972	.99973	.99974	.99975	.99976
3.5	.99977	.99978	.99978	.99979	.99980	.99981	.99981	.99982	.99983	.99983
3.6	.99984	.99985	.99985	.99986	.99986	.99987	.99987	.99988	.99988	.99989
3.7	.99989	.99990	.99990	.99990	.99991	.99991	.99992	.99992	.99992	.99992
3.8	.99993	.99993	.99993	.99994	.99994	.99994	.99994	.99995	.99995	.99995
3.9	.99995	.99995	.99996	.99996	.99996	.99996	.99996	.99996	.99997	.99997

From *Operations Management*, 9/e. Jay Heizer. Barry Render. Copyright © 2008 by Pearson Education. All rights reserved.

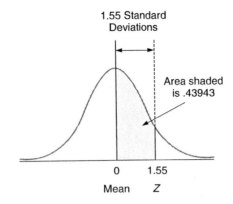

1.55 Standard
Deviations

Area shaded
is .43943

0   1.55

Mean   Z

As an alternative to Table 1, the numbers in Table 2 represent the proportion of the total area away from the mean, μ, to one side. For example, the area between the mean and a point that is 1.55 standard deviations to its right is .43943.

TABLE 2

z	.00	.01	.02	.03	.04	.05	.06	.07	.08	.09
0.0	.00000	.00399	.00798	.01197	.01595	.01994	.02392	.02790	.03188	.03586
0.1	.03983	.04380	.04776	.05172	.05567	.05962	.06356	.06749	.07142	.07535
0.2	.07926	.08317	.08706	.09095	.09483	.09871	.10257	.10642	.11026	.11409
0.3	.11791	.12172	.12552	.12930	.13307	.13683	.14058	.14431	.14803	.15173
0.4	.15542	.15910	.16276	.16640	.17003	.17364	.17724	.18082	.18439	.18793
0.5	.19146	.19497	.19847	.20194	.20540	.20884	.21226	.21566	.21904	.22240
0.6	.22575	.22907	.23237	.23565	.23891	.24215	.24537	.24857	.25175	.25490
0.7	.25804	.26115	.26424	.26730	.27035	.27337	.27637	.27935	.28230	.28524
0.8	.28814	.29103	.29389	.29673	.29955	.30234	.30511	.30785	.31057	.31327
0.9	.31594	.31859	.32121	.32381	.32639	.32894	.33147	.33398	.33646	.33891
1.0	.34134	.34375	.34614	.34850	.35083	.35314	.35543	.35769	.35993	.36214
1.1	.36433	.36650	.36864	.37076	.37286	.37493	.37698	.37900	.38100	.38298
1.2	.38493	.38686	.38877	.39065	.39251	.39435	.39617	.39796	.39973	.40147
1.3	.40320	.40490	.40658	.40824	.40988	.41149	.41309	.41466	.41621	.41174
1.4	.41924	.42073	.42220	.42364	.42507	.42647	.42786	.42922	.43056	.43189
1.5	.43319	.43448	.43574	.43699	.43822	.43943	.44062	.44179	.44295	.44408
1.6	.44520	.44630	.44738	.44845	.44950	.45053	.45154	.45254	.45352	.45449
1.7	.45543	.45637	.45728	.45818	.45907	.45994	.46080	.46164	.46246	.46327
1.8	.46407	.46485	.46562	.46638	.46712	.46784	.46856	.46926	.46995	.47062
1.9	.47128	.47193	.47257	.47320	.47381	.47441	.47500	.47558	.47615	.47670
2.0	.47725	.47778	.47831	.47882	.47932	.47982	.48030	.48077	.48124	.48169
2.1	.48214	.48257	.48300	.48341	.48382	.48422	.48461	.48500	.48537	.48574
2.2	.48610	.48645	.48679	.48713	.48745	.48778	.48809	.48840	.48870	.48899
2.3	.48928	.48956	.48983	.49010	.49036	.49061	.49086	.49111	.49134	.49158
2.4	.49180	.49202	.49224	.49245	.49266	.49286	.49305	.49324	.49343	.49361
2.5	.49379	.49396	.49413	.49430	.49446	.49461	.49477	.49492	.49506	.49520
2.6	.49534	.49547	.49560	.49573	.49585	.49598	.49609	.49621	.49632	.49643
2.7	.49653	.49664	.49674	.49683	.49693	.49702	.49711	.49720	.49728	.49736
2.8	.49744	.49752	.49760	.49767	.49774	.49781	.49788	.49795	.49801	.49807
2.9	.49813	.49819	.49825	.49831	.49836	.49841	.49846	.49851	.49856	.49861
3.0	.49865	.49869	.49874	.49878	.49882	.49886	.49889	.49893	.49897	.49900
3.1	.49903	.49906	.49910	.49913	.49916	.49918	.49921	.49924	.49926	.49929

Appendix II

Values of e^{-2} for Use in the Poisson Distribution

VALUES OF $e^{-\lambda}$

λ	$e^{-\lambda}$	λ	$e^{-\lambda}$	λ	$e^{-\lambda}$	λ	$e^{-\lambda}$
.0	1.0000	1.6	.2019	3.1	.0450	4.6	.0101
.1	.9048	1.7	.1827	3.2	.0408	4.7	.0091
.2	.8187	1.8	.1653	3.3	.0369	4.8	.0082
.3	.7408	1.9	.1496	3.4	.0334	4.9	.0074
.4	.6703	2.0	.1353	3.5	.0302	5.0	.0067
.5	.6065	2.1	.1225	3.6	.0273	5.1	.0061
.6	.5488	2.2	.1108	3.7	.0247	5.2	.0055
.7	.4966	2.3	.1003	3.8	.0224	5.3	.0050
.8	.4493	2.4	.0907	3.9	.0202	5.4	.0045
.9	.4066	2.5	.0821	4.0	.0183	5.5	.0041
1.0	.3679	2.6	.0743	4.1	.0166	5.6	.0037
1.1	.3329	2.7	.0672	4.2	.0150	5.7	.0033
1.2	.3012	2.8	.0608	4.3	.0136	5.8	.0030
1.3	.2725	2.9	.0550	4.4	.0123	5.9	.0027
1.4	.2466	3.0	.0498	4.5	.0111	6.0	.0025
1.5	.2231						

From *Operations Management*, 9/e. Jay Heizer. Barry Render. Copyright © 2008 by Pearson Education. All rights reserved.

Appendix III

Table of Random Numbers

52	06	50	88	53	30	10	47	99	37	66	91	35	32	00	84	57	07
37	63	28	02	74	35	24	03	29	60	74	85	90	73	59	55	17	60
82	57	68	28	05	94	03	11	27	79	90	87	92	41	09	25	36	77
69	02	36	49	71	99	32	10	75	21	95	90	94	38	97	71	72	49
98	94	90	36	06	78	23	67	89	85	29	21	25	73	69	34	85	76
96	52	62	87	49	56	59	23	78	71	72	90	57	01	98	57	31	95
33	69	27	21	11	60	95	89	68	48	17	89	34	09	93	50	44	51
50	33	50	95	13	44	34	62	64	39	55	29	30	64	49	44	30	16
88	32	18	50	62	57	34	56	62	31	15	40	90	34	51	95	26	14
90	30	36	24	69	82	51	74	30	35	36	85	01	55	92	64	09	85
50	48	61	18	85	23	08	54	17	12	80	69	24	84	92	16	49	59
27	88	21	62	69	64	48	31	12	73	02	68	00	16	16	46	13	85
45	14	46	32	13	49	66	62	74	41	86	98	92	98	84	54	33	40
81	02	01	78	82	74	97	37	45	31	94	99	42	49	27	64	89	42
66	83	14	74	27	76	03	33	11	97	59	81	72	00	64	61	13	52
74	05	81	82	93	09	96	33	52	78	13	06	28	30	94	23	37	39
30	34	87	01	74	11	46	82	59	94	25	34	32	23	17	01	58	73
59	55	72	33	62	13	74	68	22	44	42	09	32	46	71	79	45	89
67	09	80	98	99	25	77	50	03	32	36	63	65	75	94	19	95	88
60	77	46	63	71	69	44	22	03	85	14	48	69	13	30	50	33	24
60	08	19	29	36	72	30	27	50	64	85	72	75	29	87	05	75	01
80	45	86	99	02	34	87	08	86	84	49	76	24	08	01	86	29	11
53	84	49	63	26	65	72	84	85	63	26	02	75	26	92	62	40	67
69	84	12	94	51	36	17	02	15	29	16	52	56	43	26	22	08	62
37	77	13	10	02	18	31	19	32	85	31	94	81	43	31	58	33	51

Source: Excerpted from *A Million Random Digits with 100,000 Normal Deviates,* The Free Press (1955): 7, with permission of the RAND Corporation.

From *Operations Management,* 9/e. Jay Heizer. Barry Render. Copyright © 2008 by Pearson Education. All rights reserved.

Appendix IV

Using Excel OM and POM for Windows

Two approaches to computer-aided decision making are provided with this text: **Excel OM** and **POM** (Production and Operations Management) **for Windows**. These are the two most user-friendly software packages available to help you learn and understand operations management. Both programs can be used either to solve homework problems identified with a computer logo or to check answers you have developed by hand. Both software packages use the standard Windows interface and run on any IBM-compatible PC operating Windows XP or better.

EXCEL OM

Excel OM has also been designed to help you to better learn and understand both OM and Excel. Even though the software contains 24 modules and more than 50 submodules, the screens for every module are consistent and easy to use. Modules can be accessed through either of two menus that are added to Excel. The Heizer menu lists the modules in *chapter* order as illustrated for Excel 2007 in Program 1a. The Excel OM menu lists the modules in alphabetical order, as illustrated for earlier versions of Excel in Program 1b. This software is provided on the CD-ROM that is included in the back of this text at no cost to purchasers of this textbook. Excel 2000 or better must be on your PC.

To install Excel OM, insert the CD-ROM. The CD should start automatically. If not, click on the file named Start that is on the CD. After the web page opens, click on the Software option on the left hand side, click on Excel OM (version 3) and follow the instructions. Default values have been assigned in the setup program, but you may change them if you like. The default folder into which the program will be installed is named C:\ProgramFiles\ExcelOM3, and the default name

▼ **Program 1a** Excel OM Modules Menu in Add-Ins Tab in Excel 2007

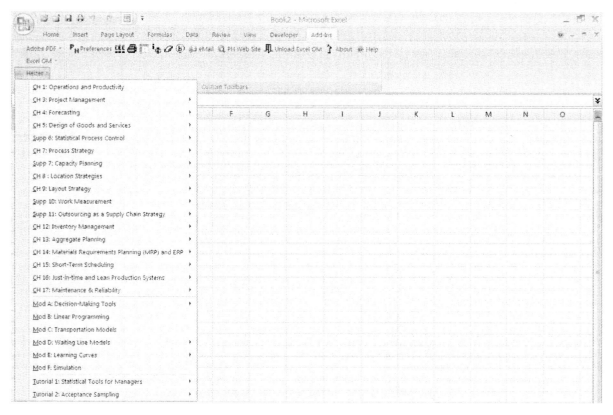

From *Operations Management*, 9/e. Jay Heizer. Barry Render. Copyright © 2008 by Pearson Education. All rights reserved.

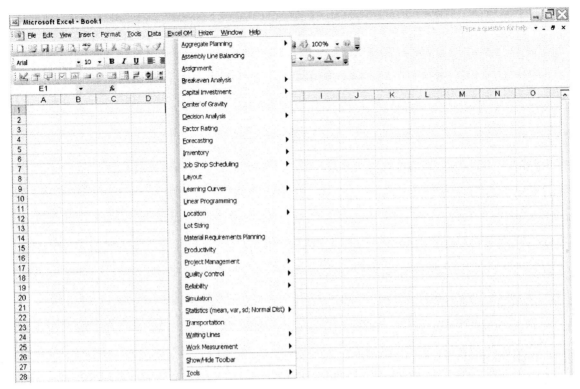

▲ **Program 1b**   Excel OM Modules Menu in Main Excel Menu for Versions of Excel Prior to Excel 2007

for the program group placed in the START menu is Excel OM 3. Generally speaking, it is simply necessary to click NEXT each time the installation asks a question.

Starting the Program To start Excel OM, double-click on the Excel OM 3 shortcut placed on the desktop during installation. Alternatively, you may click on START, PROGRAMS, EXCEL OM 3. In Excel 2007 the Excel OM menu will appear in the Add-Ins tab of the Excel 2007 ribbon as displayed in Program 1a, while in earlier versions of Excel the Excel OM menu will appear in the main menu of Excel as displayed in Program 1b.

If you have Excel 2007 and do not see an Add-Ins Tab on the Ribbon or do not see Excel OM 3 on this tab as displayed in Program 1a, then your Excel 2007 security settings need to be revised to enable Excel OM 3. Please consult the Excel 2007 instructions on the CD-ROM or consult the support site, **www.prenhall.com/weiss**.

Excel OM serves two purposes in the learning process. First, it can simply help you solve homework problems. You enter the appropriate data, and the program provides numerical solutions. POM for Windows operates on the same principle. However, Excel OM allows for a second approach; that is, noting the Excel *formulas* used to develop solutions and modifying them to deal with a wider variety of problems. This "open" approach enables you to observe, understand, and even change the formulas underlying the Excel calculations, hopefully conveying Excel's power as an OM analysis tool.

POM FOR WINDOWS

POM for Windows is decision support software that is also offered free on every student CD. Program 2 shows a list of 24 OM modules on the CD that will be installed on your hard drive. Once you follow the standard setup instructions, a POM for Windows program icon will be

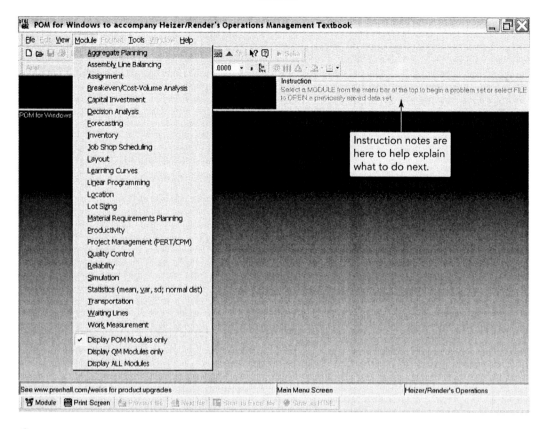

▲ **Program 2** **POM for Windows Module List**

added to your start menu and desktop. The program may be accessed by double-clicking on the icon. Updates to POM for Windows are available on the Internet through the Prentice Hall download library, found at **http://www.prenhall.com/weiss**.

Index